WITNESS
TO MY LIFE

WITNESS
TO MY LIFE

The Letters of Jean-Paul Sartre
to Simone de Beauvoir
1926–1939

Edited by Simone de Beauvoir

Translated by Lee Fahnestock and Norman MacAfee

CHARLES SCRIBNER'S SONS
NEW YORK

MAXWELL MACMILLAN CANADA
TORONTO

MAXWELL MACMILLAN INTERNATIONAL
NEW YORK   OXFORD   SINGAPORE   SYDNEY

FIRST AMERICAN EDITION

Charles Scribner's Sons
Macmillan Publishing Company
866 Third Avenue
New York, NY 10022

Maxwell Macmillan Canada, Inc.
1200 Eglinton Avenue East
Suite 200
Don Mills, Ontario M3C 3N1

Macmillan Publishing Company is part of the Maxwell Communication Group
of Companies.

Library of Congress Cataloging-in-Publication Data
Sartre, Jean Paul, 1905–1980
[Lettres au Castor et à quelques autres. English]
Witness to my life: the letters of Jean-Paul Sartre to Simone de
Beauvoir, 1926–1939/edited by Simone de Beauvoir: translated by
Lee Fahnestock and Norman McAfee.—1st American ed.
p.   cm.
Translation of: Lettres au Castor et à quelques autres.
Includes bibliographical references.
ISBN 0-684-19338-8
1.Sartre, Jean Paul, 1905–1980—Correspondence.   2. Authors,
French—20th century—Correspondence.   3. Beauvoir, Simone de, 1908–1986
—Correspondence.   I. Beauvoir, Simone de, 1908–1986.   II. Title.
PQ2637.A82Z483 1992
848'.91409—dc20
[B]   92-5068
CIP

10 9 8 7 6 5 4 3 2 1
Printed in the United States of America

Contents

Never have I felt so forcefully that our lives have no meaning outside of our love, and that nothing changes that, neither separation, nor passions, nor the war. You said it was a victory for our morality, but it is just as much a victory for our love.—November 15, 1939

From the 1950s to his death in 1980, Jean-Paul Sartre was considered everything from the moral light of his age to the most demonic threat to the existing order. Conflating the two extremes, John Gerassi subtitled his 1988 Sartre biography *Hated Conscience of His Century*. Many Americans remember him as a lucid critic of the war in Vietnam, or think of him as the author of one of the century's pivotal philosophical texts, or as the life partner to Simone de Beauvoir. By 1964, when he became the first person to voluntarily reject the Nobel Prize for Literature, Sartre was the world's best known living philosopher. In this volume of letters from the years 1926 to 1939, written mostly to Simone de Beauvoir but to some others as well, we see quite a different Sartre: the young student becoming a teacher who is trying to become a writer; the awkward lover courting his first love.

"Let me tell you about myself." So begins the opening letter of this collection, written when he was a twenty-one-year-old student at the prestigious Ecole Normale Supérieure, to the slightly younger Simone Jollivet. With self-deprecating humor, he describes his essential qualities: ambition and cowardice. He is drawn, he confesses, to the lives of great men of the nineteenth century. He recommends books to her, pouring into her all his new knowledge of literature and life. We see him doing what he feels all those with ambition must do: fending off depression, working against previous models. He is writing a novel—never finished—called "A Defeat," based partly on his current experiences as a tutor, partly on the relationship between Nietzsche and the Wagners. The hero, Frédéric, slightly pompous as a tutor should be, lends his voice to these early letters of a young person to his first love.

This first Simone, it turns out, was a tryout for the real one—Simone de Beauvoir, a student two and a half years his junior. In 1929 he met "the Beaver"—le Castor, as he ever after knew her—when she was studying for the nationwide *agrégation* exam for exceptional teaching candidates, he for a retake of it. Brilliant though erratic, he had failed the previous year. This second time around, he took first place, she a close second.

The first exam failure could only have been devastating to the young Sartre, though disaster was far from unknown to him. In fact, he was born into a family tragedy: His father, a naval officer, was mortally ill and died when Jean-Paul was a year and a half. There followed a five-year period when Poulou, as they called him, was the adored center of the family consisting of his mother and her parents. The grandfather, Charles Schweitzer came from a distinguished Protestant, intellectual Alsatian family that included his nephew Albert Schweitzer. A teacher, he devised what became the Berlitz method of language instruction. When he was three, Poulou, the epitome of precocity, was let loose in the Schweitzer library, where he would hold and pretend to read the great books long before he could even puzzle out the words.

Sartre's early years saw sudden life-changing upheavals. From the disaster of losing Jean-Baptiste Sartre, the family built a new emotional structure, which collapsed the day Charles sent the boy to the barber. Losing his golden virgin curls, the boy not only lost his childhood beauty but discovered he was actually ugly, a realization that became a given for the rest of his life. When he was eleven, a final blow destroyed the remains of the childhood utopia—his mother took a new husband. The stepfather's ambivalent, unstable relationship with the stepson leads to a memorable last line in a set of letters to Beauvoir from a 1935 Norwegian cruise: "Parents lodge like a knife in the skulls of their children, whose thoughts they cut in two." Charles Schweitzer appears in these pages only in 1934, as a senile though still virile nonagenarian.

The story of Jean-Paul Sartre and Simone de Beauvoir is well known in general terms. Their extraordinary renewable contract of primary essential love relied on total candor and allowed outside contingent loves. Intellectual trust remained their primary link, the basis of an interdependence that lasted a lifetime, whatever the competition. If inevitable flaws in the goal of complete transparency between them are visible in these pages, so too is a remarkable resilience.

Witness to My Life tracks the dynamic shifts and adjustments of their lives through the 1930s to New Year's Eve, 1939. It is a decade when they found high school teaching positions in literature and philosophy, at opposite ends of the country to begin with—Marseilles for Beauvoir and Le Havre for Sartre, with a significant year's leave in Berlin when he studied the writings of the phenomenologist Edmund Husserl. His letters describing irritation with officious colleagues give little idea of his true talents as a teacher: He would stride into a lycée classroom, hands in pockets, and talk nonstop for an hour without notes, overturning the bourgeois certainties of the young men in his charge.

It is from isolated, provincial Le Havre that in October 1931 Sartre wrote Simone de Beauvoir a letter full of images that would reappear six years later, transfigured, in his first published novel, *La Nausée (Nausea)*. On that day, he went to a public park and proceeded to contemplate a tree. In the next years, Sartre transferred this event to the narration of *Nausea*'s antihero, Antoine Roquentin, for whom the chestnut tree becomes an exemplary contingent object, existing—like his body—without reason or need, destined for meaningless death. This thought fills him with dread and nausea. But Roquentin is further troubled by the thought that his consciousness, which perceives the tree, has no substance: It is a nothingness.

Although these letters make scant mention of *Imagination* and *The Transcendence of the Ego*, Sartre's two earliest philosophic books, they do log the circumstances of *Nausea*'s writing and rewriting. And the reader receives news of its 1937 acceptance by the top French publishing house, Gallimard, as Beauvoir did, from Sartre himself, in a charming, witty letter.

The 1930s also established a lifelong pattern of travels. A handful of almost surreal letters to Beauvoir from a Norwegian cruise with his mother and stepfather is narrated with Sartrean humor that relishes eccentric detail grotesquely juxtaposed: After the ship's drag ball, Sartre—still dressed up as a golden-braided German girl—describes to Beauvoir, by light of the midnight sun, his flirtation earlier that evening with an American woman in a tuxedo. The longest single letter in this collection—almost thirty pages—was written from a Naples squalid and carnal, poised between destruction by millennial epidemic or modern fascism. Sartre analyzes contemporary Neapolitan and ancient Pompeiian social, political, and sexual life largely from visual clues, examining images of surreal, hallucinatory beauty with lucid, almost scientific language.

Deciding to avoid what they saw as the fetters of marriage and children, the couple drew in about them an alternative family, including persons who constantly reappear in these letters; Jacques-Laurent Bost, a student of Sartre's; Mme Morel, known as the Lady; Beauvoir's younger sister, Hélène, known as Poupette. Many of the closest members, among them college friends or former students, lived in neighboring hotel rooms in their *quartier* of choice, Montparnasse. As the group gathered for meals and drinks at the local cafés, the two would draw upon the details of their daily lives, turning mundane events into anecdote with dazzling skill. One friend, Marc Zuore, recognized the drawback that came with the fascination, wondering if "the pleasure one enjoys with such strong personalities isn't sterilizing because . . . one doesn't feel the need for anything else."

In this alternative family, the Kosakiewicz sisters (here called Olga and "Tania" Zazoulich), with their volatile temperaments, were a case apart. Supported by the couple on their uneven path to becoming actresses, each was for a time the object of Sartre's consuming amorous attention while remaining Beauvoir's friend. Between the lines of the stormy dialogues reported here, the reader can follow the sisters' uneasy attempts to retain a certain degree of independence.

Some idea of Sartre's tangled loves appears on the pages of parallel letters to Beauvoir and Louise Védrine written in July of 1939. So long as Beauvoir retained the position of primacy, of intellectual partner and trusted first reader, she was able to ride out the vagaries of his love life, which appear here in his letters to a few other women, and in his detailed accounts to her of his affairs.

For Sartre, 1937 was one of those banner years when everything seems to come together. Despite sporadic complaints about his unorthodox teaching methods, a favorable report from the state examiner earned him a teaching position at the top—Paris. No more stagnation in provincial schools, no more commuting to Paris for a day or two every week. Even more important, where before he had languished among the unknown and obscurely published, he now had final assurance that Gallimard would bring out *Nausea*. He writes to Beauvoir of "walking the streets like an author," ignoring the pebble in his shoe.

The year 1938 brought the sense that the world was moving toward war. Although he analyzed the European crisis with rigor and lucidity, many of Sartre's predictions proved falsely optimistic, perhaps because much of this speculation was obviously meant to allay his correspondents' and his own anxieties. The couple's visit to the Lady's Mediterranean seaside villa in

August of 1939 reads here like a mixture of *Rules of the Game* and *Beat the Devil,* as the house-party pleasures and intrigues spin out, leaving them all but oblivious to the looming war that will define their future and redefine their past.

Sartre had been reading *The Trial* and *The Penal Colony* when on September 2 he was suddenly plunged into the Kafkaesque world of a vast army waiting, seemingly forever, though actually only six months, through a war that wouldn't start, the "phony war" of September 1939 to March 1940. As part of a four-man meteorological unit, he was stationed in a series of small Alsatian villages along the German border, territory he knew well from summer visits to Schweitzer relatives. He was writing every day, as a ward of the state—looking, he said, more like a chauffeur at a country estate than a soldier: "Three letters, five pages of novel, four pages of notebook: in my whole life I've never written so much." He recognized that he was being saved by literature—reading, writing, the crystallization of a philosophy. While his comrades disintegrated from inaction and boredom, he developed ideas that would lead to the turning point of his life.

By late October he was writing to Beauvoir of the need for them to rethink and experience the war together; he had gradually realized in philosophic terms that he had been living inauthentically, without a conscious, active attitude toward his situation—growing up bracketed by two wars. Already living the new ethic before he had fully worked it out, he found it was having an effect on others. Mistler, an army clerk, confessed to a profoundly changed interest in the events around him after Sartre demonstrated how it was *his* (Mistler's) war. The teacher in Sartre was delighted to have so impressed a grown man, "a very different thing from inspiring enthusiasm in a few adolescents."

"Everything of course hinges on ideas of freedom, life, and authenticity," he wrote to Beauvoir. But as he copied it out for her in December, the early version of his new philosophy of commitment is ambivalent in its promise of freedom. A human consciousness wills itself forward to become the basis of its own changed future, only to discover on reaching the future that nothing has fundamentally changed. The mind is still confined by its own horizons, as gratuitous as before. The first vital step is there—recognition of the individual's own facticity, like Sartre's discovery of *his* life situation bounded by two wars. But as yet there is no clear picture of the personal identity achieved through making choices and acting on them, no application of the philosophy to an authentic self-determined life. Or in other words, there is no philosophic reasoning to back up Sartre's intuition that "it's not that man *is*, he *does*." These pages of philosophical essay constitute a precursor to the existentialism that would play the central role in a postwar French society still demoralized by defeat and the German occupation.

This struggle between the obligation to act and the inability to do so is the theme of *L'Age de raison (The Age of Reason)*, first volume of an eventual trilogy called *Les Chemins de la liberté (The Roads to Freedom)*. Sartre encouraged readers to consider its protagonist, the schoolteacher Mathieu, as a wartime extension of *Nausea*'s writer-observer Roquentin. Readers of the letters will recognize some features of the Kosakiewicz sisters in Ivich, of Bost in Boris, of Sartre's old friend Paul Nizan in Brunet, and of Zuore in Daniel.

The relationship between Mathieu and his mistress, Marcelle, is a commentary on traditional sex roles, and the housebound Marcelle could be said to suffer the illness of being female in a prefeminist world. If her dilemma is whether to abort or keep Mathieu's baby, his is how to arrange the abortion. Mathieu uses the freedom he craves merely to come and go in the outside world without commitment. Lying and stealing to finance the abortion, he cannot make up his mind to marry Marcelle. Nor can he follow Brunet's example of dedicated communism.

Mathieu's moment of awakening comes late. The first effects of Sartre's own self-recognition emerged in his philosophy and the fiction that he based on it. Only after returning to occupied Paris did Sartre become politically engaged. He founded a short-lived resistance group called Socialism and Freedom, whose name and aim are a fair summing-up of Sartre's larger politics after the war: to make a third way between a capitalism he rejected out of hand as trivializing and corrupt and a communism embodied by a series of hopeful revolutions that kept going sour.

This volume ends with a New Year's Eve letter full of both uncertainty and closure. Sartre's agitation and preoccupation as he finished his complete draft of *The Age of Reason* were such that he tore up the final three pages and had to patch together the smudged fragments retrieved from the coal bin. In two more weeks he hoped to be on his much-postponed leave in Paris and able to hand Simone de Beauvoir notebooks packed with writing on bad faith, violence, and nothingness that would appear four years later in *Being and Nothingness*. He tells her his joking vision of a future "dictatorship of liberty to force people, through a regime of tortures and arguments, to be free."

The material in this volume is prime Sartre; its detailed observations and conversations, sifted through the letters, became the very currency of his fiction and philosophy. Spontaneous, as Sartre promised, the correspondence nonetheless reveals the art of the trained thinker and writer.

Sartre and Beauvoir rejected the familiar address form of "*tu*" in favor of the "*vous*," good vestigial bourgeois that they remained in some habits, these startling renegades. And they developed a private language deliberately crafted of philosophical terms, university argot, slang from new American novels, colloquial catchphrases, and individual words deflected from ordinary use and made precious by invisible quote marks. Sartre insisted that this language—abundant here and spoken by characters in their fiction—*represented them*, sublimating their love while disguising it from the public. Determined to write the same language they spoke, he dismissed accusations of artificial or sloppy speech.

Sartre clamored for long, detailed letters and gave Beauvoir the same, lingering over vignettes to extend her pleasure and contact with him, including everything from philosophy to menus, budgets, critiques, and gossip. To that close, perceptive reader Simone de Beauvoir, they were also a barometer of Sartre's psyche: "How could I have seemed sad?" he retorts, before realizing that he had indeed been going through another bout of depression over "Tania."

Simone de Beauvoir is present in virtually all the letters, even when they are addressed to someone else. Sartre enjoys anticipating her response, occasionally framing her reply and even her rebuttal to the comment he assigned her, a trait that makes the letters seem more than a monologue, better than half a correspondence. And with a gift of empathetic dramatization, his habit of picturing her wearing her "little turban" at their last meeting or running down a train corridor at four in the morning makes presence out of absence, an illusion that gives way to a sudden eclipse of the reader's view during times when the two were together. This sensitive flattery, portraying a woman for her own benefit as a gesture of love, may help explain the often-asked question how so many women could have found Sartre so charming.

The sustained daily output of wartime letters, from September through December 1939, comprises more than half this volume—a proportion continued in the second, final, volume, as Sartre becomes involved in the real conflict. But for the two of them, apart and isolated by the circumstances of war, it was through the letters that they achieved perhaps their greatest interdependence and love.

This collection, edited by Simone de Beauvoir, herself not well and constrained by the tensions between Sartre's survivors, was published in 1983, three years after his death. It appeared soon after Sartre's *Les Carnets d'un drôle de guerre*, 1983 *(The War Diaries*, 1984), and Beauvoir's *La Cérémonie des adieux (Adieux: A Farewell to Sartre)*, 1984, but before the posthumous biographies written about each of them. In the French edition, critics praised the insights into the development of this supremely influential thinker, the humor and anecdotal skill, the tender side of his deep dependency on Beauvoir. But there was also protest about the missing letters, the cuts to protect third parties—omissions that may be corrected with time. This collection is mirrored by Beauvoir's letters to Sartre, found and published after her death though she had long denied their survival. She inquires and reports in equal detail, warm and solicitous, more discreet about her sexual life, less adventurous in proposing philosophic ideas, forthright and insightful in her appraisal of his writing.

The title of the English-language edition of these letters, *Witness to My Life*, is part of Sartre's own description of them, as conveyed by Simone de Beauvoir in her preface. But the phrase recalls a writer from the previous century who summed up his time in much the same way that Sartre did his own. Adèle Hugo's memoir of her husband is called *Victor Hugo, by a Witness to His Life*. Hugo's funeral was the largest for any literary figure in his century, Sartre's the largest in the twentieth century—over fifty thousand attended. The intertwined lives of Sartre and Beauvoir signal a new way of human flourishing, a peculiarly twentieth-century advance that doesn't necessitate the sacrificial destruction of the women around the totemic male. At Sartre's death, the central mourner was the strong, independent woman who lived out a mandate to be free and had the accomplishments—*The Second Sex*, the novels and memoirs, the life of struggle and reflection and production, the international following—to prove it.

Lee Fahnestock and Norman MacAfee

Preface to the French Edition

When they were young, Guille, who was Sartre's best friend for many years, liked to say, "In centuries to come, my boy, literary criticism will cite 'Jean-Paul Sartre, letter writer par excellence, author of a few literary and philosophic works.'" During his interviews[1] with me in the summer of 1974, Sartre described what these letters meant to him:

> They were the transcription of immediate life. . . . They were spontaneous work. As far as I was concerned, they could be published. . . . In the back of my mind I had the idea they would be published after my death. . . . In effect my letters were a witness to my life.

So in publishing this correspondence, I am simply carrying out one of his wishes. Of course, it would be nice if all his letters—an immense number—could be collected, but this would surely take a great deal of time. I preferred not to delay publication of the letters addressed to me—and of some others left or entrusted to me by those who received them.

They refer to a recent past, and so I did not feel I had the right to publish the entire text. I have not altered one iota in anything concerning my relationship with Sartre. But so as not to embarrass certain third parties— or persons close to them—I have deleted certain passages, changed certain names. I was the one who decided on practically all these changes. A few

---

[1]*Éditions Gallimard, pp. 228–9. (SdB).* Simone de Beauvoir, *La Cérémonie des adieux,* suivi de *Entretiens avec Jean-Paul Sartre* (Paris, 1981). *Adieux: A Farewell to Sartre,* trans. Patrick O'Brian (New York, 1984).

were requested by Mme Elkaïm-Sartre. In any case, I will entrust the original manuscript to the Bibliotheçue Nationale, which will deal with it at the prescribed time.

Despite these very minor reservations, for all who are interested in Sartre, this collection, which covers a period of almost forty years, 1926 to 1963, has the irreplaceable value of a vast "witness to my life," the "transcription of my immediate life."

Simone de Beauvoir

WITNESS TO MY LIFE

1926

To Simone Jollivet[1]

(a true letter)[2]

Let me tell you about myself—you'll understand why soon enough. You accused me of being neither simple nor true, but I want you to see whether that comes easily for me.

Basically, I'm a man of many sides.

On the one hand I'm extremely ambitious. But about what? When I think of glory, I imagine a ballroom with gentlemen in evening clothes and ladies in low-cut dresses all raising their glasses to me. It's pure Épinal,[3] of course, but ever since childhood I've had that image. It doesn't tempt me, but glory does, because I want to be far above ordinary people, whom I scorn. But, more specifically, I have the ambition to create. I must construct, construct anything at all but construct. I've done some of everything, from philosophical systems (idiotic of course, I was 16) to symphonies. I wrote my first novel when I was 8. I cannot look at a blank sheet of paper without wanting to write something on it. I get this feeling, it's ridiculous, really— this enthusiasm—only in the presence of certain works, because I imagine that I could remake them, that I could create them on my own, and if I am writing to you today it is because I have just read one such work and was

---

[1]*Whom I call Camille in* La Force de l'âge [The Prime of Life] *and whose relationship with Sartre I described at length.* (SdB) When Sartre met Simone Jollivet (born Simone-Camille Sans) at the funeral of his younger cousin Annie, she was living a bohemian, liberated life in Toulouse.

[2]A remark directed at her description of him referred to two lines below.

[3]A French town that gave its name to colored prints produced there in the eighteenth and nineteenth centuries, typically of slightly pompous military figures.

immediately seized by the need to construct something: this letter. The problem is, I don't like anything I produce, I don't have my own genre to write in, so to speak, I constantly change styles but without ever really pleasing myself. Actually I please very few others either. All this is so banal. And unfortunately, what's more, deep down, I have the personality of a little spinster. As you may not have guessed, I was born with a personality to match my face: foolishly, stupidly emotional, cowardly, self-indulgent. My sentimentality can make me teary-eyed about the least little thing. I've cried like a baby at plays and movies, over novels. I've had unjustified, implausible attacks of pity and cowardice and weakness of character, that have relegated me to the nadir of failure in the eyes of my friends and relatives.

So, those are my two fundamental tendencies. The primary one is ambition. I was dissatisfied with myself very early on, and the first real constructing I did was on my own character. I worked on two things: to give myself will and to suppress the second tendency, which shamed me deeply. To strengthen my will, I employed the method of the gratuitous act: I would do, with *no* reason whatever, something I found very disagreeable. For example, my first gratuitous act was to toss beneath the wheels of the La Rochelle tram a hat I'd been coveting for two weeks, which my mother had finally just bought me. It was stupid, but I was 14. That got me the last spanking my mother ever gave me. To master my character, I forced myself to conceal it. Previously I'd been very talkative, but the life given to me at La Rochelle,[4] which I've already told you about, on the one hand, and my desire to change, on the other, made me withdraw. I tell you this candidly: it's the first time in seven years that I have gone into it at such length, and this is because I am sure of myself now. But don't get the idea that I have stifled all these grotesque tendencies in myself: they still exist. Thus I was cowardly and self-indulgent and still am. When a dog near me barks I still might just tremble. And yet I believe that when I'm firmly decided on something, there is no fear that can make me retreat. But all this results in:

First, that these tendencies are constantly trying to reappear, and in repressing them I assume that artificial attitude you reproach me for. I am never real since I'm always searching for ways to modify, to recreate: I will never feel the happiness (?) of being able to act spontaneously.

Second, that when I feel a sincere emotion, a feeling that I think can be expressed, I'm absolutely incapable of doing so. Either I babble or say just

---

[4]With the remarriage of his widowed mother and the family's relocation to that port city, Sartre had entered a rougher world.

the opposite of what I wanted to say—or I express the equivalent of that feeling through refined, meaningless phrases—or else, as happens more often, I express nothing, fleeing all expression: the wisest course. Besides, of course, at present I keep an infinitely tighter rein on my emotions, and it takes a great deal to agitate me.

I've told you just about everything; I'll only add that I have a certain ideal of character to attain: moral health, that is, a perfect balance. I'm still very far from it. But I have reached the point of never again letting anything show through except what I wish. I'm exaggerating; to be absolutely honest I'd have to make that "almost never."

In writing out this rapid analysis I found the balance sheet not very attractive and would have liked to embellish it. I decided against that because it is preferable, once I have begun speaking about myself, to do so with complete sincerity. But I know what I'm exposing myself to: you will discover that for now I seem very little like Erich von Stroheim, your model for a "man of will." This much is sure: I wasn't born with an auspicious character, except for intelligence. For the rest, there's still not much there, yet whatever character I do have I owe to myself, which is something. Once more, I know I'm courting "rejection." You're too romantic for all this to please you, but if there weren't that risk, I believe my self-portrait would have been pure fantasy. Basically it is yet another gratuitous act. As for you, if you're more natural than I, it's because you were born with a character far superior to mine. So it's only natural that you should show it. But perhaps it is unjust to reproach me for what are—in my eyes at least—my good points.

The two young ladies in the letter[5] do not exist.

To Simone Jollivet

[Before April]

My dear little girl

You mustn't tire of this; be patient. These last few days I was all ready to see you; but a hitch due to the stupidity of one of my collaborators keeps me from giving the publisher the translation of the book that should provide me the money for my trip. I won't be able to come to Toulouse now till about April 10th. This year has seen a series of disappointments of every sort, but particularly financial ones. I dream of a year 1926–27 in which money's

---

[5]*Lost letter, the first written to Simone Jollivet. (SdB)*

less scarce, allowing me to visit Toulouse once a month, the way M. de Norpois would go to see his friend Mme de Villeparisis.[1] School[2] is particularly dreary at this point. We've just presented our Annual Revue, with some success. (You'll find it reviewed in last Sunday's *L'Oeuvre*—and a photo of me as Lanson is in Monday's *L'Oeuvre*.) And we're all knocked out by this morning after, totally hungover and punchy. Also I'm particularly affected by the approaching Easter vacation. I'll be staying by myself here in Paris. I know the pleasures of such vacations, wandering the streets without spending money—to economize so I can come to see you—allowing myself the luxury of a 3-franc movie ticket twice a week. I have just been through a battery of exams—which I passed, as usual—and now I cling to my desk, stupefied. I'm reading hardly anything. No, I am: Henry de Montherlant's[3] novel serialized in the *Journal*, *Les Bestiaires [The Bullfighters]*. Read it, it's quite remarkable. You'll find in the young man Alban the concept of love I like: the knight with the gauntlet we've spoken about. It takes place in your beloved Spain. Do you like my friends? Who do you like best? At the moment they're aimless, endlessly repeating senile little phrases, wandering from one group to the next, silently munching sugar cubes, unable to get up and go. They're always eager to confide in someone, which just goes to show how confused they are. They would like to talk about their personal traits and tell those little lies one does in such a state. My presence alone keeps them from doing so, for I hate weakness and confidences told halfheartedly, without reflection. But behind my back they must be babbling on like old women. Today Canguilhem said to me, "I like you because you're basically very sad and it's only to break out of it that you amuse yourself by telling stupid jokes and fighting with Larroutis." I don't know why that flattered me. Yet you know how I hate this melancholy. Here's a beautiful thought on that subject, from a philosopher I'll recommend when we've *spoken* about him together a bit— Alain:[4] "Hegel says that the immediate or natural soul is always enveloped in melancholy, as though overwhelmed. That seemed to me to have beauti-

---

[1] In Marcel Proust's *À la Recherche du temps perdu*.

[2] Along with Raymond Aron, Paul Nizan, and many other writers and philosophers of his time, Sartre studied at the prestigious École Normale Supérieure—the "Norm Sup"—on the Rue d'Ulm, near the Sorbonne. Its students, with traditions and a jargon all their own, prepare for top teaching posts in the state-run universities and secondary schools, the lycées.

[3] Novelist and dramatist (1896–1972). His works examine themes of sexual stereotypes— male courage, female sentimentality—while often succumbing to the stereotypes. *The Bullfighters* (1926) is about attempts to find the peacetime equivalents of the peak experiences of the war. Fearing blindness, he committed suicide.

[4] Pseudonym of Émile-Auguste Chartier (1868–1951), influential philosopher and teacher.

ful depth. When self-reflection doesn't make it right, it's a waste of time. And whoever interrogates himself answers poorly. Thought that contemplates itself alone is really just boredom or sadness. Give it a try. Ask yourself, 'What on earth shall I read to pass the time?' You're already yawning. You must concentrate. Desire languishes when it does not lead to will. And these remarks are enough to judge the psychologists who would like every individual to study his own thoughts as one does the grasses and the shells. But to think is to will." (*Propos sur le bonheur* ["Thoughts on Happiness"])

I'm thinking of very little. The notebook I kept two years ago fills me now with shame. Then I knew it all. Now I feel that I'm specializing slowly. For the past few days I've applied all my ardor and strength to solving a problem of pure psychology, a problem of detail. It's time to react. I'm giving little thought to that beautiful novel I will write for you. Yet I do think about it and I believe it will please you. Right now I live a bit too much on the admiration of others.

What is this very beautiful way you have of loving me, my dear little girl? Is there still some tenderness in it? It's your tenderness I'm particularly fond of. I'm swamped by the trappings of intelligence and weary of intellectual love affairs. What I need is warm and foolish tenderness, the kind I feel for you right now. I only want to kiss you and tell you sentimental nonsense. Put your love to the test: would it hold up if I did *only that* in Toulouse? Tell me about it in writing.

Read *Ariel ou La vie de Shelley* ["Ariel: The Life of Shelley"] by André Maurois.[5] It's not very profound or well written, but it is the novelized biography of a great English poetic genius. You'll find it interesting. I'm hardly interested anymore in anything but accounts of great men's lives; I want to search them for some prophecy of my own life. Unfortunately *by my age* they had a purity and enthusiasm I've never had. They each vow, in the forest or beside some stream, to dedicate their lives to this or that. I don't even feel like doing that, and anyway I'd be too afraid of seeming ridiculous to myself. As guarantee of my future value I have only my immense pride and a hazy sense of my life. That must seem quite incomprehensible to you: I mean the mere fact of feeling alive is a guarantee. Here is what I'll have

---

[5]Nom de plume of Emile Herzog (1885–1967), an Alsatian and student of Alain at the lycée in Rouen. Known in the 1920s as a humorous novelist, Maurois turned to history and literary biographies (of Voltaire, Hugo, George Sand, Proust). A year before his death he published the critical study *From Gide to Sartre*.

the hero of "your" novel[6] say: "I'm a genius, because I am alive. You people indirectly appear to me and no doubt suggest remarkable ideas to me, and I call you intelligent or stupid according to what you offer me. But I suppose I'm pleased that you're alive. As for me, my God! Oh how I'd love others to feel my life as I do, overflowing, tumultuous, encompassing all my horizons. I see it everywhere. If only I could express it, tear it out of me. Then I would truly be the genius that it is my right to be. One man alone lives for me: myself. And the mystery is that it is precisely me; I cannot conceive that I will die." What do you think of that? Alas, there are so many proud people in my family, I sometimes fear my pride is simply some hereditary malady.

Anyway, read *Ariel* and tell me whether you prefer your Jean-Paul to this Percy Bysshe Shelley whom women adored—or whether you prefer Shelley. He was very handsome.

I love you in every way you could desire, dearest.

Herewith a photo of me in the Revue, which was called "À l'ombre des vieilles Billes en Fleurs" [Within the Old Biddies' Grove].[7] It shows M. Lanson (me) granting an interview to a reporter (played by Péron.)[8] I danced naked with a half-naked Nizan[9] in that Revue.

To Simone Jollivet

[April]

And yet we should come to some understanding. Do you want to see me or not? I will *absolutely* not tolerate this habit of considering me the guy one writes a letter to punctually every two weeks to string him along and on whom one bestows a charitable three days a year visitation. "Not free, pointless to come Sunday." Now look, did you think *I* was free? On Friday noon I

---

[6]Sartre's unfinished novel "Une Défaite" ["A Defeat"], dedicated to Simone Jollivet, was inspired by the relationship of Richard and Cosima Wagner and Friedrich Nietzsche, as well as Sartre's experiences tutoring in the Morel household and his affair with Jollivet. The surviving version is in Sartre, *Écrits de Jeunesse*, edited by Michel Contat and Michel Rybalka (Paris, 1990).

[7]Punning on the title of the second volume of Proust's *À la Recherche du temps perdu*: *À l'Ombre des jeunes filles en fleur* (*Within a Budding Grove* in the C. K. Scott Moncrieff translation).

[8]*A fellow student at the École Normale Supérieure and specialist in English, who was quite close to Sartre and later died after being deported.* (SdB)

[9]Paul Nizan (1905–40), a close friend of Sartre's from the Lycée Henri IV and the École Normale. He wrote six books, including the highly regarded novel *Antoine Bloyé* (1933).

had not a red cent of travel money and was tied up in a dozen different directions for the Easter holiday. But I managed. By 4 o'clock I had the money and I was free. (At 4:30 I received your cheery little telegram.) When one is tied up one breaks free, simple as that. How much weight could or should be given to your idle little pastimes next to the fact that you, who claim to love me, hadn't seen me for six months?

At the very least it would have been natural to apologize, to make some excuse and write immediately. I've waited till today, and I note that you've retreated behind a complacent indifference, content at having shown me the door as you did your fiancé.

What does this all mean? Are you getting tired of me? So soon? Silly girl who just 4 months ago wrote, "I love you even more than my mother!" At any rate, you should be brave enough to say so. But you're selfish, frivolous, and cowardly to boot. "The rooster and the pearl," you said one day when, after some other such quarrel, I had acted a little frosty. But it is I who am the pearl. Who has made you what you are? Who is trying to keep you from turning into a bourgeoise, an aesthete, a whore? Who has taken charge of your intelligence? I alone. I believe I don't deserve to be sent packing like your Spanish pen pal or that fool Voivenel, whose books (*Cafard—Remy de Gourmont as Seen by His Doctor*) are total idiocies.

I'm getting tired of this nonsense. Never have I been closer to abandoning you to your own little crowd. *Let me propose this:* Let me see you at your place, or we can meet in Toulouse on Tuesday, April 13, 1926, at a time of your choice. I must have a reply before Saturday, April 10. If yes, I'll reach my own conclusions about your feelings, down there. If no, you'll hear no more of me.

To Simone Jollivet

My dear little girl,

This letter, which I'll prudently mail from Paris, is being written in Toulouse, from the Café Régina.

It is neither a correction nor a supplement to what we said last night, but simply a continuation of our conversation. Having to wait for my train, I thought to myself that I could do nothing better than write you. You are, particularly at this moment, "my little girl." You were not altogether so last night, or, if you like, you were a little girl instructing the grown-ups, as in the tale where the son teaches his parents to treat his grandfather with filial piety. You were holding over me all the superiority of your candor. The expression on your face was *very beautiful*, tender, noble, and serene, and on the way back to the station I marveled that you, with that wonderful expression, were the same person who gets drunk at dances in Toulouse. And, truly, I felt somewhat inferior to you last night, up to the moment when I saw such honesty in your eyes that I trusted you. That trust, my little girl whom I've found again, I of course lost in the Allée Saint-Michel. Anything else would have been a surprise. I'm a novice in these matters and you're so many-sided, but this letter is an act of faith. I wanted to write it, then I thought you had put on an act and I was afraid I might be handed over, bound at the ankles, to a flirt, then I was ashamed of being afraid, and finally here it is. And *I do trust you.* Last night taught me a strange humility. Imagine that Cosima sees Frédéric again after Richard's death and shows him that the brutal mistrust of women that he took for strength was really only self-protection and weakness. That's what it is. Will something good come of it? That is what I don't know yet. At any rate I now know that most of my mistrust was merely superficial shame for overly confident thoughts concerning you and a hateful fear of ridicule. And I offer you the proof of my trust in you, admitting what I didn't dare tell you out of desire to seem tough: that I want to be not the first but the *only one* in your heart, dear girl. I have known this for a long time and didn't expect to tell you. I'm not telling you now to make you change on this point, but to offer you as a mark of faith the most painful secret I could give you. (And even that is not entirely too candid: even as I write, I faintly hope that you will change, but *don't change.*) Never scorn Chaplinesque gestures. In trying to understand what Charlie Chaplin wants to be as "the little tramp," learn the psychology of my "innate soul," this sad soul that commits those follies I spoke of at the movies. My little girl, stay tender, if not for my sake then at least for yours. Harshness is not your style. From that standpoint, in those escapades that I reproach you for, you're playing a role that is anything but you. I ask no more than this: that out of love for me you apply to your world the tenderness and *candor* you have shown me. Do you understand? If not, ask me to explain; it's important. I'll tell you what I did after leaving you—you'll enjoy this. I walked to the end of the Allée Saint-Michel and found a sort of a garden which is—at least at this time of day—the prettiest thing I've seen in all Toulouse. I sat down on a bench and dropped off thinking of a mysterious rabbit hunt. I slept for half a minute and was roused by the custodian going by, a likable old man. I'd fallen asleep with my pipe in one hand and a matchbox in the other. I absently lit up, thinking that it would be lovely to spend a moment or two talking with the old man, in the state of quiet sadness we sometimes see in certain heroes of novels after an important, emotional scene (for instance Myshkin talking to Rogozhin after Nastasya's murder— more or less). Then he came up to me and said, "You're up early." I answered that I was waiting for the train, that I was from Paris, and he said, "Paris? My son just got back from there." And he told me the story of his son the captain in scraps of charmingly simple dialogue. For instance: "The colonel said to my son when he graduated from Saint-Cyr (13 years ago), 'Lazy, you haven't done your work.' 'Yes, Colonel, I have.' 'No, you haven't done your work.' 'Colonel, I believe I have.' Then the colonel said to him, 'Well, all right, I believe you, you've done your work,' and gave him his second lieu- tenant's stripes, which he'd been hiding in his pocket." I've shown you the old man. I didn't consider him senile, and I thought he was full of goodwill and simple pride in his son. It would please me to have found and, without the least reservation, recognized goodness itself right after leaving you. It'll undoubtedly be a long time before I'm in the right situation to find it again. At the moment I hardly feel sad at leaving you, and I love you with a simplicity worthy of the old custodian. I don't know if this letter is worth anything. I'm half asleep. Doubtless on rereading it in Paris I'll find it stupid, but I'm sure I'll send it to you, for it does homage to the marvelous little girl you were at five this morning.

I love you now more than I have ever loved you.

My dear little girl, I'm picking up again, an hour later. This time, to tell you that going away is terribly painful. I suppose the insomnia that makes me feel so weak right now has something to do with it. Nonetheless I have just been wandering around the town totally dazed by the pain. I know it will go away on the train, but my new ethics, however new and strong, is not enough to protect the pathetic character I am right now. Though as you've said before, it doesn't spoil my appetite: I'm eating some croissants at this very moment.

But I swear to you that this 'low' that we ought to endure together is no fun facing alone.

On the train. My dear little girl, my moral resolve has worked. I'm simply *very* happy. I love a little girl who loves me, who's precisely the little girl I need, I'm firmly resolved to return to see her before July, I trust in her, the countryside is lovely in the sunlight. Perfection. I'm stronger than in Sep- tember, when I loved you less; I went away hoping to see you soon and yet was very sad. Today I don't know for sure if you'll be able to come to Paris, I love you all the more and I'm full of joy. But that may also be because I love you more and *better*.

To Simone Jollivet

If I sent you a second letter,[1] humble, repentant, it's not that I thought your letter was written in the grip of rage, but I feared that after writing it, when you'd received my letter No. 1, seeing its futility, you might be angry at yourself for the somewhat childish act, and by adopting a self-effacing attitude, I hoped to avoid that anxiety for you.

Your last letter is delightful. You have (voluntarily?) corrected your little faults, and that pleased me very much. I don't know, for instance, what baroque desire possessed you to ask for a photo of me as a child. Do explain what got into you. It was hard to find. Up to 5 I was a gorgeous baby with the slightly conventional look so pleasing to the average mama. So pictures of me were in great demand. After 5, that ephemeral splendor disappeared along with my shorn locks; I turned ugly as a frog, much uglier than now. So nobody wanted to take my picture anymore. They feared I might cloud the photographic plate, the way shocking sights cause pregnant women to miscarry. So for those 2 contrary reasons it was difficult to find pictures of myself. My mother has a few, but she would defend them to her last breath. She leaned against her desk with the tragic air French nurses adopt when the Germans try to enter the cellar where the French wounded lie. I had to withdraw. My grandmother proved less resistant but much too curious about what I wanted to do with a photo. Finally I forced open a drawer and found this overly pretty picture giving promise of a Byron (odious man) but certainly not your humble servant. Happily, I also found a horror, the small snapshot of myself mugging, uglier even than in real life. I'm sending it on too, for you to average them out.

I congratulate my student for taking up the piano again. But why do you scorn the jazz flute? It's a splendid instrument. In the high notes it sounds like a nasal but charming human voice, suddenly produced by an instrument, as though it were coming to life; it is a kind of flower that emerges from a flute and abruptly retracts in the lower notes, suddenly sounding mechanical. The effect is surprising. The voice shatters, the instrument reappears. So try

---

[1]A *lost letter*. (SdB)

to listen for the jazz flute in the 2 blues "Lonesome Night" and "Shanghai Lullaby"—I'm sure you'll be delighted with it.

Your sadness came, so you tell me, from what you foresaw your life would be if you didn't succeed. But it won't be like that if you trust me. I want to give you a mental attitude that in the midst of a totally ordinary existence will keep your life from being botched, so that you will not be a Madame Bovary but an artist, with no regrets or melancholy. And you, you ingrate, say that I can find no outlet for your energy. So go and find it among the people who approached you and did as much for you as I have, and above all, what I will do.

So do write, don't be afraid of words, you'll do them more harm than they'll do to you. Don't worry about them. Know that no one can say exactly what he wants. The trick is to give the sentence an air of incompletion, of mystery, of the infinitely approximate, that entices the reader to do the work of completion without words. You will surely find fulfillment that way.

Practical advice.

1. Don't let your mother write too many letters to Aunt Hélène. When she came to Paris she raised doubts in my mother's heart by telling her about you and me in terms that were really offensive to me. She's always searching for gossip; she pokes around for turds the way others pluck flowers. (Forgive the comparison—it is tasteless but springs from sincere indignation.) My mother, by the way, was on her best behavior and will be as encouraging as possible about my trip to Thiviers.[2]

2. My uncle Joseph, twice alerted by me about my arrival, gives no signs of life. He has a quite indecent abscess; will he want and will he be able to put me up there? If he can't, I would have to stay at the hotel, in which case, since—quite rightly—you care about what people think, perhaps you might need a chaperon (father, mother, etc.), but that would be a last resort, for I would far rather see you alone. I'll turn the heavy artillery on my uncle, namely my mother, who will bring up the subject of pecuniary considerations, to which he is not indifferent. I'll keep you posted.

3. Don't let her know you're coming till I get there. Can you put it off until the 20th? I have some minor problems to keep me in and around Paris till the 15th. So I'll get to Thiviers on the 15th. Supposing that *by some remote chance* the trip to Thiviers doesn't work out, think of someplace else, if need be, where I could find you. We must be ready for any eventuality.

I have to confess that what delayed my last letter a little was that I did

---

[2]Town in Périgord associated with the Sartre side of the family.

it over twice. I was convinced I'd told you a story I was repeating in the aforesaid letter. I dread repetitions. Anyway, I'm arming myself with philosophy. In Thiviers we'll end up going over and over what's already been said, I know, even though we do have many new things to say to one another; forewarned, we can try to avoid that. Besides, I should have put the endlessly repeated story in my letter, which would have taught you the charm you'll find in marriage. I've seen it happen a hundred times: the husband retelling for the thousandth time stories of his youth. Learn from the marvelous behavior of wives in such cases: they smile, never taking their eyes off the old chatterbox as if it were their first hearing, and seem to appreciate his secrets, carefully concealing their own.

To Simone Jollivet

My dear little girl

For a long time I've been wanting to write to you in the evening after one of those outings with friends that I will soon be describing in "A Defeat," the kind when the world is ours. I wanted to bring you my conqueror's joy and lay it at your feet, as they did in the Age of the Sun King. And then, tired out by all the shouting, I always simply went to bed. Today I'm doing it to feel the pleasure you don't yet know, of turning abruptly from friendship to love, from strength to tenderness. Tonight I love you in a way that you have not known in me: I am neither worn down by travels nor wrapped up in the desire for your presence. I am mastering my love for you and turning it inwards as a constituent element of myself. This happens much more often than I admit to you, but seldom when I'm writing to you. Try to understand me: I love you while paying attention to external things. At Toulouse I simply loved you. Tonight I love you *on a spring evening*, I love you with the window open. You are mine, and things are mine, and my love alters the things around me and the things around me alter my love.

My dear little girl, as I've told you, what you're lacking is friendship. But now is the time for more practical advice. Couldn't you find a *woman friend*? How can Toulouse fail to contain one intelligent young woman worthy of you? But you wouldn't have to love her. Alas, you're always ready to give your love, it's the easiest thing to get from you. I'm not talking about your love for me, which is well beyond that, but you are lavish with little secondary loves, like that night in Thiviers when you loved that peasant walking downhill in the dark, whistling away, who turned out to be me. Get to know the feeling, free of tenderness, that comes from being two. It's hard, because all friendship, even between two red-blooded men, has its moments of love. I have only to console my grieving friend to love him; it's a feeling easily weakened and distorted. But you're capable of it, and you *must* experience it. And so, despite your fleeting misanthropy, have you imagined what a lovely adventure it would be to search Toulouse for a woman who would be worthy of you and whom you wouldn't be in love with? Don't bother with the physical side or the social situation. And search honestly. And if you find nothing, turn Henri Pons, whom you scarcely love anymore, into a *friend*.

What have you learned about the character of Jean Douchez? Did you find the little picture? Is he better or worse than you used to think, and what are your feelings for him?

I won't write anymore about it tonight, because I'm going to sleep, and I won't return to the letter tomorrow, as I don't like going back to an unfinished letter any more than relighting a dead cigar. I'll simply add that I have just seen a *splendid* film called *Déchéance* ["Downfall"], which you must go and see too, if it comes to Toulouse.

Yes you can indeed read that book on Edgar Poe by Lauvrière. Here's how: it's a doctoral thesis, and every thesis is distributed to every municipal and university library. Ask Jean Douchez or someone else to get it for you.

I love you with all my heart and soul.

To Simone Jollivet

How proud you are of your logic. You speak only of logical refutations, your letters are dense argumentations peppered with "therefores" and "consequentlys" that detract from any pleasure I might find in reading them. Therefore, give up logic! It has never advanced anybody one single step. Try just as hard to avoid contradictions, but if you occasionally find one, don't be afraid, they don't bite. There are so many of them! The 5 or 6 great philosophers that the university curriculums required me to study this year, well-regarded characters all, teem with contradictions. It didn't bother them in the least. Just remember that they lived only for their systems and that they could live in peace with this contradictory and ill-connected thought and that some of them like Plato and Descartes had the most beautiful lives in the world (I'll tell you about Descartes to show you a man beyond love); and who discovered their contradictions? Swarms of pedants descending on their works. Remember that logic is the daily bread of impotent intellectuals.

Try to acquire ideas in other ways, *without reasoning*. You will see how they spring up on their own, you ponder an image in your mind, all at once you feel a swelling, like a bubble, also a sort of direction indicated to you, almost all the work is done, all it needs is clarifying. But to find them you must renounce logic, which is artificial and keeps you away from the truth. We'll talk later about that. But don't inflict any further scholarly argumentation on me. I have a more serious reproach to make: you tell me you're sad, that my book saddens you. Do you expect me to soften before this interesting pose you decided to adopt, first for your own benefit and then for mine? There was a time when I was inclined toward that kind of playacting, I was saddened for general reasons, as you are, I bewailed the meanness of men, bewailed my moral solitude as a misunderstood man (!). Nowadays I hate and scorn those who, like you, indulge their brief hours of sadness. What disgusts me about it is the shameful little comedy rooted in a physical state of torpor that we play out for ourselves. Without believing them, we think things like "Perhaps in the end I am worth nothing at all" or "Maybe I will be unhappy all the rest of my life." What delightful corrupt pleasure there is in imagining a dreary life, when we actually feel assured of the contrary. We are full of self-pity. Serious effort is out of the question—working, for instance. Sadness goes hand in hand with laziness. And we feel we must make cinematic gestures for our own benefit: we let our bodies droop despondently, we let things fall from our hands, feigning indifference; we sigh in a certain way—you know, widening the mouth as though to say *ee*, we give an occasional smile of melancholy or disdain, every five minutes we shrug our shoulders like someone with no time to waste on such trifles, someone who will banish sadness— and we don't banish it. You revel in it to the point of writing to me, 500 kilometers away, who will very likely not be in the same mood: "I'm sad." You might as well tell it to the League of Nations. This state of mind is really odd. It has a thousand drawbacks. The worst is that it dulls your sensitivity. Once you've given in to this little game often enough you'll lose the ability to suffer, an ability indispensable to your goal. Assume it's a taut rope. If you continually tug on it, it will slacken. But it is indispensable to suffer at least twice a year, and to be ever prepared to do so. That changes our outlook a great deal, it deepens a knowledge of ourselves and provides real experience (not that abstract experience you get with your slave).[1] Now, I've known a lot of melancholy people. Most, gnawed by a causeless inner sadness, basically

---

[1]*Zina, a little gypsy who had been adopted as a child by Mme Jollivet and raised with Simone, whom she adored. (SdB)*

a playful sadness they don't take too seriously, are practically insensitive. The worst disasters that can befall them they accept, hardly feeling them. That's the greatest calamity. Be very wary of it. You should understand too that sadness accompanies imagination, reverie, and you should take considerable precautions against that. Remember Descartes's words: "I can say with truth that the principal rule I have always observed in my studies and the one I believe to have helped me most in acquiring some knowledge has been that I have never devoted more than *a very few hours a day to thoughts that engage the imagination* and a very few hours per year to those that engage the understanding alone, and that I have given all the rest of my time to the relaxation of the senses and repose of the mind, thereby devoting myself to emulating those who, in looking at the green of the woods or the flight of a bird, are persuaded they are thinking of nothing at all." Apply yourself to that, with the caveat that the flying bird must be *your* bird, the woods *your* woods, and to achieve this it's not that you must feel it, you must lightly transform it. A nebulous formula, you say? I'll explain it all to you. But try it without me first. Sadness, to come back to that, is the one thing in the world on which the will can do the most. If, on your melancholy evening, you'd been made to saw some wood, your sadness would have disappeared in 5 minutes. Saw away, mentally, of course. Stand erect, stop playacting, get busy, *write*: that's the best remedy for a literary temperament like yours. Get on with your novel, transform your sadness, turn it into the emotion in your writing. The results will be good. Don't object that melancholy is of your century: after all, you are living in ours. Watch out that your innocent nineteenth-century habit doesn't gradually transform you, unadapted, into a *failure*. Always be gay. If you're really in pain someday, let me know. I've learned to be consoling because, though I still don't understand how it happens, I've been given countless secrets. Actually, this is a problem I often think about—why do I attract them like this? If you have a solution, tell me, you'd be doing me a real service. At any rate, I would use all my art of consolation to help you, if necessary, just as I put all that I know at your disposal. Of course, I know as well as you that Toulouse is far from Paris, so in transit everything I write cools off; I'm saying it badly and you don't understand very well, you revolt, I'm wasting my time trying to convince you, I'll have to work fast and well in Thiviers to tell you the basics of what I have to tell you.

You've been kind enough to worry about the packages I've sent you—you want to save me trouble. Soon you will be sending me a book of stamps to save me the price of postage on my letters. Don't you see the ridiculous and deeply wounding side to that? You have one possible excuse, that you are probably embarrassed to have books around without being able to account for how you got them. Otherwise it is inexcusable. So don't feed me the odd sugar cube, as though I were your poodle. So I won't send you any more books today—I'll stop sending things until you've told me whether it is really to spare me the bother or rather to spare yourself embarrassment that you wrote me such delightful thoughts, but I do recommend one: *Les Rêveurs éveillés* ["The Dreamers Awakened"] by Adrien Borel and Gil Rotin, which appeared in *Documents Bleus*, published by the NRF.

"The student hasn't yet surpassed the teacher?" But he'll never know on his own. We always maintain a vague respect for the old teacher who berated us. When I see you I'll get some idea of what you have become and whether you've surpassed me. My final service to you will be to show you how superior you are to me.

To Simone Jollivet

My dear Myette

Today no letter from you, which makes me happy because it proves that my confidence and joy are genuine. The whole day has been one long ode to you, to joy.

I've launched into a complicated theory that I'm in the process of developing, on the role of the image for the artist, and it will be quite wonderful. Then perhaps, when it's finished, I may have a complete Aesthetics. That would please me very much. In other matters, I have finished Chapter 1 of *Empedocles*, in which Empedocles, following the order of Lenten sermons—from Hell to Heaven—plunges the wretched youth into the depths of Contingency and completely stuns him by singing him the famous *Song*. I'll copy it out for you in 5 minutes (the *Song*). For Empedocles in toto, it will be finished by April 1st and I will send it to you then.[1] For the moment, be 100 percent sure, don't forget it. This afternoon I was von Stroheim to the Tapir.[2] I called him a liar. "I beg you, sir, don't think I'm a liar." A

[1]Contat and Rybalka hypothesize that this text might have been "A Defeat" in an early draft, taking its name from the Empedocles myth, which defeated the "wretched youth," Frédéric, like Nietzsche himself, in his attempt to recast it in a new version. Empedocles—ca. 493–33 B.C., Sicilian poet, philosopher, and statesman—believed the four primal elements meld through the forces of Love and Strife.

[2]*Albert Morel, son of Mme Morel (the Lady), to whom Sartre was giving private lessons.* (SdB) In French scholastic argot, *tapirizer* means to tutor, give private lessons; the tapir is the student.

detached and skeptical air. "All right, I believe you, I believe you. Let's get back to Leibniz." "I beg of you." "But I believe you. Let's get back, as I said, to Leibniz." Then he threw some object on the floor, saying, "You have a pretty odd way of believing people." Then he began to get really testy. I went on with the lesson as though nothing was happening and then at the end, as he was still sputtering with fury and looking balefully at all mankind, I said to him, "No need to be so severe. Everybody does stupid things. Like your irrational anger just now. . . ." "Sir, it was quite justified." "Nonsense!" "If a friend had done it, I would have hit him." "Well, why didn't you hit me?" "Because! Officially you are my superior. You abuse your position to insult me and treat me like dirt." At times like this his voice gets shrill and sullen. "Excuse me, but when you feel insulted by someone, whatever the inequality at the outset, you become his equal. You were my equal, because I insulted you. So you simply had no guts, that's all." He finally agreed, and I retired with the honors of battle, giving him my sermon on lying. The charm of the whole thing comes from the fact that from the very beginning I was sure that he hadn't lied to me.

After dinner I went to La Baronne[3] with Bédé and Larroutis, who were subdued and dazed from the *agrégation*.[4] They regained a ray of intelligence only when Herland described a military law that would officially make us second lieutenants. Then I went up to Broussaudier's place, where he, Canguilhem, and I discussed in undertones and with an air of mystery Lagache's deepening vices. Here the weather has been the sort you like: rain and wind. Excellent for writing about Contingency. I'm not unmoved by the thought that in an hour the first line of the first page of *une jeunesse* ["a youth"] will be written. I wish with all my might that what you write tonight will be beautiful. Please imagine me behind you like Saint Matthew's Angel, but silently, without prompting you, less handsome, less worthy of violets, but still and all, every bit as much an Angel.

To Simone Jollivet

After waiting in vain for word of their arrival, I suppose you have not received the excerpts I sent you. It's true that with my usual practical sense I stamped them as a letter and put them in the slot for printed matter. No doubt some difficulties resulted. Stop calling my letters "little lectures." You

---

[3]A *cafe near the Rue d'Ulm (SdB)*—that is, near the École Normale.
[4]A highly competitive exam for admission to the teaching staff of state secondary schools.

know I don't want to seem like either a student or a professor. Why should you have less ability to see than I? It's enough to look, the direction hardly matters. What is this tone of humility that pervades your little card? Is it irony? In that case, my compliments, you're making progress. Is it sincere? If so, it's stupid. Why shouldn't you be proud? It's the primary condition for getting anywhere. Besides, from the standpoint of our relationship, won't you ever find a tone of simplicity as far removed from submission (feigned?) as from angry reproach? It seems to me that at Thiviers we found it occasionally—you more than I: since I know I never will.

You will always find me hard, brittle, hobbled by awkward and irrelevant phrases.

That is where you can help me: try to soften my edges. One more little lecture on moral well-being. Seen from the outside—it is the absolute liberation from all social constraints: first of all, from morality; if you are moral you obey society. If you are immoral, you rebel against it but on its own grounds, where you are sure to be beaten. You must be neither one nor the other, but above. Next, it is liberation from the social aesthetic (I told you about that the other day). Finally, from joys and pleasures that society finally tosses you like a bone. When you want a ring or some jewel, reflect that you are enslaving yourself to the ideas of its maker and seller, two fools who are exploiting you. If you're not disgusted it's because you *yourself* really do want the thing, and so you must do *anything* to get it. What particularly disgusts you, among all the pleasures society offers, is that however low one has fallen, whatever vice one has discovered, one can *always* find someone to satisfy it for money—in other words, a seller. Petty commerce is ubiquitous. That's why one must avoid falling into certain vices out of snobbery or indolence, simply because we think them elegant. One of my friends, who is intelligent and virile but weak, almost became a homosexual recently, though he didn't love men, simply because he was surrounded by homosexual friends. Since the desire didn't spring from deep within him but was imposed from outside, he would have been very unhappy and probably that would have been the end for him. I extricated him, but not without some difficulty. I'm afraid that you may be heading off in the same direction. But whatever you say, you have more will than he, you'll snap out of it. I never know how safe these letters are and how much I can say about your private life without risking harming you if someone stole them.

But you know what I'm alluding to. A certain little display, if true, was no more than weakness, snobbery, cowardice on your part; but you got hold of yourself.

Obviously we must live with others, *but never allow them (even if they are weaker than you) to have such an influence over you, to be so indispensable, that you cannot send them to Hell if you choose.*

Once you've made yourself absolutely independent of society, you must correct two major faults: first of all melancholy. Until last year I was very melancholy because I was ugly and that made me suffer. I have absolutely rid myself of that, because it's a weakness. Whoever knows his own strength must be joyful. Then, the only ideal you must hold on to is one you can attain yourself: your present ideal is to be loved by an intelligent, ugly man, someone like Charles Dullin.[1] If that should happen, which I doubt, it will be thanks not to you, but to chance, which will enable you to meet that man.

So you aren't free to realize your ideal, and consequently you feel inferior, looking for what you may never find. Give it up—at least for the moment—and take up an ideal you can achieve, such as acquiring the greatest possible power. With a will you'll surely succeed, so the ideal will amount to strength, a help to you, rather than a hindrance, a weakness. Avoid all reveries, moonlit or otherwise; they're pleasant but a waste of time. If, concurrently, you develop within yourself the force and the violence of the passions, stifling all scruples, all *pity*, you will then be *absolutely free*.

At that instant you will know *true joy*. I call that state moral health, because it is exactly like when one is in excellent physical health, one feels strong enough to bend lampposts with a single hand. Also, in that moral state, one feels bursting with health, ready to try anything, and it is an immense joy. Just like kids with twenty cents in their pockets who go from store window to window without hurrying to buy, assured and calm, entirely possessed by the happiness of *power*. You will know the joys of the incognito: faced with intimidating, revered men you will be able to imagine them as puppets you can make dance; with them unaware of your identity, you'll seem to have the hidden power to overturn them. And then, self-assured, taking much more pleasure from being unknown than being admired, you will be still freer.

So that's that for moral health. I don't have time to speak of the emotional joys open to you in this connection. Discover them on your own or ask me to write about them for you. For you mustn't think that to be morally

---

[1]Experimental theater producer, director, actor (1885–1949), later to stage several of Sartre's plays; soon after this letter, he became Jollivet's lover, and he remained so for many years. She worked on several productions with him.

healthy is to be cold. One must be sentimental (I too use my sentimentality), but in respect to yourself, not others. Overnourish your imagination, if you like, but always keep hold of the reins.

In case you didn't get my package, I'll reiterate a request made in it: I spoke frankly of my "emotional life"; tell me about yours with equal frankness and describe your fiancé (without partiality one way or the other). Tell me also what you intend to do about him. It is important, because after his general advice, Vautrin[2] gives precise and specific advice, and if you should happen to go back on the decision made in Thiviers, I would be obliged to give you other advice.

---

[2]Allusion to a scurrilous character in Balzac's *Le Père Goriot,* who advises the young hero on ways to do away with his rival in love.

1927

To Simone Jollivet

My dearest

You love me and I love you and the Llama's[1] just an ass. Everything he told you is nonsense. If he brings it up again, just ask him these three questions:

What is love?

What is a *simple* love affair?

Why are *simple* and sensual loves the only true love?

With those three *simple* questions you'll have him hoist on his own petard. But I totally understand how with Inès one might feel only the very *simple* desire to give her children. Therefore I excuse him. He has a mania for "donning the frock coat of the worldly psychologist," to quote a poster lauding a melodrama called *l'Enfer des Pierreuses* ["The Streetwalkers' Hell"]. Actually, you seemed pretty smug hearing him say, "You will never love." You're quite fond of ideas like that. I'll counter that—and at some length—in Toulouse. But that's another story. Let's discuss it: I'm longing to see you again, my dear little girl, for I love (?) you passionately. How I wish it were next Monday, May 2nd. This time I think you'll be free. Are we set for a quarter to 2 at Maxim's bar? You'll get this letter Thursday. Would you be so kind as to answer *without fail* this time, if only a quick note, *on Thursday*

---

[1]*Nickname for René Maheu, a* normalien *and friend of Sartre's, born in Toulouse, where he had met Simone Jollivet. (SdB)* Sartre kept up use of the college nicknames and fanciful caste system derived from Cocteau's *Le Potomak* [see note page 40].

night, because my travel plans will need to be firm by Saturday morning. I'll stay 4 days and 3 nights: from Monday to Thursday night at ten o'clock. Is that OK with you?

I don't like to hear you say you love me "passionately, *like La Marietta*," who was after all just a slut with a crush on Fabrice. The expression "passionately in love" sounds like some old madam trying to squeeze out the last penny. Instead, I'd like your love for me to be like Sanseverina's for Fabrice.[2] Isn't she an admirable woman?

So I don't know whether I love you but I do know I have a mad desire to hold you in my arms, dear little girl, and that in all the world you are the being I'm most attached to.

What do you think of *The Charterhouse of Parma*?

My best to Zina, whom I am looking forward to seeing again soon.

To Simone Jollivet

My dearest

I'm really sleepy, but I must write to tell you that I scarcely had the time to love you this week except in a totally conceptual way, but that just now it all came back to me. I love you as I loved you the Nils Holgerson night, with the same reserved tenderness and fear of hurting you that made me just brush you with my fingertips, which is a hundred times sweeter than the most violent transports, my dear little porcelain girl. You must look just like a little girl, with your tiny face all puckered and rumpled and your nose wrinkled up. I'm so sorry you have a headache and I give you permission to suspend for a while all the love you feel for me.

The man with the famous "power to work" is whipping himself up to work more than fifteen minutes a day. All in vain. But soon my power to work will reawaken, just as my love for you did. And if it has the same strength and youth as my love, 24 hours will not be enough, and every day I'll have to encroach upon the next, writing Monday: work 24½ hours—Tuesday 24¾, etc. to satisfy my thirst for labor.

I love you passionately.

I peeled onions at the Morels' while the Tapir was making an omelet, so my eyes are weeping as though I'd rubbed them, and my fingers reek.

---

[2] In Stendhal's *Charterhouse of Parma*.

Have you read Arbelet's *Stendhal's Youth?* Can you read yet? I pity you with all my heart.

Guille's[1] in love with Mme Morel.[2]

(Philanderer!)
S.

To Simone Jollivet

[May 25]

My dearest

I want to tell you about a gorgeous practical joke, but first, some background. A certain Lindbergh flew alone across the Atlantic in an airplane, a splendid feat. All the papers are talking about it, but you'd rather face the firing squad than hear about it. Anyway, this young man, the darling of Paris, is towed about everywhere in the wake of various officials; no honor is denied him, the Legion of Honor has just been conferred on him. In addition, you should know that on the occasion of an analogous flight attempted by Nungesser and Coli, the press covered themselves with ridicule by reporting their arrival in New York as planned though they hadn't made it at all, and are very likely at the bottom of the Atlantic. So we—Larroutis, Baillou, Herland, Nizan, and I—conceived a marvelous practical joke. In the name of the vice-principal of the École, we telephoned all the evening papers and told them, "The Disciplinary Committee of the E.N.S. has unanimously decided to confer the title of Honorary Student on Lindbergh for his feats." In no time the news was everywhere, and the VP spent two days on the phone denying it. But here's the best part. This morning's *Petit Parisien* has a note: "Lindbergh will be at the E.N.S. this morning at 9:30"; and at 9:30 there were 500 people in front of the School, a mob, guards keeping order, police, souvenir vendors, journalists. After a really good laugh, we had Bérard, who looks a little like Lindbergh, shinny down a lamppost to the Rue Rateau and

---

[1]*Pierre Guille, a fellow student at the École Normale Supérieure and Sartre's best friend at the time. (SdB)*

[2]*Whom I spoke of at length in* La Force de l'âge [The Prime of Life] *under the name Madame Lemaire. (SdB)* Known as "the Lady," she became the close friend and frequent hostess of Sartre and other members of "the family."

fifteen minutes later arrive by cab. Immediate ovation from us—we lofted him on our shoulders and carried him around in triumph. The crowd followed, and an old man kissed his hands. Meanwhile the piano and 2 violins in the music room struck up the "Marseillaise," and the public joined in. The crowd gradually dispersed, and at 10:45, when Bérard left to go to class, there was nobody left but three policemen, who trailed him all morning. This evening the papers are reporting the event, trying to joke about it, with a few jabs at Lanson. Because of this affair and his protestations and because for some time he had been wanting to leave, he submitted his resignation.

Don't you find all this delightful? If you see him, you can tell it to Maheu, to amuse him.

In another connection, Nizan bought himself a sublime thick notebook for his opuscules. I was devoured by envy but, being somewhat short of cash these days, didn't want to spend the money. He notices this, and I have just found on my table an identical notebook with

> J.-P. Sartre
> Notes
> Gift of P. Y. Nizan to his old friend Sartre
> May 25, 1927

I deeply appreciate this gesture, and am touched. True enough, he did lose 3 of my collars; usually so much the Magdalene, here he was somewhat the Martha, and this will appear on his record.

Did I tell you, this summer I'm going to Geneva? Various people will speak on the League of Nations, and I'll listen. It would be lovely if only I didn't have to put up with Lagache's company.

Chadel is in the army, buried away in Mayence.

Little by little, Mme Morel is revealing a sexuality one would not have at first attributed to her. Where will it all end? (I am speaking for Guille.) She taught me something I was not prepared to hear from you, because you touch me too deeply: it is the indifference of women toward sugar daddies so long as they pay the way and provide them the chance of *seeing things*. For three months she endured the company of a stepbrother, a gross, bloated Mortimer[3] (who in fact loves her), merely to see Florence. The Boor's continual presence wasn't any burden: she simply ignored him. That's typical of women, I believe. I must persuade myself of that so as to understand you.

---

[3]*Allusion to Cocteau's mythology of the Eugènes, Mortimers, etc., revealed in* Le Potomak [The Potomac]. *(SdB)*

I love you with serenity and joy. My life is blessed and blissful: I eat, I spend more than I can, I'm surrounded by nice, boring people, I don't think at all, I do absolutely no work, but I've earned this rest. Will I fail my exams? But what's an exam? I rejoice at the thought that in two weeks I'll be seeing my little girl again. May she feel better by then.

Love.

Today I was the prototypical von Stroheim in the Morels' living room. Through them I see other people, which is good for me.

1928

To Simone Jollivet

[Summer]

My dear love

You must be building up resentment against me, not because I haven't written to you but because you probably think I took so long about it just to get even. I know that would be "base and vile and shabby." I also know that you could have written sooner without seeming to throw yourself at me. But I haven't thought for one instant of holding it against you, because as you know, I'm on the march toward wisdom; even though, as you know, I'm an ordinary fellow in many respects. Such wisdom would consist of accepting all things in my friends with equanimity. That's already been achieved with Nizan and you. I'll tell you about it someday, but above all you will see it in the evenness of my disposition. As a matter of fact, if I haven't written, it's because I took the written *agrégation* and thereby forgot about everything for a week, including your existence.[1] I was numb—really dissatisfied—and preoccupied. But with the fair weather you've come back, for I no longer want to see you as a foul-weather friend. That's one version of those observations we used to make about sloppy couples living together (at the same time we were happily sleeping together—but with such switches in moods). Basically it is just as rotten to expose oneself morally. Only the other day I

---

[1] In fact he failed the written part of that year's *agrégration*. His friend Raymond Aron took first place. But he became acquainted with Simone de Beauvoir, a philosophy student at the Sorbonne, as they studied for his second attempt and her first. The next year, 1929, the judges awarded him first place and her a close second.

was telling Guille how we describe ourselves to one another, one speaking disdainfully of pseudo-fabulous meals at the Coq Hardi (or Coq d'Or or Gaulois) and the other vaunting the alimentary treasures of his cellar (or larder), and since he found that intriguing, I reflected that you and I had gone about it very badly, and that an atmosphere of latent drama for me and latent delirium for you was keeping us from making a beautiful game of our love. Everything I told you the evening I read you *La Ville dans les airs* (which was called something else, I think) but lying through my teeth because, with that promise of play, I wanted to restore you to a love serious as the rain. But today I'm very sincere, and above all I'm still under the spell of that last night I saw you, when I was playing Stève Passeur's game[2] very badly—and when Zina spoke to me about your birthday and when you put on such beautiful masks. I've even kept a truly beautiful image of you with that mask of a man and your legs spread and bare as far as a woman's sex permits, just like the legs of Achilles or bearded Oedipus, naked—tender and white—all the way up to the short cloak, on Greek vases. I don't know what to say about the genitals of those men, actually, because I know the Greek vases only from schoolbooks in which those afore-mentioned organs were cruelly suppressed. If I am thinking of you at the moment it is especially behind that mask and also to the extent that you look like Dorothée Reviers, who plays the prostitute in *Épaves vivantes* ["Living Wrecks"] (a sound film from Vitaphone). I love you as I might love an Erector set. But I would lend myself to every game and to the most beautiful, my dearest. Not only Stève Passeur's—but the one in *La Célestine*, too.

I found in the *Dialogues* of Fléchier (seventeenth-century author) the following line against Quietism:

Marthas are sometimes every bit as good as Marys.[3]

It's very bad—so bad I'm actually not sure I'm quoting it correctly.

I picture Zina giving her body to everything human in the neighborhood so as to wish you a birthday worthy of you. If I wanted to celebrate it as you deserve, I'd have to do the same, since I have no money. But if you were in Paris now I'd certainly buy you one of those bunches of violets because "it's

---

[2]Stève Passeur (1899–1966) wrote plays, with biting dialogue and bitter humor, often about the struggle between the sexes.
[3]A reference to the New Testament Martha of Bethany, who worked while her sister Mary prayed.

the thought that counts" and because they touched you so—they alone—when we were in Paris.

I hope to see you again soon, my dearest, since I'm thinking that the month will soon be over and you'll have to return to Toulouse. I would be so happy to see you again, and since I have been thinking of you again that is what I desire above all. You might, on that occasion, buy me a *Célestine*.

Love and kisses.

1929

The letters that Sartre wrote to me during the summer of '29 have been lost. (SdB)

To Simone de Beauvoir

Darling little Beaver[1]

Would you be so kind as to give my laundry (bottom drawer of wardrobe) to the laundress this morning? I'm leaving the key in the door.

I love you tenderly, my dearest. There was a charming little look on your face yesterday when you said, "Ah, you were watching me, you were watching me," and when I think of it my heart melts with tenderness. Au revoir, good little one.

---

[1]Partly, perhaps, because of the similarity of the English word to her last name, René Maheu gave Beauvoir the nickname "le Castor"—"the Beaver"—while they were both attending philosophy lectures at the Sorbonne.

1930

To Simone de Beauvoir

My little morganatic wife

I'll be arriving at 12:15, Gare d'Austerlitz (up to you to check the time—it will give your sister a walk. No, I take that back. The schedule's here in the drawer of the table where I'm writing; I can check it myself: it's 12:13). I'd be delighted if you could find time to meet me at the station. By the way, I hope to be in Paris for six days.

If you have free time, we might go out together sometimes.

With warm regards.

P.S.: My dearest, I've read the description of your 1st chapter.[1] If its style is as simple as the style in your letter—no more, no less—it will be excellent.

To Simone de Beauvoir

My sweet Beaver

Just a tender little note, gratuitous at best, to tell you I love you with all my heart. It's three; I could be wakened at eleven if necessary but not before.

I love you.

---

[1] *One of my novels that was never finished. (SdB)*

To Simone de Beauvoir

Saint-Symphorien[1]

My dearest

It is thundering, and I look constantly to the past, all those beautiful days with you, and to the immediate future, all those days, each one like the next, with me languishing here. I don't know whether it's possible to derive pleasure from considering, from a higher perspective, the eternal return taken as law. I know I face the prospect of an eternal return, or at least one whose cycles so far outstrip my imagination that I see it as eternal. Just think, the details of my life here are so well regulated, minute by minute, that I know for certain that in eight times twenty-four hours, at 18:15 I will take the same readings, which will begin with the same numbers, after performing the same actions. This will always be mechanical, but I know that the same thoughts will recur, the same hope and despair and all the schizophrenic fabrications which I notice I'm trusting more and more. Thus I sink into the condition of all who are sequestered.

But I wanted to tell you that the storm and this terrified contemplation of the wasteland of my future have given me a sort of nervous excitation, which is really, in the end, boredom. Boredom cannot be the lethargy I so often feel here when the hours go by unremarked. Consciousness diminishes, and the body, inert like a swimmer who realizes he is caught in seaweed, lets go and drifts along with the current, unrestrained. But if the swimmer kicks, of course the strands tighten around him, and that's what boredom's like: the stimulation that dominates you, forcing you to kick as an impalpable but sure bond draws you ever more gently to the depths. In fact in bed I kicked, stretching out, my legs thrashing left and right, driven to act in a thousand different ways by nervous irritation, and understanding that I was temporarily incapable of even the simplest actions. To try was to come up against an immediate impossibility: write five lines of some factum,[2] see what they were like and give up then and there. But even when all the forces of my being seemed to conspire to have me leap out of bed, hardly had I made the effort to sit up when I could barely arch my back, and it required a real task—sending out a report—to finally get me up. In such cases, I believe it

---

[1] *Where Sartre was doing his military service as a meteorologist. (SdB)*
[2] Sartre habitually used the word "factum," taken from the parlance of philosophers and jurists, in reference to any written analysis linked to opinion.

best to take a walk, to relax the muscles that the nerves have stirred up. But it's raining, and anyway I don't have permission to go out. So I'm writing to you: essentially my nervousness had me believing I could give universal form to all these individual little thoughts that I still had strength enough to delineate, on my current state and on a thousand other peculiar topics, I mean that I could pour them into some small poems. But I'm not hazy enough yet to be unaware that with the little strength currently at my disposal, they would barely achieve the general before dissolving into the proverbial, for the difficulty is surely to stand at the edge of the proverb without falling in, when you mean to speak about yourself to the "public" in its conceptual sense. And, on the contrary, on condition of leaving them as they are, that is, as real ideas, though specific ones, the true remedy for my edginess is to share them with you. And so you see why I said that when I wanted to but couldn't write, I found pleasure in writing you a letter.

To tell you what I am thinking, to write as though speaking, perfectly suits that middle state between power and impotence where I now am and where a snap of the fingers would turn my personal concerns into generalities, because those concerns have the heady aroma of ideas. So now you understand my daily condition here, though it's usually less intense and painful than tonight. Here is how I judge my case: I am intelligent, I sit at my table and want to speak of the case of a necessary Jean-Paul Sartre who is to my impressions and feelings what the essential characteristic of Spinoza is to the modes that it underlies. And that's it: dead in the water; I write "large hollow nostril," and I'm dissatisfied. But I'm quite conscious of it. Hereafter under similar circumstances you will receive a letter from me. It will be in arid, obscure prose, of no interest whatever to my Beaver, but it just might amuse Mademoiselle Simone Bertrand de Beauvoir, the brilliant academic.

1931

To Simone de Beauvoir

Hôtel Printania[1]
Rue Ch. Laffitte
Friday, October 9

My dearest

I found your letter here when I got in last night. I'm so pleased. I never think of you as being sad, but rather as this little person who must be having a good time—doubtless as my mother thought of me during my trip to Spain. But, O part of me that's having a good time, the rest of me isn't having so bad a time either. If you like long letters, I think this one may well be, since I have both ink and leisure. Still, you shouldn't think, as you seem to, that each one will be long. You're profiting from a complete breakdown in the literary realm. I've told you that already.

I'll skip over Monday: five hours of classes, private tutoring. Early to bed. Tuesday: typical day in the life of a young professor, so typical that Guille was doing exactly the same thing in Reims. In the morning I taught classes, as usual: I'm dwelling on psychological methods because I take my own good time about picking up certain precise information that seems necessary for going on. I tutored for another hour. At 12:50 I went to a restaurant for lunch. It's next to the station in the part of Le Havre I like so much and

---

[1]*Sartre was teaching in Le Havre. (SdB)* Beauvoir had just begun to teach in Marseilles.

which I've decided to put in the factum on Contingency.[2] Indeed everything there is contingent, even the sky, which, according to meteorological probability, should be the same all over Le Havre but isn't. How was lunch? I have no idea, because I have a cold. The stuff they bring me doesn't look too nice, and now I'm afraid that when my nose clears up on Monday, I'll taste something revolting. Briefly, in the morning I read (a Spanish habit),[3] I munch whatever is at hand, I have a coffee at the Hotel Terminus, where you spent the night. But, after that, Tuesdays seem long, since I have no classes. Accordingly, imperceptible solicitations propelled me from the Hotel Terminus to my room and from my room to my bed. To dally a moment on my bed, to imagine the Beaver in Marseilles, to conjure up the sun, to dream of the sun, to sleep. At three-thirty I awoke. I was a little ashamed because of my noble calling as a writer—all things considered, if you take the word literally, a writer should ultimately write. But that's not the case with me. At any rate, I decided to drop that damned perception, which doesn't amuse me at all, and start in on Contingency. I took off under one part rain to three parts sun, in search of the Rue Émile-Zola. Actually, I'd received a note from the Widow Dufaux, who had rented a room to Morel and whom I wanted to turn down, as you know. She didn't take it that way and wrote me a letter in which the accretion of participles referring to the object, though placed at the beginning of the sentence, antagonized me from the start. Yet the wish to save (this year I shall make an art of economy) persuaded me to inspect the premises. I reached the Boulevard François-Ier (you know it). I found a bourgeois house tucked away, I entered a bourgeois vestibule, bathed in bourgeois obscurity. Then the very double of your grandmother appeared before me, o precious Beaver. Yet another service you have rendered me. As I see it, I must say, she personifies widowhood and the abjection of humanity. The idea of living in the house of an old woman like that had me sweating bullets. I wrote a lovely letter to the Widow Dufaux. It is not to be.

Then, unburdened, I went to look at a tree. All you have to do for that is open the gate of a lovely park on the Avenue Foch, choose a victim and a chair, and contemplate away. Not far off the young wife of a maritime officer was listing for your old grandmother all the drawbacks of the seaman's

---

[2]A work that went through three separate versions and several titles, including "Melancholia," before emerging as *La Nausée* (*Nausea*). Sartre first tried to develop the idea of contingency in the *agrégation* of 1928, the one he failed. In the simplest sense, contingency involves the idea that there is no conscious pattern to life. In *Les Mots* (*The Words*), Sartre alludes to his discovery of the principle when the lights came up at the end of a movie, replacing universal order with chaos.

[3]During July the couple had traveled together in Spain.

vocation, and your old grandmother was bobbing her head as though to say, "Isn't that just the way things are." It actually could have been Mme Dufaux. And I was looking at the tree. It was very handsome, and I make bold to offer here these two precious items for my biography: it was in Burgos that I understood what a cathedral is and in Le Havre what a tree is. Unfortunately I'm not sure what kind of a tree it was. You'll tell me: you know those toys that twirl, in the wind or when you give them a spin; little green twigs rampant all over it with six or seven leaves stuck on, let's say, just so. I await your reply.[4] Herewith a little sketch.

After twenty minutes, having exhausted the arsenal of comparisons destined, as Mrs. Woolf would say, to make this tree something other than it is, I left with a clear conscience and went to the library to read M. Lancelot's *Samedis* ["Saturdays"] (perceptive remarks on grammar by Abel Hermant). After that, I went to the movies to see *Contre-enquête* ["Counter-Inquiry"], which I didn't much like. Whereas on the same day at the same hours, Guille ate lunch, slept, went to see *Rive Gauche* ["Left Bank"], which he didn't much like. On Wednesday I taught classes, then took the train to Paris, where the good sister was awaiting, all tears. You troubled her by so forcefully urging her to go to Marseilles, when in fact she didn't have a cent. I consoled her, promised her five hundred francs; she became radiant; I took her to a little café, where she read your letters with running commentary, lingering over the episode of the old Englishman, and telling me that everyone was deceiving me and that it would be far worse when the both of you were in Marseilles. I let her write you fifteen pages, I took a cab, I met up with a somnolent Guille, an alert Lady, a discreet Mops,[5] and the Tapir. We went to the Lady's place, and the people there were charming, though nobody did or said much of anything. Guille was particularly struck by the automatic duplication of our days in Le Havre and Reims. He had a good laugh, full of warmth for me. I gave him news of you, read him some of your letter. We talked. I slept there, and Mops woke me up at nine, admitting Aron,[6] accompanied, as befits him, by a flood of electric light. He stood there like an old eagle,

---

[4]*It was a chestnut tree. (SdB)* This passage appears, transformed, in *Nausea*.

[5]*Nickname of Mme Morel's daughter. (SdB)*

[6]Raymond Aron (1905—83), classmate from the École Normale with whom Sartre had a long competitive relationship. It was through this future philosopher that Sartre gained a year of study (1933–34) in Germany.

expounding on a thesis of the French instructor in Cologne while, fascinated, I panted gently in my damp sheets. Then Guille, who was going out with him, arrived. They served me breakfast in bed; Aron poured the coffee and Guille buttered the bread, as they said, "Well, you rakish widower, aren't you the lucky dog! The Beaver wouldn't have buttered your bread," etc. I left them, I searched all over Montparnasse for the Rabbit,[7] finally found her, and we made a date for the afternoon. Lunch at my grandparents with Uncle Georges. I met your sister in the Luxembourg Gardens. She was overjoyed at the prospect of going to Marseilles. And, as good fortune never arrives unaccompanied, or so she said, Giraudoux[8] was to receive her Saturday morning. She hopes he will misbehave with her. But alas his tastes go in the opposite direction. And she said, "Aha! They're pulling the wool over your eyes, little goat. They chase you for your pennies. But they're deceiving you." I took her to the Place d'Italie for a drink. She clutched the pictures of Spain under her arm, boasting, "Who do you think I am, I wouldn't lose a single one—not like that Beaver." But she spread half of them around the Gobelins, and without a Boy Scout in desperate need of a good deed they were lost forever. At the Gobelins she claimed that Guille had already resumed his baleful influence over me and I was already losing that beautifully gentle patina she had so successfully given me over the past few years. The waiter was busting his gut laughing. We took a taxi, and she dropped me at the Acropole and went off to find Gégé.[9] The multicolored bottle bottoms that cover the Acropole's vaulted ceiling were reflecting in my port. If I shook the glass very hard they became tiny and dense, and when the motion ceased they expanded to regain their majesty. I entertained myself that way for a good half hour, listening with one ear to the prophecies of a fat drunk of a woman, and your sister returned alone and disgusted. Desmoines[10] didn't want Gégé to go out, and the mother-in-law threw in a few nasty remarks; she had left Gégé pale with rage and saying, "All right, I won't go out." "Because, you see," your sister told me, "that way she gets to be the one to make a scene, which she much prefers." We took the AE bus, I dropped her at the Lutétia and scurried off to see the Lady. Now comes a bizarre incident. (I leave you in suspense for three minutes while I go to the station for my commuter ticket.)

---

[7]*My sister. (SdB)* Two years younger than Simone, Hélène de Beauvoir was an art student.

[8]Jean Giraudoux (1882–1944), writer and diplomat, began an important theatrical career in 1928 when he adapted his novel of 1922, *Siegfried et le limousin*, to the stage.

[9]*A friend of my sister's who had also become my friend. (SdB)* Her full name was Geraldine Pardo.

[10]*Gégé's husband. (SdB)*

Here's what happened. I ring the Lady's doorbell: not there. I leave, undecided. I suddenly think, though without much hope, I might find Nizan at *Bifur*.[11] There, the typist, with her delicate smile, informs me that Nizan has not been in that afternoon. I leave, I toddle back toward the Lady's. Across from Gallimard I suddenly see my Grand Duke[12] walking along whistling, with his wife three steps behind, as is only proper, burdened with packages. "Hello, Grand Duke." But the Grand Duke turns green, and his whole attitude exudes constraint and false cordiality. "Let's go with him as far as the Lady's place," he says. "We have time." But the Lady's windows were dark. Eventually he makes up his mind: "Let's go for a drink." We talk of Athens. "Just stones. Best to have gone there two hundred years ago to really see it." In the final analysis, Greece is a "fucking bore." They were bored out of their minds in Naxos. We reach the Lutétia, and my eagle eye, or rather my proprietary eye, immediately lighted upon the ice that was chilling them. Lying under some shoes and a package of cervelat on the marble table right beside the Dowager[13] I see my "honorable book,"[14] shabby and defeated-looking. I said nothing, and though I was so anxious that I must confess my fingers trembled slightly as I held my glass of sherry, I played along, letting them lead the way. They talk hesitantly about this and that, careful not to dwell on literary matters because of those damn mental associations that lead you from one thing to another. . . . Finally the Grand Duke gets up abruptly "so as not to miss the train" and, on his feet: "Ah! by the way . . . uh . . . By the way, old boy, I've just seen Robert France and there's . . . here it is. . . ." He wasn't exactly making himself clear, and I thought my book[15] had been rejected. But it seems that's not it at all, he thinks it's good and wants to take it, but it appears the preface isn't accessible enough, so he entrusted it to the Grand Duke, who in his twin capacity as editor and author's friend could see what needs to be done. That's all: they left and I paid, but I find the whole thing puzzling.

1. Why, if it's just a matter of revising the preface, was the Grand Duke so awkward and flustered?

2. Why didn't Robert France speak to me directly, which is usual when an editor wants an author to revise his work? I still hope Nizan won't eviscerate my factum without consulting me.

---

[11]A magazine that published part of *The Legend of Truth*.

[12]*Nizan.* (SdB)

[13]*Rirette Nizan.* (SdB)

[14]*The name Sartre gave to his "omoring-book"* (SdB)—that is, his spiral notebook. "Honorable book" is Sartre's pun on "omoring-book."

[15]*La légende de la vérité [The Legend of Truth].* (SdB) The name of the publisher at Rieder was actually Jacques Robertfrance.

3. If, since "L'Homme seul" ["Man Alone"] seems pretty heavy going, because of my own mistakes, and, according to Aron, *The Legend of Truth* pretty obscure, why does he choose the preface—the one part that I (and you and Nizan when he glanced at it) found lucid—to accuse of obscurity?

4. But if, on the other hand, as I had supposed, he refused my factum, why did Nizan, instead of sliding past it, swallow the hook by fervently repeating that Robert France wants to take it at all costs?

5. Nizan wound up by telling me, "Anyway, you should speak to him."

Guille ventured the quip that Nizan probably wants Carrefour to publish the book under his own name. In any case, I'll see Robert France on Thursday morning and I've set a date for Thursday afternoon with the Grand Duke. But it's really strange: all those coincidences (I nearly took a different route; I would have missed him); and the look on the Grand Duke's face—even if there's nothing behind it—was worth the price of admission.

From there I went to the Lady's place. The Llama had just arrived. He is cool to Guille and kind to me.[16] So it's likely, given his balancing act, that I'll become a Eugène[17] again in return for a few kind gestures. I'll buy some flowers for his wife. I showed them the photos, and they found Santillana astonishing. I downed a partridge, two eggs, some Brie, helter-skelter, a quick glass of red. I caught a cab with the Llama, then my train.

This morning I got a haircut and, on reflecting that everyone is so happy, I resolved, as they say in your beloved countryside,[18] to make myself a little pleasure. So I went to La Grosse Tonne for lunch, but it wasn't as good as usual, except for some exquisite haddock and a glass of 1913 Calvados less expensive than that other one but nearly as good. From there I went to read Maurois's *Turgenev* at the Bibliothèque Nationale, then came back to write to you. These eight packed pages actually represent many more.

Now listen: after you receive the check, you'll get my letter asking you to pay me back around October 16th. *Disregard it.* Things have changed since I wrote it. First of all, I have some private students (three, including a little girl, a fat little tomboy), and I just learned I can pay my nine-month commuting ticket in three trimonthly installments of a thousand francs. And

---

[16]While Sartre's release from military service was delayed by officers who wanted him to accept a commission, Beauvoir, avid for travel, took a trip around France with Pierre Guille (just released by the army) in Mme Morel's car. Meanwhile, because he was already married, she had rebuffed advances from the Llama—René Maheu—with whom she had been good friends at the Sorbonne.

[17]In the roles derived from Cocteau's *Potomak*, the Mortimers exhibited bohemian artistic traits, while the Eugènes—the philosophers' caste—were capable of stuffy bourgeois behavior.

[18]*In Limousin. (SdB)*

finally, the bank is sending me 2,750 francs, of which I will spend only 1,300 on clothes. So, if you don't wish to irritate me, do not mention the money again, all right? If you send it back to me, I'll send it back to you and so on and so forth. If you absolutely don't want to spend it, keep it for your sister in November, because it's possible I might be able to give her only 500 francs.

My dearest, you cannot know how I think of you every minute of the day, in this world of mine which is so filled with you. Sometimes I miss you and I suffer a little (a very tiny little bit), at other times I'm happy to think that the Beaver exists, buys herself some chestnuts, takes a stroll; the thought of you never leaves me and I carry on little conversations with you in my head. By the way, why not come for All Saints' Day. It's a Sunday, but we're bound to have the Monday off. And you don't teach on Tuesday. . . .

1934

Many of the letters that Sartre wrote to me in '31–32 when I was in Marseilles have been lost. Lost too were all those he sent me from Germany in '33–34. (SdB)

To Simone de Beauvoir

September 3–4

My love

You've been in Ajaccio six hours now, under I hope sunny skies. Here it's been raining steadily. The four who've taken over this sad little house tucked away under trees down a long driveway from the highway are: first of all my grandfather,[1] who stays in bed all day long whimpering; my stepfather,[2] "who is too kind" though visibly fed up; my mother,[3] and the maid Germaine. Another maid, Misandre, and I round out the household. Alas, we're constantly tripping over one another. Luckily, people come and go, taking off for Paris, except for the old man, who weeps or sleeps. He's totally senile: "It occurred to me that my son Georges must have moved my house lock stock and barrel and set it up elsewhere, though with the very same view and facing the very same houses. . . . Nothing has changed, except that we are no longer in Paris. It must be because we're both bachelors." He babbles on like a rivulet of tepid water. With the most exquisite civility he will say to

---

[1]Charles Schweitzer, descendant of a long line of prosperous, liberal Protestant Alsatian intellectuals and teachers.

[2]After ten years of widowhood, Anne-Marie Sartre married an École Polytechnique classmate of her first husband, the stern and exacting Joseph Mancy.

[3]On May 5, 1904, Anne-Marie Schweitzer (1882–1969) had married Jean-Baptiste Sartre (1874–1906), a young naval officer from a respected family in Thiviers (Dordogne). A year after the birth of his son Jean-Paul, Jean-Baptiste died of a combination of dysentery and enterocolitis picked up in Indochina in the 1890s.

my stepfather, "Excuse me, my dear sir, but I cannot seem to place you.
Would you be so kind as to tell me your name?" And to Mother (whom we
call "You," as you know), "Ah, you've been to Vichy so you must have seen
You." Last night he called us in. He was in bed, completely beside himself:
"I wish to present a problem to you. I have this brother, for whom I have
only the greatest respect. But he stole my furniture. What am I to do?" He
is kissed; he is told, "You'll get your furniture back." He is given a piece of
candy. Immediately he calms down. In another connection, the expression
"playing the lovers" took on its full meaning, revealing a cynicism in my
mother I'd never seen before. Some blood was found on the old man's fly.
A certain Miss had displayed a most persevering hand. His last days in Paris
had totally exhausted him, because of a curious regimen of hot then cold
showers. This Miss would come in the afternoon, have him discharge some
drops of blood, then leave him extraordinarily overwrought. He trembled and
he spoke of throwing himself out the window. Then Germaine, the maid
who watches him at night and who wanted her sleep, would put a powerful
dose of phenobarbital in his soup, which made him punchy. Whereupon
she would hoist him across her shoulders, or very nearly, and drop him,
tongue lolling, onto his bed. The removal of the old man's furniture and his
move to the Boulevard de Beauséjour can be traced to a devious, profound
struggle between Germaine and La Goulut.[4] Otherwise, we would have been
completely in the dark about the whole thing. But La Goulut had retired and
wanted to move into the Rue Saint-Jacques next year. She would have fired
Germaine, who counterattacked and revealed everything to my mother (except
the phenobarbital, which came to light only later). My mother decided to
press on, rented a house in Saint-Cloud, and made Germaine promise that
she would reveal nothing to my uncle, the photographer. Germaine, fearing
my mother might not be expeditious enough, though wanting to keep her
word, reported everything to the concierge, who proceeded to inform my
Uncle Georges, who in turn was seized with righteous anger and decided to
dismiss this Miss. To avoid scandal my mother shipped my grandfather off
one afternoon without a word to anyone and moved in here. At the same
time she rented the ground floor at 57 Boulevard de Beauséjour. Next day
the Miss found nobody home at the Rue Saint-Jacques. She wrote a four-
page letter, which I'll try to get hold of to show you. In it she attempted to

---

[4]*A former student of Charles Schweitzer's, who "played the lovers" with him. (SdB) She
is the "Miss" referred to earlier in the letter. The affair had been going on for at least twenty
years. At this time, Charles was ninety.*

cleanse herself of any "odious suspicions." . . . The photographer responded with talk of his own "atavistic intensity of moral rigor," which most certainly did not dispose him toward indulgence. After which, he grabbed all the furniture at the Rue Saint-Jacques, saying, "For however much time he has left to live, he doesn't need it." A family is a real pile of shit. But they're withholding the best parts, the drops of blood and a few other such details, from my stepfather so as not to ruffle his sensibilities. And that's my grandfather's story.

As for me, I'll be brief. First off, as I left the station, a befuddled passerby sent me to Suresnes, where I found a footbridge but no driveway. I suffered moments of despair as I tramped muddy roads for forty-five minutes, suitcase in hand, interrogating thirty-seven individuals, none of whom could help. Finally I retraced my steps and, around seven, located the abovementioned driveway just off the highway and not five minutes from the station. I was warmly welcomed by my mother, who reproached herself for writing to me in Strasbourg too late; she was expecting me "one of these days." They're so unpredictable. My stepfather came in a while later with a migraine and went off to bed. My mother and I had dinner while the two men slept, then we went in to see my stepfather, who talked to me steadily from eight to ten about America, from every perspective, using all the wiles of the raconteur. We went to bed, and around two in the morning I had a mild attack of asthma. I turned on the light and began to read. But here everything's family, so within three minutes the door opened and my mother entered in her bathrobe with a glass, gum balls, and aspirin—the gum balls for the asthma (who would have imagined?) and the aspirin for general malaise. I downed the lot, reflecting sadly all the while that the walls are paper-thin and that one sees a huge ray of light under the door of one room as soon as a light goes on in another. Perhaps these considerations explain why, last night, I didn't have even one moment of asthma. On the other hand, in my sleep, I always take extraordinary walks, visiting old châteaux and medieval cities. Yesterday I went to Paris. In the morning, with my mother, the Boulevard de Beauséjour. In the evening with my stepfather, who left me off at the Rue de Messine. From there I took a walk and bought myself a raincoat. My mother buys me *nothing*. So I'll have to spring for a pair of shoes. In addition, I owe 70 francs for my suitcase from Berlin. The raincoat cost 80 francs. I withdrew 300 francs from the bank and may have to take out more. However shall we live, my poor little marvel?

That's all. I'm going to do a little work now, I hope. Images. I'm thinking intently of you; all day yesterday I was wishing you calm seas and no *mal de mer*. I love you with all my heart. You looked so charming on the station platform. I caught a glimpse of you again up on the deck, but you weren't facing my way and looked a little silly. While thus involved till seven in simply getting to my family, I really regretted not going on with you.[5] I love you and send you a big hug.

Warm greetings to my old pal Guille. Again yesterday I had one or two little *Erlebnis* for him.[6] Don't forget to give him the cigars, if you haven't crushed them. Also, make sure he smokes them; he could, disgusted by the mere sight of them, simply pretend to.

To Simone de Beauvoir

My darling Beaver

I'm writing to you for the pleasure of it but I'm not entirely sure the letter will reach you, since I have no address for you. I was rather hoping for a letter from you this morning, but there was nothing. I'm very pleased I was able to send you five hundred francs yesterday and to know that you are well out of need. All the same, if you need more cash, just telegraph and I'll find some.

I was delighted yesterday to think I'd be writing to you this morning, but I was wrong: I went to bed late (I'd been to see Toulouse),[1] got up early (you know that here[2] I'm rousted out of bed by eight even if I've been up till four) I wanted to write to you from the Café Tourelles, which I rather like though the proprietor is a wretched Flaming-Cross,[3] but

[The rest is lost. (SdB)]

---

[5]As an example of the Sartre-Beauvoir private language, the phrase *vous autres*, used here, correctly refers in French to the second person plural, "you," or roughly "all of you." Sartre's use, referring to Beauvoir alone, signals his special relationship to her. In a later refinement, they frequently use the expression in the singular *vous autre*, a neologism since it does not occur in French, to heighten its intimacy. Since an English equivalent is lacking, the phrase is simply translated as "you."

[6]*In the phenomenologial sense, "lived experience"; Sartre used it to mean "emotion, pang."* (SdB)

[1]*Simone Jollivet (SdB)*
[2]*He was staying with his parents. (SdB)*
[3]Member of a far-right-wing group.

1935

To Simone de Beauvoir

7/24
Hammerfest

My dear love

My first note "from the most northerly city in the world." I'll be going ashore in a while. The cruise has turned out to be as inoffensive as could be expected, since there are 12 Anglo-Saxons on board and 18 French, distributed as follows: a monarchy of photographers whose leader is an important politician (I don't know his name); a republic of bridge players in which my stepfather is a senator; and one desert island: me. I read, I work on my factum, I do what I please. Tomorrow, the detailed description of a cruise ship. Just know that yesterday we saw daylight at midnight but no sun. A cannon was all set to blast away, but the heavenly body refused to show. This nighttime daylight is very beautiful; I'll tell you about it. I'll have to limit myself to descriptions of natural beauty, since there has been nothing in the way of events.

I kiss you with all my heart and love you passionately.

To Simone de Beauvoir

[July 24]

My dear love

I'm writing to you at one in the morning, and naturally we're in full daylight. People are chatting and munching sandwiches all around me and

46

I've just drunk a big cup of black coffee as though it were noon. This morning we sailed past Hammerfest, where, in the winter, they have two full months of night. Accordingly there is a magnificent wooden edifice above the town— the lunatic asylum. As a rule it's full by the end of that long night. After that we fired some shots in front of a "Bird Rock." The cormorants, sea gulls, eider ducks didn't get too het up because with twenty-four cruise ships in Norway during the summer they get the guns twice a day. The birds flapped around a little, on principal, consenting for five minutes to look like a swarm of flies, and then returned, their dignity intact, to alight in rows of fifty to a hundred upon their rock.

This evening a launch took us to the foot of North Cape. My parents, with their tender feet, stayed on board; I and, alas, a hundred others worked our way painfully to the top of the cliff. The purpose was to catch up with the midnight sun that we'd missed yesterday. But it got the better of us again, swathing itself in a magnificent white cloud, like Aeneas entering Carthage, and we climbed back down like dogs into the depths of the fog. We *were* able to verify from there that the earth is round (something you can do just as well from Sainte-Adresse)—and I saw a deaf-mute from Austria who is doing Norway by pedal car, plus three Laplanders. But I've already seen enough Lapps: the whole thing is one big joke. At thirty minutes past midnight we were back, I greeted my parents, still going strong, and ate seven little sandwiches and a large piece of intricate cream cake.

I love you. I love you tenderly. Till tomorrow.

There are some excellent things in *And Quiet Flows the Don*,[1] which is, however, not as good as his *Virgin Soil Upturned*. But good enough to put me to shame. This morning I tore up and threw out thirty pages about an all-girl orchestra, then I despaired of ever mastering my profession, then I wisely put off the question till later. I'll start in again tomorrow.

To Simone de Beauvoir

7/25

My love

This time we caught it—the midnight sun, I mean. It was Norwegian midnight, which is six minutes before midnight French time. You are sleeping

---

[1] *By Mikhail Sholokhov. (SdB)* Sholokhov, born the same year as Sartre, would receive the Nobel Prize for Literature in 1965, a year after Sartre declined his. He died in 1984.

the sleep of the just or at least gazing at the stars. Here all is pink and melting candy, the snow is pink, the water is pink—the sky goes from mauve to pink, like a very ordinary sunset in Rouen. And two hundred individuals in dinner jackets and evening dresses are grouped around the deck with cameras poised. Perhaps now they'll fire off the cannon. The ship has stopped and is rocking quite a bit. They helped us wait it out with a soprano or rather a would-be one who grabbed the high notes from below so as to lift them up more easily. But the notes wouldn't submit and the result for a good forty-five minutes was falsity for notes, audience, and singer. Minimal applause. Earlier (I realize I'm telling you everything in reverse order), we got off the ship (they've just fired the fateful cannon shot, and another, and another. Laughter and shouting. It's one second past midnight, the sun is rising, and we're off to bed). Visited Tromsö, also written Tromsoe or Tromsø, a wooden town, like Hammerfest and Molde. Entirely made of wood and miserable, with grim houses, preplanned streets. But here at least there is some vegetation. In Hammerfest only the garden of the town's richest man has anything beyond pebbles. All those villages are sinister and pleasing because they've relinquished any attempts at coquettishness. They have the smell of hard life. I dumped my parents and had a beer at a pleasant café, on the second floor of a wooden house; I was alone with a little girl who tirelessly played German records on a bad phonograph, and I experienced ten minutes of pure joy—that pure joy automatically produced in me by a phonograph, a café, and a foreign town.

I'm spending very little money.

I love you very much and I so want to be with you. But we're on our way back.

To Simone de Beauvoir

7/26

My love

Today we've seen nothing but sea, and it was rather rough (off Lofoten: it won't escape you that we are returning); half the passengers were overcome with languor between ten o'clock and five. Many of them didn't show up for lunch or ate only an apple. As for me, the Almighty gave me my intellectual fortitude, which doubtless resides even in my hair, so here I am beginning, just when I'd despaired, a splendid novella on a surprising topic: a little girl of ten climbs the North Cape and sees the midnight sun. I think it'll be very good. At any rate it's flowing along easily, and I'm enjoying the writing. My parents are mired in bridge, which calms them down a lot. It seems that when the cannon was being fired last night to celebrate the midnight sun, my mother blew up. Then my stepfather said, "But I do all I can to make you happy," and he stayed out on deck till four in the morning. But they were calm and sweet today. This evening we had a transvestite dance. I unwillingly dressed up as a woman and someone slapped a blond wig on me. I looked like a fallen *Maedchen* with her braids, underage, working the streets. Nonetheless I seduced an elderly Jewish-American woman dressed as a man who made me dance, then introduced me to a bunch of people. She was charming. We spoke in German. I started dancing the way your little friend[1] taught me, stepping on people's toes and getting dirty looks. Then I went back to my old ways and was told, "How well you dance." Meanwhile my stepfather, having won fifty-seven francs at bridge, passed around a bottle of champagne. It's half past midnight and I'm sitting here writing to you in my women's clothes. I had a very good time and find these Americans quite appealing. Tomorrow we're to visit Trondheim. I love you dearly and I'm going to bed. Au revoir my love.

To Simone de Beauvoir

7/27

My love

First, to alert you that the ship arrives at Calais Thursday at 13:00. So I'll reach Sainte-Cécile midnight Friday. Isn't that the time we said? I'm ecstatic about seeing you again—and also, of course, about getting away from my parents. My stepfather was unbearable today. Nervous, contradicting everything, and worst of all dispensing advice on matters that don't interest me in the least. This evening I was on edge and counting the seconds to his bedtime. Still, I managed to avoid him for a few hours. But tomorrow we're taking a side trip by car and I'll be stuck with them for twelve whole hours. I shudder to think of it.

We went ashore at Trondheim. I took a short excursion alone (in a car with three old Frenchwomen) to escape them for a while. Nothing interesting. These Norwegian cities are hideous once they reach a certain size. Trondheim is the third-largest city in Norway (50,000 pop.). I met up with my parents

---

[1]*Olga [Kosakiewicz]. (SdB)* She met Beauvoir at the lycée in Rouen, where Beauvoir taught from 1932 to 1936, seeing Sartre on weekends and vacations.

again in the garden of an old uninteresting cathedral, and never lost sight of them till now, when they've just gone to bed. I should do that, too, because tomorrow we'll be up at six-thirty, but I can't quite make up my mind to do it yet, I feel like enjoying my freedom a little while more. I've had only a glimpse of that most agreeable American from last night, but I intend to cling to her tomorrow evening after the excursion. We understand each other very badly but still it's that much more time subtracted from my parents. I've never had so big a dose of my stepfather; he used to have his factory. Actually, though I'm sweetness incarnate, I'm never far from tossing him overboard.

And you, my dearest? You are jauntily hauling your big bag around? You are shooting lots of shepherds with your revolver? Then you are violating them? You are having a good time? I hope to find bushels of letters at the Boulevard de Beauséjour. I hope above all that you're very happy. I can't wait to see you. Parents lodge like a knife in the skulls of their children, whose thoughts they cut in two.

I love you and send you a passionate kiss.

1936

To Olga[1]

[Summer]

My dear Iaroslaw

This letter, describing our arrival and first three days in Naples, will reach you only after considerable delay. You've already read the Beaver's letters about Capri and all that's happened since. So I hope you're not too set on chronological order, and I ask your indulgence.

We reached Naples on a Saturday at noon, after an uneventful trip: we'd gone to the dining car for a drink, waiting in vain for a peek at the sea, and seen the Appian Way far off, lost in the Roman countryside. We had some reservations about Naples. Our guidebook sang its praises, but who believes guidebooks, anyway? Poupette,[2] on the other hand, had found the city uninteresting: "Naples: just big, filthy houses. But filth alone is not enough." And the good Beaver and I honestly had to agree that, generally speaking, filth is not enough.

We stepped off the train into a huge, sad station, and, after depositing our suitcases in the checkroom, went outside. Immediately in front of us we

---

[1]Olga Kosakiewicz, eldest daughter of a White Russian father and French mother, had been first the student, then the friend of Beauvoir, and was involved from 1935 to 1937 in a deeply passionate affair with Sartre which almost wrecked the balance between the couple. Both used her in their fiction and dedicated books to her, and the three remained close for years, despite her feeling that her privacy had been seriously abused. She later acted in several of Sartre's plays.

[2]*My sister. (SdB)* The usual nickname for Hélène de Beauvoir, earlier identified as "the Rabbit."

saw a large dusty piazza, surrounded by banal Italian houses, with those hotels, cafés, and restaurants you find around any station; they could all be called Terminus. But you can't judge a city by its station. Even more dis-quieting, or so we thought, was that from the piazza you could see, deserted in the sun, enormous boulevards leading off to the port and the center of the city. Stretching away as far as the eye could see were buildings with flat facades, painted beige, cream, or gray, with green shutters. Not one jutted out past the others but all were lined up like barracks. We looked for a restaurant, to settle the alimentary question as soon as possible, and had lunch next to the station piazza, at the Nuova Bella—polite and perfect in a gloomy way; one of those restaurants, you know, the kind with an indefinite something in the atmosphere, in the waiters' attitude, even in the taste of the food, that tells you the people who eat here have just ended or are about to begin a train trip. But without the sad, slightly poetic feel of those railway restaurants where people linger over sad departures; instead there is the hasty comfort of traveling salesmen who don't want to ride on an empty stomach, or else families eating an hour before usual because you shouldn't leap up right after a meal and anyway the dining car is too expensive. We got up, weighed down by food consumed too quickly, and commenced our promenade.

We left the wide boulevard behind us on the right and took a left, because our map of Naples shows a mass of narrow little streets in that direction, and we hoped against hope they might be rather attractive. We were immediately surprised and delighted.

My dear Iaroslaw, I'm afraid this letter may bore you just a bit; it might seem too much of a "Letter on . . ." Still, I'm going to describe, all in one go, those little streets that make up about three-fourths of Naples. I really want you to feel a little how the city looked all around us, the atmosphere we were steeped in, and I don't think I could make you feel that by describing events and things we did chronologically. So I'm going to tell you what Naples is like. Naturally we didn't see everything or understand it all that one Saturday afternoon. It came little by little. Nonetheless, everything was already there around us and we could hazily intimate what there was to understand. So here we go. I'll get back to chronological order later.

There are very few broad streets. A half-century ago, for the health of the city, they put through the Corso Umberto, which still has a rational and antiseptic air about it. It runs straight as a rod, from the station to the Piazza Trento e Trieste, and it has the dry scowl, the sinister dustiness of countless wide streets in the South, and in the French Midi too (around Toulouse or Albi). There are also the Via Roma, the Via Duomo, the Via Diaz, where they have erected the new Postal Palace, a huge modern building in black imitation marble, totally out of place in Naples. It is the perfect fascist monument and would look far better in Littoria, the city Mussolini built from scratch in the Agro Pontino. But the delightful part is that all those gorgeous new streets don't make up a whole neighborhood; they're constantly crisscrossed by hundreds of sordid little streets. If you stray only slightly, you find yourself smack in the middle of overpopulated Naples and feel a hundred miles away.

Of course I should now tell you about the people in those streets, the Neapolitans. They are perhaps the only people in all of Europe about whom a foreigner can have something to say even if he's been in their city for just a week, because they are the only ones whose lives you can *see* as they're being lived from beginning to end. I suppose that nowadays they go into hiding to make love: *nowadays*, under fascist authority; but twenty years ago, they must have done it on their doorsteps, or else, with the doors wide open, on their vast beds. How generous they seemed to us in their immodesty, the day we arrived, compared to the Romans. Alas, they are neither handsome nor appetizing, so the spectacle of their intimacy is somewhat repellent. From afar they often seem gorgeous because they dress up in brilliant rags. The Beaver will tell you about the tattered old woman with her golden slippers. I can still see a young woman and a little girl in a steep street, halfway up a staircase—the girl in a purple dress; the woman had tossed on top of her nightgown a coat in a green that would have set your teeth on edge. You often happen on children wearing pajamas of multicolored light material printed with greenery or huge flowers in vibrant colors, but when you get close, you see faces mottled with eczema, impetigo, scabies. Almost all the children have dirty red scabs on their faces, and the adults aren't spared, either. In addition, the heads of many of the little girls have been completely shaved to get rid of lice. Nowhere have I seen so much infirmity. There are all sorts: first, people with rickets, then hordes of dwarves. I remember a little hunchback of about ten, horribly pale and thin, wearing his father's old shoes, enormous clogs that made him look monstrous. He was standing on one foot, right in the middle of the street. With a look of solemn despair, he was trying to fasten the shoe on his other foot. But you see so many other miseries too: empty eye sockets, rotten teeth, enormous warts, stumps. The other day a woman, her left arm amputated above the elbow, was brandishing her stump in the air, in a fit of indignation, striking it with her right arm, the way others would beat their chest. Just imagine, amid all this wretchedness, an extraordinary freedom, if not sexual then at least carnal: all the children up to five or six and often older run around bare-bottomed. I've never seen so many infant rears in all my life. Everywhere children, everywhere behinds and quivering little genitals shaking every which way. When they crawl up stairs scraping their genitals on the steps, I have the same painful sensation I felt at the Hamburg zoo with the Arabian baboons, when I was afraid they'd squash their members. All those dirty backsides and genitals—it does seem awfully animal. Sick suffering animals, a teeming species, yet in the process of petering out. The dirtiest thing I saw was a five-year-old girl, head shaved, sitting on a staircase with her legs spread open. At least a dozen flies had lit on her naked genitals, and she was shuddering but didn't seem able to brush them off, and it reminded me of the defense-lessness you see in a horse when flies buzz around his eyes and all he can do is shake his head to drive them off. Well, there is a certain carnal natu-ralness in this display of dirty flesh, a pagan promiscuity, which might be appealing in handsome bodies that are whole and healthy, but is troubling and embarrassing here. The mothers kiss their children's bare bottoms. The other day a man about fifty, all wrinkled and tanned by the sun, wearing a leather apron and a gray cap, was kneeling in front of a boy of five. One gnarled hand, complete with dirty fingernails, was on the child's bare belly, while the nails of the other were lightly scratching the kid's genitals. Yesterday the Beaver pointed out a twelve-year-old girl crossing the Via Roma carrying a child upside down. She had one of the kid's feet in her mouth and was sucking on it. The slightly older boys forever play with themselves through their pants, and the little girls scratch away under their skirts. When a boy decides to urinate, he doesn't face the wall or unbutton his fly, he simply hikes up his pants, pulls out his member till it's slightly beyond the pant leg, and relieves himself in plain view. Everywhere mothers are nursing their babies in front of everyone, chatting with the neighbors. Of course, they do that in Rome too. But in Rome it was nastier, more fascist: it was the matron's chaste immodesty, the lesson to the celibate, the severe reminder of moth-erhood's precious role. Here, it's animal, it fits in with all the rest, with that all too contingent flesh digesting and breathing as one, all those bodies freely exchanging their fleas and their microbes—which becomes tragic when you recall that this population was decimated by cholera at the end of the last century. That was when, along with other sanitary measures, they put the Corso Umberto through to give the city some air. But you get the feeling that none of that would prevent new devastations, that these people have been marked for epidemics, that the "destiny of Naples," as Aron would say, the meaning of all this human swarming, is plague, cholera, diphtheria. And it is this tragic underpinning that gives the beautiful streets I've spoken of their full significance and profundity.

Yet Neapolitans don't look at all proletarian. Taken as a whole, they seem not a class but a flock. And their true social milieu is their street. They don't seem to contemplate their situation at all, to judge it or consciously suffer from it. I don't think they look very cheerful (the Beaver says the young people do), but they *are* insouciant. We even concluded that many of them must be happy: humanists in their own, almost animal, way, they live their whole day squeezed against their fellow men, whom they love, even in the flesh. They earn little, but everything's so cheap they aren't in need. For instance, with the liras we've just tossed him, the strolling musician buys a big slice of watermelon. And they do eat their fill. Filthy, misshapen children eat all the time, at all hours chewing on enormous chunks of bread stuffed with cooked peppers. And then, when Neapolitans aren't eating, they're sleeping. It's no myth. In the afternoon certain entire streets fall totally asleep—it's like Sleeping Beauty's castle—and the sleepers stay in the position where sleep overtook them: three musicians are asleep in a street of stairs, leaning against a wall with their instruments beside them, wrapped in gray covers; a young man curls up in the flat basket used for the fruit he sells, and sleeps among the green leaves and dry dirt from the fruit. Waiters, in their black vests and white jackets, sleep on tables in the same spot where they will lay out place settings an hour later. Others sleep against walls, against lamp-posts, on the ground. On the beach, a sailor was asleep beside a boat, one leg raised, foot hooked on the gunwale. Those who aren't sleeping have reddened eyes and a pensive look, as though remembering one dream or just embarking on the next: they are always between naps, always a bit vague. But then when the moment comes for stealing or begging, an amazing vivacity overtakes them—a vivacity, by the way, without the least intelligence.

The Neapolitans aren't intelligent; they're beneath good and bad taste. It wouldn't occur to them to arrange a market stall or a street to make it attractive or agreeable. Of course, they do put plants all over the place, but they love them as they love children's backsides: in an animal sort of way, because they're green and alive. They have no depth at all: in Rouen, in Paris, poverty gives certain people a look so strange and profound, you want to get to know them, to know what they're thinking. But it's all too obvious that Neapolitans don't think about anything. Yet their streets, the things they use, the way in which things are arranged, everything is delightful and pro-found. That is because of the filth, which has settled on things just as the sun has settled on Turin's houses or the years on the columns of the Roman forum. The wood of their long water barrels, of their wine vats, their doors, the iron of the locks, of the tools, it is all a beautifully intense and carbonaceous black. As they get worn, rusted, dirtied, broken, all these objects take on a meaning far beyond their original one: they're not merely a tool, a plate, a utensil; they exist for themselves and are absolutely indefinable, inhuman. And it's also the indolence of the Neapolitans, their sense of letting go, that permits all those things to maintain on their own a mass of relationships that are totally beautiful and unintended. A basket of fruit beside a barrel organ, a plate of tomato paste drying beneath a picture of the Virgin, an oven drawer laid on a rickety chair and filled with glowing coals: all of that is the successful product of chance. But everywhere in Naples, chance is master, and it flourishes. It flourishes even in horror. On Sunday I saw a young girl walking in the bright sunlight. The entire left side of her face was contracted to overcome the blinding light. Her left eye was closed and her mouth grimaced, but her right side was absolutely still and seemingly dead. Her right eye, wide open, pure blue, completely transparent, radiant, sparkling like a diamond, reflected the rays of the sun with as much inhuman indifference as a mirror or window pane. It was quite awful but strangely beautiful; of course, the right eye was glass. Only in Naples can chance thrive like that: a filthy sun-dazzled girl with a gleaming mineral existence amid her impoverished flesh, as if her eye had been ripped out, to adorn her the more sumptuously. In fact, I think that in ten days we must have seen eight or nine Neapolitans with a glass eye.

Of course, there are some Neapolitans who are simply handsome. They have svelte tan bodies and handsome sleepy Oriental faces whose eyes both caress and scheme. Most of them sport thin black mustaches that make them look like villains in American movies. They know they are handsome, and they strike poses, in a manner that isn't always graceless, like the young Neapolitan singing, sprawled on a horsedrawn cart, his shirt wide open across his tan chest.

I must emphasize to you that the Neapolitan's bodily filth isn't the dingy filth of the Rue Eau de Robec,[3] but rather a swarthy, gilded filth. Actually that isn't always true: Naples is the only city in Italy where I saw inexplicably wan bodies and faces, flesh like plucked chickens. I think the explanation must be that the laziest and sickliest huddle like mushrooms in their stifling, shady streets, never venturing into the sun.

So that, my dear Iaroslaw, was the impression these streets made on

---

[3]A very poor street in Rouen. (SdB)

us. They often reminded us of the Moroccan streets of Tétouan, because of those sick bodies wrapped in resplendent fabrics, because of the street life, and also because they make up a sort of separate city, as in Tétouan, an indigenous city surrounded by European-type boulevards. But in Tétouan the sumptuous quality had more grace, a lighter touch, and there were happier landmarks of the human will. Besides, the Arabs are far more pleasant and likable than the Neapolitans.

So I'll resume with Saturday afternoon. We were exploring the alleyways between the port and the Rettofilo. It's the most sordid neighborhood in all of Naples; there's simply nothing like the filth and poverty of these people. There were many, incidentally, who seemed mentally defective. The houses are totally squalid, and nearly all are on the verge of collapse. As for the odors, my dear Iaroslaw, I don't feel obliged to linger over them. But because of all this, it's one of the most interesting parts of Naples. It is a veritable den of thieves, and yet you can still hear the sound of trolleys and cars on the Rettofilo; many of these alleyways terminate at the Rettofilo itself, which appears at the end of these swarming hives like a deserted flaming furnace. The Beaver was in heaven. She wanted to follow each little street, and I was hard at my map trying nonetheless to keep to a set direction for our walk. I was overwhelmed by a sense of responsibility, because we take turns as tour leaders, and it was my turn in Naples. After a while we tried to get to the harbor, to our left. We were hoping to find docking areas, as in Le Havre, or masses of boats behind a long breakwater, as in Marseilles. But the port of Naples is off limits, since it is a military port. It is from there, you may recall, that the troops embarked for Abyssinia. We saw nothing but walls stretching as far as the eye could see. Once, discovering a door, we went into a sort of shed, but no sooner had we glimpsed a little murky water at our feet than some soldiers came rushing up and chased us away. So we went back to our narrow streets, which grew shorter and shorter and cleaner and cleaner, because the sanitizing boulevard crosses the city diagonally, moving closer and closer to the port, until finally the dirty streets are squashed between the harbor and the boulevard. Soon there were only short stretches left, and it took considerable ingenuity to avoid constantly winding up at the docks or on the Rettofilo. Then there were no more at all, and we emerged through a triumphal arch into the Piazza Municipio. It is there you see the sea for the first time. The harbor wall stops and you suddenly see it, and across the water, there is Vesuvius, emitting a steady wisp of smoke, calm and persistent. The Beaver has undoubtedly described these natural beauties to you. That's not my role. I'll simply say that it was very pleasing and that a heat haze veiled the other side of the gulf without concealing it completely. This said, I'll return to my part, the Piazza Municipio. It was strangely shaped, what with the sea to the south, offices and shipping agencies to the north and east, and a charming old castle with two crenellated towers to the west. It struck us with an instantaneous feeling of *seaport*. Till then, in the little streets of old Naples and facing the docks rimmed with walls, we had not seen that. But there, facing that contingent, incomplete square, with the sea entering as a sumptuous, indispensable element, we really felt we were in a seaport. Not simply by the sea, but in a city that lives from the sea. We took a street bordered by arcades and found ourselves on a small square crisscrossed by trolley lines, the Piazza Trento e Trieste, in the heart of the city.

We sat down and had coffee in a pleasant brasserie with a narrow little terrace, the Gambrinus. And we had some really splendid orange *granitas*. To the north we could see the somber entry to the Via Roma, the city's major thoroughfare. We got an impression of prosperity, totally surprising after all the dirty little streets. Men in white linen suits passed by. And beautiful women, much fatter than the Romans, with hair black as night, thick, bestial lips, and a look of brutish sensuality. We left; we were already very fond of Naples, and yet we didn't know a tenth of its narrow streets. We followed a long promenade beside that luxurious sea, and it is that sea, with its sparkling blue and the charming contours of its gulf, which makes you think of a Riviera of palaces like the ones in Nice and Juan-les-Pins. But the narrow, silent promenade that borders it, with its dark little garden, wasn't remotely like the Promenade des Anglais. It was poor and decent, it was unremarkable; Naples is a city of failed luxury, and it is very moving and appealing, when you think of everything that predestined it to play the role of an Italian Nice. Naturally there was nobody yet along the walk except for two men on a bench in animated conversation. But on the beach was a band of half-naked fishermen, some asleep, others playing cards or repairing nets, some children, a few men and above all some handsome old men, dark as American Indians, with white hair on their bare chests and white mustaches. So, on our left was the sea and the far shore of the gulf, very white, so clean from a distance that we said, the Beaver and I, "That's the palace side" (it was a serious error: it was the pasta-factory side, Iaroslaw), and, above that white line, the cone of Vesuvius. Across from us, far away, veiled in haze, the Isle of Capri. On our right, below a little elongated garden, the city in tiers, with an ugly white palace visible from every direction, very high above our heads, and a charming bright red house with a tall arcade. After a while we left the seashore and began to climb toward the upper city. I remember a street of stairs, long and cool, with walls painted blue, with creeping woodbine, and women delousing their children. It could have been four-thirty, but the temperature was lovely and soft, hot with a gentle cooling breeze. We turned back across the hillside toward the Via Roma and the center city, through prosperous streets. They were very appealing. You remember how you noticed in Le Havre that French houses by the seashore grow lighter, almost—but not quite—becoming vacation houses. That's what happens in Naples to Italian houses, to those long flat houses without peaked roofs. And it's very pleasant, I assure you, to see the severe houses of Florence or Turin soften, lighten, and begin to look like glorified shacks where you spend a month or two. In those tranquil, gracious streets it wasn't the Southern Italian, or Neapolitan, side that dominated, it was more something that both Naples and Genoa have in common with them: the slightly languid, slightly sneaky sweetness of the comfortable areas of Italian ports with their indefinable feeling redolent of that cinnamon cream they use in their pastries. I wasn't quite acclimated: I was just coming from Rome, and my tourist's eyes were looking everywhere for beauty by the square inch. But what was really needed was letting go, giving in to the artful sweetness of the ending of the day. White walls, creeping woodbine, balconies, carriages passing close by, the sound of horses' hooves almost as pleasant as the sound of water in fountains and wells, occasional glimpses, down dark little streets, of blue sea. A bit farther on the houses closed in, the street grew darker, and we came upon another of those impoverished districts that I described a while ago. We stayed there as long as possible, but finally had to leave, exiting onto the Via Roma, a wide thoroughfare full of people and shops. We wanted to find the post office and a hotel. According to one guidebook, the hotel was on the Via dei Fiorentini. But the Via dei Fiorentini has disappeared along with many other little parallel streets; walls have been demolished. They have been replaced by vacant lots and fences. It is the beginning of the end of old Naples. Certainly the fascists won't need more than twenty years to transform it into a squared-off city with streets that intersect at right angles and big healthy apartment buildings ten stories high. Thus we were all the more moved, as it is something that cannot go on living. If it stayed as it is for very long, cholera and typhus would take charge of its destruction. Actually, however, Mussolini will destroy it much more quickly than cholera. Thus it is caught between the two perils of epidemics and fascism. We are very pleased to have seen it: perhaps by our next trip, scarcely any of it will remain, perhaps it will have become a Milan by the sea. So our old hotel no longer existed: there must have been three walls and some wallpaper left. We looked for the post office and found, as I said, a huge black-and-gray fake-marble structure. The interior fulfills the promise of the exterior. There are huge halls with masses of service windows. Each hall has tables for writing, with nickel-and-red-leather stools. When you sit down on the stools, they sink slightly and the writing-table lights come on. I sat down on one of them to compose a telegram to Zuorro,[4] who was asking for our address. An old woman with a bandanna on her head came up to me and laboriously explained that she wanted me to compose a telegram for her too since she couldn't read or write. You can imagine the impression that made: modern fascist Naples, the illiterate old woman in the glorious Postal Palace. I have to confess she wasn't satisfied with my services and approached others. After that we went off to look for a hotel and found one near the station, modest but clean. In the closets a large sign read: "Our esteemed and respectable clients are requested to disregard the disloyal bellboys and rivals who resort to a thousand ruses to prevent them from staying with us and who go so far as to use our name in order to lead them to hotels in the lowest category." With everything else now settled, the Beaver's stomach became imperious. I didn't want to eat, and the Beaver, left to her own devices, succumbed to the picturesque and dragged me into a little pizzeria on a piazza near the station. It was a tiny white room with a counter and four tables covered with white cloths. In the back of the shop they made the pizzas (you know, those Neapolitan crêpes with cheese and tomatoes). When ready, they were carried out to a stall set up in the street, and there a man would sell them to a clientele of mainly women and children. But the better-off people came in and sat at a table to eat their pizzas while sipping glasses of wine. Clearly the shop wasn't made for anything else, it was solely for the delectation of pizza. But to flesh things out a little they'd added a few dishes to the menu, such as pasta and veal scaloppine. The good Beaver caused a bit of a sensation by asking for pasta. The waiter, who looked exactly like the faithful old servant of a noble family down on its luck, nonetheless accepted her order. But when I, wanting neither to eat anything nor to occupy a seat without consuming something, asked for some mineral water, he exploded: "One does not drink mineral water in Naples, sir. One drinks water." But then he placed in front of me a bottle of warm mineral water, in which one sensed, from a vaguely

---

[4] *[Marc Zuore] A friend of Sartre's from the Cité Universitaire, a professor of humanities. I spoke of him at length in* La Force de l'âge *[The Prime of Life], under the name Marco. He was Sartre's inspiration for certain characteristics of Daniel in* Les Chemins de la liberté *[The Roads to Freedom]. (SdB) Sartre lived at the Cité Universitaire, a student residence enclave on the southern borders of Paris, during the 1928–29 academic year while preparing for his second* agrégation.

dusty sensation on the tongue, that it might once have been effervescent. But the Beaver's spaghetti was another matter. They undoubtedly had to get it from some old box in the cellar, which took time. We were politely seated, the Beaver and I, and watched fat navy officers in white uniforms consume their pizzas with glasses of red Vesuvius wine. Every five minutes a cook would cross the little room with a platter of piping hot pizzas, which he placed on the stall. And through the store window and the open door we could watch the pizza vendor, with red hair and long decaying teeth, surrounded by a mob of kids to whom he'd hand out the pizzas. Then, when he'd sold them all, the kids would go off, leaving him alone. Then he'd turn around, come up to the door of the restaurant, and vaguely scan the interior, rolling his eyes and smiling like an idiot. After a moment or two he would return to his stall and we would hear him singing, in an odd and very Neapolitan sort of nasal singsong, with flourishes and scoops, to attract customers. Then a mass of tattered, squealing little boys would crowd around him; the cook, a handsome young Neapolitan with a black mustache and a smug and vapid manner, would bring out the steaming pizzas, and the whole thing would start over. At each new order, the idiotic vendor would take up a pizza, fold it in two, and put a thick slice of cheese inside. It's more rudimentary than in Rome, where the cheese is melted into the pizza. But where was the Beaver's spaghetti? When the old waiter finally brought it, it was inedible. We left the pizzeria, disappointed, with empty stomachs, and the good Beaver accused me, not without some injustice, of wanting her to die of hunger. Next to the pizzeria, there was a cinema that seemed inviting. For one franc you could see, from the best seats in the house, three movies, each an hour and a half long, plus the news. It was a small old theater, very touching, a survivor from the silent era, with charming photos, the kind of pictures that seem to date from the time of daguerreotypes, glued onto the red cardboard billboards. The photos themselves are completely worn, almost indecipherable, crisscrossed with white cracks that look like traces of tears. (Don't think, by the way, from the looks of this handwriting, that I've become a systemic paralytic: I'm writing to you on a Sicilian train on our way from Palermo to Messina.) One of the movies they were showing was about the end of the world, and another was a detective movie. That was the one we wanted to see, and we had the good fortune to arrive just as it was starting. We climbed a narrow staircase to a small gallery with some twenty chairs scattered about. It was terribly hot and humid, with the kind of heat you find inside every building in Naples. Of course, the film was as bad as could be, but that didn't matter at all: the charm of little old movie theaters is totally unrelated to the movies playing in them. The poor Beaver left, completely dazed by the heat and with a growling stomach. So we got some fresh air and ate some brioches on the terrace of the Gambrinus, which I've already mentioned to you. Then once more we saw the Bay of Naples. When darkness hides the city and the lights shimmer all along the coastline, there is nothing more sumptuous in all the world. There is even a small column of lights in the sky—the cable car on Vesuvius. And who would believe that the other lights are from lampposts and the houses of the poor? There was a cool breeze, and we saw a lot of light coming from the crenellated terrace of the fortress in the Piazza Municipio. Looking closer, we made out a stage with little characters moving about, and the wind even wafted some fragments of music our way. We would really have liked to go, but it was a festival of Neapolitan song. Neapolitans create songs, *canzonnette*; it comes naturally to them. Like the people, the songs seem lively yet lazy and caressing beneath the liveliness. At times they have the harsh accent of a Sevillana, but it immediately dissolves into syrup. They are like bullfights to the Spanish: a national sport. There are enthusiasts who judge them rigorously, and every year grand festivals of the canzonnetta are held at La Piedigrotta, a suburb of Naples. Later, they sell the most popular songs under the title "Canzonnetta of La Piedigrotta 1935," or '36, etc. We were afraid, the Beaver and I, of being unable to savor all the fine points and so went off to bed.

The next day, Sunday, we walked down every little street we could find, and then went to the museum to see the mosaics and frescoes of Pompeii. We were entranced by the mosaics, but the frescoes gave me an odd feeling. As you know, they are sections of painted walls. The people had very small rooms, with little more than a bed in each. But they had the walls painted with care. There are some charming motifs, arabesques in a beautiful brown with a tiny bird or a small pitcher in beautiful

[*passage missing*]

What put me off at first was the Pompeiian way of fictively enlarging their tiny rooms. The painters did it by covering the walls with false perspectives: they would paint columns, and behind those columns receding lines that gave the room the dimensions of a palace. I don't know if they allowed themselves to be taken in, those vain Pompeiians, by the trompe-l'oeil, but I would have been horrified: they are the very sort of pictures you can't take your eyes off when you're slightly feverish. And then I was rather disappointed by the frescoes of the so-called best period with their mythological characters and scenes. I had hoped to find in Pompeii some kind of revelation about real Roman life, a more youthful life, more brutal than the one we were taught about at school; it had seemed to me impossible that these people weren't a bit savage. And I held the eighteenth century responsible for the whole Greco-Roman stereotype I found so boring in school. . . . So I'd expected to rediscover the real Rome. Whereas these frescoes soundly disabused me: you could already find the Greco-Roman stereotypes at Pompeii. You get the feeling they'd stopped believing long ago in the gods and demigods they painted on their walls. The religious scenes were only pretexts, but the Pompeiians didn't pull free of them. Going through these halls filled with frescoes, I was hypnotized by a classicism full of hackneyed drawings. I would see the same scene from the life of Achilles or of Theseus ten times, twenty times over, and it was frightening, a city whose inhabitants had nothing but that on their walls, just that alone, and it already seemed a dead civilization to them, a condition far removed from their preoccupations as bankers, merchants, and shipowners. I imagined the cold refinement and convention-laden culture of those people, and I felt very far from the beautiful, bewitching statues in Rome. (The Beaver will no doubt already have told you that a few days later we did discover on the ground floor of that same museum a mass of bewitching statues, with copper pupils. But they were from an earlier era.) As we left the museum, I had lost almost all desire to see Pompeii and felt a rather disagreeable mixture of curiosity and revulsion for those Romans. It seemed to me that even in their own time they were already Antiquity, that they could have said: "We, the Romans of Antiquity," like those knights in some farce: "We, the knights of the Middle Ages, are off to fight the Hundred Years' War."

[passage missing]

All those streets[5] are so narrow that the rooms opening onto them remain dark at noon despite the violent sun. Dark but not cool. It must be warm there, the kind of warmth that brings out odors in things and people, since from each dark room wafts a powerful complex of odors, the smell of sweat, of fruit, of frying, of cheese and wine, which swept over us as we passed by, and we would leave one odor only to plunge into another containing the same elements but in different proportions. *It is the streets* that are cool and shady, though one glimpses the implacable sky above the roofs of their tall

---

[5] *In Naples. (SdB)*

houses, or else, at the very end of the street, steamy sea gleaming in the sunlight. On the ground floor of each house they've cut out a mass of small rooms that open directly onto the street, and every one of these small rooms contains a family. (These are very poor and dirty people, like the population of the Rue Eau de Robec.) They are all-purpose rooms, where they eat, sleep, and work, but because they're warm, dark, and odorous, and the street is convenient and cool, right there at the same level, it attracts the people. They go outside for the sake of economy, so as not to have to turn on the lights, and to be out where it's cool, but also, I believe, from a humanist impulse, to be out and moving around, feeling alive alongside others. They drag their chairs and tables out into the street or to the doorways, half in, half out, and it is in this intermediate world that they perform the principal acts of their lives. So there is no longer any inside or outside; the street becomes the extension of their rooms, they fill it with their intimate odors and their furniture. With their history, too. Imagine, walking down a street in Naples, we pass a clump of people sitting outside, busy doing in public everything the French do in private, and you can just make out behind them in a dark lair all their furnishings, their armoires, their tables, their beds, the bric-a-brac they love, the family photographs. And the outside is organically connected to the inside, it always gives me the feeling of a slightly bloody membrane pushed outside, accomplishing their numerous little gestations. When I was working on the PCN,[6] my dear Iaroslaw, I read that the starfish, under certain circumstances, can turn its stomach inside out, extruding it to digest food externally. That disgusted me. But the image forced me to feel the generosity and organic obscenity of the streets of Naples, where thousands of families turn their stomachs inside out (and even their intestines). Everything is outside, you understand, but everything remains contiguous, interlinked, organically connected to the inside, to the shell: the thing that gives meaning to what happens outside is the dark cavern behind it, where the beast returns to sleep at night, behind thick wooden shutters. In the evening when we go for a walk, everywhere we see people who have carried a table outside and are eating dinner in the street. From time to time the wife gets up and goes into the room to fetch a dish or a bottle. Yesterday I saw a father and mother dining outside, while inside the baby was asleep in a crib beside the parents' big bed, and at another table the oldest daughter was doing her homework, by the light of a gas lamp. As for the bed itself, you couldn't say whether it is outside or in. No doubt around eleven they return to the heavy odors of

---

[6] The examination for a course of study in the sciences.

the room, close the shutters, and go to bed, marinating in that atmosphere of musty smells. And at that moment, contact with the outside is broken off, the body has reingested its stomach: from outside you can no longer see anything but solid shutters, fastened by iron bars; you would think there was nothing there but shops abandoned for the night; you would be oblivious to all the breathing and all the digesting going on in the dark. But when a woman gets sick and stays in bed all day, it happens in broad daylight, and she is there for everyone to see. Yesterday we saw a sick woman, very pale, lying in the big double bed, her face turned to the street, watching with her large, feverish eyes the people passing by. And then, a bit farther on, a convalescent who had just gotten up, sitting on the doorstep in a long night-gown, and, behind her, the unmade bed. Births and deaths, I suppose, must happen like that, in the open street.

The artisans do their work in the street too. There is a cobblers' street, with all the cobblers out in it. Pairs of shoes by the hundreds hang from the open shutters of their rooms. They sit at a table by their doorstep, hammering soles and wielding awls. The carpenters and the wrought-iron workers are also interesting to watch. The charcoal workers too. They're totally blackened, and the room where they work is darker than all the others. The street, too, around their shops is black with soot. But the finest shops are the wine merchants'. The casks are outside, and so are the bottles in their water buckets, enjoying the fresh air. But inside, by the light of a lamp that I'll speak of later, you can just see other casks, wicker-covered bottles, and above them the ornate receptacles used in France for expensive liqueurs, such as Armagnac and Calvados, but used in Naples for the commonest wine, the coarse red Vesuvian that smells of rotting earth: they are huge green glass demijohns or immense bottles with slim necks that must contain a good ten liters. Those shops give off a splendid odor of wine that wafts into the street. We also saw a flock of merchants dealing in paper dresses and paper hats. Women make them outside, stitching multicolored sheets of paper. They hang outside, and their vibrant colors lend enchantment to the dark cavern where one can just barely see a pile of them; in those streets, of course, no "stores" as such exist. The most beautiful demonstration of this mixture of crafts and private life so far was a deserted room I saw last night. By the cloudy light of a red lamp one could see a bed and, in the foreground on the gray slat flooring, a monstrous heap of watermelons. They were deep green and looked like stones; you'd think a disaster must have just struck, that an avalanche of watermelons had fallen on the city, crashing through the roofs, cracking the skulls of the inhabitants, and that a hundred of them had tumbled, helter-skelter, into the deserted room, whose proprietor had had his skull cracked open in some other part of town. Some of these huge green living pebbles had rolled almost into the street. Yet in these immodest rooms, there is a small personal mystery, the mystery of faith. All these Neapolitans are pious, with a naive piety that I confess I found appealing. On the innermost wall of their rooms they all hang an icon, the picture of a saint or a statuette of the Virgin, illuminated throughout the day by a single bulb placed right below the picture or the statuette. The icon is always attached to the back wall at eye level, and the lamp illuminating it, generally red, is the only light in the room in most cases. The result is that the darkness of those rooms isn't a black half-light, but a reddish, devilish glow that confers on these caves an indefinable, secret aspect. I remember, the first night we were spellbound by one of those red-black holes with the icon's red light, all the way at the back, looking like the devil's fat ass, while on a table covered with oilcloth an enormous doll was giving the fascist salute. In another house there was neither Virgin nor saints, but the lamp—yellow this time—lit up the framed portrait of a man with a mustache, doubtless the dead husband or brother. Sometimes the lamp's light isn't strong enough to color the walls of the room, which remains a deep black, especially after nightfall. But all the way back, in the farthest recesses through layers and layers of shadows, you can see the light bulb and its little pink glass shade, the only visible thing, like an undersea flower. This morning I saw an old one-eyed woman, her nose raw with eczema, grumbling away in her room, gesturing toward the wall. I really believe she was telling off her personal Virgin.

It's very hard, my dear Iaroslaw, to recount in a letter like this everything that contributes to the charm of these streets. While you're walking around you discover loads of new things: for instance, everything you've just read I wrote last night. This morning we made a few little discoveries. For example, we have seen that glove-making is widely practiced in all these streets. We've seen countless women sewing on gloves inside-out. And then I saw a blacksmith hammering iron outside on a charming little anvil that was black with grease and age, on a tripod made of pink-white boards. They usually light their fires in the open street, and that's one of the things I like the most: you suddenly feel a puff of moist heat that has nothing in common with the heat of the sun, you turn and see nearby, beside the wall of the house, a stove, an oven, an oil stove, or a simple metal box filled with hot coals. And the fire, the flames, the glowing charcoal have that special yellowish color and the somewhat devious look flames have in full daylight. The Beaver remarked that ultimately the rooms are never—or almost never—exactly at street level.

Almost always you have to take a couple of steps up or down to get in. But in any case, the steps are inside the room; they're already a part of the lodging; that's what highlights the cavernous quality of all these excavations dug in the walls: they lie wide open to the street.

As well as the stationary occupations, which are limited to going in and out of their shells like snails, there are also masses of intinerant trades, entirely cut off from fixed bases and shells. The streets are full of them; they're on friendly terms with the small workshops. They are often reduced to the barest necessities, and that is what gives them their charm. Take, for example, a lemonade vendor; he's got a bucket of water, four lemons, two glasses, and a lemon squeezer. The guy sits on a chair, dozing as he waits. You give him two cents, he wakes up, squeezes the lemon into the glass, pours in a bit of water, and *voilà*: lemonade. The day before yesterday we saw a delightful object that was just as rudimentary: a small wooden vat with two handles. Across the rim was a big block of ice, and wedged between the ice and the vat were four or five little bottles of sparkling orangeade. A filthy little girl was watching over it. It's a small enterprise, selling a dozen bottles of orangeade a day. Or again, a guy is lying on a sack beside a flat basket containing some figs and a Roman scale. That's a fruitery. There are more sumptuous ones, there are also handsome stalls of fruit, artfully arranged, where they alternate the bleeding pink of the watermelons with the cucumber green of the honeydews. We saw a lovely one, with wheels painted blue and pretty paintings showing a crowd of little characters talking among themselves and arguing about the fruit. The handsomest stalls are certainly those of the lemonade and frozen syrup vendors, small box shelters in the middle of the streets decorated with garlands of beautiful lemons, their leaves still attached. There are also stalls for cakes and for cheese. In a general way, the streets are running over with food for sale: nuts, boiled ears of corn, grilled fava beans, fish, crustaceans, small squid. The Beaver says that Rome is a city without a stomach. Naples' stomach, on the other hand, is everywhere. Old women watch over all the comestibles, absently waving fly switches, which are bamboo handles with strips of colored paper stuck on the end. When the street is sunny, you also see thick tomato paste, tannish red, drying in the sun in a bowl placed on a chair or on the ground. There are also onions, fat red onions or strings of straw-colored onions, completely dried, that look like thick ropes. Now and then you come upon a simple old man absentmindedly cranking a barrel organ. We saw a charming old woman telling a young man a lengthy, very animated tale, waving her left hand in the air while her right turned the handle, eliciting from the instrument a jerky melody that would stop and start according to the rhythm of her story. Other times it's a trio of musicians, one singing while the others back him up on the guitar.

In the same way that the small open-air enterprises are an extension of the sedentary trades tied to the houses, there is a religion of intersections— icons at street corners—that extends and perfects those little private religions. Often you see very crude paintings on the walls—a rigid Virgin, with large crossed eyes, carrying her son in her arms. Then there are plaster Virgins and saints under glass, at the street corners. In Venice, in Rome, we'd seen such Virgins, but there were far fewer, mostly neglected; at night most of them weren't even illuminated. In Naples, each street has its Virgin or saint, lit up day and night by rows of electric lights. The votive statues are in large cases of multicolored glass that remind me of the verandas of old provincial houses, and the windowed boxes are topped with small glass roofs that extend beyond them like eaves. Most of the saints are ugly, but some are magical and full of mystery. This morning, for instance, we noticed a huge painting under glass showing a dark sky dotted with dim stars and in the middle of this sky a sort of haze in human form, a phantom riddled with stars that seemed to rise mysteriously into the heavens. The other evening we saw an uninteresting statue of the Virgin surrounded by a wall painted with a great royal blue sky and stars that gleamed like suns. And you get the strong feeling that each of the figurines reigns over the odors, the filth, and the food of its street, protecting the public life as those of the dark rooms protect what corresponds in Naples to private life.

Of course, the life of people in the upper floors must be rather different, since they can't push their armchairs and tables out onto the street. We don't know much about the way they live, or about any differences between them and the people on the ground floor. We do know they tend to bring their lives as close as possible to the life of the street. In Naples the balconies are like nowhere else in Italy, not Turin, nor Milan, nor Venice, nor Florence, nor Rome. Each window from the second floor up has its own personal balcony, overhanging the street, a small loggia with grillwork painted light green. And these balconies are quite different from those in Paris or Rouen: they are neither ornaments nor luxuries. Rather, they are respiratory organs. They allow people to flee the warmth of the room, to live outside a bit; they are like a very small portion of the street hoisted up to the second or third story. And in fact they are occupied, almost all day long, by people doing on the second or third floors what the Neapolitans of the street do: some eating or sleeping, some vaguely watching the theater of the street. And communication occurs directly between the balconies and the street, without having to *go back into* the room or use the stairs: a small basket is lowered to the street on a string. The people in the street empty it or fill it according to the need, and the person on the balcony hauls it up slowly. The balcony is quite simply the street in the air.

So far this has been explanation, dear Iaroslaw. But what I really hope is that you'll be able to get a general image and feel of the streets—not the anecdotal side but the totality of the first glance as you enter one of them. So, imagine a street darkened by looming buildings under a blue sky, a narrow street without sidewalks. The houses have entirely flat facades, as in Rome or Turin; their roofs are invisible and they stop abruptly at a straight line level with the top-floor ceiling. That goes for all of Italy. But then there are all those light-green balconies that jut out over the street and seem to converge at its end. The houses are generally a handsome pink, a real candy pink, but dirty, peeling, cracked, with missing pieces here and there. Still and all, the first colors the street offers are always pink and light green. There are also some with no definable color, dingy or simply dirty. But, different from Rome, what lends depth to the colors of the houses is never the sun, because the sun never enters the streets: it's the dirt. But, against this background of pink and light green, there is a play of nuances, because of all the things hanging there. For a street in Naples gives the impression of being filled with hanging things, which live and gently stir at every level. First because of the plants: creeping woodbine grows on every balcony, twining through the bars and hanging downward to form little arbors between the floors. And every leaf stirs at the slightest breeze. And then because of the drying laundry. On every street, at every story, laundry's hanging out to dry. Sometimes a wire or cord is run between two facing houses, but usually a long stick is fastened to the wall or driven into a crack, and from the top of the stick two strings are stretched to the wall and attached, one to the right and the other to the left, making an angle bisected by the stick. It's on those lines that the wash is hung. The wash is what you notice right away in a Neapolitan street. First there are rich colors (red, violet, gold, white), and there's so much laundry of all sorts that you wind up with the impression of walking down a street covered by a multicolored cloth. That's what gives the daylight, in the afternoon, its special and complex color. And yet, the moment you look up, you see blue sky, so you get the paradoxical impression of being in full daylight and, at the same time, under a tent, which is altogether unique to Naples and corresponds to the constant mixing of outside and inside. That's what gives the street its direction: it *hangs*. That's what always causes a street in Naples to be seen from top to bottom. As they are very rarely horizontal and often rise (Naples is a city of changing levels), you get the charming impression of streets that rise from the bottom and descend from the top.

And here is the essence of a street in Naples: a cool chasm full of nauseating odors, with shadowy holes to the right and the left, a chasm teeming with agitated people milling around, exactly like the Rue Mouffetard, while above people's heads objects hang and sway, their movements on the upper stories echoing the movements of the people in the street. And then, from time to time, a great white sheet hanging out to dry overhead swells like the sail of a ship. And shutters, handsome painted ones, a few with a complete little tale to tell. In a sense all the streets are alike. Yet they are also extremely varied. First, immediately after furnishing a general view, they scatter into countless little anecdotes, so you can walk through the same street a dozen times without recognizing it. Unlike Roman streets, they lack a unifying sense of the whole street that's strong enough to distinguish it from all the others or even impress itself on the inhabitants. That's because, unlike Roman streets, they're not made of walls, almost unbroken by windows, whose color, height, and direction constitute the intrinsic meaning of the street: they're made up of people, of itinerant vendors, of wash that hangs out all day long and disappears abruptly when it's dry, of things that come and go, they are bits and pieces in flux, that coalesce and dissipate incessantly. If you remember how the Rue des Charrettes in Rouen is different in the afternoon, when it is almost deserted, and in the evening with all the sailors cruising up and down, then you can imagine what happens a hundred times a day in the streets of Naples, so that while we walk around, we never know if we are seeing a different street or another view of the same one. We would have liked to walk around in each of them at all hours—in the morning, when the artisans are outside; during the hot hours of the afternoon, when the people are asleep in their chairs, sitting astride them, their arms resting on the back and their heads on their arms, and the mothers languidly delouse their children; in the evening, when the tables are dragged out into the street and the people eat; at night, when all the blinds are closed, all the stomachs retracted, and there's nothing left but a deserted trough between two tall naked walls. Depending on the day too, the sense of the street changes: on Saturday long strips of lights had been hung between the walls, and we were enchanted, as we strolled in the evening down the long Via dei Tribunali, to see on our right a clot of dark streets leading down toward the sea, decorated at ten-meter intervals with blossoms of fire. Clusters of sailors dressed in white were moving through, laughing and singing, so that each street looked like a charming mysterious avenue of bordellos. But that was an illusion: we saw no bordellos in Naples. Fascism has tidied things up there, and prostitution must be in hiding. Today, Sunday, around five in the afternoon, the Via dei Tribunali was less crowded than usual; the people suddenly seemed to prefer their interiors to the streets; most of them were resting in their dark rooms. Passing by, I could see on the bed the slipper-shod feet and dress hems of dozing women; young people were playing cards at the tables, or else, with all the doors open, they were dancing in the back of the room to the radio. We managed to distinguish among districts (it's easier than with streets). There's the impoverished and almost frightening port area, the central commercial district, and the slightly more prosperous, slightly more intimate quarter in the northeast.

All these streets intersect at right angles or very broad angles: there are almost no open piazzas in those districts, and that is the great difference between here and Rome or Venice. But in Naples there is something altogether unique: the blind alley. To all appearances it is simply an impasse like any other. You still see the balconies, the rooms opening onto the street, the drying laundry, etc. But, since the people live outside, life there appears to be a bit more closed-in than in other streets: instead of losing itself in the life of the next street, of giving the impression of incompletion, of always being open, it closes in upon itself. All these people who know each other, and live together, look as though they communally own their dead end. And I'm sure that's how they feel, from the way they proudly chase a stranger away, saying, *"Chiuso."* That's undoubtedly why the blind alleys are the most appealing areas in Naples, something like animal colonies or coral reefs.

Then we went up to the Posillipo, a hill above Naples with a fine view across the whole gulf. From above, Naples seemed white as a Moroccan city, spotlessly clean and luxurious. It's astonishing how this city is so dazzling white the moment you see it from outside. Each time we saw it from a boat, coming and going to Capri, and the evening of our departure for Messina, it presented the dazzling whiteness of a new city. And the moment you're inside, it is a somber, filthy city with pink walls. That day, from high up on the Posillipo, we didn't let ourselves get carried away, we already knew the truth. But we found ourselves enchanted by that hypocritical, girlish ingenuousness. We walked down again, taking a pleasant private lane, completely pink and paved with flagstones, which took us right down to the seacoast in ten minutes, two kilometers from the city. We had a drink there, on a café terrace, just above the water between two public bathhouses. We left at sunset and of course went back to the movies.

The following day, Monday, we took an early-morning train to Pompeii, crossing the entire southern suburbs of Naples, which had appeared so luxurious the previous evening but are actually, despite the pompous names (Portici—Torre del Greco), no more than a strip of big industrial buildings. An hour later we got off the train and onto a white, deserted road. There were two hotels by the roadside, one large and handsome, one small. We had to take a path to the left and climb for a hundred meters or so till we reached the "Excavations of Pompeii." We went through an automatic gate and the large portal of the Roman ramparts, repulsed the offers of several guides, then ducked into the little museum for a few minutes to give a group of tourists time to move off.

There was almost nothing in the museum except two or three cadavers of Pompeiians—all twisted with pain and verdigris—which the lava had taken by surprise and engulfed. There are another five or six in the houses of Pompeii. Some are simply castings poured into the imprints that the bodies, long since disintegrated, left in the lava. The others are real cadavers, and you can see their white bones sticking through the bronze flesh, where a piece of foot or leg has broken off. Some are raising their arms in front of their faces, while others are protecting their genitals with their hands. I thought of them again a few days later, on top of Vesuvius, when we saw the lava flows reaching out across the countryside like the fingers of a black hand. It is from up there, I believe, that the astonishing history of Pompeii assumed its full meaning. As the Beaver said, "This city had to be totally destroyed for it to remain preserved today." When the tourists' voices faded away we cautiously left and entered the city.

To Simone Jollivet

September 15

Dear Toulouse

We got home yesterday. First to obey you and then for pleasure, I read the aforementioned "Captain."[1] As reading matter, it is actually rather pleasant. But I'm filled with apprehension, since I can't really judge its theatrical value. If you have two hours, I will tell you about it, scene by scene, and translate passages for you. There definitely is a delightful role for Dullin, a totally original and appealing character which he could do something with.

---

[1]A German play [by Carl Zuckmayer], The Captain of Köpenick, which Simone Jollivet hoped to have Sartre adapt. (SdB)

We dreamed of treating you both at Pierre's, but we've returned from Italy without a stitch of clothing; I don't have any shoes left and I'm shuffling around in white espadrilles in the rain. So we'll have to put off the "formal" dinner till October. But if you can have me over (I'm free and at your disposal) we'll try to be entertaining as though at dinner and charm you with the tale of our trip without making you jealous. Let the Beaver know—71 Rue de Rennes (VI)—which afternoon or evening you're keeping for us.

We'll be very pleased to see you.

For Simone Jollivet

[Autumn]

A PLAY FOR THE YOUNG

Julius Caesar is a play for the young. An old play; but one that hasn't aged. The civility of love that we find in Racine is a bit out of style now. His Titus and Bérénice are dated—not because they are Romans, but because they belong to the court of the Sun King. In Corneille's work even heroism is cast in molds that have since been shattered. But anyone seeing *Julius Caesar* on stage is surprised to see and hear men very much like himself; this illusion is a terrible anachronism and the most exquisite "local color." From secondary school on we hated the Romans: it seemed inconceivable to us, so malign was their syntax, that they could speak as we do, order wine at a bar, tell a woman they loved her. Doubtless the fault lies with all those yellow- and green-backed books where we learned to declaim annotated expurgated Horace and Virgil. But any traveler who visits Pompeii suddenly feels his hatred for the classics dissolving. Or rather, the Romans that he imagines in that rediscovered city are no longer classics: they are men. Here rich merchants gave fine dinners, housekeepers went shopping for fish or meat, drunken sailors caroused. It's this freshness, this violence of life, that you find in Shakespeare's *Caesar*. Not so long ago it was thought necessary to burden the play with gorgeous sets. That was a mistake: crushed by the grandiloquence of the palaces, of the public squares that had been extravagantly recreated, it lost its familiar everyday character. Dullin tried to render its true flavor: *Julius Caesar* is a harsh and terrible drama that convulsed *the daily life* of the Romans. He admirably evoked everyday Rome; streets that look like those in Pompeii, a somnolent and bored Senate, interiors that have a barbarous charm, all serve as backdrops for the action, lending still greater force to the brutality and grandeur of the drama.

Thus Shakespeare, well served by a cunning modesty, moves us directly. I am not saying that Caesar, Cassius, Casca can without any transposition evoke our political concerns. In some respects that should please us very much. Yet the dissensions and factions of the expiring Roman Republic have furnished an eternal political substance for our reflection. These people move us; for reasons that aren't our reasons, they have fits of anger, uncertainties, disappointed ambitions, abrupt bursts of energy that we can recognize.

The young, particularly, recognize themselves there, though most of the characters are mature men: if youth is the age of generosity and mistakes, what more generous and irreparable faults can one find than those of Brutus— if it is the age of friendship, what friendship could be more tragic and beautiful than that of Brutus and Cassius—if it is the age of pure respect for great men, what respect could be more beautiful and intolerant than that of Brutus, who killed his idol Caesar to keep him from decaying—if it is the age of great ambitions, what more moving than to feel Caesar's immense and terrible glory, than to see the youthful fortunes of Antony and Octavius come alive while those of Brutus abruptly shatter? But youth, said Claudel, is above all the age of heroism, and that is why, I believe, young people have been flocking in such great numbers to the Atelier these past three months: *Julius Caesar* is a drama for heroes.

1937

To Simone Jollivet

[March]

Dear Toulouse

The note to Gallimard produced the anticipated effect.[1] At least as far as the Gil Blas. As for the La Fontaines, my mother clutched them, all six, to her breast, and I saw that only by trickery could I gain possession of them. Tomorrow you'll receive some "Sartre-Beaver" correspondence, as gracious supplement. Plus some Néguses.[2]

Would you be so kind as to leave with your concierge a candle decorated with aces; it would help me a lot with a rather superbly black mass I'm contemplating;* I can't thank you enough. Of course, if you would attach, as exchange of courtesies, the "Toulouse-Sartre" correspondence, you'd be even nicer, and my gratitude would be boundless. So I'll come by tomorrow, Monday, during the day, to drop off the correspondence and candies with the concierge. The Beaver's very tired; I had the doctor come by but don't yet know what he said.

You made a real conquest with the Lady, who came back dazzled by you. She said, "I have a veritable passion for Toulouse," then, blushing slightly, corrected herself: "One never has passions—but a very strong affec-

---

[1]When in 1937 Sartre resubmitted his manuscript of *Melancholia*, Dullin wrote a note, which proved very helpful, to his old friend Gaston Gallimard.
[2]Candies.

*I'll tell you a bit about it when I see you.

tion, yes." I really hope she pleased you too, though her timidity and the spell you cast over her reduced her to the role of enthralled listener.

I send you warmest greetings.

To Simone de Beauvoir

From Laon[1] [April]

My darling Beaver

I'm delighted to be writing to you, since it gives me the chance to call you that. Spelling out that name made me feel years younger, and I saw Saint-Germain-les-Belles again, not as it was, but as I imagined it while writing to you from Vichy in 1929. Now you seem like a young girl again and I want to write you a courting letter. Of course, my little grumbler, you will say that it's the ingenuously good husband in me trying to make the conjugal relationship attractive. But that is, in essence, bullshit, as you know.

I had a good trip, slept well, was thinking of you fondly. I ate a sandwich downstairs, but the radio was emitting *Faust* and not those charming Tartar melodies that so moved me the day before yesterday. A career officer woke me up this morning, washing his feet in his washbasin; I hated him, but managed to rack up my eight hours of sleep anyhow. I'm delighted to think you'll get this letter with your breakfast tomorrow. Insist on it, for it will be there; have the boy with the jug ears go downstairs; I did some research, and a letter mailed in the morning in Laon may even reach Paris *that very evening*. Just like that.

Do you feel well, are there roses in your cheeks? Don't forget to take a little walk around your armchair. And when you've had a good trip around it, sit down in it.[2]

Adieu, I'm about to talk to them about Gide. From 11:15 to 12:15 I'm writing to the T.P.[3] Zazoulich. From 4 to 11: Les Statues volantes [The

---

[1]In the fall of 1936, Sartre's teaching assignment had been transferred from Le Havre to Laon, about an hour northeast of Paris by train, allowing him to return a couple of times a week.

[2] *I was convalescing. (SdB)* Beauvoir missed a whole term of teaching, recovering in the South of France from a collapsed lung and exhaustion. Since the autumn of 1936, after the Naples trip, she had been teaching in Paris at the Lycée Molière.

[3] *Toute petite [the youngest], meaning Tania, Olga's sister. (SdB)* Zazoulich is the name given to the sisters in this correspondence.

Flying Statues].⁴ Tomorrow from 10 to 12: St. V. From 1:30 to 3:00: T.P.Z. From 4:15 to 5:15: T.P.Z.

I love you.

To Simone de Beauvoir

From Laon [April]

My darling Beaver

This letter will be short as there's not much to tell you. My spirits are high, though nothing's happening. I was quite surprised, on reaching Laon, to think that you weren't at Le Dôme or La Coupole with little Zazoulich but on some big important train speeding toward Marseilles. I didn't like leaving you before your departure; I'd like to have seen whether you had only a sad little corner or your own glorious banquette. This morning, as I woke up, I was also very surprised because I'd been in the habit of thinking of you with some superiority during the 10 minutes I devote to reverie between 7:25 and 7:35, imagining you asleep with your little fists clenched and looking worried. But this morning you were up, bright eyed, perhaps a little rattled inside, but all poetic and joyful and, doubtless, your nose glued to the window to see everything all over again. I hope you have lots of sunshine. Here it's all gray and gloom.

Young Bost¹ was at the station, glowing in his white sweater. He said, "It's hell, the Laon train," pointing toward two or three hundred people crushing their way into the car. I answered, "I hate military men." At which he smiled with some superiority. On seeing which I timidly replied: "But I've devised a theory to pardon me for hating them." He said, "Of course. What is it?" So I gave him my theory and he simply answered: "Pffft." Yet, earlier, young Bost had astutely discovered an empty compartment toward the front. When two soldiers came in later, two boneheads with tiny eyes and fixed stares, Bost was quite willing to agree that if that's the military, well, I might not be entirely wrong. Then without a transition, he went sad: "You realize, I'll be with guys like that for two years," then cheered up: "But maybe they'll reject me for active duty," then, turning poetic: "When I do my military

---

⁴ "La Chambre" ["The Room"]. *(SdB)* Under this new name, the short story appears in Sartre's collection *Le Mur (The Wall)*.

¹ Jacques-Laurent Bost, youngest son in a prominent Protestant family, was a student of Sartre's at the lycée in Le Havre. Bost became part of the Sartre-Beauvoir "family," remaining close to both all their lives. He later married Olga Kosakiewicz.

service I'll get to know some gangster who'll take me under his wing, and all the other guys'll quake." I said curtly: "But you'll be in the noncombatant service." At first he tried to deny it, then found a better defense: "There are gangsters even among the noncombatants . . ." "No, they're all screwed up." "Well, he'll be a screwed-up gangster with a pistol." Then we did the *Paris-Soir* crossword puzzle without using the vertical definitions. Then we made a resolution, and shook on it: next September we'll buy ratty clothes at a thrift shop, put them on, and with ten francs each go off together for a week. We allow ourselves to beg, open doors and steal. But all other resources are forbidden. We'll sleep in shelters, on the Salvation Army barge. For tobacco we'll pick up butts. I'll sing in courtyards. We had fun imagining the whole thing: we'll make new friends, tramps and disreputable types; we'll fear the cops. We'll fear everything. "It will be disgusting," he said rapturously. "Dirty old men will want to paw *us.*" Caught up in the story, I didn't have the heart to challenge that flattering and inexact "*us.*" We agreed that if we held out for a week, we'd be unapproachable and reek for the rest of our lives. We won't see you during that week, but on the eighth day, we'll invite you to Pierre's and tell you the whole thing in detail, which you'll suffer through. We concluded, not without some melancholy, that you wouldn't take this project seriously so long as it isn't realized that you'd discourage us by your doubts and mocking. But we'll stand pat. We won't take you along because— as young Bost vehemently insisted—"We don't want any *old bags* with us." Then we arrived; we drank and ate at the poetic little café. Of course there were military types there. "I hate the military," said young Bost. We went to bed at midnight and I slept for six and a half poor little hours. I taught 3 ½ hours of classes and found a certified letter at the concierge's lodge. Just imagine my curiosity and my joy. It was a summons with costs from the tax collector. But I'll hold off till the 15th. They don't act until after the second summons.

Bost came to pick me up at the lycée. He told me two nice little details about the relationship with Zazoulich. The first: yesterday they played at insulting each other, "stinker," "louse," etc. She walked out, in the heat of the game, calling him dead meat. Ten minutes later she came back. Young Bost, still playing: "Fuck off, get lost." She looked at him with wide offended eyes and ran off and shut herself up in her room for two hours. The drollest part, I think, goes to Bost, who stayed in his room, placid and incurious, for two hours. Round two: still at it. She said to him gently, "You know, I went to see Dumas—he'll come to see you at six tonight. Oh, it's nothing, he simply wants to chat a bit with you, because you're his former student." "But why?" "No reason, just because." Interrupting, I said to Bost, "You believed her." "Me? No." I insisted, sternly: "You believed her." "No. Just for a second." "A long time." "Two seconds." He said to her, "If you don't tell me why you went to see Dumas I'll have a fit." She, gently, "But you *don't have* fits. You're just a little senile and forgetting everything." Then she clapped a hand over her mouth, as though dumfounded by what she'd said.

That's it. My darling Beaver, I'd really like to have a little note from you, because things are still idyllic despite the distance between us. I'm delighted to think that you've already begun your little solitary activities, but I'm a bit scared you might tire yourself out. (The character facing me is muttering, "I'd sell my soul for one good sneeze.") I grabbed young Bost by a jacket button a little while ago and sang your praises, for the pure pleasure of talking about you. I love you, my darling Beaver.

To Simone de Beauvoir

Tuesday

My darling Beaver

Young Bost has just left. It's seven o'clock and I'm writing to you from the hotel lobby. Light as that young man's presence is, you feel something like a vacuum when he goes. This lobby becomes awfully gloomy as I think of you so far away. Last night and this morning I felt a slight pang thinking I won't find you at the Hôtel Royal-Bretagne Wednesday night, and that we won't go off arm in arm, to the Auberge Polonaise or some such place, and *that* I find totally absurd. At Laon I don't miss you too much, because you've never been here, but in Paris I will certainly feel your absence. But, my love, don't come tearing back like a whirlwind; this is just a gentle little melancholy, with its own charm, that lets one know when one is fond of someone. I'm extremely fond of you, my darling Beaver, and you are here before me, in the flesh, with your little white raincoat and blue hat. And so you see when you ask if I have any images of you, I do, Beaver, I do indeed, and I think they'll keep till your return, for they seem so very solidly imprinted. Are you on tenterhooks? Are you having good weather? Are you strolling around like an ant with visions of rocks? Yesterday it was your yesterday letter I was longing to see, but today I would like the one you're writing at this very moment, because, even if you had a slight headache, I think it must be gone by now and you are all joy. I so want you to have good weather. Eat well, my Beaver, turn your back to the sea, walk three little kilometers, then sit down.

So, yesterday around four I mailed my letter. We settled down in the lobby and worked on our respective factums. He was disgusted because he'd lost his fountain pen and would scowl as he dipped a stick pen into a half-empty inkwell. As for me, at first I felt tired and quite incapable of laying out the words (for lack of sleep), then was overcome with frenzy and wrote six pages with a feeling of total satisfaction. Their comparative worth (at least in the eyes of young Bost) you will soon discover. We dined. I made him laugh till he cried by describing my feelings for Z.: "I love her in God." (If you hate me calling Zazoulich Z., write me. It isn't out of repressed hatred that I cut it short, nor to destroy her symbolically, but because when I spell out her full name I have to think about each letter in turn.) We talked very little over dinner, because each was lost in his factum and a bit groggy from two hours of mental exertion (tapioca soup—poached eggs Florentine—squab ragout and dessert). But after dinner came the show. We'd returned to our seats (the two by the desk). We were face to face, with the pouch of tobacco on a little shelf between us. Little by little the armchairs in the lobby filled: the old Catholic bitch was knitting, so was the good little girl beside her, the crabby mother was sewing, the art teacher came and sat down, and then, to her left, a young veterinary officer in a green velvet kepi, with a face both flaccid and nervous, looking like pink meat, his weak sensual mouth frozen in an eternal smile of unconcern that seemed vaguely insolent. He'd planted himself in the rocking chair with his head thrown back, rocking away to express even more clearly his casual insolence. His friends, three officers his age (indistinguishable to me now as I sit here writing) and, settled into the smoking room, a fat captain with a mordant wit, and a whore for a wife (cheap perfume, diaphanous blonde, wrinkles, flowery hat, fortyish. The garish makeup and frills on her dress seemed little more than old habits; the dominant impression was a bad-tempered decency and a ladylike ease, which seemed to come from far away). This flowery blonde briefly stood behind the young vet and rocked him gently in his chair, but like the mother of a friend, nothing more. Fat M. Bihan, owner of the hotel, prowled around, straddled a chair, threw a word or two toward the ladies, disappeared, reappeared, toddling, his stomach great as with child, concentrating on his posture (he has that naturally comic nobility of fat men from the Midi). Then someone came in, at first I couldn't see who. Then I heard an eruption: it was M. Bihan and the newcomer busting their guts laughing: "She's just playing all by herself. She said she's just playing all by her lonesome. She's saying stuff that would make a sailor blush." And the art teacher was protesting, "I do not know what you're trying to make out of what I said, but this nonsense has to stop this instant." Indignant and lisping as usual and thinking she was

concealing her fury behind the lisping, the way an ostrich thinks it's hidden
when its head is in the sand. I took a look at the newcomer, the one they
call the man of law, who is in fact a judge in Laon. He's tall and thin, with
a short, slightly snub nose, an insolent look in his eyes, incipient jowls, streaks
of steel gray in his hair. He's maybe twenty-six. He paced back and forth,
turned on his heels, "crossing the stage" at each remark. Then he and the
art teacher began exchanging venomous observations in the general silence:
"Have you been dancing?" he asked. "I know you're a splendid dancer."
"Oh, Monsieur Noël, I don't have any such pretensions—you know that."
(He claims he dances very well, and taunts her.) "But with patience, you
will, you'll learn to dance." "Perhaps I will, but not from you," etc. The
young vet looked at the judge with hatred; I didn't yet understand why. "And
Mlle Quint," said Mlle Bouvet, the art teacher, treacherously. "Have you
seen her today?" "Mlle Quint?" queries the chorus of officers minus the vet.
"Who is Mlle Quint?" The judge: "A young woman who likes me. She has
a crush on me, and Mlle Bouvet tried to warn her off me." "I never did any
such thing." "You never said there's a dirty so-and-so in the hotel you should
avoid?" "No, no, I said there's this phenomenal creature at the hotel. But,
M. Noël, it's perfectly possible to be a good phenomenon." I was trying in
vain to write, but the judge kept brushing past me, pirouetting as he replied,
his voice deep and booming. But his words were sounding retreat, and he
masked the rout with bombast and meaningless noise, heavy on the vowels.
Suddenly he turned on the veterinarian: "You must have tons of sex appeal;
you've conquered Mlle Bouvet. See, it's ten o'clock and she hasn't left." The
vet adopted a superior air and, very much the hedonist, rocked back and forth
in his chair. "You have bedroom eyes," said the judge, pirouetting. "The
ladies must find you attractive; they love caressing glances." "And you,"
replied the veterinarian, with false air of indolence, "you have a wicked look
in your eye, or at least you want to look wicked. Because of your dark eyebrows,
you can almost get away with it. But take it from me, nothing can top the
truth." M. Bihan interrupted: "But you take it from me, he *is* like that." The
judge, pirouetting: "Yes, it's true, that's the way I am, I am wicked, very
wicked." Mlle Bouvet: "Yes, he *can* be wicked." A pause. The judge passes
by to sit among the other officers; he speaks to them softly, then suddenly
booms: "M. Francis"—the veterinarian—"Do you like getting sketched?"
"What do you mean?" "Do you want to get sketched till you're blue in the
face? Mlle Bouvet will do it for you. She loves to do it to men." Mlle Bouvet
was livid, lisping as always, but shrilly: "M. Noël means that I began his
portrait but had to stop midway because of his conduct; he frightened me."
M. Noël, pretending not to hear: "Are you unmarried, M. Francis?" "Yes."

"Well, Mlle Bouvet is too. You're sitting next to a very marriageable young woman. She may have designs on you." Mlle Bouvet, indignant, blushing, her face heavier and older in her fury, her chin tucked into her collar: "M. Noël, please do be quiet—after all, there are limits." But he keeps it up. Lucie, fretting: "You'd think he's jealous." Mlle Bouvet and the vet chortling together: "Good Lord, you might think he's jealous." The judge, sharply: "Me, jealous?" But the art teacher quickly loses the slight advantage because the chorus of officers, delighted to see their friend Francis cornered, line up on the side of the judge, giving him the upper hand. Chorus of officers: "But what on earth's the matter with Francis"—"Our friend Francis—he's trans- figured"—"It's love that's changed him"—"Ah, Mademoiselle, you've per- formed a beautiful metamorphosis"—"There's no one left for him but you"— "Do you like blond men, Mademoiselle?" Then, a solo from the depths of the smoking room, the somber, caustic voice of the captain (the whore's husband): "Love is the child of Bohème." Near hysteria, Mlle Bouvet turns to Francis, trying to distance herself: "It seems to me they've got you cornered." The vet (above it all): "No indeed, Mademoiselle, it is you they are aiming at through me. I"—he plays with his gloves, leans back—"I'm only passing through." At that moment Bost and I turned our chairs to face the action and were doubled over laughing. The bellboy (whom the fat captain had that afternoon called the "gro-om," hiccuping with laughter yet looking as if he'd said a dirty word) and the kitchen boy Bouboule were sitting on the edge of the stairs, listening open-mouthed, in a state of silent hilarity. Following some remark or other, the judge began to describe a friend of the art teacher's, a certain Buchez, whom he called "La Buchez." "Call her Madame Buchez." "She's got beautiful breasts, La Buchez has, but a flabby rear and too much armpit hair." "M. Noël, someone should give you a good slap in the face," said Mlle Bouvet, tearfully, still lisping. "See? After stroking me she wants to fight. Women!" Then, serious, even threatening: "In any case, if you say anything at all about me to Mlle Quint . . ." "Oh sure, M. Noël, go ahead, try to frighten me." "You understand, Mlle Bouvet, if you say one word to . . ." "You've already scared me once before, M. Noël. You know when." "If you say one word to Mlle Quint . . ." "Don't worry, M. Noël, she's already judged you, she already knows you," etc. This went on from eight o'clock to ten-thirty. Around ten-thirty, Mlle Bouvet got up and left. When she'd reached the stairs, the judge called her back: "Baby! Baby! You're leaving without even a handshake." "I'm not speaking to you, Monsieur Noël." She paused on a step. "Show off your legs to M. Francis—they're so pretty." The young girl with the sewing-bee look, who so far had kept mum, to Mlle Bouvet: "Tell him to show us his garters." Mlle Bouvet: "I wouldn't want to see them; you don't have very nice calves, M. Noël." M. Noël: "And M. Francis? You're not going to shake his hand?" "I am doing so in my thoughts, M. Noël. But not yours." She left, and the judge, patronizing and chummy, admonished the unconcerned vet, like an older man who wants a younger one to profit from his experience: "It's true, she's twenty-eight and still wants to play the ingenue. You should've consulted me, my friend. You wanted to have a little flirtation, a little fling; you're a little too sentimental; but I could've told you you'd be wasting your time." And the veterinarian smiled and rocked as he replied: "Oh, is that so?" in the most insolent manner imaginable.

We left them and went upstairs, for a little peace and quiet, to young Bost's room. He was scandalized and delighted. During the conversation between the judge and the brazen young woman, he was dying to thumb his nose at the judge. At one point he had me worried, and I made him see that he would merely seem to be siding with widows and orphans. He thought of an elegant solution so as not to appear merely partial to the wronged. He wanted to say to the judge: "Excuse me, Monsieur, don't you see that you are being a pain in the ass to all these jerks?" Finally, docilely, he followed me to his room and did nothing at all. But throughout the day today he would give a start as he thought of M. Noël. In the room he showed me his short story, which is really good—badly written but even better than the first, and charming. I congratulated him, then had him read the three pages you've seen and four others I did yesterday, which filled him with stupefied admiration. I think they're good. He gave me some good criticism, which I took (oh, I can see you beginning to storm, Beaver. But it was good advice, I swear). Today I'm bursting to go on, but—see how much I love you?—I'd rather finish this letter.

Today I've seen little of young Bost, because I had three and a half hours of classes and he was leaving at six forty-five. But what I saw of him was delightful. He sang me a song in English, played the bartender bouncing a drunk (me), boasted that he's too good and suffers for it (but I chided him when he claimed to have been *good* with Zuorro), and he lovingly spun out the following fiction: he has twenty-seven women. From me he took Tania and you, dear Beaver; he actually refers to you with great respect. He also has Poupette and de Roulet's[1] lady from Oran, Gégé, etc. He buys back the Hôtel du Théâtre from the proprietors and sets himself up with his women, one to a room. Only you have the right to go out, to exchange your books at A. Monnier's. The woman from Oran is in the kitchen; Bost sometimes

---

[1] Lionel de Roulet was a student of Sartre's in Le Havre. See note p. 91.

says to her with an avenging ferocity: "So, you've let de Roulet paw you. Well then, shine my shoes." So she throws herself at his feet and licks them. Poupette sleeps in the cellar. Toulouse is at the door coaxing pretty women in. All those who enter refuse to ever leave. The Lady alone goes in and out, calm and serene, sometimes laughing right in his face as she explains that all the women are frigid and only pretend to enjoy doing it—and sometimes takes pity on him by saying: "You're the sole victim in this whole business, it's all Sartre's fault." Etc.

Out of kindness to you and Guille, he had me write to Paulhan[2] what he dictated; submitting to his imperious charm, I therefore wrote:

"Monsieur,

"From Pierre Bost[3] I have learned that you are willing to see me. I would be happy to submit several short stories that I have just written. I venture to offer my address, in the eventuality that you might have the kindness to grant me a meeting.

"With my very best wishes, Monsieur, and my thanks."

What do you think of that? He stamped and pocketed it. It will be in tatters when he gets to Paris, where he plans to mail it. Why didn't he mail it from Laon? Because he didn't want to. I took him to the train, and we'll see each other again Friday afternoon; he'll meet me at the station, we'll take a long walk. Enough about him.

Good news: I've been inspected by the academy inspector, a doddering fool. An inspection at this stage means, I think, promotion. They send the academy inspector to see that the beneficiary hasn't become senile, vicious, or dangerous now that they've decided to reward his zeal. That'll be 1,800 francs for Guille.

There. I've been writing to you since seven and it's now nine-thirty, I only stopped half an hour for dinner (pea soup, filet of brill Bercy that smelled so much of woman I had half an erection—but just like a dog that raises his head a little, then goes back to sleep on seeing that he was mistaken and it isn't his master after all—shepherd's pie and dessert), my hand is damp and trembling. I have just enough strength left to tell you that I love you with all my heart, my darling, tender Beaver, and I think of you all the time. And you will see how much when you come back. I love you.

You'll have a very brief note tomorrow and a long one Thursday.

---

[2] Jean Paulhan (1884–1968), editor of *La Nouvelle Revue Française*, or NRF, distinguished journal and precursor to Gallimard, where it still exists as a magazine and literary imprint.
[3] A novelist and editorial reader at Gallimard, Jacques Bost's older brother.

To Simone de Beauvoir

Laon, Wednesday 25 April

My darling Beaver

Just a note today to tell you I love you a lot and that I rejoice at the prospect of finding word from you in Paris, which will tell me about your trip. It is 4:20 and I'm taking the 5-o'clock train. Fortunately I have little new to report to you since last night.

So, I went to bed after mailing the letter and slept well, though I did wake up with a start from a nightmare, which wasn't very serious. We were at the Balzar, you and I, lying on a large divan fifteen feet above the ground. Beneath us two homosexual men and two women, leaning over a balcony, were signaling to the passersby. You said, "What a nasty bunch." Then an Algerian entered with a revolver and demanded payment from all of them. When they refused, he killed them one by one, but from time to time his shots strayed perilously close to us. When the danger was too great I prudently awoke with the feeling that I was a big coward for leaving you alone back there with the Algerian in the dream. Disgusted at myself and moved, I spent a loving half hour with you, then went back to sleep.

This morning I taught two hours of classes, then was waylaid as I was leaving by the son of the vice-principal, the Thomist, who took me to his room. He is clumsy, has heavy extremities, and a nose that goes on forever, long and sad, tipping up at the end, shocking, like flamboyant clothes on a tramp. This hardy soul wears a skullcap that he never removes under any condition whatsoever and that makes him look like a sad Pierrot. To greet someone, rather than take it off, he raises two fingers (the index and middle) to ear level in a gesture reminiscent, in some ways, of a bishop, the bestower of blessings, and in others, of the cavalry captain, martial and condescending. He has heavy lips, feverish and insolent. He apologized for "disturbing my solitude" several times: "Because I know you don't see a great deal of your colleagues, you're so independent." Then he interrogated me on pheno-menology, though he didn't listen and interrupted to explain the Thomist view of the question. What's more, he belongs to the A.F.[1] and handed me six typed pages he pompously calls "good pages" but which are simply the

---

[1] Action Française, right-wing group active during the first four decades of the twentieth century.

outline of a book he hasn't written on Maurras[2] and Saint Thomas. I struggled a bit with his insect thinking, but halfheartedly. He is both insolent and timid, but, as with his insolence, his timidity rings false. From time to time he would interrupt himself to take care of some neurasthenic activity, saying, for instance, "Excuse me, I've just cut myself, I've got to use the styptic pencil," and disappearing behind a screen; or, as he was about to leave, "Excuse me, I must go check whether I left a burning match on my desk; it might touch off my papers." Meanwhile I was thinking with horror, "The guy's praying"; he seemed more crayfish than anything else. He told me, "I am sincerely orthodox." I said, "But you've been excommunicated" (since he's in the A.F.). He answered with a heavy laugh, "Don't believe that—we have more than one trick up our sleeve." And with a laugh he quoted a mess of pontifical and episcopal texts to justify it. Then, with sudden gravity, as intensely labored as his laugh, "I may joke, but I beg you to believe that for me it is, in all senses of the word, a matter of life or death." Handing me his tract on Maurras, this lowly soul said, rather like Guth, "I'm lending it to you, though I know you can be harmful to me. But I trust you because you don't seem the university type." I fled and went off to read *Marianne* for a while, then worked some in the hotel lobby—not enough. I had lunch (fried dab—steak and dessert), and, from a nook in the lobby, heard the epilogue to Monday night's performance:

Mlle Bouvet bid an emotional farewell to the blond wench, who was leaving: "So, till we meet again, Mademoiselle." "Till then, Madame." Then she had a cup of coffee with the veterinarian and another officer. "Have you seen the Degas exhibit?" she said. "You really must. But how hard he is on women!" "In a modernistic way?" asked the vet. "No," she said, gazing pensively at the ceiling. "I think he simply saw them that way. Now, from the point of view of painting and composition, they're really interesting." "I don't see much in those big modern things." "I prefer the classics, I must admit," said the veterinarian. "Oh? So you're in agreement with Commander Chanté?" The judge came in. Shook hands with the officers. He offered his hand to Mlle Bouvet, who silently refused it. "What's the matter?" No reply. "All right, all right," he said nonchalantly. "We already quarreled once but we'll make up." He went to sit in a corner, whistling. Mlle Bouvet said goodbye to the two officers, who were leaving that afternoon, and went out.

---

[2] Charles Maurras (1868–1952), writer and political theorist of the right, whose ideology of "integral nationalism" was similar to fascism; author of a collection of philosophical short stories, *Le Chemin de paradis*; imprisoned after the Second World War as a collaborator, but released the year of his death.

Then the judge talked for a moment with the officers and left in turn. The two officers had the last word. As they took leave of the proprietor, M. Bihan, one said, "That judge is a weird character, while Mlle Bouvet is a delightful companion, though you can't ask too much of her." And the other: "He's a judge, see, so he's always judging."

There you are, my darling Beaver. Next an hour of class on neurasthenia, 45 minutes in the lobby writing to you, and here I am on the train, where I'm finishing the letter during the stops: hence my shaky penmanship.

My dearest, my darling Beaver, I'll stop there, because I want to mail the letter the moment I get to Paris. I love you with all my heart.

I'm finishing at the hotel. There's no letter from Tania. There's no letter from you! But that doesn't matter, I love you dearly anyway. I kiss your gaunt little cheeks, my love.

To Simone de Beauvoir

[Paris] Thursday [April 26]

My darling Beaver

I'm very sad—one of your letters has been lost. You refer in the one I've just received to one it seems you wrote the day before and which I never got. Fortunately Zazoulich had a note from you yesterday and told me about your arrival. It seems that you dozed comfortably in the train, that you had a whole banquette to yourself, and that you were groggy at Bormes during the afternoon. Today's letter seems filled with joy. It would be pointless, I think, to tell you that you're doing *too much*. So I'll simply hope that you aren't tiring yourself too much and I'll be happy about your little walks. I read everything twice, unjust Beaver, and I struggled to imagine the wild brush country and the properties that look like the brush, and the sun-scorched moors. It's not so much that it interests me directly, but I'm feeling such tenderness for you I want to feel as intensely as possible the things that happen to you and the objects surrounding you. So I'm going at it with gusto to the point of doing exercises à la Loyola.

You should know that I was a bit annoyed last night at Le Dôme not to have received a letter from you or the littlest Z. I've been to buy a stamp and an envelope (that little ass of a Bost is playing the purist, insisting that one must always say "I went" instead of "I've been" and "we" instead of "one." It sets his teeth on edge to read "one has been" for "we went"), and

I saw Z. going into the tobacco shop, while I was standing up writing your address. Morose, deciding that she hadn't seen me, I let her continue on. But she must have seen me, since she turned back. I was very friendly, and we went to the 2nd floor of La Coupole, the one for a Welsh rarebit and a yogurt, the other for *choucroute* and plum tart. Z. was strange and sweet; she saw nothing—contrary to her usual self—in anything, and even looking was an effort. She didn't hate me, and even looked at me with a certain tenderness and almost regret, but the way one sees in a drawer the faded garter of a woman once deeply loved. She permitted silences to come between us, but out of mild indifference more than constraint. When she told me how she'd spent the time since you left, I realized she'd stayed in bed all Monday and Tuesday till Bost arrived. She'd slept and reawakened every two hours "to read *Samedi soir au Greyhound* ["Saturday Night at the Greyhound"]" . . . so she said. But I could see she'd profited from that supine position to construct a cavalier attitude toward her life and destiny. A pessimistic attitude, of course. As we went downstairs at La Coupole I told her, "You look as though you've ruminated over your whole life." Of course, she gave me a candid look of astonishment: "How could you know that?" I told her that in her case it was chronic and always came from physiological origins or was brought on by some annoyance unrelated to the thing itself. She agreed, admitted that her meditations had not been happy, then hastily changed the subject. But I had learned several little things: for instance that she was disgusted by her aborted attempts to write her short story—which proves that nothing escaped her review—and also that she realized, as she herself admitted, that it wasn't fate but the way she is that's spoiling her life. I believe she also thought that she'd lost me through her own doing, that it seems too irremediable for her even to regret it, but that she does accuse herself of it with a sort of passive remorse, that I seem to her distant, poetic, innocent, from the past. I'm delighted, because of Tania, and I truly hope her attitude won't change. She was actually charming, with a graceful tenderness, playing (but you know how Z. plays) the crushed flower. I think she was pleased with herself, feeling graceful and thinking herself, with a comforting sadness, the crushed flower. All her gestures, the play of her features, had a moistness that was ever so slightly unctuous and also, alas, ever so slightly comic. Alas, poor Beaver, a month and a half ago I would have found it all quite simply bewildering. We took a walk along the Seine, beneath the bridges. She scarcely looked at anything, complaining that compared to those at Rouen, the boats here weren't as at home on the river, weren't at one with it. That's reasonable, of course, but the main thing was she just didn't want to see anything, with her gentle cut-flower sadness coming between herself and the world like a dirty pane of glass. And yet there was a ship's prow piercing a patch of red lapping water and on that red patch a low black boat bobbing up and down: "That was worth the trouble," as your mother would have said. She noticed hardly anything except the long streaks of light sweeping the sky, because they were trying out the lights for the International Exposition. But I thought of it more as a diversion, and, to tell the truth, I wasn't very pleased to see the spire of Saint-Germain-l'Auxerrois gleaming as though whitewashed. Aside from that, Paris was charming. The Place Dauphine looked like deep forest and smelled pungently of spring. We crossed the Seine and followed the Rue de la Harpe and the Rue de la Bûcherie. The little oriental restaurant near the bordello was glowing with warm, suggestive colors. Snatches of laughter and Arabic music reached the street. Through a small patch of clear glass (all the rest is like stained glass) I saw a woman's face that was quite attractive, reminding me of the Moon Woman. We had a drink at the bar of the little café across from Notre Dame, and then of course Z. felt tired; we went back to Montparnasse, had another drink at the bar of Le Dôme, elbow to elbow with Stefanopoli, and headed home. It was about eleven forty-five. She wanted to read the 11 new pages of my factum, and we went to get them in my room. Then she left. I'm seeing her again on Saturday; I'll take her to lunch at Androuet's, since she likes cheese, and we'll go for a stroll, God willing. I went to bed thinking that it's definitely impossible to live a bit and tell what you're living, because I was thinking all sorts of things about the Thomist I told you about, that I'd really like to write them down, and of course that's impossible, I must limit myself to simple accounts of facts. Just think, I've already filled four pages, I still have all of my day to tell you, and it's already ten past seven.

This morning I shaved meticulously, taking advantage of your absence to make a mess of everything around me. I suddenly caught sight of your little postilion's hat and I felt a pang, because I'd thought you'd taken it with you. So it was almost as though you'd returned. Actually there are lots of haunted objects in your room, haunted by you, of course: you know how everything of yours moves me. In its way it's also an animation of inert, unpolished existence. It's all very well to say that it is pure continguity, but that's absurd, since the kind of emotion it provokes is very different from the sort your real presence might give me. It's a different type of existence, a bit of you *become a thing*. Well then, you'll say, why isn't that funny? Perhaps there is something almost funny in it. And besides (I'd say with just a trace of bad faith), let's confine ourselves to simple accounts of the facts.

When I went downstairs, I naturally found the box empty of any letter from you or Tania. There was simply a note from Paulhan that I'll copy for you:

"Sir,

"I would be pleased to meet you—and most impatient to read the stories you promise me. Would it be possible for you to come by the *NRF* one of these evenings, for instance tomorrow (Thursday) around 6 or Friday around 4. I will be expecting you.

"With best wishes

"Jean Paulhan"

I find that rather cordial. All the more so since he answered instantly. Bost mailed the letter on Tuesday and Paulhan answered on Wednesday. It was written by hand this time, a curious script that seemed inscribed letter by letter. I had thought to go this very day, but Poupette had only typed "Erostratus" and half of "The Wall." So I'll go Friday at four with the three typed short stories; Poupette will press on with it tonight. Copying it out, I realize that perhaps it's a letter that requires an answer (because of the "I will be expecting you"). But never mind. I'll say I was out of town today.

Saw de Roulet. Anecdotes about the young lady from Oran, etc. Nothing new. He has read my stories and of course prefers "Disorientation" and "Erostratus" to "The Wall" "because there's a study of signification in D. and of humanism in E." He is mistaken, poor man, thinking that Erostratus was a sympathetic character, and, with that feeling, he read some of it to the girl from Oran. Of course, she said, "He's disgraceful," and de Roulet, undone, beat a hasty retreat, saying: "It's a case study." He spoke to me about your stories,[3] saying he likes Lisa and Renée very much, but denigrating Anne after saying: "Of course, I'm a great admirer of the Beaver's talent." Here are the complaints: Mme Vignoux's interior monologue good but too long, with obscure passages (in vain did I tell him they were intentional), too many characters in the first part (he only read the first part and half of the second), too many children, Mme Boyer is artificial, the picnickers conventional; Chantal, too intellectual, is merely there to satisfy a need; we don't see the "spare, brisk" style of your other stories. That's it. I think most of the criticisms are insignificant; nonetheless, Anne does seem the weak point in your factum. I don't think you should give a damn; just leave it as it is.

I stayed till 1:30 and gave him a long lecture on the relativism of values.

---

[3] *Collected under the title* Primauté du spirituel [When Things of the Spirit Come First]. (SdB)

I left him with his back to the wall but satisfied. I'm seeing Poupette tomorrow and having dinner with the two of them at de Roulet's next Wednesday.[4]

(I'm writing in the train now, waiting for it to leave. Wherever I sit down, these days, I write letters, and I still owe some—one to Tania, one to my mother, one to the Boxer.[5] It's what you might call epistolary over-exertion.) I left him smiling and went to have lunch at Demory's (two frank-furters, sautéed potatoes, dessert). It was charming and serious, two guys pontificating on politics, one flabby, one jittery. Flabby rehashed the argu-ment of the Croix-de-Feu Algerians to Merleau-Ponty: "In Algeria the French worker earns 18 francs and the native worker 6 francs for the same work. And that's the way it should be." Long pause. Then, serious, in conclusion and emphasizing every word: "Yes, yes, that surprises you, that shocks you, it's paradoxical. And yet it's right." A pause. "And I'll tell you why." Here followed the argument you already know. During it all I was correcting the typos Poupette had made on "Erostratus." Around four I left on foot, alto-gether charmed by Paris, and went to the hotel for my manuscript of "The Room," which Z. was to leave in my box. It was there, and with it a letter from Tania and one from you. Yours was very short, my darling Beaver, but so blissful it was a joy to read. Tania's was long (about like the previous one) and very appealing. That girl seems to have a lazy but considerable intelli-gence, because each of her letters shows progress over the previous ones. I'll send it to you as soon as I've answered it. I was a bit worried by the thought that when she brought back my factum, Z. had seen her sister's letter and the sight of the guilty object might have reawakened her anger; I was em-barrassed and overjoyed to have my letters, and the manuscript Z. returned with the comment "far more than honest." So I got on the elevator without picking the key to 65 off the hook. Upstairs I of course found the door locked, was too lazy to go back down, and shut myself up in the bathroom to read the letters in peace: it is a well-lit place and you are sitting down. Later I went back downstairs and off to work at Le Dôme.

My darling Beaver, I'll still have to tell you about how Mardrus[6] came to find me at Le Dôme around six o'clock and the strange ideas he related to me ("God committed suicide after the Creation, that's my starting point").

---

[4] Lionel de Roulet, a steadying influence on all the "family," had met Poupette while he was still in Le Havre and she visiting her sister in Rouen. The two were married in Portugal during the war.

[5] Alphonse Bonnafé, who taught with Sartre in Le Havre, where they would often box together.

[6] A *friend of Gégé's.* (SdB)

He's an ass in no way superior to Carteret except that he's epileptic. I was very cool to him. But I beg you, don't hold it against me if I keep you in the dark about this episode, don't accuse me of "never telling you anything about Mardrus." Bear in mind, rather, that it's 11:10, that I'm at the poetic little café finishing this letter and dying of fatigue. My head spins when I think of the number of pages I'll have written to you between now and your return. I really must love you.

To Simone de Beauvoir

Friday 30 [April]

My darling Beaver

Herewith the outcome of epistolary overexertion: I was planning on writing you a carefree note today, with nothing to report, limited to some small endearments and reflections on the world in general. Instead, though, I must inform you I have something indeed to report: I spent all afternoon at the NRF. If you'll excuse me from describing my morning in Laon and my trip, I'll tell you right away that *Melancholia* is as good as taken and that M. Paulhan wants to run one story in the NRF and another in *Mesures*. I'll start with the facts. I would also like, if I could, to describe the bizarre and, more precisely, pleasurable inner state in which I find myself, but the revelation of my states of mind will undoubtedly be precluded by the lack of available time. (I'm to see Poupette at 9.)

So let me tell you that the train got into the Gare du Nord at 2:40. Bost was waiting for me. We took a cab, and I went to the hotel to pick up "Erostratus." From there we went to Le Dôme, where we found Poupette, who was correcting the other stories: "Disorientation" and "The Wall." The three of us set to work, and at precisely four o'clock it was done. I left Bost in the little café where I waited for you the day you dejectedly went to pick up the rejected manuscript at the NRF. For distraction he had only the sight of Mme Martin-Chauffier, an old bag. I made a quite glorious entrance. Seven seedy individuals sitting in the hallway were waiting for Brice Parain,[1] or Hirsch, or Seligman. I gave my name to some woman handling the phones at a table and asked to see Paulhan. She picked up a phone and announced me. I was told to wait five minutes. I sat down in a corner on a little kitchen chair, and waited. I saw Brice Parain pass by; he glanced at me vaguely

---

[1] *A philosopher, friend of Nizan's, and reader at Gallimard. (SdB)*

without seeming to recognize me. I began to read "The Wall" for something to do, and also somewhat to comfort me, since I found "Disorientation" so appalling. Then a brisk little gentleman appeared. Dazzling shirt, tiepin, black jacket, striped trousers, spats, bowler tipped back on his head. Reddish face with long sharp nose and hard eyes. It was Jules Romains—really; it wasn't a lookalike. First off, it was natural for him to be there, rather than somewhere else; then he gave his name. After a while, when everyone had forgotten about me, the telephone woman peered out from her corner and asked the four other guys still there for a light. Not one of them was equipped. So she got up and, coquettishly impertinent, said, "Four men and none with a light?" I looked up. She saw me and said with some hesitation, "Five." Then, "What are you doing there?" "I've come to see M. Parent—I mean, Paulhan." "Well, go right up." I went up two flights and found myself facing a big swarthy guy with a blackish mustache on its way to gray. He was on the heavy side, dressed in light colors, and seemed to me somehow Brazilian. This was Paulhan. He led me into his office; he speaks in a distinguished voice with a high, feminine pitch, quite soothing. I perched on the edge of a leather armchair. Right off he said, "What's all this mixup with the letters? I don't understand." I said, "It began with me. I'd never thought it would appear in the magazine." He said, "That would be impossible. First off, it was far too long, it would have run for six months and had the readers out of their minds by the second installment. But it is splendid. . . ." There followed several laudatory epithets that I leave you to imagine: "so personal in tone," etc., etc. I felt quite ill at ease, because I was thinking, "After this, he's going to find my stories awful." You'll say it hardly matters what Paulhan thinks. But to the extent that I could be flattered by the fact that he'd found *Melancholia* good, I was annoyed that he would inevitably think my stories so lousy. Meanwhile, he was saying, "Are you familiar with Kafka? Despite the differences, I see no one but Kafka to compare this to in modern literature." He got to his feet, gave me an issue of *Mesures*, and said, "I'll give one of your stories to *Mesures* and keep one myself for the *NRF*." I said, "They're a bit . . . uh . . . uh . . . free. I touch on questions that are in some sense sexual." He smiled indulgently. "In that area, *Mesures* is very strict, but in the *NRF* we publish everything." Then I told him I had two others. "Well, then," he said, looking delighted, "give them to me. That way I'll be able to choose, to match them up with the issue of the review, you see." In a week I'll take him the two others, unless my correspondence keeps me from finishing "The Room." Then he said, "Brice Parain has your manuscript. He and I are not in total agreement. He feels there are some slow passages and some dull ones. But I disagree. I feel that shadows are needed, to set off the brilliant parts." That pissed me off. He added, "But your book will certainly be taken. Gallimard cannot not take it. Anyway, let's go see Parain." We went down one floor and ran into Parain, who's the spitting image of Constant Rémy, though livelier and hairier. "Here's Sartre . . ." "So I was just saying to myself . . ." said the other cordially. "Anyway, there's only one Sartre." And he began to *tu-toi* me on the spot. Paulhan went back to his office, and Parain led me through a lounge full of leather armchairs with guys in them to a garden terrace in the sun. We sat down on some white-enameled wooden chairs at an enameled wood table and he began to talk about *Melancholia*. It is hard to report in detail what he said, but in general here it is. He read the first thirty pages and thought: Here's a character like something out of Dostoyevsky. It has to keep on like this and extraordinary things must happen to him, because he is outside human society. But from page 30 on he was disappointed and irritated by things that were too dull, the populist stuff. He finds the night at the hotel too long (the one with the two servant girls), because any modern writer can do a night at a hotel like that. Also too long: the Bd. Victor-Noir, but he does find the woman and the guy who give each other hell on the Bd. first-rate. He doesn't at all like the Self-Taught Man, whom he finds both too dreary and too caricatured. But on the other hand, he's very fond of the Nausea section, the Looking Glass (when the guy glues himself to his mirror), the Adventure, the doffing of hats, and the dialogue of the good people in the Brasserie. That's as far as he's gone; he hasn't read the rest. He finds the genre false and thinks it would be less noticeable (the journal genre) if I hadn't been preoccupied with "welding" the "fantastic" parts with sections of populism. He would like me to cut as much as possible of the populist stuff (the city, the drabness, sentences like "I ate too much for dinner at the Brasserie Vézelize") and the welding in general. He likes M. de Rollebon. I told him that in any case there is no more welding after the Sunday (there is nothing left but fear—nausea—the discovery of existence—the conversation with the Self-Taught Man—contingency—Anny—and the ending). He said, "Here if we think something in a young writer's book needs changing, we generally give it back to him, in his own interest, so he can touch it up. But I know how hard it is to redo a book. See how it goes, and if you can't, well, we'll make our decision anyway." He was rather protective, very much the "young older brother." As he had things to do, I left him, but he invited me to have a drink when he was through. So I went off to play a little trick on young Bost. As I had inadvertently kept my manuscript of *Melancholia*, I went into the café and without a word tossed the book on the table. He looked at me and turned a bit pale. I said,

"Rejected," with a glum and falsely stoic air. "No! Why?" "They think it's dull and boring." He sat there looking stunned, and then I told him everything and he was overjoyed and quite amusing. I left him again and went off for a drink with Brice Parain. I'll spare you our conversation in the little café on the Rue du Bac. Brice Parain is quite intelligent, nothing more. He's a guy who thinks about language, like Paulhan. That's their business. You know the old stuff: dialectics is merely logodisputation, because you can never exhaust the meaning of words. But given that everything is dialectics . . . etc. He wants to do a thesis on it. I left him. He'll write me in a week. I met up with Bost again at the Deux-Magots and we set off under beautiful sunny skies. We went as far as Montparnasse, where he left me to go find Z., who is leaving on Monday for Laigle. I came back here and right off saw Madame Llama and the Tapir dressed to the nines at a table facing mine. I went over to shake their hands, and committed three or four gaffes in six or seven words. Then an hour later, Zuorre, in a strange yellow shirt and red tie all dotted with *birds*, came up to greet me. He claims to harbor the warmest regards for us, but simply finds himself very absorbed in his work and family. He lives in the suburbs (at their place, Kremlin-Bicêtre. He will certainly not return to the hotel in May). It seems he ran over to your place Sunday evening about eight with the dough only to learn you'd just left for the Gare de Lyon. I will be going out with him Sunday about four-thirty. We're to meet at Le Châtelet and go for a walk.

Phew! That's all, my love! Now I'm off to see Poupette. Your long Monday letter isn't lost—I found it in Laon this morning. It made me very happy. I love you dearly, but I have absolutely no time left for states of mind. If by some extraordinary circumstances there is nothing tomorrow, I'll send you an "interior-landscape" type letter. But a brief one, my darling Beaver. Because I must write to Tania and would like to finish my story as soon as possible. In addition, I'm taking Z. out from noon to four.

I love you. I'm happy because I think that this letter will please you. As for revising *Melancholia*, I will of course wait for you and together we will decide what must be done.

To Simone de Beauvoir

This is Saturday's letter. But I'm writing on Sunday morning because I had no time last night. Nonetheless I have quite a few little stories to tell you. But first, my dearest, know that I'm very anxious about you. What is this new illness? If it continues, I beg you to go to *Marseilles* for a good—

expensive—doctor. I don't even want to hear about that twenty-franc doctor. And I also feel that you're doing too much walking. You're acting rashly. The Lady says it certainly won't hurt your lungs but you'll strain your heart. I'm dismayed and anxious about being away from you. I'm also worried about writing to you at La Garde-Freinet, because you might have had to stay at Bormes, but I rather hope that in that case you'd have the good sense to write to La Garde to have your mail forwarded. So I'll keep on writing to you there. I have several little items to tell you. But I'll simply mention them and go into greater length tonight.

1. The evening with Poupette. Story of the Swede and Giraudoux. Very funny.

2. Saturday afternoon with Z. Idyllic. She was so affectionate I was emboldened to tell her, "You remember how uncomfortable you felt with me because you couldn't speak to me about Bost. Well, though the details are quite different, the same is true for me about Tania." She said: "I feel the same way, though I hoped that with time it would go away." And she began to tell me snippets about her sister. She's leaving tomorrow. I'll fill you in.

3. At seven I saw the Llama for a half hour. Story about Nizan and Simone Téry. I'll fill you in. A breathtaking monologue by the Llama that I'll reproduce for you verbatim.

4. Last night—nothing: I write to Tania from the Sélect till 1:30.

5. This morning—young Bost. As I went out I found a strange, despondent letter from Gégé; I'm sending it on.

6. Phone call from Toulouse. I'm seeing her Wednesday evening (instead of Poupette and de Roulet).

7. I'm hard pressed financially, because your mother hasn't sent me anything. Write her or send her a telegram to hurry.

My sweet Beaver, I love you anxiously and fiercely. Wire me your news; if you aren't well and if you need me, say so—I'll leave next Friday if you like.

I love you. I'll write tonight.

To Simone de Beauvoir

Sunday evening May 2

My darling Beaver

I'm very worried about your illness; I want to know more about it, but the letters I'll find at the lycée tomorrow will already be several days old.

What reassures me somewhat is that there is absolutely no connection between the stomach and lungs, at least not in this case. Perhaps it's just a minor liver upset. Eat well but watch your diet. I imagine that the day after tomorrow I'll have news from you, and I think it will be much better. I love you dearly, and hate to think of you suffering perhaps even as I write. I'm in Laon, in the poetic café; it's eleven o'clock.

Since I'll obviously have nothing new to tell you tomorrow, I'm going to split up the work. Tonight I'll tell you about my Friday evening with Poupette and Saturday morning right up to Z.'s arrival. Tomorrow I'll relate the rest of Saturday and Sunday.

So, Friday night I sealed my letter, left La Coupole, and went to Le Dôme. Gégé was there, sitting on a banquette in front of a bowl of porridge. Poupette was facing her, perched on the edge of her chair, to clearly indicate that she was going out with me alone. Gégé looked very poorly, her eyes bright with fever. We exchanged a few words, and as Poupette was conspicuously picking up her gloves and purse, which she'd left on the table, I thought it kind to take the lead. I said goodbye to Gégé, I got up, and we left.

She told me a rather nice story. On Monday afternoon, coming home quite late, she finds the Swede waiting for her. "I saw M. Giraudoux," he tells her. "Giraudoux?" "Yes. He came to see you. He knocked. I told him to come in; he looked surprised to see me here. I said, 'I know who you are and I admire your work.' He was as charming as I'd imagined him," etc., etc. Poupette dashes to the phone. Giraudoux answers from his place in a ceremonious voice, and when she invites him to come by her studio the following day, he replies, "You say that your exhibition runs through tomorrow morning, Mademoiselle. Very good. I'll be by tomorrow morning without fail." And hangs up after a few banalities. The following morning, he simply drops by. He'd parked his car at the end of the block, like the guy we saw the other day coming out of the brothel. She invites him in, he kisses her. She wants to show him her paintings, and he agrees to look at them, but with an arm around her shoulder or her waist. "I was very cool with him," she told me. "He was playing the great lover with me, and it doesn't suit him. He looked silly." He examined every object in the room with concentration and consideration, taking care to comment on each. Such as: "Well, well. *Marie-Claire*.[1] I hadn't seen *Marie-Claire*. But it's quite new. And you get *Marie-Claire*, do you, my dear?" Then, when he'd completed his inventory, he drew Poupette to the divan and took her—she was cold as ice, she told me. While they were eating lunch, she asked him what he

---

[1] A women's magazine.

thought of the Swede. "What Swede?" "The one who let you in yesterday." "But I didn't see anyone. I simply slipped my card under the door and left." At which Poupette began to laugh innocently. "I think he must have stolen it. That's how he would have known you'd been there. Of course he'll make use of it in one way or another." And she begins to tell him the story of the Swede. But Giraudoux remained serious. "And yet, old boy, you'd have to say that it's a most amusing tale!" she told me. "Well, he wasn't listening. I had to cut it short." When she was through, he said to her seriously, almost sobbing, "I'm terribly worried about that card, my dear. Please do try to get it back by any means." She promised. He got up, not so calm, and asked her somewhat anxiously as he left, "Do I have any lipstick on my face?" I told her, "He sneaks in here as though it's a whorehouse. Just like that. Or else he took you for easy pickings when you told him you loved him three years ago. If so, he's soft in the head or he'd realize that in three years you'd have changed and have had other affairs. Or else he thought you loved him enough for him to take his own sweet time: three years. In that case it's disgraceful of him to treat you like a whore." She agreed indignantly. But when I added, "Next time, just show him the door." She answered, "Yes. . . . Well, at least I'll say to him nicely: so you only come here for that?" It seems that the Swede sticks to his guns about seeing Giraudoux and speaking to him—and that Giraudoux looked constrained and a bit shifty as he denied seeing the Swede.

Le Dôme was packed. We were beside the bishop of black masses, who was drunk and blustering. At one point he got up, and I vaguely saw another man just as drunk, stumbling, grabbing him by the jacket and demanding a cigarette in a menacing tone. I raised my eyes and saw the Magus, who has let himself go soft and fat, passively shaken like a package as he said in a curt but not very confident voice, "Remember the American who punched you in the nose a week ago?" I could only see the back of the guy doing the shaking. He had a real cat on his shoulder, a superb Siamese. He turned around: it was Z.'s former Russian teacher, looking gaunt and gray. He saw me and shook my hand, releasing the decrepit practitioner of black masses. I asked him, "What have you been up to?" "I'm walking my cat," he said, and turned his head toward his shoulder, trying to bite the cat's thigh. He was charming. The cat was unflustered and content. Some women took possession of the Russian, petted the cat, and they all disappeared. The exophthalmic was there, with the curly-haired woman you find rather pleasant, who was roaring with laughter at his banter. Gégé claims, it seems, that the exophthalmic is Man Ray. But I don't believe a word of it.

Later, without Poupette, I saw within ten minutes: a huge, bearded, limping man and a small black woman, who took four chairs and three tables onto Demory's empty terrace, lined them up before the eyes of two flabbergasted policemen, and made a large black dog jump from one to the other, calling out, "Hop! Hop!" After which the large man let out a laugh that rolled like thunder in the mountains, the woman replaced the tables and chairs, and all three exited, man, woman, dog. What I also saw: loads of charming old women, cafés, whores—of course. And finally this: as I was walking up the Rue de la Gaîté, I heard a fart behind me. Nothing out of the ordinary in that—I didn't even turn around. But other farts followed, resounding and by the hundreds. I turned around to see the fartomaniac, a guy in a cap with a pale, unhealthy face and enormous red hands. He began to *bawl out* his farts. He told them, "That's enough of this shit out of you jerks. You bore the crap out of me," etc. When he yelled at them, the farts would stop. But as soon as he shut up, they'd start up louder than ever. He said, "You're torturing me!" *"It's something you gotta believe so we can laugh about it together."* He was certainly mad. Lagache studied the role of exhalation in hallucination, but he certainly didn't think of studying the role of farts. It was grotesque but rather terrifying, because the man was suffering and looked as nasty as can be. I went home to bed. He passed right by me, farting and grumbling away, and said as I was ringing the bell of the hotel, "So, am I an unlucky bastard or what?"

My darling Beaver, it's midnight, and I'm going to bed because I'm getting up at seven tomorrow. I love you.

To Simone de Beauvoir

Monday, May 3

My darling Beaver

This morning at the hotel I found your letter of May 1st. It pleased me no end, because I see that your illness is over. It was just a little attack of God knows what. But you speak so lightly of the 20 kilometers it seems you've gone, and that's not all, you kept on walking after you stopped counting. That's not good for you, crazy Beaver. Not at all. You should do five little kilometers in the morning and five more in the evening. Otherwise we'll be a wheezy Beaver and everyone will scorn us. In other respects it was a very nice, very tender letter, my darling Beaver. I love you passionately too, and if I don't have lizards to fan my affection, I have your hats, your coats, all your little belongings. I have an involuted need for you. Totally undefined, of course. But always present. At the height of the joy that is my almost constant state, it seems to me that there is something I'm missing, that ought to be there. And it's you, darling Beaver. But you are an idiot about letters. I'm sending this one to Saint-Raphaël but haven't yet received the one from you alerting me to write to Saint-Raphaël, which must have been written on April 30. God knows where you sent it. In any case, write to La Garde-Freinet to have my letters forwarded, because if you leave there today you can be sure a bundle of them will arrive after you leave (I sent three there on Sunday and they'll get there Tuesday. They contain: a letter from Gégé, a letter from Tania, and a bunch of funny stories). Since you'll get this one before the others, I'll mention specifically that this will cover Saturday and Sunday.

On Saturday I got up too early for my liking and went to La Coupole to write to Tania. Though groggy, I wrote a long dissertation on loyalty (she had asked if we should ever be loyal and what I mean by that), a dissertation that, subsequently I never sent. At noon I went to pick up the daughter of the Cossacks[1] at Le Dôme. She showed up, idyllic, of course, and her face as always informed by sadness (her botched life, etc.). She had rediscovered or even discovered a lot of charming facial expressions, and I felt in real sympathy with her—but, an important counterproof, a benign and pleasant sympathy. It simply muffled my gestures and tone. Unhappy Z. was not herself. It's not simply her botched life or terrible headaches (due I think to undernourishment) that had defeated her: there was worse. She had *also* discovered a bedbug in Bost's room and wanted to leave the Hôtel du Théâtre immediately. But with such misgivings! The hotel was so pleasant—the old woman liked them so much. Z. felt almost guilty about giving in to her aversion to bedbugs. But in spite of everything, it won out. But now a new difficulty plunged her into new anguish: the previous evening she and Bost had scoured all the hotels in Montparnasse and hadn't found a room. I portrayed the situation as grave, explaining that all the hotels in the neighborhood were filled because of the International Exposition. She rather lost her composure, after not wanting to believe me (she never believes in collective phenomena, since she can't grasp them), and finally we decided to try the hotels around the Gobelins. The idea of living near the Demory and the Rue Mouffetard was obviously seductive. "And then, in summer, distances are shorter. I'd be closer to Montparnasse," she said, thereby demonstrating

[1]*Olga. (SdB)*

that, for her, heat contracts bodies. We had lunch on the second floor of La Coupole, and she ate very well, squirming a bit, a hamburger, two salads, and some Cheshire cheese. (For me: scrambled eggs on toast, *choucroute*, and dessert.) She described an animated cartoon, talked about my factum; I gave her the next section (which you haven't read yet), which enchanted her. And I told her about my meeting with Paulhan. She looked at my hair and laughed enchantingly because I was, it seemed, completely myself and gave her (pardon, I'm quoting) an impression of perfection. We walked down the Boulevard Port-Royal under a gorgeous sun, and she went into several hotels that unceremoniously rejected her. No room. One woman, right in front of her, snapped up the last available room in a hotel on the Avenue des Gobelins. After that, of course, she rebelled and refused to go on. So we went for a drink at Demory's, in the left corner, by the window. Demory's was deserted, a lovely reddish brown, flamboyant in the sunlight. We could hear them singing "The International" outside, and all of it—the deserted bar and the singing—gave a splendid holiday impression. That's when I said to her, "There's something bothering me. May I tell you?" "Why yes, Kobra." "Well, I feel that everything is perfect between us right now. But you remember how embarrassed you were in January because you couldn't speak to me about Bost? Today I'm the one who's embarrassed, though it's completely different, because I can't talk to you about Tania." She immediately seemed forthcoming, without any hypocrisy at all. She said, "I was uncomfortable too, but I hoped it would pass in time." And after a bit of conversation on other subjects she blushed, scratched her head, tugged her hair, then: "I was think-ing . . . about Tania and my mother. . . . Did she write you that they wanted to have her get married?" I said she had simply written, "My parents have been doing some planning for me behind my back." She went on, "It's that young man, the little homosexual. It seems he comes to our house all the time, with his mother. Tania has just written me about it. My mother is discreet, but she feels an obvious fondness for the mother and son. Tania's furious." Then she launched into a long description of the young man: an idiot, splendidly dressed, with a modicum of charm because of some gangster details to his clothing and because he's a good dancer, rather a shady character. Tania and he caused gossip at a tea dance in Laigle. After a moment I said, "Did you tell me all this to be a little disloyal?" She seemed sincerely upset and said, "No, I swear. How could you think that? He's nothing at all, the young man, a zero. If I wanted to be disloyal, I'd try for something better." I also told her that the night when our conversation was so painful I was somewhat annoyed with her because I thought she'd done something disloyal to make me quarrel with Tania. Without a trace of anger she said, "There are times, Kobra, when you're completely mad. How did you think I could have done that?" And then we talked of other things. I was very affectionate and told her, "You know, Iaroslaw, I want you to stay my best friend." We were rather tender with each other. With the result that either she adopted a pose—I don't say a perfect pose, since it wouldn't surprise me, but a constant one—or else she really had calmed down about that business. Is it because she doesn't take it seriously? Or else she thinks she thereby does not lose any of her sister or, in the long run, me? Of course, I asked Bost the next day how she was when he saw her again. It seems she was in seventh heaven and spoke of me in glowing terms. I left her at six and went to say hello to the unapproachable Lady, whom I found in her room, scratching and fussing and rummaging around because she was leaving the next day for La Pouèze with Pelote.[2] From the living room came the sound of male voices alternating with a female voice. The Lady said to me softly, "That's the Llama and his Llamess; they've been here since three-thirty. You *can't* not go in to see them. Guille is there, too." After a while I went into the living room. The Llama had just come back from London to pick up his wife and son. I saw the son, pale and tall for his age, with Proust's eyes and a deep voice. He is six. He adores his father, slaps his hands then kisses them passionately, on the soft fleshy spot between thumb and index finger, fills his mouth with it. The Llama plays the papa, takes his son by the waist with his long fingers and speaks to him with gentle gravity, tilting his head slightly to listen carefully when the little fellow answers, as though he were listening to someone through the wall. He immediately discovered the tone that best says *father* (and not at all big brother. That would be tactless and moreover ignore what the situation can give him by way of rights and possibilities of play). He's already quite good at lacing rational explanations that could stimulate intelligence with the fibs you have to tell to put yourself within reach of a child's mind. We stood around him, mouths agape, and it was a magnificent show. He even put his son up on his shoulders and gravely walked around the room. Boudy[3] was there, pink-cheeked and jumping around. I'm not worth two cents to her since Guille's come back. It's as though she holds a secret grudge against me because she betrayed Guille with me while he was gone. Little Maheu went up to her, pointing to me: "That's your papa." She let out a burst of scornful laughter and said loudly, "Oh no! Not that one." The Llamas

---

[2]*Albert Morel. (SdB)* Also known as the Tapir.
[3]*Mops's six-year-old daughter. (SdB)*

wanted to invite me to dinner, but I pleaded a rendezvous. Actually I wasn't meeting anyone but did have to write to Tania. I nonetheless went with the Llama by cab as far as his wife's dressmaker. It's there that he told me about seeing, the morning he left London, a fat little man in glasses who was waiting for him: "It was Nizan. He said to me with perfect simplicity, 'Hello, old man, it's eight years since I've seen you.' And he spoke to me as though we'd just parted the day before." He found him unchanged to the point of confusing him with the man he had been at the École, only with sagging cheeks. He'd gone to London to report on the strikes and the coronation. Did you know he's the editor in chief of *Ce Soir*? Aragon and Bloch[4] are directors. He said to Maheu, rubbing his hands with childish glee, "I'm directing a paper with a circulation of two hundred thousand." Maheu was shocked by the rather astounding self-satisfaction: it sounds too like a young man. He would have preferred greater arrogance, a worldly air of languor. As for the Llama himself, I won't describe him, I'll do better, I'll give you verbatim his monologue, that'll be enough. He wanted to bring me back by cab and asked me where to drop me off. I said the Hôtel Royal-Bretagne. So he asked the driver to drop us off at the corner of the Rue de la Gaîté and the Avenue du Maine. Then, turning to me, "Let's walk a little way together, my friend. I never get out in the fresh air anymore. Except in the morning, with the Prince de Beaubourg, in the gardens of his house." (I don't guarantee the name Beaubourg, since he nonchalantly chews his words all day, as others do gum.) "Hey, old man," I said, "I don't know the first thing about princes, but it seems to me you've got some pretty spiffy acquaintances." Then he: "He's a real prince. His family distinguished themselves in the thirteenth century during the crusades. They were made princes in the seventeenth century. He's a man I like a lot. He's a bit senile, but so aristocratic. I like him for a resemblance, you see—a very poor reason—I like him because he looks like Fontanges, by Bella. With this small difference, which I appreciate tremendously, that he doesn't talk to me about hunting or horses, about which I know nothing." That's all. He exulted at length, all the way down the Rue de la Gaîté, because we've all stayed so much ourselves and our futures seem made to order: "Take Boivin," he said. "Boivin's dying of cancer of the anus. The doctors have given up on him. Once a week he comes to his office, he stays on his feet, if he sits down, he sits on one cheek. He'll die of the anus and as principal private secretary to Jean Zay:[5] isn't that a perfect end for

---

[4]Louis Aragon (1897–1982), surrealist, Communist, poet; Marc Bloch, historian.
[5]Minister of Education, assassinated in the summer of 1944.

him?" He reviewed a couple more: Nizan, etc. He concluded, "Ah, life, my friend, life far surpasses all our novels." I left him then and went to Le Sélect, where I wrote from 8 to 11 nonstop, except to look around a bit at the other people, who were appealing. At 11 I went to finish my letter at Le Dôme, which took me up to 1:30. Next to me was the pleasant frenzy of a drudge of a whore chatting with a waiter. "And I'm telling you your son will cash the whole thing in when he comes of age," said the waiter. "Never in a million years," she said, thundering but shaken. "Since I tell you it's written in the documents. I said just what I wanted. I'm leaving everything to him but I want him to get half of it at twenty and half at twenty-five. It's signed, I tell you." "No signature can hold up," said the waiter authoritatively. "The question is whether he'll be reasonable. If he isn't reasonable, he'll make a clean sweep of it. How many fathers does he have, your son?" "He's got just the one," said the prostitute. "And what's his name?" "His name's Monsieur de My Groin," she cracked. I went home. On the way I saw a drunk bawling out two policemen. "Beat it," said the police. "Well, arrest me," said the drunk, "but I'm a citizen, and I won't beat it for any cops." Then they chased him off with a rain of blows. He'd take a few steps forward propelled by the blows, then turn back on them, his finger raised, sometimes friendly, sometimes threatening. The charming thing about Paris in the spring is the vast number of such little goings-on. You see little dramas everywhere, particularly around one in the morning. To close today's account, I still must tell you that Toulouse called me at the hotel, and since I wasn't there asked to have me call her back. So I called around eight (after leaving the Llama). She wanted to see me the next day, but I said I wouldn't be here. So I'm seeing her on Wednesday. She didn't say anything else. She was stern about the Néguses, and I played it humble. I promised to bring some on Wednesday but can't—I didn't even have enough to pay my hotel bill in Laon, because for some unknown reason it came to a heavy blow of 759 francs. Have your mother send me 600 francs posthaste; she forgot to give them to me, the bitch. Here are my figures: 600 francs to the Lady—628 to the Hôtel R.Br.— 600 to Laon on account—150 to Z., another 20 to Z., 20 to your sister, comes to 2,018. I'm left with 80 francs and change. I spent the rest (200 francs in 4 days or 50 francs a day). I may have a pure heart but I can't pay for my railroad commuter ticket.

Let's get on to Sunday. Bost picked me up at the hotel around 9:30, and we went for breakfast at La Coupole. Downstairs I found a letter from you telling about your stomachaches, poor darling Beaver, and Gégé's letter, which I sent on to you. In case you haven't received my Sunday letters, I'll tell you that hers was a cry for help six and a half pages long: I'm in a mess, things are going very badly, there's no one I can say this to but you, etc. In the end there was nothing good in the letter, nothing really new, but the painful part was that she has *never* been overwhelmed to the point of calling for help; she is too proud. I'll write to her in a bit, and I'll see her Friday evening. We wandered around, and at a small café I saw Georges Izard, completely bald, and his wife, a large insipid woman. We pretended not to see one another. Bost was charming, of course. He's coming to Laon tonight on the 8:20 train. He'll stay till Wednesday. Then, till 4:30, parents. I'll skip over it because they were simply themselves. Lunch (*choucroute* and dessert), walk in the Bois, tea at the Pré Catalan. I said that next year I'd write a long article vilifying Jules Romains. My mother said with some concern, "Aren't you taking on a tough customer?" I guess at that moment I seemed to her like a pug yapping at the heels of a mastiff. At 4:45 I was in the lobby of the Salle Pleyel waiting for Zuorro (and not at the Châtelet—the meeting place had been changed). He arrived full of charm and explained his actions thus:

My good Beaver, that's enough for today. My fingers are peeling from so much writing. I'll finish tomorrow.

My love, I love you most tenderly, and I send you a kiss. Have a good time but be careful.

To Simone de Beauvoir

Wednesday

My darling Beaver

I have to admit, I didn't write yesterday. It wasn't because of young Bost, who was here though discreet as ever, but because of my factum, which kept me absorbed all day. It was going well, and since for once it was clicking, I thought I'd better take advantage of it. Please forgive me, my sweet little Beaver, and reflect that, all things considered, I was more or less in the right; after all, I always send very long letters filled with funny stories. I won't do it again. I love you dearly, and I enjoy talking about you to young Bost, pretending that you terrorize me and that you're a woman of steel.

I'll finish with Sunday. So I saw the Zuorre at the Salle Pleyel and we went for a drink at the Francis on the Place de l'Alma. He told me that he feels very warmly toward us. "I didn't think you hated us," I said. "But I think that you wanted to completely reform your style of life and that, of necessity, you had to drop people you used to see in your unreformed life."

He said, "That isn't exactly it, but I wondered if the pleasure one enjoys with such strong personalities isn't sterilizing, because it's enough in itself and one doesn't feel the need for anything else." I said, "My dear Zuorro, you're either crazy or a hypocrite." He laughed and put things in another light: "When someone is in your world, it's impossible to get out." Ultimately, that was what I had been saying. I said, "Taking that idea of a world, there are quantities of people who live in worlds different from ours, like Toulouse or the Lady, and with whom we have the best of relations. I think that among ourselves we must eliminate the mixture of worlds and everyday life. There can be relationships between one world and another, even if they are a bit formal." Looking satisfied, he said, "I'm glad to see that you take it that way, and I agree that relationships are possible." Which means, stripped of all versification, that he wants to see us less often, not to be immersed in our affairs, but never wanted—or has ceased for the time being to want—a total rupture. He was handsome and full of good health, with a touch of pink cheeks beneath the tan (which disappears slowly). He was still wearing that necktie decorated with guinea hens, not in the best of taste. He had hardly any stories to tell. He wants to learn twelve roles right now, and that naturally delays till October the moment when he'll confront Rouché.[1] He lives in Kremlin-Bîcetre with his sister and brother-in-law, who's completely crazy. The third day of their visit to Paris, he took them to *Julius Caesar*, took them backstage to Dullin's dressing room to introduce them and to ask for some free seats: "It's not that we couldn't buy them ourselves, but my sister and brother-in-law would be very appreciative of the kind gesture." He asked me if he had overdone it. I of course said no, but I'll apologize tonight to Toulouse. Z., to whom I told the story that very night, snorted indignantly and said, "Not very civilized of him." I stayed only awhile with the Zuorre; we junketed all around town in a cab to find an open pharmacy because he wanted to get a calmative for his brother-in-law. As it was a kind of narcotic, he was turned down everywhere. So he went into the Hôtel des Écoles to steal some stationery with a doctor's heading (a black doctor who stays at the hotel) and make up a prescription himself. I left him at the Rue Vavin and went to Le Sélect, which was crawling with people, to wait for Z. The clientele of Le Sélect has acquired fresh blood, as has Le Dôme, because of springtime and the International Exposition. They're Americans, Hemingway types, beautiful girls, rich people, who prefer to sit at the bar. On the terrace were the Sunday bumpkins. Z. arrived late, but charming against a dark back-

---

[1]*Director of the Opéra. (SdB)*

ground. She went with me to the station. She couldn't finally make up her mind to leave her dear Hôtel du Théâtre. They, Bost and she, only made timid protests to the good woman, who severely scolded them: "It could be that you were the ones who brought in those bedbugs." Satisfied, she decided to leave Monday for Laigle and come right back—to the Hôtel du Théâtre. We had a nice cab ride to the Gare du Nord and said farewell with a wave of handkerchiefs. So much for Paris.

About Laon there's little to say. Three things, nonetheless.

1. An invasion of June bugs. They're repulsive. These gigantic idiots ferment and marinate underground for five years. The fifth year they erupt by the thousands. But they don't know how to fly, they crash into everything, get knocked senseless, and die. It's asinine and repulsive: it's Nature, no doubt about it. And it's Spring. Monday night they were swarming everywhere, in our rooms and outside around the lampposts. You couldn't walk under the gaslights because they were burning their wings in the flame, falling and landing right on your face. Young Bost was in terror of them. He'd jump aside with a shriek. He mistook a dog for a June bug. As for me, once I was back in my room I put my raincoat on a chair and it fell while my back was turned. I thought it must be a monstrous stubborn June bug and nearly shrieked. Yesterday and today, same thing, belly up and stiff-legged, littering the streets, croaking. You walk on them and they go "crrr." One day sufficed for them to do themselves in down to the very last. And all's quiet for another five years.

2. The discreet presence of young Bost. He put an ad in *Paris-Soir* saying: "Young man w/o spec. knowl. good app. accept any empl. Write J. Bost, 11 Rue de l'Abbaye."

He hopes thereby to attract some old bags. He bored the hell out of me all day yesterday buying *Paris-Midi* and all the editions of *Paris-Soir* and even the previous day's *Paris-Soir*. His ad hadn't appeared yet. I advised him to put one instead in *Vie Parisienne*. Right now he is sweet and has calmed down. The three girls in my class poke one another with their elbows and burst out laughing when they see him.

3. A minor conspiracy against me at the lycée. A vile old lout named Neveux with the ugliest wife in Europe, a disaster, came to give me some friendly advice yesterday morning. He was obeying obscure motives in which a liking for me obviously played no part. Nonetheless it seems that a certain Jollivet, first form teacher and "head of a clique, Monsieur," thinks ill of the fact that I don't attend the honor-roll meetings. It seems there were a dozen of them at the last meeting, in March, who said in front of the headmaster,

"But do we really even have a philosophy teacher at all?" "Does he really exist?" "One never sees him," etc., bouncing it back and forth. I knew nothing about it, of course. Yesterday was the April honor-roll meeting, and on top of that they were to hold the election for the teacher who would represent the faculty for the Fiftieth Anniversary of the school and give a speech before the Minister (another aspect of the question: it was Boivin, a former teacher in Laon and principal private secretary to Jean Zay, who organized the Minister's visit and who undoubtedly persuaded him to come, to impress his colleagues). Whereas what the old lout—full of gripes and secret resentment (for reasons unknown to me)—revealed to me is that Jollivet and his gang had decided to vote for me (they constitute a majority) to piss me off, oblige me to be present at the Fiftieth and have me make a speech to Zay. There was another reason for their choice: the academic left wing had their candidate, one Laigle, a teacher of arts in the senior class. In short, I went to the honor-roll meeting duly warned; I helped the headmaster's secretary count the votes, and I fixed them. There were eleven cast for me, eleven for Laigle. I marked down 13 for Laigle and 9 for me. Laigle will make the speech. After which I departed with dignity. Anyway, I intend to corner this Jollivet one day and threaten to kick his ass. But the bowels of the Laon Lycée were revealed to me at a glance.

My darling Beaver, I'll stop here, because I'm off to lunch. Tomorrow you'll have a beautiful long letter on my evening with Toulouse. I love you.

Don't bother your mother about the 600 francs. She sent them to Laon.

To Simone de Beauvoir

Laon

My dear love

First, here's a piece of news that will surely please you: the factum has been taken and I'll be getting a contract. Here's the letter I received this morning:

"My dear Sartre

"I have finished *Melancholia*. From about page 130 on (when we really enter into the action) I find it splendid, inspired. So I am going to advise acceptance, and I hope that we will finally take it. But if you see even the slightest possibility (of reworking it) try to trim it a bit: I feel that if it moved more rapidly, it would be unassailable. As for me, I feel its truth as though the book were addressed directly to me.

"Brice Parain

"*P.S.: After conference, it has been decided that we will take it. I will draw you up a contract.*"

I found the letter this morning at the hotel, and it was with a glad heart this time that I went to de Roulet. But let's not get ahead of the story: first, I took the train last night with young Bost—the seven-o'clock train, since I had no Beaver to be a little impatient over my arrival. On the train young Bost of course lost his beautiful new story, which he has the infuriating habit of folding up in old newspapers. Right on the spot, fiercely determined to rewrite it, he wants to buy himself an "honorable book." We wandered around a bit on the Bd. Rochechouart and I went to buy some Néguses for Dullin at the top of the Rue des Martyrs. Then I went up to Toulouse's place. She'd gone off, leaving a note in red pencil that her maid handed me: "My dear Sartres (sic), I have to go to *Numance*. Come meet me at the Théâtre Antoine at intermission. I'll have a ticket for you." I went there on foot, across a dark, cool Paris, peopled by very strange individuals, each one an individual little story. But it would take twelve letters to tell you about all of them, and it saddens me to think that all their nocturnal traits will be lost. I found Toulouse in a strange mood, dazed and ominous, in a black flowered straw hat. She was wearing a tailored suit open across the bust and showing a blouse printed with Marie Laurencin[1] figures. That was the surprising thing, because when one looked carefully at the blouse, one saw the faces of good little children suddenly materializing all over it like images in a puzzle. She said to me, "You know, that's what won me over. I'm very pleased, because I think that many people won't notice it at first, then one day, talking to me and gazing absently at my blouse, they'll suddenly break off and say: 'But it's a face!' "
I reluctantly followed her into the Théâtre Antoine. There was a full house: it was the closing night, and the audience was peppered with "personalities" who hadn't been able to come to the opening. There were Simone, Genica, etc. Should I talk about *Numance*? It was a botch. In a word, this Barrault[2] wants to give the theater a language of its own, a language of gestures and attitudes, and he tries to make the figural and pantomime dominate the delivery of the text. At the same time, inspired by Chinese and Japanese art,

---

[1] Painter, printmaker, stage designer (1883–1956).
[2] Jean-Louis Barrault (b. 1910), renowned actor (*Les Enfants du paradis*), director, producer; student of Dullin's.

he gives symbolic gestures an essential importance. You remember those hands striking Christ in the monk's cell at San Marco, as though the personality of the torturers had no importance and only *the act of striking* was important. There are lots of signs like that in *Numance*. For instance, to indicate that the two Numantins who broke through the city ramparts are running at night, toward the sleeping Roman camp, they have them run in place, downstage. And to indicate that they've finally reached the Roman camp, the Romans come toward them, by which I mean the bodies of the sleeping Romans come out of the wings naked, lying down and rolling on the ground. Except that the schematic pantomime often borders on the ridiculous. The sculptural quality and the movements aim for beauty, without reference to the action; there's an abundance of symbolic characters (the plague, illness, the God Mars, etc.) that muck it up. Jean-Louis B. is thin and supple, with a nice little round paunch (rounder than mine)—the face of a modernist instructor just out of Saint-Cloud. The actors play like pigs. Another example of ridiculous symbolism: all the Numantins have rather beautiful costumes, simple and sober, but there are two Numantins who represent romantic youth (a young man and woman) and someone decided to give each one a garish costume that sticks out from the others and represents Youth and Love. The young lover is dressed in a white jersey like a coach from Joinville, and his partner is dressed in tulle and silks like a fairy princess. The sets are truly ugly.

We went back on foot to the Ballon d'Alsace. I was doing most of the talking. Toulouse was still quite somber. She finally admitted that what was bothering her was the thought that Dullin was going to get a divorce next year, which she thought would provoke a bundle of problems for her. She's afraid that in their own circles she'll be blamed as the cause and agent of the divorce. She phoned Dullin, and he came to meet us with that vague cousin of his who follows him everywhere. They've revived *Atlas Hôtel*, and he'd just finished the second performance. We spoke for a moment about *Numance*—he listened to us, slumped in his chair looking crafty. He liked *Numance* very much, but he didn't mind hearing us vilifying Barrault a little, once we'd clearly credited his generosity of spirit—the great man who helps the young. Then they began talking about personal trivia, and I left. Toulouse will surely not go to Greece with us, because *Plutus* will probably be opening in September with rehearsals in August.

I slept well but little. At nine I went downstairs, found that letter, and went to celebrate at La Coupole over a coffee and croissant. I feel more at home with this sort of pleasure than in what comes to me through the bounty of a good woman. I'm not a cad, but I feel poetic and think well of myself.

I went to see de Roulet. Nothing to say. Or rather yes, there'll be little anecdotes to recount about the girl from Oran; we can discuss her case, which increasingly confirms our ideas about that sort of virgin. But I think that this, as well as, incidentally, a detailed description of *Numance,* will keep for your return. At noon I met Gégé at Le Dôme. I anticipated gloom, or an even gloomier show of false gaiety, but she was fine: she denied nothing, recognized that she was still sad, but said she was more or less happy today because she wasn't thinking about it. We took a lovely walk along the quays and in the Saint-Antoine district, all around the Rue des Rosiers (without ever finding the Rue des Rosiers). I rather like strolling around Paris with her—she takes a good look at everything and quickly gets a good sense of it. We saw loads of charming objects (streets, little shops, and people), but it would take fifteen pages to describe them: struck from the program. At four I took her to eat at "Dominique's." The room was quite dark, and the street, through the window, took on a blue cast. The owner, dignified, beautiful, and generous, was sitting in her smock on a bar stool. A waiter was standing by the far end of the bar, stirring a cup of coffee. Almost no customers except for a foreigner, a nervous-doll sort of a woman, the kind that knows how to say Daddy and shut her eyes when laid down on her back, with her male. Gégé had on her handsome new outfit, and for the first time she had on makeup, because otherwise she'd look too unhealthy. She was very amusing.

I took her up to my room to pick up my suit for the cleaners (hypocritical little man, the good Beaver will say. Good Beaver, I was pure, I swear it), and then "I was true to you, Cynara, in my fashion." Just like that, because that's the way it turned out, that's the way it was to be. I kissed her on the cheek, she kissed me on the mouth. I took off her jacket, she took off her dress and her underpants. I slept with her. She said she loved me and I didn't believe a word of it. I told her I like her a lot and she believed it. She said, "I almost enjoyed it." Then I gave her a copy of "Erostratus" in thanks.

We went back down; she treated me with the thoughtful little gestures of a happy woman. I returned her to the care of her husband, I had a drink at Le Sélect, I took the train. On the train I read a book on the German theories of Value (Miller, Freyenfels, Scheler, Hartmann, etc.), asinine but with some practical information. I got it from de Roulet.

And there you have it, my sweet little Beaver. I found mounds of letters from you in Paris—you seem so happy that I was moved to tears. I'm so fond of your solitary little activities, your strolling, reading, and sometimes drinking your little carafe of wine. I love you. I can't wait to see you. But I haven't in the least forgotten your dear face. Have you gotten nice and fat?

To Simone de Beauvoir

May

My darling Beaver

Here are two letters in one. This one is Sunday's letter, the other was Saturday's. It is seven in the evening; I'm at the Closerie des Lilas. Windows and doors are open, people are swarming around on the terrace, but inside there's almost nobody but myself and other scribblers. I love you very much and constantly long for you, I'm in a hurry to get to Friday. We'll have a lot to tell each other. I'll take you by your plump arm and we'll saunter about, chattering away all day long. How's that? You'll have landscapes to describe, and I'll listen to your descriptions, kissing you a bit to keep me occupied. And, as well-informed people full of experience, we'll comment on all the events of these past two weeks. I'm very delighted about it. Today I felt like a widower. My parents left me at five o'clock, it was too late to work (I had to write to Paulhan, to Parain, to Denoël and Steele), I wandered about like a lost soul, eating *petits pains au chocolat*.

Yesterday evening I arrived at the de Roulets' in rain and thunder. I found a nest, with soft lights and knowing shadows. Poupette was in the kitchen, cheerful and busy; Lionel, in shirtsleeves, let me in. With great care he extracted a Château-Laroze 1905 from a basket, he put on a few records, and the conversation dragged a bit. Poupette, with pink cheeks and blue apron around her waist, brought out some croque-monsieur. "Don't wait for me," she said. I sat down on the green divan, feeling very small, well below the level of the table, of normal people. Poupette served us tournedos Béarnaise and sat down beside me. Then de Roulet, who had seen Sonia again (the one for whom Sylvère had dumped Mme de Coninck), told me the Sonia version of that old story. I'll tell you immediately who Sonia is, because I caught sight of her that evening at Montparnasse. She's the rather beautiful girl with long frizzy hair we could easily have taken as Algerian. Well, here's what she claims. Six months after their marriage, Mme de Coninck and Sylvère met her in Montparnasse. She had strongly attracted Sylvère. She innocently failed to notice. "Were you a virgin?" asked de Roulet. "That," replied Sonia, "I couldn't tell you." Sonia left for Switzerland, and the Sylvère couple went to live in Chamonix. But memories of Sonia continued to torture Sylvère. Then, in the spirit of Corneille, Mme de Coninck invited Sonia to Chamonix. Sonia went, unaware of what was expected of her. Then, over a three-month period, by means of allusions that grew progressively more precise, Mme de Coninck explained the role she'd play. Sonia refused. Then one day, under some pretext or other, the three stayed overnight at a hotel, in the same room. They got undressed in front of each other, and, when they were in bed, Mme de Coninck caressed Sonia most precisely and, judging her sufficiently aroused, pushed her toward Sylvère. But that night again, Sonia resisted. Finally after three months the act was achieved and even so well achieved that a while later Mme de Coninck, totally abandoned by Sylvère and in despair, left for Paris, leaving Jacqueline and de Roulet to Sylvère. Sonia claims that Jacqueline de Roulet wanted to sleep with her and kept appearing before her in the nude under the most varied pretexts, that Sylvère was slightly in love with Jacqueline and Jacqueline rather in love with Sylvère. That would explain her fierce hatred for Mme de Coninck. The whole story is lovely but seems to me a web of lies. After dinner, he held up a copy of *Semaine à Paris*. He wanted to go to a dance hall with me, to a show or even a bordello. In other words, "go out." But I, with only 35 francs in my pocket, hesitated and suggested a beer on the terrace of Le Sélect. My idea prevailed. Poupette left us, and we went to finish off the evening in Montparnasse. I'll give you a brief account of it tomorrow.

I send you a kiss, my dearest, and I hug you tight.

To Simone de Beauvoir

Sunday, 11 o'clock

My darling Beaver

I wanted to write to you last night after visiting the couple. But since de Roulet released me at one-thirty, I thought it would be just as good to write to you this morning and that my letter would thereby doubtless gain in lucidity. On that last point, I think I was mistaken. I'm a bit in a daze, though blissful. The skies are gray but beginning to clear. I'm at La Coupole, of course. The place is full of young girls, really young, because it's the day for First Communion. They're with little girls smothered in white muslin, and I think they're wearing dresses they used last year when they were maids of honor. What do you think? There are four of them in particular, laughing and joyful as they shuttle back and forth between a table on the terrace and the washroom. All together. And when young girls are together you notice them. They seem springlike and guileful, the springtime of buds and June bugs and larvae with a touch of something martial that makes you think of field maneuvers. Now there are more girls here, just arrived with an old lady, but they're not taking their First Communion. They're like the others, but in addition they seem slightly corrupt, about to blossom. Funny. Once again, my darling Beaver, you'll prevent me from getting a haircut: usually it's by your presence, today it's by your absence, by the letter I'm writing you. My family is after me about it, particularly since I think my mother gave me twenty francs, last Sunday, to make sure I'd go to the barber. Let's get to the news.

Friday evening, yawning away and fuzzy-headed, I went to bed around eleven, weaving slightly. These days could I be like that managing director I used to see at the Guillaume Tell, who'd fall asleep the minute he was alone? People get to me, good Beaver. I went to sleep, but not without reading a letter from you telling me about your walk at La Sainte-Baume. You're such a blissful Beaver it's a joy just to see the way you write your lines, slanting up toward the corner of the page. They are letters a bit too full of nature for my taste, but since it's you who's seeing the nature, all of it interests me and I conscientiously continue my exercises according to Loyola. I went to sleep, therefore, surrounded by a mass of maritime pines and a brilliant blue sky overhead. I awoke around nine, beneath a sluggish brooding sky. I got up, I worked a bit at La Coupole, and I went to see de Roulet (he profits from your absence by gaining more of my time). He was delighted with a story about Sylvère, Sonia, and Mme de Coninck that he wanted to tell me in the evening, over dinner. He was keeping it in reserve, allowing himself only mouth-watering allusions. He had scarcely worked. Spring exhausts him. These days he talks about his "state." "In my state," he says. He compelled me, through his questions, to distinguish between meaning, significance, essence. But I'm not too unhappy to have done it; it's easy. Meaning is what you grasp directly about the object: for example what is immediately given by a Japanese mask hung against a gray curtain. It is also the theme of functional unity that makes up the individuality of the thing. The significance is grasped and often constructed by the intelligence: it is what refers to other things—to layers that are physical, historical, social. For example: the significance of the mask is that it is Japanese, of a certain period and style, that it corresponds to Japanese needs and aesthetic tastes, clearly derives from certain religious beliefs, from certain theatrical customs. The essence is the structure of the mask without which it would not be a mask, and surely it is a totality that melds within itself the meaning and significance and other factors. Individual essence must be distinguished from general essence. But all objects do not have individual essence. Now it would be good to study the relationship between these different terms and their connections. If I've bored the hell out of you, I'm sorry.

Leaving de Roulet, I went by bus, prudently, to meet Zuorro at La Coupole. He was there. Very sympathetic. He was delighted this time when I told him that the factum had been taken. But he was annoying, of course, because I felt he was scrutinizing me to see if I'd become vain. He admitted it, but added that he didn't feel I was reeking with it. So what did he think? That's another matter. The other day, in a puckish frame of mind, he called Mlle Gruber, Mme Fourestier's[1] housekeeper. He'd counted on chance to provide him with the opportunity to play the prankster. In a woman's voice he asked to speak to Mme Fourestier. "Is it you, Mme Djannel?" asked Mlle Gruber. "Yes," said Zuorro. "That's strange, I don't recognize your voice. . . ." And with that to go on, Zuorro took off: "Alas, my poor Mlle Gruber, how well I know that my voice is changing. It's an appalling disaster, and that's why I would like to see Mme Fourestier. I had some hormone shots during my trip to Switzerland. They were male hormones, and now look: my voice is sinking, I can no longer maintain the register that Mme Fourestier assigned me." "But what is this?" said Mlle Gruber. "It's not true, Mme Djannel, it's not possible." Then Zuorro, in dramatic tones: "Alas, Mlle Gruber, *it's not my voice alone* that has changed." With that, Mlle Gruber, transfixed, asks naively: "Oh, Madame Djannel! It is not you on the phone!" "It is I, yes yes, it is I." "I can't believe it." "Well then, call me back in five minutes and you'll see, I'll be here and I'll repeat what I've just said." He hangs up, calls Djannel, who was in bed. "She must come to the phone immediately, it's urgent. A message from Mme Fourestier." Djannel picks up: "Mme Djannel, this is Emma, Mme Fourestier's maid. A dreadful calamity has just occurred, Mlle Gruber has gone mad, and you are the source of her madness. She believes you are a double personality, male and female. She is going to call you." "Heavens no!" says Djannel. "Shall I come?" "No, it wouldn't help. Just be very kind with her if she calls." Zuorro added, "Excuse me for having disturbed you. You were tired, I believe." "It's nothing," said Djannel. "I'm lying down, I'm resting. But it's for *perfectly normal* reasons, Emma." Zuorro hangs up and asks for Mlle Gruber again. "Well, you didn't call me." "Yes I did; I just called," said Mlle Gruber firmly, "and I was told that Mme Djannel didn't want to come to the phone, she had gone to bed. This is not you, Mme Djannel." "Don't say foolish things, my good Gruber, I am Mme Djannel." "Well, if you are, tell me what your last concert was." "Now whatever is the point of such questions? You know very well that I sang in Amsterdam in April," said Zuorro, who had seen a letter from Djannel at Mme Fourestier's house. "Tell me, too," said Gruber,

---

[1]Mme Fourestier was Zuorro's voice teacher.

shaken, "why you were in bed when I called. I'll know if you're lying, because your maid told me." "Well, my good Gruber, you are beginning to annoy me. You know very well that I am indisposed." "Then it is you, Mme Djannel," Gruber exclaimed, convinced and in despair. "But in that case what a terrible pity. And with Mme Fourestier not here! I'll tell her as soon as she comes in," etc. Finally, the next day, there must have been an exchange of calls and misunderstandings, because Djannel had dinner at Mme Fourestier's, something she never does. Two days later, Zuorro telephoned Mlle Gruber, putting on a woman's voice. "Hello," said Mlle Gruber. "Is that you, Mme Mahé?" "Yes, it is I," said Zuorro. "I'd like to know when I should come for my next lesson," etc. After a moment, he asks: "But tell me, what are these rumors going around, about Djannel?" "It's nothing," said Gruber dryly. "It's a bad joke that gave us a lot of trouble." That's all for the moment. Zuorro has an idea that he's under suspicion, because Mme Fourestier hasn't breathed a word about the affair to him, whereas ordinarily she tells him every bit of gossip. And now here's Zuorro's version of his break with Palle.[2] It seems he told him one day, out of the blue, "You were extremely important to me for two months, when I was going through a difficult period; but you shouldn't get the idea that it will go on. I don't want to see you anymore." Young Palle went pale with anger, and said, with a tense grin that Zuorro obligingly imitated for me, "Well then, you can just look for someone else!" and he left. "I couldn't bear to take him along skiing. With his terrible reproving personality, after twenty-four hours he would have wanted to correct my snowplow." I find that version clearly inadequate. It doesn't explain why Zuorro gave me an urgent call two days before the vacation to keep me from lending my skis to Palle. If he really shook off young Palle like dust from his shoes, he had no reason to get even with him later. He threatened me with dire sanctions if I spread the rumor that he was homosexual. "But," I said to him, "you're going into a milieu where it's more or less accepted." "That makes no difference, I don't want it said that I'm homosexual. Furthermore, I'm *not* homosexual. Last year I told you that I wanted to do a bit of homosexual experimentation. Well, I did, and it didn't work out; and that's that." "Well," I said to him spiritedly, "now revert to women." He also said, "You think I hate you, and it's the Beaver who gets you worked up." You see the source of all this: the Lady—Guille, Guille—Zuorro. I said I thought he'd been hating me, and that you had nothing to do with it. He denied it, so I quoted one of his notions: "Sartre's pituitary

---

[2]*A former student of Sartre's, friend of Jacques Bost's. (SdB)*

gland should be removed and those two poor girls put in an asylum." He was a bit dumbfounded and didn't say a thing for a minute, then, looking up: "Yes, but around that time *they* were telling me, 'Don't you think that over the past two weeks Sartre has been going totally senile?' " I laughed without answering: usually his fibs are better than that. Then he concluded: "These verbal rages don't mean a thing." We went up to his place, he sang a bit, in really superb voice, then, so I could compare, he had me listen to a Tita Rufo record. I left around five-thirty and went to work at Le Dôme. Young Bost came by to say hello for a moment. He had had a letter from Z., affectionate and a little sad, saying nothing. "I'm sorry not to be seeing you," she wrote. She says she's already bored in Laigle. Nothing about her sister. Armand waved to us as he went by. He'd fallen off a low roof the day before "while performing a break-in" ("robbery with forced entry," he said with simple pride), and he was still completely dazed. He'd been spitting blood. Bost left for Le Havre; he'll be there three days. As for me, I worked on the passage where the statues begin to fly. It's difficult, but it will work out. It isn't there yet. It will be finished by your return. After which I caught the 91 in pouring rain, with thunder and lightning, and went to Lionel's.

My love, I'm stopping here because I must go to my family. I'll write another letter tonight. I love you, I wait for you impatiently.

To Simone de Beauvoir

My darling Beaver

I received two very pleasing letters from you this morning. On second thought, it was only the one, which you continued several hours later. I regret that you're still weighing only 49 kilos. You won't be a choice morsel anymore, but no matter, there'll be celebrations for you because we're longing to see you again. It must be I'm no longer cut out for the bachelor life. It's fine to write you all my petty doings, but I'd like to tell them to you while blowing pipe smoke in your face and watching their effect on your dear, pretty little mug. Beaver, my good Beaver, I love you dearly. Skinny though you be, we'll still be able to grab onto some part of you, a shoulder or an arm, and that'll be better than the precious little phantom Beaver that accompanies me everywhere without being much company. You've given me your addresses so cleverly I have to send this one to Marseilles, where you'll find it on Thursday along with tomorrow's. I think it's pointless to write the following day, but on Thursday I'll leave a note for you at the Hôtel Royal-Bretagne, in the letter box for 65, so that you'll find it there to welcome you on Friday when you get in.

So, Saturday evening I went with de Roulet to the terrace at the Sélect, because the rain hadn't cooled things off. I went to bed, then went to see my family. Not much to say: we saw *Love Is News*, rather implausible, but not unpleasant. Loretta Young is very pretty. The leading man[1] is rather insipid. I left them at five, went home to change and then to La Closerie des Lilas to write you. The weather was heavenly. I also wrote to Paulhan, to Brice Parain, to Denoël and Steele, then trotted down to the Seine, where I caught a cab. Return by the 8:20 train reading detective stories that I'd stolen—yes, good Beaver, stolen for lack of cash from a sidewalk book store display. Today practically nothing: classes; the headmaster called me in to show me my inspection report, unreserved praise ending with: "From now on M. Sartre is ranked among the prime candidates for a post in Paris." He congratulated me and seemed to think it's all set.

I worked, wrote some to Tania, even though I've had no letter from her, because if I find a line from her on Wednesday I won't have a minute from now to Sunday or Monday to answer (you'll be here, my darling Beaver). "The Room" is practically finished.

This evening telegram from Toulouse: "Prepare documents *Captain of Kopenick* for Wednesday evening we'll devote all evening." So be it. Between you and me, I could easily do without it. I was counting on taking the 6:45 train and going straight to her place. I'll have to take the five-o'clock, which is slower, and treat myself to 25 minutes on the Métro to pick up the book. Furthermore I have no idea where it is—I'll have to turn your whole room upside down.

Goodbye, dearest, I send you tender kisses. I'm very happy and very eager for your return.

To Simone de Beauvoir

Friday, 9 o'clock

My darling Beaver

Your Tuesday letter really moved me, and tears came to my eyes thinking that there had been tears in yours. Even at such a distance, it must be

---

[1] Tyrone Power.

contagious. I love you so. We'll see no one Friday, you can count on it, I don't want to any more than you, except perhaps for M. Paulhan, because he wants to see me. This is what he writes me today:

"Dear Monsieur,

"Your three stories are very beautiful. I'll put one ('The Wall,' I think) in the NRF July 1 issue. I will suggest 'Dépaysement' ['Disorientation']¹ for Mesures.

"Melancholia is off to the printers. Even more than the actual reading, my recollections of it allow me to evaluate its power and its reasoning.

"I would be delighted to see you again. Some evening, without causing you any inconvenience, may I come by the Hôtel Royal-Bretagne? Most cordially yours, Jean Paulhan.

"P.S.: I don't know whether you have thought about other publications: however let me ask you for 'The Wall' to be your first work published in a magazine. In a few days you will have the galley proofs."

So now we're rich, thanks to the good M. Paulhan. I wonder if I should see him? Calm down, naughty Beaver, just kidding. I'll say, "Any day you like but Friday." OK?

Not much has happened since last night. I sealed my letter, mailed it, and came back to go to bed. Slept. Three and a half hours of classes, lunch, train. What can I say? It was all very dull, but deep down I was very pleased, still poetic and gentle. I fervently hope this state lasts till you get back, for you will benefit from it: whoever was present at the sorrows must be there at the honors. I have a strong suspicion that this uneasiness I've been feeling these past days—which I was attributing to subtle causes—was quite simply because Melancholia hadn't as yet been conclusively accepted. But today, I walk the streets like an author (I'm ignoring the pebble in my right shoe).²

Young Bost was at the station, in fine fettle. I led him through the streets (Bd. Barbès—Porte de la Chapelle—Rue de la Chapelle Gare de l'Est—Rue du Faubourg Saint-Martin. At Le Châtelet he offered to pay for a cab). The weather was gray and gloomy, perfect for our tour. He was delighted with Brice Parain's letter, which I showed him. A little later, having

¹A short story that Sartre considered a failed attempt to capture the signification of poor neighborhoods in Naples; it appears in the posthumous Oeuvres romanesques ("Works of Fiction,") ed. Michel Contat and Michel Rybalka (Paris, 1974).

²About a year later, in April 1938, after eight years of work under several titles, the book was published as La Nausée by France's leading publishing house, Gallimard. Gaston Gallimard himself suggested the title. As of 1991, the U.S edition alone has sold 680,000 copies.

read Paulhan's letter (which we found at six, dropping by the hotel), he said, "He'll bore you out of your mind, that guy. Don't let him get started." "He'll see me once every six months." "But he feels friendly toward you, he admires you." I said, "I discourage guys like that. I can't please them, and they take a dislike to me." "But by then," he said, "his admiration will be set." I left him at 6:30 and took a brief and aimless stroll: I was going in circles. I finally decided to go to Le Dôme to work on "The Room." (Which Bost wants me to call "Sans repos" ["Without Rest"].) Mardrus was there, the pig, he got hold of me and bored the hell out of me for thirty-five minutes. I dumped him, saying I was headed for the Lady. But the Lady wasn't back from La Pouèze. So I came up here (the ground floor is filled up) and am writing to you. I've slept very little these past months and I'm droopy. I'll go to bed as soon as it's appropriate.

I love you, my sweet little Beaver, I so want to see you again, to tuck your little arm in mine and take a walk. I send you passionate kisses.

To Simone de Beauvoir

Tuesday [May] 11

My darling Beaver

This is my last letter before your return. I would really like it to be long and ceremonious, but I have nothing to tell you and pomp isn't my way. What to tell you? That I love you dearly, that I've had no letter for two days and don't know what's become of you, but that I'm hopeful about your health and happiness; that I'm hurrying to finish my factum so you'll find it done on your return, and that I'm scared I'll mar the ending in my haste. All of that is nothing. I'd happily try moods, but moods have given way: I'm blissful, a little bored but not much really, I'm waiting for you. A chronology wouldn't do any better. Last night I wrote to you too soon after dinner and thought I'd die. To recover I had to walk my letter to the station. The June bugs have come back, or perhaps it's their ghosts. They're still buzzing around the streetlights, but they're more cautious and less numerous. I followed the road the cars take on my way home. It's a route I hadn't used since the day I arrived, in other words for seven and a half months. Quite naturally I thought, What changes! All of them, or nearly all, pleasing. From a distance, actually, this confused year is beginning to fall into place somewhat and take on some meaning. It has less force and charm than last year, but more changes and adventures, and it's a turning point. I went home, the hotel lobby was dark, everyone had gone to the movies. I got into bed with pleasure; this bed is slightly country-style, you know: wide and deep with a huge comforter—I have a weakness for that kind of bed, I just let myself go in them, I surrender with sweet confidence, and you know how rarely I surrender to anything at all; at any rate, in the flat beds of Paris hotels I drop off with one eye open, and that's that. I pampered myself a bit by staying in bed and reading a detective novel which you might buy for your return: *Erreur sur la personne* ["Mistaken Identity"]. Then I slept till 8:30, because it was Tuesday. I worked some, then went to teach my class. I have a corrupt liking for the Sunday-to-Wednesday semicaptivity, with long, empty stretches, they restore my sense of time, and to tell the truth they're restful. I'm fresh and eager, I sleep, I eat. I do everything slowly. It is I (not you, my poor bag of bones) who'll be the morsel fit for a king. You will be allowed to partake. What else did I do? I talked for three quarters of an hour with the Thomist. Shame, shame, you say? Not at all: assume my Laonais point of view, the life of indolence and leisure (the provincial life of yesteryear). Well, you have to know how to be a bit bored, you have to feel the slow passage of time. Besides, I was the one who did the talking this time; he had to pay his share: I told him he's an ass. Of course, he doesn't believe a word of it, even after I'd said my piece. But it was enough that he didn't know what to say except "Obviously I haven't given this enough thought." The conversation took place on a second-floor landing; we were leaning over the railing, and from time to time, every five minutes, he'd excuse himself and duck into a classroom whose door was open, and I could hear him abusing the students he was supposed to be supervising. He made this bold generalization: "Among Marxists there are numerous manic-depressives, and among Thomists numerous neurasthenics." Which means, I think, he feels neurasthenic. In fact, he has the look, the strange remorse. For instance, after three months of patronizing me (actually I'm not complaining), he comes every day to apologize for "not acting with due respect toward me." He told me that elites are necessary. I answered, "I talk to you because you don't have the *agrégation*. If you had it I wouldn't come near you." Actually he isn't a total idiot. I left him. I ate lunch while doing the Renée David crossword. I left and taught two and a half hours of classes. At four I had a cup of tea and finished the detective story—regarding which don't worry, I'll be as silent as the grave—then I worked a bit. The flight of statues is now done and passable. But the end of the story lacks energy; I was rather too peaceful when I wrote it. Right now I need a breaking heart or must confine myself to humor.

It's six o'clock and I am writing to you. I'll take this letter to the post

WITNESS TO MY LIFE

office and come back for dinner. Tonight I'll finish my short story or my letter to Tania.

Farewell, dear little Beaver, I'm all impatience to see you. I love you.

I must also write to Z. I promised.

To Simone de Beauvoir

September 15[1]

My darling Beaver

I got your two letters, which conveyed a strong and pleasant sense of you all alone in Strasbourg; the evening I telephoned, it had seemed somewhat pitiful, since the dining-room cashier told me there wasn't a soul in the room and I imagined you in that huge place, discreetly seated among the empty tables, tired from the trip and disappointed. But now I'm completely reassured, and I feel you show a wise, poetic little nature, turning everything into a variety of joys, and that you don't seem old at all, but rather taking lively advantage of everything that comes your way. I'm all moist with tenderness for you; throughout the night and day while you were alone in Marseilles, on the train, in Strasbourg, and while I was alone in Paris, I never ceased feeling one with you deep inside, as though I were talking to you, and it seemed as though I were telling you my every thought, or rather that you were thinking it along with me, it gave me profound pleasure on the train, because I was imagining two consciousnesses melded into one, floating that way toward Lyons, between earth and sky, and two little robot bodies, looking occupied but vacant, one striding along the streets of Marseilles and the other the train corridor. Just now I don't feel quite the same way, and I feel you slightly less present because I can't bring to mind anymore the things you're doing, and then you're with Zazoulich,[2] and your every fleeting thought is directed toward her, as is only right. But I love you dearly, as a person who is not me, and I long to see your little face, my darling Beaver. I dearly hope you're having a pleasant trip, but I'm very scared for you because here it's cold and rainy. I caught a terrible cold the last night on the boat, and with

---

[1]With Sartre's new teaching assignment at the Lycée Pasteur in Neuilly, just outside the city, he and Beauvoir were both living in Paris at last. During July and August, they had traveled in Greece, returning to Marseilles by boat, whence Sartre had journeyed home by train.

[2]Beauvoir had invited Olga to join her for a short trip in and around Strasbourg, where the Kosakiewicz family had lived during Olga's lycée years.

this gorgeous weather my cold is blossoming, I'm coughing up my lungs.

Here's what I've done: I watched you disappear, and that made me heavyhearted. I expected you'd be able to turn your solitude to the poetic, but weariness could have worn it down to gloom, and that would have been wasted time, wasted Marseilles, and wasted Beaver. I went back to my compartment, read *Marianne*, then felt very cold and wanted it to be warm. The Good Lord answered my prayers, but not in the way I'd hoped: I was asking for a blanket, and he mercilessly denied me; even in Lyons I saw nary a pillow vendor. But then he provided me abundantly with animal heat: at Avignon four hearty souls burst into my compartment, warm as toast, three men and a young woman. I drank abundantly of their organic warmth but paid for it by absorbing their outbursts and joyful conversation. They were "provincials going to the Exposition on a budget ticket." From that standpoint it was rather entertaining, because you could observe the living animal—read "provincial"—who goes to Paris once every five years for a solemn occasion. They explained they'd reserved their rooms a month in advance, they discussed the theater and entertainment offerings at length, and they wondered whether the Bobino was a chic dance hall. There was no question of Montparnasse: always Montmartre, Montmartre, they thought that Bobino was in Montmarte. Five to a compartment isn't so bad, after all; I couldn't stretch out flat, but I could spread out, which was something, extend my feet as far as possible from my head. I put an old pair of flannel pants across my knees, I girded my kidneys with a pair of Bost's, and I dozed. Let's say five hours (you'll add two, you most cunning little thing, thinking I slept like a log all the way). By morning it got a bit tiring, because the train, which wasn't listed on the timetable and had no set schedule, never seemed to get there. The disheartening part was not being able to say: It is now so many minutes behind schedule. No, it was all indefinite, it would get in when it got in. It would stop every fifteen minutes in barren countryside. I finally went to wash up, to shave and change, in the first-class toilet, and also decided to drop in on Zazoulich before going to the hotel. As it turned out, we got in at nine, and I caught a cab and reached the Rue Pascal at nine-twenty. That was the start of a weird morning, it too rather indefinite. First off, Paris, seen from the cab, seemed formidably poetic—as Strasbourg did to you—because it looked like a city in the North (I'd already had a good chuckle near Laroche as I suddenly caught sight of a very French bit of countryside, cultivated to its fingertips and smelling frightfully of man). It reminded me of Berlin, actually. Gray sky, wide streets, and houses dedicated to protecting their inhabitants from the cold while for two months we had just been seeing houses that protect people from the heat. Naturally it made me feel totally disoriented, I felt I was nowhere. Thereupon, carrying my bags, I walk up to the sixth floor of the building, I knock, I ring the bell: no reply. I hung on for a long time, because I remembered Poupette's story and vaguely imagined Zazoulich dead drunk on the other side of the door. On the next door a sign gave me ironic encouragement: "Knock loudly." After five minutes I went back down and asked the concierge what was up. "Mlle Zazoulich? She won't be back for a long time. Just to show you, I got a letter from her this morning asking for her mail to be forwarded." Quite a blow. I left, feeling vague and undecided. It was particularly that letter that intrigued me; it seemed to indicate some morbid intention on Z.'s part. I took another cab to the Hôtel Royal-Bretagne. Another blow. The fat blonde slumped back, surprised to see me: "You should have alerted me. I don't have a room—all the Montparnasse hotels are full." She finally decided to give me a note to another hotel, the Mistral, on the Rue de Cels (off the Avenue du Maine, near the Rue Froidevaux), where she keeps some rooms for clients who show up without warning. I said I'd go there later and left my bags in the hall. The old lady was there, bubbling with kindness; she shook my hand and asked about you in an affected throaty voice. I went out again and immediately wired Zazoulich: "Telegram doubtless astray. Please return Paris today if possible. Anyway call Sartre Dôme noon. Beaver waiting Marseilles." It was then ten in the morning; this pinned me down to the neighborhood till one. I had lunch at La Coupole, reading the papers. A gray, deserted Coupole: just me and the schizophrenic drawing his little flyspecks with an air of total madness. Around eleven I went to 216 Boulevard Raspail to find Zuorro. The concierge vaguely directed me "to the courtyard . . . hall . . . fifth." I got lost in a maze of buildings, then when I wanted more information the woman had disappeared. It was eleven-thirty, and I felt my presence in Paris to be more and more absurd. I went to Le Dôme, where I planned to begin my quest for money. I phoned the Lady: sound of ringing in an empty apartment. Toulouse: sound of ringing in an empty apartment. Bost: a woman's voice; "We haven't heard a thing." The Moon woman:[3] a woman's voice: "I hope she'll be back someday." So I felt fiercely forsaken in this world, precisely in Heidegger's sense, and embarrassed about myself, with an overlay of anxiety concerning the money to be found. I ordered a coffee to wake me up and consulted *La Semaine de Paris* to see what was on at the Atelier. I saw that *Volpone* wouldn't open till the 16th, which removed my last hope. Just then I caught sight of a tall figure in a cowboy shirt, dashed out, and dragged in

---

[3]Marie Ville Girard, whom Sartre had known in Berlin.

Zuorro, who was at first ever so slightly chilly but then all at once cordial and charming as he knows how to be. I'll tell you right off that we've been on the best of terms since then; he even paws me a bit. The money question: of course he couldn't lend me anything, but I was reassured to see he had a thousand-franc bill on him. I did think he could lend me something for a day or two, which would give me the chance to "bounce back" (I put it in quotes because it's an expression I hate, like "getting the upper hand," etc. But in quotes it looks even uglier). We chatted while I waited for Z.'s call, and up to that point he told me nothing significant about his life: he hadn't been to Vichy, was a bit tired of Mme Fourestier, felt he had no more need of her and even that she hampered him a little (because each time he gropes a bit and tries to adapt her advice personally and in a slightly original way, she stops him, believing he's mistaken, and not seeing that these experiments are conditions of any further progress). He had stayed in Paris throughout, had seen the Lady until August 15th. Guille married her daughter and is putting in some military training time, which makes mincemeat of his vacations. At present he's with the Bel Eute,[4] doubtless in Corsica (the Lady in La Pouèze,[5] of course). Zuorro saw Toulouse: first for lunch at La Coupole. Second time, a day at Férolles. He's definitely signed on for *Plutus*.[6] At the moment he pretends to find her charming, and perhaps in fact he does find her better than that (but I also think he's maneuvering because of course he thinks I'll try to manipulate his relationship with Toulouse according to dark and Machiavellian designs). All the same he was candid about her intelligence. "I feel she can't be judged according to our preoccupations and our ideas. They are two separate worlds, and I wouldn't want hers. But if you judge intelligence by the richness and solidity of the world constructed, she's intelligent because she has a world that is truly hers, very strange but coherent." Already his imitations of her are delightful. As it turns out, Dullin knows Rouché very well and will say something to him. For the first time, by the way, Zuorro has told me, "Seriously and frankly, I believe that I am completely ready and can join the Opéra tomorrow." The day at Férolles seems to have been surprising: Toulouse would leave him every fifteen minutes to tend to some mysterious needs, perhaps to have a drink. They have a goat named Corinne. Meanwhile time was passing and Z. hadn't called. At one-fifteen I despaired and we left, having decided to lunch at Zuorro's. But first I phoned Laigle, asking Z. to call me at Le Dôme at 4. Thereupon,

---

[4] *His wife's nickname. (SdB)*
[5] The ancestral home of her invalid husband, near Angers in the Loire Valley.
[6] *An adaptation by Simone Jollivet of Aristophanes' play. (SdB)*

outside, the real Zuorro revealed himself, with his cortege of little adventures. An old woman in a white smock threw herself at him: "Have you seen Paul?" Zuorro, affable and dignified: "No, Madame. What's happened to him this time?" "Ah, Monsieur." She was white with anguish. "He was seen with some criminals. And then they found a set of skeleton keys in his room. They won't take him back. You know, you should speak to him." "Well, Madame, I'll give him a really good dressing-down, this very day, and I'll come by to talk to you at the drugstore." The woman left. "Who is Paul?" "Oh, Paul isn't important, but there's someone else who's interesting—Williams." Anyway, one day when Zuorro, after some hard work, was in an adventuresome mood, he saw a tall young man about 17, blond and—as he said quite emphatically—very ugly, crying buckets in front of the one-armed bandit at the bar of Le Dôme. He went up to him. The young man—though surprisingly of an economical bent, or so he said—had spent the last of the 117 francs that were to see him through the month, by inserting them into the machine, twenty centimes at a time. Zuorro took him off for some *choucroute* and made him talk a bit. A sly customer, rather stupid, three years of reformatory, and, to boot, both pitiless and pitiful. For several days he had him take care of his place, for a small sum, then, irritated and mercurial as he sometimes is, had him hired as a salesperson in a drugstore to get rid of him. "Yes, but tit for tat," said the cashier, the very one who'd come up to us, "only if you hire my sister as your housekeeper." Which he did. She's a shrew, but capable. Then quite often Paul would fail to show up at the drugstore, etc. I saw him (I'm anticipating) the night before last. He is blond and rather ugly (though not too); he stammers, with a look of embarrassment, insolence, and extraordinary craftiness. But from that moment on I knew he wasn't the interesting character: Williams was. I didn't see Williams that day, nor learn anything significant about him. We went to the butcher to buy a steak, to the grocer for a bottle of wine, to the dairy shop for some butter, to the bakery for some bread. Zuorro enjoys his role as a householder, argues about the prices: "Why is it, Madame, that you sometimes charge me 70 centimes for the bread and sometimes 80 centimes?" "Because you don't know anything about it, Monsieur, and without noticing, you sometimes take one quality, sometimes another." Or else: "Four francs fifty? Then I was robbed. My salesperson charged me 4.90." At the grocery they offered us a choice of two grades of potatoes. Though Zuorro was hearing the names for the first time, he shrugged his shoulders as though there could be no question: "The Dutch, of course." "That woman in the grocery doesn't like me," he confided, "because I only go to her when the other is closed." At the butcher's he inquires precisely how many minutes the meat should be cooked. But if the figure is too high he explodes, once out in the street, "Those idiots, they say that because they have gas stoves. With an electric oven it cooks much faster." In fact, the next day it took an hour and a quarter to cook a shoulder of veal that should take, according to the butcher, forty minutes by gas. After all this, laden with packages, we climbed the stairs to his place. There is a grimy door (black iron fittings against a white wall, frosted glass panes) just above and beside the movie theater at 216 Raspail. A long dark corridor leads to a court. There's one building to the right and another straight ahead. We took the stairs in the right-hand one. On the fifth floor (there's one door per floor; the stairway is lit by large bay windows) you can see through the window to the right of a laminated door, a small open window with a bottle of milk, butter wrapped in waxed paper, and two little jars of yogurt, all resting on the sill. It's Zuorro's kitchen. We went in. A tiny entrance hall opening onto a kitchen to the right and a huge room with a ceiling that's not actually very high (I mean in comparison to immense studios in other parts of the building), white walls, a huge bay window looking out onto the Boulevard Raspail. In the room in a corner to the left a divan-bed lent by the Lady. A small Norman hutch center right, a splendid black Steinway grand at the far right. That's all. I should add a Smyrna rug, dirty but with splendid colors, notably a turquoise blue. A couple of bookshelves on the wall. It seems monastic and luxurious. The Lady was so charmed by the place, it seems, she wanted to come to do her needlework every afternoon while Zuorro sang. At the far left, opposite the piano and the bay, a door opens onto a handsome bathroom with built-in tub and a bidet with running water. 6,000 francs a month all told. The piano is on lease-purchase, meaning that a rental fee of 400 a month also constitutes a purchase payment. When it is all paid up (a long way off, since the piano is worth 50,000 francs) the piano will be Zuorro's. But beyond that, as a special condition, he can return the piano at any time and the amount paid in can go toward any piano of his choosing. That's what he expects to do, when he has worn out the Steinway. We went to the kitchen, since there's no other table, and Zuorro gravely cooked our steak, while of course accusing me of finding the whole thing grotesque and re-pellent. We ate between the stove and the sink, seated on two Louis XV chairs. The table service consisted of two forks, a single knife, and four cracked plates belonging to the Lady. We washed up, I told him a bit about my trip to Greece, and around four we went back down. But don't get the idea, mind you, that my relationship with Zuorro remained that good-natured and su-perficial: I have *loads* of funny stories to tell you, though it all took place only the following night. At any rate I want you to know that chances are good we'll have very cordial relations with him this year. From four to five

I waited in vain for a call from Z. At five they call me downstairs: without giving her name, a young woman had told the operator at the Laigle post office that she was *expecting* a call from Paris, but she left after half an hour. I had to call Laigle again, explaining that she should call me collect. I'll tell you right off that the messages to Laigle, the telegram, and the two phone conversations to Strasbourg cost me 72 francs: how love adds up on the accounts of an old man! Besides, I was annoyed and torn, because I was waiting for that call but also wanted to meet the six-o'clock train on the off chance that Z. would be on it. At five forty-five, Zuorro kindly offered to meet Z. for me, while I waited for the call. I accepted, though dreading in anticipation the effect that meeting would have on Z. and possible consequences for me. At seven to six they called me downstairs, and Tania was on the phone. A little voice, rough and appealing, with long silences. "Hello." "Hello, this is Tania." "I'm very pleased to be hearing your voice." "Me too. You know that my sister is on the train." "Good, I'll run and meet her. Things going well with you?" "Not too." "Why not?" "Just because." "Are you working?" "A little." "Will I be seeing you the 18th?" "I can't." "Why?" "It would take too long to tell you—I'll write. Briefly, Violette Brochard is on vacation. But I'll come to Paris on the 30th." "You'll stay at my hotel and we'll never be apart. OK?" "Sure." "Goodbye. I'm very fond of you." Long silence. "Hello there, silly, at least say goodbye." She laughs a bit. "Goodbye." Whereupon I tore off and ran till I thought my lungs would burst, all the way to the station. I got there at 6:03 (late by three minutes, but the train was late by four). At 6:05 I saw Z. ambling along.

My darling Beaver, I have to leave and get back to my family. Already I'm going to be bawled out because I was to have had my hair cut and I spent the time I should have devoted to the barber writing to you. Tomorrow I'll tell you the rest, which you'll find amusing. I give you a big kiss, dearest of little ones.

To Simone de Beauvoir

[Summer]

My darling Beaver

Yesterday I really enjoyed writing to you, but this morning I'm in a foul mood. I went to bed late and was mercilessly awakened early, as is the custom here. I got up dazed and unconsciously wandered toward the bathroom, where my stepfather was shaving. I saw his back, beat a hasty retreat.

But they were already vacuuming the study, with windows wide open. I had to wait in the toilet, the only place left to me. After that I would have liked to write to you from the Café des Tourelles, but my mother begged me to stay in the dining room as an experiment, to see whether I could write here. She is cunningly nursing the hope that I'll "hop over" in the hour between classes and work here (I'll have a key, won't even have to alert anyone, etc.). She'd even like me to board here with them for lunch. I'm resisting as gently as I can, but I'll avoid it at all costs, because I've discovered that they sadden me. Whenever I'm with them for more than two hours at a time, I become irritated with myself, I'm conscious of my every gesture, which profoundly disgusts me. There reigns here an atmosphere of slow, decent death, expertly established by my stepfather, that would drag down anyone at all. And then they surround me with their image of me, and I of course must play that image, bend to it somewhat, under threat of conflicts. I feel I'm a decent lad (perhaps even a "good sport"), a little crazy, with a bit of the devil in me (not too much, just enough, a bit less than Mme Emery's son, who has a sports plane), but who adores his mother. An honest lad, too, who messes around some with ideas—small wonder, he's still young—too clear-sighted to be a communist, but a nice little anarchist surrounded by his books, basically very serious-minded, a young teacher of merit. Someone who still has a lot to learn from life but is starting out well. And he writes, in his free time. He turns out little stories and more serious articles on philosophic questions. A nice amateur talent. I swear to you, my darling Beaver, that it even takes away my desire to write. Twelve hours a day of submitting politely to their image of me: it's enough to do a person in. And I still have two good weeks to go. I know that seeing you I'll come back to myself somewhat, but that won't be tomorrow. Look, just try this one: my stepfather tells long stories I already know, riveting me with his brilliant eyes, I nod "yes, yes," I feel myself nodding "yes, yes," I feel a smile of respectful attention on my lips and long to get the hell out. Aside from that—and perhaps it's the worst part—they are very nice.

But I'll get back to my account. So I found Z. at the station. I was trying to catch my breath when I saw her coming, glassy eyes in a wide pale face. I instantly understood that she had been crying on the train. She said hello without surprise, but coolly, and with an air of not seeing me. She was full of complaints, which came out softly, faintly, with a lilting politeness. In a word, she reproached us for coming back too late, she was no longer expecting us. She had expected us around the 4th. Hence this clever arrangement: she left for Laigle with instructions to the concierge not to forward her letters, meaning that all the letters (two from you, one from me) giving her details of our return lay waiting in Paris. Hence twelve days in Laigle with no news; she went off the deep end and gradually turned bitter. I insisted that we had written, poured on the affection, and at La Coupole, where she had some Welsh rarebit, she relaxed a bit, not without a few flashes of hatred against me, because *I* had been the one to see Greece with you instead of her. She spoke morosely about Bost, but that was part of her general mood, because later she spoke of him more tenderly and revealed that she had had her mother make a belt for him. But I felt that her departure for Laigle on August 31 had been something of a rout. And then she spoke of people in a certain way, with pretty, ironic thrusts of the chin suggesting that she fully comprehended in one way or another the absurdity of all creation. Finally everything came out on our way back to the Royal-Bretagne so I could pick up my suitcase, on the Rue Delambre which has seen so much, so much fury, so much crying. It all came out without any help from me, since it was eleven, I was dying on my feet, had to get up at 6:30 to take her to the station, and realized that it would take two good hours of talk. So, we were walking up the Rue Delambre, and I said, "I do hope you won't catch cold, either one of you, in those shelters and in this weather." She shrugged and said, "The Beaver has been vaccinated; she had pleurisy. As for me . . ." with a funny look. "You mean you have an iron constitution?" With ironic emphasis, "Yes, that's it." I said, "No, that's not it. You seem to mean that in your state, it's not a little thing like a chill that counts." Then, weak but annoyed, "Of course not." "What's the matter? Have you seen a doctor?" "Of course not. You see a doctor when you *feel* sick," in a lilting Russian tone as she emphasized "feel." "You mean there are hopeless illnesses in which one *is* sick but can walk about and tend to one's affairs? Is it mortal, Zazoulich?" Burst of ironic laughter; thereupon we fetch the bag and go to a small café so I can show her the recording, the mill, and the pencils. For a while she discreetly plays the role of someone for whom everything seems extraordinarily absurd and Lilliputian because she is already consumed with death. Until, irritated, I say, "So what is it? You are tubercular and spitting blood?" That was it. A small touch of pink showed up in her saliva one day when she was brushing her teeth or rinsing her mouth. I took a deep breath: faced by these anxieties and reticences, I had thought for a moment that she was pregnant by Bost and determined, naturally, to kill herself. It would have cost us 1,500 francs. There followed, of course, a description of night sweats, pain in the shoulder blades, swollen glands under the arms. I begged her to see a doctor. At first she said no, then agreed, with an ease that proved she had already made up her mind to. That's where things now stand. She said she would talk to you about it. I do hope, darling Beaver, that you won't be anxious about all of this. The upshot of what she said is that she feels poorly at times, agrees she should see a doctor, and will take better care of herself. She'd been crying on the train because after first looking forward to the little trip with you, she'd suddenly been struck by its futility as against the threat of death. On the outside I was sensitive and good, along the lines of holding hands in a long moist embrace, in intimate conversation, but inside cold as ice and even hostile, because I've had enough of imaginary invalids and long meditations on impending death and youth nipped in the bud. The funniest part is that she repeated point by point the business about Bost, which gave her a good laugh, and on top of that, she has just reread the spitting episode in the short story he wrote. I took her back to the Rue Pascal by cab and had myself taken to the Rue Cels and the Hôtel Mistral. It doesn't look very promising, has a shabby stairway and motheaten halls, but the rooms are large, clean, and much better furnished than those at the Royal-Bretagne, with a sofa, rug, bookshelves on the walls. For the largest they want 350 francs a month plus service, and 300 for the smallest. I'd like you to go and take a look when you get back. On the other hand, at the Royal-Bretagne they are offering me a large room on the seventh floor (for you or me, whichever). They wouldn't give a price for this winter, merely assuring me that they would make it as low as possible. Of course, they would have a second room, but still indefinite.

I slept little, had myself woken up at 6:30, and at 7:15 I was at Z.'s. I had set an early hour because I was sure she wouldn't be ready. And, indeed, she wasn't. I had to go back down and wander around outside for a while, and we finally left at eight. The weather was superb, though it later changed. Z. started out charming, became irritated, then dreamy, glum, and unresponsive. Finally she volunteered the admission, in an effort of goodwill, "When I leave Paris I'm always atrociously jealous of those who are staying. It was the same with Bost on the 31st of August." I told her gently, "But you're leaving because that's what you want; you want to go on a trip with the good Beaver." "Yes, but I'd like to be everywhere at once." Up to 8:30 she was radiant at the idea of leaving, and she must have been so again as soon as the train left, but a five-minute wait on the platform and one ray of sunshine were enough to have her begin missing Paris again. When the train started up, we fluttered our handkerchiefs. I came back to Montparnasse on foot, very happy to be taking a walk and thinking that everything I was seeing at the moment I'd be able to see every day for the rest of my life.

Around 12:30 I went to meet Zuorro (after a long walk and a brief letter to Tania, written at Le Dôme). Right off I'll tell you that I didn't leave him for a minute all day—except for an hour from seven to eight while he was seeing Williams. We had lunch together at his apartment, a shoulder of veal and green peas. As he had gone off leaving me alone, I opened the portfolio he was to give Z., which was full of letters. I found some letters from Guerrieri and some addressed to Williams: "Dear boy, your poor Auntie Louise—as you used to call him—well, she died, a great sadness for us all." And a letter from a certain Simone: "Since you're so close by, I hope we'll keep up our friendship. Don't write here—my parents open my letters." When Zuorro came back I said, "What are Williams's letters doing here?" He said, "I put him up here for more than a month—I tossed him out only a short while ago." And he showed me a photo of a very young man, quite handsome, laughing and showing his pearly whites—dimples, of course—hustler shirt without a jacket, and, so it seems, hazel eyes. Zuorro insisted that he wasn't at all a Montparnasse pansy, boastful and hollow "like that street trash Armand." He turned serious, as when he wants to convince you or me about the intelligence or special qualities of a close friend, and said in a simple tone conveying inner fire, "He is altogether intelligent, and he is tough in a very pleasant way, I've never seen anyone so tough, and he leads quite an interesting life and he's already come up with loads of ideas, many of which struck me as profound; he's wily as a monkey." At that point he simply told me how he had met him one day with Armand at the bar of Le Dôme. Armand was giving him advice on "how to defend himself with queens." But Williams, who is no pansy, has a profound contempt for Armand. The next day Zuorro took Armand aside: "A hundred francs if you introduce me." And they met that very evening. "I'll tell you everything about him," he added. Meanwhile the conversation took another tack. With a sardonic smile but no anger, Zuorro learned that Bost was with us in Greece: "So, Bost went to Athens and dropped you a note to let you know he was there. Then he has certainly changed. In the past he would never have allowed himself to descend unauthorized on a city where you were spending your vacation." Thereupon the conversation turned to Bost, and he spoke of him without apparent bitterness but rather profound contempt, explaining, 1st, that Bost and Z. were worthless because without any resistance they accepted the world we had built up and drew their value and nourishment from it; 2nd, that Bost considered the people he saw as "passing stages." I noted that these two points didn't go too well together, but he disagreed, and I let it pass. Then I told him that in any case, even if this story of "steps" and "stages" is true,

I found it quite normal that a young man should take mature individuals he meets as people to use and also as stages to outgrow and that we would have done as much. First he answered, "Perhaps, but not emotional stages." And he told me that if at twenty he'd met someone like me or himself, he would have either hated him or given himself to him without reservation, forever. But that answer didn't satisfy him, since he thought it over and promised another, which is pending. Then we launched into a comparison of our youth and Bost's, which I found somewhat painful, making me feel we're no longer spring chickens. I'll spare you. I only remember that at the moment Zuorro stared at me and said, ferociously, though under his breath, "Because each of us thinks himself more intelligent than the others. Thus, however much I esteem Guille and you, I consider myself much more intelligent." It made me laugh, and I said, "You've always hidden that; it would have spared me from irritating you so badly last year." He laughed too. "Ah yes, that was on the Rue Damrémont, when you said (imitating me, or rather imitating the Lady imitating me), 'The good thing about you, Zuorro, is that you don't care about being intelligent.' " But while we were taking up these burning issues we were still engaged in agreeing that it was all in the past and we were purified. And in fact I believe he is more or less sincere, because he is perfectly pleasant right now and it's a pleasure to be with him. He told me this little anecdote, probably doctored but rather amusing. One day it seems he said to Bost, "Deep down you have some sort of genius," and Bost replied with a look of finality, eyes downcast and half-closed: "For all the good it might do me!" Then he spoke about Roquentin,[1] which he has read this time and claims to like very much. He made a few pertinent criticisms. That evening we went to the movies to see *Trafic d'armes* ["Arms Trade"]. Excellent. Then we went back to Le Dôme and embarked on a long conversation that I'm sure he later regretted. First he spoke about Williams, giving a delightful account of how Williams had calmly settled in and made himself at home. The way he would say in the evening, "Zuorro, we're going home," as early as ten, and Zuorro, a bit sad to be going home, would think that at least it would mean a long night and a good sleep, but hardly would they be in when Williams, stretched out on a panther skin on the floor, would take to singing terribly off-key till one in the morning; how Williams—who before Zuorro adopted him had first slept at his old sugar daddy's "without letting himself be touched," then under bridges, on benches, in stations—had brought bushels of fleas into the apartment and went around saying, "It's not bad at

---

[1]The protagonist of *Nausea*.

Monsieur Zuorro's, but it's overrun with fleas." Then one day Zuorro said, "strip down." Williams stripped and Zuorro sprayed him all over with Fly-Tox. He also mentioned Williams's language, full of slang and charming expressions. For example, one day Williams came out of the bathroom just after Zuorro had rubbed his head with sulfur. He said with a sniff, "Hey, buddy! Did something die in here?" Zuorro portrayed his relationship with Williams as completely straightforward, without a ray of tenderness. They even fought, because Williams, raised in the country among solid peasants, conceives of friendship as a continual exchange of blows. Zuorro beats him up, but with great difficulty. All the same, Zuorro put him out because he was in the way, gave the cold shoulder to friends who came to see Zuorro, and told him, "You know, you wouldn't have to pay me to get rid of all your buddies, you could simply let me do the entertaining." And annoying, dead set on his proud, unshakable little male convictions, a little terror. For example: "She wanted me to pay for her Métro ride, but I said I didn't have the money. The broad that'll call the tune for me ain't been born yet." And when Zuorro wants him to change his opinion, he says slyly, "You argue like an old fag I lived with." Knowing he'll wound Zuorro and also because of his conviction that the moment another man is interested enough in him to offer advice and want to influence him, it's sex that he wants. The next morning he came to ring Zuorro's doorbell, rather pitifully, to pick up some of his things. "Where did you spend the night?" "At so-and-so's"—a friend, but for some reason Zuorro knew it was impossible. He changes his clothes and underclothes, and Zuorro sees suspicious stains on his pants. When he has left, Zuorro looks at the pants and shirt, which he finds full of sperm "with suspicious gray streaks as though they'd been used to wipe up something." When Zuorro next sees Williams: "You've slept with some guy, don't deny it, I saw your shirt," etc. Williams listened, head down, without saying a thing, then after five minutes he looked up. "No, old boy, I didn't get laid. I didn't go see my buddy, that's the truth. I went up to sleep on the landing above your apartment, and I beat off to pass the time." And Zuorro insisting that he had never given himself away and that after all there was no proof. Anyway, 1st, the boy never sleeps anywhere but at the sugar daddies'; 2nd, having stolen three thousand francs from a drawer the day his grandmother died (?), ordered up a superb pansy suit, with rear-hugging trousers, etc.; 3rd, changed his prosaic name—Dupont or Durand—to Williams, just like an actress or hooker. Zuorro is visibly eager for him not to be a homosexual, and it's true that the queen whom he stayed with before he knew Zuorro admits he never got anything from him. Williams says, too, that the first guy who took him in was an aviator, a wartime ace. At night the guy propositioned him, but Williams went off to sleep on the floor and the other didn't insist. During the night, Williams is woken up by the creaking of box springs. He says, "Why're you masturbating?" and the other answers, "My friend, under the circumstances it's the only thing left for me to do," in a tone of charming courtesy. He also slept at another place, a sort of homosexual dormitory with six or seven beds in a huge but miserable apartment where lots of young guys like Williams would come for the night. After a while the host was fed up and fled to Geneva, leaving the furniture for them to divvy up. Williams got a mattress and an armoire, which he sold for fifty francs. Finally he stayed with a homosexual Arab—the one who openly admits he never had any success with him. He has kept up with him, and Williams tells him about Zuorro. "He wants to lay you," says the older man. "No, no," say Williams, "he's a guy that writes novels." "Oh sure!" says the other. "And he told you he wants to research the scene? But I've said that too, sweetie. Many times, in fact. So look, don't hand me that." Zuorro told this as he always does, with irony, and using the irony to adopt a superiority over the Arab, so it would be clear that the guy was mistaken, that he was indeed a novelist and asked no more than information from Williams. As for me, I told Zuorro that doubtless it was possible that Williams had slept with no one but that his familiarity with the queens, his pansy clothes, his great care to swear that he wasn't a hustler, proved at least that he was strongly tempted and toying with the idea of offering his ass. Agreeing, he turned sad and spoke no more about Williams. We spoke about homosexuality in general, and he told me it was incredible how many men had been in love with him. "I was never in love with Larroutis, but when he touched me like this"—as he spoke he gently took me by the shoulder—"he had to put a hand in his pocket to hide the evidence." And Guerrieri? "Guerrieri is surely in love with me. Nowadays he puts his head on my shoulder and says, 'Oh, you! You!' "

My darling Beaver, I've just received your telegram, and I'm cutting this letter short to send it off to you. Count on the 50 francs in Strasbourg.

I love you very much, and I'm a bit melancholy without you.

To Simone de Beauvoir

[September]

My darling Beaver

I long to see you and talk with you. So I'm going to tell you a whole bunch of things; I hope you'll find this letter in Strasbourg, along with the check. But instead of going chronologically, I'll tell it to you in small stories, because you'll probably want information on each.

1. *your relationship to me and mine to you*: idyllic. I constantly think nice little things about you. You've been very good and have written often; but I'd have liked letters every day, even if there were nothing in them, for the pure pleasure of holding something from you in my hand. I love you very much. When you get here, there'll be a note for you at Le Dôme giving you a precise time for our meeting, probably for the evening of the 22nd.

2. *question of money*: it is my mother who has provided everything and will also provide the 50 francs you'll find in this letter. These days she's being very nice to me. My stepfather will cash the endorsed check from the NRF for me. I've received a notice of payment for the two courses on cooperation I taught in Laon (you remember?): a hundred francs. But the check that arrived on August 20 was returned to the sender. I've written to the Centre de Coopération de l'Aisne, and I'm counting somewhat on the dough for your return. While waiting, I live ten francs at a time, I let others pay, I eat as often as possible at my parents'. It's not always fun but it's food. No *bachots*[1] in sight. But I received (and sent back, corrected) the proofs of *La Transcendance du moi*,[2] forty pages. That should mean five hundred francs, perhaps payable in October. That, together with the *bachots* from Lille, will help us a lot. Meanwhile, we'll have to tap a Toulouse or a Gégé for three hundred francs on your return. Perhaps after all it would be good to suggest to Zazoulich that she go home to Laigle for five or six days. I'm living very well on 10 francs a day; tobacco, matches: 5 francs; 2 Métros: 40 cents; the rest goes for drinks (1 beer, one coffee). My mother gives me my ten francs every morning.

3. *reading*: I find you a bit severe about the adventures of Ellery Queen. There is a story of a mirror reflecting a clock that appealed to me. You, on the other hand, would be enchanted by *Mystery of the Match*. Buy it when you get back. The solution may be a bit weak, but it's engaging. I'm going to buy *The Waves*[3] when possible, because I think it would be astute to do two parallel articles, (A) *The Waves*, (B) *Eyeless in Gaza*.[4]

4. *personal works*: I'm doing none at all. But I'm full of ideas (surfaced while rereading *The Transcendence of the Ego* for *La Connaissance de Soi*). I only await landing in some propitious location to start it. Between now and

---

[1]*Baccalauréat* exams to correct.
[2]Published as *La Transcendance de l'égo* (Paris: Vrin, 1937). *The Transcendence of the Ego*, trans. Forrest Williams and Robert Kirkpatrick (New York, 1957).
[3]*By Virginia Woolf. (SdB)*
[4]By Aldous Huxley.

October 15 I'll do only criticism for the *NRF*, which I'm waiting to begin when you bring back *Eyeless in Gaza*. It seems an article in praise of "The Wall" has appeared someplace. But since I heard the news from my mother, who heard it from another, it's pretty vague. I tend to believe it would be on *Imagination*[5] and she got it all wrong, but who knows? My Englishwoman informs me that "The Wall" will appear in *Life and Letters To-day*. She'll send me one pound Sterling (140 francs at the present exchange rate), "which," she writes me, "you will be kind enough to accept." Several people have protested that it's not enough. But at least it's something.

5. *Poupette, Tania, Gégé, the Kaufmann woman*: I haven't seen Poupette. I haven't seen Gégé. Bost told me that she was so proud of your letter that she showed it to the entire Kuntz atelier. And each of them read it, noting with admiration that your writing is so illegible or that you could walk so many kilometers. He also told me that she had beaten up a guy who had put an arm around her waist as he went by on the street. She threw herself upon him and punched his face so thoroughly that his nose was bleeding all over the place. The funniest part is she was carrying a little parcel, which she carefully put down before launching in and picked up when she'd won the round. A guy in a cap with wrestler's shoulders shook her hand enthusiastically in congratulation. Another time (this I also heard from Bost) she ran into Zuorro. Now Zuorro had told Poupette that Gégé was tubercular, and Gégé was furious to hear of it. She feigned the greatest cordiality, walked around him saying, "But how bald you're getting, Zuorro. I tell you this in your own best interest. What a lot of hair you've lost since the last time I saw you! Here, and here, and here," pointing, "there are places where the skull shows right through. . . ." It seems he was very displeased. —As for the Kaufmann woman, she wrote to me here, of course, a letter that isn't even funny. I'm not sending it on to you because I can't even remember what pocket I stuffed it into. She simply says in postscript, "If it would amuse you, I'll tell you a ridiculous story that concerns you: Wolff wants to sue you if . . ." I can pretty much guess what it's about, and it's truly funny: having gotten no answer to his letter, that poor buffoon of a Wolff is afraid that he's revealed himself and that I might want to use the precious points he gave me on his own theory of images. He will sue me if he finds any trace of his ideas in my upcoming books. Enough to split your sides. But how annoying that Kaufmann is, the one time she has a slightly amusing story, to drag it out

---

[5]Sartre's first published book, *L'Imagination* (Paris, 1936); *Imagination: A Psychological Critique*, Trans. Forrest Williams (Ann Arbor, 1979).

WITNESS TO MY LIFE

so. Unless she's holding back to entice me. But that still won't be enough to make me want to see her. I haven't felt up to writing her. Anyway, I'm fiercely resolved not to go and bore the hell out of myself for three days with her. I'll see her in a day or so, on September 30.

6. *young Bost*. I've seen him twice. Once on Friday afternoon, once last night, Sunday. Pleasant as usual. Without any great revelations. Young Bost wrote then tore up 37 pages about a stowaway in a hold. He is working a bit at philosophy. Yesterday, after a rather unrewarding effort to read the Brunschvicg on causality, he was quite seriously resolved to dedicate himself to colonial agriculture. On the other hand he doesn't doubt that he'll pass the Philo-géné[6] in November. The other day he went back to the Pierre Bosts'. It was dark in the deserted apartment, and he found only one of his sisters—"the one for whom," so he told me, "I had an incestuous passion"— hidden away in a dark corner, looking extremely vacant. He turned on some lights and put on some records, and they danced. After a while she blushed, stopped dancing, and said to him, "I have to tell you something." But she immediately took it back and said, "No. It's just stupid. Let's dance." After an hour she started in again (she's unmarried at 30) and suddenly said to him, "Jacques, I think I'm going to take a lover." He asked her nothing but enthusiastically encouraged her. Two days went by, and it must have happened on Saturday evening (that alone makes it seem pitiful), because she slept away from home that night and stayed in bed till six in the evening on Sunday. Bost found her asleep on the living-room divan around that time. Her purse, stuffed with change, had been tossed on a table. He reached out for it, but she sat up and said plaintively, "Who's that?" Apparently she didn't look exactly glowing, and Bost fears it was a fiasco. Friday we joined the authors at Les Deux Magots. Bost was painfully shy—"This is one place I'd never go alone." But the waiter wasn't too scornful with us, because I was carrying corrected proofs (of *The Transcendence of the Ego*, which I was returning to the printer Boivin. Will you think me senile if, through association of ideas, I tell you that the other Boivin just suffered an atrociously agonizing death?). Right across from us, holding forth at the center of one group, was a magnificent intellectual woman, with thin, sinuous lips and light-rimmed glasses, who knew how to challenge the others with a penetrating stare. In forty-five minutes she reviewed all the current films and books, emphasizing her points with cramped gestures of her forearms and hands only, her upper arms glued to her sides. But we didn't see any of the great

---

[6]First of four certificates required for the bachelor degree in philosophy.

stars. They're still away on vacation, I suppose. Last night, with 100 sous apiece, we treated ourselves to promenades at Bobino. We saw the inevitable Charles Fallot, even more repulsive at Bobino, because he tries to look like a leftist. And a dumpy little person who can sing but has no charm at all: Lyne Clevers. Behind us there was an idiot (a complete nut case, said Bost), laughing wildly but understanding nothing in the show. While Fallot sang, he began to laugh and suddenly shouted, "Land of sunshine!" while holding his sides. Since he was right behind me, I discreetly moved out of reach. We guess that he took Charles Fallot for Lyne Clevers, actually confusing the latter with Lys Gauty. We also jointly bought *The Mystery of the Match* (see #3).

7. *Toulouse.* I phoned her on Tuesday. She was there. With some unknown demon prompting me, I said, "Is this *Madame* Jollivet?" At that mistake she mistook me for someone else and prattled fifteen seconds of nonsense, to have me believe that she was the maid and that Mme Jollivet wasn't at home. Then I said, "It's Sartre." "Oh, hello, Sartre," she said enthusiastically, "I'm awfully pleased to hear from you. Come to the Atelier tomorrow. We're rehearsing *Volpone.*" So I left Wednesday evening under pouring rain (but see #8a) and got soaked changing buses, finally reaching the Place Dancourt at 8:45. Our meeting was for 9:30. I went into the little café-tobacconist and sat down across from the bar. I had a rum as I mopped off my neck and spent a happy hour there. There were the cashier (still young and not too ugly) and two women, of whom one, young and wearing makeup, was knitting; a mob of young people from the neighborhood came in, who all knew each other and the two women. They chatted, played billiards, then others came in with more chat. I felt steeped in Paris and fascinated by all the people, who became almost likable. It took a great deal of effort to wrench myself away from the bench and leave. I reached the Atelier, slipped through the wings, quite intimidated, and sat down in the dark house. They were rehearsing in costume. Right now Marchat is playing the role of the freeloader. He does it superbly, though his pretty clinging breeches, instead of molding to his delectable little pansy derrière, dangle lamentably at his heels. But that takes no more than a pair of pants to fix. To general laughter and with good humor, he said, "I'll marry you to a Spaniard among my friends. He has a name long as the Grand Canal, five or six first names, and he does it only with men." Dullin superb as always, all crafty and whining, with a hunted look and beautiful flashes of meanness; it is his best role. Toulouse was talking in undertones with a young woman in glasses, a niece of Dullin's who takes care of the costumes. She finally saw me: "My dear Sartre"—she came over

and sat beside me—"I confess that I'd completely forgotten about you." Then immediately and without too much fuss, "Listen, do me a favor. Tell Dullin you came back several days ago, because I didn't want to tell him Zuorro came by in Férolles, but"—she added obscurely—"I had to say someone had been there because of the maid. So since he doesn't give a damn, I said it was you." We spoke very little, because she was beset as always. The most fervent was Georges Auric,[7] whom she accurately describes as looking like a duck. Me she calls, justly too but more crudely, Boubouroche. She told me, "Perhaps I'll have Auric do the music for *Plutus*." Me, surprised: "Why not Milhaud? He's much more talented, and you were very pleased with what he did for *J. Caesar*." She, squirming: "Exactly—since I've always worked with him and think highly of him, that makes me want to be unfaithful." But a bit later she confessed that Georges Auric was courting her in order to get the big deal, which flattered her: "Because, you see, when I was a little girl, if they'd explained to me who Georges Auric was, I would have taken him for an important gentleman, and it would have amazed me if they'd predicted he would one day be courting me to get something from me. So it amuses me to be disappointed to see that he's so low." She also told me that she would get Poupette to adapt, according to her ideas and under her direction, the scenery and costumes by Touchangues for *Plutus*. "It will serve as apprenticeship, and she'll be paid." Meanwhile she was yawning like crazy. Dullin came up and shook my hand. But a rather painful scene interrupted our effusiveness. An old actor called Gildès is playing the Judge. His former talent has given way to senility. Already Dullin had deeply humiliated him by openly saying, "Do take off your wig, Monsieur Gildès, play it as you are, it'll be far funnier. There, there! Just like that. And right then you . . . you'll get a laugh, right?" etc., at length. But now, in the big scene of the third act, Gildès began to forget his role at random, once here, once there, never the same place, confusing names, particularly those of Volpone and Leone. He was frantic, because he fully realized, the poor old man, that this was his last chance; he glanced around him painfully. And of course he was saying his lines more slowly, giving himself time to recall them. And Dullin, sounding false, went up on stage and took his hand: "Now look, Monsieur Gildès, an old actor such as yourself, you mustn't be scared. Now then, take it again from Leone's entrance. Don't worry. You'll see, it'll work. And a bit faster, please." He came back to sit on a folding aisle seat near Toulouse and

---

[7]Composer (1899–1983), best known for film and ballet scores; member of the group Les Six.

whispered to her, "It's very annoying. He's slowing down the scene. It has to be played fast. Well, there he goes again, he's dropped his line. He's screwing the whole thing up." And Toulouse told me with a laugh, "They put a ladder in the wings for him to climb up to his bench in the second act; but he gets vertigo, they have to push him up." But I didn't laugh much; it was rather painful. If you have feelings, you'll be happy to hear that after all of this he later chalked up a personal success at the dress rehearsal. Toulouse asked me a few questions about our vacation, then, very slowly and nasally, as though sulking, said, "You know, I don't much like to hear about trips. I listen to please the Beaver . . ." I was about to retort indignantly, "But you don't mind giving *your own* travelogues," but she saw it coming and said it herself with a laugh (incidentally, I haven't yet found anyone to listen to our Greek trip except in snatches. But my soul is at rest, for I've recorded it in detail in a number of little epistles).[8] The conversation was very disjointed, because we had to listen to the play (it was actually very amusing, though *Volpone* isn't a terribly good play: its effects are too facile and predictable, and Volpone's character isn't well-defined). Toulouse was yawning like crazy. As they were changing the set we went for a drink on the Bd. Rochechouart. Toulouse had a kirsch for kicks and a half bottle of Vichy for her liver. She was circling around the Zuorro story and finally said tentatively, "I saw Zuorro . . ." "I know," I told her. "You even paid him a compliment about his voice that touched his heart." She laughed, curious and flattered. "Oh? What did I say?" I carefully repeated it back to her and she said, rather coolly, "Yes, I do like his voice a lot." "And what do you think of him?" "He's amusing, he's very much the young Italian lead, very Monadelschi, with a whole other side that makes much ado about nothing. You know, he told me his whole life story without my asking a thing. He says he's not homosexual, but it's glaring, and he talks of nothing else." She took a moment before adding, hesitantly and yet with conviction, "He's got a nasty tongue." "What did he say?" I asked somewhat anxiously. "I'd rather tell you the whole thing, someday when we have more time. But you swear you won't tell him?" I swore. She spoke a bit about *Plutus*, but reluctantly, like the times she's late or something's troubling her conscience. But it seems that Dullin is enchanted and predicts a big success. (On that score, Zuorro, to whom Toulouse predicted more than a hundred performances and who will earn 32 francs a night, is already thinking of reserving the right to disappear on days that suit him, and even for good if need be. I fear he might scrupulously

---

[8]See "Lettres à Wanda," in *Les Temps Modernes* 531–533, October–December 1990.

attend each rehearsal, let them depend on him, then leave them in the lurch at the last minute. He nonetheless talks of finding them a replacement.) We went back to the Atelier, and Toulouse confessed with a squirm that she'd done some little thing that didn't look so good but was basically not so bad as all that, because it could help her career and it's better to do a bad play if that paves the way for lots of other good ones—and she said I shouldn't be too severe, etc. In short, she'd accepted Salacrou's *Savonarola*. I roared, "*Savonarola?*" "Yes, but you know," she said, frightened, "Savonarola hardly appears." I had to take a taxi home because it was raining cats and dogs and the last Métro was long gone. Which meant that the next day I had to put the touch on my mother for the daily ten francs. On Wednesday the 22nd I'm to call Toulouse again. I'll set up a meeting for the two of us, not too soon, never fear: Saturday or Sunday. I didn't give her the photos, which are still at the de Roulets'.

8. *Miscellaneous:*

(a) My mother gave me a superb suede-cloth raincoat (225 francs), which was the envy of Williams and the Moon Woman. On other matters, Williams hates me more and more, because Zuorro convinces him that I take him for an ass.

(b) I went to see my lycée, an immense red brick building "like the Château de Versailles," according to my mother. In a sinister and airy neighborhood where the girls must have their periods a week early if it's true, as Nizan says, that in the XVth they have them a week late. But I don't give a damn: the 43, which leaves from Montparnasse, puts me down at the door of the lycée in 27 minutes. So I'll be closer than you to the Lycée Molière. Did I tell you that my mother wouldn't have minded at all if I boarded with them for lunch? It seems there's a terrible EG bus line that makes it to Neuilly-Passy in 10 minutes. "You'd just have to hop on . . ." Fortunately, those beautiful birds are also rare birds: the EGs go by every 45 minutes. And then my stepfather, who is in a crushing mood, bawls me out continually and seems ready to take a real dislike to me. So I convinced my mother that it would be quite enough if I came for lunch on Tuesdays and dinner on Sunday evenings. She asks only a brief bit of afternoon for herself, which is reasonable, because these days she's being extremely kind. All the more so because with my stepfather unbearable she's afraid I'll be fed up with the household.

9. *The Moon People.*[9] They had to track me down, since of course

---

[9]Marie Girard and her husband, André. See note 3, p. 124.

they'd lost my address. They went to my grandfather's concierge at 200 Rue Saint-Jacques and peremptorily asked to see M. Schweitzer. The concierge told them with great dignity, "M. Schweitzer has been in the cemetery for three years now." Then he softened and gave them the address of my uncle the photographer, lacking mine. They phoned his office: "Poulou? I haven't seen him for six months." He nonetheless gave them our address, and they called me twice before reaching me. "This is Girard. Have you given a thought to our furniture?" And I heard the Moon Woman, who was herself too dignified to call, laughing at the other end of the line. I set up a meeting for Sunday morning but admitted I had no idea who might want their furniture. Meanwhile, on Saturday I mention it to Zuorro, who jumps at the idea. "I need a divan and a table." The Moon People will give him all that, chairs, etc. So on Sunday when I found them seated very politely at La Closerie des Lilas (they griped at getting up so early; the Moon Woman had said to André, "The annoying thing about Sartre is that he is so energetic"), I triumphantly announced I had a taker for their furniture. But this news left them cold. "Good, good. Agreed. He'll have to sign a paper." It's that they were already absorbed by other projects: would they adopt that little 12-year-old Spanish girl the Moon Woman had seen in Mosset at her mother-in-law's, and who said "Yes, Madame" so nicely, looking her in the eye and holding her hand for more than two hours? I said, "Why not?" "But the upkeep is so steep," said the Moon Woman, while André went down to the rest room. "Not that much," I said cautiously. "But the lycées?" "Well, the lycées are free." "Oh yes? André," she cried out to her husband, who was on his way back up, "he's advising us to take her." "Well then, let's!" said André, lighting his pipe. In other regards, they were thinking about going to the United States because a priest had told them there were good jobs to be had there. "I thought of you for three hours in Nice, Jean-Paul, and I was downhearted to think that not even you are trying to do something great." "But what?" "Oh . . ." she said with a vague gesture. She's had enough of being poor and traveling third-class; she had severely taken me to task for sleeping out on the deck of the *Théophile Gautier*.[10] Actually she is as profoundly and delectably stupid as ever. She said to me, "You know that my father died two months ago? When I learned that he was dying, I decided to go and see him. I'd always told myself that a guy who has been a son of a bitch all his life would have no reason not to admit it as he lay dying, since he'd have nothing to lose. So I was very curious to see my father admit his faults. It

---

[10]*On our return trip from Greece. (SdB)*

was an experiment, you see, because I'd never seen anyone die. So I show up, he was all alone in his apartment, in bed, there was just a dirty old woman taking care of him. He says to me, 'Ah, there you are! For a week I've been stuck with your husband.' I say, 'What?' He begins to play an imaginary bugle and says, 'It's all the bugler's fault.' They'd forgotten to tell me that he had tubercular meningitis. When I saw he was crazy, it really disappointed me, because of the experiment I'd wanted to do."

My darling Beaver, your telegram has just come, and I'm very pleased to be seeing you tomorrow but very sorry that you have had to cut your trip short by a day. I'll tell you the rest tomorrow. I send you a kiss, I love you very much.

P.S.: You'll find the fifty francs at the post office under "Principal Receipts" because the central office, God knows why, doesn't accept telegraph orders.

To Simone de Beauvoir

[September]

My darling Beaver

Your telegram arrives just as I was about to send this letter to Strasbourg. So I'll leave it at Le Dôme for you.

Tomorrow morning I'm going to the Palais de la Découverte[1] with my stepfather.

I'm seeing the Moon Woman at 2:30. I promised because she said, "I have to see you."

I was to see young Bost at 6.

I'll cancel young Bost right away and meet you at Le Dôme at 6:00— I'll spend the evening and a long part of the night with you.

I love you, darling Beaver.

Try to borrow 200 from your parents if you're going to see them. We haven't *one sou* between us.

---

[1]At the International Exposition.

1938

To Simone de Beauvoir

Sunday [July]

My darling Beaver

It's around eight. I'm at La Coupole and I've just had some lovely roast beef with green beans and a fruit tart while reading a detective novel. I don't know whether Tania has arrived, since I didn't want to go up to my room a while ago for fear of running into them. If she comes, Zazoulich will leave me a note. I didn't much like saying goodbye yesterday, you absurd little globe-trotter; you'd still be with me right now, full of good little smiles, if you didn't have that strange mania for gobbling up kilometers. Where the devil are you, anyway? This morning I was mourning for you because it was gray out and I imagined you at the summit of your little mountain looking up, with a stubborn expression, at a sea of gray clouds, like a fisherman gazing at his cork bobbing on the water. And then after that I imagined you piercing that gray carpet, eating the cotton balls and risking a broken leg, but now I'm happy because I picture you eating cabbage soup, totally blissful, drinking your half bottle of wine. I love you very much, absurd little thing. As for me, I went to see the Lady. We chatted away in the dark, she laughs when she thinks of you, she says, "The Beaver makes me laugh" and "I find her so funny." She wouldn't think of climbing mountains either, but the idea seems appealing to her nonetheless; she explained that you were "well organized." She's very insistent that I should give you a child: "To see what it would be like," she said. She will raise it. She was feeling bitter about soon having to leave Paris, while the weather is so beautiful, though, on the other

145

hand, she hadn't so much as stuck her nose outside all day long. I suggested a walk, which she accepted with pleasure. We went down the little Rue Férou, where we had been so happy, we two, you and I, and I told her that we had been happy there—then other streets and the Rue Bonaparte and the Pont-Neuf, and we strolled around Les Halles, full of baskets and smells and people with weary faces working silently. There were baskets crowned with roses that smelled of strawberries at twenty paces, and other baskets, more muted, coiffed in white and electric blue; there were enormous baskets of watercress, the cress arranged in funerary wreaths; we saw a one-armed man, a real or seeming corpse, loads of people sleeping, prostitutes, everything one ordinarily sees, but with that odd unreal color that comes from the piles of baskets and white wooden crates all lit by yellow lights. We came back through dark still streets filled with warmth, like a July 14th evening without the revelers, and the Lady was indignant that there were so many shopkeepers and stalls: "Basically," she said, "now that I think of it, I must be antagonistic toward commerce." I took her home, and she wanted to make me up a bed in the living room, but I refused because of the light. It was one-thirty, and I slept till ten-thirty, when Lucile[1] woke me with a phone call. With red and swollen eyes, I went to hear her slow, thick voice and her affectations: "I stopped by to see you yesterday, now that was nice of me, wasn't it?" I was rather curt. She said, "Nothing else to say?" "No, goodbye." There was a letter from my mother (from Piana) and a translation of that Dutch article you've heard so much about. Such praise! In fact the article is genuinely more intelligent and more serious than the others, but when they praise me so much, I can't take it seriously. Anyway, I'm fed up with my book and with writing. I don't hate it that Tania's coming, and that the vicissitudes of gallantry will make me forget the whole affair in a while. A letter from Lionel, very nice. However, I won't send it to you. I went to get dressed and resolved to use my freedom with a certain style. Work, movies, and who knows what else? But the programs were not very tempting, even for a widower wanting to dabble in vulgarity, and I had no wild desire to work. The night before, the Lady had invited me to her place, so I went. Mops and Isorni[2] were there. For six francs Isorni had bought a review copy of Nausea with the dedication page cut off. Zuorro came in; he had seen Lucile at Le Dôme and she was looking for me. He told her I'd repeated everything to him, and she blushed a little, but not too much. He asked her, "Who won the game?" She replied,

---

[1]A student of Dullin's. (SdB)
[2]Mops's husband. (SdB)

"He might have imagined he did." We had lunch, then I drew gnomes and fairies for Boudy, while Zuorro, out of pure perversity, made us listen to a rebroadcast of *Mignon*. We rumbaed a little, Zuorro and I, then did some other dances, and around six-thirty we left the Lady and went off to play a new game at La Rotonde. Ah, what a lovely game, my darling Beaver! Like the others: full of little electric tops and bells, but if the ball touches a certain peg, it leaps gracefully into the air and spins like a mad thing in its box. Yet after a while a person finds the game traitorous, but I relished the thought nonetheless of playing it with you on your return. When we left there, Lucile was at Le Dôme; she hadn't budged since 12:30, waiting for me. I spent fifteen minutes with her. She was bittersweet: "You want to trifle with me," she said, "but I can spot you a mile away, like those detectives with their yellow shoes." I told her, "I swear, you don't interest me enough to trifle with you." She laughed, saying, "Ah, Sartre! Sartre! You are beginning to appeal to me." Of course, steeped in mystery, the eternal feminine and all that. Her Egyptian arrived at this juncture and relieved me of her. After which I came back here, ate, and now I'm writing to you. And then what'll I do? Alas, my poordearlittle Beaver, even I don't know. I guess I'll go to the movies after all. Farewell, good little person, most charming of all little people. I'll go on with this tomorrow.

To Simone de Beauvoir

Monday 11:30 Coupole [July]

My darling Beaver

First, two little items of information: 1. I love you very much. 2. The schizophrenic is not dead. He is across from me with his twin, and he even seems to be better, he is looking around with lively interest. But that liveliness may just be a part of the act.

I can't picture at all where you are anymore, and that irritates me. I don't know why, but I see you in an open field with your espadrilles sopping wet. I want you to know I found no movie fit for consumption yesterday, though I carefully checked *La Semaine à Paris*. As I left La Coupole, Zuorro ran after me with his all-seeing concierge eyes: "What's up with Lucile?" But I had nothing to tell him. He's seeing her at 3 today and taking her to his place. I have no idea what kind of strange game he's playing. I caught a cab (it was 9:30) and had myself dropped by the Opéra on the off chance, then went up the boulevards looking at all the movie marquees. Nothing to see:

La Présidente, Barnabé, Raspoutine, who knows what else. I saw Patri with his good wife (bags under her eyes, a serious look, black merino hat, on the hideous side), his arm around her shoulder with a blasé social air of proprietorship. He didn't see me. I ducked into the obscene little alleyway across from the Musée Grévin, but everything was closed, dirty bookstores and peep shows, or I'd have put my twenty sous down some slot. All dark like that, the alley looked completely respectable, of course. Around eleven I finally took the Métro and went back to the hotel. No letter from the Charrachboufftigues.[1] I was a bit annoyed. Zazoulich's room was dark, no key in the door. So I began to downplay the fun I'd have the next day with Tania, through a compensatory phenomenon I know very well by now: ever since the Olga affair I immediately blot out anything with the slightest resemblance to passion, be it no more than jangled nerves, in a sort of abiding fear. It's not just with Olga but with the whole world that I have "counter-crystallized." So I went to bed regretting, as part of the act, that I wouldn't be able to work the following days if Tania should come. And I stuffed little wads in my ears so as not to be so much as tempted to listen to the noise. I did fall asleep but around 12:30 woke to the sound of footsteps and sat bolt upright, turning on the light to see if there wasn't a note slipped under my door. Nothing. In my pajamas I went as far as Zazoulich's door: still no key. I went back up and stood by the window in the dark, a little blissful, because it was poetic to see people coming in. A fat old guy in a cap, looking shifty, was pacing up and down. A woman on the seventh floor across the way was undressing, I could see her going back and forth in front of her window, more and more naked. At one o'clock I closed the shutters again and went to bed satisfied, reasoning thus: since Tania was supposed to come that evening, Bost must have gone over to the pastor's,[2] so Olga wasn't with him. If Tania hadn't come on the six- or nine-o'clock train, Olga would have gone to meet her at the midnight train and, furious at having missed her, automatically returned to her room around 12:45. Since there was no one in her room, most likely Tania had come on the six-o'clock train, and they were together someplace. I slept till ten-thirty and did indeed find a note from Tania setting up a meeting at Le Dôme for two o'clock, and downstairs a note from Olga asking for money. I slipped fifty francs under her door (was that enough? It's for her trip, she's leaving this afternoon), and I heard them talking. Then I came

---

[1] *Zazoulich.* (SdB)

[2] Bost's father, Charles, a minister, had been chaplain of the school in Le Havre where Sartre taught from 1931 to 1936.

here, I read a bit, and I'm writing to you. It's noon now, I'm going to work a bit on the factum, and I'll write you a note this evening.

To Simone de Beauvoir

Monday evening [July]

My darling Beaver

It's ten to seven, Tania's resting in her room, and I'm writing to you while awaiting some fried ham *jardinière*. The weather is rather lovely and idyllic. All day Paris has seemed like a garden. You'll say, then what's the point of hating real gardens? But then, is it my fault if all day long I've been having flashbacks to heavy, poetic afternoons in the presbytery garden in Grunsbach?[1] And I don't scorn stone gardens. The thing about it was that the merest shrub, the skimpiest bush in a pot or tub, was shown to particular advantage by the heat and for all the senses. It was hot but bearable, and in the cafés very cool, very dark, very intimate. Chronologically there is little to say. I went to Le Dôme around one-thirty: Olga and Tania, who was wearing a charming little blue blouse, were on the sidewalk terrace, but I didn't want to disturb them. I went down by the phone to leave my things and there ran into Lucile, full of melancholic ardor, looking like a girl from Martinique with a little madras scarf in her hair as she tenderly cuddled against my breast. I was gentle with her, and she spoke of staying in Paris for me, but I replied I was tied up for two weeks. At which, despair. She made me smooch her stubby little hand, and I left to join Tania, who gave me a very friendly welcome, all alone on the terrace. We left almost immediately to take more cash to her sister (a hundred francs all told), who was discreet and gallant, and we walked to La Rhumerie. There we found Olga again, in despair, and she had a white rum with us while waiting for Bost. She'd sent her *pneumatique*[2] too late and hadn't been able to reach him. Though Tania was a bit drunk, our threesome had a pleasant enough time. We eventually let Olga work it out alone and went off toward the Rue Mouffetard, affectionately entwined. We had an espresso at the place your sister likes, near the Gobelins; we walked a bit in the Jardin des Plantes, then a cab, and here I am.

---

[1]During his year of study, 1933–34, in Germany.
[2]Familiar blue notes—the *petit bleu* or *pneu*—dispatched across Paris through rapid pneumatic tubes and hand delivery, to those without phones.

To Simone de Beauvoir

July 14

My darling Beaver

It's Bastille Day, and is it ever! It's five in the afternoon and I'm at Le Dôme. Outside, on the Rue Delambre, there is a delightful fellow on stilts, wearing a top hat, and whirling around as he plays the accordion. He was twirling so fast that at first I thought he was costumed in green and orange stripes, but when he stopped I saw they were harlequin diamonds. It's cloudy today, gray and terribly republican, as in the Bastille Day paintings by Manet and Van Gogh. Here, a long interruption of my letter by Péron, just back from the Popular Front parade, with a little red card stuck in his buttonhole: "Fidelity to the oath. Enactment of the program. Long live Republican Spain." He held forth at length about his wife, then, since she is Russian, on the Slavic character in general. I was boiling: he wasn't preventing me from writing to you—because I was determined at all costs to get rid of him long before that—but from working on the Factum once the letter was written. Alas, poor Factum, when will I finish it? Perhaps at La Pouèze. Le Dôme is cool and dark, and I love you very much. More than once I've thought of your little trip, I've imagined you reading *Plume*[1] in your cozy corner, and then this morning at 4, having dropped Martine Bourdin at her hotel, I was about to take a cab when it came to me that it was four, that the day was breaking, and you were at Culoz, awake and running the length of the dark train with your little bag. That set up a simultaneity so close and so real that I went home on foot, imagining all the way the dark and distant Alps under the same mauve sky, a little train in a station, and you, my love, so small beside that little train. I loved you very much, I was totally with you, separated merely by the fact that our heads weren't heavy with the same kind of drowsiness at all. I love you. I long for Morocco[2] and you, I'd be very happy if I could simply finish my story. Ah no, there is one shadow: Beck and Godet[3] have the effrontery to be claiming their due (925 francs). But I think that I'll quite simply not pay them. To be done with subjects by fits and snatches, you should know that today at four, back from my parents, the fancy took

---

[1] *By Henri Michaux. (SdB)*
[2] With Beauvoir on a walking trip in the Alps with Bost, and himself in Paris, Sartre was planning their August trip to Morocco, postponed from the year before, when Beauvoir was still too weak from her winter's illness.
[3] *Sartre's tailors. (SdB)*

me after that dull day to knock at the door of the wild Zazoulich for a bit of fun (from her sister no news at all, she's sulking, I guess). A drowsy voice replied, "Who is it?" I, excessively affectionate: "Me, my good little Zazoulich—may we talk for five brief minutes?" "No, Kobra, I'm sorry," she said in a dejected acidulous voice, "I overslept and I'm just getting up." "Are you still leaving tomorrow? There was no note." "Yes, but I haven't been to the station, I'll write this evening." "Do you still feel abandoned?" "I haven't thought about it since then," she said dryly, "but yes, I suppose I do." "Now now, you resentful little dear." Silence. After a moment I said to the door, "Goodbye then," and got a vague and very muffled farewell in return. So much for that.

Let's move on to the Bourdin affair. It's going too well: yesterday I kissed that fiery girl, who pumped my tongue with the force of a vacuum cleaner (it still hurts) as she coiled against me with her whole body. She seems very pleased with the turn of events. But no oath has been exchanged, rest assured. But let's take things in order. I met her at 9 at Le Mathieu because for no valid reason she'd gone to find me at Le Dôme. Her aunt had left during the afternoon. Little Bourdin had seen Merleau-Ponty[4] and Jean Wahl.[5] Merleau-Ponty had reproached her: "Don't keep Sartre up to all hours—he doesn't like to go to bed too late." He also told her pensively, "In theory Sartre is a very good guy, morally speaking, but I wonder if he's as good in practice." She considered it a warning. She had been given another by her aunt, who had asked, "Why are you staying on?" "To see Sartre, a very fine man, a professor who is advising me on my thesis." The aunt cried out, "Sartre! Beware! He lives with Simone de Beauvoir as husband and wife, and the Barrys tell me that no woman can resist him." As for Wahl, he was waiting for her in a light gray suit, plus fours, with a pink tie and a pink shirt. He sat her down in a chair, saying, "I'm going to read you a poem about yourself." He read it to her, skipping the passages that referred too precisely to her body. She remembered one line, worth a long poem in itself: "Martine, the schoolgirl, whom I called Cécilia."

After which, he told her something like: don't try for the *agrégation*, your gifts lie more in bed. The whole of it with a trace of the smug. He

---

[4]Maurice Merleau-Ponty (1908–1961), France's leading phenomenologist; during their final year he and Beauvoir had been the two top students at the Sorbonne. He was a teacher before the war and an officer during it. Co-editor with Sartre of *Les Temps Modernes*, 1945–52.

[5]*Jean Wahl, a well-known philosopher. (SdB)* His writings on phenomenology placed him in the same field as Sartre from 1936 on.

clearly seems to feel he has a chance. She left, seething with anger and profoundly humiliated. To console her I suggested as subject for her thesis "Time in Bergson and Husserl." As for Boutang,[6] no news. She and I chatted for quite a while, then had a drink at Les Deux Magots. Paris was intolerable, with "unfinished" written all over it. There were ladders and scaffolding everywhere and loads of people vociferating and dancing around, who seemed to be having a good time amid the flats of a stage set not yet entirely in place. Many of them were carrying lanterns that lit their faces from below. I told her she was basically riffraff and that she snagged men with a "Won't you help me along, Monsieur?" She agreed, then for over an hour she became unbearable, vulgar and nervous. So I gave the little speech you can imagine: "The other night it was nicer because Boutang was between us. Could it be we can't bear being alone together?" And of course I spoke, not unfairly, about "goodwill"; she said, "I'll get there," and sat there wise and calm, a tender look in her eyes, as I talked. We went to Le Dôme; I took her hand and said, "I've got a taste for you. You've unleashed my rough side, which is rare, since I'm rather thin-blooded. Unfortunately I don't know what to do with you, I'm no Boutang to make you false promises. You came into my life like a dog into a game of ninepins; I wanted to take you without having the least *need* for you, which is even more flattering. I have three days to give you—let's take them and try to make the most of them." Shameful little speech but delivered with all the artifice of Thucydides, which doesn't show to its best here, perhaps, but which worked wonders. The next minute she was in my arms, and we kissed all the way back, she silent and all mine, with an enchanted smile, and I from time to time trying, as usual, to say something. I suspect she wanted to ask me up to her place, but I didn't want to recognize it, because I don't want to sleep with her. I came back on foot, with the poetry that you know in my head (on rereading, I find that phrase disgusting). It was five when I got to bed.

Friday afternoon: Catastrophe. The Merly-Ponteau[7] is in love with Martine Bourdin. And rather deeply, it turns out. Last night I was a bit heartsick about it, and this afternoon I'm somewhat uneasy because I'm going to have a meeting with Merloponte. Yet I have a clear conscience, and the Lady has granted me her absolution. But see what you think: I saw the strapping girl last night after writing to you. She was beside herself. France,

---

[6]*An ultra-right-wing writer who had been in love with Martine. (SdB)*
[7]*Merleau-Ponty. (SdB)* Similarly, subsequent variations.

the wolf-trap[8] she lives with, had left her that afternoon in tears (jealous of me), and when she entertained the Ponteaumerle, Martine was all stirred up with stifled tears. Thereupon Merleau-Pont shows up and she tells him she has broken off with Boutang, which seems to leave him absolutely cold. Thereupon he suggests she go out with him that evening: "But I'm going out with Sartre." "Oh, Sartre doesn't bother me," he replies candidly. So she tells him she'd rather see me alone. Apparently, those simple words are enough to make him furious. There's a long silence, then he says to her, painfully, "If I'd asked you the day before yesterday to kiss me, what would you have done?" "Well, I don't know, since you didn't ask me it means you weren't eager enough or else you felt I didn't want to. . . . In a word I guess I'd have said no." At that point he stammers and seems on the verge of tears; she too. He takes off his jacket and goes out onto the balcony, and there he says, "Basically I don't love you—no, I don't love you, I don't think I love you." Tearfully, then, "I think I'll never love again . . ." and then, "I have no easy explanation, but last week I slept with a woman I didn't love, it was awful." He comes back into the room, sits down, and with great pain in his voice says, clasping his hands and studying his thumbs, "You don't realize that you have extraordinary charm." After which he spoke of me: "What Sartre did is rotten, he's basically like all the rest; he said he was watching out for you because he's interested in you for your mind, and ultimately this is what he wanted." After that he turned anxious: "But what are you leading up to, you two? You haven't given it enough thought; where will you end up?" She said that the whole thing was coming to a crashing halt on Sunday. "But that's crazy—you're counting on a separation to settle the question, which isn't very brave of you." He also said, "You know, Sartre isn't the kind of guy who'll hold your hand and kiss you: he'll simply ask you to sleep with him. Is he in love with you?" "I don't know. Perhaps—in any case I don't give a damn." Then he said: "You should go a few days without seeing each other, so you can really understand what you mean to one another. At any rate I'll be spending the night at the École, and if you need me, you can wake me up at any hour." And he left, worn out and pale. Whence it was evident, first of all, that he considered me a bastard (and I am not indifferent to the judgment of the Pontaumerle), secondly, that he had immediately thought there was passion between Bourdin and me. I was very uneasy, because I was afraid she too might have gotten that impression. A painful conversation followed in which I told her, dotting the i's and crossing the t's, that I was

---

[8]*The Lady called gays and lesbians "wolf-traps." (SdB)*

in love with her but that there was no place for her in my life, and in which I spoke not only about you but also about Tania. Of course she said with a heavy heart, "But I knew all that, you don't have to rub it in." But I went on to the end. I asked her if she thought I'd acted like a bastard. "No. We both knew that the other was touched. You'd have been a bastard if you hadn't kissed me." "For how long have you thought that you would let me kiss you if I asked?" "Since the first night, at Gabriel Marcel's[9] place." Nonetheless, after that she began to sulk, on the pretext that I'd told her I loved her. "I can't get used to that, I can't help it. You'll be like everyone else if you're in love with me." You'll soon see the real reason for her sulking.

Saturday. My love, I won't have much time to put in the sweet things I'm thinking about you if I want to tell you the rest of this story. But do realize that I love you very much; I'd really like to get a letter from you. But this morning there's nothing from you (nor from Tania, who is doubtless furious). On the other hand, a card from Roger Martin du Gard:[10] "How to write to you after reading you? One would be too afraid of sounding like the *Self-Taught Man* . . . or, worse still, being pigeonholed with the bastards. All the same, it's truly splendid, your book. And I'm happy that you *exist.*" A book from M. Aimelle: *Propos d'un défaitiste* ["Thoughts of a Defeatist"] (1917–1919), with a dedication: "To the great, very great author of *Nausea*, to Jean-Paul Sartre, in remembrance of Barrès's spanking,[11] in insufficient homage of total admiration (this is no mere turn of phrase)," and a note from Paulhan promising me Dos Passos and "Intimacy"[12] for August. I'll get back to my story.

So she sulked and I griped. We went to the Falstaff and I gave her a good scolding. Whereupon she fell, like a tree uprooted, right into my arms and invited me to take her to my place, which I did. She spent the night there (and again the next night—and she'll spend the coming night; she's leaving the following morning, Sunday). We played around together on the bed in complete silence, which shortens the account of the night. Except for

---

[9]A *Catholic philosopher. (SdB)*

[10]Roger Martin du Gard (1881–1985) wrote the long novel cycle *Les Thibault*, conflating the story of one family with the social and philosophic history of their era. With the series all but complete in 1937, he won the Nobel Prize.

[11]*Nausea*'s hero Roquentin dreams he is a sailor and with two mates spanks the right-wing prowar writer-politician Maurice Barrès (1862–1923).

[12]With Sartre about to be commissioned to do a monthly column in the *NRF*, he had already begun book reviews that drew wide attention for their audacity. He called John Dos Passos "the greatest writer of our time." "Intimacy" was to become part of Sartre's short story collection *The Wall.*

sleeping with her, I did *everything.* As her figure rather suggests, she is what Boubou[13] would call a "great lover"; in addition, she is delightful in bed. It's the first time I've slept with a brunette, actually *black-haired*, Provençale as the devil, full of odors and curiously hairy, with a little black fur patch at the small of her back and a very white body, much whiter than mine. At first her slightly violent sensuality and her legs that prickle like a man's badly shaved chin surprised me a bit, and half disgusted me. But once you get used to it, it's rather powerful. She has teardrop buttocks, solid but heavier and more spread out at the bottom than the top, with a few small pimples on her chest (you well know that sort of thing: the little pimples of an ill-fed, not very well groomed student—rather endearing). Very lovely legs, a muscular and absolutely flat stomach, not the shadow of a breast, and, all in all, a supple, charming body. A tongue like a kazoo, which unreels endlessly and reaches in to caress your tonsils, a mouth as pleasant as Gégé's. On the whole, I'm happy as an undertaker's assistant. However, read herein the expression of my satisfaction with *the night just passed*, which was perfection on the emotional side, unlike the previous night, which was more strained because something was bothering her. I didn't want to be too encouraging, and anyway my pronouncements had deprived me of the means, and she didn't want to say she loved me, particularly after the things I'd told her. All by itself the music of the open-air orchestras on the Avenue du Maine created a bond between us, I mean an auditory bond. At one point they were playing "Some of These Days"[14] under my windows. It was just what she'd wanted to hear, and I said, "There's 'Some of These Days.' " We didn't have to say much else. She wanted to sleep in my arms, which meant I didn't sleep a wink all night. In the morning she said, "I'm not jealous of Tania, I would never accept what you offer her. I'm jealous of Simone de Beauvoir." A reasonable feeling, in my view. You see, in her eyes you don't seem at all a dupe or some old well-trod path.[15] On the contrary, she told me, "I've always wanted to be with some guy the way you are with Simone de Beauvoir. I think it's great." I told her she was absolutely capable of it. After that she turned nervous and wriggled around on the bed, her head buried in the pillow, while I got dressed to go and meet Zazoulich. Tomorrow I'll tell you about the conversation with Zazoulich and the meeting with Ponteau-Merly. But I do want

---

[13]Fernando Gérassi, painter friend of Sartre and Beauvoir, who became the model for Gomez in *The Roads to Freedom.*

[14]The song appears as a recurring theme in *Nausea.*

[15]*A woman Sartre had rejected reproached him for preferring "an old well-trod path" to herself.* (SdB)

you to know the cause of Bourdin's griping and nervousness: she thought me a coward because I didn't want to sleep with her. But I held to my word on that score, as you'll soon see. You must realize, my darling Beaver, that I'm muddling through in the midst of all these storms to stay as one with you. That's not obvious from this letter, because I have too much to say.

I send you a tender kiss, my darling little Beaver, and will tell all at length tomorrow. I love you.

Expect a telegram from me bidding you to be in Marseilles on the 29th. The Lady might very well try to dine with us, after all, on the 29th. She seems sincerely eager to.

To Simone de Beauvoir

[July]

My darling Beaver

Alas, how tired I am. I've slept six hours in three nights. Passion is behind it all. I'm barely holding on, and yet before nightfall I have to see the Boxer and Gégé. I've just seen your sister and before that Hoffmann[1] about his thesis, and my parents. That's the way my day went. This morning at six forty-five I put young Bourdin on her train. The departure leaves me with a slight sense of pathos; this young person is perfectly well-behaved, I feel, and very touching. I had two beautiful and tragic nights with her that plainly moved me, and I'm left with the slightly bitter regret of having absolutely no place for her in my life. The sad part is that she had begun to love me passionately ("at least as much as Mme Canque"), and she wanted to give me her virginity. I'm not quite sure whether I took it or not. In these matters doubt is well advised; in any case it seemed like a profoundly difficult and disagreeable task. You will say that the whole thing was imprudent. On the contrary. Everything's settled; she left cheerfully and without the slightest hope.

Friday the 15th I put Zazoulich on the train. The two of us were at the Café Rouge, and since young Bourdin was conspicuously lingering in front of the counter with eyes wide as saucers, I told Zazoulich, who was eyeing her intently, about the night we'd just spent. Zazoulich—who knows why?—was moved, found the story charming and M. Bourdin appealing. I took that advantage to tell her in a confidential tone that Tania wasn't writing

---

[1]A former student of Sartre's. (SdB)

to me—that she must be jealous of Bourdin and that she, Zazoulich, might set things straight as a good friend. She was terribly flattered and felt devastated when, gazing off into space, somber and restrained, I said in a monotone, "Make no mistake about it, your sister is the apple of my eye." "If Tania has acted like an idiot," she instantly replied, in a tone protective of the two of us and our newborn love, "I'll try to straighten things out, I promise." (And in fact she kept her word, talked till six in the morning with Tania, from whom I received a letter this morning overflowing with tenderness.)

I smothered Zazoulich with special attention and coddling. She was a bit nervous about leaving but not sad at all, instead kind and very good to me, scolding me about the Bourdin episode, very much the debonair big sister. The train left and we waved handkerchiefs. Then I went by to see the Lady, whom I found under the thumb of the Tapir. The guy is overwhelming. His anecdotes have become even more long-winded than his brother-in-law's, and now he's particularly taken to telling old jokes: "Have you heard the one about the vegetarian and the abortionist?" etc. He was packing his bags, running back and forth but always showing up in time to say his bit. It seems I looked like a kid caught with his hand in the cookie jar, and in fact that's how I felt: I deeply regretted taking Bourdin away from Montaumerle and was feeling as criminal as all get out. I got to Le Dôme around four and, while waiting for the guy, wrote you the letter you found at Chamonix; then Hoffmann came to warn me that the Gontiers had kicked out Cauchois,[2] first because they'd discovered he'd failed his exams, then because of a rumor about some hanky-panky in Rouen. Cauchois had written Hoffmann the inevitable letter of the great solitary, with a lot of teeth clenching between the lines, and Hoffmann made me read it, then, boringly patient, explained Cauchois's case (he of course made it another tale of evasion). Finally, after I'd seen Gégé for a few moments and made a date for this evening, came the Merloponte, ever fresh and spruce amid the heaviest of storms. We cordially launched into conversation and beat around the bush for a while. Eventually the Pontomerle said, "Listen, about Martine Bourdin, I didn't say you were a bastard, I only meant . . ." "But, old boy, I'm not here to accept your explanations but to offer my own." "But, old boy . . ." "But, old boy . . ." After rounds of these civilities he finally said, "But why on earth don't you sleep with her?" It wasn't coming out easily, and I suppose he was driven to ask me the question less for his conversation with M. Bourdin than by his taste for the definitive and for logic (which at one time led him to religion).

---

[2]*A former student of Sartre's. (SdB)*

I explained why. I'll spare you the reasons. (You, of all people, know I wasn't sleeping with her because you'd forbade it when you said, "Don't put yourself in a bad situation.") "It surprises her," he said kindly. "She thinks I'm a coward?" "I wouldn't go so far as that, but it does surprise her. She had said to her Aunt Nène, 'Sartre is good. If he asks me to sleep with him I will.' And she's awfully surprised that you asked nothing of her." "I'll do whatever she likes," I said, a bit disconcerted by these strange family relations. There followed a long psychological discussion of the relationship between sleeping together and desire, properly speaking, a relationship that I find very lax, as you know. I felt I was tiring the Pontomerle, but I thought it was a healthy fatigue and that the brain is a muscle which, as the Lady says, must be exercised. Then the Pontomerle told me that she's jealous of you. "And it's understandable," he added, and asked me with intense curiosity whether you hadn't become mine (*sic*) at Tours during my military service. "Why, no," I said reservedly. "Oh? Because at the time Simone wrote to me, 'On my return perhaps I'll have news for you and perhaps not.' " What on earth did you have in mind, oh Beaver? And he began to question me about Bourdin's jealousy, about my relationship with you. I told him what you thought, that it was for keeps, and on a level where we wouldn't worry ourselves about my little spring fevers. "I always thought that was the way it was," he said. All the same he was shocked that I wasn't sleeping with Bourdin, and I saw that he was drawing conclusions from that, the way an ant drags a splinter behind it. But for the moment I couldn't tell what they were. "Hasn't she transferred onto you her love for B.?" "That's very possible," I said modestly. "Do you get the feeling that Martine could have transferred that love to me if I had been in your place?" "Well, why not?" I saw that he was listening to my replies. You'll see in due course what use he makes of them. We left—I reassured and, without my guessing why, he almost smug—and I caught a cab to go and see M. Bourdin. On leaving him I said, as when one is charged with a difficult task, "Well, I'll do the best I can," meaning: I'll screw Bourdin or not, as the occasion provides. He replied with his familiar tender smile, "You're silly." I answered, "Nonetheless, that's how it is," and he, dreamily, "Nonetheless, it's true, that's how it is." What can I tell you? I was thinking, with considerable candor and a bit of nastiness, that he had recovered and didn't love Martine Bourdin anymore. I reached the Maheus' in fine fettle.

My darling Beaver, I'm sending this disjointed bit of a letter, that lacks, above all, the least little *Erlebnis*, so that you can have it sooner, because I imagine that you are more avid for stories than declarations of love. Nonetheless you should know that still and always there's a constant moiling in my heart for you. I'll tell you everything in detail on Wednesday but don't have the time to write before that. I love you, my good little Beaver.

To Simone de Beauvoir

Wednesday [July]

My darling Beaver

This is my letter day, I have a dozen to write. I'm beginning with you, very happy to have the time at last to tell you I really do love you, I love you very much. All true, not trivia, lots of fleeting instants in which I picture you again, at Montroc for instance, at this very moment, or else on the Zugspitz, and it's all set to satisfy the most demanding heart. The thing that annoys me is that I'm imagining you white as a little turnip with your hair down, as you were when you left, and I know you're tan by now. The Lady can't mention your departure without laughing: "Beaver was so funny," she says, chuckling. Beaver, my darling Beaver, I pine to see you again.

Now listen to me. I have so much to tell you—but most of it bores even me (everything I've done since Bourdin left is so boring). I'd like to tell you right away about the oddly tragic look of yesterday's Paris (King and Queen of England), but that cannot be. So I'll take up again at Friday evening when, leaving Merleau-Ponty and properly reprimanded by him ("sleep with her"), I go to the Maheus' and find M. Bourdin. "So," I say to her—or just about—"you want to sleep with me." I don't mind addressing her with *tu* and *toi*, because she's from Provence, and it goes well with her dark-skinned look. "No, I don't want to anymore. Because I love you too much." So be it. To grasp the sense of that reply you must know that Bourdin oscillates between two very different concepts of her virginity. In the first and natural one, when she is "inside," if I may put it like that, it's her totem, her manna, the initial and final term of her complexes, the most beautiful gift she could make a man. So at that moment, the man, for his part, must give her all of himself. Result: she retains her virginity indefinitely and can't freely play around as she likes. Ah, if I weren't still a virgin, how I would flit from prick to prick, lighthearted and gay. From this contradiction comes the second concept of virginity: the reflexive concept. Rising above the complex, a woman is outside, and she says, "What is this virginity but a nest of complexes and other crap? Granting so much value to that membrane is exactly what the complex is. So let's to bed at once and with anyone at all. Free of virginity I would be done with the complex as well as the illusory belief in the value of virginity." When she met me, since I appealed to her, she thought, "Why not him?"—the reflexive plan and concept of virginity. Then, as things turned more serious, she naturally left the terrain of reason and sank to the depths of the complex: if she loved me, of course, she would be giving me an enormous amount by sleeping with me; her love abruptly changed the meaning and value of her virginity. Not without reason, because as she felt more drawn to me, I could no longer be the clean, healthy, moral lad who rid her of a slight encumbrance the way one has a tooth pulled. But if on the other hand she loved me *too much* to ask me to play the surgeon, she didn't *yet love me enough* to give herself to me totally. Naturally, in that intermediate period, with moments of near-paroxysm of love, of returns to reflexive considerations and reason, she was unbearable and hardly once throughout the whole night knew what she wanted, tossing her legs right and left and making a battlefield of the bed. As for me, I naturally said nothing more about it. That night she gave me a very intimate kiss or two, and as I was surprised, I said, "Aren't you horrified by the male organ?" "Horrified, yes. But not by yours. Which is how I now know I love you." For she has that tendency of gauging her feeling for someone by the barriers that a spontaneous burst has allowed her to break through: "I must surely love him, since I'm kissing his penis." "And with B.?" "With B., too, I caressed him the same way, because I was in love with him." "And with who else?"—"No one ever." But she has shared the bed of several guys, notably that Norman, of whom she said that he had such a big tongue. Nonetheless we slept for four hours, from five to nine, and at nine we woke up. With eyelids shut and a charming smile on her lips, she threw herself into my arms, saying, "It came to me in my sleep, it came to me in my sleep." "What?" "That I love you so much." "You love me more than during the night?" "Much more. You know, just as I was waking up I felt my love for you, without being able to name it or think anything about it, like an enormous weight, and then suddenly I realized that you were there, you whom I loved, and it seemed marvelous and a little frightening." We played around on the bed, of course, till about eleven, and then she went to see "some people" at Corbeil, while I went to my family, where I stayed till about three, dazed and rather weighed down by the night's activity, without much ability or will to overcome it, smelling her near, like the dark heavy odor of truffles. At three I went to Le Dôme, where I found the Boxer, with Lili and a little girl, a cousin of 12 they have had with them for a whole year. Affectionate greetings from them. The Boxer is superb, he has the body of an 18-year-old, with extraordinary lightness, still wiry, with a torso that swivels on his hips as though it were a separate part turning freely on an axle; his hair is black, sprinkled with lots of silver; he still has that set little face, like a handsome kid's, with most noticeably the lips of a charmingly spoiled child, you know, the upper lip protruding voluptuously, and the lower receding, hiding as if in a pout, all the way down to the chin. Except all the other features have hardened, the bones clearly visible, temples lean and hard, the cheekbones prominent, and beneath the handsome-child face one begins to see the crude physiognomy of a peasant. He was charming, Lili too; we put Lili and the little girl on their train (they were leaving for Dunkirk) and strolled back to the Latin Quarter on foot in beautiful cool weather. He was his usual self, launching as passionately as ever into his pet subjects, except that his pet subjects were no longer the same: he is no longer a vegetarian, "because after all it isn't more natural to eat carrots than steak." But his primary preoccupation is heroism à la Corneille, whose modern representation he sees in Roquentin. He gave me again the whole of Alain's theory on the love-oath and explained that his for Lili was just like that. He admires her as much as ever, and his greatest joy is to have her untiringly repeat the same smutty stories of her adolescence, how she had herself mas-turbated by the guys, etc., not out of vice but, on the contrary, to send up to the heavens a hymn of gratitude: "That's the way she was, and now this, this is the way she is." He scans and judges their common past and individual pasts from the standpoint of their present happiness and wisdom, and it gives him a feeling of necessary and constantly renewed adventure that is the basis of his extreme beatitude. He speaks of it pleasantly, actually he finds it very good but is conscious at the same time of the extraordinary role played by chance. Yet from time to time he shyly explains that the good are always rewarded. When he isn't stark naked next to a naked Lili, listening to her stories, he's reading Corneille or Mallarmé, or he's walking, almost always on the same mountain above Hyères. From all this I realized what a classic is: a guy who rereads. That's Bonnafé, he isn't perpetually longing to go on beyond and see something else, but a plot of land, one page of one book, is enough: he's in the presence of something equal to an inexhaustible and demanding theme. And then you dream a little of anything at all, before that necessary and unchanging object that glows through dreams at times, like the sun between two clouds. There is a justification and validation of the reveries, and then abruptly all the clouds break up, you reread a line, perceive it in its hard, eternal being, and that dazzles you, etc. The same goes for landscapes. To see little, read little, think little, but always return to the same landscapes, the same books, the same thoughts, eternally encircling them. I'll spare you the rest, darling, because it's rather boring (it would take several pages at least, and anyway I realize that I haven't clearly said what I wanted to), but may it suffice for you to know I had never felt that classicism is a doctrine, a direction of the will, or a historic development, but rather a type of Mediterranean man, with his passions, his reveries, his vague sadness, etc., but all of it "classicism," or in other words, that it needs 1st to be rehashed, which is to say warmed over, 2nd to be rehashed *in the presence of* an inexhaustible object (in this sense, temple columns seem to me the most inexhaustible, because they mean nothing—and the most classic), 3rd for one to taste a certain sensual pleasure in the very absence of change in certain objects, while one is changing, indolently and calmly, right in front of them. You see that it leads naturally to happiness—not at all your variety, which is violent and instantaneous—but the happiness whose descriptions abound in the writings of the fifteenth, sixteenth, and even the eighteenth centuries. Bonnafé is absolutely like that, and it happened all by itself: he sees nobody, never budges from Sète, reads only the classics, gives Lili his sworn love, and gives the impression of always being terribly busy and tremendously happy. From time to time he commits a cry of enthusiasm to paper:

"Autumn comes, the wind takes the leaves, night falls: I wish I could thank a God."

Which, after all, is not so ugly and very slightly resembles the mad Hölderlin's poems. But then a person must have a power of enthusiasm and admiration, to be classic, which makes me wonder, which is totally foreign to me in any case. The governing object-themes must be clearly beyond the human, present domain: hence the Ancients for our classics. I tell you this because I play the role of Ancient for Bonnafé. I'd never seen such happy admiration and would be extremely embarrassed about it if I didn't understand that it is in his nature. He ponders, talks, gets all worked up when I'm there, whiles away the time, relaxes, grows indignant, talks nonstop as though in the presence of Virgil. He asks me only to be there, to keep quiet and let an occasional phrase slip out that is inexhaustible, like a column or a verse from the Golden Age. "How can you do it?" you'll say. Well! I say what I think, having understood that all is always inexhaustible so long as a person has a classical character, that is, the sense of depth. Then he moans a bit, squints because it seems to him I've suddenly given off a bright light that dazzles him. "Ah ha! yes . . . yes . . . you are showing me the light. Oh, that's it! I was going astray, adrift without purpose, and there!—one sentence did it, would you just repeat it, how exactly did you put it? . . ." I've said enough to make you sense how charming and sensitive he is, but boring because deliberately lacking coherence with me—classic behavior, filling the moments with babble whose meaning or direction I know I can totally reverse with a single word. But how sympathetic and pleasant he is to watch. He lives at Pontremoli's,[1] at Pontremoli's expense, whom he pays by saying, "Excuse me for being frank, but I consider you a repulsive ass, and your writing's garbage." "I'm well aware of that," says Pontremoli, "and I thank you for reinforcing my convictions. But that should not prevent you, please, from staying in my most unworthy house." "I'm quite willing," said the Boxer, "but on condition that you don't set foot in it this afternoon, because I would like to show it to Sartre." "I'm on my way," said Pontremoli, "I'm on my way. By the way, I'm dining this evening at an excellent restaurant. If you have nothing better to do, I would be so happy to treat you." So I saw the Pontremolis' apartment, on the seventh floor, near the Porte d'Orléans, very bright, very cheery, its only trace of gloom supplied by the inhabitants. But I was shown Muriel's[2] paintings, and, believe it or not, she is *talented*. For a long time she did lots of ordinary young women, gracious and sensual, posed here and there, near a window, on a beach, in the countryside. And it was sensual and lighthearted! I couldn't believe my eyes. Now she's taking lessons, and I saw a serious painting of hers, a graceless but extremely well-painted nude. She has only to regain the charm of her first paintings while painting well, and I think that what she does will be very pleasing. I left the Boxer at 6:45, and while waiting for Martine Bourdin at Le Dôme, I happened on the following newspaper item, which I find *tremendously* funny.

Death of M. Paillu

Our fellow citizen M. Paillu, having inadvertently touched a high-tension wire, experienced slight tremors on returning home. The physician called to his bedside diagnosed a benign fever, but toward dawn M. Paillu gave unmistakable signs of carbonization. Around nine in the morning he died, burned to a crisp. Our sincere condolences to the family.

Thereupon M. Bourdin appears and sits down practically in my arms: "I haven't once stopped thinking about you." "Nor I. So let's go off to bed." Which was done—around seven-ten, you see. There were M. Bourdin's suitcases which had to be picked up at her hotel on the Rue Cujas and taken to the Hôtel Mistral (she was leaving the following morning at eight), but we decided to go and fetch them at eleven in the evening. Caresses and frivolities.

---

[1]*A Sorbonne friend of mine and Sartre's. (SdB)*
[2]*Pontremoli's wife. (SdB)*

But with a touch of pathos: she was charming, and if I reflected that this night was our last, I could easily join M. Bourdin in a feeling necessarily sad and somewhat stifling. Seldom has any affair in my life seemed so gratuitous and so necessary. Around midnight she suddenly became very nervous, pushed me away then drew me back and finally said, "It bothers me that I'm not yours. I would like you to enter me." "You want me to try?" "You're going to hurt me, no, no!" But I tried gently. She moaned, and I said, "Look at you: if your hand were hurting as much as I'm hurting you right now, your pride would keep you from crying out, but now because of some vague fear, you're not ashamed to groan." She smiled and said, "Anyway, you aren't hurting me at all . . ." But after a moment she said louder, "No more, no more, let me be, please." I stopped and said to her, "But you're no longer a virgin." And I think it's true. But she squeezed me tight without saying a word, covering me with kisses. She was beaming because, as she told me later, she was thinking, "Here's the first guy I love enough that I really want him to possess me." We walked all the way to the Place Médicis (it was two in the morning), and she dryly revealed motives for remaining a virgin that were so profoundly shabby I finally said, "You're out of your mind, you know that." Then she fell sobbing into my arms, saying that was true. We went to Capoulade, which was just about to close, and I told her she was really splendid, and she gazed at me through her tears, her eyes filled with wonder, saying, "And you! And you! You're terrific. I never imagined there was anyone like you." Thereupon we went to pick up her bags, we made a terrible racket in the wretched hotel, asleep and totally dark, getting the wrong room, then hauling huge bundles of books down the stairs. We took a cab and came back home, indecently leaving all of her suitcases at the foot of the stairs. Then we slept a little and at seven left for the station. She was charming at the coffee counter of the Gare de l'Est, radiant as she said, "I'm happy." I told her, "Remember that we'll meet again in September, and we'll only finish our affair on October 1st." And she answered, "Even if it had to end at this very instant, I'd still be profoundly happy. I know I love you with all my might. As much as Mme Canque." With that we ran to catch the train, because she had only a minute left. She got on just anywhere and stood on the steps, out of breath, and gracefully bent over as she gazed at me silently. When the train started up, her eyes filled, but she never stopped smiling. That night when I went home, I found a bit of blood on my sheets.

My darling Beaver, I've just come from seeing Paulhan, who announced the following pleasant news to me: 1. I'm hired for sure to do a monthly column starting in November: 350 to 400 francs a month. Eventually to be raised to 500. The column will be about anything I like. 2. It seems there's much talk of me for the Prix Goncourt. Gallimard, who hadn't wanted to propose me, thought better of it because it seems to him I have the best chance.

That's how it went. Tomorrow I'll tell you how we spent the afternoon because of Bel Eute. For now I'd like you to know that I'm weak with longing for you, that I miss my little one, that it's ever so slightly painful. But you send such pleasant letters and seem to be having such a good time that I'm quite content. I'm at the Café Rouge, Marie Dubas is singing "Mon Légionnaire," and I'm thinking once more of your dear little attentive expression the day I was crying like a baby, and then I see you again with pleurisy, so skinny and grim, sitting up in your bed, such a pathetic little Redskin, and I think that if the music hadn't abruptly stopped, I would again, all alone and far from you, have wept a tear or two.

I love you.

I'm not going to La Pouèze.

Something that will amuse you: an official and very serious teachers' journal is doing a long article on Paulhan's *Dictionnaire des mots retrouvés* ["Dictionary of Rediscovered Words"], taking everything at face value and advising teachers to use it in class. "Show them," it says, "that the duodenum—an insufficiently known fact—was formerly, like the barbecue, a war machine." Paulhan, who is a socialist and, as such, pro-teacher, is very put out.

Giono has gone mad.[3]

To Simone de Beauvoir

Sunday morning, 9:30 [July]

My darling Beaver

I'm writing to you in haste while the youngest Zazoulich is putting on the finishing touches at "Le Petit-Mouton."[1] I saw her on my way down, already wide awake, and I doubt I have much time. But I did want to greet you and tell you a few sweet nothings because I love you so. I endured a

---

[3]Jean Giono (1895–1970), a novelist of rural Provence and a pacifist; the habit of protecting his privacy through a prodigality of misinformation and self-contradiction must have caused the report of madness.

[1]*A hotel in Rouen where I stayed for several years. (SdB)*

stormy dinner last night at L'Opéra[2] and thought of ours, which were so idyllic and, at times, contained such elevated conversation (for instance on value or the nature of mathematics). I imagined you saying "dear man," and I loved you very much. I had the leisure to do that because the other, on the verge of tears, never opened her mouth. The incident causing the dispute: she'd looked at the menu and, with a stubborn air that portended disaster, ordered a Chateaubriand. After which, when the waiter had left, she asked, "What is a Chateaubriand?" "It's meat." Alas! So then she emits a shriek: meat!—and gives way to despair but stubbornly refuses to change her order. Whence thunder and lightning and you can just imagine the arrival of the enormous Chateaubriand, looking insolent and sensual with a pint of melting parsley butter, a piece of meat that had "meat" written all over it. She ate it, teeth clenched; sitting there on its plate, it looked as out of place as the grand piano in that schizophrenic woman's garret, and on seeing it I even had the gall to snicker. Then it appeared that everything was my fault: if I hadn't looked determined not to crack a smile, "one would have asked for information on Chateaubriands, but one hadn't really felt like it"; actually it had always been this way with me—when she went to a restaurant with other people they knew how to advise her discreetly. "But what other people?" "Once, Violette Brochard in Caen. And then I really don't know . . . Madame Blanc." She ate three-quarters of her meat, half nauseated and sobbing, "It's worse than snails." Or else, in an inimitable tone of voice, "But is one supposed to chew this!?" But if I said, "Leave it," she would immediately put in her mouth a piece big enough to choke on and say firmly, "No, no. I must get used to eating it, the doctor told me I would be seriously anemic if I didn't have meat once a day." Then she dabbed at the butter on her lips, saying, "They do a lousy job of cooking here." The Chateaubriand weighed on the evening till about 12:30 (nerves, reproaches: I'm all right, I'm not all right, etc.) and it ended very happily with three hours of kissing, in a little room in the Petit-Mouton. To tell the truth, I gain territory each time. Instead it was I who was cold within, because my heart teeters.

While we're on the subject, the day before yesterday I saw Lucile, whom I took to dinner at the Bouteille d'Or. She was in a tender mood, and the sight of Notre-Dame inclined her toward sensuality, so she asked me to stroke her arm as we ate cassoulet. These alimentary games seemed all the more repellent to me because we had seen them performed, the Lady and I, just the evening before, at La Grille, by an unattractive couple, old and fat.

---

[2]*The Brasserie at the Opera House in Rouen. (SdB)*

So I laid hold of her arm like a handle and it went at it lovelessly. "Your caresses lack any subtlety," she told me disdainfully. After which she relaxed completely and said, "Sartre, my own little Sartre, I'd like you to run your fingernails across my stomach and breasts." I said, "I have a rendezvous at eleven o'clock"—with the Lady—"but from ten-thirty to eleven I can render you that service." We took a cab, she went straight over to lie down on the divan, drawing me onto her. Of course, she didn't want to be kissed, but she said, "Hold me tight, I want to feel so small, so small, so small." I felt like a total idiot. I conscientiously hugged her for a few minutes, then said gently, "You know, I'm bored to death." Then she sat up, shoved me away, and began to sob: "The one time I'm being myself with someone, I'm told, 'You're boring me to death.' " Then she looked at me gravely, saying, "It's tragic, Sartré, it's tragic." We went back down, and I told her, "Well, what do you expect? You fend a person off and offer yourself at the same time, how do you expect to keep a man? What did the others do?" "The others loved me," she said, crying, "and when I let them caress me, they were only too happy." "But you know very well that I don't love you," I said. "So what an odd tactic if you wanted me to love you: you don't catch flies with vinegar." She started to whimper again: "I do know you don't love me, but still it's always painful to hear." So I played the whore and addressed her tenderly. "I had no idea you could be such a sweet talker," she said, glowing. She wanted to stay with me for a bit, but I was to meet the Lady at eleven, and I left her, but not before requesting and receiving a peck on the mouth. As I went off, I said as whorishly as possible, "Well, you did find the soft spot in my heart, my butterball of a heart!" (because she was complaining I had no heart). I gave the Lady a good laugh, telling her about all this.

Sunday seven o'clock: the letterhead on this stationery will indicate I'm just back from Rouen. A day of passion disturbed around noon when I gave Tania a playful tap on the behind. She made a fuss; I blew up the whole incident; she sobbed; I was wretched. The balance sheet is as follows. It is understood that I'm a master manipulator, there's even talk of blows and kisses mixed. She doesn't try to hide the pleasure she gets out of it. On the other hand, I asked her, "Do you love me?" at the last moment, and she was disturbed because it's a pledge that commits her, and she didn't want to reply beyond "At the moment I love you," promising to give the pledge later. I've found it very awkward to readapt, these past two days, because I'm used to easier women. Last night, I even wanted to dump her. But ultimately, of all those who have honored me with their ardor these past few months, there's not one who's been so pleasing physically and so moving in the realm of passion. So the thing is done.

My love, I received your long letter and I love you. Rest assured, there will be as many little *Erlebnis* on my side as on yours, and they will pile up together and we two will love each other very much and passionately. I am furiously longing to see you again, my sweet, and to talk with you about every last thing and to cover your dear little dark Queen of Sheba face with little French kisses.

I'm overwhelmed by all there is to tell. I think I'll have to make a selection. First, didn't I forget to tell you that the day after our discussion Merleau-Ponty wandered into Martine Bourdin's place, all pleased with himself, and gave her to understand that he was not in the dark about her love for him? "Basically," he said, indulgent and amused, "in your business with Sartre, there's no love on either side." And he explained: she did not love B. because she had so rapidly transferred her feelings to me; she didn't love me because it was only a transfer. Very much at ease, he let her hope, in roundabout terms, that he would reward her the following year for her discreet love. She was seething with rage and confusion as she told me this. And what's more, soon after she arrived at Le Dôme on the last evening, he reached her by phone, while she was virtually in my arms, to assure her of his feelings. Since then he has written her a postcard to La Ferté, which I'll enclose here, very unpleasant and conceited—"Empty, more than anything else," says the Lady—and a long letter whose contents are completely unknown to me, because M. Bourdin mentions it only in her little snatches of love talk, but which is more pleasant, so it seems. And there we are. I met him yesterday at the College Inn, and tomorrow I'm to see him at Le Balzar from 2 to 4. That's it for him.

Another matter: the Nizans. I saw them from 8 to 2 in the morning on Tuesday evening. Nizan had brought me *La Conspiration* ["The Conspiracy"], with dedication as follows: "To J.-P. Sartre, particularly page 92, his friend P. Nizan." I dashed to page 92 and there was: "Commander Sartre, who was a complete idiot . . ." I said that in my review of his book (which will appear on October 14—I'll write it in Meknès,[3] poor Beaver, along with my review of *Maïmona*[4] and an article on Husserl) I'll put: "A single error: the portrait of Commander Sartre." We dined at La Grille, and they got

---

[3] In Morocco. See note 12, p. 150.
[4] By François Mauriac (1885–1970), journalist and author of novels based on provincial life and questions of faith. Mauriac was awarded the Nobel Prize in 1952.

themselves treated to a movie that was "very Nizan," as Toulouse would say, I mean an American movie on the Spanish war: *Blockade*, with pacifist tendencies, boring as hell, favorable toward the Republicans but all the Republicans turned out to be spies. To reach the Olympia, where the film was showing, we made our way through a dense, tragic crowd on the Boulevards. The crowd was there, under bright green trees lit from below, beneath English and French banners because of the celebrations, because the King of England was in Paris. No other possible connection between that crowd and the king, since the king was at that very moment ensconced in the Élysée. But the crowd was demonstrating. The faces were ennobled by military passion, by a sinister gaiety. One could quite easily imagine a few bombs released over it all, from a Junker overhead, and then the Grands Boulevards completely dark, completely still and deserted. And Nizan repeated in a monotone, "It's 1914 all over again—we'll have war in three months." Aside from that they were boring as hell; tired—me tired—we dragged along.

And now the Guilles. I dined with them at La Grille on Monday evening. Colorless and insipid. The big topic of conversation, "Trip to Greece," having receded into the past, we confronted a total void. We were very affectionate but had no idea what to say. I took them back to the Hôtel Mistral, and they slept in Zazoulich's room, which still smelled of her. On Wednesday I wander over to the Lady's place and I scrounge a few leftovers in the kitchen with her. Around four-thirty, Guille turns up (letting himself in with his key without ringing), completely weird. He seems embarrassed to find the Lady at home, chatters awkwardly for a bit, and finally says, "I didn't want to disturb you and I'm sorry to find you here, because I have to give you a shock: I'm about to call all the hospitals in Paris, because the Bel Eute, who was due back at twelve-thirty, isn't home yet." She'd gone to do some errands in central Paris. Of course, the three of us were overcome by groundless terrors while he tirelessly called the various hospitals. The Lady drew me into a corner and said, "I saw her dead this very morning." You know she predicted the Bel Eute would die in the year following her marriage. The prediction was expiring that day. If nothing happened, the Bel Eute was saved. During the morning the Lady had spoken about it to Simone de Stoecklin and said, "I think she will die today." Mysterious, the Lady: to what degree did she wish it, one wonders. Finally I was sent by cab to 101 Bd. Saint-Michel to see if the Bel Eute had come in. I found her there, safe and sound, but in a terrible state of nerves because the concierge, an artist in off-hours, had told her that Guille had gone to look for her at the morgue. She had simply been delayed by the king's procession and the impenetrable crowd stagnating for days in the center of Paris. But what shocked the Lady was that she had been delayed *on the way there,* in other words she reached her dressmaker around 1:45. So right then she could have telephoned the Lady or taken the Métro and given up her errands, which would have put her at home around 2:15. "Since I'd gotten that far," she said, "I preferred to do what I had to do." Of course the Lady said, "I'm very pleased to have been wrong, to be mistaken. But the Bel Eute is a child of six, she doesn't think of anything!" It seems that Guille, when he heard us come in, the Bel Eute and I, wanted to bawl her out, but the Lady dissuaded him. After which I served them two glasses of Calvados to pick them up, and they sat slumped in their chairs, sighing. It was rather dreadful. From there I went to Paulhan's. You know the essentials of the conversation, which for once was animated. He introduced me to Jean Grenier, who emphatically advised me not to go to Morocco because of the heat. He had just returned and claims that the nights are as hot as the days. We'll see soon enough. It also seems that there's still a risk of typhus in the old parts of Marrakech. But I wouldn't be surprised if he was thuper-thenthitive.

My love, what more to tell you? Lots of little encounters of no great interest (the Boxer had Lili dance for me, in the nude, of course); scraps of little happenings I'll tell you about on the boat. I'm leaving soon for La Pouèze, where I'll stay until tomorrow. The day after, I'm off to Berck. I love you, I'm feeling a sort of departure anguish right now, the whole year's behind me. I'd like to be with you, my love, only you can give me the impression of living in a new present, O charm of my heart and my eyes, mainstay of my life, my consciousness and my reason. I love you most passionately, and I need you.

Don't forget that I'm arriving *on the morning of the 30th.* Meet me at the station cafeteria. Plans with the Lady have fizzled.

To Simone Jollivet

July

Dear Toulouse

You've been dead silent for too long, alas, and we're on our way. To be precise, the Beaver has already gone. She is someplace on the peaks of Savoy. I'm still in Paris, but only for a short while longer; an article on philosophy earned me a most flattering affair with one of the students at the

Atelier[1]—from whom you borrowed a pencil one day during a rehearsal of *Plutus*—and I'm exhausting its charm before rejoining the aforementioned Beaver in Marseilles.

Many thanks for pushing the sale of my book a bit. By tomorrow I'll drop off on the Rue Navarin the maté pot and drinking tube,[2] which have arrived at last from Argentina. I'll add a quick note to Dullin including: 1, discreet allusions to the great esteem in which I hold him, the affection I feel for him; 2, clearer allusions to the gratitude I still feel for his energetic and decisive actions with Gallimard; 3, clear and indiscreet remarks on the use of these instruments—which is not so simple as you might think.

Adieu, dear Toulouse, we bitterly regret not having seen you. I'll be in Paris, alone, around September 15. Call me at the Hôtel Mistral as soon as you get back, and we'll go for a walk, the two of us, if you like. We'll write to you from Morocco. "You on your side," as Chrémyle says, send us a word or two to General Delivery in Fez, if you want to make us happy. If you write to us, we'll bring you back some trinket. And in any case, we'll think of you with much affection.

My greetings and salutations.

To Simone de Beauvoir

Tuesday evening [end of July]

My darling Beaver

I just got your telegram and will send the letter. I love you very much, and in this heat I long to be with you in some Morocco of our own, oh Lovely Human. More and more, little Zazoulich displays the mental faculties of a dragonfly, and I'm finding it heavy going. I so wish you were here, I want to feel your arm in mine and tell you little anecdotes and hear your comments. Last night was painful. She was all upset by her reconciliation with Olga and then Olga's departure. I was deliberately very affectionate with her, first on La Butte, and then at the College Inn, but all in vain. There at the end, my tenderness made her shudder with displeasure. When I kissed her on the mouth, walking down the Rue Delambre, she claimed to be horrified by any kiss that did not simply make contact, that this one did more (she meant it was a penetration—hardly true), that perhaps she wasn't made

---

[1]*Martine Bourdin. (SdB)*
[2]A device used in Argentina for sipping tea.

like everyone else, but that's how it is. "And yet in Rouen . . ." "What are you doing, bringing up Rouen at a time like this?" At her door, she wasn't too eager for me to leave her in that state. Eventually we went in, but we couldn't find the light switch. I struck matches without any luck, then she broke into a sort of berserk laughing fit, and there we stayed—between light and darkness, the door open onto the lighted hallway, the window open onto the moon—sitting on Olga's unmade bed. Then she explained that she didn't know what sensuality was, that this saddened her, because she couldn't have a complete relationship with me and because she'd never be an artist, since a person must be sensual to succeed in the arts. I calmed her down as best I could, tipped her back on the bed, and kissed her. After a moment she freed herself and I left in a fury, though I could hear her dash to the bathroom a second or two later to vomit, as she'd gulped down white rum and sherry, which had upset her stomach. Physically appealing aside from that, in an angelic little jacket and with her hair down. I slept beautifully till 12:30, and went to meet her at Le Dôme at two. She was embarrassed but also intimidated, and I froze her out all day, abruptly dropping my game and declaring that we were through unless she became more loving with me. She promised anything I wanted—and this took place at an attractive café in the Palais-Royal, where I intend to take you, my lovely Beaver, for why the two Zazouliches and not you? There she explained that she derives complete physical pleasure merely from contact and a few kisses (with Brochard and with me). That's what she calls not being sensual. I walked the girl, who was anxious and disoriented by the vague threat that "we're through," back to her hotel room, where I found your telegram. I'll mail this letter tonight and begin another tomorrow, in case I should get another address.

Farewell, dearest Beaver, come back, come back soon. What you've left me here in your place is meager fare, and I'm so fond of carrying on this bit of correspondence with you in the evening that I'm already imagining the raptures of really talking with you. I love you, little one, I love you passionately.

To Simone de Beauvoir

[July]

My darling Beaver

I won't have the time either today or tomorrow to write you a very long letter. Nonetheless, here are two or three little items for your amusement.

1. I love you passionately

2. the director of the Paquet Co. turned out to be a schoolmate from La Rochelle and a real sweetheart. He's giving us a 4-person cabin for the two of us and is telegraphing Casablanca to do the same for our return.

3. All at once I've found the subject for my novel, its proportions, and its title. Just as you hoped, the subject is freedom.[1]

So there's the title (the 2nd volume will be called *Le Serment* ["The Oath"]).

Adieu, little one, I'm working on "L'Enfance d'un chef" ["The Child-hood of a Leader"][2] and will finish it in time. I love you.

To Simone de Beauvoir

[September]

My darling Beaver

I'm writing to you under a beautiful cold Sunday sun. I love you passionately and have not ceased to feel that I am with you. My relationships with people here seem totally unreal, and they notice it. Paris is deserted and abstract, despite the good weather. The few people I know at Le Dôme look like survivors—the Magus, some unremarkable women, Foujita. But as for our close friends, they're too many, and I don't know how I'll see them all: there's Bonnafé, whom I saw last night and will again later; Boubou, who is leaving again this evening and whom I'll see in a while; Toulouse, whom I'll see Monday. And the Moon People, back last night and wanting to get together. Also Lucile, back in Paris for the revival of *Plutus*, just called me at the hotel. Fortunately I wasn't there. Incidentally, she's tenacious, that girl. I'll also see Feldman, who wrote me in tragic tones that she was "crossing a minefield" to see me, but I'd never asked that much of her—and Poupette. I don't know how I'll get any work done. Still, I began an article on Nizan that will almost write itself.

So, I found my compartment, exhorted and supported by the Moon People, and noted that we were only four, each of us claiming a corner—two women, another man, and myself. We did our best to stretch out, and we slept. But around three in the morning it got so cold we woke up. We moved around a bit and more or less warmed up, but I urge you to rent *blankets* for both[1] of you, on your way back, even if it's hot in Marseilles,

---

[1] Planned as a tetralogy, only three novels were finally written, published as *Les Chemins de la liberté* (*The Roads to Freedom*): in 1945, *L'Age de raison* (*The Age of Reason*) and *Le Sursis* (*The Reprieve*), and in 1949, *La Mort dans l'âme* (*Troubled Sleep*).

[2] A short story included in *The Wall*.

[1] *Olga and myself. (SdB)* They were on a walking trip in the French Alps.

or you'll freeze to death. When I got in, I found José and his wife[2] here, torn between the extreme pleasure afforded by my return and the fury produced by Chamberlain's trip. José wants to fight at any cost and right away. He handed me several letters—one from a Swiss cousin who wants to translate *Nausea* into German, a contract from the *NRF*, a second notice for income taxes, a bill from Beck et Godet, etc.—and he came back up a few moments later to say timidly, "My wife and I would like to offer you some café au lait." I thanked him effusively, and now we flash knowing smiles whenever we meet. There was a note from Boubou, sorry to be leaving without seeing me, and another to tell me he'd put off his trip and hoped to see me. So I went by their place yesterday morning. I found Baba[3] in a pink nightgown and Boubou in pajamas, perfectly in character. Of course, he wants war immediately, like José, and rages against the cowardice of our government. Baba was eyeing me critically: I was no longer Sartre, but the intellectual petit-bourgeois Frenchman who has lost interest in politics and must be forced to face reality. She finally said, "How nervous you are, my boy, you seem all at sea." I wasn't in the least; quite the opposite, I was in excellent spirits. But my efforts to convince her were in vain. We talked about hardly anything else but the unfolding events while sipping some of her tolerable coffee. Boubou doesn't foresee a victory for the Republicans in Spain anymore, or for Franco either. He believes an agreement will put an end to it, within about a year.

Then I saw my family, not too worried and counting on France's backing down to preserve the peace. My stepfather wants us to resign ourselves to becoming a second-rate power and live for several years cowering behind the Maginot line. Aside from that, kind, interested in Morocco. So they did rent a little house, but each took me aside to say it was a nuisance and had been done only to please the other. I stayed with them till around five and worked on Nizan till about 9. At 9 I saw the Boxers. They'd been in Paris for a week, trying to elude Pontremoli. They hadn't read the papers from August 1st to September 13th. On the evening of the 13th, to see the write-up of a sports event, the Boxer buys *Paris-Soir*. He reads "Ultimatum for Sudetens,"[4] etc. "Hum," said he. "That could mean an air raid tonight." They went to bed, slept, and woke the next morning completely surprised: "So nothing hap-

---

[2]*Hotel employees. (SdB)*
[3]*Stépha Gérassi. (SdB)* Her husband, Fernando (Boubou), was back from the Spanish front.
[4]*The Sudetenland was a part of Czechoslovakia that Hitler claimed for annexation, because it had a German majority. (SdB)*

pened?" "The heroic part," the Boxer added, "was not buying the papers either that day or the following days. We walked around, we studied people's faces, we said to ourselves: still nothing. So what happened to the Sudetens?" Finally Pontremoli returned, called back to the Conseil d'État because of the international situation (now that's delightful), and he filled them in. Whence the Boxer, pursuing his deaf-and-dumb meditations, convinced himself that the Germans are on firm ground in the matter. As you can see, there's no lack of diversity of opinions here. You can just imagine Le Dôme, buzzing with political conversations. Foujita is not the least agitated. She seems to have had (she's at the next table) a big debate on the war at Les Deux Magots. When someone insulted her, and her companion of the moment wanted to intervene, she said, "You're not my father or my brother or my lover. Just a friend. If you get mixed up in my fight, you become my enemy, because you don't have any right to speak for me."

Perhaps this is the place, my darling Beaver, for me to slip in some information about the current situation. You know that Chamberlain, who arrived at Berchtesgaden to haggle over a plebiscite, found himself facing some demands of Hitler's that exceeded his expectations: annexation of the Sudetens, pure and simple—and after that we'll talk. So he headed back to London to inform his colleagues and the French ministers of the German proposals. Meanwhile Hitler had agreed not to resort to force before his proposals had been officially accepted or rejected. Hence the relative calm that allows you to continue your trip. At the same time, Henlein[5] committed the blunder of proclaiming the Anschluss and getting the hell out, soon followed by 23,000 of the most agitated Sudetens. The result is that the other Sudetens, leaderless and at a loss, calmed down, and the Czech government proclaimed the dissolution of the Sudeten party and regained control of the situation. Naturally the 23,000 Sudetens formed up as a legion at the German frontier, ready to try and lend a helping hand. This hastily constituted legion seems to indicate that Hitler, perhaps impressed by Chamberlain's assurances (England will enter the conflict in the case of German aggression), still contemplates, among other means, settling the question through a civil war between Sudetens and Czechs, which would deny France all pretext for intervention. For the time being the legion is holding still while awaiting

---

[5]Konrad Henlein (1898–1945), Sudeten-German politician. In September 1938, after the Czech government ignored his earlier demand of autonomy for the Sudeten-German areas, he demanded that they be ceded to Germany. With his party outlawed at home, he fled to Germany. There the Nazis appointed him commissioner for the Sudetenlands, which were ceded to Germany by the Munich conference.

London's decisions. Meanwhile, here is the official situation in London: the English, who have not guaranteed the integrity of Czechoslovakia, discuss Hitler's demands and decide: "We, who are only indirectly involved in the affair, can go only so far"—up to now it isn't known what they will concede to Hitler. Doubtless almost everything: even a pure and simple annexation of the German majority cantons, with a plebiscite for the regions where the Germans are a minority. In return, England would undertake, with France, Italy, Russia, and Germany, to guarantee the integrity of the new, neutralized Czechoslovakia. There has been friction in the inner core of the English government, because several ministers refused to take on new responsibilities in central Europe. But if this were done, the English Prime Minister could say only: We, we have guaranteed nothing. It is the French who have a mutual assistance pact with the Czechs. So the lead goes to the French government. Whence Daladier's and Bonnet's[6] invitation. But this is only the official version. In fact it seems certain here that the backing down is coming from the French. It is at Daladier's request that Chamberlain left for Berchtesgaden, and from that moment on doubtless Daladier was ready for any concessions. Spain's ambassador to Czechoslovakia was convinced of that fifteen days before the events. Incidentally, the fact is that Daladier and Bonnet, on arriving in England, declared themselves in complete accord with the English proposal. And, on their return to Paris, the entire council of ministers approved the plan. So this puts an end to the legend of opposition by Reynaud and Mandel within the ministry: everyone backed down.[7] Just now, there's new information on the proposals we will make to Hitler, and here it is: annexation of the areas with a German majority, autonomy of the others arranged without plebiscite by neutral commissions, neutralization of Czechoslovakia, which loses its alliances with Russia and France (a neutral country has no right to enter alliances) but is guaranteed its integrity by several powers, *not including Russia*. You can see that this plan, if it is the real one, concedes absolutely everything to Hitler: on the one hand cession of the richest areas of Czechoslovakia; on the other, abandonment of the politics of alliance that made Czechoslovakia an advance bastion of Russia. Incidentally,

---

[6]Édouard Daladier (1884–1970), Radical Party politician who served in numerous governments from 1924. As Premier he signed the Munich Pact. Georges-Étienne Bonnet (1889–1973), Foreign Minister under Daladier.

[7]Paul Reynaud (1878–1966) and Georges Mandel (1885–1944). Reynaud was Minister of Finance from 1938 to 1940, and Premier from March 1940 to June 1940, when he resigned rather than agree to an armistice with Germany. He was kept in captivity till the Liberation. Mandel, a Jew, fled to Morocco, but was arrested and delivered to the Germans in 1942, and after imprisonment in several concentration camps, was shot on orders of the Vichy government.

Russia, which was not even consulted, is thereby removed from the "concert of European powers." Victory for Hitler all along the line.

At that price we may have peace *but*

1. Czechoslovakia still must have its say. After all, the country would be deprived of vital areas. So without even mentioning national sovereignty or dignity (and from that point of view the Czechs seem uncompromising), it is rather difficult to imagine their agreeing to allow such reduction to misery. Will they say no? The latest news from Prague leads one to believe they'll choose to fight. But in that case, what will France and England do? England, which is under no obligations, can withdraw from the game. And France? It will undoubtedly not take up the fight without England. Russia has declared that it would not intervene alone. So then? A general backing down. Is it conceivable that we could stand by and complacently watch the crushing of a nation whose integrity we have guaranteed? On that point the future is uncertain. Perhaps by the time you get my letter it will all be settled. On the other hand, it is difficult for Benès and Hodza[8] to decide alone. No doubt they will convene the Czech parliament. But in that strange parliament "the minorities are the majority," and it's highly doubtful that Slovaks, Poles, Hungarians, etc. will agree to fight, while they're all more or less insisting on their autonomy. So the Czechs will be left to stand alone, a majority in the parliament now that the Sudetens are gone, but a fragile majority. Ultimately it is also rather difficult to imagine a government lightheartedly throwing its country into such a conflict, *without even the slightest hope.* Finally, people point out that if England and France fought beside Czechoslovakia, *either* they would be defeated and Czechoslovakia would disappear from the map, or they would be victorious, and England would probably not let Czechoslovakia continue in its present form. If Czechoslovakia, consulted first, refuses the proposals, how will these plans turn out? Will the powers present them to Hitler after all? It seems nothing can be predicted on that point.

2. It is highly possible that in case of a refusal, Hitler would return to his first plan of civil war, with a "Sudeten legion" and 100,000 German "volunteers" who will cross the border. In that case, will we in France look the other way?

3. The consequences of this retreat are the following (in the event that Czechoslovakia would allow itself to be devoured):

---

[8]Edvard Benès (1884–1948) and Milan Hodza, respectively President and Prime Minister of Czechoslovakia.

Sooner or later Yugoslavia, Romania, Hungary fall under German hegemony.

Russia breaks off its alliance with France. Lots of people here are saying that it will then turn toward Germany, which is not impossible. As a matter of fact, the German representative in Moscow, who had left Russia with the whole embassy, suddenly returned by plane.

The democrats have lost all hope of making Hitler retreat. It is a true victory of fascism, not only on the level of international politics but also within the different nations. Hitler emerges stronger from the affair. The result is obviously new arbitrary demands and new threats; the conflict is no doubt simply put off for several years.

There, my darling Beaver, you have the picture. As you can see, as yet it's not a very rosy one. The risk of immediate war still exists, though of course greatly diminished. But even in the event that war is avoided, it's not a very pretty picture. All the same, people are calmer here, happier: it seems to them that perhaps they'll have a reprieve of a few years. As for me, I ask no more than that for the moment; we'll see soon enough. As for you, if Czechoslovakia refuses, I think tomorrow I'll call you back here by telegram. In that case you won't get this letter. If it accepts, or if the possibility of negotiation remains open, you can blithely go on with your trip.

I've just seen Boubou. He is leaving in despair. He thinks that the retreat of the powers will bring on the defeat of the republicans. Probably, he says, Mussolini will be encouraged enough to mount a decisive effort. I don't happen to believe that, but whatever I think about it is of little import to you. He said he had seriously blundered in going off to fight, that he didn't know why he was fighting, since defeat was certain, and he hoped for one thing alone, to return as soon as possible and get the hell out of Europe. We parted with real emotion, less perhaps out of true friendship than from a realization that we didn't know when or how we would see each other again, and because we sensed a sort of total uncertainty about the future.

Monday

While I think of it: *Le Journal de Lausanne* lists me as favorite for the Goncourt.

I saw Lucile, "down in the dumps."

I saw Toulouse, looking splendid; she'd been hiking with a backpack in the Causses. The account of Moroccan misery opened Dullin's eyes onto untold depths. Reticence on the reasons leading to the acceptance of *Savonarola*. "Financial?" "Noooo . . . it's rather that there wasn't anything else."

How lovely. She wants 2,000 francs, which she'll return in a month. So tomorrow I'll go by the NRF to tap Hirsch. With an air of concentration she said about the war, "A war is always unpleasant. Besides, Hitler's a mystic."

My dearest Beaver, I received your letter and feel a deathly pall because you're so sad. I too am sad to be far from you, and nothing much appeals to me because you aren't here. But I imagine that even as I write, you must feel more confident and calm. After all, there's a good chance that an immediate conflict will be avoided. I love you, my Beaver, I'm still completely with you, and the forty-five days in which we were so tenderly united weigh heavily on me, I'm not forgetting them, I assure you. I felt deep stirrings of emotion for you again as I told Dullin and Toulouse about our trip. I didn't take along, but did promise, the trinkets to a dazzled Toulouse. Every day Dullin sips his maté through the tube and claims to be enchanted with it.

Tuesday

No letter from you or telegram; I have no idea where to send this letter. A note from Tania, who has just endured two weeks made terrible by fear of war. "Now," she says, "it's over, but I got so tired out, I'm sleeping all the time."

In the latest bulletins it seems that Czechoslovakia is accepting the Anglo-French proposals. But that's from official sources only. What seems certain, in any case, is that it won't raise objections on principle. My darling Beaver, I so wish that you could have brought yourself to read the news, which has been somewhat reassuring in spite of everything, and that you'd felt a little hope and joy. I love you. I'm not closing this letter. If I get an address today I'll mail it, but otherwise I'll go on with it while waiting to know where to send it.

Your telegram has just arrived, my darling Beaver, and I'm sending this letter off as quickly as possible. I've just found a letter here from de Roulet asking me lots of metaphysical questions and ending with an urgent request for our presence on the 27th. He says that around October 1st his family (aunt and perhaps mother) will be here. So if you could come home, barring new complications, around the 26th, all would be well. I've just been to the NRF, and I found the article in *Paris-Midi* in which the guy—who tears me apart in other respects—writes: "Already the sound of new titles is wafting their way"—the Goncourts. "Have they read *Nausea*, by J.-P. Sartre? They must read it, even if they don't want to. Several critics and some leading lights have and found there the scent of a masterpiece. The papers are saying so; it is making the rounds by word of mouth. They even say that several among the Ten, without giving names, out of discretion. . . . In short, a favorite, as they say, since editors have 'stables' and the prizes are 'races.' "

Adieu, my darling Beaver, I'll take this letter to the post office. You *cannot* know how much I long to see you.

This letter isn't a whole lot of fun, I think. You'll have to forgive me, given the circumstances.

To Jean Paulhan

Monday [autumn]

Dear Sir and friend

I have just received your letter and also one that you sent to me in Fez, which came back to the *NRF*, and from there to my place. I'm extremely sorry not to have been able to reply. In it you spoke of "The Childhood of a Leader." I realize that the milieu of the A.F. [Action Française] is more complicated than I say. But I wanted to show it only insofar as a young man who is profoundly corrupt and not particularly observant could discover it, in his effort to gain his salvation through social means and privilege. One could imagine—by taking a hero from a more intellectual level of the bourgeoisie—the same story with an ending in which the young man enters the Communist Party, and, similarly, in that case communism would have to seem simple, because the only thing required of it is to bolster an existence that is collapsing.

As for my short stories, in July I sent a table of contents to Chevasson. The necessary order seems to me: "The Wall"—"Erostratus"—"The Room"—"Intimacy"—"The Childhood of a Leader." In any case, I definitely like 1–3–5; as for 2 and 4, clearly their order can be reversed. Nonetheless I would prefer to have "Intimacy" come after "The Room," because of some indefinable priority of the tragic over the grotesque. The date that M. Gallimard has proposed surprises me somewhat. Indeed, Hirsch, whom I saw last week, stated that the decision had "always been" to have me published on January 10. He thinks that the publication of my short stories before the Goncourt would definitely compromise the slim chance that remains to me. To tell the truth, Dear Sir and friend, I do not understand a great deal about these tactics and I'm simply not very eager to get mixed up in it all. And I believe you share my view. So, may the book appear at the time judged best. I contemplated doing a brief preface to explain that I was not "playing around in the muck" etc. and that the stories represent a precise moment in a general plan. *Nausea* defines existence. The five stories describe the various possible escapes from it ("The Wall": death—"Erostratus": the gratuitous act, crime—"The Room": imaginary worlds, madness—"The Childhood of a Leader": privilege, the social), showing the failure of each, with "The Wall" to mark their bounds. No possible escape. Then I'll offer a glimpse of the possibility of a moral life at the core of existence and with no escape, the life I want to define in my next novel. I've had enough of being called deliquescent and morbid, when I am precisely the opposite. But before undertaking that preface (about two pages) I would appreciate your advice. Would you be so kind as to tell me whether you think it necessary to "explain oneself," or if it would be better to keep quiet and let them say what they like? After what you told me about the very special success of "Intimacy," I can imagine the bundle of garbage I'll receive on publication of *The Wall*.

I received *Les Liaisons du monde*[1] and I thank you for it. At first glance the book seems to me rather daunting, but I'll apply myself to it. Will I soon have the great pleasure of reading *Les Fleurs de Tarbes* ["The Flowers of Tarbes"]?[2]

Most sincerely yours

---

[1]*Les Liaisons du monde: roman d'un politique*, by Léon Bopp (Gallimard, 1938).
[2]*A work by Jean Paulhan. (SdB)*

1939

To Simone de Beauvoir

[June]

My darling Beaver

Please forgive me, I was just on my way to meet you when I ran into Tania. I was terribly sorry not to be able to say goodbye to you, dear one. But an argument started up immediately because I suspected her (that was a mistake) of not having left Paris or of having come earlier than she said. She was bitter and kept on denying everything till midnight, showering insults on you, you and her sister (I loathe them both, etc.). And then suddenly she sobbed and said, "I just pretended to leave." Here's what happened: she really did sleep at Vlasta's[1] the second night because her sister was at the Swing Club; except that in telling Olga, she didn't mention that the night before she had voluntarily shared Vlasta's bed for the first time. Then she told Olga— two or three days later—but Olga, innocent in this whole affair, had already given you an account of it. Then, it is true she told Olga she was leaving on Wednesday. So the older sister hadn't lied to you. It simply remains to be seen whether Olga went with her to the station. But that would be a harmless fib. The fact is that Olga believed Tania was leaving. Thereupon Tania, disheartened about leaving but ashamed to face Olga, drops her suitcases at the baggage room (she still has 100 francs), returns to Montmartre, and takes a room for two days at her old hotel. She goes underground, sees nothing of Olga for two days. She sees only Vlasta. I bawled her out, she cried but

_____
[1]_A girlfriend of Tania's._ (SdB)

182

bawled me out too, reproached me for M. Bourdin, partly to defend herself
with whatever she had at hand, partly to externalize grievances she must have
been mulling over in Laigle. There's something more bitter and harsher about
her since yesterday, but more passionate too; no doubt there are more surprises
in store from all this. I'm being cold. I do miss you. I much prefer the life
of the mind to personal obsessions.

Adieu, dear one. I'm about to take my pipe and go to see Maurice
Sachs.[2] Have a good time on your trip and don't do anything unwise. I love
you passionately.

To Simone de Beauvoir

[June]

My darling Beaver

Are you truly in Bellegarde, my sweet? In Bellegarde *Basses-Alpes*? I'm
all a-tremble, for I've lost, God knows where, my notebook with your address.
We'll chance it and trust to God. You must be having a sad time, my poor
dearest, and more than once I've found myself very moved as I imagined
your fragile little iron-willed self on wet roads, completely stubborn and
completely soaked. I'm eager to have a note from you. Tomorrow I'll drop
by my place. I love you so much. I hope your eyes will be soothed by the
time you get back, poor little thing with the pitiful eyes, and I long to hold
you tightly in my arms.

Lots of goings-on here, but as you know, goings-on that are cataclysmic
and inconsequential. I'm leading an odd life. Wasted time, of course, tremendously wasted, but consensual waste. Whence an odd dreamy state, not
too unpleasant. Of course, there were storms and despair and clamoring on
Saturday, because I got in at nine o'clock. Or rather I found a prostrated
creature bearing all the pressures of the world. "What's the matter?"
"Nothing." "But what *is* it?" "Nothing." "But?" "But I already told you, it's
nothing!" A little scene: she goes to the washbasin, puts cream on her face,
powder, lipstick. Silence. And then finally, in a good-faith effort: "All right,
I came in without looking in my letter box. I waited impatiently till 8:45,
and only then did I think of going down to see if there was something for
me." "And that's when you found my *pneumatique*." She nodded, and then

---

[2]Author (1906–1945) of the memoirs *Witches' Sabbath* and *The Life and Times of "Le
Boeuf sur le Toit,"* about bohemian, artistic, and homosexual life in Paris.

dryly, "Well, whaddaya want, that's the way I am. I get tied in knots waiting. But that's the way I am, that's all. It's not my fault." And I, of course: "If you were telling me you hated me till 8:45, all well and good. But after you found my note at 8:45," etc. etc. This goes on awhile longer. Thereupon, impatient, I say, "Come on, let's go out!" We go out. Outside, silence. I say, "Listen, I'm not angry at you. Let's stop all this." But no, not in the least, she felt like going on: "But you forced me to go out before things were settled, and now you want us to work it out with all these people around, in this . . . vortex!" So we walked down empty streets. The Rue Pigalle, the Boulevard Haussmann, which was in fact completely dark, and then she said, "I'm tired," and we went into a big café with music, the German café-konditorei sort and more specifically, you may remember, like the one in Hamburg, near the station, with a balconied second floor. There were gypsy musicians, a clientele of widowers and respectable adulterers. As it was so profoundly gloomy, she suddenly perked up, and rubbed her head against my shoulder, and things were turning rosy when, after forty-five minutes, a soprano drove us out of the café. Then Tania got a headache. She wanted us to go to the Café de Flore. Upon which her mood turned sour. This sort of dialogue in the Métro, punctuated with long silences: "I've got a pimple on my chin, I'm furious." "What from?" "You gave it to me, with your bad food; you're full of them, I told you to change your diet but you refuse to listen, I won't tell you again," etc. At the Café de Flore, where Léon Daudet[1]—I think that's who it was—was sitting, I finally got mad.

"Look," she said, "it's all right, I'm in the wrong. But why do you insist on pointing it out to me? It ties me up in knots to admit I'm wrong." We went back by cab, and then came the obligatory reconciliation in my room (the tiresome part is that, down to the minute, one can predict the reconciliation). Naturally she didn't sleep a wink, I slept four hours, and in the morning there was some quarrel or other. Out of weariness. Nobody felt like pursuing the argument to its end. I left her at 12:15, after letting her know that the week I was spending with her would be poisoned, that I had hoped for a certain flair. To which she replied, "It's as though you're doing something out of the ordinary, spending a week with me. But it's just something natural, and you should have done more of it during the year." Then she promised to be charming. And with that I went off to be with my family. Without a fuss. Around 8 I found Mouloudji[2] and Tania, radiant, they had talked it all

---

[1] Journalist, novelist, polemicist of the right in *L'Action Française* (1867–1942).

[2] A young French-North African, at the time acting in the play about Savonarola staged by Dullin, Salacrou's *La Terre est ronde* ["The Earth Is Round"]. After the war he became a popular singer.

out, there was nothing the matter, nothing at all, it was my fault in fact, and Mouloudji was a charming child. The charming child left (by the way, he eavesdrops at doors and peeps through keyholes) and Tania, now lively and lighthearted, came over to sit on my knees with dubious intentions. I'm always so suspicious of her demonstrations of affection. She mussed my hair and plied me with a thousand affectionate gestures, we left by Métro for La Coupole, she was charming, and then around midnight she gave out and I took her home by cab, where whe slept like a log till eight. In the morning (it was Monday) I took her by cab to Poupette's. I'm seeing her again today. That's when I sent you your money order. I looked in the phonebook for the Département, but there are six Bellegardes—Ain, Haute-Vienne, Basses-Alpes, etc.—and I know neither geography nor your itinerary. I took a chance and sent it to Bellegarde Basses-Alpes. Thereupon Tania wandered over to Demory's. And there occurred a most extraordinary conversation.

Alas, my dearest, I can't report the conversation to you now. It's late and she'll show up any minute.

My darling Beaver, I love you enormously. I'm spending a little time away from you—quite absurd and contingent. I would so like to see you, my stubborn little thing, and tell you my stories and hold your hand. You are my love, you good little being. Far from you I measure the nothingness of the flesh, and I'm not having much fun. Till Saturday, you, my little sweet, I send you a big kiss.

To Simone de Beauvoir

My darling Beaver

I saw you, so appealing, leaning against the railing at the station gate—did you see me?—then it was over, I was back in the bosom of the family. They're sweet and kind, but that doesn't matter, it's so oppressive. We went through Gien, streets decorated, their fair in full swing; it amused me a bit to think that five minutes later you would come upon the same acrobats, behind the same band, that delayed us for so long on the main street. And then after that it was all nature, an aqueous nature, green and spongy, full of those green plants that look as though they'd ooze milk if you squeezed them. I was gloomy in spite of myself. We reached Saint-Sauveur at five, and I put my suitcase in my mother's room; she immediately opened it only to find a woman's hat, feminine underthings, a little notebook of knitting instructions, etc. I'd taken some poor lady's suitcase and left my own in the train. I know just about how it happened. I put my bag on top of another as we started up, because the rack was filled. The woman must have needed something; she picked up my suitcase, then her own, then quite naturally she put her suitcase back on top of mine. Since my suitcase was brand-new and actually looked a lot like hers, I didn't notice the change. My stepfather was triumphant, my mother upset. In the long run it isn't too serious. There were heaps of books and my toilet articles, but not one line of my book, which is all in Paris. And in addition, the woman has my address (because there are piles of envelopes addressed to me in the suitcase) and she'll surely get in touch with me. I'll call Gien in a bit. Only I was left without a single book to read. We went for the evening walk, one of those ambles when the talk rambles too and you pay no attention to what you say, but just enough to prevent thinking about your own little affairs. We came back, still at a saunter, had dinner, then played bezique till ten. At ten I came to sleep here, in a gloomy inn. It's from here that I'm writing to you. A large common room, calendars and apéritif ads on the walls, tiled floor, oilcloth on the tables, but it doesn't add up to anything very appealing. The effect is waiting room. Last night I finally found the sole curiosity of the place: a chamber pot, which I contemplated at length, that actually has a grinning eye on the bottom. I read a piece in *La Petite Illustration* and I slept. I had myself woken up at 7 this morning to linger over my only hours of independence, and finally got up at eight-fifteen. There you are, my darling Beaver. When I remember that I'm stuck here till Tuesday, I cringe. I *know* that you love me and that I'm happy, but it does me no good, except perhaps to make my presence here seem more absurd. I love you dearly, you darling creature, I thought of you all day yesterday, imagining you running around Gien, but you would have found it dull (there's an idiot here, she's sixteen, the owner's daughter, she goes, "Beuh, beuh!"). My dear one, I'd be so happy to be with you at this very moment: it's mild out and beautiful, it must be so nice to walk around Paris. Well, at least there's one day down. But they're so hard to kill, so tough.

Farewell, my darling Beaver, I do so love you, I yearn so to be near you. Write me often. Love.

> Sartre
> General delivery
> Saint-Sauveur (en Puisaye)
> Yonne

To Simone de Beauvoir

Tuesday [July]

My darling Beaver

This is just a brief note to tell you that I love you with all my might and that you're my little sweet. I received your good letter, and I'm sad to be away from you, my flower. I'm a bit less gloomy today because I'm working, and also we've gotten out some. Yesterday afternoon we took an excursion to Auxerre, about which there is nothing to say, except that it filled the day. This morning I worked, right now we are going to the Émerys' for lunch, it will be torture, but basically no worse than a lunch with the family. After which we'll go to send off the young woman's suitcase. Digging through her things, we discovered her address in Saint-Étienne. The saddest part is that I have no books. I await the NRF as if it were the Messiah.

Farewell, my darling Beaver, my little flower. I think so intently about you, every day, nothing but you, and I would so like to be near you.

To Simone de Beauvoir

[July]

My darling Beaver

I forgot to ask you in this morning's letter if you would kindly telephone the Lycée Pasteur for me to find out the exact time and place when the prizes are to be given out.

Farewell, I love you very much.

To Simone de Beauvoir

Wednesday [July]

My darling Beaver

Here's my daily letter (but you, naughty girl, you aren't writing to me every day: there was nothing from you this morning). There's not much to say, except that I'm bored to tears. Put more precisely: I'm being flayed alive with boredom. I've never seen the likes of it, and in Saint-Étienne's apogee. Just imagine: from 12 noon to 10 at night with neither let-up nor relief: family. We take short walks along the banks of a pond, we play bezique in the evening and then go out again for a short turn around the village. My stepfather gets nervous when my mother drives, etc., etc. What can I say? It's deadly. Yesterday evening we went to see Colette Willy's house, a beautiful large house on a rise, with a double flight of steps at the entrance and masses of windows. At the end of the street there's an ivy-covered wall, and above it the château terrace with the ruins of a castle keep. It's not bad. And across from our house on the little square is the school from *Claudine à l'école* (*Claudine at School*)[1] precisely as it was, with precisely the same little girls taking the same secondary school courses, we see them after dinner, lined up, when they go on their little walk as far as Moutiers (1.4 km). We don't go all the way to Moutiers, not us. They are ruddy, glowing peasant girls, with glasses, most of them, as a sign of intellectuality. The place is overrunning with anecdotes about Colette. Did you know—did I tell you?—that Sido, Colette's famous mother, poisoned her husband so as to marry M. Colette, a handsome local heartbreaker? Here are the facts. The husband liked to drink, but drink was forbidden him because he had cirrhosis of the liver. M. Colette appeared on the scene, and from that day on, Sido's husband found within reach, placed everywhere by devoted hands, flasks of eau-de-vie and white brandy, bottles of good Burgundy, glasses of absinthe. He died happy, and Sido married M. Colette.

Yesterday we went to the Émerys' for lunch. The fare was fine, but spirits sagged. We stayed till 3 in a beautiful terraced garden under a parasol. After that we wandered by car along a pond. Afterward, the few hours of agitated torpor that I've seen nowhere but here. After that, dinner, walk around the village, step by tiny step, and bezique. To top off the bad luck, I have asthma. Still it's Wednesday, moving along. Tomorrow, Thursday, I'll be halfway through my stay. I'm working. Without a doubt I'll have finished the chapter at the Sumatra[2] and begun another chapter. But it seems like stubborn folly to work here. Everything seems dismal and meaningless, and a person can't really see a reason to do anything but toddle around or play bezique. I love you so, my darling Beaver, I so long to see you again, and have some fun with you. You don't seem at all abstract to me. I feel you very close and think with joy I'll see you soon. But it is pure time that separates

---

[1] By Sidonie-Gabrielle Colette, later called simply Colette (1873–1954); this romanticized version of her schooling was published in 1900 under her early pseudonym, "Willy." *La Maison de Claudine* (*Claudine's House*) (1922), another evocation of her childhood, opens on a description of this same house.

[2] The bar in *The Age of Reason* favored by the young student Boris, his sister Ivich (based on Tania), Mathieu, and the cabaret singer Lola.

me from you, time swallowed like individual spoonfuls of cod liver oil, with the feeling that everything will be disgorged all at once.

Do write to me, and often. Your letters are my only pleasure. I love you so.

To Louise Védrine[1]

[July]

My dear little Polack, my love

All day Sunday I was thinking about you being in pain—and by Monday I already thought you'd be feeling a little better. Right now I'm imagining you still flat on your back, so pale, with your lovely hair framing your face. But I imagine that your poor little eyelids aren't fluttering anymore, that you aren't suffering any longer, poor little martyr. I'm really relieved; a whole stretch of my horizon was clotted up with real pain, made worse because I myself couldn't feel it. And now it's over. I imagine the good Beaver sees you every day and you aren't too bored. I would so like to see you, my love, to sit down beside your bed and hold your little hot hand and see one of your gentle smiles. All that will come soon. Next Wednesday. I love you. The Beaver will tell you that I'm not having fun every day but working a bit; I'll bring you the end of the chapter on the Sumatra. I would really like to know what you think of my novel. Dictate a note to the Beaver.

Goodbye, my love, till Wednesday. In the meantime the good Beaver will convey a heap of little messages from me. I love you with all my might.

To Louise Védrine

[July]

My love

Your first little letter arrived inside one from the Beaver. I was really moved to see your poor shaky handwriting, so like one of your wan smiles last Sunday; it tugged my heart strings. I love you so, my love, poor little martyr. Then this morning I received your second letter, and that hurt, too, because I sense that you're so unhappy, with your "little head dealing with

---

[1] *A friend of mine with whom Sartre started a liaison, soon broken off by the war.* (SdB) A pseudonym, used in the French edition of these letters, for Bianca Bienenfeld.

things that are interesting and unpleasant and have to do with love." You know, that seems to me a bit like those long sequences of reasons one has in nightmares; I can so well imagine all the mechanisms and gears churning away behind that pale face. My love, how I long to be near you to stop them for a while. Besides, I know how tragic we feel when we're flat on our backs, the moment we are a thing with no prospects beyond those of other people, entirely dependent. My love, I don't quite know what to tell you about the Beaver's departure. But there is one thing I do know well, in any case, that *our* future is *your* future; there is no difference—and that the Beaver lives in a world in which you are everywhere and always present. As for her departure, I can also imagine so well how empty Paris can seem for her, and how impatient she can be to see the country for a while. You know that around the month of June a terrible, imperious need to see green overcomes her. Personally, I don't really understand it, but I accept it. It's a need as violent as the need to eat when she's hungry. She gets restless, she doesn't sleep, she becomes obsessive and rather sinister. And if you weren't ever so slightly sad, I'd think she had every reason to leave and would feel quite comfortable about it. But above all, my love, don't take what she's done as lack of affection. I know, more than you can, how much the Beaver loves you. I say "more than you can" because there are certain things you don't see. You forge ahead with your great generosity, without wondering about others, and when you do wonder, it's during slightly withering setbacks. My love, you must be happy. I would so love you to be radiant always. I love you.

I love you with all my heart, you know. I want to be sitting next to you, beside your bed, stroking your hair. I'm bored out of my wits here, days on end, I'm going to pieces from boredom. I now know pure time, with nothing in it. I think of you all the time, I'm healing along with you, every hour I imagine your strength increasing. I almost never leave you. You won't see me Tuesday, because I'm taking the 6-o'clock bus that gets me to Paris at 10 at night, but you will right off *Wednesday morning* and from then on every day as long as your mother allows. I love you, I need you. I'm so pleased to think that you are your old self again. Goodbye, little charmer. Do write to me. Have you read my novel? What do you think of it? I kiss you with all might, I love you passionately.

P.S. You're right, you know, we must always tell each other everything, and right away. I can't see any harm in that. (?)

To Louise Védrine

[July]

My love
      Yesterday you promised I'd have a letter, but there was nothing from
you this morning. That bothers me, because I want to know how you are.
After lunch I'll drop by the post office again. Since yesterday I've been totally
enervated, because I'm thinking of you as miserable and sad, it's so gloomy
to think of you flat on your back in your bed, unable to budge but your mind
whirling, whirling every which way all at once. My love, I so wish you could
at least feel how I love you, how passionately attached to you I am. Please
tell yourself that my every moment not working or talking with my parents
was spent thinking of you. I have never left you. From the beginning to the
end of this visit, there was Paris like an enormous void at the far edge of the
village, and you in Paris, and a violent suffering within you. How much I
preferred when it was a suffering in your little bruised body. I'm so unhappy
now to think you're so upset. My love, my little passion, can you feel from
afar how much I love you, at this moment as I write to you? Listen: about
the Beaver, I won't say anything now, because I'm not there, I don't really
know what both of you said and thought, and I didn't get a letter from her
this morning either, because her letters have to go through Paris first and are
only then sent on this way. I want to see her and see you. But what I want
to stress is that the Beaver loves you as much as you could wish. If I understand
it correctly, you had the beginnings of an argument, which your mother
interrupted (the Beaver told me that in a scribbled pencil note, but I don't
know the details; I know she was unhappy not to have been able to explain
it thoroughly to you). So I beg you not to torture yourself and to await our
return, both of us. Can't you trust in that? You know how you always say
that Simone is perfect. Well, this the moment to believe it and to wait. I
think that I, for one, would not have left. But I feel that doesn't prove a
thing, because I'm not Simone. Today is Saturday, my love. You'll see
Simone on Monday, so wait two days, just two days, and you'll be able to
air things out. And if you're slightly hurt in your love for Simone, think
anyway meanwhile that I love you passionately. Remember you are my dear
little Polack, my little purity, and that I do not want you to suffer.
      Goodbye, I'm off to family lunch. Tomorrow I'll tell you what I've
been doing here, though it's not a whole lot of fun.
      With all my love.

To Louise Védrine

My love

I'm furious, it's Sunday and the post office is closed. But the mailman, who has just stopped by my parents', tells me there are five letters for me. Surely there will be at least two from you, since I didn't get any yesterday. As they are stuck in General Delivery, he claims he can't give them to me. It's idiotic—if I had simply put J.-P. Sartre, c/o M. Mancy, Saint-Sauveur, they'd have brought them here to me at the house. Now it's too late. We'll know that the next time, but I hope there won't be a next time for a good long while. I'm a bit anxious about you. I'd like to hear your news. Tonight at six I know there's an employee at the post office, and I'll cajole him as I put this letter in the box. I'm bored out of my wits being away from you, it's just too much. In the newspapers I saw that the Lycée Saint-Louis award ceremony was yesterday. If I'd known, I'd have said that mine in Neuilly was taking place tomorrow, Monday. Anyway, it seems it will go down on my record, not in heaven but here on earth, in my relationship with my stepfather. But it's hard, I'm haunted by your pale little face with your lovely dolorous eyes, the remorse is painful, though I have nothing to reproach myself for regarding you, I swear, except being away from you while you're miserable. This morning as I was waking up it seemed to me you were here and you were holding my hand, and I thought, "Yes, yes, it's Louise, she's come to see me because I've been operated on for a polyp." And then you weren't there; my heart was so heavy when I opened my eyes because the room was empty. My love, I love you passionately, I so want you to be happy.

I'm bored here to the point of sentimentality. I mean, the other day, as I was reading a mawkish scene in a lousy piece in *L'Illustration*, tears actually came to my eyes. I was totally surprised, but I think that I'm both reticent and stubborn here, and full of silly mawkishness, which is the other side of things. What am I doing? Well, till noon I wander from café to café (there is one called the Canary, which is at once jaunty and strictly village— that describes it). I drink black coffee with dead flies floating in it and write my novel. I'll bring you seventeen pages, which will finish the chapter about the dance hall. It is there that I write to you and to the Beaver. At noon I put in my appearance, and that lasts till 10:30 at night. It is deadly, because my stepfather is sick and edgy, I talk when I can't avoid it, most of the time I emit distracted little remarks, courteous and complicitous, in which I repeat the last words of my stepfather's sentence. Example (recent):

My stepfather, at the window: "Well now, who's that stopping there?"
Me: "Who's that stopping there?"
My mother: "Is it the Émerys?"
My stepfather: "No, it's some people who've stopped to consult a map."
Me: "Oh! A map?"
That's it. My mother asks me every five minutes: "You're happy here,
Poulou?" "Yes, Mother." "Hmm? Not feeling well?" (Searching look.) Me:
"No, I'm fine, Mother." Then a vigorous and decisive thrust of the chin, an
optimistic look: "Anyway, it does you good, it's healthy." What do we do?
We have lunch. Then, at 1 o'clock, it's newspaper time, because at 1 the
bus brings the papers from Paris. I leap off to get *L'Oeuvre* and *Le Matin*,
because that means three and a half minutes of solitude. I bring them back
and we read them. At three o'clock we get in the car and doggedly go off in
search of a pond ten kilometers from here which we never find. I pick foxglove
for my mother; we sit down on the grass. We get up, we come back. Around
six o'clock, we walk to the village: to watch the planting of "the liberty tree,"
to buy some salad greens from the plasterer's wife, "to see Colette's house"
(but it scarcely changes from one time to the next. Although this morning I
did notice a small round marble plaque: "Colette was born here"). We go
along "the station road." Then we have dinner, for five minutes we stay out
on the wicker chairs in the garden, and then another walk along "the station
road" "to Colette's house," etc. We come back home and play Chinese
bezique till ten-thirty. At that point I go to bed thinking that I've already
made it to tomorrow, one more day done with. The terrible part, as the
Beaver must have told you, is that I lost my suitcase (I switched it by mistake
for some woman's). So I have nothing to read, except for a few back issues
of *L'Illustration* that I've already read five times. Inside, I feel mummified,
and, obsessive, I try to catch my parents in mistakes, as if I were constantly
thinking, "I can take affability just this far and no further." That seems
Protestant and contrary, which disgusts me, but I can't help myself; I mean
that if I felt that the sight of me gave them pleasure, I would be sugar and
honey inside and out. But if they do feel any pleasure, I swear they hide it
completely. They're surly, or rather my stepfather is surly and my mother is
enslaved to someone surly, so I feel I'm boring myself for nothing. So I drown
in gloom and then, abruptly, I wake up, I tell myself, "While I'm at it—"
and I turn nice and attentive by fits and starts, which would surprise some
but not them, for the secret of the whole thing is that my stepfather doesn't
give a damn about what goes on in my head: he's bored here, he feels that
my mother forced his hand in making him rent this house, and he wants me
to be bored too. As for my mother, she derives no pleasure from seeing me

with my stepfather, but she wants me here because he wants me here. Anyway, the day after tomorrow it's all over, and on Wednesday I will see you. I'll figure out some way to get there at 7 Tuesday evening. And even that's not certain. In any case I couldn't see you. But Wednesday morning I'll arrive with the dawn. My love, I love you so. I think the best is that I see you in the morning and the Beaver see you in the evening; that way you'll have two visits instead of one, and then we'll each see you for a while alone, I long to see you alone. I love you passionately, little virtue, dear little Louise. I'll write to you again tomorrow.

I love you with all my heart.

To Simone de Beauvoir

[July]

My darling Beaver

Just a word or two to say hello. I have nothing to tell you, since here it's pure time, still. Tuesday, then Wednesday, then Thursday. Today is Thursday and I persuaded myself "fallaciously" that it was the exact halfway point of my stay. Fallaciously since I still have five whole days before getting the hell out. The thing is, I'm working. I'll have finished the chapter on the Sumatra by the time I get back and begun the conversation with Brunet.[1] Yesterday the weather was bad. My parents dozed all day in their chairs and I wrote. Oh, wicked girl, I really could use the *NRF*. How can you have no pity on me who has *nothing* to read? Fortunately yesterday was Wednesday and I read *Marianne* and *Candide*. But today is a black hole. This evening we're entertaining Mme Émery, and we'll play *bridge*. Can you imagine?

I want so much to see you, my sweet, I need you. I too love you in a slightly tragic fashion. As for what you tell me about cash, never mind. But I'm sure you didn't owe 2,400. About the rest, we'll find a way. So let's go to the Pyrenees and Portugal, they'll be less expensive.

I love you very much, my darling little Beaver.

---

[1]In *The Age of Reason*, an orthodox Communist friend of Mathieu's, loosely based on Nizan.

To Simone de Beauvoir

[July]

My darling Beaver

Just a quick note, because we're about to go on an outing with Mme Émery—we're going to Sancerre. It annoys the hell out of me, because if the old girl's beside me in the backseat, I won't be able to smoke my pipe.

This morning I received your penciled note, and it certainly pained me to feel you disenchanted like that. By the time you get this, my dearest, we'll be very close to seeing one another again. I love you so much, my dearest, so much, so much. I am so happy when I'm with you, I long to spend the days in Paris with you, we'll see a lot of one another, we won't part. I love you.

Adieu, my darling Beaver, my mother is after me to finish this. I'll write more tomorrow. The NRF arrived and I read it. What Clara Malraux said is a riot, and the story of *Seduction* isn't bad either. But I've done nothing else this morning, because, for lack of a place to go, I was stupid enough to come to my family thinking I could work. I was instantly recruited to wash the car. I did; it's not a bore but it is a waste of time.

Farewell, I love you very much.

To Simone de Beauvoir

[July]

My darling Beaver

When it comes to you, my little darling, everything is idyllic. I got both your letters at the same time. You've finally read Heidegger,[1] it's worth your while and we'll talk about it. The day after tomorrow I'll see you, my love. I can't sit still. I have little stirrings of hope now (I was logy and drowsing) but I'm also more nervous. Now I can tell you that prospects weren't at all rosy these past days. When I arrived, there was fear of war for *the following day* (there was an aborted coup in Danzig, the papers are now calling it the July 2 coup), and I was petrified that war would erupt while I was still at Saint-Sauveur. Do you realize what that means? And then later, on Tuesday,

---

[1]This remark was in oblique response to Beauvoir's statement that, visiting Bost in Amiens where he was doing his military service, she read Heidegger to fill a frustrating wait for him to get off duty (Simone de Beauvoir, *Lettres à Sartre*, Vol. 1 [Paris, 1990], p.77).

things calmed down. But then on Wednesday I got a letter from Tania that annoyed me, pure delirium of passion on my part. And then I calmed down. I'm so nervous and out of sorts here that yesterday, while reading an idiotic and sentimental scene from a piece in *L'Illustration*, suddenly I was teary-eyed. With no thought or qualms on my part but due, I think, to the strangely larval, overagitated state in which I find myself. But it's over. On the other hand, I think I've done some excellent work. You'll be the judge of that.

I love you with all my heart, my little one. You are my haven, and I need you.

I send you all my love.

To Simone de Beauvoir

[July]

My darling Beaver

According to your letters and my calculations, this is the state of our finances for August and September: I am paid 4,000 on July 12. You 3,000 on August 1st. The two of us 7,000 September 1st, makes 14,000. *But*: I need 3,000 for my trip with Tania and you need around 1,800. Gégé wants 1,200 and undoubtedly Poupette 700. Cost for the 2nd half of July: 6,600. So it behooves us to negotiate a loan of 3,000 francs repayable September 1st. That will leave 3,000 for August 4,000 for September. Which should about do it, because 1, at the Lady's we'll spend only 100 francs a day or even less, we'll tell her so right away; 2, from September 1st to the 20th that makes (for the 4,000 total) 200 francs a day—and after the 20th, there must still be 1,000 to come from the NRF (I hope more)—. But that *absolutely* prevents our leaving France. Since I don't want you to be deprived, here's what I propose: when we leave the Lady's, a fifteen-day trip *on foot*, which would take us back to Les Causses, l'Aigoual, Cordes, Albi. Following that a trip by bus* in the Pyrenees, from Foix to Pau. Does that sound good to you? You can think it over between now and tomorrow evening. Don't be morose, my dearest, I'll walk as much as you want, I'll be a completely open and attentive boy. Incidentally, I'll suggest to Tania that we stay in Paris. We will spend 200 francs a day and that would make a 1,000-franc saving. Except if she refuses, I'm bound to go on the trip.

There you have it. The whole thing is somewhat sobering this morning,

---

*by that I mean: going partway by bus.

it sets up barriers on the horizon. But it would be impossible to love you more than I do, and, mired as I am in my worries here, I'm tremendously happy to be seeing you again, dear little thing, for I love you very much.

N.B.: I won't be writing again. Meet me at the cafeteria in the Gare de Lyon at 7 o'clock (the cafeteria that's also an exit and leads directly onto the sidewalk—*not the one* where we stopped for coffee that last Sunday while waiting for the train to Saint-Sauveur). If by chance (with my parents one never knows. They are to drive me to Gien, but Lord knows what can happen at the last minute) I should miss the train, meet me *at your place* at 10:30 or 11 o'clock. If that happens, I'll send a telegram. Meanwhile, kisses.

To Simone de Beauvoir

Monday [late July]

My darling Beaver

I'll be leaving soon, at 1 o'clock. I'm writing while Tania's getting dressed. It's 10:30. I was about to commit the monumental stupidity of going to pick up my bag at the Gare de Lyon, whence I would have brought it here, when I realized the economy of simply getting it five minutes before leaving. So I came here and am writing to you. I haven't left your side. My "personal obsession" isn't unpleasant, but it's on the insipid side. Up to yesterday—Sunday—we argued for 3 hours, and since then it's been the flattest of flat calms, with lilting barcarolles. Yesterday afternoon I took her to the Weber (the bar), which she liked a lot, and then from there I went to see Monnier,[1] who entertained me from a chaise longue and told me a hundred malicious stories about everybody. You should know, though I fear it won't amuse you that much, that the beautiful Vittoria Ocampo[2] carried off Roger Caillois.[3] So now they've actually gone off to Argentina, the two of them. You should also know that Denis de Rougemont, since he has extolled the mad virtue of fidelity in *L'Amour et l'Occident* [*Love in the Western World*], is exposed to all the temptations and seductions of the reigning queens of high society. He does the best he can: "I want to go and see my son," his wife said to him in front of Monnier. "Can I leave you alone for three days?" "Oh, three whole days, no! No, it wouldn't be wise."

---

[1]Adrienne Monnier owned a bookshop and lending library in Paris.
[2]Latin American intellectual who founded the literary magazine *Sur*.
[3]A writer, teacher at the Ecole Normale Supérieure.

The women showed me Gisèle Freund's most recent photos, notably one of Virginia Woolf that I found extremely interesting, a mixture of the angelic and the intellectual, with the good Anglo-Saxon mouth (stupid, naked good- ness) and some indefinable old woman's harshness beneath so much gentle- ness. And an air of having suffered from everything—but then all rethought. Long, frail face, altogether a thinking reed for Britain. G. Freund told me that wherever she has shown it (in London or at J. Cain's place, opposite Colette), my photograph (the beautiful one you haven't seen) caused a sen- sation. I say this without having it go to my head, since it's all in the lighting. At 7:40 I met Tania at the Danton, mad with fury and fatigue, I took her home, she slept a bit while I did a crossword puzzle, and then we went, on foot and by bus, to the Rue Mouffetard and Demory's.

Farewell, this is just a bit of a letter, I'll write more and better tomorrow. I love you and am totally with you, my dear girl; I'm living an oddly absurd time here.

To Simone de Beauvoir

[Late July]

My darling Beaver

Here I am at Aigues-Mortes after one rather pleasant day traveling (Monday), and one hellish day (Tuesday). We had our bouts of nerves; we were tired, as you can imagine. I had to exert great pains to keep a completely straight face and attentive consideration when it was explained to me, in tones of aesthetic reflection and a grasp of essences, that Avignon was "infernal and tragic" and that the Fort Saint-André at Villeneuve-lès-Avignon was "ominous and hallucinatory." Apart from that, one hour of quarreling, from 9 to 10 in the morning—four hours of quarreling from 4 to 8, two hours from 10 to midnight. Will it surprise you to hear, nonetheless, that she[1] is much nicer all in all than I was expecting! This morning, for the first time, I slept with her. The result was that I left her on her bed, all pure and tragic, declaring herself tired and having hated me for a good 45 minutes. But it is totally unimportant, it is a groundless hatred, since basically she is more or less grateful to me for an initiation that, in her eyes, will have the effect of putting her in circulation. By which I mean that since one of her fondest recurring aspirations is to become a prostitute, she had hitherto been slightly frustrated

---

[1]Tania.

due to the fact that prostitutes, according to conventional wisdom, aren't virgins. Now, there is nothing further to stand in the way of daring late-night pursuits of enticement and blackmail and skillful, artful domination, of weird adventures, etc. As for me, I've been clever enough to indicate that I'm offended by the ridiculous situation that falls to the guy in a devirginization, and from time to time I find myself about to say, with feeling, that I must love her as I do, having lent myself to the sordid task.

Last night, at a moment when things were going well between us, she did all she could to make me say that I wouldn't repeat to you, if the occasion should arise, what she was about to tell me about Olga. (You know that I had told her I would tell you everything.) I managed to look disconcerted and finally swore: If you gain by it, I'll gain too. I believe she has undertaken to gradually tear down the "friendship" I bear for you. It's rather amusing.

What can I tell you? I'm having the greatest difficulty balancing my budget because the trains are much more expensive than we'd anticipated, as you, incidentally, must have noticed. So we scarcely eat: I haven't set foot in a restaurant since we left. We're living on fruit and sandwiches and yet, including the buses, it will still cost almost 160 francs a day. We sleep in the same room, still for reasons of economy, and that entails hateful squabbles because she needs 45 minutes in the evening to get ready for bed. I have to stay outside, but in Avignon and yesterday in Aigues-Mortes, we were staying in small early-hours hotels that closed at 11. We would come back late and I wouldn't dare wake them up twice, so I'd go in with her. I would wander around the dark halls of the hotels waiting for her to open the door, trailed by the night watchman who would cry out (in Aigues-Mortes), "Who's there?" Twice this vagabondage ended in the john, the only place where my presence wouldn't look suspicious, and there I read Nietzsche for 15 minutes facing a Turkish-style toilet. So that's it. We won't go to either Arles or Les Baux. In a while we're going to see Le Grau-du-Roi, and after that we'll go back up to Nîmes and reach Marseilles by evening.

And you, little one about whom I know not one thing, what on earth are you doing? I'm so eager to be in Marseilles and to find your letters there, I love you so. I have lots of leisure time, I swear, to think about our vacation, our little trip to Portugal. My darling Beaver, little perfection, I love you with all my heart.

Farewell, my little dearest. I'm so eager for your news that I'd even lap up descriptions of walking trips through the great outdoors.

To Simone de Beauvoir

[Late July]

My darling Beaver

I received your two delightful letters, which I read without skipping a single one of the descriptions (which are very spare, incidentally), and I was very moved by your small compliments. Dear God, how nice you are, my Beaver. You fill me with regrets and longings, and yesterday I was completely morose not to be with you. Who wanted this? you will ask. I did, probably, but without you it's like Paradise Lost. I love you.

For now I'm relentlessly devoting myself to my personal life (we said it better, I think: personal doggedness), but personal life doesn't pay. To tell the truth, Tania is almost always charming and affectionate, and it is very nice sleeping with her, which happens to me morning and evening, for the moment. She seems to get pleasure out of it, but it kills her, she lies on her bed dead to the world for more than 15 minutes after her revels. The thing is, it takes the violence of arguments or the touching quality of reconciliations for me to feel alive. Last night we had a terrific argument, but it was worth the effort. We were talking about fidelity, and the tone had gradually risen. She finished by saying, "I cannot understand how you could have had an affair with M.B. if you cared for me." "But I didn't care for you anymore just then; I was excluded." "Nonsense! Sounds like a guy playing for sympathy." We were near the cathedral of Marseilles, sitting on the stone parapet of a sloping, poorly lit street (it might have been eleven at night). A wave of anger comes over me—and, as with so many others, I can't remember whether it was fake or sincere (a snake biting its own tail). I jump down off the low wall: "Idiot!" I say. She sneers, and I stalk off saying, "Come on, let's go!" All of this in a tone of darkest violence. I go a hundred paces in the direction of the Vieux-Port and realize she isn't following me. I turn around and see her in front of me, walking away. I call her, and she stops beneath a streetlamp. I say to her through clenched teeth, "What's gotten into you? Now you don't even follow when I say 'Come on!' " She, sneering: "Well now, would you listen to that! Giving me orders! And in such a tone of voice! You're going crazy." There follows a long and hateful staring match, which goes deep into our eyes, then I: "You're nothing but a whore." And she: "And you're a dirty bastard." I: "I'm sick of the sight of you. Here's 500 francs. Get on the train." I take the money out of the wallet and throw it on the ground at her feet. She: "I don't need your money, it horrifies me and you disgust me, I'll manage without you." Me—anxious because she didn't have a sou: "If you don't take that money, I'll smack you!" She takes a step, closes her eyes, and collapses. I catch her in my arms and thereupon: "My dear little Tania . . . " "My Sartre," etc. but the anger had been so strong that I suddenly went totally blank, which kept her terrified for an hour. It seems I had the sinister and vacant look of a congenital cretin, and there was nothing but fog in my head. Upon which we went back to the hotel. I waited in the john as usual while she washed and got undressed. I went back and lay down beside her: "Good night," she said, moving toward me. "Good night." "How're you feeling?" "I'm not angry at you, I'm simply all played out." "Oh! I knew it had to end, our affair is over, I'm leaving tomorrow for Laigle," etc. "No—now I'm not played out anymore." "Yes you are, you're always played out." "No." "Yes." Whereupon we made love, then went to sleep. Today all was bliss from morning till seven this evening (as I write to you). There were a few slightly dull moments, notably at Le Cintra from five to seven, where she was asleep on her feet, because we go to sleep at three in the morning and she wakes up—and wakes me up—at seven. In addition, we're a bit in a daze, as we eat only one meal a day. In those vague and mortal moments I talk to her about Michel Leiris. The guy's book[1] is fascinating, you'll have to read it so we can discuss it. I'll finish this letter quickly, because I'm afraid she'll show up. Herewith a few details to amuse you. We're staying on the street by the station, the first hotel on the right as you come down the stairs. A shabby little hotel, but we were bored with the idea of looking for something else. We're on the fourth floor on the street side, where a hellish racket reigns all night. I get up around ten—Tania has already taken a little tour around the port and its fruit market, totally naked under her coat; she wakes me up. Generally we make love once, then I quickly wash and I'm at Le Café Riche or La Taverne Charley around eleven after a clandestine trip to the post office to pick up your letters. She shows up around noon and we go for a walk down La Grand-Rue and neighboring streets. Today we went to Le Château d'If. Then Cintra from five to seven. Then she spends an hour in her room resting. I wait for her till eight, then we go for dinner at Charley's, then sit on planks by the Vieux-Port watching the lights. We won't go to either Aix or Martigues.

Adieu, my darling Beaver, she has just arrived and I am finishing right in front of her. You know my feelings, but I don't dare write them, because it's not that difficult to read upside down.

---

[1]*L'Âge d'homme [Manhood]. (SdB)* Michel Leiris (b. 1901), novelist, memoirist, ethnologist. This book was probably "as great an influence as any" upon Beauvoir's memoirs, according to her own testimony (Deirdre Bair, *Simone de Beauvoir* [New York, 1990], p. 284).

To Simone de Beauvoir

My darling Beaver

Do you recognize this little bar? I feel very emotional, recalling that we dined here, the two of us. That time I ordered ragout of cod. Incidentally, all of Marseilles is full of you, and it makes me very happy to find you here. It will help to cleanse it of this strangely unbecoming otherworldly atmosphere. I love you very much. Your two little letters arrived at the same time, the sad one and the serene. I want you to know that I quickly tore them up (I've torn them all up, even those you wanted me to keep—it's impossible to hold on to them: we share the room and Tania wanders around every morning while I'm still asleep). I regret rather a bit not seeing you every day at Juan-les-Pins. As Sorokine[1] would say, I have a faint need for you, and you know, though I may need to have my ear tweaked and might drag my feet on vacations, for me it's a powerful and pleasant time, because I'm with you, little one, all day long. But as you know it will be only eight days, and I think it will be a delightful time for you, and as you also know, it won't be subtracted from our solitude together but from our high life at the château. What I think, however, is that we should definitely stay at Juan till the 20th. I believe the Lady is really counting on our visit, and it would be rather cavalier for you to say at the last minute: I have my own plans, I can only come for two days. But since, basically, you already foresaw that possibility, it shouldn't annoy you overmuch. Besides, I'll already have done a good bit of work, and I'll be with you the whole time, and we'll carve out our own little private sessions. There you are, I think you should consider it as something pleasant that's happening to you, and you're a little silly to have blown it all out of proportion.

So. Here Tania is transformed, all is perfect love, gazing into one another's eyes, holding hands. She's really charming and even touching, but I don't know why it bothers me so terribly.

Adieu, my love. I love you with all my might.

---

[1] A former student, whom I call Lise in my memoirs. (SdB)

To Louise Védrine

August 4

My dear little flame

I was so counting on a letter from you this morning, August 4, and General Delivery had only a note from you to the Beaver. But I am sure that you have written to me, I have such confidence in you. I simply imagine the letter must be lost or they couldn't find it at the post office. But I'm left with a feeling of great emptiness, because ever since my last glimpse of your little hand waving at the window of the bus, I've had nothing more from you—only memories. I love you passionately. So, you know the good Beaver was right there waiting at the station, and on the dot of 5:25—as you would have been yourself—so dark, her nose and arms peeling from sunburn and awful raw skin on her neck, charming little monster, all tanned and healthy, it gave me a pang of joy to see her, because, as I told you, I had done a lot of worrying. She had on her pretty little pink and blue dress, she grabbed my arm, I checked my bag in the luggage room, and off we went for a walk. And what a lot there was to tell. You know, we never once stopped talking all day, and I did most of it. The Beaver wanted to know all about my stay at La Clusaz, how you were, etc. You know, it happened just as I predicted: at some moment during the day when you were thinking of us, we were thinking of you, we were talking about you. We strolled around the town, which was just waking up, Canebière, old streets, then we went by the post office, where I found a wire from young Bost. They were making him take his leave on August 3rd, Zazoulich of course told him she couldn't leave Laigle because they were taking care of her nose; he asked, afraid of spending a gloomy week—alone in Paris, without money—could he come to Marseilles. I telegraphed: "Come on down." After that we wandered all over; every five minutes I would reflect that the Beaver was not on some precipice in the Basses-Alpes, but really and truly there, at my elbow, and I was overjoyed. We took a room in a hotel on the Vieux-Port, a pretty little room, slightly fussy, with a superb view out over the quays and the water. It is beautiful, at night particularly, with great luminous puddles dancing against the window from the harbor water. Perhaps it affected me this way because I lack depth perception. Toward evening, you know, we had an immense philosophical conversation in which you were intimately involved. First I explained to the Beaver the new method I had used to tell you about my life, and, one thing leading to another, we argued about the value of psychoanalytical-Marxist-historical explanations of a guy's life and their relationship to freedom. Then, still talking away, we had dinner by the Vieux-Port, Beaver had a fish soup, and the beggars fell upon us like grasshoppers, we would hand out a few sous and keep on talking. I told her that Lévy[1] would say, "A person never knows what he's doing," and that you and I didn't share that opinion. But she brought me back to my senses, showing me that it was Lévy who was right. In broad terms, here it is: a person is thrown into the world, in a situation that's inherently irrational, for example the sexual situation with its links between sexual pleasure and childbearing, and whatever you do—abstention, abortion, or on the contrary childbearing—you can only conceal the irrationality of the situation for a moment, but not cancel it, because it defines your being-in-the-world. Thus even the guy who remains chaste all his life takes a position on this question of births—and a position just as irrational as the one that makes children or that imposes an abortion on a woman. And, looking within myself, I understood that this was what I should think, and we then agreed that we should dissuade you from your rationalism because you have the optimistic tendency to believe that it is possible to confront irrational objects with rational conduct, which can there-fore—without eliminating the irrationality of the object—purge you, sub-jectively, of all irrationality. Instead it is the being-in-the-world that is irrational, or in other words, an original connection between you and the object, from which issues concurrently your "you" and the object, and nothing can change that. So it's Lévy who is right, but we had supposed that he reached the correct view by pure logic (thinking something like this: to do X is irrational, *so not to* do it, being the opposite, is irrational too) instead of seeing the concrete. After that we went to sit beneath the plane trees at the Place de la Préfecture, on the terrace of a café named Le Pélican. It grew dark, a mild night without streetlights, darkness falling from the trees, we could hear people going on about their lives but we couldn't see them, it was cool, it was so poetic, and we talked about philosophic reality and we became existential and I looked at an illuminated ad on the opposite sidewalk, and I perceived it as existential. And then we went to bed, completely blissful, heads still full of words.

Yesterday morning we had breakfast across from Le Café Riche (the Riche is Marseilles' handsomest café), as though to sneak up on it. And then we moved over to Le Café Riche to read the papers (I was doing the reading; the Beaver only understands fashion sheets) and to write to you. But scarcely

---

[1]Raoul Lévy, a historian, former student of Sartre's at the Lycée Pasteur.

were we installed when what should appear but a lady, bubbling over, with two bespectacled brats: Mme Nizan. They were heading for Ajaccio as a family, had gotten off the train and were taking the boat at 3 o'clock. The Grand Duke (Nizan) shows up next, fresh as a daisy, not at all surprised to see us. We all had a drink. The conversation dragged somewhat, since Nizan, being very relaxed, didn't feel like making the effort. They always manage to look totally bored, but it's a ruse, because they're not. The proof is that around 11:45, he sounded us out: "Where are you having lunch?" with an evasive look—and we replying: "Nowhere in particular," in a waiting mode: "So, let's eat together." The two of us, suitably casual: "Why not?" Thereupon they led us off to buy a rubber boat for the children in a department store. Then we had lunch at La Rascasse on the quays—a good little restaurant. We were right outside in the street, the cars were grazing past us, and the beggars fell upon us like flies; the Nizan family quickly polished off a bouillabaisse. We plied them with questions about the people they know whom we find entertaining, Agnès Capri (you know, she runs a cabaret—I'll take you there next year), Marianne Oswald (the one I thought you resembled when you were "the little V." to me). But, looking off vaguely, they would answer, "Oh yes . . . well, we've forgotten. We *tu-toi* Agnès Capri, but we haven't kept up with her." Or else, "Marianne Oswald came to weep at our place till three in the morning, but we don't remember a thing she told us." The children, meanwhile, were unnaturally well-behaved. As we had spoken for a good hour the day before, the Beaver and I, about child rearing, we asked them how they did it. "Sometimes I beat them and sometimes I bribe them," said Nizan. And Mme Nizan said, "I cry and say, 'Look what you're doing to your mother.' " It's what you might call the "any means at hand" method. After that, we strolled along the quays with the children at our heels, and then a great devil came running after us: "There you are!" It was Bost. He'd been here since morning and set himself up at a brasserie, sure of finding us sometime or other. We went for a drink at Le Cintra, and then the Nizans left. We installed Bost in a handsome, sordid hotel on the quays. When he came out again, we went for a stroll. We saw a lively crowd around a drowned man (it was in the local papers this morning) and all sorts of scenes typical of Marseilles. Young Bost, just back from the Ardennes, was in a daze for lack of sleep. "What a racket," he'd say. And so there was. You know, we might even go to a bullfight if the Lady doesn't show up before Sunday. (We stop by General Delivery three times a day, but there's no word from her.) This evening, through an appalling stench, we climbed to the sixth floor of Bost's hotel, where there was a balcony. And there we stayed for a long time, watching Negroes arguing on a little square, watching the neon signs and their reflections on the water in the harbor, watching the rising moon. "How quickly it rises," Beaver said. And then, as young Bost was caving in to sleep, we bade him farewell and went home. He's a good companion, he has a great tan, and would you believe, my love, I've lost mine? Bost and the Beaver compete as to which one is tanner, and it would never occur to them to include me in the contest. "Yes, you are quite golden," the Beaver deigned to say to me. And she hastened to speak of my moral qualities to console me somewhat and change the subject.

There you are. We miss you so. You know, I'm sad not to have gotten the letter. I would so like to know about your return, how they treated you, whether you had much trouble: I love you so much. I think you can tell me about it in a few words in your next letter, because I've lost all hope of getting your last, it must be lost. My love, what a long time it is till September 25th. But you know, I haven't yet lost your face; on the contrary, it is clear as day, and I feel a little pang each time I see it again, beautiful little eyes, dear little mouth. I love you passionately.

To Louise Védrine

[August]

My love

I suppose this should be the day of the official letter, but I can't write it just like that, coldly, I love you much too much. It will be the next one, I promise. I got two little letters from you, so tender I want to answer them first. Soon, you will tell me, I'll receive others just as tender. That's true. But it seems to me I haven't told you forcefully enough how much I love you; from time to time it seems to me I didn't know how to make you feel it; it is when I am so sure of your love that I have only one desire, for mine to give you something strong and forceful, something present. You aren't here, but you were able to write me so appealingly that there's something right beside me, it is the way you love me. It is really a *thing* and a thing that is present, it has no face but is like a weight. I like my love to be weighty for you too, my little wonder, I love you so much, I value you so highly. It horrifies me a bit to think you've suffered from our separation and that you're still unhappy from it. I would give anything at all for that to end, and yet I'm happy you're that fond of me.

I'm writing to you from Le Cintra in Marseilles, and believe it or not,

Zuorro, in splendid form and sitting across from me, is writing to some young bewildered male souls. The Lady finally arrived. But let's take one thing at a time.

The day before yesterday the three of us went to Martigues in the rain, and Bost and the Beaver ate Pascal's celebrated bouillabaisse, beneath a veranda roof pelted by a steady rain; from there we could see the pond of Berre, totally gray, its dark mountains plumed in rain. Then the rain let up, and we strolled along the inlets; you could see clumps of little pink houses with green doors. The fishermen nail seahorses and starfish to the doors, and they look like strange little skeletons, dusty and crumbling. And everywhere there are black fishnets and boats on the calm inlets. And also wastelands surrounded by inlets; some guys were playing boules on the still-drenched ground, the balls rolled through puddles and spattered the spectators. After that, as the sun had slightly dried Martigues, we stretched out on huge stones along a dike, then skipped pebbles on the pond, Bost and I, while the Beaver watched us. Bost can skip them better than I. The poor good Beaver gripped a stone firmly in her hand, then threw it stiffly. The stone dutifully sank right to the bottom. Not unreasonably, the Beaver concluded she had no knack for such an undertaking. We went back by bus and were annoyed to discover there was no letter from the Lady. (No letter the next morning either. We sent telegrams all over the place: to La Pouèze and to Juan-les-Pins. We were a bit anxious, as our money was rapidly running out.) After which we took a long delightful walk around Marseilles, which was cool and violet from the afternoon downpour. We followed the Corniche, then climbed up one of those widely scattered large, colorless crags that give some parts of Marseilles the look of a chalky quarry. As evening fell, we found ourselves in a suburb, perched very high above the city, from which we could see the lights of the harbor between the houses. Suddenly we caught sight of an old movie house, small and very poetic, called L'Impérial. Two horror films were showing, the second one in color: *Calibre 9mm* and *Le Voilier maudit* ["9mm Caliber" and "The Cursed Ship"]. Never mind the color,[1] young Bost was dying to go in. So in we went. It had a charming interior that reminded me of the silent era, with seats that folded up with a snap when you got up to go. During the intermission women circulated with baskets full of ice cream cones. The two films were superb, they really put you through the wringer, they had murders, mobsters, madmen, natural phenomena (cyclones, etc.). After that, we went home, partway on foot, went to eat on La Canebière,

---

[1]Sartre hated color films.

which suddenly went out "like an eyelid closing" (Lucretius) and became a huge, gray, lifeless trench. Then off we went to bed.

Yesterday, nary a word from the Lady. But we nonetheless subtracted 75 francs from our poor nest egg to see a bullfight in the Prado Arena. Over breakfast, I explained to Bost at great length all the marvels of the corrida. But it turned out to be a bad show and made him queasy. "I was sure he'd be indignant, that Protestant," said Beaver. Bad bulls, bad matadors. I can hear you say that speaking of "bad" bulls is as shameful as talking about "lazy natives," since they actually demand nothing of us and it is we who seek them out. Agreed, and that's just what made Bost indignant. "You told me the bull played a part in the contest. But he's totally uninterested." And it is a fact that the ideal toro, with whom the torero "does as he pleases," is a sort of bull version of a military cadet: irascible, heroic, stupid, forever charging this way and that. But the ones they produced for us retreated at the first flash of a red rag, raking the dirt with their hooves and bellowing lamentably. There was even one they couldn't manage to kill: he just kept dodging. So they brought a calf with bells into the arena and the calf peacefully led the bleeding bull along behind him. The matadors made correct passes, but they killed badly. The beasts bled all they had, and it took four tries to kill them. The ineffectual sword stuck in the back of their necks was yanked out with a cane ("Why not use an umbrella?" said Bost, furious), and another was plunged in, and so forth, until they fell. And at that, the beasts still had to be polished off with a knife. The public was ugly: inept Marseillais, preoccupied solely with hiding their discomfort by nonstop jeering. Four seats away from us, a youth of twenty-five, terrified, felt faint. He left, ashen-faced, held up by his aged father. It bore no resemblance to the bullfights in Spain, yet it was fun for us because it reminded us of Spain. That evening we went to bed early, because we were dead tired, and this morning, when we went to the post office, we found a pile of telegrams: one from the Gentleman, one from Isorni, one from the Lady: "Arriving Monday 10 o'clock on the *Gueydon*." We bade Bost an emotional farewell; I think he had an extremely good several days of leave. Then we went to the docks by cab; we reached a pier, from which I saw boats coming into port, loaded down with people leaning over the railings waving handkerchiefs; it was delightful. And then, around 12:30, the *Gueydon* arrived and I saw people fluttering hankies, *for us*, this time, Zuorro, Mops, the Lady, and Boudy. We fell into each other's arms. The Lady immediately asked for news of you and was delighted to know you are your old self again. I'm writing to you while she washes. Zuorro, charming but somewhat pale (he was seasick the whole way), is writing across from me; we are leaving for Juan-les-Pins around 5 o'clock. Write to me there.

My love, I love you passionately. You know, I can still recall your little expression anytime I please, and there are even times when it comes without my bidding, and that always gives me the same little shock. It will be a long time before I forget it: it was the same I saw on you when you left me at Annecy, I think it's been imprinted on me. My love, I would so like to hold you in my arms. I see people and things, and I'm happy, yet it's odd but I can't help being impatient and counting the days.

Farewell, my little wonder, I kiss your two little eyelids.

I forgot to tell you: the Lady is furious about her stay in Cavallo. She had the mothers of both Zuorro and Guerrieri in her hair the whole time, and she couldn't even go camping. While she was helping Mmes Zuorro and Guerrieri with the cooking, the dishes, and the laundry, Zuorro, Guerrieri, and Zuorro's little sister would duck out onto a boat all day and come back only for meals. She's obviously miffed at Zuorro. Boudy is exhausted from the heat, and Mops has a case of sunburn that has just about finished her off.

To Louise Védrine

Sunday [August]

My love

What a long time it's been since I last wrote you. I wanted to do so two evenings ago and then again all day yesterday, but our stay here is corrupting. It's happy sloth all day long—with the addition of terrible tension among all the visitors, two by two, which is probably typical of country houseparties. In every nook and cranny, someone's either whispering about someone else or cursing someone out. Alliances are formed and dissolved. But I'll explain it all in good time. First, I'd like you to know that if I'm at fault for not writing yesterday I'm fully aware of it and very much bothered by the thought that tomorrow you'll go by the post office and find nothing, and that you'll leave, sad and uncomplaining. I love you so, my love. The Beaver showed me the snapshots you took at Annecy, and they brought back that whole day. You're so appealing in the photos (and so beautiful in the other one, the big one where you're nude. Who took it? Your father, of course). I love you most passionately, I would so like to have you here beside me, and believe it or not, I do get some help—a slight added something— from the thought that you were here at Easter, that you too looked at this sea, these pines.

It wasn't easy to get here, you know. First, we had to telegraph all over to get news of the Lady. And then on Monday morning, there was a telegram, followed by their arrival. That much you know. What you don't know is that the tension among the group was already high. Zuorro was pointedly keeping aloof, Mops, rather unbalanced, was screaming at everybody, and the Lady was enraged at the Zuorre. I didn't yet know quite why. Thereupon there were marches and countermarches, and then we decided to leave at six in the evening. The Lady's car was in a garage in Marseilles, and when, around four, she went to pick it up, wouldn't you know but the batteries were dead. The garage was at fault. A Marseillais came to tell her, with the calm assurance of a high-ranking military officer, "Never mind, Madame, we'll recharge them for you. All will be ready at seven." At seven we go back—after a long argument to settle which bags we were sending by train and which were going with us, an argument that broke off without agreement—and the Marseillais declares confidently, "So there you are, all ready." "Fine," says the Lady, who fortunately has the idea to turn on the headlights and blow the horn. The horn peeped and the lights blinked a dirty little yellowish haze that didn't reach beyond our car wheels. God knows what they'd done, but the batteries were deader than ever. The Marseillais garage mechanic didn't get riled up over such trifles: he first cast aspersions upon the honesty of the battery manufacturer, then said in the same calm tone, "We'll start all over again. Come back at ten and they'll be charged." Meanwhile Zuorro, who feverishly and inexplicably wanted to leave Marseilles, was studying the schedules to find out the train times for Juan. The last was at 9. But the Lady was determined to wait for the batteries to be recharged. So I took them to La Taverne Charly, where they ate salade Niçoise, in a lingering atmosphere of tension, inexplicable to me but which I well recognized for having felt it a thousand times at the Lady's place. Then little Boudy fell asleep on the bench and the Zuorre mysteriously disappeared, saying he was going to settle with the hotel (where they had taken a room for the afternoon) and would be back right away. After an hour we left the Mops and Boudy and went to the garage, the Lady, the Beaver, and I, passing the hotel. There we learned that the Zuorre had never shown up. From there we went to the garage, where we were told, "The car is absolutely ready." Thereupon Zuorro and Mops arrived, and Zuorro explained that he had just been sleeping for a moment, which was untrue, since five minutes earlier the room was locked and the key was hanging on the board. The car started up obediently, and we stopped it in front of the hotel. There, new and lively conversation about the baggage. We were in the entry hall, six individuals taking up so much space with our bodies and voices that the hotelkeeper finally asked us to move to the parlor. Which we did not want to do; we preferred to block a whole street, arguing stubbornly, with Zuorro sitting plunk in the middle of the sidewalk, surrounded by his suitcases. Then, after an hour of arguing, we simply returned to the initial plan. Zuorro and I went by cab to register three bags, and we stuffed the rest into the car. Finally departure. It was midnight. Zuorro, who two hours before had been so anxious to leave, was suddenly furious, thinking we would have done better to sleep at the hotel and leave in the morning. As a matter of fact, it was pure folly to leave at midnight with only two hours of recharge in the batteries, when it's at night that you use the most electricity (horn and lights), and on top of all that, it was drizzling, which required the use of windshield wipers. At the same time Boudy, exhausted by her Algerian trip and falling asleep on every available bench, really could have used a bed. But the Lady has a veritable complex about hotel beds. She claims that all French hotels have bedbugs and that even in the best the sheets are disgusting. For her, one night in a hotel is a night of sleepless martyrdom. So she prefers to travel at night, whatever the cost. For twenty kilometers we drove along smoothly, but then the horn went hoarse and the headlights dimmed. Whereupon the Lady panicked and began to fiddle with the levers for the headlights and inside lights, so thoroughly that three kilometers past Aubagne and twenty-five from Marseilles, the car stalled. Zuorro and I got out and struggled with the crank. No go. Then the Lady had us push the car every which way, hoping the engine would catch. Still no go. A group of girls walking home from a dance kindly pushed the car to the top of the hill. There, the Lady made a U-turn and coasted back down with the car in gear. Joy. We heard it starting up. But once down the hill it died again. We struggled with it a bit, but after fifteen minutes we looked at each other helplessly, breathless, and the Lady said, "I'm going to sleep in the car." "Me too," said the Mops. "And I," said the Beaver. For Zuorro it was a disaster: he would be sleeping on the ground. It was drizzling, and how would he ever get his hot water in the morning, how could he shave? He picked up his overnight bag and said, "I'm going to the hotel." There was, so the girls had told us, a hotel three kilometers away. A glacial silence from the Lady. Then she said, "Fine. You men go to the hotel. We women are staying," stressing the "women." It was the umpteenth episode in her squabble with Zuorro; she was outraged that he would abandon them on the road. So I said to her, "I'll stay with you." But I was a bit irritated, for it was actually the Lady's obstinance that had caused us to leave at midnight *knowing*—or very nearly—that there would be a breakdown, and, on top of all that, there was hardly any reason for our staying: they were well protected from the weather, closed up in the car, on a little village square, and we would have had to sleep on the ground out in the damp. All the same I thought I should stay. "No, don't," said the Lady. "Yes I will, Madame," etc. We argued courteously for a while. Meanwhile Zuorro was mum, standing there so tall, so dark, so grave, slightly removed, like some great sepulchral figure, his case beneath his arm, and with fury and terror at the idea of a night out in the open. Finally the Lady said, with scornful irony, "You've got to go along with Zuorro, my boy. You don't imagine he'll manage three kilometers at night all by himself." So I left, promising to return early. And we did the three kilometers in the rain. For me it was more or less a lark, resigned as I was not to getting any sleep. But after a bit the houses became scarcer, and finally we were walking through open country. At that point the Zuorre panicked. He tried hitchhiking to Aubagne or even Marseilles. But seeing two grim guys alone on that road, the cars speeded up instead. Then he pointed out to me that we had taken off in this direction simply on the word of those girls, that they could be mistaken and then we'd be lost. He would peer into the rare hovels we passed, saying in an anguished tone, "Perhaps it's a hotel." I prevented him from turning back, and finally we entered a little town, Roquevaire, dead to the world, with a few flickering lights and, oh joy oh rapture, a hotel. We pounded on the door crying out "Hotel! Hotel!" and finally a shutter cracked open and a hideous shrewish face appeared. "We would like some rooms." Ten minutes later the door opened and we entered a huge house with a certain gloomy charm, tile floors throughout, wide stone staircases and vast coun-tryfied rooms where enormous keys hung from immense locks. We took a room with two beds, and Zuorro, his equanimity completely restored, ordered some beer and sandwiches and began to chatter as he ate and drank. Then I asked to have us waked up at seven (it was now three in the morning), and we went to sleep. At seven they woke us up, but Zuorro wanted to wash and shave. I waited for him downstairs drinking bad coffee, and finally at 8:45 he appeared. We were lucky enough to catch a Roquevaire-Aubagne bus, which put us down at the very spot where we had left the Lady. But there, no car. We looked all around, inquired of the merchants, and learned that the butcher, just leaving on his rounds with his truck, had gotten the Lady started up twenty minutes earlier. She had driven off in the car to find us, and we must have passed her in the bus. After a while she showed up, furious that we had come at nine in the morning but holding Zuorro alone responsible for our delay (for good cause, actually, but still a little out of spite). She said nothing, actually, or next to nothing, except "The butcher said to us, 'You mean that you weren't afraid to stay there all alone?' And I answered, 'We were with some men, but they went to the hotel.' " Thereupon Zuorro, wounded, huddled into the back of the car with Boudy and the Mops, I settled into the front between the Lady and the Beaver, and the trip began. Just imagine the atmosphere: the Lady tired and vindictive, constantly saying "I'm about to lose control of the wheel" (we stopped twice to have her consume large bowls of coffee); Zuorro sulking and mute; the Mops, tired and insisting on her rights, demonstrating through her every statement that she basically wasn't well at all, but dead set on refusing my seat, which I was dead set on offering to her; while Boudy, punchy with weariness, was crying angrily like any exhausted child. I was in high spirits, singing my whole repertoire, since the Lady had begged me to make noise to keep her from falling asleep. Aside from that, the car was running smoothly, and the road was very beautiful, the Route de Brignoles. Here is a map so that you can see what I'm talking about, little you who so appreciates details. As you see, we didn't for one

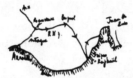

moment follow the coast. We grazed it at Saint-Raphaël-Fréjus, only to go back up into the mountains. Incidentally, that Fréjus-Cannes road is wild and splendid, it's delightful to think about all the comfortably moist luxury hidden at the foot of the mountains and on the seacoast. Finally, at 12:45, we reached Juan-les-Pins. It's just possible that if we'd left Marseilles at 6:30, after spending the night at the Hôtel Lafayette, we would have arrived around 11. I was very sleepy and permeated with the harsh, disheartening taste that trips with the Lady always involve.

My dearest, I'm stopping here. I'm going to join the Beaver, who's in swimming. I want you to know that she can now keep afloat all by herself and that tomorrow or the day after she'll know how to swim. She's very happy and proud of herself. To be continued day after tomorrow; I'll describe the villa and tell you funny stories, for I assure you that life here isn't simple. For the moment I only wish you'd think and feel very intensely that I love you passionately, and that almost all the time I feel a real need to see you, and that I associate you with everything I do either by thinking that I'm going to tell it to you or in imagining that one day we'll do it together. You would be in seventh heaven in this villa. Goodbye, and with my deepest love.

To Louise Védrine

Saturday [August]

My love

I'm just back from a swim, so as I write to you, my fingers are sticking to the page. I'm really proud of myself: I've doubled my speed at the Australian crawl. Thanks to Zuorro. He has me doing a helix movement with my right arm that is gracefulness itself. But I've swallowed buckets! The water plays delicately across my eyes and into my ears and mouth. I'm constantly going "chchch," and a little fountain arises in the middle of the sea from the water I spit back, like a dolphin. I did my kilometer again this evening. But after five hundred meters I was scared of the Beast. I've told you about it—the horrible beast that lives at the bottom. I imagine it lifting an immense crab claw and drawing me down toward its twelve pairs of legs. So I did the return five hundred meters at top speed (using the helix movement) to flee the Beast and myself. Result: record time. As for the obsession, don't worry, it's just one of those semiserious, neurasthenic obsessions. But it is tenacious. Though only when I'm alone in the sea. Otherwise not. This evening I was all alone on an empty sea, it was almost like a roller coaster under wraps because the fair is about to move on. The sky was gray, with a crescent moon (it was seven in the evening), and on the beach they were busily folding the steamer chairs and taking them in, I could see that from far off. Not a single bather. Aside from the Beast, it's a lovely time to swim, with the water warmer than the air. On my return I found the Beaver, still a terrible swimmer but making notable progress. Just imagine, she does ten meters effortlessly. But she's lazy as can be, and I scolded her this evening; she said, "I'll do better tomorrow."

Right from the terrace of the villa we've been seeing the French water-skiing championship. This morning it was "jumping and speed"; the world record was broken at 78.5 kilometers an hour. The guy who came in second hurtled off into the air at 82 kilometers an hour. His skis whirled and pinwheeled around him. This afternoon it was the slalom. Generally boring except when the champion came on, Lévy, who went through all the gates, down and back in 43 seconds (the others average a minute). It's monotonous, but sometimes entertaining. The champion is beautiful to watch on his skis. Zuorro said, "He must be really something," and ran off to inspect him more closely. On that subject, the Beaver said to me the other evening, in a bar in Cannes that's a pickup joint for male hustlers, that she preferred female prostitution, because it's an honest deal, usually with indifference on both sides, while the sale of some little guy entails reciprocal hatred. The hustler hates the one who humiliates him, and the john hates the one on whose behalf he's humiliating himself (this latter is the less frequent). But this evening, on seeing Zuorro run to the gate to see Lévy, I showed Beaver the other side of the coin: the frank admiration that is often, in the homosexual, the beginnings of love. There's more of a taste for reverence, with a sort of gullibility (Zuorro's is boundless), than for domination. No equivalent at all, except in the lowest reaches of male prostitution, to the battle of the sexes. I remember how Proust demonstrated that so well with Charlus and his Morel. Zuorro amuses us: there are a lot of guys passing through here, friends of Pelote Morel, 25 years old, 30, handsome guys, tanned and athletic. With all of them he plays the old coquette, he looks them over and laughs in their faces. For the moment he's not overjoyed, because for lack of space a regimental friend of Pelote's, Chantrelle, has to sleep in his room. It's typical in this house: a guy shows up and says, "I was in Cannes, at the hotel, but I have five more days' vacation and ran out of money. Could you put me up?" "Why, of course. We'll have a bed made up for you." Whereupon Mme Rialland shows up, the mother of a young photographer from Cannes who is a classmate of Pelote's: "May I come to your place? I haven't seen my son for two years." "Poor Madame Rialland! Of course; Jacqueline Parodi can sleep in Mops's bed." Etc. Yesterday there were ten of us at the table, and it was all idle chitchat. Has anyone told you about a smarmy Jewish fellow by the name of Samuel Nathan? He's a vague acquaintance of Isorni's. Isorni-the-son-in-law invited him here (but he sleeps at the hotel) in a gesture of defiance: "Why can't I invite my friends, too?" But for the moment he doesn't know what to do with him. The guy's crude, a jerk, totally insignificant. The type you want to kick in the ass. But since he's a lawyer, wouldn't you know but the Lady has got it into her head he's sniffing around the place to gauge the discord in the Isorni household, and will later serve as witness for Isorni if he should want a divorce. So she ordered, "Be on your very best behavior with Nathan." And so here's this worthless character, abruptly surrounded by universal consideration, basking in it and playing the local dictator. It's awfully funny, particularly since the witness story is nonsense and the guy attributes the respect he's getting to his personal merit.

That's the news for the moment. We'll stay here till the 22nd, at Sull'Onda, for the sake of economy, though the good Beaver is boiling with impatience: this houseparty life barely even half suits her. But I worry that the letter you would send on receipt of mine might find us gone, so write to each of us c/o General Delivery in Foix. Write me a long letter; it seems a century since I've had the slightest contact with you. I often look at your photos, but that's not enough, I want to see you. I want to touch your little face and kiss your mouth. You know, here there are lots of dresses that are wide at the hem and pleated at the hips, like yours (except they open, obscenely, in front for a glimpse of thigh); each time I see one from a distance or from behind, I get a little pang, as though I'm seeing your dear little body. I love you passionately. You write delightful little letters, you must keep it up. You don't seem too sad, and that pleases us so much, we'd be horrified to think that you are miserable. Farewell, my love, there's only a month and five days separating us from you.

I dream of hugging your little body close to mine.

To Louise Védrine

Tuesday, August 22

My love

How sad to spend three or four days without your lovely little letters. I'm sure we'll find a handful in Foix. I like to imagine us walking around that appealing town, asking the way to the post office, and finding everything from you at the service window, and going off to some little café to settle down and read your letters. Which doesn't stop me longing for you right now, with nothing to read from you, no fresh news at all. I'm sure that nothing bad is happening to you. But it's like a pure time for you, flowing along there, and we'd like to be involved with that pure time. I love you so much, you know. Last night I went, with the Lady and the Beaver, to the Masséna, in Nice—I'll tell you about it in a bit—and I left them, the way I left you one morning—for just five minutes, to buy tobacco. And those five minutes were filled to bursting with you, it was as though the Beaver and you were waiting for me on the café terrace. Incidentally, Nice was bursting with memories; we saw the streets again where we'd looked for a hotel, the square where we caught the bus for Avignon, and you were there the whole time. Aside from that, the city was deserted and a little melancholy, like a huge abandoned fair whose carousels were going round and round, completely empty.

The Beaver wrote to you yesterday, so you know that Isorni beat up the Mops. He dragged her by the neck onto the garden path and banged her head against the ground, while the Lady, flat on her belly, poked two fingers in his eyes and pinched his nose shut. That was the only authentic event amid all the psychological chitchat and what you called "the war of whispers." The good Beaver was really upset by it all, because she'd seen Isorni's long, greenish, unshaven face as he went off, knees trembling, the deed done. Solicitous Zuorro was at his elbow; the role of consoler becomes him, his eyes grow handsomer than ever. And as in Hollywood movies, there was a thunderstorm at that very moment. But this house is a bog into which events immediately disappear. At the time, the Lady had said angrily, "If I were you, Mops, I wouldn't stay a moment longer with a madman like that," but then reverted to her original indecision: "But what should we do, dear boy?" she asked me. "Whatever should we do?" The rain, the gray clouds scudding across the sea, the sophisticated but, beneath it all, horror-stricken look of the guests at the table, the empty chair for Isorni, who was upstairs wringing his hands—everything contributed to the sense of departure and autumn in the house. And indeed we were about to leave, we really felt we were going to leave, and it seemed strange to allow this drama to unfold in our absence. We would learn almost nothing more about it; it would close in on itself. In Paris the Lady would bring us up to date in very general, discreet terms, and that would be that. Then we were all restored to the calm of exhaustion. The Lady had violent pains in her shoulder and her chest, her heart was giving her pain, she's supposed to avoid violent emotions. Mops's neck is swollen— she can't turn her head. As for Isorni, you'd have laughed that afternoon, seeing him sitting on the ground, his chin resting on his knees, hugging his long legs with his thin hands and looking vacantly at one Ramel, a painter and notorious homosexual (the sort that gets chased out of town after some scandal), whom they honor and invite to the villa because he knows how to make bouillabaisse, bourride, and fish soup. Ramel, under Isorni's dull eyes, was hammering with all his might at a stockfish, a cod dry and hard as wood, to break splinters off it. A mournful gathering, Mops, Isorni, Zuorro, Ramel, Mme Rialland (a dull old fool), ate the stockfish that evening at dinner; it seems it was scarcely more tender, once boiled, than before. But *we* didn't eat it. We kidnapped the Lady and took her all the way to Nice in her car. She was extremely tired but gave in to her fatigue with a sort of bliss. We turned over, fingered, commented on, and scrutinized the event as though it were simply a stockfish. The Lady had no idea anymore what to do, since Mops doesn't want either to get a divorce or to stay with her husband. We dined at a charming little place facing the Vieux Marché, where the Beaver and I had tried in vain to go at Easter, and then we went down on the shore below the Promenade des Anglais to watch the sea because there were waves. "Real waves!" said the Beaver, who complained of not having seen enough of them at Juan. After which a glass at the Masséna, and then, as fate would have it, back at the car, which we had left at the Place du Vieux Marché, we couldn't start it up, the batteries were dead. So I had to perform the usual ceremonies, the crank, etc., push the car a hundred meters, call on some workmen to help, etc. The Lady was insistent on finding a slope, and in vain did we explain that Nice is flat as a bedbug. Finally we went, the Beaver and I, to fetch a cab to tow the car with a rope, and when we came back with the taxi, the Lady was nowhere to be seen. At last far off we saw a little car creeping along looking dubious and pathetic, with dying lights. Two Dutchmen had pushed it with all their might, and eventually it had started. We drove home minus lights and horn, but it didn't matter, since there were streetlights all the way. It was two-thirty. The house looked ominously dark, with one solitary light on at Mops's window. It appears that Zuorro had closed himself in for the night, because his shutters, which he ordinarily leaves open on principle, were hermetically sealed. We learned that Isorni's first act after his "fateful deed" was to shave, because either he'd glanced in a mirror and gotten scared or he didn't want the Mops to find, when she looked at him, the murderer's face she'd glimpsed earlier. This morning the house is doleful and the weather too, everything smacks of departure more than ever, the war of whispers has begun again. In her nightgown, the Lady sketched out the situation for us at length and in two or three contradictory ways. What muddies the waters is that Isorni, who yesterday was humble and grim, showed up this morning looking defiant and said to the Lady, "I'm leaving tomorrow, I've had enough of this nonsense!" as though it was he who had been beaten. "As you wish, Jean," said the Lady. "In any case, I think it would be best for you to separate from the Mops for six months or a year." "No, no," he replied, "I've had enough. Anyway, I'll talk to you about it later." Which seems to indicate that he has made up his mind for divorce. But, as I said, Mops doesn't want that. This morning she asked anxiously, "A woman can't be forced to get a divorce against her will, can she?"—fiercely resolved to keep up the appearance of conjugal submission and even to exaggerate it. That's how things stand. Zuorro seems set on a little tour of Marseilles for a change of scene; we leave this evening, Jean Isorni tomorrow. Finally the Lady and the Mops will perhaps stay on alone. The whole thing seems ominous and contingent, and we are enchanted with the thought that tomorrow we'll be in a quiet little town in the Pyrenees. When you get this letter, my love, there'll be only a month till we see each other again. I'm so impatient to hug your slim little body. I love you passionately.

Farewell. Write to us at Hendaye, Basses-Pyrénées, from the 24th to the 28th (we'll stay on there the 29th and 30th, and from there we'll give you new addresses).

To Louise Védrine

Thursday [August]

My love

     I am totally ashamed and quite upset because you write in your dear little letter you were sad not to have any mail. Henceforth I'll write you short letters every two days. With those from the Beaver, that will almost give you your daily letter. But do consider, I beg you, the debilitating way of life here, and I chose to write you vast letters because four pages wouldn't be enough to describe seven people and their interrelationships. Incidentally, I don't know whether the Beaver brought you up to date on everything. There's so much going on here, and you were the one who wanted to know all the details. I get lost in it all, there's enough for a four-hundred-page novel. Or rather, you see, it is the ideal setting for the crime in a well-made detective novel, because each individual has a secret and personal duplicity. But soon we'll be leaving here, and you'll get pure letters, not filled with complicated intrigues but ones in which we will talk about mountains, old towns, and narrow streets. And the Beaver about me, and I about the Beaver. Today I would above all tell you that I love you to a passionate degree. You are present here. I saw your hotel, and I am so happy that you stayed here, that you've seen our villa, it's a really miraculous bit of luck that among so many places where we are going without you, there is this little concrete link with you here. When I see something you have seen, it seems as though my eyes are caressing you. I love you.

     I do lots of exercises, you'll be pleased to hear, enough to win the admiration of more than one young man. "How conscientious you are!" says one to me. —"How energetic you are," says the Lady, in a reproach mixed with praise. —"What good wind you have," Isorni tells me. Alas, I'm not slimming down, my love. But my muscles are growing taut and bulging beneath my skin, I'm in much better shape than before. I swim too. Around this time of day I do my kilometer. I leave from the diving board at the Provençale and do five hundred meters along the coast, passing the Casino, the villas and cafés, it's quite pleasant. Here's my schedule: I get up at nine-thirty (picture me sleeping under a beautiful pink mosquito net, which the Beaver covets. She's also jealous about my room's sea view, which I don't appreciate enough, she's decided, whereas she, poor little soul, would enjoy it so). Then there is that very pleasant moment when I put on anything at all, sometimes a bathing suit, and go out barefoot onto the terrace, which is still shady. After a good search I find an old mustached maid, who brings me some café au lait on the terrace. Picture this: a green steamer chair, a green garden table on a marble terrace ("Marble's very cheap here," says the Lady modestly), a tray laden with victuals placed on the table, and me in the steamer chair, and then the sea two steps away filled with the growl of the motorboats towing water skiers. I eat my breakfast watching the skiers do jumps. Some pretty pitiful, others beautiful. After they fall, you suddenly see a head emerge and then, some distance away, the tips of their skis. It is a fascinating entertainment, you know, monotonous yet moving, you could watch it indefinitely. So much for that. Suddenly I hear someone calling me from upstairs and I see heads appearing from second-floor windows, it's the Mops, the Lady, Jacqueline Parodi. We exchange greetings, then the Beaver appears, sleepy and already set on her program: she wants to have her swim. She goes swimming twice a day, you know, stays in the water for three hours, and that's it, she now knows how to swim. This evening, with me right beside her, she'll go to a spot that is over her head. Everyone admires her, but there's a terrifying expression on her face when she swims. The other day Zuorro watched her with a look of mingled repulsion and anguish, then when she stood up again he said, "And yet usually you've got a rather kindly face." After that, there's a charming interval of vacant animation, people wander up and down the stairs; when we can catch the Lady in some corner, we carry on a snatch of a conversation, soon interrupted by a jealous Mops, who takes her mother by the hand and leads her away. Then we go back down, and the Beaver dons her bathing suit again, quite humble compared to the complicated two-piecers of the ladies around here, and she puts on a blue bathing cap of Jacqueline Parodi's which is very becoming (if you want to picture it, this is at eleven-thirty). She goes to the beach, and I work till one-thirty (I've completely changed the chapter that was boring, and the Beaver finds it very good). At one-thirty I get into my bathing suit and do my exercises on the terrace in the full sun. I sweat, if you only knew how I sweat, it tickles all over and the sun burns my eyelids. Then I go inside, trembling, and I take a shower and make myself presentable. Finally around two-fifteen, lunch, always under almost unbearable tension, either because it's silent or there are wearisome annoyances—because of the relationship between Mops and Isorni, between Zuorro and the Lady, Isorni and the Mops. Recently a character appeared who is mysterious and very Jewish (in the classically anti-

Semitic sense), by the name of Nathan, a lawyer who calls himself a friend of Isorni's. Isorni is suspected of wanting to get a divorce and of bringing him in here as a witness, to direct the divorce to his own advantage, meaning the custody of the little girl. In fact they did take the kid into the corner and interrogate her, and Nathan tried to pump the Lady. To win her over the other day he bought a marzipan cake, which he cut into seven portions, giving one seventh to each of us. Quite often he does all the talking at the table. We leave the table at four, and then I go for a walk with the good Beaver, who is simultaneously surprised, scandalized, and not a little pleased by this life of leisure. She feels as though she's discovering something. At seven we go swimming together, I take her by the chin, and I lavish advice on her. She was nice enough to say that it was I who had taught her the best. As I say, as of now, she can swim. After that I leave her to paddle around, and I go do my kilometer in really warm water, while the sun sets. It's wonderfully pleasurable, the water and sky darken, and finally you're in an odd wet world that licks you all over. After that I shower and we go in to eat. Fatigue from the day's activities and uncertainty about the evening's arrangements make dinner even heavier going than lunch. There's scarcely any talk. But it doesn't sadden us; instead, all that tension actually amuses us. Afterward, sometimes, on rare occasions, responding to our chiding, the Lady—whom we almost never see, as you know—walks with us as far as Antibes. We climb onto the ramparts and sit there talking, at the edge of the quays. Last night was one of those times, and we loitered there till two in the morning, eating ice cream and chocolate, and then after all that, instead of going home we just lingered on white enameled wicker chairs in the deserted pine grove, watching one or two very active couples—spying on a pair of guys in caps, very out of place here, whom the Lady—who knows why?—suspected of being cocaine dealers. Other times we stay on the terrace, listening to the sound of the sea and the jazz from the Provençal, which we can hear remarkably clearly. Another time I went to Cannes, to that gyp joint the Beaver must have told you about. If not, I will, day after tomorrow.

So, my love. You can see these strange times, empty and teeming, all leisure and exhausting tension—magical to me. But I imagine the Beaver likes it much less. My love, my little pearl, I hope you'll get this letter very early. I got yours at noon, it's four now, and I'm writing to you. I love you with all my heart, I have all the time in the world to think about you, to think how much you love me and to gladden my heart with that. Listen: The night before last, it was two in the morning, I was sitting astride the terrace wall, gazing at the sea and the lights at the Casino (when the dance lights are on, you can see the dancers from the villa, like great fiery butterflies). It was very still, and then at the Casino dance they were playing our song: "Bei mir bist du schön"—and it touched me as though you were sending me a signal. I love you passionately, and I have a mad desire to crush you in my arms. The Beaver showed me the photo with your beautiful little body, so slim, stirring me deeply with desire.

Farewell, my love. I'll write the day after tomorrow.

To Louise Védrine

[Late August]

My love

It delighted and devastated us to hear your weary little voice on the phone. We know what anguish you're going through, all alone in Annecy, unable to find a single reasonable person to talk to, and feeling cut off from events, with everything happening beyond your reach. During the first few days, we got our information from the local country papers, we experienced the first events out in the country, and like you we know that waiting in the country is passive, you wait for the news without anticipating it or even trying to.[1] If you were here, you'd be much calmer, and it breaks our hearts to think of your anxiety from lack of information, your devastation. My love, we would have had so much pleasure hearing you this morning. But the long-distance lines were cut off, the government is using them for its communications. We telegraphed you immediately, but when will the telegram reach you?

And yet I would have liked to reassure you. I can scarcely endure the idea of leaving without seeing you again, and I can well imagine that it must be even more painful for you, because *I* am the one who is leaving, you have to put up with the forced passivity. But listen, perhaps I never thought to tell you: I am *not in any danger.* If anyone is to come home from this war, it will be me. Almost a shirker, if you get my drift. Just remember, I'm a meteorologist at Essey-lès-Nancy. You have to understand what that means. It means that someplace two or three kilometers from Nancy is a little hill and at the top of the hill a little house with meteorological apparatus and *real beds,* and that's where I'll be. Nancy is way behind the front lines, and I am scarcely at risk from shelling. As for air raids, they will aim particularly for the town, the station, and the airfield. I'm very far from all that. So just

---

[1]The buildup toward war; the signing of the Hitler-Stalin nonaggression pact.

imagine my life as a gloomy bore, with the work of a very lowly civil servant, no more than that. I know the work, incidentally—which is done hourly, and I know I'll have ample time to do my own work and write to you. The good Beaver calmed down considerably when she managed to see a possible war as a separation, perhaps long, but temporary and not as though linked to the permanent possibility of death. Do you understand, my love, even if there were a war, there would be an *afterward*, for the three of us. Of that I am absolutely certain; our life will go on.

For that matter, I don't really believe in the war. Obviously this letter runs the risk of arriving at the same moment as the announcement of general mobilization. Nonetheless I venture to say that I don't think it will. There was a guy with one arm at the Café de Flore who was saying today, "I'm very optimistic, but watch out, with all the bullshit that goes on, anything can still happen." That's exactly my view, with this proviso: I'm not so sure Hitler is a fool. Think about it: craven Spain and Japan, clear-cut attitude of Roosevelt and the American press (they'll help the democracies), Italy's panic, Turkey's fidelity to the commitments made. Add to that the significant distribution of ration cards in Germany. Schacht said one day: "If worst comes to worst, you might finish a war with ration cards, but you do not begin one that way." What's more, the German people seem anything but enthusiastic. If you ask me, the big blow was to have been struck on Friday or Saturday at the latest: as he announced the German-Soviet pact, Hitler was counting on disarray among the democracies and internal troubles in France. He thought that by invading Poland then, he would reach Warsaw before the French and English governments could react. All the correspondents of French papers in Berlin are saying that the attack was planned for Saturday at 5 in the morning. The plan misfired, whence Saturday's braking action. Note that the foot on the brake belongs to Hitler himself, who called together Coulondre and Henderson. Naturally he is too involved to yield, and particularly not in just any which way. Hence his negative response to Daladier's letter. But this should not make you unduly anxious, since from the start it is with England that he has sought a basis for negotiations. Beyond that, he has always been hostile to the idea of *direct* negotiations with Poland. He needs an intermediary, a third power, which will of course be Italy. Bear in mind that the point of view I have just put forth is the one shared by everyone here. People are very calm, not very anxious at all. Obviously there is still the possibility of "bullshit." There is nothing to be said about it, since its nature is to be unthinkable. Excuse all this lecturing, but I think that if you were here, we would have talked about it, and I would have given you my opinion. So there it is. My love, I swear to you that what torments us the most these days is the concern you are feeling. We talk about it all the time and we would so like to take it on ourselves. I love you with all my might.

Here is a synopsis of our doings. We arrived at Foix on Friday morning, and things looked bad. So we decided to go home. I hardly dared propose it to the Beaver, who cared so much about her little trip, but she too had thought that it was the only way to see you, and she almost beat me to it. Upon which we reached Foix. It's a charming little town, on a hill with a large and beautiful château and a most luxurious restaurant, the Hôtel de la Barbacane, where, firm in our resolve to return home, we gave ourselves a costly lunch (hors d'oeuvres, trout, cassoulet, foie gras, cheese and fruit, with a local wine). While there I revealed to Beaver how Brunet, in the fourth volume, disgusted by the German-Soviet pact, would quit the Communist Party and come to ask for Mathieu's help (necessary reversal of the situation laid out in the first volume). I had just about made up my mind about the war at that point; it was as though something in me had frozen. And it was very odd and pleasant in that situation to wander through the placid little town that would in no case be touched by war. We went to doze on the grass at the foot of the château around three o'clock, and the Beaver, in a modernist frenzy, tried to ridicule the Albigeois of bygone times, totally intent on waging their little wars with crossbows and taking themselves seriously. But I vigorously deterred her from that path, which could lead her a long way off. After which we wrote to our parents and settled things as best we could, then went for a walk along a river. I will keep enchanted memories of that day in Foix. After that, things were not so much fun. Around 19:30 we took a train for Toulouse. There we were to change and immediately catch the Paris train. But it was packed. For two and half hours we had to stay in that crowded, very dark station, with small violet stars at distant intervals for the only illumination. The second train arrived late, and as there were five hundred people on the platform, we definitely expected to travel standing up in the corridor. But, thanks to our joint initiative, we got *four* corner seats. The Beaver regretfully gave up her two, and she registered her disapproval for my choice by vomiting a bit during the night. But don't worry, that was the exception, and the rest of the night she slept rather well. Me too. And we arrived on time.

Paris was very strange. Everything was closed, restaurants, theaters, stores, because it's August, and the neighborhoods had lost their individual character. There was only one totality left, Paris itself. A totality which, for me, was already a thing *of the past* and, as Heidegger says, retained and upheld by nothingness. And then little by little, insinuating memories as well as the news in the papers had us tossing out possibilities, out beyond the stones and gratings. For the Beaver it was quite odd, because she was foreseeing her whole life for the coming year, but for a moment or two it gave her the feeling that she too was past and dead. And then toward evening we were completely thawed out. Yesterday too was a somewhat enervating day. We called you, we wandered about, we went to the movies, and throughout there was a disagreeable feeling of hope. Today, God knows why, I'm totally calm and serene. The Beaver almost as much as I. It is this calm that we would so like to have you share, my dearest.

Goodbye—the Beaver will write to you tomorrow and I the day after. At this moment I would so like to see you, to kiss your dear little face and hug your little body. But I'm sure I'll soon be able to.

To Louise Védrine

August 31

My dearest

You're a strange little politician. You get everything mixed up. You cheer when Hitler sends Daladier a stubborn reply whose clear aim is to throw responsibility for the war back on the French—and you get all panicky when real negotiations are about to start up. That doesn't matter: though your sadness may be ill-timed, it is no less painful than if we were the ones feeling it. I'm furious that I can't be there to explain things to you a bit. God knows what papers are available to you at Annecy. Above all don't read *L'Intransigeant*, the organ of the Munich-oriented Chautemps. Read *L'Oeuvre*, *Paris-Soir*, and *Le Temps*. Don't lose heart. It's impossible that Hitler is thinking of starting a war, given the mental state of the German population. It's bluff. Perhaps we'll go as far as general mobilization, but this is the moment to remind you of the phrase—which was unfortunate in its own day, incidentally—"mobilization is not war." My love, we so wish for you to stay calm. We scarcely dare tell you that despite our worries about you, our poor little friend, and the debilitating frustration of waiting, we're having a good time here. We could scold you, little idiot, for not coming! Alas, there was nothing else for you to do but what you did. To be an altogether, altogether perfect little Louise, you must resist the tendency toward jeremiads and be totally calm. It is anything but a new life beginning for the three of us, it's simply two months of downright nuisance. You'll see, we'll have our own life together this year in Paris, and we'll go to the beautiful Chalet du Mont d'Arbois to ski.

We love you passionately, my love, and we're sure we'll see you again soon. Farewell. I kiss your swollen little eyes and your dear little mouth.

To Louise Védrine

September 2

My love

So the bullshit triumphed.[1] I'm leaving tonight at five o'clock. The Beaver will go with me as far as a square called Hébert, at the Porte de la Chapelle. In the middle of that square is a lamppost, around the lamppost are police, and those police will ship me off via a cargo station two steps from here. My love, I don't fear for my life, I'm not even afraid of being bored, and I don't too much pity the good Beaver, who is absolutely courageous and perfect, as always. What tears my heart is your solitary pain way off there in Annecy. It is to be leaving without seeing you again, taking along a few little photos of you in which I can barely make you out. My love, it wouldn't outwardly be too different if you were here, but we would have experienced the end of all this *together*, and that would be one more bond. But it is neither your fault nor mine, poor little marvel. Now listen, I will come back to you. I'm in no danger, I'm the faithful type, and you'll find me again when the time comes, exactly like the person you left at the station square in Annecy. Nothing can change us, my love, neither you, nor the Beaver, nor I. This is a wretched moment *in* our lives, but it isn't the end of our lives. There will be a peace and an *afterward*. I'll write to you as early as tomorrow, my dearest, telling you how things are going for me. And after that I'll write you as often as possible, perhaps every day. Right now I'm going to sleep for three or four hours. But I'd like you to know that I love you passionately, *forever*. Goodbye, my poor little marvel. I can imagine how things are in Annecy, and my heart sinks, but that too will last for a time only, and the Beaver asks me to tell you that she'll go see you before the end of September, perhaps even as soon as communications are reestablished.

Farewell. I cover your little face with kisses.[2]

---

[1]The day before, Germany had invaded Poland, and on September 3, France and Britain declared war on Germany.

[2]*This is the last letter from Sartre that was kept by Louise Védrine, whose parents took her abroad soon after war broke out. (SdB)*

To Simone de Beauvoir

Saturday, September 2

My love

I'm writing to you from Toul, where the train has been standing for twenty minutes. Who knows when it'll get moving again. At the moment they're loading gas masks onto the baggage cars. A train has just left for Paris, filled with women and children. Someone in our compartment called out, "Say hello to Paris," and then: "And what if we just went back?" Alas, the Kafkesque journey continues. We have been on our way now for seven hours, and there must be about fifty kilometers left to go. The train stops every-where—though it's a *rapide*, it's acting more like a local. There are quite a lot of women and children. In our compartment, we have an old woman, the Mme Canque sort, whose maternity or femininity seems stimulated by the reservists.

People still have individual destinies. Each has *his or her* station: Toul, Lérouville, Bar-le-Duc, or Nancy. They get off, like real peacetime travelers, except you get the impression that each one feels a special little something. They take their musette bags and say in an odd tone, "Well, here we are. Goodbye, everybody." And those remaining, still optimistic, say, "Well, here's hoping we'll meet again on the way home." "Absolutely! Here's hoping. It's not like everyone will get killed." Actually they are mostly quite cheerful and steady, but not carefree. At the stations they talk to the soldiers on the platforms. The soldiers are in uniform, and we'll be in military clothes before the day is done. And yet, there's one small difference. We are civilians. We are traveling in compartments made for humans. They're traveling in cattle cars. Actually, they seem to be a whole lot better off than we, but that doesn't matter. We cling to our human dignity. We cling to it for yet a little longer. I'd promised myself I'd fraternize, but I can't, and I've bitterly reproached myself. Friendly banter doesn't flow easily for me. Through the windows I looked out at a tent pitched in one of those little gardens that give provincial stations their charm. It was run by the Women of France. "First Aid Service." Inside we could see a whole pharmacy, and there was a woman in a white blouse puttering at a table outside. A guy in a cap came to lean on the window bar with me and said, "Just get a look at that pretty little woman. I'd go to war if they gave me something like that . . . " And it so forcefully reminded me of the timorous horniness of soldiers in garrison that I didn't answer. I felt a twinge of guilt. Even more so when I heard him say to another guy, who was actually as tight-lipped as I, "I didn't sleep a wink all night, I don't feel good, so I gotta talk, no two ways, gotta talk, or I'll start worrying."

I slept a bit, finished *The Trial*, read *The Penal Colony*[1] and three or four newspapers that were lying around. And then I began to wait. At some station or other, I realized I was going to wait like this right to the end of the war. There were soldiers on the platform waiting. Officers too. The train crew was waiting. Everybody was waiting. It will keep on like that. At Lérouville there were masses of soldiers, they hadn't read a newspaper for two days. We passed one over to them. When will they read their next? Actually, thinking about the wait doesn't affect me one way or the other: I'm stymied. From time to time some small memory surfaces—generally a walk with you. But then it bursts on me. I feel very peaceful. Slightly impatient to get there, but it feels odd because in the end it's my body that's impatient: my legs, which want to limber up, my throat, which is thirsty. But *me*, in the long run I'll never feel better than on this train.

5:10—Things aren't Kafkaesque at all anymore, it's back to Courteline.[2] I got to the camp at 3 o'clock, with a little thump in my heart, even me. I said to myself, Here we are. And in fact there we were. At the station they told me, "Take the Number 3 tram." I took it along with three other reservists, and went right through a typical provincial town from one end to the other. At the last stop, I latched onto a guy, or rather he latched onto me. He was rather nondescript, the perfect type to have along when you're joining your regiment. He offered me a can of beer, I offered him a beer. He offered me another beer, I offered him another beer. And from beer to beer, we reached some large dreary buildings, far off in the countryside. I said to the guy, "You see, here we're still civilians, and on the other side of the fence we're not." He said, "Yes." And then we went in, we went from building to building. They said to me, "Sartre, you're with Z 11. But Z 11 has already left." Where to I don't know. What I do know is that they're going to "forward" me. Z 11 is a meteorological unit. It can't be far away. They gave me a pair of fatigue pants that are too big for me, explaining that I can simply roll up the cuffs, and a cap that's also too big but pretty jaunty. Upon which I became an unclassifiable phantom. I wander around with a card, and everyone says "Z 11? Z 11? Never heard of it." Finally I sat down on the floor, on a straw

[1]*Both by Kafka. (SdB)*
[2]Pen name of Georges Moineaux (1858–1929), who wrote *Le Train de 8 heures 47* ["The 8:47 Train"] and other satirical comedies.

mattress where I'll sleep tonight. Some guys seated around a table are discussing the political situation; another is putting on his new fatigue pants. I feel profoundly absurd and very small. But it won't last. They'll send me someplace or other and things will settle down. For the moment, the worst of it is I don't have a clue where you can write to me. I don't even have an envelope for sending this letter. I'll search one out.

As for my feelings, not only have they not changed since I saw your poor little ravaged face for the last time, on the other side of the gate at the Gare de l'Est, but they are all-consuming and almost painful. For now, I will have to live a long, long time without seeing you. My love, that will be the most difficult. If you were lying on the little straw pallet beside mine, everything would be fine and I'd be lighthearted. But you won't be lying there, it'll be some guy snoring away. Oh, my love, how I love you, how I need you. Farewell. Your whole little day runs through my head, Le Dôme, the telephone calls, the movies, I am living it hour by hour in addition to my own day. Now I'll write two brief notes, to my parents and to Tania. I love you with all my might.

To Simone de Beauvoir

Sunday, September 3

My love

I'm still waiting. I was issued fatigue pants and a kepi, but it's not quite enough to leave. Others have secured complete outfits and are leaving this evening or tomorrow morning in various directions. If by evening I've seen nothing coming, I will discreetly remind the authorities of my presence. Otherwise I can see the day coming when I'll be employed here cleaning out latrines. Last night, after writing to you, I went to the canteen with three or four guys from the Vosges. Family men. One of them was rather grief-stricken. This morning he's raging because war hasn't been declared quickly enough. Overall, opinions here are in real flux. A courteous camaraderie prevails, willing, superficial, and indistinctly addressed to *man*, an interchangeable creature. And at the same time each man is isolated by his own life, this is nothing like the animal colony that is a dormitory of twenty-year-old guys doing their military service. They are neither crude nor grumbling. Proper. In the canteen we sat down around a large table and drank coffee from white bowls. Then they found comrades from military service and hollered out to them. One guy had a photo showing all of them during their military service fifteen years earlier. It was rather sad seeing them so young in the photo in fatigues and then, in identical fatigues, in real life, hardened, fatter, their faces lined. They talked among themselves, and I left them. I went into the courtyard (there's a huge yard with a vast number of buildings). The sky was pure, it was dark, I walked around completely alone, and I understood that I would be absolutely alone as long as it lasted. I don't mind experiencing this solitude that you, my dear little one, have always spared me. I went back to the barracks dormitory, because I was tired and then because it is characteristic of army camps that even the most inventive spirit in these matters will fail to find there a favorite haven, a *querencia*.[1] It is truly "solitude in common." We're hemmed in by the human, in the German sense of the human, big guys who shit, wash themselves, snore, and smell of man. And yet a person is alone, unable to do a thing with his solitude. I was scarcely on my bed when a Corporal First Class came to courteously order us to put out the lights because of possible alerts. "Put your masks at the foot of your beds. And if you hear the alarm siren, put on fatigues and masks." We replied, "We have no masks." He answered pleasantly, "Fine. All right. Then you'll croak like rats." Cheered by that prospect, we went to sleep after one of those lapping barracks conversations, in which the lapping fades little by little, each phrase rising through the silence then falling, fading more and more gently, on dozing ears. Then silence, then suddenly a "funny" thought, then weary sleepy laughter from guys who finally get the point. For instance, they complain halfheartedly about the beds. "Puts a crick in your back. Can't sleep on the thing." Then silence, then someone: "Ah, the old lady's rump was a helluva lot softer." Laughter, then someone: "Yeah: rump and plump tits." Then silence. Except after that, till three in the morning, reservists kept on arriving every ten minutes. They would turn on the switch and the dormitory would be flooded with blinding light. We'd groan and ask, "Where you from?" "Such and such." "Is it evacuated?" "Yes." Etc. The guy would spot a pallet, take off his jacket, turn out the light, and go to sleep. Ten minutes later two or three more guys would come in. Same deal. There was one, a forty-year-old Alsatian, who said pleasantly with a heavy accent, "Excuse me, but I'm going to leave the light on for a moment to eat." Which he did, without for one second suspecting the mortal hatred I bore him. Finally I must have slept for five or six hours, then this morning at six-thirty I woke, washed, and went to the canteen for coffee. And here I am. I loaf, I wander through

---

[1] In Spanish, a favorite spot, haunt. Hemingway, among others, adopted the word from its bullring use for the place where the bull feels safe, a haven of sorts.

hallways, I write to you, I'm just one of the guys. Yesterday or the day before, they had to assume a stance of heroism or despair, but now that's all over. They know it's not asked of them. They're asked to be here. They are, that's all. Today is Sunday. But I can't go out: we're confined to the camp, and anyway I have no uniform. If this afternoon is like this morning, I'll get to work on my novel.

There you have it. I think of you all the time, but I mustn't put you in a frame or see us doing things together, or it breaks my heart. For instance, last night, untying my shoes, I imagined that they were *your* ski shoes, and how much we like to ski together (a bit, you can see, like Poupette in front of a ski store), and that wasn't very pleasant. But if I think about you as you are, and that's all, the way you are solid, solider than Paris, the way you are my life, the way you were perfect yesterday as I left Paris, that leaves me with a strong feeling of pleasure. I love you. Farewell, my dear little one, be good, read the papers, take out a subscription at Sylvia Beach's,[2] read books about the world. Don't get bored, don't be too sad. Please be ready to send me books the minute you know my address. But that address I cannot give you yet.

I send you all my love.

To Simone de Beauvoir

Monday, September 4

My love

There's something new. Guess whose house I'm staying at. A priest's. An extremely worthy man from a small parish, who gallantly let us a room in his house. We, that is the four men of the meteorological unit under Corporal Paul, of which I am now a member. Yesterday around four, I despaired of ever leaving the camp, I would have chosen to be anywhere rather than in those gloomy courtyards. I went to see the authorities and they said, "You'll have to wait a bit, buddy. We can't send you on right now." Then we learned about the declaration of war, and it was as though a wall had risen behind me to separate me from my former life. For now, that's it, I'm cut off. I went back up to the room, where an Alsatian of about forty was tearfully telling his story: the previous morning they'd mobilized him and evacuated his wife. Since he'd been sent to a different unit from the one

---

[2] Shakespeare and Company, the bookstore on the Left Bank in Paris frequented by an international literary clientele.

entered in his service record, his wife couldn't write to him, and he had no idea where she was. I stretched out on my bed, feeling not as though I were at war, but as though I were doing my military service all over again. Where-upon a small blond man wearing glasses, with the air of a timid and humiliated intellectual, wanders into the dormitory: "You don't have someone here named Sartre?" I leap to my feet. "That's me." "Pleased to meet you. Paul here. You're leaving with us tomorrow morning. Meteorological unit." I followed him, and he introduced me to two others, a big, well-fed guy of forty, a slackard if ever I've seen one, and a curly-haired Jew, in women's hats, the soul of resourcefulness. I moved into their barracks. All the equip-ment was ready; I didn't even have to go to the commissary. And this morning we left by truck. I had put on the uniform you know, but I replaced the beret with a kepi, actually far too large for me. Nonetheless, I look much more military than before. Is that because we're at war? From the truck, I caught sight of myself in mirrors, and I approved. Finally after 22 kilometers we reached a handsome little village where we were billeted on the locals, thanks to the Jew, who knows how to talk to the officers. We have a thousand francs for subsistence, a bicycle, the weather station equipment, and for the moment nothing to do, but that will change. We undoubtedly won't be staying here. But you can write to me care of M. l'Abbé de Ceintrey, Meurthe-et-Moselle. This morning we had breakfast at a restaurant, and that delighted me, seeing as I hadn't eaten anything for two days but bread and sausage. We went for a walk down the road, and the Jew managed to fix a stalled car filled with refugees. He's rather fat, with a nervous cough, and always on the go. His secret is he likes to ask favors. And he puts so much ingenuity and pleasure into his requests that so far no one has refused him a thing. He's the real head of the team. The other, a physics instructor at the Collège de Bar-le-Duc, a pessimistic, offended soul, is nominally the one in charge. An odd bunch. Who knows how many years I'll live with them? They aren't unlikable. Right now there's neither war nor peace. Rather than soldiers, we look like chauffeurs at some estate. Nothing in the village makes me think of war. On the other hand, this morning Nancy, crushed, reeked of war. Write to me soon. I'm beginning to get anxious about you. They say here that London has been bombed. If that's true, Paris will be next. Do be reasonable, dearest love, and leave the moment it gets dangerous. Now I'm beginning to realize that behind the lines too, life will really change, I fear that something quite different and rather ominous might be in store for you. In any case, don't worry about me. I love you very, very much. I didn't need this war to realize that. But the fact is that since I left, I'm cut off from everything that made up my former life—alas, even writing—except for you. You, you are truly me. My love, we are simply one, despite the distance, and that gives me a great deal of strength. Here, oddly, most of the guys are married. They wax tender about "the kid" or "the little one" or "my son," according to their social milieu. Never about the wife. I say nothing, I let them say, "You're a bachelor, you have fewer worries," but I know that I'm attached to you with all my soul.

P.S. I: The moment you get my letter, my love, send a small package of *books*.

P.S. II: I am going to get back to writing today after all, though still only with my head.

To Simone de Beauvoir

Tuesday, September 5

My darling Beaver

Here absolute tranquillity still reigns. A strange sort of life: that Jew, Pieter, is invaluable. It's thanks to him that we're billeted with the priest and eat at the house of an old retired cook, who for forty francs a day—the forty francs of subsistence funds—provides us with excellent meals. We still have nothing to do. We wait, we walk in the pleasant countryside, we pick plums (circumstances are making me something of a rustic). A strange solidarity is developing among us, due neither to esteem nor to sympathy, but rather to our identical situations. No one was waiting for us here, they have no idea what to do with us: from time to time a captain comes to look at us out of curiosity and goes away shaking his head. We get along very well with the priest, who is 89, and decided out of gratitude for his loyal services to go to mass on Sunday. I have gotten back to writing my novel, with already twelve pages of rough draft. It seems as though I might be able to keep it up, seeing that at most we will be asked to do two or three readings a day. But if our individual personal lot for the moment is an easy one, I feel a general, grave solidarity with the people at the front and in the cities that will be bombed. I would like you to give me news of young Bost—I often think of him with a sort of horror about his lot. If you give me his address, I'll write to him. We're waiting for a captain in the air force who will decide our fate. We read the papers, but they are mute. In the street outside the window of this dark room in which one of us is sewing, the two others are reading my Kafkas, and I am writing, soldiers go by, soldiers and horses. It makes for an oddly peaceful life, but within that very peace, a constant whiff of nightmare. I heard that there has been an alert over Paris. Is that true? I am beginning to worry about you.

Farewell, my dear love, I love you with all my might. When I am alone, which rarely happens, I look at your little photos. But I think it will be a long time before I forget your dear drawn face on Saturday morning.

To Simone de Beauvoir

Wednesday, September 6

My darling Beaver

Today is just like yesterday and, I suppose, tomorrow. The day after that things may change, since an air force captain left for Nancy to have them settle our fate. Meanwhile we take walks around the village and across the green countryside, and I write my novel, dutifully. It's like a slightly restricted country vacation, but a country vacation nonetheless. It costs the state ten francs per day per guy. We walk side by side, or else the four of us stay in the room. We don't have much to say to one another and we don't force the conversation. They showed each other pictures of their kids and their wives, they teased me because I write three letters a day, and, after commentary on the events, we fall silent. We're in somewhat the same situation as the village gossip who watches the doings in the street through her windows. "Oh my, an orderly is just ringing the doorbell across the street!" "So they've billeted an officer there?" "Ah! That would be the captain who got here last night," etc., etc. We are under the command of an air force captain who looks like a very good sort and who respects professors. Incidentally, there's an inspector general of German here who is a captain and wants to see us. Corporal Paul, who has an unfortunate personality, is fretting about whether he should be addressed as "Captain" or "Monsieur Inspector General." I think I told you I had perceived in his glassy eye that he is a believer, but didn't know whether it was in the Catholic faith or socialist. Inquiries have been made, and it is the socialist faith, which suits him. As for the Jew, he's the perfect incarnation of the radical[1] spirit, a schemer, he's been around. The incarnation of Heidegger's *des Man*,[2] I would

---

[1]Referring to the Radical Party, liberal and secular, under the Third Republic (1871–1940).

[2]"The they" is the English translation given in *Being and Time*.

add. Truly, from the look of him, I don't imagine that he could have been touched by the existential for one instant of his life. Actually I imagine that right now you civilians are much more existential than we are. It seems to me that because we skipped out right at the outset, we've attained the childlike simplicity of tuberculars, which de Roulet described to us. We have become pure hearts. Somehow it is a defense against the waiting. As a matter of fact I am now waiting for nothing beyond the immediate. For example, I had just begun this letter when we went off for lunch. After lunch we took a walk, during which I naturally had to "be my possibilities"—but the only one I was, was to finish this letter. It was my way of being with you, of waiting for you, talking to you. Through a sort of substitution it was you waiting for me in my room, and I was as happy to come in as though it had been to see you again. And then from time to time we have a patch of chatter and innocent laughter, comparable I suppose to those of the Carthusians, on the one day a year when they're permitted to speak. Last night, for instance, a glass of red wine had something to do with it. As for the novel, it's coming along: in the barracks at Nancy I had to force myself, but now it's smooth sailing. When I remember my peevish despair about my period of military service, I think it was a result of my bad will. Extremely justified bad will,[3] actually, but in spite of everything it proves that liberty exists. I mean that by a free effort, I have completely narrowed the circle of my universe, and I feel everyone is doing the same. But you can see that we're a long way from the far-reaching existential considerations of last September or March. Perhaps they'll return with the first cannon shot. And you, my love? Are you very dutifully writing in your little journal? Did you dutifully troop down to the cellar the other day? If I'm impatient, I am so only about receiving your letters. How are you managing your solitude? If I thought that you were peaceful, I believe that everything would go along well for a long while. Incidentally, I wonder what effect your letters will have on me. You know, it must be a bit like the times when you spend five days alone in the mountains, and you find the world again at a general delivery window.

Goodbye, my dearest, my darling Beaver. My love to you.

Until further notice, write to me care of the priest.

---

[3]*Mauvaise volonté* has been translated here as "bad will." Sartre later settled into use of the more familiar *mauvaise foi*, or "bad faith," the state in which a person is untrue to his own perceived situation or historicity.

To Simone de Beauvoir

Thursday, September 7

My darling Beaver

Nothing has changed. In any case, today I know my permanent address. From now on you should write to: "Private Sartre, Sector 108." That's all. Don't put a stamp on it, put F.M. on the envelope. I also know that I am leaving with the artillery on Monday. It is not for the air force but for the artillery that I'll be doing the readings. It's more of a bother, because we have to determine the "ballistic wind," and the calculations are complicated, though we follow the balloon to only a thousand meters instead of six thousand. What to tell you about my life? Yesterday we were presented to the colonel, who has a large white mustache and treated us with consideration because of our capacity as "specialists." Next we opened the sealed cases, took out and set up the theodolite in the room, then threw ourselves upon the instruction manual, trying to learn our specialty. It didn't take too long. After that I worked on my novel. I am at the moment when Mathieu slips into Lola's room to steal Boris's letters. I'm having a good time. Since we do a reading every three hours, I think I'll have a lot of time to work and, even if the war is short, to finish volume one during the war. If it goes on for long, I'll begin the second volume. That way I would actually gain time on civilian life. Around seven we went to have dinner at our cook's place; she's a bit annoying but she does make us fricassee of rabbit, chicken with cream sauce, and immense plum pies. My sole worry is I'll get fat. Aside from that, her conversation and noisy swallowing remind me quite of bit of old Madame Marcellou. We went to the other end of town for a coffee, at a place run by a one-armed man who also serves the officers, and there we read, like true soldiers, an old *Paris-Soir* that was lying around. After which we went back through the pitch black to the priest's house. I wrote a bit more, and we went to sleep. Unfortunately the snores coming from Pieter and Keller seem destined to prepare me for gunfire. Keller, who is profoundly and maliciously stupid, has a happy disorderly snore, with something sedentary about it. Pieter breathes heavily and from time to time bellows like a beast. As for Paul, the corporal, he sleepwalks. Today he confided in us that for ten years his constant recurring nightmare has been that he is buried in the wreckage of a collapsed house. He sees in it a portent of death, but I think rather it's such a lovely dream to psychoanalyze. It goes so well with his humble, desperate pride of the failed professor. And so well too with his mother's horrible puss, which he showed me yesterday in a photograph. We sleep on two mattresses, Pieter and Keller on one and Paul and I on the other. They are strange nights in which we wake up ten times (I've never had so much desire to pee), in which ten times we grope our way in the total darkness to the window to open the blinds and pee into the street. Nights that we extend far into the day, since we get up at eight in the morning. As you can see, we're still on a country vacation. This morning we had a breakfast of bread, foie gras, and red wine, then I studied the meteorological texts, read a bit in *The Castle*—which, in the end, I like a lot—worked on my novel a bit. The others disturb me all the time and marvel that I can work amid the noise. It's lucky I got used to it in cafés during my civilian days. I'm not at all put off by such mention of peacetime because, in the long run, this war still seems a phantom war to me. Simply put, in my eyes it has a slightly retrospective character; it's as though I were writing a historical novel. I was in a good mood this morning, the way I told you I was yesterday, but slightly enervated because I am beginning to wait very concertedly for your letters. Just think, since Saturday I've had no news from you. In the ten years I have known you, this is the first time that has happened. Anyway, we must be patient amid our setbacks; Pieter, who is just back from the post office, says that the postmistress didn't receive any letters for the village either yesterday or today. My love, how I would like to know what you're doing. Now, your letters are you. But I don't expect to get much before Sunday. But are you getting mine? I want you to know that this is the sixth I've written.

Goodbye, my dearest, totally charming Beaver, who "has given me ten years of happiness." I love you very much and kiss you with all my might.

To Simone de Beauvoir

Friday, September 8

My love

Three lines today, because it is a bit discouraging to write without knowing if the letters are reaching you. Here, no mail at all. I'm not anxious about you, because I know that the alerts have been innocuous thus far, but I would still like to know what is becoming of you. I saw that from the 10th or 12th on, they are making "high-speed" trains available to travelers. Will you go to Laigle? To Quimper? Who have you seen? Have you thought of seeing the Moon Lady? She might be amusing, who knows? I'm afraid you may be terribly bored. What if you went for a swim? It's annoying, my charming Beaver, not to know how you are managing your little life. I'd so like for you to have as little unhappiness and as much interest as possible in this new life. Don't forget to go often to the Café de Flore and scrupulously note down everything that's going on. Do they finally believe that this is serious? Perhaps not yet, and to tell the truth, the news bulletins may lend themselves to that illusion. Have you called my mother or gone to see her? And how is little Sorokine faring? That's a lot of questions, my love. And I know that the answers will head my way at very slow pace. But it is more or less to show you the preoccupations that roll around in my head all day on your behalf. I saw some photos of Paris during the morning alert, and they generally reassured me: you could see lovely salesgirls laughing as they went toward the shelters. My guess is that they chose ideal Parisians, the way they show model factories in Russia. But still, it looked like good weather there, and then there was that little whiff of Paris to it. Here everything's still the same, I haven't had news from anybody. Our little group is splitting in two: Pieter, fearless, optimistic, resourceful, materialistic—and on the other side, Keller, enormous, lazy, fearful, with Paul, idealistic, timid, appallingly pessimistic. I think that his pessimism, which obviously derives in the first place from his offended personality, also occurs to him as a duty. The other day he was laughing and abruptly broke off, saying, "If someone had told me a week ago that I'd be laughing now, I would have been disgusted." He feels that to contemplate his lot serenely while his buddies are getting killed would be unpardonable puerility, and, lacking the means to experience a condition as dismal as the guys in the infantry, he makes himself consider his own in such a way that it finally appears gloomy to him. So he interrupts conversations inopportunely with a sigh, eyes to the heavens, and disillusioned words. Example, Pieter to me, joking: "If they chop off your legs, you get the Croix de Guerre?" Me, also joking: "I'd rather do without the cross than my legs." And Paul with a sigh, completely serious and in the mawkish and civilized tone of the universitarian: "Alas, I'm afraid we will neither keep the one nor obtain the other." I ranted at him a bit, pointing out that he was temporarily enjoying such exceptionally good fortune that, on the contrary, it would be shameful to be sad. But I didn't convince him in the least. Like many physics professors, he likes to recite lilting prose, generally from Barrès, in a melodious tone ending in whispers. He annoys me some, but not too much. Above all he is inoffensive. Finally, I seem instead to have taken a vague liking to the "materialist," the schemer Pieter, who has just now meticulously drawn up his will but is always cheerful and fully anticipates a safe return. As for Keller, the fat weakling, I don't hate him, particularly since I realized he looks like an elephant seal. Aside from that, last night we had dinner, we took a walk in the dark, we slept very well. This morning we stayed in the room, and I worked on my novel. The draft of chapter XI is done, and I've begun the fair copy. We had lunch, we went to stretch out on the grass on a riverbank, and they bucolically picked Alsatian and mirabelle plums while I smoked a cigar. And here I am.

My love, this morning I gazed for a good long time at your photos. I don't want to pine to see you, simply to get your letters. But about that I do feel desperate. And then you must know that I am tremendously happy that you exist. For me you are solider than Paris, which could be destroyed, solider than anything: you are my whole life, which I will find again on my return. I love you passionately.

To Simone de Beauvoir

Saturday, September 9

My darling Beaver

I have nothing to tell you. We are waiting, we are leaving the day after tomorrow. We are still living the strange idle life, restricted on all sides by the war. Corporal Paul is gloomier and gloomier—he gets a bit on my nerves—and Keller more and more slothful. This morning Pieter gave me a long exposition on anti-Semitism. I said "yes" every two minutes, drawing on my pipe, and he seemed satisfied. Aside from that, trivial worries absorb us: the priest, the priest's maid, the sexton's wife (who cooks for us), the blacksmith, that's the company we generally keep. We endlessly discuss petty incidents. The blacksmith didn't want to lend us a key for our sealed case, and the captain threatened to requisition it. That's enough to keep more than one conversation going. While I think of it, here finally is a complete address—but I hope that the letters sent to other addresses won't be lost:

Private Sartre
Meteorological Post
Artillery General Staff
Sector 108

I have been worrying about you since this morning, because I haven't received any letters. The colonel called us together today and said, "Should your information prove useful to us, gentlemen, I will so inform you, as encouragement." We have a captain and a lieutenant, who are splendid guys.

There is no difference here between the men and the sergeants; everyone's on familiar terms. Fortunately we are very far from peacetime discipline; the locals are beginning to hate us, some because we are soldiers, others because we aren't yet at the front. Particularly the sexton's wife. This morning she said to Paul, putting some badly cooked potatoes on his plate, "Eat up. That way you'll dic fat." She thought for a moment after that so delicate remark and added, "But it's true that you're not like the others. You're not exposed." "Same with your son-in-law," answered Pieter. "He's been mobilized in a factory." "Oh," she said, "but it's certain to be bombed." Last night we sat on a bench across from the priest's house. We hardly fit, because of Keller's elephant-seal behind. There wasn't a light in the whole village, because of the passive defense regulations, but the sky was very bright and filled with stars. We could see hesitant shadows pass by; from time to time officers lit their flashlights every ten paces. Down the street a guy was singing "J'attendrai" in a rather nice tenor voice, and all of last year's songs. All we needed was mandolins. We weren't saying very much—our camaraderie is anonymous. We communicate on the extreme surface, but each of us is distanced from the others by his whole life, like the spray of a bursting shell, if I may put it that way. Pardon this first philosophico-military joke. Again this morning I worked a bit; I'll send you what I've done, chapter by chapter, in a registered letter, the moment the postal service offers reliable guarantees of security. I'll keep the drafts. I'm dying for a letter from you, my sweet. But it's a desire without impatience, because nothing allows me to expect it on one date rather than another. I would also likc some books; by tomorrow I will have finished all those I brought. I don't know whether it's because it is so much in keeping with army life, but I liked *The Castle* a lot.

Goodbye, my charming Beaver, I so want you to be neither anxious nor sad. I love you with all my heart.

I must admit something: if I bear up cheerfully under the separation, the wait, the life I lead here, it is because the war *interests me*. I feel I'm in a foreign country, which I'm going to explore bit by bit. Like when I was in Berlin five years ago.

To Simone de Beauvoir

Sunday, September 10

My darling Beaver

I've received your first letter, and it gave me incredible pleasure and a short of shock. For a moment the ice was broken, and it was pleasant and painful. I have read and reread every detail you gave me. I love you so much. In another letter I'll answer everything you've told me. *That might not be tomorrow.* We've leaving tonight, destination unknown, and I won't go into it further because we're up to our necks in bundles. I love you. I'm extremely sorry that your little *querencia* at the Café de Flore is closed. Are you going to write your novel? I am furious because if I had stayed here, I would certainly have gotten a letter from you tomorrow, instead of which now I'll have to wait a long time, however long it takes to forward it. Keep on writing to Private Sartre, Readings Post—Artillery General Staff—Postal Sector 108.

I hug you with all my might, my charming Beaver, my dear little wife.

I'm furious at my mother's ridiculous comment.[1] I wouldn't have thought her so stupid.

To Simone de Beauvoir

Tuesday, September 12

My darling Beaver

I didn't write to you yesterday. I wonder when you'll get this letter. I've reread yours several times, and each reading seemed like a new one. Particularly the part where you say how you are bound to me. Believe it or not, when you wrote you would not survive me if there were some disaster, I felt a profound peace: I wouldn't like to leave you behind, not because you'd be a free little consciousness sauntering around the world and I'd be jealous, but because you've persuaded me you would be in an absurd world. It would be the ultimate cleansing, as though the two ends of the severed worm were annihilated. But don't worry, I was thinking about all that in the abstract, since I'm in a charming Alsatian village, very secure and comfortable. Besides,

---

[1]"It'll show him a bit of life, it'll do him good" (Simone de Beauvoir, *Lettres à Sartre*, Vol. 1 [Paris, 1990], p. 91).

I also think, in the long run, that I'd definitely want you to go on with your own little life without me: to me, a life cut short does seem, after all, a loss of something good. The fact is, in any case, I've never felt so intently that you are me. That has deeply moved me over these past two days. I love you so, my darling Beaver. Besides, when two people have lived together for ten years, and thought with each other and for each other, without anything serious ever coming between them, it has to be more than love. Now, tell me, you speak of only *one* of my letters and you say you're happy because communications are reestablished between us. But in fact, as of today I've written ten, counting this one. Have they reached you? Please tell me. It strikes me as very strange and a little sad that you're so alone in Paris. I hope Zazoulich comes soon, and that you go to Quimper. And why not call Rirette Nizan? It'll be a great treat to see her, and, alone and in a panic, she'll talk. Everything you told me kept me really entertained. Always tell me everything in detail—you can't imagine how much it interests me. I'm afraid Gide's *Journal* must be lost if you sent it to the priest's. Don't forget to send me Dabit's *Journal*.[1] Add to that the September 1st *NRF*, four pads of paper ruled in squares like the one I brought with me, and fifty regular envelopes. If any new Masque and Empreinte detective novels have come out, send them along too (I have the latest Empreinte: *Le Mystère de la Falaise* ["The Mystery of the Cliff"]). Thanks.

Tomorrow they're finally going to give the address of Sector 108 to our central post office, so I hope I'll get five or six letters from you all at once. Also: has there been any mail for me? Don't forget to stop by the *NRF* and ask for my money. At the same time you could ask, 1, if *L'Imaginaire* will appear anyway;[2] 2, if the *NRF* is still publishing. If you've already been there, telephone, in my name, to find out. The novel is moving along like clockwork. If things stay quiet for a while, I'll have it finished in *four months*. When you come right down to it, I'm working more here than in Paris. After the four months, if the war is still going on I'll begin the second volume.

I didn't write to you yesterday because I had no time. Here's what's been happening: Sunday night at one forty-five, reveille. We loaded our possessions on our backs: helmeted, gun on the shoulder, mask slung across the chest and four musette bags apiece. We looked splendid, I must admit. Alas, there was no one to photograph me in my outfit. In addition on my

---

[1]Eugène Dabit (1898–1936). His *Journal* was published in 1939.
[2]Gallimard published it in 1940; it later appeared in English as *The Psychology of Imagination*.

left arm I was carrying my overcoat and a fruit basket Pieter's wife had sent him. Overwhelmed by these burdens, I went to a narrow street to join around fifty men who were slipping through the village in the dark of night with the look of conspirators. Then, since war is ultimately part of military life, we waited, for no reason, about an hour. Then we went down to the railroad embankment. There, another wait, with several handsome compensatory nocturnal human touches: one time it was the beam of an officer's flashlight, which abruptly plucked several helmets out of the darkness in a halo of light, another time it was the blue headlights of a military car suddenly revealing fifty heavy and heavily burdened men, gray-black, marching between two rows of poplars. From there we crowded onto the platform of the small station. And more waiting, this time with no compensations, beside a very short train (three passenger cars, six cattle cars), which did nothing but lurch backward and forward in front of us for an hour. A false order had us climb up into the cars "for men," but immediately an officer had us get off: "You think these're for you?" Great, I said to myself, we get the cattle cars. Not unappealing, actually. But finally, at five-thirty, we were piled into some second-class cars, like grown-ups. Pieter and Keller were in one car, Paul and I in another. I had a corner. I was enchanted seeing the gray of dawn rising across all the dozing men in the trim compartment. I pondered the wartime world and conceived the project of writing a journal. Would you send me, in the package, a strong black notebook—thick but not too tall nor too wide, ruled in squares of course.[3] The dawn revealed a photo of Rouen attached to the wall. I saw the Rouen quays again, photographed from the left bank, and suddenly I felt very melancholy and yet full of good feelings for Olga. She seemed precious, and I felt happy to have had that affair with her. Upon which sleep overtook me, and when I awoke, there was a blazing sun, it was eight in the morning. We traveled till two-thirty at—I do not exaggerate— an average speed of eight kilometers an hour. When it was moving the little train managed a good forty, but it didn't move often, nor for long. We passed other trains of soldiers who were eating—as for us, we had empty stomachs— and then trains of refugees, old people, women and children, who'd been on the train for *twelve* days. The thing is that when there are military convoys—which naturally have priority—they park the others on the side tracks, where they wait, sometimes for as long as twelve hours. We handed them

---

[3]In all Sartre would fill fifteen notebooks during the "phony war," writing from September 1939 to March 1940. Five survive and were published in Paris in 1983 as *Les Carnets de la drôle de guerre* (*The War Diaries* [New York, 1985]).

some cans through the door. During that whole time I neither read nor talked, but I wasn't bored: we were still in a state of military waiting. When you see me again, my love, I certainly won't be embittered or changed, but from time to time I may have the same heavy gaze and wooden expression—we've been seeing it recently even on Bost—that I see every day; in civilian life, I'll still be waiting, mistakenly, out of habit. Suddenly the train stopped in open country and we were unloaded. We waited an hour at one spot, then they had us go eight hundred meters and we waited for two hours at another spot. It was very nice. There was thick grass beside the road, and we stretched out: above our heads were pine woods on a steep slope. On the other side of the road, a parapet to keep people from falling into the railroad gully, and on the far side of the track, a sheer red cliff, topped by an oak forest: through the treetops you could see the sky. Finally at 10, two trucks came to get us. There wasn't room for all the men, and Pieter stayed behind with a dozen others and a lieutenant. Supposedly the truck would return to pick them up an hour later. We had a nice excursion through an area I know well, and I rediscovered smells of the Alsatian countryside I'd completely forgotten. Following which we reached a village at nightfall, and they lodged us temporarily in the boys' school, with the clerks of the AP [Artillery Post], rather pleasant guys (the staff sergeant, an enormous Fatty Arbuckle, is a government architect in private life). We slept on straw, and it's very pleasant, I prefer it to the priest's mattress. I slept like a god. This morning, great activity: they had to find a place for the weather unit. We went around ringing the doorbells of the most attractive houses, but in each one the vacant rooms were taken by officers. Finally a rather appealing woman gave us a room looking out onto her garden, with permission—I'll forgo the pleasure—to eat her plums. We quickly had our kit loaded on a truck and brought it here, because the colonel looked as though he might change his mind and was already talking of having us do readings in the schoolyard. We are well thought of. It is understood in high places that we "lack military demeanor," but they appreciate our competence. To tell the truth, what we know is of no use to anyone, but we're the only ones who know what we know. Right now we're settled into the woman's house. Her husband is a soldier and, by an extraordinary stroke of luck, was sent here, just like us, from his mobilization center in Nancy. They gave us mattresses and are nice to us. I ate some corned beef with the clerks at lunch—it's very good—and then I worked on my novel for a while at the school. Then I returned here and began to write to you, but the lieutenant came to find out once and for all what he should think of our capabilities. He had us show him the theodolite, we set it up and took it down, after which we were dazzling about the psychrometer, the Nord Lambert, the hand-held anemometer. Edified, he departed, and I'm writing to you. There isn't a table yet in this little room, which is cluttered instead with photographs and objets d'art, but I'm writing to you sitting on an equipment case with my paper resting on the other case, which is higher. Keller, the elephant seal, is babbling away beside me, but I don't reply. Now I must write to Tania. I'm going to smoke a pipe and chat with Keller before getting down to it. Farewell, my dear love, I love you passionately, you are my totally charming little Beaver.

Please Turn Over

I forgot to finish the story of the trip—we waited in vain for Pieter all last evening. He got in this morning: the truck arrived only at eleven to pick them up. They'd waited in the dark, the lieutenant got impatient, went off for information, fell headfirst into a ravine, bashing his skull.

To Simone de Beauvoir

September 13

My darling Beaver

Today I was hoping to receive at least ten letters, but nothing came. It reminds me of the compulsory isolation they imposed on us during the first two weeks of military sivice. It's nearly two weeks since I left you, and I've had all of one letter from you. From my parents, from Tania, nothing. No packages either. Fortunately this morning Paul went to the village and brought back two detective novels from Masque. I've just read one—it wasn't great. So, once more I'm waiting, and I think—by what some are saying—that I'll have to wait five or six days more before I get any sign of life from you at all. I'm also resigned to finding out that several of your letters have been lost. That's the way things go here. Nonetheless I'm really dying to know what you're up to, dear Beaver. In any case I know that Paris is very quiet, and I strongly suspect that you never go down into the shelters during the alerts. You must be bursting with stories about everyone right now—how I'd like to hear them! Perhaps you've had news from Bost. I'm afraid you may have received none of my letters (except for one) and you're anxious. I love you very much, my little dearest.

Since yesterday there's really very little new to say. We had dinner at an inn packed with soldiers, after checking seven cafés and restaurants in a vain search. Everything was filled with soldiers, and we were told there wasn't a crumb left. Finally, as we were despondently buying some bread to eat back at home, the proprietress of the bakery, who also owns an inn, said, "In ten minutes there'll be four free chairs at one table—I'll make you an omelette." So we waited a moment and then squeezed into a table for eight that already had six occupants. I was squashed against an enormous Alsatian who could easily be taken for a Bavarian and was silently drinking his sixth half-bottle. After which he began to indulge in a range of meditative and puzzled expressions, which made me think of the *Oseille* and the Bar Océanic. Meanwhile we were eating heartily in an incredible haze of smoke and ruckus. I wasn't saying a word, for I was separated by a table width from Pieter and Keller— and the noise was such that the width of that table was as good as a hundred meters of countryside—and because I was on the side of Paul's bad ear, he would occasionally send me the smile of the deaf. But I was blissfully happy. My ears were filled with noise, I was watching the fat Alsatian drink, I was watching Paul eat, and he eats heartily but with the finicky delicacy and slow steadiness of a universitarian. And I thought in passing of Bost's novel, where he tells how his father used to eat. And at five to nine we replaced our helmets and masks (slung across the chest, of course) and went back home to bed. The mattress I share with Paul is so small I spent the whole night teetering on the edge and twice found myself on the floor. This morning I worked, quite well, and we went off for lunch in pairs to another rather pleasant inn, where we had the following mysterious dialogue with a fat Alsatian. He said, "It bugs me that I'm going to be sent to the rear." "You'd prefer the front lines?" "Of course!" "You want to fight!" "Oh no!" "Well then?" "At the rear, pal, you've got the planes." We went home, sauntering through the little old village, so trim, so varnished, with green and pink houses, completely surrounded by orchards loaded down with fruit, and so here I am. Yesterday there were neither tables nor chairs. Today there's progress: we have two chairs. Tomorrow we'll give our packages of lentils and rice to the landlady in exchange for a table. Tomorrow we'll have some hydrogen and will start right in with the "trial" readings at the rate of one a day. The other day a guy said, "For all that we're at war, you'd think we're on field maneuvers." And that's certainly the way it is for us. I'm smack in the middle of the military world, and I do nothing but guess about the world of war. In one sense, if I weren't writing, I wouldn't have kept that little civilian obstinacy that makes me a bit impermeable, I'd be like a barometer. But I prefer to be slightly less permeable and to write. My three companions respect my writing, actually, and arrange things so I can work in peace. There's a bit of a running battle between Keller and Pieter, because Keller—meek and lazy and slightly stingy too—would like to eat at the field kitchen, depend directly on the officers, and not give a damn about anything. He's scared of freedom. On the other hand, Pieter is jealously protective of our solitude and wants to eat in restaurants. Pieter wins, but Keller has a formidable power of inertia. To tell the truth, I feel a little swindled, after setting off with a sort of stoicism, to find myself among these three scared rabbits and manipulators, against whom stoicism is useless. But no doubt you would congratulate yourself for it, my darling Beaver.

Goodbye. You see, I had set out to do only short letters, and I'm writing long ones. That's because I love you so, and I love to write to you. Now I'm going to write to Tania. That's no fun, because the other day I realized anxiously that if the war were to last three years, as the English think (but I do not), I won't ever see her again: she'll be dead, crazy, or gone off with some other guy. So, for my own peace of mind, I consummated an interior provisional breakup with her. But all of this is on the back burner. There is no one but you, my charming Beaver, now and always present. I love you.

To Simone de Beauvoir

September 14
Private Sartre
Readings Post
AD General Staff
Sector 108

My darling Beaver

Nothing really new. I went into town this morning to get a tank of hydrogen at the weather station. A charming little town, one that would be pleasant to explore in different times, with German-style taverns and houses with steep roofs. The barracks are pink sandstone, like the church in the village where we are living. We went there by truck, Corporal Paul and I; I sat in the back, pipe in mouth, helmet on head, jouncing with each bump. We carried the heavy hydrogen tank to the truck on our backs, then before going back we did our errands. Tobacco, tobacco pouches, candy for the daughter of our landlady, newspapers. We had a glass of wine in one of the taverns—tables of pine, mid-height pine partitions, low arched windows— then we went back. I had bought a leather notebook for my journal, and I started in this morning. Everyone here knows I write. Paul told the colonel, and this morning a captain who saw Pieter said to him: "And your friend the novel-ist, has he written much since yesterday?" Taking another tack, the colonel suggested I give him philosophy lessons to round out his general culture. Otherwise, royal peace. We had a splendid breakfast this morning, and of course we drink the local white wine. Keller feels we're spending too much and there'll soon be repercussions. He still doesn't give a damn about anything and seems intent on keeping it up. He'd like all four of us to do the readings, because then he'd be the fourth, which is to say the fifth, wheel on the wagon. But I'll stand firm on doing them two by two, because that way I'll only have one or two a day to do. It seems I'm acquiring that military air, because this morning the local bookstore proprietor asked me, "Was it quiet for you last night at the front?" "All quiet," I replied. I'd just read it in the papers. I'm still in excellent spirits, and there's just one hitch: still no letters. We'll stay here for two weeks and then go to a place that's even quieter, where, perhaps, I'll be able to do a bit of skiing this winter. I love you very much, my darling Beaver, and right now, I'm no longer hoping, I *know* I'll see you again— just as though I were back from a long trip. Be totally confident and calm.

I love you tenderly.

To Simone de Beauvoir

September 15

My darling Beaver

Today I scarcely have time to write to you. It's six-fifteen; we've just done the first reading, a trial reading. It took us exactly four hours. First it took an hour to install the theodolite on *true* north (because it is set to magnetic north). Then we released and immediately lost sight of a first balloon, much to the ironic pleasure of two state police. We inflated another, we released it, and it was a hell of a job to do the analysis. Naturally we'll get the hang of it, but in any case it takes much longer than I thought. Aside from that, I'm living like a king. This morning roll call was at six forty-five, after which we went to a tavern for breakfast, then I worked awhile on my novel, then I went to take a bath at the hairdresser's, right after my captain: the tub was still hot. After which, lunch at a restaurant—salted beef, salad, plum pie. And then the interminable reading, which wore me out. I have some hope of getting your letters at dinnertime. The postal clerk left this morning to get two bags of mail in town and hasn't reappeared. Either he's dead drunk in some ditch, or else there really were letters hung up in transit.

Goodbye, I still love you very much and very tenderly, and I kiss you on your dear little eyes.

Soon I'll have some photos of me in my helmet; I'll send them to you.

To Simone de Beauvoir

September 16

My darling Beaver

There's a package for me at the post office. A small one. From you? That would be the first sign of you I've had since Ceintrey. Except that for me to get it the postal clerk has to sign a discharge, and of course the postal clerk isn't there. Letters, none. There were 100 this morning for the whole division but not one for the AD. That's already some progress. Our first sergeant hasn't had a letter in twenty-five days. This silence is beginning to weigh on us. I think that our existence would be different—perhaps more vulnerable—if we had daily news from our civilian lives. I'd so like to know what's going on in your life. I get the impression that after some few days of gloom, Paris is beginning to come back to life. Am I wrong? Have you gotten back to your novel? And are you giving a little attention to "the social life"? For me, I feel out of touch with social matters. This war is so disconcerting— still Kafkesque, and rather like the battle in *The Charterhouse of Parma*.[1] It defies thought; I struggle valiantly to catch it, but ultimately everything I think holds good for field maneuvers, not for the war; the war is always screened, elusive. Actually there's nothing new. I'm calm, but the calm doesn't much satisfy me, it isn't a calm based on good reasons, and I justify myself in my little black notebook. Whoever reads it after my death—for you will publish it only posthumously—will think that I was an evil character unless you accompany it with benevolent and explanatory annotations. In short, I'm morally a bit disoriented (don't worry, moral preoccupations don't spoil my appetite), like the guy who, getting ready to lift a heavy barbell, suddenly realizes it's hollow and, at the same time, that deep down he was hoping it was. Needless to say, he finds himself flat on his ass.

[1] In Stendhal's splendidly ironic scene, the naive young hero, Fabrice, riding in a detachment escorting Marshal Ney, blunders his way, uncomprehending but lucky, through his first battle—Waterloo.

In five days we'll be in our tents and doing readings for an artillery school. That means more field maneuvers, but I enjoy the camping side of it. Here they're quite blunt about it and call sleeping bags meat sacks. It's the technical term. We're the meat. It rained today and we couldn't do any readings. We'll have to do three tomorrow. We stayed in the room, and I'm rather pleased with what I wrote. The other days I was dubious. Oh, how I miss you, good little adviser. And not only for that. I'd so like to see your nice little face. But I don't think about it too much, and as I say, I'm calm.

With all my love, my little dearest.

To Simone de Beauvoir

The 17th of September

My darling Beaver

This morning a letter from you (written the 12th) and this afternoon another letter (from the 8th). There are more missing, but you can't imagine how it enlarges my life to regain some contact with you. It is like when the movie suddenly comes up on the big screen. Now once more I have solid and—I must admit—slightly painful ties with Paris. And particularly, *concrete* links with you. I can imagine your life so well. I don't find it a whole lot of fun, my love, it upsets and saddens me, and I realize that it is I who have the easier role because—until further orders—I don't have to be anxious about you. As far as I'm concerned, you can be *absolutely* reassured, my love. I'm not part of the artillery but of the artillery General Staff. I probably cannot give you details, for fear of censorship, on the reciprocal positions of the batteries and the General Staff, but in any case you can consider that I am in complete security. There are also other security reasons that I cannot explain here at all, but they are decisive. Believe me, my love. If ever I am exposed, you well know that I will tell you: you, you are me, I wouldn't want to risk danger without your knowing it. I received three untroubled letters from my parents, the Gide, which enchants me (you must know that now I would like Dabit's *Journal intime* ["Intimate Journal"]. But until further notice you won't have heavy costs on books for me: our work on the readings, my novel, my notebook, and three letters a day absorb the greater part of my time), and finally a sad little letter from Tania, which stirred my heart. She writes to me every day (but of course this is the first I've received), she seems terribly dejected. My love, do all you can to have her come to Paris (without ruining yourself). Reimburse M. Bienenfeld[1] with the money from the *NRF*, and if that isn't enough, don't worry, ask for delays. And try to give a thousand francs a month to the two Z's, perhaps they'll be able to get along on that, particularly if Z. is to live with you at the Pardos'.[2] Anyway, I trust you to work it all out; I'd feel truly guilty leaving Tania in Laigle.

For us there's still no change. We conscientiously try to do the readings, but the balloons leak the moment we blow them up; they're rotten. So the colonel has ordered a halt to the readings to save hydrogen, until the new balloons arrive, and for a while we'll fall back into our lazy waiting again. My dearest, my darling Beaver, your letters have given me back a whole realm of feeling that had been frozen. I'm so sorry about your life, and I long to see you again. I love you passionately.

(1) Write to me again giving very exact details on your visit to the *NRF*, and tell me what I must write them.

(2) I am pleased that you're staying in Paris.

To Simone de Beauvoir

September 18

My darling Beaver

I'm writing every day in my little notebook: the misadventures of a Stoic; you can guess what they are: the circumstances are too ironically easy and favorable for the worthy Stoic that I am. And that should reassure you too. I've also written that in order to feel this phantom war in all its sinister gravity, I had to read your letters. You were feeling the war much more than I, my poor charming Beaver. Here it's still and always field maneuvers. Since the order stopping the readings we have nothing left to do all day long. My three acolytes yawn, wallow in bed, and though not hungry eat the peaches in the garden, which are half rotten and full of worms, and they wail, "It's so fucking boring here!" Whereas I, unable to avoid a slight feeling of superiority (which I also noted and condemned in my notebook), I'm writing for all I'm worth. In three days I'll have finished my chapter XIII. Then I'll have to confront the problem of the mail service. To keep it here would be to risk losing it or getting it all screwed up. To send it would be to risk having it go astray or that the censor might see some coded message in it. After what people have

---

[1]*The father of one of my very good friends.* (SdB)
[2]*Gégé, married then to Pardo, lent me her apartment, since she had left Paris.* (SdB)

seen, along those lines, in Shakespeare's plays, I wouldn't be surprised if they found a long account of military operations in my works. Aside from that, one day is lamentably like the next, but that doesn't bother me. One disappointment: I am still without three of your letters, those of the 9th, 10th, 11th (since I got those of the 8th and 12th), three letters from Tania (the one you sent me and two others), and a letter from my mother. In all, seven letters, at the most conservative estimate. I'd hoped that some would arrive today—or else, at very least, the next ones, from the 13th on. But I got nothing at all. I hope there won't be a single one lost. I am having a very good time reading the Gide. Enticed by what you told me about it, I began with 1914 and really enjoyed it. In the long run you're not facing great expenses for books, since I'm reading little; when I have the time I prefer to write, and the time will surely come again when I'm taking weather readings, and then I don't know if I'll have more than an hour or two a day for my book. What else to tell you: if this goes on as is, this war will change me neither for good nor ill. It will be—not even a test—a withdrawal from the world.

My love, your letters touch me more forcefully, more profoundly than you can know. They are like a slight warmth that suddenly thaws me, then I freeze again. I'm eager for more of them. As an instance: I learned from your letter of the 8th that you were going to have Z. come, and then from your letter of the 12th that you are sharing your "apartment" with her, but I don't have any background on her arrival and your explanations. Write me everything in detail—the smallest detail of your life is terribly precious to me.

I love you, you who are me, most passionately.

To Simone de Beauvoir

September 19

My darling Beaver

I'm writing to you in the large study hall of the boys' school, sitting at a light-colored wooden desk, my gas mask behind me, two typewriters beside me. The windows with blue-spattered panes are open, the electric lights are on, it's raining outside. It's five o'clock; in the house next door a radio is broadcasting Hitler's speech in German, and even over here I can hear him shouting, I can hear the crowd's *Heils*. The Alsatian staff clerks went downstairs to listen, but they soon came back: "Always the same thing, waste of time." So right now Hitler is talking to himself in the street.

I've spent the whole day here, because it's a good place to work. Of course, there is a perpetual bustling of officers and noncommissioned officers. But I'm used to cafés. And then the mails are supposed to be imminent, and I wanted to get your letters as soon as possible. In fact, around noon, I did get three letters from you, three letters from my mother, and one from Tania. Your letters are from the 10th, 11th, and 14th. I think the series is complete, since you must not have written on the 13th, and I have the ones of the 9th and the 12th. My love, how precious it is to me to know about the daily details of your little life. Now Paris exists again for me. It is so full, so filled with you. I don't know if it's because of that, but this afternoon a few little recollections surfaced like bubbles to make me rather sad. This rain reminds me of our last days in the Pyrenees and Bourg-Madame, when we arrived in the evening and you went to buy your chocolates at the grocery. My love, how poetic that seems to me. How much I loved you, how much I love you. My little dearest, today I'd gladly sacrifice a finger to see you again for five minutes and *tell* you that I love you. But that will come. It seems that the system for home leave might take effect on October 1st. Of course, we can't expect that I'll get one right away. But maybe around Christmas, or at the latest in March. In a bit I'll write to the NRF to have them send you some money.

Tania's letter is moving. She writes this sentence with a touching naiveté that I understand so well: "If it all were to stop in time, I think I'd attain perfection, in my work, with you, with everyone; I'd be limitlessly, truly happy my whole life through." Everything depends on what she means by "in time." It amounts to an invocation to God: "My God, if you get me out of this, you'll see how good I'll be."

Today we tried on our masks, because they're going to make us go through the gas chamber. I was scared to death, because I was suffocating in mine and almost fell over backward. It was because I'd forgotten to take the cap off. In fact it works beautifully. The ugliest thing in this apparatus is the guys' *foreheads*, which become red and bestial. I worked well all day. Everyone around me has the same feeling that it's a phantom war. A fat senior sergeant shook his head this morning: "This is an odd state of war." And he added, satisfied, mysterious, "It's a political war."

Adieu, my dearest, I love you passionately, and I feel it very strongly and very painfully, today. Write to me every day.

To Simone de Beauvoir

September 20

My darling Beaver

Today I got your letter of the 15th in which you tell me about Bienenfeld's[1] claims. I'm afraid my answer will reach Paris only after your departure for Quimper. In any case, I agree with you all along the line. This is not at all because your absence made me more loving. But, quite reasonably, I don't see what she has to reproach you for. For God's sake, we're at war, and that presumes a mass of petty annoyances that could keep you in Paris: to stay with Z., who is worrying about young Bost and his immediate future, is not futile; rather, it would be wretched to do otherwise. And also it's quite natural that you wanted to stay in order to be reassured on my account—inasmuch as you run a good risk of getting no letter during your whole stay in Quimper. This said, I quite understand her panic and her longing to see you again. But actually it's not a question of not doing that, but simply of putting your trip off awhile. In writing all this to you I seem like the Gentleman writing to the Lady, giving her lengthy reasons for her having done what she has done: same absence, same powerlessness, same ratiocinations. Essentially, I don't see how anyone could blame you at all.

Like me, you don't appear to be "realizing" the war, making it seem real. (I put the word in quotes because there are lengthy arguments about this problem in Gide. I consider it indispensable, as he does. I don't see any term to take its place.) I suppose this is our common fate. I'm actually persuaded that this is because it hasn't really begun, and also because we're *bracing* ourselves to realize the war of 1914 while adapting poorly to the one of 1939. I really think it will be a phantom war with a minimal consumption of human matériel. I'm happy you're keeping up your interest in your novel, as I am in mine. I do think that the question of conscience still ranks above considerations of war. And above all it seems to me that it is somewhat our role to maintain that *primacy*, at a time when minds are particularly sensitive to anecdote and mise-en-scène. I think an air raid can seduce a novelist only through its immediacy or picturesque quality—or else through the portrayal of conscience that it brings into play—but then not more than any other subject. Simply, when you take it up again, you may perhaps have the

---

[1] *A former student who became my friend.* (SdB) Bianca Bienenfeld is the real name of the pseudonymous Louise Védrine.

impression, as I do, of writing a historical novel, something like the *Thibaut*[2] of '39 (leaving aside the question of value, my poor good Beaver). Keep on with it to the best of your ability. You're doing enough for current events by keeping your journal.

I read today that Pitoëff[3] died. It gave me a rather unpleasant "end of an era" feeling. Now it is over, and come what may, the Cartel of Four will never again dominate the scene. And the others, particularly Baty and Dullin, aren't young either. At least one will certainly die during the war. I was thinking yesterday how strange it is to see my whole life as a youth and a man squeezed between two wars, and how that now seemed to constitute *an era*. Whence lengthy considerations in my notebook, which I'll show you.

Last night Corporal Paul, who is a sleepwalker, gave us quite a scare. Already the night before, terrorized by the same nightmare that has been recurring for the past ten years when he's overtired (he dreams he's trapped beneath wreckage), he got up in the dark, sound asleep, went to crouch against the fireplace, and scratched my feet. But last night it was worse. We go to bed, I insert Quiès earplugs, which I've dubbed DAK (defense against Keller, because he snores), and I go to sleep. An hour later, I wake bolt upright, the light was on and Pieter and Keller were struggling with Paul, who was half sitting up, his eyes open, livid and crying out, "The roof! The roof!" They got him to lie down, while he grumbled, "I thought the roof was caving in on me." Here's what had happened: Pieter and Keller couldn't get to sleep because our landlady's dog was howling uncontrollably (God knows why). They finally thought there was someone in the garden and rather indiscreetly turned the light on. When they got up to take a look at the garden through the window, they saw Paul, with a terrifying expression on his face, trying to get up, tangled in his covers, kicking like a fly in milk, yelling "The roof." They put him back to bed. He went back to sleep, I think, without having understood what had happened to him. This morning we told him everything, and he blurted out "Oh! Ohs!" and "Reallys" of embarrassment and apology. We went to the village, both of us, and he confided that he was terribly unstrung. "Pieter too," I told him. And it's true: Pieter is falling to pieces. His nervous tics are consuming him: he sniffs, coughs, clears his throat, and shakes his head all day long. As for Keller, he is wallowing in

[2]An eight-volume social-psychological novel about the Thibaut family, which won the Nobel Prize for Roger Martin du Gard (1881–1958).
[3]Georges Pitoëff (1884–1939), Russian-born director who introduced many modern foreign plays to French audiences; one of the major theater figures, along with Louis Jouvet, Charles Dullin, and Gaston Baty.

the flaccid sadness of a starving elephant seal. Paul replied, "Yes, only you have stayed completely yourself." And that pleased me. But there's an explanation: it is neither fear nor regret that is overwhelming them, but boredom. And literature is preserving me. Forgive me, my darling Beaver, but I really think I'll copy out that anecdote, word for word, in the letter I'm going to write to T. right now. It seems to me that, sensitive to feelings as I can be, there's nothing wrong in that, since it's actually impersonal, and I would tell it aloud in just about the same terms to you as to others. You know, it's hard work writing three letters a day. Three letters, five pages of novel, four pages of notebook: in my whole life I've never written so much. I got the letter from F., about which there is nothing to say, and the letter from Catinaud (did you understand that it was Magnane?), which amused me: he is contemplating writing a novel at the front (though invalided out and far removed from any army discharge board), because he knows I'm going on with mine in the army. The attempts at imitation continue, but clearly from a great distance. I wrote to Gallimard to send you a check—the letter went off yesterday. What more to tell you? This afternoon we tried out the shelters. Ours is a repulsive little cellar, where the temptation to put on a gas mask, even without an alert, is very real. Actually we live at the other end of the village, and I think that in case of danger (but there will be no danger) we would be more likely to go to the trenches belonging to the police, who are our neighbors.

There you have it. It has been a joy to write this letter, because it's the first time I've *answered*. "We're chatting." My love, you are always my conscience, my witness. Each thing that happens to me I think of putting in a letter to you. This little notebook I'm keeping is for your eyes only. I cannot be separated from you, because you are like the very consistency of my being. I love you tremendously, dearest creature.

Did you hear Giono was locked up?[4]

Tomorrow I'll write to Bost, whose address I found today in one of your letters.

If you have Tania come to Paris, tell her it's with my money from the NRF.

---

[4]He spent several months in jail for antiwar activity.

To Simone de Beauvoir

September 21

My darling Beaver

Today I got your letter of the 16th and your package. Thank you so much, dearest creature: everything I get from you moves me to tears. Perhaps today the package even more than the letter, because it—or at least the notebooks within it—is a *thing* and had something of the imperviousness of a presence. Through it I can feel you. It is on *your* paper I'm writing to you today. It arrived just in time: I had only seven or eight sheets left and was despairing. I'm writing to you in Paris, since according to your letter, you must be in Quimper today. I'm happy you're with Bienenfeld, because I think she must be feeling very blue. Except that for several days I won't hear anything from you. Basically, however, the timing is rather good, because on Monday I'll be leaving, to help out the Artillery Schools with my readings. I won't be going far from here, but chances are it'll be in the middle of nowhere, in a tent, with no mail. It lasts five days, then I'll be back.

Nothing new aside from that. My three acolytes are beginning to get on my nerves. Someday I'll have to tell you about it in more detail. They stick to one another and the trio to me like leeches, and, probably out of military solidarity, they cannot conceive the possibility of separate activities. As might be expected, they annoy me first off with their noises: suckings, snifflings, inhalations, exhalations, mastications, garglings, all the unconscious sounds in creation. The noises are increasing right now because they're bored, so I duck out on them as best I can. The moment we woke up this morning, on the pretext that one of us always has to be present at General Staff (where the clerks are more human), I tossed on my puttees and said, "I'm off." But Corporal Paul got up too, saying, "I'll come with you." He was hoping for some letters—which are distributed there—and above all, wanting breakfast at the café, he is terrified at the idea of having it alone. I won the race, and he could only say, "See you there." I hurried so much that my half-wrapped puttees were slipping farther over my heels at every step. I was hurrying because as I got up I was certain that if I had a moment of solitude at the inn, I would have some of that poetic joy I love so. It didn't fail me. I leafed through a Swiss magazine, some guy behind me was singing a popular song, it worked. After which, Corporal Paul arrived, undertakerlike as usual, and I took off to go and "stand watch"—which simply meant to sit down at a desk in a far corner of the study hall and there, cool as a cucumber, read Gide's *Journal*, write in my little black notebook, or work on my novel. In general, up to noon, I'm as gay and lively as a lark. Besides, we're waiting for the mail, which gives meaning to the morning. We lunch at the inn, and then the afternoon is a bit slower. But not by much. I wash, I write some more, I read and take care of my letters. I've begun Dabit's *Journal*: insipid whimpering. He was obviously an ass. In October you can send me Green's *Journal*,[1] and I'll be finished for a long time with intimate journals, unless Kafka's, which has been announced from Stock, appears despite the war.

Till tomorrow, darling Beaver. I love you as much as humanly possible. You, I haven't lost you in the least, and then I have my lovely little photos of you. I send you tender kisses.

To Simone de Beauvoir

September 22

My darling Beaver

No letters from you this morning, but that's natural because you must have sent them from Crécy. I'm very curious to know what's become of Toulouse and Dullin and what relaxing effect the stay will have had on your poor, constrained little heart. I love you. Two letters from Tania in which she apologizes for the note she sent to the Hôtel Mistral and you forwarded, and which I haven't yet received. She's nice and more intelligent than I'd thought. She writes, "I used to think myself a little center of the world, all my fears were poetic and superstitious, and I thought that in my life nothing really terrible would happen that came from outside, nothing beyond my own responsibility. And now, on the contrary, here I am feeling smaller than a flea, I fear all sorts of catastrophes; instead of being the center, I'm caught up in the gears." It seems that for once a Zazoulich, helped by circumstances, will have clearly seen within herself. Perhaps the war will do her some good, if it doesn't last too long, by teaching her that there are misfortunes other than magic catastrophes. But let's not anticipate.

My mother wrote me a card on the 18th; she hasn't heard from me since the 10th. Mysteries of the military mails. Yet it seems that everything finally reaches us.

Now for a story about cows. A thousand poor guys who lived near the German border were evacuated, and they brought their cows along with them.

---

[1] Novelist Julien Green (b. 1900). Publication of his journals began in 1928.

But since they had a long trip ahead, they left off the cows along the way, in other words here, after an understanding with a peasant who bears the pompous title "Chairman of the Commission on Cows." They are leaving the cows to a certain number of farmers who agreed to feed them and give them back at the end of the war, in return for which they can have the milk. This said, yesterday, as I came in to my landlady's to pick up my stationery around four in the afternoon, my ears were struck by horrible bellowing. The Chairman of the Commission on Cows had penned up *a hundred* cows in a small rectangular enclosure separated from my landlady's garden by no more than a fence of rotten wood. Right off we simply said, Keller and I, "We'll be hearing quite a concert out here tonight." And I said, "I'll insert my earplugs with utmost care." Upon which, I go off to write in a little café, sipping a schnapps, then I pick up my acolytes and we dine at the inn. A fifteen-minute walk, and at eight-thirty, a half hour before the regulation army lights-out, we're returning home under a beautiful moonlit sky. A kilometer from our house, desperate mooing. We find our landlady and her mother on the doorstep, at their wits' end: "They've broken everything, gone through the fence in three places, there are some of them in the garden and some on the path." Immediately Pieter, with his usual resourcefulness, said, "We'll go get the police." And Paul, timid and anxious, "But it's already nine o'clock. If we're nabbed in the street after nine, it's the guardhouse." "Be that as it many," said Pieter, "I'm going to talk to the state police." The state police make the rounds at night, and they have the reputation of being tough. They nabbed a guy in Ceintrey, and it wasn't very nice. But that's another story. They live next door to us. We sight of one of them, broad-shouldered, helmeted, peeing at the side of the road, and we explain the situation. "Can we walk as far as the police station?" He replies, still peeing, "And just who would turn you in?" "Well, you, for instance," I told him. He turns around, crimson with rage. "I'd never screw the army, see? Two guys on guard duty last night, they were playing cards at the café, I just made believe I didn't see them, there's your proof." I blurted out, "You're quite a guy!" "We're off?" said Pieter. "Go on," said the policeman. We walk through town to the gendarmerie. Another type of farm animal, if you'll permit a little military joke. They open cautiously: "What is it?" "We're here on a civilian matter," says Pieter. "Come in." We run through the thing again for the three cops. "So what did you want us to do? We're not paid to mind cows." "But the poor woman . . ." "Sure, fine, we'll go wake up the rural police and we'll follow you." We set off again, bumping into officers in the dark; we get there after passing a man who was leading back a cow found on the highway. We find the woman, still desperate, negotiating with three Cow Keepers, who are half drunk and furious. A conversation embellished by the abrupt coming and going of capering cows. Everywhere you could hear mooing and clumsy cavorting in the dark, and then you would suddenly see a vast white body hurtling by one inch away. "Oh," said Pieter, "I'm from Paris, I don't like this, I don't know cows . . ." And he sprints up the front steps, opens the front door, and waits on the doorstep, ready to lunge into the vestibule and shut the world out behind him. Meanwhile the guards were running after the cows, hollering, and shooing them back into the fold one by one. But for every one they'd corralled, three were breaking loose. Finally Paul and I joined the posse. Paul had picked up a heavy stick and was prodding them back with the tip, and I, making a stand in front of a gap in the fence, scared them back by clapping my hands like an Arab in the Djemaa El Fna Plaza. Then, in a frenzy of emulation, I wanted a cudgel of my own and picked up a thick round stake the cows had ripped off. I laughed to myself, thinking of the look on your face if you'd seen me playing cowboy by the light of the moon, nobly leaning on my prod. The police came, saw the devastation, shrugged, and left, imperious in their black capes. Finally, the three cowherds and ourselves, together, rounded up the cows and set up the fence again, splicing it together with wire. After which our landlady, overcome with gratitude, offered us great mugs of kirsch, which went right to Corporal Paul's head. Today they evacuated the cows. But last night I experienced a moment of strong, pure joy, chasing after them.

This morning an equally diverting ceremony: the gas chamber. We put on our masks and trooped down, in groups of fifty, into a cellar. Imagine the semidark and a circle of fifty chumps with snouts. An officer in sky-blue uniform, sleek and terrifying as an insect, from his feet right up to his shoulders—but with a pig's snout—fired two revolver shots. Gas canisters are fitted to the gun barrels, and they let go. Thereupon the fifty masked individuals in single file, their hands on the shoulders of the guy in front, begin to walk in a circle. They're supposed to sing, but you hear nothing beyond a frightening gurgle that made me think of the sounds Kafka's Gregory emitted, thinking he was speaking. The weird part is the sense of being in a venomous, verminous space yet remaining unscathed. When you speak to your neighbor, you have the feeling the words are passing through a poisoned world; when you look at your hands, you have the feeling they're surrounded by a haze of poison, and yet you're unharmed and almost at ease. We were strongly urged to raise our masks slightly on the way out "to see the difference." But I prudently abstained.

So there's the latest news, darling Beaver. Believe it or not, I feel slightly abandoned because you aren't in Paris. Quimper is too far, with the new "war distances." It's as though you'd just left me. My love, I love you with all my heart. Everything that happens to me I immediately want to tell you. You and I are simply one.

(1) This morning I finished a chapter 30 pages long. I think I'll go on with it. And then I'll rework this one because I'm not yet entirely happy with it.

(2) Did you enjoy the headline in the newspapers about the military operations on the French front: "Period of strategic delay"?

To Simone de Beauvoir

September 23

My darling Beaver

From Tania, nothing in three days. Precisely the exact span, allowing for the mail, that her sister has been back at Laigle. From you a madly entertaining letter about Toulouse, her mother, and Dullin. You can imagine how much pleasure I got from what you reported on Chonez.[1] I feel so forgotten as a writer—and rightly so—and I'm even forgetting myself so much that my two published books are what I've left farthest behind. It seems as though the novel I am writing now is my first novel. So to suddenly come upon someone who still thinks from time to time of one J.-P. Sartre, writer, and who deplores dispassionately, solely for the good of things literary, that I'm gone, warmed the cockles of my heart. Because of that I wrote to Paulhan to propose "Reflections on Death," which I may write in October and November. "Keeping secrets from me," I can hear you saying, "thinking about Death?" Yes, good Beaver, but not about mine. It came to me, I'm embarrassed to say, at the time of the supposed death of Lola in my novel. But anyway it immediately takes on the flavor of current events. How kind you are, you, to write to me at such great length. You cannot know how much it pleases me. I have a nice little note about you in my journal. I explain that Death cannot damage our relationship retrospectively, whereas if yours or mine should come about abruptly, our whole past would be marred,

---

[1] *A writer and journalist who had done an interview with Sartre. (SdB)* Chonez had told Beauvoir she would give the lives of ten ordinary people to save Sartre's (Simone de Beauvoir, *Lettres à Sartre*, Vol. 1, p. 122).

because the only thing that is not unfulfilled and that represents achievement, perfection, and repose is our relationship, our love. I added that so far I have achieved only that in life. The rest awaits. I'm still reading Dabit. It's side-splitting when I myself am right in the midst of a war to read the journal of a guy who passed his last years scared shitless about the coming war and who finally died of scarlet fever.

What else to tell you? We did a brilliant reading a short while ago before six respectful soldiers. We continue to be a separate unit, respected, on familiar terms with the sergeants, exempted from fatigue duty, calm, specialists in all accepted meanings of the word. We'll do two readings a day for the Artillery Schools but we'll be staying here.

Till tomorrow, my love. I'll probably get one more letter, then nothing for a few days, as letters from Quimper take *eight* days to get here. With all my love.

To Simone de Beauvoir

September 24

My darling Beaver

Nothing new today, so I'm only sending you a short letter. We did a reading before the authorities, colonel, major, captain, lieutenant—and answered their questions easily and loquaciously. From tomorrow on, Artillery School, 2 readings a day, at 7:30 and 13:30, or two hours of work, that's not overdoing it. And we're staying here; the firing practice takes place nearby. But how we'll get it in the ears! In one sense it's rather funny: I haven't heard cannon fire since November 11, 1918, which was also the first time I heard it.

Received one letter from you written the 19th, the day you left for Quimper, together with the letter from that idiot. But I know the name of André Masson. Don't you? I'm amused that C. Audry has married Minder. But I've seen that hearty guy, and I pity her. I've nothing else to tell you, except that I love you with all my might and that I am still one with you. It's good of you to write to me at such length each time, it feels as though I am living everything you tell me. I have finished chapter XIII (which I reread yesterday and today) and I'm going to begin chapter XI and chapter XII (Boris, Boris and Daniel, Daniel and Marcelle). By now the whole division knows that I write. That will mean readers after the war. Nothing from Tania, which is rather distressing.

Goodbye, my love, till tomorrow. Tomorrow I won't get your little daily letter (nor the day after, nor following days: nothing before the 30th or the 1st of October), but I know where you are and what you're doing, and I'll wait till then.

Love.

It smells like Sunday even here.
And yet God knows!

To Simone de Beauvoir

September 25

My darling Beaver

First day of Artillery School. There are seven or eight guns very close to the school. We stand in the window and watch them fire. They are lined up beside the road, and along with their crews they look like cardboard toys. They fire across a curtain of trees, into a long undulating field. Beyond the field are blue mountains. The weather is beautiful. First we hear a sharp, dramatic noise: the powder. And after that an odd indefinable, liquid hissing; it's what is conventionally called the "whistling" of the shell. That's the most amusing part, you really feel that the shell splits the air and that the air itself is a *medium*. When you don't see the guns, from the schoolroom or the cafés or on La Place de Marmoutier, you simply feel it's Bastille Day. They asked us to do two readings a day, and today they were superbly executed. At 7:30 and at 13:30. We're getting to be old hands at it. I don't put in more than 45 minutes on a reading. And of course I worked very well all day. The only problem, we have to eat lunch at two in the afternoon, but the advantage is that the inn's deserted. Something else: in nosing about the village, Pieter found a hotel which will rent us a splendid room with two beds for 6 francs a day, the military price. And it is the main hotel of the village. We immediately took it for Pieter and for me. The two others will stay on with Madame Gross. I'm not unhappy to be sleeping in a bed: for two weeks I've been sleeping on the ground wrapped in two overcoats and a blanket, my head on my knapsack. That isn't too bad, but a change won't hurt, particularly since the odors are beginning to get pretty dense. Keller smells of feet and Paul smells sour. And then, most important, I'll be able to work quietly during the day. I asked my parents to send me 300 francs a month.

Yesterday I was very much impressed: I had dinner with six infantry guys. Things are changing. They are *lost* ones (I don't mean "destined to die," but rather "the beyond"). The obsession about "going up," which they wind up wishing for, is the heroism of impatience. I can't tell you much more here. I'll fill you in later. I have lots of things to tell you that I can't put down here. Basically all the interesting parts. I'm cut off from Tania, because she isn't writing to me anymore. The whole thing is a part of the past in the process of dying away. There is only *You*, my love, you alone always with me and dear and with whom I constantly contemplate an *afterward*. It would seem that lacking my regular salary I would perhaps be entitled to a substantial "compensation." Find out about it. It would help to support you and to have the two Z's come to Paris. I'll make inquiries at my end.

I've grown a necklace beard like Stendhal's, carefully shaving my upper lip. Don't shriek in horror—you won't see it. It's for my personal edification, and I'll shave it off if I come home on leave. But if it's unpleasant for you to even think of me with a beard, tell me: I'll immediately do away with it. It will be given the same treatment as the little white tie you threw into a garbage can that day in Marseilles I always remember with such love. I love you.

To Simone de Beauvoir

September 26

My darling Beaver

First, excellent news: I am to get my salary. This morning I received a note from the school bursar[1] that my mother sent me. I must have her send an *assignment* authorizing a person to cash my civilian pay (or rather the difference between my civilian pay and my military pay, or 3,000 francs minus fifty centimes). So I "authorize" you to receive it. Can you go by around the 1st or 2nd of October? That would be best. Now we can make plans. I'll probably be paid 3,200 minus 14%, or about 2,800. With that you could: 1, send me 500 francs a month. 2, for the month of October, perhaps, repay M. Bienenfeld (the rest of the money will be supplied by Gallimard, I hope). 3, after November 1st *have the two Zazouliches come to Paris*. You'll also have to find out whether those who've been mobilized still pay taxes. It's likely when it's a question of government employees, since they keep their pay. In that case, from time to time you could subtract 300 or 400 francs, and when it adds up to a considerable sum, send it in on my behalf, asking

---

[1] As a lycée professor, Sartre was a government employee and as such entitled to his salary while mobilized.

them to be patient about the rest. That way you'll reach June or July and all will be paid up. Olga won't have to look for a job, she could perhaps wait calmly for the chance to make a film, and Tania will have something to live on. It seems to me that if you give them two thousand francs a month they can get by. I can't tell you what pleasure this news gives me. As for you, you'll have your salary for yourself alone, more than 3,000 francs, which means that while spending freely you can probably put aside a little money. The future brightens, and I have no further worries. If Paris should become untenable, you would send Tania off to Rouen or Marseilles and you could do with the other Z. exactly as you see fit. My love, you don't know how much that relieves and pleases me. It is a bit as though I had only myself left to worry about. I'll know that all of my little family has enough money and security, and I won't have the feeling—which was really beginning to gnaw at me—that it is you who are supporting the burden of the whole community.

So do go there around the 2nd. You need only an identification card. Nonetheless, do take along the paper I gave you, on the off chance. And as soon as you have the money, send me 500 francs by telegraph order. No answer from the NRF as yet. In a week I'll write again. All's well, it's a pleasant day. As for me, I woke up this morning so sleep-surfeited that I committed a thousand stupidities over the reading, lost the balloon ten times, and confused the azimuth with the elevation. The results were nonetheless consistent with reality. It's beginning to get cold: +1 degree at 6 o'clock in the morning, my hands were frozen. A bit of hoarfrost on the grass of the meadows, a clear sky, pleasant. I biked over to give the results to the officer in command of the guns, which weren't even firing yet. At the top of a hill, two guys burst out of a hole in the brush with leaves on their helmets shouting like asses, "We've got a prisoner!" They were camouflaged observers, whom I know, a first sergeant and a private. I don't know why that poetic little scene reminds me of the second act of Copeau's *Rosalinde*. At 10 o'clock I got two letters from Tania, very nice. At 13:30, another reading, then Paul and I managed to get the necessary documents for collecting our salaries, and finally Pieter and I went back to settle down in our 6-franc room at the inn near the station. It's from there I'm writing to you. It's on the second floor. From the windows we can see the whole countryside; there is no running water, but two good peasant beds facing each other, in which you can't help but submerge as though into butter. Lots of mosquitoes, but if it goes down to −2 tonight, as it did the other night, they'll die of the cold. I've begun a new chapter. The one I've just finished (I finally went over it again, while I was at it) is 35 pages long. I'm not sending it to you right away; I'll send you a hundred and fifty pages at a time; it takes a war for you to be reading one of my novels like a normal reader.

My love, no letter from you today, but that's natural, I wasn't expecting one. Perhaps tomorrow. I'm still writing in my journal. The fourth volume of my novel will be called *La Guerre fantôme* ["The Phantom War"]. Pretty title? And topical. But perhaps you aren't aware of that. That's what I don't know: I don't know the state of mind on the homefront. At the front lines it's very strange . . . more and more like Kafka.

I love you with all my might, my dearest, my darling Beaver. Till tomorrow. When I've finished this letter, I'll gaze at your little face in Ri-alland's photos.

My necklace beard is slowly thickening. It gives me a hard and skeptical look. My acolytes think I'm an ass because I'm always looking at myself in the mirror.

To Simone de Beauvoir

September 27

My darling Beaver

Just a short note. Empty day. Autumn has begun. The sky is hazy and overcast, it's cold. The guns of the Artillery School bang away constantly. Our landlady's dog is sick from it, he shivers and refuses the sugar we give him. Yet the noise isn't much louder than a firecracker. Last night Pieter and I slept in beds. Strange beds, but it was the first time in 25 days I've slept in a bed. The day had been a bit long, because I am doing drafts—you know, the times when you waste page after page and throw up your hands in disgust. I can't work long when it's like that. So I dragged around. They moved the clerk's office of the Artillery Division. For now it's at the Hôtel des Postes (while the post office employees are at the boys' school); it's much less convenient for us. It has "office" written all over it, no more tables for me, and just a crate to rest my bones. Fortunately the taverns are almost empty, and I spent my day at the café. In fact I was quietly happy; it was the aftertaste of yesterday's joy (from the news I'd be receiving my salary). My dearest, I don't think there's any way for you to come and see me, since you're not even supposed to know where I am. The women you told me about must have been legitimate spouses—of officers—and it must have been in the very first days of the war. In any case—if you *did get* my last letter—I can do no more for you than that. I would so love to see you, you can be sure of that. Perhaps Jacqueline Audry's[1] husband could help (you would need a permit, of course). Do everything you can. But there is something else: I have no idea whether we are staying here or if we are leaving in four days. You know that this uncertainty is my daily lot. That is what we have to accept if we don't want to slip into despondency. In any case it'll have to wait a bit. But then it will be lycée time for you. It's true that anyone can be out sick for a day.

Till tomorrow, my love. I got a letter from you this morning. I clearly understood what you mean when you write that happiness seemed a privileged way to seize the world and that it no longer seemed so necessary to you, now that the world's face has changed; you're wise as can be. You are the only true Beaver. I send you my dearest love.

To Simone de Beauvoir

September 28

My darling Beaver

This morning I got your second letter from Quimper. It seems tremendously poetic to me that you are there, that you're getting around by bus, just as we used to on our peacetime vacations, that you're staying in that little provincial town.

If I get eight days (and not six), I'll spend six with you and two with Tania. If I get six days, I'll spend the whole time with you. So on that point don't worry. I settled all that in my head a long while back. Here, everything's still the same. Today reading, cannon fire (nonoffensive—Artillery School), novel. A letter from you, a letter from T. It's odd, these days that pass one after the other, I scarcely feel them going by, I'm not bored, I don't find time dragging, and yet it seems that an eternity separates me from the 3rd of September last. I am no longer the same: my personality hasn't changed, but certainly my being-in-the-world has. It is a being-for-the-war. (Long development on that in my notebook.) And then, how odd it is to live with men. How dense man is! It's incredible.

---

[1]Sister of Beauvoir's friend Collette Audry. Jacqueline's husband, a general, was said to have the authority to grant passes for women to visit husbands at the front. (Simone de Beauvoir, *La Force de l'Âge* [Paris, 1960], p. 452).

They are all afraid of turning into clods. Not I. My novel and my journal keep me alert. And, I have to admit, I have much more time to write in wartime than peacetime. Send me regularly, would you, *Marianne, Candide*, the *Nouvelles Littéraires*, and of course the *NRF*. I love you tremendously, my love. You are very specifically a part of myself removed from the army zone. We are simply one, my dear little Beaver, my little beast, you are my tender love.

I am a considerable topic of amusement for my three acolytes because of the way I put on my puttees and because I'm always losing one of the collective properties granted me by the state. Yesterday Pieter said: "Sartre is like us, his physique does him disservice. When I caught sight of him the first day I said to Paul, 'Oh! What have you come up with now? He's half asleep, your guy.' " Today at the hotel I search in vain for one of my socks. At two o'clock I find it at our landlady's house. I had taken it there in my pants. And the acolytes howled with laughter. They seem to me a bit like K.'s assistants in *The Castle*. Someday I'll tell you about them at greater length. Right now I'm going to dinner. I cover your dear little face with kisses. My mother speaks of you in all her letters. Go to see her when you get back, it would be kind of you.

To Simone de Beauvoir

September 29

My darling Beaver

I've just received your letter of the 23rd. I was shocked that you got some of my letters at Quimper, since I am sending them to the Rue Cels. You are having them forwarded, but isn't that a bit unwise—some will be trying to catch up with you.

That frigidity you speak of I share. You'll tell me that it doesn't change me. Still, I think as you do that it is a way of closing things off. But right now, for me, it's no longer a question of barriers: the state of war is *natural* to me. There's neither tension nor repression: that's the way it is, and that's that. Today, military life closed in on me somewhat because, 1, we are on "subsistence," that is, we are now eating military food. It isn't bad—it's awfully dreary. I'll take the opportunity to lose some weight, since I've put on some fat. 2, As some guys have screwed up, the cafés are off-limits during the day. It so happens that the rooms are cold now (0 this morning at 7 o'clock), and

I wonder where I'll work (since the clerks moved to a poor little hole where we aren't welcome). Surely it will all work out, it will only take a little ingenuity, except that just as it happens each time I feel the *presence* of the military world, each time possibilities are taken away from me, for a moment I have felt undone. For now that's over. The readings are over too, the firing over. Tomorrow we have nothing left to do, unless they invent tasks for us. It seems we should be staying here yet awhile. It's also certain that I won't fear a thing throughout the war. I cannot explain why, but take my word for it. I'm delighted that you are going to see the Lady—it seems to me that should do you a bit of good. Why don't you stay two days if you are starting classes only on the 9th? To get back and draw your pay, perhaps? Don't forget to draw mine. Your financial plans seem reasonable to me. As I said: repay M. Bienenfeld with my first allotment, and have the Z's come on November 1st. But you could just as well repay him a thousand francs and have them come in October. That way you won't be alone, since ultimately Z. is somewhat resourceful; I will be pleased to know that she is in Paris near you. My love, now I have received *all* your letters, all your little journal. It is indispensable to me. Thanks to them I can imagine you hour by hour, I feel you. I love you so much, my love.

Here are the titles of some books to send me (no use sending them all at once. Some, I believe, aren't out yet):

Lucien Jacques: *Carnets de moleskine* ["Moleskin Notebooks"]

Hermann Rauschning: *La Révolution du nihilisme* ["The Revolution of Nihilism"]

Marcel Aymé: *Le Boeuf clandestin* ["The Clandestine Ox"]

Cocteau: *La Fin du Potomak* ["The End of the Potomac"]

Drieu la Rochelle: *Gilles*

Martin du Gard: *Épilogue aux Thibault* ["Epilogue to the Thibaults"]

Vindry: *La Haute Neige* ["Deep Snow"]

Jean Cassou: *Quarante-huit* ["Forty-eight"]

H. Troyat: *Dostoïevski*

I haven't yet sent the Gide to Bost; I am reading it slowly and with interest. That guy knows how to write.

Goodbye, my dear love, my charming Beaver, I kiss you with all my might because

I love you very much.

It seems so strange that you are moving out of the little Hôtel Mistral. But you would be far better off at Gégé's. It's an excellent idea to put the Z's at the de Roulets'.

To Simone de Beauvoir

September 10

My darling Beaver

I'm writing to you at the Rue d'Assas.[1] Funny to think you'll be living there. It's a nice little place. That's where I'll stay when I'm on leave. It also makes me happy to think that as I write you, you are at the Lady's. I can imagine what things are like. Maybe they gave you the bungalow—but then again maybe not, because of the cold. In any case, I remember the dining room well. The Lady must be there, and the Mops and Boudy too. Several times today I actually imagined your conversations. You'll still be there to-morrow, and the next day you'll be in Paris. It almost feels as though you'll be going back with me, I don't know why. Because your letters will get to me sooner? At any rate the mail service has improved: today I received your letter from Quimper dated the 25th.

A long time ago, my love, I stopped objecting to my quietude. It has changed, incidentally, and become something natural; as I was saying yesterday, I think being-in-war is my nature for now. And yet, three-quarters of the time the war eludes me. At the moment I don't have much to write in my little notebook. It's the same with the others here: when you don't know them terribly well, you have loads to say about them; then, when you begin to get to know them, nothing. I've become hardened too, my love, very much, and all the more so in that since I'm living with men, I don't even have to pretend to be tender. You see, on top of everything else, I feel no regard or friendship for my acolytes: I simply put up with them. They complain I'm always criticizing, and it's true, but I don't want to attain a state of

---

[1]At Gégé's. (SdB)

goodwill toward them that would amount to simple resignation. And would be, it seems to me, a sort of betrayal of all the really nice people I've known. I'm quite curt and probably even pretty disagreeable, but they don't take too much offense. They don't seem to have affectionate personalities. Nonetheless I'm not alone, I live in my imagination with you and the others, Tania, the Lady, even Bost, often. I make laudable attempts to think of Guille, of Zuorro, but it's hard, and my horizon is limited. I'm happy to know they're safe, because that frees me from meditating like Loyola about them. I think about Toulouse and Dullin too. Sometimes these people appear as they were in my past, sometimes as in their present lives, but never in our future lives. Did you know that at the last minute Nizan, like a rat, abandoned the sinking ship?[2] I read it in the papers. Could you confirm this for me and give me any more information? And you: periodically, searing remembrances of things we've done together recur, and in those moments my love for you is painful. Usually, I feel a fulfilling tranquil satisfaction, just thinking that you exist, that you're not unhappy, not unlike those times when you were leaving for a little walking trip in the Alps. And my daily life, moment by moment, is either routine, or else the black hole of the war's end disarms it and makes it something not worth having lived through, or else I experience it as though already past, from the vantage piont of the war's end (a rapid, happy end), and then it turns comic and pleasant, and I tell myself something like what Desmoines said to himself as he looked at the photos: "OK for memories." What's impossible is to live it like a human present in which you are your own possibilities—future possibilities. Or else—I guess I was forgetting—like a sort of momentary joy like Gide's. There you have it.

Yesterday I was a bit anxious. I had no idea where to stow my carcass. Everything worked out, thanks to Pieter's cleverness. He knows how to rouse the bakeshop proprietress, and, unable to let me stay in the café, she allowed me to work in her dining room upstairs. So this morning after breakfast, I went up there. There were two well-behaved blond kids looking at pictures, and the grandmother, almost a double for my Aunt Caroline, though not so camel-like, who was making pies. I was there, I wrote, I listened from time to time to the grievances of the old woman against her eldest daughter, who wouldn't invite her to Angers—and it is there, for example, that I couldn't help considering my presence in that dining room unusual, given the memory

---

[2]A French Communist Party member for twelve years, Nizan announced in September 1939, soon after the signing of the Nazi-Soviet Nonaggression Pact, that he was leaving the party.

it will become once I'm back in civilian life. I was filled with well-being. I worked very well (on Daniel). Around 10:30 I had a bath at the hairdresser's, then we went out in the garden to eat our army rations. It wasn't bad at all (beef with carrots), then we had coffee and went to roll call, and I came back up to the hotel room. I have the window open wide, I can see a garden with a birch and various other trees I can't name, and then, in the distance, vineyards on a hill, I hear an airplane motor, it's sunny.

You must immediately send me *some envelopes* (2 packages of twenty). Don't forget to go to the bursar at the lycée when you get back. No news from the *NRF.* I'll write again soon. Today I wrote to Bost, the letter just went off.

The colonel did a report on the target practice for GHQ, in which he praised the readings post.

I love you with all my might, my little dearest.

I see that I'm not answering your question: I was reproaching myself for silence because—as long as I'm at war—I wanted to do it authentically. But that isn't so easy, because it is a phantom war.

P.S. Soon they're surely going to dress us up in khaki. My beard's ridiculous, a goatee, I'll shave it off very soon.

To Simone de Beauvoir

Sunday, October 1

My darling Beaver

I am writing to you from the café downstairs in "my" hotel (funny to be telling you about "my hotel," as though I were on a village holiday). It's dark and hazy out. Because of wartime economy or stinginess, the innkeeper doesn't turn on the lights, so I'm wearing my eyes out. It came rather close to being a somber Sunday. This morning the fog and, at the same time, the boredom of Sunday, the feeling that Sunday was infiltrating everything. Isn't it odd they still have Sundays around here? Perhaps we keep to Sunday rhythms out of habit, like those creeping things in aquariums that still live to the rhythm of the tides. Or else it's because of the laudable efforts of the sparse civilian population, which carried out both a burial and a procession this morning within two hours. The fact remains that the military people felt a sort of oppressive ennui all day long. I shook it around noon. In the morning I wrote above the café. Through the second-floor window I could see a red banner embroidered in gold bobbing along the street, toted by some invisible altar boy, and beside me the grandmother was making pies, just like yesterday. The little blond girl was howling imperiously in the next room. Small effects of mighty causes: every morning the general leaves home at eight sharp. Every morning at that moment the bugle blows and a small detail of men present arms. The general paces back and forth, inspecting each man in turn. But the daughter of this house is in the habit of sleeping till ten, and the bugle wakes her up. Consequently she's unbearable all morning. I worked badly, and I left the bakeshop around ten, a bit disoriented. I ran into Pieter and Paul, I wandered about a bit with them, then back to Madame Gross's house, where I read Gide's *Journal* some, while Paul was doing exercises. Around noon, out of curiosity and idleness, I dragged Pieter off for lunch to a small restaurant a fat sergeant had told us about: "The food there is better than at the bakery café—a pity it's such a whorehouse." Disappointment all down the line: the food wasn't better than at the bakery café, and it wasn't even a whorehouse. Following which we went back to the bakeshop for a slice of plum pie followed by a cigar. Then roll call at 13:30. I was already feeling much better, and I worked well from 2 to 4 at the clerk's office. Peiter was there, fluttering about tiresomely; he was passing out popped weather balloons to the officers to use for making tobacco pouches. At four o'clock I went back up to my hotel room; it wasn't too cold. I read some Gide, wrote in my notebook (already 60 little packed pages—but there must be much more in yours), and now here I am. No letters from you—no mail at all actually, probably because it's Sunday, which increases the Sunday feeling. And then you'd warned me I wouldn't get anything for two days more. And letters from Tania reach me very arbitrarily. That's that. For the moment I'm in excellent spirits, and I love you fiercely, I feel it in a very tranquil way, confident, content. It's fantastic how fast the days go by here. Probably because I'm writing. But I had a brush with boredom around noon, and I have the impression it must be awful if you have nothing to do. My love, send me some books *immediately* (for example, if you would: the October NRF, Green's *Journal*, and [Fyodor Dostoyevsky's] *The Idiot*). Later you could send *La Carrière de Beauchamps*,[1] which I'll gladly reread, and [Max] Scheler's *Nature et forme de la Sympathie* [*The Nature of Sympathy*]. One of these days go to visit my mother. She's phoned the hotel I don't know how many times. I realize it's not a whole lot of fun for you, poor darling Beaver, but she's a poor woman. I scolded her a little for saying "That'll teach him about

---

[1]*Beauchamp's Career*, a novel by George Meredith.

life," and then I reflected that it must have been one of fifty daily thrusts of her chin to hide her anxiety.

Adieu, dear little Beaver, my dear little one, my sweet little one. I love you with all my heart, and we two are one.

To Simone de Beauvoir

Monday, October 2

My darling Beaver

I'm writing to you from the hotel café. It's 6 o'clock, and there's only a stingy glimmer from the single bulb. And then, my two neighbors (who settled on my table though all the others are empty) block it each time they drink (raising an elbow and ducking the head). Enough of that—I gave them a friendly smile and moved. I can barely see any better. No letter from you yesterday or today. At least I suppose so for today, since Pieter, who left at three to get the mail, hasn't returned. You are back home in your little apartment. Did we need to have a war for you to get a little place of your own? You must have found some letter there from me. In case one of them is lost, may I *remind you* that I'm getting my government salary, that I've delegated you to go to the bursar, and that you must see him as soon as possible. Of the money paid out, send me five hundred francs, and work it out as best you can with the rest, for your benefit and that of the Z's. Something else: perhaps there's a risk I'm still receiving letters (of the literary variety) at the Hôtel Mistral. Would you have them sent to you (and you'll send them on to me) or else forwarded directly to Sector 108? Finally, along with the books (NRF, *The Idiot*, Green's *Journal*), please send me the *Mariannes* and the Masque and Empreinte detective novels, some envelopes, and two packages of Waterman blue-black fountain pen cartridges. You can also go by the Rue Amélie, to see if *Europe* still exists and tell them I'll continue my columns if they send me the books as they are published (that will save you money). I'll soon be through the Gide, and I'm very impatient for new books. Whew, thus endeth the chapter on errands. Alas, sweet Beaver, what else to say besides that? I dread reaching the end of my letter too. I'll take advantage of the fact that there's no deluge of new events to make you thoroughly understand the way you are bound to me. First of all, I'm slightly detached from my whole past life, now I clearly see that the war could be long (which is not the same as saying it will be), and that I'll find a completely changed world with perhaps other values and other people (not the Nazi values in any case, which have once and for all seen their day. If I wanted to sound like Aron, I could say that whatever happens, Hitler is already ideologically defeated). So every day I close myself off a bit more, alas even for my poor little books. Those I've written I've forgotten, and though I still have the same relentless eagerness to write the others—on that point I'm reassured, it's my nature—who knows when they'll be published. But there is one thing that does not change, nor can it change: whatever happens, whatever I become, I will become it with you. If there had been a need to feel how much we two are one, this phantom war would at least have had the virtue of letting us see that. But it wasn't necessary. All the same it answers the question that was tormenting you: my love, you are not "one thing in my life"—not even the most important—because my life no longer belongs to me, because I don't even regret it, and because you are always *me*. You are so much more, it is you who permit me to foresee any future and any life at all. We cannot be more at one than we are now. And you must realize, it's a miracle: I see all the guys here, they're married, and well, they hardly miss "the old lady." They've left behind those shabby households, a bit like Isorni's, that we know from the outside. How many of them I've heard say, "Oh, if it were just my wife . . . !" and then they speak tenderly of the little ones. Pieter said to me yesterday, "Women are all the same. My wife doesn't realize that I miss the life she's a part of. But if she came to spend five or six days with me, it would be appalling." Whereas you, my love, if you could come! But I don't see how you could: it takes a pass, and in addition you're *not allowed to know* my address. A woman who tried to get through without a safe-conduct pass spent forty-eight hours in jail. If you were to simply ask for a safe-conduct pass and by an effort of intelligence and close reading you learned my address, you should, of course, not say you were coming to see me. Another problem: we might leave here any day now. Well anyway, look. There is a hotel here— my hotel—where you might stay.

My love, I love you with all my heart—and just to say I love you is not enough.

To Simone de Beauvoir

October 3

My darling Beaver

Just a little note: unexpectedly we have been ordered to leave this evening, all of us, for parts unknown (though not very far away). Farewell to the lovely plan of seeing one another I was beginning to entertain. I don't know when you'll get this letter, and yours will probably be delayed. I'll write to you tomorrow in detail. Yesterday I got your little letter from Douarnenez, which melted my heart. I love you with all my might.

There will undoubtedly be delays in the next letters—don't worry. Write to me at the same address.

To Simone de Beauvoir

Wednesday, October 4

My darling Beaver

Nothing from you today, or yesterday, but I'm not worrying. A charming letter from Toulouse, who claims that Dullin loves me "very much and very tenderly," which continues to surprise me. A gloomy letter from Tania: Mme Zazoulich had another heart attack.

As you know, I left yesterday at 19:30 by truck. I was hankering for adventure and glad to be leaving. We were headed 20 kilometers away, to make way for some Negroes. The whole village was troubled, less at losing us, I think, than at seeing us replaced by blacks. "They won't come up here," said the mother of the bakeshop proprietress. "This is *my* room." We did up our bundles, said our goodbyes, then at six-thirty gathered at the square in front of the church with the clerks of the AD. We were to leave by truck. No trucks. There was one bus on the square, but it's reserved for the officers. An officer goes by: "You counting on a truck?" He breaks up at the farcical notion that we could be so naive. "Well, if it doesn't come in fifteen minutes, go to the south end of the village and we'll commence on foot." Upon which, he leaves: consternation among the clerks and orderlies. Paul is furious: "*They* promised us a truck, *they have* to move us in trucks. I'm not budging." Despondency on the part of Pieter, the fat Jew: "I have a hernia—I can't walk twenty kilometers." I was disgusted with them, all the more as we see the departure, in the dusk, of long columns of light infantrymen who had done 35 kilometers of forced march during the day and were taking to the road again all the same. We were rather heavy laden, but I felt a sort of joy in facing the challenge ahead. I feel the strange obligation—philosophic rather than humanist—to do everything possible so as to feel the war as intensely as possible. Constantly restrained, of course, by the acolytes (you'd think they were the Assistants in *The Castle*), and perhaps really happy to be restrained.

In short, after confabulation with a sympathetic reserve captain, they had us get into the bus reserved for officers. Here, an anecdote I myself will censor. But after that, the officers already seated in the bus fly off like doves, or rather they move away like Americans who desert a whole city block because some blacks have rented one apartment. I had a good seat, my back to the driver; I put my feet up on the folding seat across from me. A long wait, then the bus slowly sets off by fits and starts in the darkness. I was overjoyed. We slowly passed column upon column of dark shapes, the light infantry. Here and there you could see the red glow of their cigarettes and then, behind us, the blue headlights of seven or eight cars in single file. Numerous stops. At one of them, the lights of one of the vehicles projected against the back window the dark silhouette of a walking man that grew larger and larger, till it loomed, gigantic. At nine o'clock, arrival. I always get a tight feeling in the chest during these military arrivals, because you never know what awaits you there. They billeted the four of us with three orderlies in an extremely comfortable hayloft with two beds and straw. The four of us took the beds, the orderlies took the straw. The dog barked, the street resounded with marching feet, shouted orders, laughter, etc. From time to time a burst of light in the window beside my bed: a passing car. Paul, the sleepwalker, leaped like a carp next to me; Pieter, in the next bed, cleared his throat and coughed. Four times over, soldiers came in, shone their flashlights on us, and claimed places. We drove them off. But in spite of it all, I slept like a log, and woke at six-thirty. This morning, search for a *querencia*—though, it appears, we are to leave tomorrow night (alas, good little Beaver, no chance at all to meet for the next few days). The village was so quiet, very prosperous, with splendid farmhouses, rough-plastered in white with dark beams, each swathed in its Alsatian egoism, charming but dried up by the highway that bisects it from one end to the other, so still I was surprised not to find war there, without really realizing that war is what *we* are bringing with us. The grim look of a billet comes from *us*, it conceals the charm of a hayloft. I'll explain that better later. They'd said to us: village with the worst reputation in the whole area, you won't find a thing. Yet at eleven o'clock we found a *querencia* in a room of the Hôtel du Boeuf d'Or. I unloaded all our cases into a handcart (eight trips). I entertained myself imagining what Guille would think if he could only see me! And I imagined myself, fallaciously of course (as you would note), having a martial air as I pushed my little cart. After which I shaved off my beard, which hadn't been entirely satisfactory. Then I worked, and here I am, writing to you in the café, where a drunk wants to bust another guy's puss. He's red-faced, shouting his lungs out, telling a sergeant trying to calm him down, "You don't know who I am, boss: in civilian life, I'd have pumped him full of lead." Not bloody likely.

My love, I love you with all my might. I was quite put out not to have a letter today. I hope for one tomorrow. I send you a kiss, my dear little flower.

To Simone de Beauvoir

October 5

My darling Beaver

Another departure. Scarcely arrived, and it all begins again. We're going twenty kilometers away. Yet I would really have liked to answer your delightful letter from Angers, my love. I'll reread it tomorrow and tell you everything. I'm so happy that you are with the Lady (no, that's not right, you're in Paris now). Give me the Boxer's address, I'll write him. I wrote loads of things in my notebook, and I'm *making real progress*; I'm very pleased about it, as you might guess. Oh, yes, my dear love, you are living *my* life for me, make no mistake about it. In fact I wrote that to you, it seems to me. My love, I so like the little photos of you in Juan-les-Pins. Do write me *everything* the Lady says; that'll keep me entertained.

Till tomorrow. There'll be a little surprise for you in my letter, if I can swing it. I love you.

To Simone de Beauvoir

October 6

My darling Beaver

I'm a civilian now, or rather not civilian so much as abandoned by my division. First, picture how, per usual military custom, the previous order was quickly countermanded, and we learned around 6 in the evening we were to leave the following morning (that is, today) at 7. Then as we were loading our baggage that night we realized that instead of a 3-ton truck, they'd given us a little one that holds only eight hundred kilos. So we loaded only half the cases, and it was agreed the truck would return the following day for the rest. I offered to guard it. I wanted to see the quiet village return to its peacetime self again after the disturbances, because it's obvious that it is we who bring the war with us everywhere we go. So last night we went back to sleep in our hayloft, a night intercut with orders and cries, with lights and sounds of marching feet, like the night before that. Suddenly Paul was dreaming he was on top of a tower and the tower was crumbling. Upon which he sat upon our bed howling. I sat up too and grabbed his shoulders and calmed him down while the six other occupants of the dormitory shone their pocket flashlights on us. Paul fell back on the mattress and could only say, "You make me drink too much white wine," then went back to sleep, while the six others, since they were already awake, went in turn to pee off the balcony onto the manure pile in the courtyard—and he wriggled all night long. Though I scarcely slept a wink, I was exhilarated on rising, because of the windfall of solitude. I left around 6:45 and went to take possession of the premises we'd occupied two days in a row. It's an odd place, a ground-floor storage room, dark, damp, with a low ceiling, separated by a courtyard from the hotel (which is at the same time a model farm—if only you could see how well the pigs are cared for there!). In "our" room there's some of everything: a bad stove, some coal, jazz band equipment with a bass drum, horse harnesses, a trombone, and a screen. Aside from that, there's the bare floor and four walls with dangling shreds of wallpaper. I first went into the big room of the inn—where the previous day I'd had a long philosophical conversation with my colonel (he'd said to me, "You're taking notes on the war. You are certainly right, it can always be useful")—and I had some coffee, some bread and butter. After which, since it was cold, I made a fire in the stove—an operation I accomplished on the first try, to my great astonishment, but which resulted in intolerable billows of smoke: in an instant the whole room was filled. I threw windows and doors open, and so much smoke was pouring into the courtyard that an old man came in, poked at the fire in the stove, and roundly scolded me in Alsatian. I felt embarrassed, and stayed there with all the windows open in the middle of the smoky room, condemned in the eyes of the passing villagers by the smoke as if I were pilloried. Though I was left like a turd upon the road by my division, my human dignity was reborn, and my military insouciance disappeared along with my anonymity. For now, in this civilian village, I am no longer anonymous, I am "the village soldier." They should issue me bells, as they did to lepers in the Middle Ages. I worked till noon, I was very happy, but no civilian: rather, a man without a country, knowing only too well that my real place was a few kilometers away. At noon, my eyes weepy and rather like smoked ham, my jacket exuding smoke, I returned to the large main room of the deserted inn (yesterday it was packed with the military; today you'd think it a village dance hall after the ball was over) and lunched on an omelette and sausages, reading Gide's *Journal* and Dabit's. After which I returned to be smoked some more as I worked in my lean-to. After a while, all the same, I took a stroll around the village. Disappointment; a few soldiers are still here, still being loaded onto trucks. The military's as hard to get rid of as lice. But in the main street, women were reappearing on their doorsteps; at the blacksmith, civilians have showed up again, fat men in work jackets, they were swearing as they shoed a horse. The cocks were crowing at the top of their lungs (yesterday, it seems to me, they didn't crow). Only token of "our" passing: on a picket fence the words "postal clerk" scratched in chalk and topped by an arrow. And me with my pestilential eyes trailing behind me a whiff of war wherever I went. I turned back, I felt odd: lost in space and time. I began to write to you. Last night the staff sergeant said to me, "We'll be back for you. But you know what military transport is like. Just don't get impatient." So I'm not, there's a mattress in my lean-to, if they don't come back this evening, I'll sleep here, rolled up in my cape.

My love, my darling Beaver, forgive me, you won't have the surprise I promised you the day before yesterday. This is because I was still in Marmoutier and I wanted to send you a flower petal symbolizing a whole bouquet. But here there are no flowers: only manure. And why the symbolic bouquet? Because it's a day of celebration, my love; when you receive this letter it will be exactly ten years since we were married morganatically, and for the first time, my little flower, we won't be together to celebrate our anniversary. My love, you have given to me ten years of happiness (and I to you, if I am to believe the charming little dedication on the photos—I too love you very much, sitting like that on the front steps). My dearest love, I immediately renew the lease for ten years, fervently hoping I'll be there next October to ratify the renewal out loud. My dearest, you're the most perfect, the most intelligent, the best, the most passionate. You are the little paragon, and I feel altogether humble before your dear little self. I love you with all my heart, and you are never gone from my thoughts. When I write in my little notebook, it is for you. I love you with all my might, you are my darling Beaver.

1. Tomorrow I'll respond to what you wrote me, that it is strange that consciousness failed to create a world to its own scale. I think I have a few little ideas on that.

2. My continuing silence on the subject of Henry James's *Portrait of a Lady*, which I was never able to finish, should lead you to understand that I see no other way to deal with the book than consign it to the crapper.

3. Your last letter was so badly scribbled that despite three readings, I couldn't decipher Isorni's assignment.[1]

4. You must send me ink cartridges *immediately*. I would love to have *La Jeunesse de Théophile*[2] ["Théophile's Boyhood"]. Thank you.

I love you.

I find that soldier's attitude very strange.[3] But it can be explained as the military mentality.

Safely arrived. Received 4 letters all at once from you: one from Quimper, three from Angers. You're a little charmer. I'm happy you're so blissful—most of the time, anyway—at the Lady's place. I would indeed be pleased to have Daniel Defoe's *Colonel Jack*; try to get *Moll Flanders*, same author.

Desperate letter from T. Their mother had a heart attack, and several deaf-mutes are going to be lodged on them. So you're quite right: reimburse M. Bienenfeld by the month and have them come as soon as you've cashed my paycheck.

To Simone de Beauvoir

October 7

My darling Beaver

So the little truck came, they loaded me onto the back with the baggage, and after a charming ride from dusk on through the night, I reached an affluent but dark town (3,000 inhabitants). I saw the Assistants running after the truck. They'd done good work and found two rooms in a private house. I went to bed in a splendid, hospitable German-style room, with inscriptions embroidered on the cushions—and a complete run of *Marie-Claire*. I didn't want to sleep with Paul, but Paul didn't want to sleep with Keller, who is too fat, a bad sleeper, snores, and smells bad. To settle it, we put the mattress on the ground for Paul, and I slept on the box springs. We were extremely comfortable, and Paul hollered for help only two or three times during the night. And then came the pleasant surprise: *four* letters from you. My love,

---

[1] Beauvoir had reported that Isorni was in an extremely dangerous position, with a machine gun unit (*Lettres à Sartre*, Vol. 1, p. 146).

[2] By Jouhandeau. (SdB)

[3] A soldier known to friends of the Lady had met Beauvoir's late-night train in Angers and forced his company upon her (*Lettres à Sartre*, Vol. 1, pp. 143–44).

how charming you are to write to me so often and so nicely. You cannot know what your letters mean to me, and how impatiently I await them every day. This morning I stalked from one end of town to the other from 6:30 on, all alone and eluding the Assistants. It's as German as can be, full of new architecture, bold and in awful taste, but with a comfortable feeling that is also German and delightful. There must have been a lot of interchange and German influence in this part of Alsace. I'd gladly stay here throughout the war. Unfortunately we're leaving tomorrow and will probably go to a small evacuated village, much less comfortable. I'm writing to you from the school study hall, modern too and gleaming. Here they give us heat. Excuse this incoherent letter; sleep overcame me around 3 o'clock, and I have to struggle to finish all my letters (I'd like to write to Catinaud [Magnane], Toulouse, Tania, my family). I am putting off till a more lucid day writing to you about consciousness and the temporal-spatial dimensions. But I would like to respond to you on another topic. You tell me you're embarrassed because you have the better role, and, if you could choose without our knowing it, you wouldn't be sure of not keeping it. But, my love, don't be so hard on yourself: you are certainly better off than Bost, but not more so than I, since basically although I don't see you, you don't see me either; you have lost your way of life and the happiness you had last year, as I have, but you're freer now— but I am, too, and almost completely so. But you are anxious about me, while I, for the foreseeable future, am not so about you. You are still in Paris, of course, but I'm experiencing something interesting enough so that I don't overly miss that diminished Paris, plunged in darkness from 7 o'clock on. In reality, my love, you "are-at-war" no more nor less than I am. This is something I've understood very well these past two weeks. Nobody escapes the war. You extend my life, by proxy you stretch it as far as Quimper, as Angers, but it is my *present life* you are extending. The other, last year's, disappeared along with the peace, both for you and for me.

My love, till tomorrow, you are my little flower, my darling Beaver, and I love you with all my heart.

I got a letter from the NRF, which will "transmit my request to the department of authors' accounts" and which will publish my book on images, but they don't know exactly when.

A letter from Poupette too. If you have cashed my paycheck, send me 500 francs quickly. I have only 20 francs left. Please wire it if possible. Love.

To Simone de Beauvoir

October 8

My darling Beaver

No letters from you today. And I'm writing just a short note because there's nothing new here. A letter from Tania after two days of silence. She writes: "I love you very much anyway, but you seem rather from another planet." I'll have to get used to seeming more and more from another planet. However slight the chance that the war will drag on, I'll never find her again. That's frankly an unpleasant prospect, but I want to get used to it. In wartime, you simply have to reach a sort of impoverishment—extremely moral, according to Gide, and sometimes even pleasant. My love, you always write me long letters. You say nothing about the Lady: what are her reactions to the war, what is she thinking about Zuorro, about Guille? Does it bother her not to see them? What did she talk about? What exactly is her new wartime life like? Does she consider it disastrous or restful to be at La Pouèze?

Today I wrote in my notebook and finished a chapter of my novel. That makes fifty-four pages written. Lunched (we go to a courtyard to get food, it's not bad, we eat in our schoolroom, and I do the dishes in cold water). I cleaned myself up a bit and went for a coffee. Then I worked a few moments longer, and now I'm writing you. Let me know what the Lady thinks of my novel (in detail). And do tell me about yourself, my love. Nothing could be more precious to me. You are me, my little dearest. I love you.

I'm not too pleased you left my novel with the Lady, who loses everything. I would prefer she return it to you, and that you have several copies typed by your sister, who has a typewriter and offered to do it for me. At that point you could send one to the Lady, one to me, and keep one. All right?

To Simone de Beauvoir

October 9

My love

Here I am without a letter from you for two days. I'm not anxious yet—there's so much messing around with the mail—but I'm not far from it, you're such a darling eager Beaver and you write me so promptly that I'm afraid you might be ill. All the more so since, if you got back to Paris on Friday, I should begin to get your letters from the Rue d'Assas. I've just received a letter from Seeligmann (*NRF*), dated October 2, that reads as follows: "For a few days M. Gallimard will be away from Mirande, where we are now installed. As soon as he returns, I will ask him to look into sending the balance of your account to Mlle Simone de Beauvoir as soon as possible." *Note that he will send it to the Hôtel Mistral.* Have you definitely given them your new address? In any case, there is a balance. That's something already. You could instantly send it to M. Bienenfeld. All in all, financial matters are working out for the best. A letter from Tania, very warm. A note from my mother, who is in Saint-Sauveur. By now she must be back. You really should go see her.

Not a lot new here. We're still ready to leave at a moment's notice. But we never do. So much the better. Life is good and beautiful here, the schoolroom is heated, and I can write all day. My novel's coming along well. I want you to know that we are staying with a warden of an insane asylum. He was mobilized, but came back home to his wife yesterday, and we found him there when we got in. He was to take off again during the night. Naturally we shared a drink; poor Corporal Paul looked shattered. He hates red wine and had to drink *five* brimming glasses to be polite—and the conversation took place almost entirely in German, which he doesn't understand. The whole night through he suffered agonies of heartburn and a desire to pee, which he refused to satisfy by simply pissing out the window as I do. (While I think of it—my parents tell me that they got a letter from me with some passages censored. Do you know what it was? I was simply explaining what a reading is—the kind of thing you can find in any meteorological textbook. They're not joking. The thing is, they censor approximately one in fifty letters.) This morning I went to have breakfast at the inn, my head was a little logy and I a bit morose—but no more than I would have been in civilian life on waking. After which I worked on a new chapter of *The Age of Reason*: the one where Boris and Ivich are alone together and talk. It's easy and fun. Afternoon, same thing. Pieter and I are going to have our pictures taken in uniform tomorrow morning, and soon I'll send you some photos that will give you a good laugh. Already, despite every effort, I'm the filthiest soldier in the division. It's my lot in life. A little bike ride, and here I am: the mail is in, no letters from you. My love, just so long as you're not sick. I can imagine how worried I'd be about you if Paris were bombed, since I have been somewhat worried over two days of delayed mail. I love you so, my dear, you are so many things to me. Take good care of yourself, darling Beaver, remember with modesty and pride that you're the most precious little person in the world, since I'm a bit of an absolutist. My love, I'd so like to see your good little face. Till tomorrow, when I do hope to get something from you.

Don't forget to send me:

1. A *package* containing a vast quantity of envelopes, 2 packs of blue-black fountain pen cartridges, books (*The Idiot*—the October *NRF*—Green's *Journal*—two detective novels)

2. A money order for 500 francs, if you've cashed my paycheck.

I kiss your dear little cheeks.

But now I've forgotten again to talk about our being-in-the-world. Sorry.

I just remembered that you started classes today. That must have seemed strange to you too. Will you be at Camille-Sée or the Lycée Molière?

To Simone de Beauvoir

October 10

My love

Another day and no letter from you. Tonight I'm anxious. One letter might have been lost, another delayed. But three! That's the one hitch in this daily correspondence (which, by the way, I find of immense value): if one day is missing, a person gets very worried—and it bothers me to think about the anxieties that would assail you some time from now if my mail should be delayed. Well, what reassures me somewhat is that when last I heard you were, all in all, comfortably ensconced with the Lady. If you got sick, you'd be cared for, and they'd write to me. But what worried me right off is that—today—I got another letter from Tania, sent the 5th. So it seems to me I should have received something from Paris. In any case, since for the time being my life with you is your letters, this adds up to three days of life without you—today, worse still, it's a world where you don't exist. So how little the other letters count, my love, and how desertlike it all seems. Because now I won't get anything until tomorrow. And I'm not allowed to send a telegram.

Otherwise, life goes on as usual. A quick trip to the medical officer this morning: he wanted to make sure we'd been vaccinated. A marvelous package from my mother, with gloves, sweater, underpants, all the things I lacked. A letter from Paulhan, who is anticipating my "Reflections on Death" and will publish the Giraudoux "within two months," which means four, I suppose. A long charming letter from young Bost, who gives me news you already know via Z. and who is in almost precisely the same state of indifference as I am. For now he doesn't seem to be in any kind of danger.

My love, that's all for this evening. Tonight I'm on guard duty at the officers' headquarters. It's not arduous. We sleep on straw (I like that) and we have to answer a phone call or two. As compensation, I'll have light for quite a while and be able to write.

Do write me, darling Beaver. It is the anniversary of our marriage, so of course today of all days, I got no letter from you. Melancholy anniversary. I send you my passionate love, my little flower.

Please send some paper too. This kind.

To Simone de Beauvoir

October 11

So now I've received a token sign of life. Don't worry. I'd gladly have started over on this letter so as not to alarm you, but it's too long and philosophical, so I'm leaving it as it is.

[Added later by Sartre at the head of the letter. (SdB)]

My darling Beaver

Still no letter from you. Now I'm really upset. Where are you? What can you be up to? It's very worrisome. Without you, my courage collapses. It's because of you-there that I can go on. I really feel that, without you, I wouldn't have even the energy to write, everything would go to hell. I recognize that this sense of calamity is all in my head; four days are nothing at all, given the military mails. There must have been a bottleneck somewhere. But that doesn't negate the fact that I'm spending days without you. I haven't heard your daily hello for four days, and the world just isn't the same. For the first time I feel deprived and captive, a rat in a trap; I feel all my powerlessness; if I wanted to write to the Lady to ask her for news (since I'm not allowed to telegraph) it would take over ten days to get an answer. If I get nothing from you by tomorrow I'll write my mother asking her to stop by the Rue d'Assas and see what's happened to you. I'm sure I'd get her answer in a week. But I honestly hope that long before that I'll be deluged with delayed letters.

Last night I worked for you. I was on guard duty in the officers' headquarters. It's not bad: you sleep on straw in the middle of an office. Sometimes a phone call wakes you up, but only rarely. Before going to sleep, you have the office all to yourself. Pretty little tables with individual lamps. I sat down at one, turned off the ceiling light, lit the individual one, and there in the midst of the darkness was my own little civilian *querencia*. Then I took my little notebook and wrote down the answer to your question from Douarnenez. This is the question you asked me, my love: "At the Pointe du Raz, beneath a starry sky, I wondered why human consciousness constructed a world with stretches of time and distance, with masses, that are not to man's measure; Brunschvicg would speak of the progress of consciousness, and the fact that the Greeks thought the world finite, etc. But what I mean is that it's odd for consciousness itself to lead to inhuman constructions." And this is what I wrote in my little notebook: "What you call 'the measure of human consciousness' is the measure of human *activity*, not consciousness. The man behind each consciousness is, *for* that consciousness, like the world, and there is a being-in-man for the consciousness just as there is a being-in-the-world for man. But the disregard of man—which is what surprised you—is because consciousness creates for itself a finite representation in an infinite world. And it is possible to show that it cannot be otherwise. For consciousness, as we intuitively conceive it after phenomenological reduction, naturally encompasses the infinite. That is what must first be understood. At every moment consciousness can exist only insofar as it refers to itself (intentionality, etc.), to the infinite; and to the extent that it refers to itself it transcends itself. Therefore each consciousness encompasses within itself the infinite to the extent that it transcends itself. It cannot exist except by transcending itself and cannot transcend itself except by the infinite. But instead of completing one another, finite and infinite repel and oppose one another. Therefore human reality is both the consciousness held captive in the body and the body itself—the acts that are "objects" of the consciousness and the spontaneity that sustains those acts. In itself it is both disregarded in the inifinite world and creative of its own transcendence, which sustains the infinite world. All of man's *acts*, being accomplished by means of the body, are registered finitely on a double infinity—of immensity and minuteness. And from that fact, all consideration of objects as *implements* brings human reality to the consciousness of its own disregard. For what Heidegger did not see is that the infiniteness of the world surpasses its implementicity in every direction. Whence your astonishment at the Pointe du Raz: the pre-ontological comprehension of anything at all always presupposes the understanding of it as *implement*: to see a mountain is to understand it as "climbable." If the vast distances of the stars produce a stupor akin to Pascal's terror, that is because it comes from the transcendent infinite of the transcendental consciousness—

and, at the same time, the perception of the stars necessarily includes an attempt at their implementation[1] which conflicts with their "out-of-reach" quality. Heidegger didn't see that his world for man—which is indeed immediately and pre-ontologically an implement—is coincidental with man and not with the transcendental consciousness, and that it is completely surpassed and disarmed by the world for consciousness, which isn't capable of receiving implementicity, across which implementicity slips without being able to grab hold. And the conflict between implementicity and the infinite margins of non-implementicity, between the pragmatic and the theoretical, between the finite and the infinite, is at the very source of the disregard of the human. Thus the transcendental conscience, in making itself human reality, inevitably constructs its own disregard in the midst of the world. Do you agree? Are you satisfied?

My darling Beaver, still not the slightest word from you, but I've just found out that a money order for 500 francs has come. As only you could have sent it, I know that you're alive. So there is simply some incomprehensible delay in the mail. Now I'm completely cheered up, my love, and very much relieved. I somewhat suspect Keller—with whom I had words this morning because he hadn't cleaned the mess pot and bowls—of stealing my letters today from the clerks. Because there were no letters from *anybody*. The first time that's happened since September 15th.

I think we are supposed to leave tomorrow.

I love you with all my heart, my dear little morganatic wife. And joyfully, this time.

My love, send me the package quickly, if you haven't done so. I have *no more ink* (last cartridge today), *paper, or books*. I have nothing left.

I love you with all my heart, my little flower.

I bought myself a lighter that I already love like a son. It is absolutely handsome. Here's what it looks like

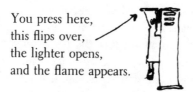

You press here,
this flips over,
the lighter opens,
and the flame appears.

---

[1]From *ustensilisation*, taken as "make an implement of."

To Simone de Beauvoir

October 13

My darling Beaver

A small package from you. No letters, but that doesn't worry me, nobody else had any and I had none from anybody: a bottleneck in mail service someplace. Nonetheless, it means a day without its small pleasures. I love you so, my love.

Here, nothing new. Last night I invited Pieter out for dinner with your five hundred francs, and we ate marvelously well, across from a very distinguished infantryman (chasseur)—in dry goods—who told us about his mistresses from the Bal Tabarin and his fine dinners in Paris. He wears a little packet hung from a cord around his neck with photos of civilian life (women, cars, himself, and even selected shots of scenery, tucked in back). He takes them out when he feels low. Petite mustache, bedroom eyes. We talked for two hours. Strange how you find yourself talking to just anyone at all. On that score, Pieter, the fat Jew, for once made a rather perceptive remark. I pointed out, as we were leaving, some negative detail in the guy's attitude, and he said: "That's the third time you've nailed something that way. You're shrewder than me with that sort of thing." As I demurred politely, he added, "The thing is, you can point out the flaws because you're independent. If guys don't appeal to you, you write them off. While I, being a businessman, always notice the good side because I have to be in sympathy with them." *This habit of looking on the good side* interests me; it explains a lot of things. A self-serving habit, of course. But I can see him sizing some guy up: "Now what does he have that I can like about him?" In another vein, my acolytes are more and more like Kafka's Assistants: I spare them no rebuff, out of a moral pedantry. And they come right back, exactly like the Assistants, silent, laughing, mischievous children. This morning we had to go for some rifles. I can't remember exactly what they did wrong, but I told them, "You lousy bastards. Go on without me, you can bring mine." Because I keep a firm grip on them. Then I went off for lunch all alone at the inn, reading *The Idiot*, writing in my journal. And at one o'clock, there they are trooping into the inn, winking and smirking. They brought me some little cakes. —So there was a package. Thanks, sweet Beaver. I'm delighted to be reading Agatha Christie. The Green seemed a bore, but only at first glance. I'll see. I still have a volume and a half of *The Idiot* to read. I'm surprised at how contrived and clumsy it all is. And the Idiot himself is dull enough to make you puke.

There are excellent passages on the comic side. But, at least so far, I like the touching sections less than I used to. They smack of artificiality, they're too frenetic for my taste. The translator, who's actually an ass, calls attention to the fact that if you take the indications of tone and gesture literally, you'd think you were in a madhouse. "With a gesture of dread" . . . "In a terrified tone of voice." The truth is that you shouldn't take the notations as directions for gestures but rather as "rests" (in the musical sense) and as veiled indications of *feelings*. Basically, to differing degrees, everyone does that. Only once they've rubbed your nose in it, you can't help noticing it, and in the long run, at least in the case of Dostoyevsky, you find it irritating. Which doesn't prevent it from being good work. I think you can send me, in a month or two, *The Brothers Karamazov*, which is better, so they say. I'd like to see for myself. As for that whole question of "shadowy recesses" in the characters, etc., it's all very interesting, but what a heap of claptrap has been said on the subject, and how basically simple it is. As long as you aren't mired in deterministic psychology, you can understand what he has in mind. There are no shadowy recesses at all. There's psychology, that's all.

Aside from that, my love, nothing new. It's raining, every day they tell us that departure is set for the next day, and then the next day we're still here.

My love, how sweet you are to me. How tender your little letters are. I feel so *supported*. You are my dear dear Beaver.

To Simone de Beauvoir

October 14

Still no letters from you. I think the rhythm's established: three days without letters, then four letters on the fourth day. So there's pleasure one day out of four. But this time I'm not worried anymore. No letters for four days from Tania either, but that could be because she hasn't written me. Nothing new here. It's irritating: every day we hear we're to leave the next day, and every evening we hear we're not. Yesterday the army gave me 120 francs for a blanket my mother sent me. So now I'm rich. I used the opportunity to have my picture taken. The photographer was working in a small courtyard filled with soldiers who, one after another, would strike becoming poses. I had myself taken with and without the forage cap. The gaze is aquiline, the mien martial. My greatest wish was not to send you a mate to that awful little photo you had during my military service, where I was heartrending. But oh how fat I've become, I can't get over it, my face too round, though no paunch. But you'll see: we'll get the pictures tomorrow and I'll send them right off. Last night I spent a while at the inn with Pieter. He confided in me. Last month he told me, "I don't take marriage lightly. I've been faithful to my wife for the seven years we've been together." But last night, with the aid of a bottle of Gewürztraminer, he changed his tune. "My friend," he said, "I caught my first dose of clap at thirteen. And it hasn't stopped since. Finally the doctor told me, 'Don't accuse the women anymore. Your duct's so narrow all you need is a different woman for the inflammation to flare up again.' I'd had it with love, man. He told me, 'Only one solution . . . marriage.' So married I got. And that's why I'm faithful to my wife . . . any change would screw me up. It seems any change in the blood at all would irritate me. So it's just no, you see. Since my marriage I haven't allowed myself anything—or else just minor stuff, maybe, a couple of blowjobs." But fifteen minutes later he was talking about the moral value of fidelity, the home, the child's lot in divided households. Discreetly, though, since he isn't completely stifled by morality. We went home making our way with my pocket flashlight, a present from my mother—though it really has very little power left, the battery's dying. Lovely nocturnal effects, a bluish sky, black houses, and here and there a mournful light seeping through blue windowpanes. But by now you're as familiar with that effect as I am. I came back to the school, where I took guard duty again for the sheer pleasure of it. But I wasn't so lucky, I had to share my office, and then around eleven I had to take an urgent message to the colonel. I didn't know where he was staying, dark night, my flashlight was flickering, it was raining. Finally, after sinking up to my knees in hundreds of puddles and wandering around in total darkness, I completed my errand and went back to sleep under my blanket, my head hidden while the mosquitoes serenaded me. Today nothing really new: I finished the third chapter I've written since September 2. Or 72 pages. But are they good or bad, O my little judge? It's up to you to say. If this goes on—and it will, for even if I do readings six times a day there'll still be time left—the novel will be finished in its first version by the 1st of January. At that point I'll tend to my "Reflections on Death," another article, on Gide, and some slightly fantastic trifles. Perhaps the *Histoires pour l'oncle Jules* ["Stories for Uncle Jules"]. Do you remember, my love, when we were in Marrakech and in the Atlas Mountains, and I told you those tales, the one about the Arab who peed upward, the one about the sergeant who hated flies. I get all emotional when I think of our little trip. I love you so. It was ten years ago, my darling Beaver, ten years ago, I was leaving with Aron and Guille for the Fort de Saint-Cyr. While waiting for Aron's car, we were sitting, you and I, on the terrace of the Mahieu, and I'd caught sight of Gégé for the first time, I thought she looked like Chadel. From time to time, like this, I'll tell you what we were doing ten years ago (like *Paris-Soir*, each day describing the corresponding day in 1914). I've finished the first volume of *The Idiot*. There's some very fine stuff in it after all; and I found some entertaining things in the Green. For instance this, which made me furious: "We are talking" (with Malraux) "about the new crop of writers, those twenty to twenty-five, and how little of interest there is in what they're doing." (This is written in 1930, when I was 25.) "What can you expect?" asks Malraux. "They grew up in peacetime, they haven't experienced the disruptions of war or revolution, which prove to have been so useful to us." Such an ass. In the end that jerk really gets on my nerves (Malraux, not Green). One fine day he'll have to be told just what he really is. In the meantime, I hope and pray he's *invalided out* because of nervous tics and that a whole generation of new writers call him an old fogy and pity him because he wasn't in the grrreat war of '39. At first glance Green seems a lightweight ass. But I'll take a closer look. Ass he surely is. But what kind?

Here I'm having a very odd experience: a socialist government employee at loose ends. I mean my corporal. You couldn't keep a straight face. Ultimately they're as worthless on the left as on the right. Of course you have to judge the leftists on peace and the rightists on war. There's a lot to be said about that, for example: our officers are really *nice as can be* and so affable that the distances are blurred though not forgotten. They all read *Candide*, *Gringoire*, and *Le Jour*. The thing is that a friendly paternalism, which can make a worker furious, turns into gentle forbearance for the soldier. Not that anyone is hard on him, nobody is; the sergeants are treated like the troops, rank doesn't count except from first sergeant on—and not much even then. Except that the private has no human dignity left. None whatsoever. Which is both good and bad. And it is not *men* who strip him of his dignity, but the system. Incidentally, you can live extremely well without dignity—better, in fact. That's something Alain probably wouldn't understand. But all this will seem thoroughly vague to you, my darling Beaver. Hang on to this part alone, that everyone is courteous and agreeable—and accommodating.

Till tomorrow, my little flower. I would so like to receive your letters. I love you with all my might.

I'm not writing to Tania anymore, since my letters would reach Laigle after her departure. I'll wait till I know her Paris address. That frees up my days somewhat.

To Simone Jollivet

October 15
Readings Post AD
Sector 108

Dear Toulouse

You made me very happy by writing to me. If you occasionally have the time, you should start sending me lots of details again on what's happening to the two of you. Do you know that you seem solid as an oak and that we have often spoken of you, the Beaver and I, as one of the rare people that we will find unchanged, undaunted, in the midst of the worst upheavals and any postwar situation. Your letters always seem like peacetime news, whereas other people's are only news from the home front. In exchange, of course, I'll send you all the exhortations you might wish: to begin, continue, or finish your novel. But, if I have understood you correctly, these would still be premature.

As for me, the war has not yet begun. And I don't know if it ever will. For the moment I am no more than a very overaged pupil in the study hall of a primary school whose teacher is a puny, extremely courtly first sergeant. Imagine me writing to you at one of the school desks, all my little possessions at hand, tobacco, lighter, cigarettes—my novel within reach (I've written 73 pages—fair copy—since October 3). My acolytes are at other desks similarly absorbed in leisure tasks, reading, writing, sewing, drawing. The sergeant, at the teacher's desk, with raised eyebrows, his lips pursed, and an air of extreme application, is reading a detective novel I gave him. The 2 blackboards are covered with sines and cosines, because he sometimes explains the secrets of artillery to his aides. As you see, anyone would take it (minus the sines) for a reeducation center, like Ville-Évrard, for the mentally retarded. There is just one gas mask lying on a table beside a licentious engraving (owned by the first sergeant), which gives the room some slight suggestion of a surrealist exhibition. I'm here all day. I read (I've just finished *The Idiot*, which disappointed me—Gide's *Journal*), I'm writing my novel and keeping a "War Diary"; from time to time I take a bike ride around the town to clear my head. It's a small town, with low white potbellied houses held up by black beams, with long, steep roofs. The restaurants and cafés have the mysterious (and German) look of bordellos and are, in fact, becoming just that. So far it seems Venus has wreaked far more devastation within our ranks than Mars has. Yet the troops keep complaining that bromides are being put in their coffee. Otherwise, where would we be? The war gives all my acolytes a childish charm. Most of them are ill-shaven, getting chubby, and pretty mischievous. I'm getting fat too and that upsets me.

Dear Toulouse, you asked me what I might need, something that would combine the pleasurable and the useful: of course, only your letters can meet that definition. Please give all my affectionate regards to Dullin. And I trust I remain your very faithful friend.

To Simone de Beauvoir

October 15

My darling Beaver

Today I got your letter of the 9th. I'm missing three. One from the 6th in which you must have told me that you were settling into the Rue Vavin[1] (which means that my October letters *all* went to the Rue d'Assas) and the two from the 7th and 8th. Your letter of the 9th makes me very sad. How on earth could you still imagine that Emma[2] might go with you? I thought her answer was final. At any rate, since her mother allowed you to take her to the Midi, it seems to me that she would allow you to go one more time, *if the occasion should arise*, on November 1st, as long as you alert her ahead of time—because she's touchy—that you have not made any mention of permission from her. On that subject, you haven't told me what sort of a welcome Emma gave to Bernard and René Ulmann when they called on her; I wouldn't want her to have had the same disappointment as last month when Maurice, Adrien, and Thérèse Héricourt, who had gone out of their way for her, found no one home.[3] To repay all those good people who went to such lengths you should invite them to your place. *Don't forget to forewarn her mother that you aren't mentioning any authorization from her.* In any case, my poor dear Beaver, I'm very sad for you and I was completely undone reading your letter. I would so like to be near you.

---

[1] On October 9, with Gégé unable to give her the apartment on the Rue d'Assas after all, Beauvoir told Sartre she was moving to the Hôtel de Danemark, 21 Rue Vavin.
[2] *A fictional person Sartre used when speaking of the possibility—or impossibility—of my coming to see him. (SdB)*
[3] *The initials of these fictional characters spelled the name of the town, Brumath. (SdB)*

Here, we're still all set to leave. Perhaps you thought we'd settled in permanently? Not at all. We never will. The annoying thing is that we've been here a whole week. Except that each morning they tell us we're leaving that evening, and every evening it's off till the following morning. In fact, I think that without the bad weather we would already have left. All of this is irritating as hell.

Aside from that, nothing new. In two other little envelopes I'm sending you my two photos, given to me today. I read and I write but I'm morose: I received only one poor weary little letter from you, my love, and nothing from anyone else for four or five days. I feel a bit neglected, and I really would so like to see you.

Till tomorrow, my love (till tomorrow means that I'll write to you tomorrow, for with the wretched, inexcusable blundering of the mail service, I don't even know whether I'll have a letter from you). I love you with all my heart.

P.S.: Have you thought to *include in my manuscript* the chapter I wrote at Juan-les-Pins (Mathieu-Brunet), which was in my suitcase? If not, please do, my dearest.

I have written chapters X, XIII, and XIV and half of chap. XV.

To Simone de Beauvoir

October 16

My darling Beaver

Three letters from you today, 2 from Tania, 1 from the Boxer, 1 from my mother. Oh joyful deluge! They say the mailing of free packages to the troops tied up 7 *million letters* for the soldiers. Now they're dribbling through, and it will all get back to normal. But I really hope you got mine. I wished us a happy anniversary, good little creature, and you didn't know it at the time. Finally by now you are probably happily showered with letters too. I love you with all my might.

I have loads of things to tell you—not about my life here, which remains idyllic and almost too dull. Just picture a slightly comic village notable exchanging greetings with each and every one—and each and every one brightening up as they see him go by. The notable is me, and the villagers are the military personnel of every rank, it's crazy how many of them I know. They bust their guts laughing when I go by, because of my puttees and some general oddity in appearance that must have dogged me from civilian life into the warrior one. You'll be able to judge for yourself from the photos I sent yesterday. So this is my life, bourgeois and lacking in the picturesque: I work and I shake hands. They call me "flier." "Hey, flier, still not a fuckin' thing to do?" I reply, "Still waiting for my airplanes."[1]

But let's get down to serious business.

1. You cannot yet use the information you got about Emma. You probably understand that. But it might not be impossible for you to proceed with it come November. In any case, I imagine you'll be alerted.

2. I'm not enchanted with the idea that Tania might come to live at the Hôtel de Danemark because of the letters I send you there. If there's no way to have her stay elsewhere, can't I write to you at the Lycée or at Gégé's? This is important. Settle the problem as best you can, my love. While awaiting your reply, *I'll write to you at the Rue d'Assas*. So go and pick up my next letters (5 or 6) at Gégé's.

3. I have a sudden desire to read Dickens. Can you find me—but only when you're making some future shipment—*Barnaby Rudge* (NRF). I think you read it and found it entertaining. Also, within a few days, you can send me some paper. I very much want *Colonel Jack* (and *Moll Flanders* if that can be) and *Les Enfants du limon* ["Children of the Silt"].[2] I like Queneau a lot. As for Julien Green, half of his *Journal* is suppressed; perhaps he's more interesting as a homosexual. I think he's the banalized reflection of Gide. No one else is so strongly influenced by him. Don't forget *Mars*.[3] By the way, whatever has become of Alain? Here's a little item from *Candide*, which I'm copying down without understanding it:

> Two students of Chartiers',[4] two *normaliens*, meet at Saint-Germain-des-Prés.
> "You know?" asks one.
> "I know," replies the other.
> "Poor old master!"

---

[1] Unlike the khaki-clad soldiers of the artillery division with whom they were stationed, Sartre's meteorological unit wore the blue uniforms of the air force, their initial assignment.

[2] *By Raymond Queneau, published in 1937. (SdB)*

[3] *Mars ou la guerre jugée*, 1921 [*Mars: Or the Truth About War*, 1930], by Alain (1868–1951), the philosopher, who opposed the buildup to the Great War but at its outbreak enlisted in the artillery. On and near the front lines he wrote several important books, including *Mars*. A model for Sartre.

[4] Émile-Auguste Chartier was the philosopher Alain's real name. He was prosecuted along with others in 1939 for signing a petition for peace.

It's true that Chartier's students conferred an affection on him bordering on veneration. His disgrace, only mentioned in undertones, is the object of excited comment.

These days fate is hard on everyone.

But similar fates don't inevitably lead to confusion.

There are scoundrels and good folk. Some rouse our indignation, some we pity.

What does it mean? Find out, please.

4. My interest was piqued by what you say about our passive responsibility toward the next generation. You are absolutely right. It's all terribly complicated, my love, and I'm thinking a lot about it. War is certainly an odd thing. Each one of us has *his* war, just as each has his death. There is absolutely no question of submitting to it as a disaster, but we each have a being-for-the-war (different in each case, and often pretty suspect) just as we have a being-for-dying. And *right from the start*.

5. I'm so happy to hear you've resumed your novel[5] and that you're interested in it again. I agree it's a subject that absolutely does not suffer from current events. Your self-criticisms are quite just, but they won't be very hard to correct.

Bits and pieces: I find Gérassi a really first-rate comic character. The right to good humor is a fairly inspired contrivance. But still and all some kicks in the ass do go to waste. I think you can be much more explicit about everything he tells you. The worst that could happen, if the censors open your letters, is that they might blacken something out with their brushes. But the letter would arrive all the same. And you can just imagine how much that would entertain me. For me it's not the same, as you can imagine, because I'm *Private* Sartre. Your story about Sorokine is odd.[6] What attitude are you taking? And what is she doing in Paris? I thought the Lady was adopting her. Has she found any money? Here's my little anecdote on Keller, which is old, but I believe I haven't told it to you. Keller is the elephant seal. He gets up (this was in the school room in Marmoutier) and says, meditatively, "I think I'd like to take a crap." Silence. He stands there, scratching his nose, "Yes, I feel like taking a crap." Another silence, during which he evinces signs of great nervousness (for an elephant seal, mind you). "To crap or not to crap?" Another silence. He knits his brows and seems unhappy. Then his

---

[5] *L'Invitée* [*She Came to Stay*]. (SdB)
[6] Natalie Sorokine, a former student of Beauvoir's who became a close friend. She had taken Beauvoir's journal, then thought better and returned it.

face brightens all at once: "Oh well, shit, I've got plenty of time." And sits down again.

My love, no more this evening. I love you with all my heart, my little flower, and I'm blissful today, after the gloom of these past days, because so many letters came. Till tomorrow, I think of you most tenderly.

Give me an immediate answer on Number 2. And remember: next letters *Rue d'Assas*.

To Simone de Beauvoir

October 17

My darling Beaver

Two letters from you today, a red-letter day. First, I want to respond that I enthusiastically approve your idea of setting the novel in 1938–1939. That ties up absolutely everything—excellent decision. It makes one more theme to develop, which, if you take it up, must be a constant undercurrent. But that's a very small difficulty against lots of advantages. Only, I see one great inconvenience: doesn't your conclusion imply the *end* of this war? It's true you can end in the midst of the war, but the effect would be more uncertain. Let's simply hope the war ends soon enough to jibe with your novel. Tell me when you write whether you intend to finish *during* or *after* the war.

I find your relationship with the Moon Woman very entertaining. She's an odd, totally unfocused person with snatches of the bourgeoise and snatches of passion. I knew the story of Tania's spanking. I believe it false, first because Tania told me quite naturally that the guy prided himself on it (there followed a believable telling of their relationship which I've now forgotten); then because the following day she was rather proud of having known how to keep him at a distance, saying "with that kind of person, you simply have to . . ."; and finally because I believe she would have taken to hating the Moon Woman and wouldn't have wanted to see her again, which never happened. And then it would have seriously shaken her up—which after all never happened. She was revolted for a day, and that's it. But the story of the purge, which she is naturally unaware of, is rather funny. She writes to me regularly every day and, depending on her mood, I am either "distant as a little puff of smoke" or else "her security." What you tell me—that I'll find her again after the war—is quite possible (although she is capable of infatuations). But, so as not to hide anything from you, I'll mention that it gives me little satisfaction. I give very little thought to the postwar, and I only foresee—basically—finding *you* there. Whereas it would be unpleasant—from here, powerless as I am and with only a dreamlike impression of that distant life, which lends itself particularly to the passionate—to feel her becoming progressively detached from me and fooling around with others. And that is what will inevitably happen. So I prefer to cut myself off, something I always find easy. I haven't written her for five days—out of laziness and under the pretext that I don't know her address. Nonetheless I'll do it today and send the letter to the Hôtel de Danemark. If she isn't staying there, it would be very kind of you to have her sister tell her to pass by and pick it up. Don't forget what I told you in my last letter and am telling you again today in case my last letter doesn't reach you: find me an address where I can write you (Camille-Sée?—Gégé?—Rue de Rennes?).

We are still here. It seems that events are moving along more rapidly now. We hear gunfire at night, and it makes quite a racket at this distance. In that case we may leave, but it's also possible, even when the division goes into action, that we'd stay. My life is incredibly humdrum, a bureaucrat's existence. I get up at six o'clock (my own choice: reveille's at 8, but I don't feel like sleeping too much, or eating too much; with a war going on it seems like wasted time. There is a passage on voluntary asceticism in Paulhan's *Le Guerrier appliqué* that's very true); I go to the inn for my breakfast. At seven-thirty to work (novel. Generally I write my war diary at 7, at the inn) till 11 o'clock, when I go back to the inn, where I read as I eat a 7-franc lunch. At 1:30, roll call in the courtyard of the town hall. We go to the school, I write till three with growing impatience because I'm waiting for the mail. At 3, mail. I answer it from 4 on and often as late as 7. I don't eat dinner; I just have a little red wine in my cup, and I work a bit more, till eight-thirty. Then, according to what the evening brings, I stand guard or go to bed. Yesterday I went to bed, Paul stood guard, I had a good bed all to myself. Today's my turn on guard. I'll work if that's possible, because there's a lot of commotion in the area just now. And I'll sleep on the straw.

My love, I won't copy out my 73 pages. At least not now. Here's why: so long as I have the chance to write new material, I'd better. One never knows, I could be prevented from further writing for lack of adequate conditions. It's not likely, but there will always be time enough for copying when the novel is finished—and it is beginning to draw to a close. Perhaps by that time I'll be going on leave, and I'll bring back the whole thing clutched to my bosom.

My dearest, how forcefully I feel your love at this moment, and how it moves me; what enormous support you are for me; I was able to see just how enormous the other day, when I was missing your letters. Everything good that I am is because of you. I love you. The Moon Woman is perhaps right in saying that I overestimate you, my little flower.

I love you passionately.

To Simone de Beauvoir

October 18

My darling Beaver

I've received a jumble of letters from you and they've thrown me for a loop. One written the eleventh in which you love me so much, my love— and toward the end you seem totally distraught, it would have scared me if I hadn't received some more recent ones the day before, in the end it was only a metaphysical intuition—and then another from the 15th in which you say: "I'm not sad, but I'm not very happy either today." Hey there, my poor good little Beaver, how I'd like to hold you in my arms. If you only knew the tenderness I feel right now for your little self, so slim and strong. It won't amount to much, it isn't one of those moments of feeling that we are one or that I'll find you again, solid as a little rock. It's just tenderness; I'm picturing your face and I'm also very aware of the space you filled in my arms when "I held you prisoner." My love, how I long to see you. I love you so. I feel sad about that return to Paris (hastened because of me, my little sweet). I gather from rereading your letters that you felt nothing there but the disorientation of the early days and our separation and the war. Run off to Provins. Revisit La Pouèze (maybe at Christmas. Unless you're going skiing), and after all Zazoulich is there now. I wonder what help she'll be.

Since yesterday, we've been feeling that the real war has started. We hear constant but very distant gunfire. And there was a funny little episode last night, a thunderstorm mistaken for bombardment, that I'll tell you about some other time and place. It actually kept me from sleeping. Not that I was fooled, but they woke me up (I was on guard duty at the officers headquarters) because of it. A fat sergeant—among others—got dressed, completely bewildered, and went out to the street in the middle of the night. It was really funny to me, but today I'm tired. I got your package—paper and books. I'm delighted to be reading *Colonel Jack* and *Les Enfants du Limon*. Read a bit of the *NRF*. The article put together by Vaudal isn't too lousy. Obviously his initial criticism doesn't hold up: just because the character telling his own story adopts various points of view doesn't mean the author can go and do the same. It is this alone I held against Mauriac. (My early works seem worse than dead to me, they strike me as *classics*.) But when he says that "my liberty is the liberty of nothingness," he's right, so long as nothingness is understood as pure consciousness. He does seem to understand it that way, since he says that "all eventualities can issue from that nothingness." Paulhan's article literally made me howl. He writes: "To the question 'Why are you fighting?' arrange it so that each one of them can answer, 'So that one day I'll be happy and honored.' " —If he only knew how remote the thought of ever being happy and honored is to the guys here! I find Pourrat's comment much truer: "A war we'll wage the way we approached a page of writing when we were very young. Something annoying that nonetheless has to be done." That's the general opinion. I don't get the feeling anymore that the soldiers feel themselves endowed with rights—like your guy at Youki's[1]—now it will occur to them perhaps as they rub elbows with civilians. Here they aren't at all unappealing. And if they hear talk about someone with a cushy job, they actually say quite frankly, "The lucky dog," calmly and still with good humor. It's as though we're like children playing together nicely, who become unbearble the moment the grown-ups appear. As for the civilians, if you go by the writings of Béraud, Dorgelès, and associates, they are screamingly funny, embarrassed about themselves. They've been taught that they shouldn't play the great old songs of 1914, but they still want to give a big slap on the back to the soldier boys. And then they say, trying to seem quite natural, "We won't tell you a thing, we have nothing to tell you." The surprising thing about this war is that everything in it is *an attitude of denial about 1914*, from the conduct of operations to the personal behavior of each man. It's a war that's been perfected after the dress rehearsal. It seems like a difficult war, too—in the same sense that we speak of difficult music. You know what I mean, we have the feeling that we're constantly telling ourselves we won't fall into the same errors as x, we won't dwell on this, which was developed at length by y, etc., Brunschwicg's war, in other words—with thoughts about thoughts.

A note from my mother, which I'll answer. I'm glad you found her so nice.

Re the Moon Woman: your last letter made me rather cocky. I'd figured

---

[1]*Foujita's ex-wife, married to [the poet Robert] Desnos. (SdB)*

it out all on my own and in Berlin told her she'd been violated by her father. She denied it then, but with more crankiness than vigor.

Till tomorrow, my dearest, my dear little flower. I send you my kisses and imprison you with my arms.

I'll send some books to Bost, but not the Gide, because I must do an article on him.

To Simone de Beauvoir

October 19

My darling Beaver

No letter from you today. And I won't be able to write very much because I have nothing new to tell you. A huge change for us, but will you appreciate it?—the painter has smeared blue over the windows of our school-room. They're like stained-glass windows now, and we work all day long in an ecclesiastical atmosphere. For a civilian happening in, it must seem pretty surreal, this bluish classroom where balding, potbellied soldiers work away at tables like schoolboys, their gas masks beside them on the desks. We're so used to it we don't actually notice it anymore, and for us its "hodological"[1] space has changed. There is none of that movement directed from individual work tables to the front desk, but rather a sort of balanced stagnation distributed equally in all directions, as in a living room. And then for us the tables no longer exist as *separate*. For each of us there is a *round querencia*-object made of four or five tables surrounding the one where he is seated—because we put our things down there, within reach. But the thing I wanted to say is that the smeared windows create a home for us in the evening; around seven o'clock, generally, we used to be chased off the premises, unable to turn on the lights. Now we draw the white curtains and stay here in bright light, all our lamps on, till nine o'clock. The officers are gone; the Artillery Intelligence Service, who share the room with us (three guys), are gone too. It is quiet and pleasant. We won't go back to the café at night anymore. But I do go there for breakfast in the morning and go back there from 11 o'clock to 1 o'clock. It seems sure now that we'll stay here *at least* till the 1st of November, and perhaps a bit later.

This morning our captain—the one I discussed politics with for over

---

[1]Characterized by the ways that tensions are resolved.

an hour one night when I was on guard duty—had us give him a demonstration of our readings. He watched everything, had everything explained, then said glumly, "Four men lost to the army." Would you believe that irked me? So much so I wrote six pages about it in my journal. You'll laugh when you read them. The notebook's almost filled, my love. Only 30 little pages to go. I've already written on my flyleaf: *War Diary I September–October 1939*.

That's all, my love. Here are today's events: Up at 6:30—breakfast at the inn—return—one hour of work—readings—two hours at the inn: 11 to 13—13:30: roll call—then a rather annoying hour waiting in a loft above a stable so they can do God knows what to our gas masks. The ammonia gas was thick enough to cut with a knife, it was coming from below, from the horses. "Very giving," said Keller, an expression I rather like, to express "it stinks," because of the generosity it lends to the odor. At 3, agitation about the mail, which came in small bundles—and without any letters from you. Then from 16:00 to 19:00: worked on my novel. At 19:00 I ate a bit of Muenster on army bread, right here, with a cup of wine, then I read a bit of the Agatha Christie. And finally, here it is, a quarter to eight and I'm writing to you.

How's that for a sober little life? It is totally filled with love for you, my little flower. You're all around me. Maybe more than I am for you. I mean that in this studious void I feel you less as a lack than as all the tenderness and poetic meaning of my life, whereas Paris for you, necessarily, is Paris without me. Remember how calm you were at Pouèze. Here there's a bit of that monastic calm, filled with you. I love you.

(1) Tell me if you have gathered all our friends together, as I suggested, and if you were able to make them chat a bit.

(2) You see, there's still a bit of hope for poor little Emma.

To Simone de Beauvoir

October the 20th

My darling Beaver

I received two short letters from you today, written the 15th and the 16th, telling me about your first classes. Good Lord, you lucky little person, how I envy you for being a prof at Henri IV,[1] and particularly for walking

---

[1] Sartre had been a student there in 1915–16 and again in 1920–22.

in the morning from Montparnasse to the Panthéon, a dream of mine, as you know. I can see exactly what you pass and which way you go, and it moves me. I was scared when I read they were talking of sending you to Bordeaux, but the moment Monod told you he'd prevent it, everything was fine. What exactly is he doing at the ministry? Has Davy been called up? Funny thought. My love, what a full docket you have. But in the long run you have two days free plus a morning and an afternoon when you can work. No, my darling Beaver, I won't construct a system here, at least not until the fourth year of war.[2] I'd far rather reach an understanding of what war is, and particularly *this* war, which is certainly not typical. I think I'll manage it bit by bit. And then, I like to understand it in a historic mode (I mean, history of my thought), through my moods. Besides, my novel is enough to keep me absorbed. By November 1st there will be a hundred pages; if all goes well, you'll be able to take them with you—as well as the first little black notebook.

Nothing new today. Except that I'm overcome with drowsiness, I don't quite know why—perhaps because of the guard duty, which I take on slightly too frequently for the pleasure of it. Actually, it's a sweet poetic drowsiness, filling me with tender little scenes. A while ago I was completely steeped in Paris in November, I saw a narrow old street near the Bourse, with the hazy yellow (peacetime) lights of its boutiques. Only it's harmful for my novel. I wrote 30 pages of rough draft but I don't have time to do a fair copy, and then when I do have the time I'm sleepy. Yesterday there was a reading and the masks. Today for four hours I copied down in order the geodesic coordinates of local sites, and now I'm sleepy. I got six letters; I'm pleased when there are a lot of them: an insipid one from Catinaud—who is going to sign up, because he doesn't have a conscience serene enough to bear up under continued shirking—one from Tania—one from my mother—two from you. I really like it when there are a lot of them; as I read them I had the feeling that my whole little world was in order. I'm very pleased you're back to work. I suppose you need a full life, my little one—complain as you may that it lacks spice.

What more to tell you? Wasn't it funny that Mauriac fished the word *querencia* out of Hemingway, as we did? Don't forget to send *Mars* in the next package of books (and also *La Dictature du nihilisme* ["The Dictatorship

---

[2]Beauvoir's letter of October 16 (*Lettres à Sartre*, Vol. 1, p. 195) praises his of October 11 (above), with its clarification of his philosophical positions, and suggests he construct a philosophical system. Fairly close to his time prediction here of "four years into the war," *L'Être et le néant (Being and Nothingness)*, written in occupied Paris and partly based on his meditations during the "phony war," was published in 1943.

of Nihilism"] by Hermann Rauschning.[3] Has the latest Ellery Queen announced by l'Empreinte come out yet?

My dear, my darling Beaver, I embrace you with all my heart and love you more than ever.

Why is Zazoulich gloomy? Bost? Her work? Give me details about what's happening to her.

To Simone de Beauvoir

October 21

My darling Beaver

I'm writing to you very late this evening, it's almost eight and lights-out is at nine. But you will lose nothing thereby, though I may skimp on the letters to others somewhat. Actually Tania hasn't written me; perhaps I'll allow myself not to write her at all. The reason I'm writing so late is that I wanted to move forward at a good clip on my novel, which had been dragging a bit of late.

I got a letter from Emma. She says it's quite probable—though one never knows—that she can entertain you there in November. Entertain you in a manner of speaking—you know that the poor dear has work to do, and I advise you not to accept if she speaks of putting you up. You would be better off staying at a hotel; there must be one near the station. You'll be able to see her quite often, though she has her work: mornings from eleven to around one o'clock, and in the evening around five, when she leaves her office. She tells me that of course she'll cook up some scheme to give you a bit more time—you'll see once you're there. In short, this time all the difficulties will be on your side and not hers, since you aren't sure your mother will allow you to see her. Do the best you can. She writes me that she'll be pleased to see you. And she seems truly sincere.

I'm writing to you in a strange atmosphere: the schoolroom's empty and my acolytes have gone out for a drink. But the first sergeant, who has just learned that his father is dying, is sobbing his heart out at the teacher's desk. I'm being careful not to look up, for then I would have to say a few words of consolation, as offensive to say as to hear. So I'm writing like one

---

[3] A personal friend of Hitler's, who turned against Nazism in 1935 after local Nazis established a dictatorial regime in Danzig, where he was president of the senate.

possessed, and I light my cigarette with lowered eyes. It's weird how family-minded all these men are.

On the subject of family-mindedness, my mother has handed me a beautiful example. Yesterday she writes that finally my stepfather has found a way of "serving," that they are offering him the management of an important undertaking, that I must immediately and personally congratulate him. Thereupon, animated by the most praiseworthy zeal, I take up my pen and congratulate him with all the stops out. I mailed the letter this morning, then received a short note: Above all do not congratulate him, the deal fell through, he's glum, it would be a terrible gaffe. I can only fold my arms and wait for the repercussions.

Aside from that, nothing new. I'm a bit worried about you, my little flower, because you seem to have lost your good spirits. I'd so like you to regain a modicum of calm, without being morose. I hope that bit by bit you'll grow used to this way of life. My love, if only I could give you some *support* and keep you from being sad.

I was just interrupted and called out to the officers' room by Mistler and Courcy, who were organizing a mosquito hunt, squashing them against the ceiling with the pole of the French flag. I gave a few polite ineffectual smacks against the wall. Mistler and Courcy are appealing, and I find them entertaining. They are clerks who occupy the classroom next door. Wednesday we'll all go out for a quiche and some Riesling. Yesterday was Pieter's birthday, and he'd brought back two bottles. We drank. I'm doing some serious drinking these days, and it cheers me up. My love, I don't really think the war will last long: a year, a year and a half at most. I'd be surprised if it goes past two winters. The Germans are seeking peace too relentlessly for them to feel very confident about maintaining the war for long. I'm confident. As for us, we may make our winter quarters here. I could ask for nothing more, for the town is quaint and comfortable and I'm used to it, I already have my little *querencias*.

The acolytes have just come in. Goodbye, my love. Have you thought more about inviting some friends, as I suggested, to a small party—Bernard and René Ullmann, who have been so nice to me, with Marcelle Allier? Why not Thérèse and Henri, too, if they're back? Tell me if you have. I embrace you with all my heart, dear little flower. Oh! how I'd love to see you.

To Simone de Beauvoir

October 22nd

My darling Beaver

Your poor little letters are so sad, it breaks my heart. I'd so like to send you back a little joy. Listen: first, you are going to see Emma in Orléans, it's more than likely. Then there's some chance that a system for leaves will be set up soon, and between now and Christmas or January you just might see me again. Isn't that good news? As for Emma, she writes me that we shouldn't be too confident—you know that her mother has the wanderlust. But here at last for a week now there has been no more talk of leaving, and, at All Saints, you could go off for a little outing there. Write to tell her the probable date of your arrival, and do make a date at the Auberge du Cerf, where we went together. Give her a big hug for me. How morose your life seems to me, with nobody around but a depressed Z. and the Boubous. Can't you find something better? Can't you get out a bit? I say that, but I know it isn't easy, my poor little flower. At least I'd like you to know that I am all love and tenderness for you. I attribute your gloom partly to the disappointment[1] that came right after your return from La Pouèze. But I think if things worked out as we wish, you would no longer feel this way. Isn't that so?

Here my life has settled down. Today was Sunday; you'd scarcely know it. Three of us went to Mass, and then during the afternoon everyone, except for me, made a bit more noise than usual and talked politics. I meanwhile was finishing the 90th page of my novel. These last few days, I've had the slight impression of a drying up as I worked on it. You know, when you're in the middle, you have two hundred pages behind you, two hundred pages ahead, and you get to seeing it as a world, and then, when you get near the end, as I am (there are about four chapters left after this one), the world freezes up, and you get the impression of a vast machinery, well constructed but without too much flesh. You know all the highways and byways, you have the impression of the *finite*. I thought an impression of the finite was *acquired*, you know, like that of the *infinite*, by a conceptualization of the primary notion of the *indefinite*. Nothing is more difficult than to think, for instance, that there is a finite number of inhabitants on earth, a finite number of days I have lived, a finite number right now of tobacco pouches or match-boxes. It seems so false. It's not that you think exactly that there is an infinity

---

[1]*The impossibility of going to see Sartre. (SdB)*

of them, but rather a number that doesn't end. Well, I think that at the point where you are with your novel, which is where I was in mine when I left you, a person gets that impression of the indefinite: it seems that the complications of the plot, the feelings of the characters, their reciprocal relationships, etc., are indefinitely numerous. That produces the feeling that you are working at great depth. And then a bit later, suddenly, it seems a finite object, which is surprising. But I realized that to the readers it will seem indefinite longer than for me—particularly at first reading, which for me is the one that counts most (for the ex- or im-pressionist—and we are among them— it is the first, because we want the words to catch fire. For the classical— among them Gide—it is the second or the third). But for me nothing equals the moment when the words themselves organize the reader's vision. I'm not of the opinion that we must give him work. Or at least not that sort of work. And I have always analyzed your novel from the point of view of the first reading. And then it begins again to seem complicated and rich, but in another way, like a piece of well-constructed machinery. It seems to me that if I have succeeded, the reader must have, at the point where I am with it now, an odd impression of simultaneity: "While Mathieu . . . ; for her part, Marcelle . . . ; and on the other hand Ivich . . . ; and Lola . . . ; and Boris . . . ; and Daniel . . ." You tell me, my little judge. And well, I finally think I've said just about what I intended. It's an odd impression: I now *know* that this novel, which I never expected to finish, will be finished. Except that I have no idea [censored] when it will be published.

That's enough about that, but I'm really up to my ears in it. I suggested to Paul I do guard duty tonight for him so I can work some more.

Aside from that: a poetic breakfast 6:30–7:30 at the Taverne de la Rose— work—noisy lunch (because it was Sunday) at the Taverne de Boeuf Noir, work in the midst of political conversations—a letter from you—a letter from my mother—dinner of a Muenster sandwich in the schoolroom, and I'm writing to you. The distressing part of it is that I'm taking the guard duty to stay up late, and drowsiness has just grabbed me by the scruff of the neck.

I'm delighted for you that Le Flore has reopened.

I'm surprised and furious, along with you, at Gérassi and Ehrenburg's behavior,[2] though a careful examination of the events and clever recourse to *theory* would allow a justification of their point of view (by stretching the point, if I may put it that way).

---

[2]Férnando Gérassi, along with the Soviet novelist Ilya Ehrenburg (1891–1967) and others, had reverted to an early September attitude of disdain toward current events which Beauvoir found annoyingly superior and untenable (*Lettres à Sartre*, Vol. 1, p. 201).

That's all for today. I had a funny little idea (at least I thought it was), then drowsiness stole it away. But don't worry, it'll come back and I'll tell it to you tomorrow.

My love, I love you so, I would be so pleased to see you again, I love you passionately, poor little Beaver. You are my beautiful little flower, my little self.

Ah yes, here's my little idea. It isn't funny at all. I was thinking about that guy who interviewed me for *Marianne* ("Would you prefer a monastic cell with the freedom to write, or life without writing but with its . . . and its . . . etc.?"). He made me answer that I would prefer, if it was absolutely necessary to choose, the Benedictine cell. I thought I had said nothing of the sort, but the very fact of having left myself open to the attribution of such an answer has brought me bad luck. Because at this very moment I have that Benedictine cell. It's a Benedictine war I'm waging. A philosopher's war. Meanwhile Petitjean, so Paulhan writes me, is leading his men in the charge: to each his destiny. It seems to me that thus far I'm waging the war that is the most in line with my destiny: seeing things through a keyhole and living in an overheated room.

To Simone de Beauvoir

October 23

My darling Beaver

Just a short note tonight, because I'm dead tired. I did guard duty last night, as you know, in place of Paul, and slept only five hours. And as luck would have it, it's up to me to take it again tonight: it's actually my turn, this time. I'm writing to you from the officers' room, very affectionately but in a daze. What will I be like tomorrow?

However, short though it may be, my letter will please you. Yesterday they officially announced on the radio that we will get a ten-day leave every four months, with travel time: either 12 or 14 days all told. The rotation will begin on November 1st. Of course, the 3 acolytes, being married and fathers, will depart before me, but I'll certainly go on leave before Christmas. What with this and Emma's coming on November 1st, doesn't that fill up your life a bit? I'm so happy, my love, so pleased to be seeing you again. Till now I was waiting for nothing. I had military patience. But now things are different, I'm beginning to be expectant again. How I do love you.

Here, nothing new, never anything new. I was so sleepy this morning at 7o'clock I had a violent argument with a staff sergeant. But we recognized our reciprocal errors thanks to the soothing intervention of Pieter and became once more the best of friends. At noon I lunched at the inn with a prison guard and a butcher from the abattoirs. The guard (from Clairvaux in l'Aube) was a kinky-haired blond kid with pug nose and loose-looking grinning mouth. His buddies razzed him good-naturedly: "Guess where this one's from?" And since we couldn't guess: "He's from where there's no further!" "The guillotine?" asks Pieter. "No, just before." "You oughta write a novel," the other tells him. "Some have. Didja know Dieudonné?" "Dieudonné?" asks the kid. "Come off it," says someone else, "he was two years old! Dieudonné, the innocent jailbird, from Bonnot's gang!" "No," says the kid, "he ain't from anywhere near us." All the others begin to laugh. "Hey, you hurt them bad, you bastard?" He answers gravely, "With us they don't suffer. They suffer because they don't have no more freedom." And with one finger raised, "Freedom's the prime thing because it's the thing man loves best." He doesn't get worked up, in fact, and eats with gusto. The butcher sees his chance when the other's back is turned to swipe a piece of his steak. He takes the meat in his hand like a small live animal, with a sort of tenderness, he seems to have a sort of special affinity with it, like the sailor and the sea. He tells us he's a butcher at the military abattoir and he's got a veal kidney sitting on his dressing table and he'll give it to the inn to cook. Meanwhile they're still poking fun at the kid: "Is it true the prisoners that behave can become guards?" "Don't say that to him, that's how he did it." But he laughs patiently. Nonetheless when the butcher calls him "lousy prison guard," he protests: "I've asked you not to call me that." "But you gotta have some name in there, right?" And the kid, with modest pride: "They call us supervisors." That's when it almost turned sour. One of them said to him, "So then you're a government employee?" "Yes, I'm a government employee." "So you get paid while we're getting screwed here for free?" "That's right!" "Bastard!" They think it's hilarious he's a jailer, but they're a little pissed at him for being a government employee.

There you have it—the only events of the day. Two little letters from you, a telegram from Tania to give me her new address. I've entirely stopped writing to her: I'll take it up again when her letters come more regularly. Actually I'm rather pleased. I'd like to write to the Boxer, to Bost, and to Guille, but I'll wait a bit because I'm absorbed in my novel, I'm at a thrilling moment, as they say, and I'd like to have finished a good chunk by November 1st.

I don't know whether I told you that I'd like you to have a party for all the friends who've been so good to Emma and me. You could invite Bernard and René Ullmann, if they are still there. Phone Marcel Arland too. Of course you should include Thérèse Héricourt, who wrote me such nice things again just yesterday. Let me know if you've done it.

My love, I can't wait to come on leave and see you. Your letters stir my soul, poor little flower. But if we can see each other every four months, it won't after all be quite the same as the present total separation.

I love you with all my might.

To Simone de Beauvoir

October 24th

My darling Beaver

How much I loved you this morning around noon. I saw you again, when you were so young, sitting beside me in the Luxembourg, it must have been in July of '29 or in October. We had our feet up on the stone balustrade of the terrace and our bottoms plunked on armchairs. I have no idea why I thought of that, but you made it seem so touching and so fragile. Oh my love, I love you so, my little paragon, I feel such grief knowing you're so far away, so drawn. You suffer more than I from this war. But how about yesterday's two pieces of good news? In fact you must have learned the lucky break about leaves from the newspapers, so you might be feeling rather blissful today. And then, about Emma, it seems to me almost a sure thing—barring some destructive caprice on her part, as often happens, alas. As you have no way of knowing her moods, you'll have to risk it, and it's just too bad if it fails.

I'm afraid I've lost your little surrealistic knife. I'll go look for it at the inn tomorrow, but I'm very much afraid of not finding it. I'm mourning its loss. It came from you and I loved it. And then it really was surrealistic, its handle was a small leg with a finely turned foot. A corkscrew, God knows why, came out of the calf. I'm telling you all this because I doubt you ever looked at it closely. My love, it was our last peacetime afternoon—and the peace was certainly crumbling. You should know that today we joined up with two clerks, Mistler, who resembles Grock, and Courcy, who reminds me of Nizan, for some chicken in the back room of a bakery. We ate it, and I must have pulled out my knife at that point, I don't know why. Now, at

1 o'clock, the hour when the cafés expectorate their soldiers, we were having coffee, with the little glasses of brandy still to go. We stayed till 1:15, when suddenly the patroness came in screaming, "The cops, vamoose, through the kitchen!" It was a rout, we grabbed up our masks and berets and vanished through the back door. In the confusion I must have left my knife.

Aside from that, it's been an incredible day of work. It had me completely exhausted around 5 in the evening. I had worked from 8:00 to 11:30 and from 1:20 to 5:20. No letters. From anybody. Must mean another jam-up. So I worked nonstop. Morning on my novel, afternoon on a 17-page note in my journal on grounds and motives. With that my first notebook is done and I've started on the second. Aside from that, nothing new. Things are turning a bit sour between the 3 from the Artillery Intelligence Service and ourselves, because the guys are bored. I was the one who took the first step over my spat with Staff Sergeant Naudin, who's actually a good guy, on the subject of packs—in other words about nothing. It was in the morning, during a morning slump. (The 17 pages on motivation actually stemmed from that incident.) What surprised me was that the 2 acolytes with brains, Pieter and Paul, backed me up, through a sort of family solidarity. The last acolyte is coming closer each day to the mineral, after leaving the zoophytic level. It's the food that's killing him. It's his vice. Today he ate seven helpings of meat (four this morning because we weren't having any lunch—and three this evening because Pieter and I dined on tuna sandwiches). He confided to Mistler that he shits three and even four times a day, which doesn't surprise me. At this point his face is flaming red and his cheeks are crowding out his eyes. So he abstains from these murderous struggles. But the rest of them are looking for trouble. This evening it calmed down somewhat. On the other hand we've struck up a friendship with three clerks, Mistler, Courcy, and Hantziger, all three Alsatian and really very decent.

There, my dearest. If the war goes on at this slow lulling rhythm I'll have written three novels and 12 philosophical treatises by peacetime. I've never thought so much, and my brain is curdling. Emma will explain my thoughts on historicity to you; it's too long to set down on paper.

My love, this makes several times I've written you, but if you've received my letters on the subject, you haven't said anything about it to me. I would really like you to gather all those people who were so kind to me as I was leaving: Bernard and René Ullmann, if they haven't been mobilized, Marcel Arland, and, if you can reach her, Thérèse Héricourt. Tell me if you can get them all together.

My dearest best little Beaver, I so long to see you. I love you.

To Simone de Beauvoir

October 25

My darling Beaver

How sad your little letters are, how I wish I could see you. I love you so. Every day I hope that you're back in good spirits, and every day there you are all gloomy, and my heart breaks. My dearest, won't it change things just a bit for you if I come on leave every four months? Won't you then have some sort of direction to your year and something to look forward to; it will make all the difference. Just in feeling how much it will change me, I sense that it will change you too. I'm waiting impatiently for the letters you'll send me when you've received the ones in which I talk about going on leave. Oh my love, above all don't think it's your duty to be sad—but I don't believe you think that—it is in having a good time and being happy that you'll give me, here, peace at heart. I have never thought of you with more happiness than when I knew you were really calm at the Lady's in La Pouèze. I'd so like you to be able to go and see Emma at Quimper. She's dying to see you and it seems to me that would help you a bit. You were separated *before* the war, which means you haven't thought through this war in common and felt it in common; you are both isolated within it. It is a bit as though what you feared had happened: as though you had died without witnesses. But all it will take is for you to see her one or two days for this war to become your war, for both of you, a milieu that will unite you as much as it separates you. And then, after that you'll be able to imagine her life. And that's tremendous. And then if I come home *at the end of November* on leave (December 1st at the latest) that will give you a slightly busy November. After that there's Christmas (won't you go back to La Pouèze?). And I do not think, my love, that it will go on for years. A year and a half at most. I don't think the Germans will endure for more than two winters.

Here, it's an odd day, I was tired out from working so much yesterday, with a moment of bathos à la Keller the elephant seal, at the inn between 11 o'clock and 1. And then it passed. It was my eyes that gave out. Today I worked less, and wisely put aside a slight dawning of thought on our *Unwelt*. I did scarcely anything but write my novel. And my handwriting in my notebook is too small. Write larger, you'll say. Yes, but it wouldn't be so pretty. I finished the 1st notebook and began the second. When I come on leave we'll work *together*, you on your Journal and I on my notebook, at night before going to bed. My love, it will be a bit sad that we'll have to hide, but we will love each other so much and be so happy to see each other that everything will be all right and we just won't give a damn. Anyway I'll have eleven days. I will spend 8 with you and we'll *admit* to two, so we can go to the hotel and the Café de Flore, etc. And I'll spend the last three with Tania. If anyone speaks to you about leave, shrug and say that with the military, it's hard to say, ten days is a maximum, that anyway it won't work for me since I am not "at the front lines." In fact I am, but I won't say so. You know, we'll still have Montmartre and the Boulevards and La République and Le Temple and all that. I think, for instance, that it's almost impossible to hide my first leave from my parents. At any rate take a look, check out the lay of the land with my mother, say that you don't know much about what's going on, that I seem to be saying that, not being on active duty, I won't have the privilege of being in the first batch. One hitch is I'd really like to have a civilian suit for this first leave. But I stupidly left mine at the Avenue de Lamballe.[1] Do you see some means of getting it back? Or procuring another for me? If I ever do see my family, actually (but make no mistake about it, my good little one, this is not to prepare you gently: if it's possible to avoid it, I'll do so gladly) I will see them for lunch and leave them by three o'clock. There are already some people around here who are preparing to leave on November 1st. But I won't be among them: being the only childless bachelor from the Readings Post, I'll leave last. For that matter, I proposed it myself, even though, of course, none of the three cares as passionately as I about seeing civilian life again.

I had two nice letters from Tania today. Here is a passage about you: "Thereupon the Beaver arrived, handsome as a young Hindu with a turban. We exchanged a snatch of easy conversation; except that, after a brief silence, near the end, we both began to talk at the same time, which immediately plunged me in despair, because this evening I'm an anxious restless soul." (It was the night she had just arrived, I think.) I'd love to see that turban. And the camel-hair coat. Go on, buy it, please. Listen, little Beaver, please write to the NRF and say you are speaking for me. I'd gladly write again, but it would take too long, whereas this way they'll have to answer you. Here's the address: NRF Mirande—via Sartilly. Manche.

My dearest, I love you passionately. I beg you don't be sad, or else I'll have failed in my life's purpose: to make you glad.

I'm really annoyed you're not getting all my letters. Yet *one single day* hasn't passed that I haven't written you. If you're going to see Emma at

---

[1]*At his parents' apartment. (SdB)*

Quimper, take the books she asked you for. If it's not possible for you to go to her place, send them to her.

To Simone de Beauvoir

October 26th

My darling Beaver
   I hope your efforts succeed. I received your little photo, which brought your dear little image to life for me. My love, how far away you are. It seems to me you are a bit more serene today. My love, if my letters bring you any succor, I'll try to make them as long and as plump as I can. Alas, nothing's happening. Or so little. It's all in my head. My eyes have been a bit tired these days, and after some thought we decided—the acolytes were suffering as I was—that it came from the electric lighting. We have cleaned off the blue from 12 panes out of the 108 in the windows, thanks to which we can work by daylight, and already things are better. That was the reason for my weariness the day before yesterday.
   I wrote another 10 pages on historicity. I'm beginning to find my way around in it. You'll see it all at one go when you read this little notebook; you'll follow how I arrived at all this. There's a good bit of change in my ethics, you'll see. But none that you wouldn't approve. I'm no Ghéon,[1] worry not, I have not yet found God, nor the self-righteous foundations of the Society. I have loads of ideas right now, and I'm very happy to be keeping this little notebook, which brings them to life. You don't mention yours anymore. You must dutifully keep on with it, or you'll be caught off guard, which mustn't happen. Doesn't it give you, as it does de Roulet, a sort of exteriority toward your life? It does me. It reveals an entire life concealed above the other, with joys, anxieties, regrets, half of which I wouldn't have known without this small black leather object. The essence of my remorse is what we talked about in Marseilles: that a person is thrown into a situation involving quantities of irrationalities, and it isn't by masking them that you eliminate them. By and large, to mask them means simply adopting an attitude of inauthenticity toward them. We listed many of them (birth, death, generation, social class, etc). But there is also the war. And I realize I was in a state of total inauthenticity about that. I was masking it, and what I wasn't

---

[1] Henri Ghéon, pseudonym of Henri Vauglon (1875–1944), dramatist and poet, and a convert to Catholicism.

seeing was that our era (1918–1939) derives its meaning from nothing else (in its totality and its smallest details) but a being-for-the-war.[2] So it seems to me for twenty years and at the very core of my nature I had, in spite of myself and unknowingly, an inauthentic being-for-the-war. What should have been done? To live and think this war on the horizon as a specific possibility of this era. Then I would have grasped my *historicity*, which was to be destined for this war (had it even been avoided in '39 and forever, it was no less the concrete meaning of the whole era). Of course, you shouldn't believe that this means I should have resigned myself to it or accepted it. But only considered it as my fate, understood that in *choosing* to be of this era, I was choosing myself for this war. You will answer: You didn't choose this era, you fell into it. No indeed. I will explain that we chose it—and I don't mean that in the metaphysical sense of intelligible choice. But in the concrete sense. There you have a totally schematic—and perhaps unintelligible—sketch of what fills pages and pages of the notebook. I don't for a second think that this leads to swinishness or dubious humanist alliances.

But we'll discuss it. I'd so like to talk with you about all of this. As of now the home leaves are about to start officially, but there will be bedlam at first and it will take patience.

I haven't yet sent the books to Bost; I still have one or two to finish. I'll send: *Colonel Jack*—*The Trial*—the 2 Greens—*The Castle*—*La Jeunesse de Théophile*—*The Idiot* and a few detective novels. Will that do it? Don't forget to buy me *Mars: Or the Truth About War* and that *Carnet de guerre* ["War Diary"] (I've forgotten the name, but it's in my letters) prefaced by Giono, and the Rauschning; I need to read it all. Also the Dickens and the Ellery Queen. Perhaps you would rather take them first to Emma. But she should read them quickly. In exchange she'll give you the first little notebook that I've entrusted to her and 130 pages of my novel. On that subject: in November try to squirrel away a little thousand-franc note for my leave. When I've alerted you (perhaps in December) of my arrival, *simply don't repay* the Lady or M. Bienenfeld for that month. That'll be the best way.

Today, total void: breakfast at the Taverne de la Rose—work (on historicity)—lunch at the Taverne du *Cerf*, on the main street, facing the post office, it's quiet and lonely; I wrote a bit more in the notebook. Conversation with Mistler. Back to the school: work (my novel from 2:00 to 4:00), then letters (1 from you, 1 from my mother, 1 from T., whose return to Paris

---

[2]Not to be construed as prowar, but rather meaning that life's energies had been and were being determined by war.

seems to ignite a rebirth of ardor for me. I haven't written to her for 6 days; I will in a bit). I read the letters, and I am answering you.

I'm pleased that you're sending me the unexpurgated letter you mentioned. We'll see. I expect to do as much tomorrow or the next day. But it isn't certain, because ultimately there's so little to say—or else myriad details, which you'll read in my notebook or I'll tell you in person. On the subject of the Moon Woman, I count up 7 lovers: her father—some guy I've forgotten—a big affair with a Turk—her husband before she married him—me—a guy from Vienna—the Corsican. I think that's seven. Perhaps she meant she had more? I haven't written to Bost, but I will. To Guille too, to the Boxer, to the Lady: it makes for a flood of letters, particularly since I'm resuming my correspondence with T., and it somewhat overwhelms me. Particularly since there's *nothing* to say to any of them.

From tomorrow on we'll be working: ONE reading a day at 7:30 in the morning. That won't kill us. I wonder whether I've given you a clear idea of what my life is like here. Monastic but with every convenience, central heating and running water. But as in households with budgets below 40,000 francs, the pleasures are mainly intellectual. In addition, the possibility of setting off for almost anywhere (for several days there was a rumor going around that we were bound for Turkey!—that was false), which deprives this monastic and bureaucratic life of any roots, any possibility of sinking into routine. And then, swamping all, this ungraspable war. And then, a sort of diverticulum of myself: you. With Paris all around. But not a Paris that gets me out of here, as it was with my military service: a wartime Paris. Odd. And so consistent with me. It's truly *my* war. That's what I was noting in my book.

My love, I've tried to make the longest possible letter so you'll have longer to enjoy reading it. I'll make myself do the same every day. I tend to put down everything that passes through my head, but I think that will be nice for you. As though you were chatting with me. I love your little photo. Pieter's camera has come and he'll take five or six of me. I'm wearing my beard again, too lazy to shave, but I'll get rid of it before seeing you.

I love you so warmly, so tenderly, my little flower. It irritates me to say "passionately"—it's a debased word; for me right now it's like saying, I hug and kiss you hard. But you are my very life.

To Simone de Beauvoir

October 27

My darling Beaver

Now your letters arrive very regularly, which is a hell of a lot nicer. I so love to have a little piece of you each day. In your last letter you explain how much I am *within* you. But you're *within me* too. Or rather, you are on the horizon of my every thought. Everything I think or feel or write is for you. Even my novel and my journal, which other people will eventually see, are first for you, and only through you for others. You are like the objectivity of this world that surrounds me, and that otherwise would be only mine but is instead ours. You are there all the time. And then you are not only that, you are also the slim turbaned Hindu I want to hold tight in my arms. My love, you are still thinner in your photo. But that turban is so becoming. You'll have to wear it when you visit Emma.

As for what may come after the war, when I return triumphant, since you are already worrying about it, have no fear, I won't let myself be chewed up. Having been bored out of my mind for *x* number of months, I will refuse to submit to any more boredom for the rest of my life. I'm already counting on using a soldier's rights with my family: my stepfather stopped dead at the headline "leave" as he read the papers, and naturally concluded I'd come before Christmas. He so informs me in a letter worth anthologizing. All well and good. But I simply will not stay with them and I'll see them only from noon to three o'clock, there's nothing they can do about it. And I'll begin to tell them that I'm sure to get only five days.

You ask whether I run any risk in case my division goes into action. First of all, my love, the question depends rather on whether the division across the way from us goes into action. Should that occur, I will tell you that we are not beyond cannon range—heavy cannon. So there is a slight risk. *But* the sector is quiet and, if there's no change, will remain so throughout the war. The configuration of the area scarcely permits an attack around here. Don't forget that no one ever undertakes a bombardment for the fun of it. Perhaps you read in *Match* that one 155 shell costs 150 hours of work. So nobody's wasting them. All of the artillery's work aims at preparing the infantry's, whereas the infantry's job is made totally impossible by the frontier on the Rhine, which is impassable. The Rhine *and* the Maginot, that's too much. Which is why the guns around here are silent. Now, will I change sector? I have no idea, but surely not in winter (unless that crazy rumor about sending us to Turkey has some truth to it. But I tell it as a joke and to show you all the false reports in circulation around here). Moreover we *are* in action—which doesn't mean we're active: the batteries of our division are in position. So, as you see, I'm hardly in danger though actually serving on the front lines just like anyone else. Don't forget that this war's a phony war, "an unfindable war," Paulhan says, not without reason. You also know that a German offensive is less and less likely, since winter's almost here—and it seems instead that until spring the operations will take place on sea and in the air, no doubt in the direction of England. Now, if I should change sector, I could be farther from the front, but *never closer*—or else by just a kilometer or 2. And also our division is a reserve division. It's not made for the big strikes. It's in support. Will the censor pass all this? It seems very innocent to me, but you never know.

It would be best to set some cash aside for my leave, which will surely be around the 1st to the 15th of December. I'm taking mine last. As you know, I'll admit to five and will officially be spending two with you. Do you know what's on my mind? Let's stay at the Hôtel Mistral. It would delight me, and there's almost no chance the Z's would show up. And too, I could live there in civilian clothes without anyone pestering me. We'll go to A. Capri,[1] my love.

Wouldn't you know I got pissed off again today? This time at Paul. We spent five hours without talking to one another. He has just made the first overtures: "How many pages did our argument provide for your notebook?" "Not much . . . half a page?" I was sure he'd come to me, because he likes to "keep up appearances." But it scares me that I fight so much. It isn't nervousness (I'm very calm) but moral pedantry. Gentle Pieterkowski tells me, "You have to take people as they come." Yes, but I'm persuaded to my core that it's not that people *are*, they *do*. So, this morning around 7:30, stormy reading, the balloons hid maliciously behind chimneys, and we chased them, weighed down with our theodolite. Then work. 120 pages of novel so far. On November 3 there will be 140, and I'll finish by the end of December. On that subject, you tell me nothing about the Mathieu-Brunet chapter that I wrote in Juan-les-Pins in August. It was in my suitcase. Did you keep it or hand it over to the Lady with the rest of the manuscript? If you didn't give it to her, remember to take it out of the suitcase and keep an eye on it. You'll be able to add on the pages I'll bring when I come on leave.

---

[1] One of the many small night spots where Beauvoir would go with her friends, this one featuring a new batch of wartime songs performed by the proprietress, Agnès Capri (*La Force de l'âge*, pp. 216–17).

I'm reading *Colonel Jack*, and having a ball, it's delightful. I also like lots of passages in *Les Enfants du limon*—particularly those on the insane. He says they're authentic, and it wouldn't surprise me. In any case he imitates them perfectly. And one—the guy who ends with "Men are little walking suns"—is great.

I received a letter from a student named Geoffroy, which made me happy (but neither Lévy nor Kanapa has written). Here are a few choice lines from my stepfather's letter:

"Now let's speak about you. The 'paterfamilias' that I am—as you have upon occasion regrettably forgotten—does not lose his rights to give advice.

"I believe that the first point is this. At war one must *keep up one's health*; everything else is in the hands of the gods. You must have everything that might be useful," etc. etc. There are four pages more of the same. Irritating. What I would have most wished for is that he lose his rights to give advice. But it is erroneous to suppose that the war is an emancipation. On the contrary, it constitutes a considerable rejuvenation. All of that to advise me buy a pair of boots. Since I'm the one who would be obliged to pay, I'll say that wearing them is forbidden to lowly privates.

Have you finally received my missing letters? In one of them I must have asked you what happened to Alain. For it seems that something did happen to him.

My sweet, I love you with all my heart and I pine to see you.

On rereading this letter, I tell myself that the little joke about Turkey might just be the kind of thing to worry you. *Don't take it seriously*, my sweet. And then if you want to suppose, regardless, that it's true, begin by thinking that before sending me out there they would give me twenty-one days of leave.

To Simone de Beauvoir

October 28th

My darling Beaver

An annoying piece of news: the government is studying a plan to allocate an allowance for government employees, which means that very soon it's likely I won't be getting my total pay. If so, who cares: if need be you'll send Tania back to Laigle for half of each month. In any case, Zazoulich the elder must be kept on, since the courses at the Atelier have started up again. But

I don't want you to cut back too much *on yourself*. Your little life is miserable enough as it is. Tomorrow I'll write again to the *NRF*.

So much for the bad news. Let's add, to end the list, that Emma writes saying she still fancies running off again. But she doesn't seem really serious to me. In any case, if she followed through and you visited her after she'd departed, she would leave you her address with her landlady, Mme Vogel—she would never go off very far. *Worry not*. She will subsequently send you that complete address, I can't give it to you today, I don't have it.

My dearest, I would prefer to balance this bad news with something good, the way I used to. Alas, we're at war, which means there is no good news. Except that my eyes, which have been worrying me somewhat, are much better. Paul, after hollering ferociously in his sleep last night (he was unhinged by our fight), decided this morning to sleep all alone in the school-room like a leper, so as not to disturb our kind landlady. This morning there was more shouting, about the cleaning of a bicycle, but I wasn't involved, the sparks were flying between Paul and Pieter. And then in the end I bawled out Keller (but with universal approbation). He had gone to fetch our masks at a mill where they are slightly mangled from time to time in order to justify the presence in the division of a lieutenant who is a specialist in gases—and he had purposely brought back only Paul's and his own. All this shows that the wrangling continued. It is the total emptiness of the days that makes for irritable moods, and about nothing at all. Finally I'm on rather good terms with the fat Jewish guy, Pieter, and the two others are alone in their corner. This afternoon "the whole class," sergeant, first sergeant, observers, and meteorologues (except for Keller, who was belching away in a corner), zestfully tackled social problems. It's curious how war develops *envy*. The reserve noncommissioned officers' envy of regular army noncommissioned officers who draw their pay, the non–civil servants' envy of the government employees who draw their pay, the peasants' envy of the workers in the rear who draw their salaries. First Sergeant Naudin—who is a great guy but childishly envious, being a peasant, a reserve sergeant, and, naturally, not a government employee—envies everyone at once. I said my piece, explaining that we couldn't expect a war to eliminate inequalities. But it is true that it shifts and unmasks them, because it claims to reveal a fundamental equality of *function*. Meanwhile I was putting final touches on chapter XVI. I think that by November 3 there'll be one more than I expected.

So there's my day. It's now seven-thirty. I'll write a brief note to Tania and then go to sleep alone at my landlady's house. If you only knew how impatiently I look forward to the beginning of November, my dear love, and how I wish for everything to go well. I hope this letter doesn't make you sad.

Here bad news hardly saddens anyone. We turn our backs on it and stay very calm. I'm only vulnerable from behind (which could be the motto of a heroic pansy). I love you with all my might, my darling little creature. You are a little flower.

Send me the books as soon as you can. Tomorrow I'm sending all mine to Bost.

To Simone de Beauvoir

October 30

My darling Beaver

I was going to begin answering you when suddenly the siren started wailing. The skies are clear today and the planes are out, like snails after rain. We saw three of them going over—ours—before the alert, and we heard antiaircraft firing. Then, as I said, around four o'clock, as I had just read your letter and Tania's, the sirens. Since the trenches were full of water they advised us to put on our helmets and sling the masks across our shoulders, then said we could do whatever we liked. We went down to the schoolyard and looked up at the sky. We could hear the cannon, but since we couldn't see a thing, we came back in. Pieter began a letter to his wife with these words: "I am writing to you during an alert." I said to him, "Don't think you're impressing her—they've already had at least a dozen in Paris." He answered, "Yes, but it sounds nicer." I suppose he intended it as Maheu did when he told me, "My wife writes to me, 'At this moment I can see a white sail out at sea.' The wonderful naiveté of love." Thereupon the siren gave the all-clear, but he stubbornly went on with his letter in the present tense ("I hear the cannonfire," etc.). Basically we are all vaguely proud to be associated, however slightly—without any danger—with this war that the civilians and newspapers tell us so much about.

Aside from that, well, I finished a chapter of my book; last night after writing to you, since I was on guard duty, I slept in the schoolroom on a splendid straw mattress, but I slept little because of an infernal clock ticking away just above my head. Tonight will be a repeat of last night, but I'll stop the clock. This morning a beautiful reading under clear skies; then, since I was on guard duty, I lunched here—on one piece of bread, to keep my figure. I'll go out for dinner in a while. I'm mulling over a central idea that will finally allow me to eliminate the unconscious, to reconcile Heidegger and

Husserl, and to understand my historicity. But it is altogether circular, with neither doors nor windows; I don't know where to pick it up. I have the time. This afternoon, Pieter photographed me with my beard (which I'm keeping, out of laziness, since I'll take it off for November 3rd). I'll send you the photo. He'll take some others, without the beard, with a helmet, beside the theodolite, etc.

So, if you're going to see Emma, meet her at Le Cerf. You ask me what to do if she doesn't show up. Wait a moment while I refresh my memory of Quimper's layout,[1] to show you where Mme Vogel lives. When you're on the main street, coming out of Le Cerf, take a few steps to the right and you'll find a covered entry that makes a vaulted passageway. Go through that entry and you'll find a sort of huge, open, unimproved square in front of the boys' school. To the right, follow the street leading out of Quimper, which runs past the boys' school. The second or third street on the *left* (150 meters beyond the school) is lined with houses on the left and a field on the right. You take it, and the third house belongs to Mme Vogel; her name's written on the door below the bell.

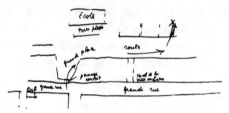

The home leaves won't be starting till November 15. We got official word today. That puts me in Paris perhaps on December 15th, or the 20th, which might simplify things with Tania. For instance, we would let her go off, and four days before my departure I'd send a telegram, which would mean that she'd come back the next day, just for the last three. Theoretically I should leave the 3rd, but if it works out for Christmas, I'd try to take the 4th leave, for instance.

My love, till tomorrow. I love you and I love your little letters so much.

What a thing is man's heart. They're showing a movie just for us. Guess what? *Jungle Jim!* Well, I certainly won't go. So there!

---

[1]*He was actually talking about Brumath. (SdB)*

To Simone de Beauvoir

October 31

My darling Beaver

I thought there was no letter from you today, then . . . there it was, a fat Jewish guy handed it to me. I already had one from T. via the usual route. We had another alert today but didn't even budge. Except that the three observers, Sergeant Naudin, First Sergeant Courteaux, and Private Hang, who reconnoiter the roads on motorcycles, came back very excited. They'd ridden through a village where everyone was wearing gas masks, they'd whiffed a mustard odor and donned their masks, Hang hadn't known how to get his on, and finally someone in the artillery told them a nearby village had been hit with gas shells. Their accounts of the event itself disagree: Sergeant Naudin is convinced he went through a patch of gas, the proof being that his eyes are stinging. The first sergeant maintains there was no gas at all, and he offers the proof that civilians were wandering around without masks. On the mustard odor they also varied: it could simply be the motorcycle exhaust. Finally one hypothesis seems logical: they'd passed through a village where the army was going through a gas mask drill. But their excitement hit a fever pitch. You see, it's always like this, when you get a little whiff of war, you bang away with all you've got, you want the whole thing. But the war won't be bossed around.

As for me, I tried to take a bath this morning, but in vain. There were too many people. I reserved a place for seven tomorrow morning; I want to be clean for November 3rd. If you only knew how impatiently I'm waiting. After that I landed at the Taverne du Cerf, where I attempted a reconciliation of Heidegger and Husserl. It didn't pan out, but I stuck to it doggedly, and I feel quite woozy after six hours' effort. The whole thing must be done over. There is still this entirely circular idea and I don't know where to pick it up, so I grab at it, and it slips through my fingers like a ball of grease. You'll see, it makes for odd little notebooks.

I'm happy that my leave seems *real* to you. It is, you know, and I've been delighted by that for a long time. But for reasons of position on the roster that are too boring to go into, I don't think I'll get it before January 1st. I'll explain the reasons anyway. The complement of those who leave must never exceed 15% of the total. But since we are a separate group of four, we thought we'd also be considered separately. And since you cannot take ⅖ of a soldier and send him off on leave, keeping the other two-fifths, we thought we'd go off as 1 out of 4. That is, that the pace for us would be

25%. But we've just learned that they'll have us leave with the others, and there'll be one sole rotation plan for all. Therefore we come back to the original 15%. Since in addition it only starts on November 15th and I'm not among the first, that doesn't help matters. Except that, on the other hand, with our own system I was to leave fourth and last—whereas with the general classification I leave third among them, that is, I must be in the third quarter of the large grouping. So you see that would put me fifty days after November 15, or around January 5. Of course, nothing in all of this is definite.

You ask me to tell you about Tania. For the moment there isn't much to say. She writes me rather nice letters. She said something marvelous in yesterday's. In some café or other she saw some Poles, and she pitied them because right now they are "so mortified." On the other hand, today she put in something rather nice about Poupette's departure: "I felt overwhelmed with melancholy"—on entering her studio. "I can't tell you the impression it made on me. I was feeling nothing for her, I was stony: that in itself scared me, and I was anxious and upset till nightfall. I waited, chilled, slumped in a green armchair, for her to finish liberally sprinkling everything with moth flakes; it felt like a real first-class funeral, and I wondered what was going on meantime behind the fresh and busy expression on her face. I imagined the studio with the door shut tight. I could already smell the rats and bedbugs."

Those two examples just about give you the extent and limits of her feelings. She has screwed up her courage to face a year of war, seems happy in Paris, with last year's brand of anxieties, and considers the war a marvelous adventure, sometimes gloomy, sometimes beautiful. That's all I know about her. If anything entertaining comes up, I'll pass it along. She tells me nothing about you.

That's all for today, my wise little Beaver. I love you with all my might and hug your dear skinny little body close to me.

As for the leave, I don't think it would be such a good idea to say that you came to see me for five days.[1] Think of something else; I'll think about it here too. On the other hand, I agree completely about spending 5 days with you, then three with T., then another two with you. Incidentally, on the days I see T., I'll still see you from noon to 2 o'clock, saying that I'm going to see my parents.

I kiss you again, my little one. Oh, how I long to see you!

---

[1]To hide the fact that unknown to family and friends she would be staying with him for five days, while the papers made much of ten-day leaves, she proposed saying she had returned to the front with him.

Have you told Z. that you're going to see Emma? I'd like to know so I can tell Tania, or rather you can say I asked you to tell her, because of the censor.

To Simone de Beauvoir

November 6th

My darling Beaver

How sad it was yesterday to leave that little person all alone in the darkness.[1] For a moment I thought of turning back, then reflected, "What's the use? It will be for five minutes, and then afterward it will be all the harder to part." I walked to the school very fast, knowing all along that the dear little person was still there, five hundred meters away; it kept me from reading for a good long time. But you know, basically, I was profoundly happy. You understand, it shook me up, those five days, to the core, and then I was falling back to earth, but it's really marvelous, all the things it gave me. Actually it gave me just one thing, plain and simple, but unequaled: your presence, all alone and totally naked, the little expressions that cross your face, the tender smiles, your little arms around my neck. My love, it is so true, what we've said so often, that I could live with you anywhere at all. Afterward I was somewhat anxious, not entirely sure of myself, and then I wondered how you were faring, if everything was going well for you; I imagined that dark, cold train. The acolytes were there, annoying accomplices. Pieter asked me, pretending detachment and discreetly swallowing his words (though he was actually alone with me), whether you had gone. I wrote a bit in my notebook and then we went off to bed. Mme Vogel had moved us. We are now in a walnut-paneled living room a bit like the Bel Eute's but with more garish colors. They set up a bed for us there that looks very much out of place. Paul trembles for fear that in his sleepwalking he might break some vase, shell, candy dish, or other of the knickknacks that overrun the room. But he was very good. This morning he went out to get some cylinders of hydrogen with Pieter, and I was alone all day. I went to La Rose around 6:45, and the fat old woman snickered at me, saying, "Ah ha! you're alone now!" I read *Un Rude Hiver* ["A Bitter Winter"],[2] middle and end, which

---

[1] I'd just spent a few days with Sartre, at Brumath. *(SdB)*
[2] By Queneau. *(SdB)*

disappointed me. Actually there isn't enough there to make a book. It's probably abridged. I was completely enveloped in tenderness but didn't want to let myself go, it's pernicious. All the same, I was constantly wondering whether you'd truly felt how deeply I love you and what you mean to me. Oh my darling Beaver, I would like you to feel my love as much as you feel yours. I came back and all morning long scratched away in my little notebook. But not about the things we'd said; basically it is so simple: I was profoundly and peacefully happy, and now I *don't want* to have any regrets, that's all there is to say. All day I felt ready to look at my situation with new eyes, but I carefully closed those eyes. Now, because of being closed, they have turned inward, as the eyes of a mole would. That's what I didn't write. But I went on from 9:00 to 11:00 (after a weather reading executed with Keller only) setting down on paper reflections on my adolescence—and then a bit more at Le Cerf (where they asked me the necessary polite questions) from 11:00 to 12:00. Then I lunched (veal, to symbolize mourning—they also suggested some salsify, but I didn't want deep mourning so ordered some hash browns), and Mistler came in with Courcy. Roll call. Then I did more scribbling till now. Paul tells me his wife is a teacher 7 kilometers from Tréveray, and that she's very accommodating. So you have only to tell me what you want. That's that. No letter from Tania—she must be furious; I'd be curious to know the dénouement of that story. A kindly letter from my mother. That's all, it's like the day after a holiday, it's a letter from you that I would have wished.

My dearest little flower, we were as one, were we not? I love you so very much, and I can feel it so well. You were a little charm, and you reminded me what true happiness can be. I kiss you on your two little cheeks.

To Simone de Beauvoir

Tuesday, November 7

My darling Beaver

No letter from you today, of course, but I miss it, I'd have liked to get one as early as yesterday, it is my daily bread, but I'm so eager to know about your return trip, whether you've kept your little hoard of happiness and if you love me very much. Or rather, I know you love me truly but I'd like to read your tender little messages, now while the expression on your face when you say them is still so present. My love, I can see your eyes again so clearly, your smile, your little turban. Lord, how I feel the emptiness of these days and my solitude more intensely, I have to steel myself against a sort of melancholy. But it's only for two or three days, and besides, I had so much happiness seeing you, and something lingers on, a sort of presence of intimacy.

Today I wrote some more on social concerns. I'm growing disgusted with myself from all this writing about me; besides, I am tiring, and what I'm writing is no longer very good. Anyway, it will be done tomorrow and I'll be able to get back to my novel. I feel like getting back to it, now that several days have gone by. Instead, I think that through the familiar seesaw effect, barring the unexpected, I'll give up my notebook for a while; it smells of the organic. I had a hasty breakfast this morning at La Rose, because Paul had forgotten to wind up the alarm clock and we woke late. But discipline has relaxed because the light infantry has left. You wouldn't recognize the town, it reminds me of a fashionable beach in October, slightly forlorn. We thereby gain a modicum of tolerance. No more guards to chase soldiers out of cafés. So we lounge about till 1:20. I worked all morning, lunched on an excellent steak at Le Cerf while reading the mad vociferations of that ass of a Suarès[1] in the *NRF* and then a few sweet notes of idyllic dotage in Tolstoy's *Journal*: "A while ago, after my walk, I went to see Semyon, I talked with him about his health and I was pleased with myself; later, passing Alexey, I scarcely answered his affable greetings. I noticed it right away and reprimanded myself. Now that is something that can make one happy." You will definitely murder me when I'm in my seventies. At 1 o'clock I saw Hantziger approaching, the impassioned albino with white hair and transparent cheeks, the one, you know, who's getting a divorce. He explained to me that he was feeling down and had obtained permission to play the piano, on his blue days, in the back room of Le Cerf. I followed him, and he told me that he didn't know how to play the piano, just knew a few tunes by ear. The piano was out of tune and quavering. He began to play a few old-fashioned melancholy waltzes. "It clears my head." In a drawer I found a 1918 foxtrot called "Là-bas sur l'Atlantique" ["Far off on the Atlantic"]. The cover showed a man with a mustache, in evening clothes, dancing with a woman dressed in twenties style, with a very high waistline and a diadem in her hair. Song titles were printed on the back, with the first bars of the refrain. "La Marche de Verdun": "And Verdun the glorious/ Returns a cry resounding/ Sending echoes of the Meuse rebounding:/ No, no, you shall not ever pass." "Your turn to play," said Hantziger. I played the foxtrot. It reminded me of "Le

---

[1]André Suarès (1868–1948), essayist, critic, and Christian mystic utilizing themes from Celtic mythology. He adopted the pseudonym Caërdal and published a "Chronique de Caërdal" in most issues of the *NRF* for 1939.

Pelican" and "Le Tango du rêve" ["Dream Tango"] and the early '20s. It gave me a lump in my throat. After that Hantziger declared that he would go in search of a violin (he does play the violin) and the two of us would make music. "And then back in Paris, wait and see, we'll assemble our own little orchestra." I get a kick out of playing the piano a bit with him. After that I came back here to work. At three o'clock, alert. We went to the schoolyard "to see the airplanes," the way you go to watch trains in the country. Of course, we didn't see any. Someone insisted he'd seen a German plane, completely white in the full sun, with a black cross, but that elicited scornful laughter. On the other hand we did see the smoke of the antiaircraft shells in the sky. They were little white puffs, like those that used to be left by the disintegrating word "Citroën" written by planes in the skies of 1935. Next I washed. I now have such an obscene hole in my pants that when I walk I cover my belly with my hands. At 3:30 the mail. Nothing from Tania, she must be crazy with anger; if you hear anything that throws light on this, pass it on. And that's that. I'm going to have a piece of bread and chocolate, and then I'll write my mother and a brief note to Tania.

My dear love, my little flower, never have I loved you so much as in the past few days and today. I would willingly spend ten years here if you were with me. With all my love.

We were so intent on love that I forgot to take the money. So you'll have to send it, my little one. But you've probably noticed the oversight yourself. I've borrowed a hundred francs from Paul, and have enough till Saturday.

To Simone de Beauvoir

November 8

My darling Beaver

This won't be a very long letter because it's late—I've been working right up to this moment and concluded my study of myself; it leads to some felicitous results—and besides, I really have nothing to tell you. This is one of those days that are buried the moment they're over, and you can never find in your memory. Nonetheless there'll be a letter about it, and when I read it again I'll be totally surprised that it existed. I went to La Rose, I asked for butter on my rolls, but they didn't have any. I worked till my eyes almost fell out of my head, while the acolytes stood at the windows watching the puffs in the sky from the antiaircraft guns through field glasses. From time to time I'd holler, "You aren't transparent," and they'd answer, "Haha!" We did a reading; the captain who had said "Four men lost to the army" came to watch. I said to him, "But watch the balloon yourself, Captain, you'll enjoy it." He said yes, and, just as I was hoping, he lost it. He didn't immediately admit it, but we could see the binoculars weaving about desperately at the tips of his fingers. Then I said to him, "But if you like we can blow up an 18-gram balloon for you—that'll be easier to follow." We blew it up and released it, Pieter trained his sights on it, and the captain lost it again. Pieter found it for him twice. Finally he was able to follow it. But he won't call it a childish game anymore. The whole thing without malice on my part actually, because he's a good guy, but he needed wising up. "Yes," he said sheepishly, "I don't yet have the right reflexes." After which, I had lunch at Le Cerf and saw marching down the street the burial party of the division's first casualty. Two nights earlier he, still a healthy paterfamilias, had said to his friends, "Gimme the candle, I'm going out to take a crap." To which his buddies, already half asleep, had said, "There's no candle." Then he said, "Shit!" And those were his last words. He left the barn where they were staying, and his friends went back to sleep. The next morning at roll call they ralized he was missing and they found him in the Zorn, already slightly green from prolonged immersion. I said to Paul, "Now it's your turn." He's only too willing to agree. Afternoon—work, my eyes burning. But now it's done: 70 pages on the subject. Then I ate a chunk of bread with some Gruyère and some chocolate, then Keller and Pieter went to play cards with the clerks, and Mistler came to our place, to quaff any good words that might fall from my lips. We explained to Paul that the postwar period would be a propitious time to establish the reign of liberty. I sketched out a dictatorship of liberty in which I would be the supreme dictator and would have his feet sizzled till he declared himself free. The gentle Mistler, the one who brushes his teeth with a spiritualistic toothpaste, was himself a little scared by it. He wants man to regain his human dignity after the war. I didn't follow him down that track. Paul listened gloomily, his head buried in his hands, and then afterward he walked up and down for a long time. And here I am, writing.

When this letter arrives, you will be with Bienenfeld, my love. I hope you're both very happy. My little Beaver, I received nothing this evening, but I'm all joy because tomorrow your silence ceases and I'll have news from you. Nothing from Tania, who must be frothing or who couldn't bear to write to me while you were here, not realizing I'd receive the letters after your departure. There you have it. My love, till tomorrow, tomorrow will be a day of celebration, there'll be a little letter from you, I'll know whether you had a good trip, if you are still clinging to a bit of joy. I would so like you to be happy. Blissful, if at all possible. In any case, for you to feel how worthwhile and important your life is and how

Your little husband loves you.

Since you don't read *Paris-Soir*, here is the headline of a thoroughly repellent article:

"English Christmas dolls had German eyes. From now on they will see the world through British eyes."

To Simone de Beauvoir

Thursday, November 9

My darling Beaver

Today two little events: one military, one private. The military was a ceremonial parade under arms and a decorations ceremony that took place right beneath our windows. Everyone was very excited, clerks and acolytes pressed against the windows, they looked like civilian secretaries watching a military parade from their office, they let out hysterical little giggles and came over to whisper secrets in my ear. Paul sulked for a moment, then he couldn't hold off any longer; he picked up some binoculars and peered at the generals. Word went around that General Gamelin himself would attend the parade, and the reason given was that a truck had brought in twelve Alsatian women with large bow headdresses and regional costumes such as you only see now at Chez Jenny or L'Alsace à Paris, and a little girl beribboned in the tricolor with cheeks-to-be-kissed-by-a-prefect. The whole town was there. A general appeared and the following dialogue took place between Mistler, Pieter, Paul, and me, seated at my table writing (in a bit I'll tell you what it was). One of them: "That's General Gamelin. That has got to be General Gamelin. He does have a white mustache, doesn't he, General Gamelin?" "Yeah, he's got a white mustache." "Then that's him." Mistler turns to me: "You see, Sartre, you were being the skeptic. But that is General Gamelin." Me: "Hand over the field glasses." I go to the window, I look, I say, "Not General Gamelin. You can clearly see that this one has a white mustache." The chorus, disappointed, "Yes? OK, you're right, it's not General Gamelin." They were decorating a civilian, a young man about seventeen; his mother and father were standing behind him. He was standing very straight, tall and blond, with a heavy pouting mouth; he looked awkward and rather likable. The photographer, who was bowing in retreat, bumped into him with his rear. After that, the general kissed him and the accolade was photographed. But as the kiss was not sufficiently photogenic or the photographer had missed his shot, the general had to do it again. Three army guys were also decorated. We simply had to know what the young hero had done. A diverse set of rumors made the rounds: some saying that armed with only a pitchfork he had prevented two strayed German aviators from taking off again, others that having seen a German aircraft land, he'd dashed off and warned the inhabitants of the neighboring village. Which, as you see, is not exactly the same thing. Finally, still others saw it in more romantic terms: the plane lands, the German gets out of the cockpit and asks in his native tongue, "Where am I?" The little Alsatian answers fearlessly, "Alsace!" The German, insinuating tempter: "You've got an independent sort of a mug. Go get me two jerry cans of gas so's I can fire up my machine." The young Alsatian, struck by a heroic idea, says, "Be right back!" He runs off in search of French soldiers and the two cans of gas. The French soldiers crawl through the Alsatian underbrush and surround the plane under cover. The Alsatian youth returns with the gas cans, offers them to the German with one hand, and grabs him by the throat with the other. The French soldiers dash up and capture man and machine. Whatever happened, it seems above all a display aimed at raising the morale of the local inhabitants, because he'd been given a lot of publicity and every house was draped in bunting all day like Bastille Day. As for me, I was meanwhile taking down, word by word, all the conversations of the acolytes and the clerks. I read it back to them afterward. They were half laughing, half furious.

As for the little private event, it will bring you down from your plateau: I'll never again set foot in Le Cerf, I'm angry at the patroness. You know I agreed to join Hantziger to play the violin and piano in the back room. Today I was all alone in the inn, and the idea came to me to play a bit of piano. I say to the tall dark-haired woman, "May I play a little?" "Well, you know, we're not too crazy about the idea." Following that, some bad justifications that incensed me. I clapped my beret on my head and said with an offended air, "Well then, goodbye, Madame." From now on I'll go to L'Écrevisse. The chateaubriand won't be so tasty, but who cares. Between the military event and the private event, the morning was over. The afternoon was uneventful.

That's the news, my darling Beaver. Right now I'm alone in the teacher's office, because it's my turn on guard duty. The others are gone, the captain's asleep on a folding cot in the next room. It provides a delightful opportunity to write to you. I believe you're with Bienenfeld now and that you are completely happy together. I love you with all my might. Till tomorrow, my dear little one.

To Simone de Beauvoir

Thursday, November 9

My darling Beaver

I'll add this brief note, my dear love, to tell you that I finally have news from you, and that your letter, so sweet, had a heart-wrenching tenderness about it. I love you so much, my little one. I'm also reassured about your trip home; try as we may, we still begin imagining things; once or twice I thought of you on damp straw, and that was frankly unpleasant. It was, of course, just my imagination. But everything's under control, and there you are running around Paris like a rabbit, and Paris seems completely present and reassuring to me. My dear little one, how I love you and how pleased I am that you have remained more or less happy. I clearly pictured you, standing "straight as a stylite" on the station platform, lost in your thoughts, and I loved you very much. Just as you do, I feel and think that the war is everywhere. Right at the outset I felt it, and that's what made me distinguish, in my notebook, between being-in-war (as universal condition) and making-war. I also wanted to tell you that Tania wrote me a long impassioned letter. She's floating on air and wants to go to Toulouse, to see Emma. She was indignant at my saying, "You have to admit that it wasn't you who had the idea," and she says, "How can you say that? That's a terrible injustice. Then I would be a bitch to have written you my last letter. I want you to know that I thought of it *all by myself*." So she'll go if she's lucky. She seems to have a real fondness for you. She writes, "I spent some deeply poetic moments listening to her tell stories, which really impressed me."

My love, you don't know how much I have been feeling your presence these past few days. And with your letter on top of all that, it's as though you were here.

To Simone de Beauvoir

November 10th

My darling Beaver

First, here's a snapshot where I look like a Velázquez gnome. The object I am holding is an anemometer. *For the censor who may read this letter I would point out that the objects photographed—anemometer and theodolite—are in common usage and in no way part of army matériel. It would therefore be useless and scandalous for him to destroy these pictures.* In the second one I look pretty likable. There'll be two more, and you'll also get the little one of me in the beard. Don't lose them—we'll chuckle over them in a few years. Everyone's fighting for the one where I'm a gnome because "it's so like" me. Of course Mistler ordered one. He's rapidly turning into a disciple. I've never had such an old one, but the war makes everyone younger (he's 37). Do you realize that I have lots of little pictures of you: one from Greece, with you looking so ferocious, a charming little one in which you are oddly dignified, with Sorokine on the balcony, one taken in the Forêt de Fontainebleau by Bienenfeld, one in the basin of the Lycée fountain with Krivitsky beside you, the little one with you in a turban, and all the ones from Juan-les-Pins. Last night when the others had gone (I was on guard duty) I looked at them one by one, and laughed affectionately. And your large beautiful ones by Railland are so moving. You are a love. I love you with all my might. Your letters delight me, even today's in which you seem somewhat less cheerful, because I feel you stored up a durable reserve of happiness at Emma's. My love, how I would like you to be happy for a long time. I want you to know I'm doing excellent work at L'Écrevisse on our plans. All will go well.

So, I read a bit and went to bed on my pallet, I was in a lovely mood and slept well. I had a strange dream but alas forgot it. This morning I woke up Captain Munier, who was sleeping in the next room, and then I did a thousand little housekeeping chores: swept three rooms and a hall, then washed with lots of water, then did reading. After that I worked a bit on chapter XVII,[1] quite well I think, but boldly. You'll be the judge; it'll have them saying, "Lotta lively descriptions." Around eleven o'clock I went to L'Écrevisse with Pieter, to a back room they reserve for us now. You know

---

[1] Unwilling to father a child, Mathieu steals money to pay for his mistress Marcelle's abortion. She, deciding to have the child, gives up Mathieu.

I'm angry at Le Cerf. It was odd. At a large table with a cloth there were
only the two of us and then a woman with yellow hair, middle-aged and self-
contained. She was in a hurry to eat her lunch, and her little car was at the
door. She was going on another fifty kilometers, all alone, probably to see a
soldier, and she seemed poetic to me because I could so well imagine—
almost from experience—what was going through her head and how she saw
us. In the sky, beautiful wisps of vapor made by a plane that some called
French and others German. We came back at 1:30 to do a reading to a height
of five thousand meters for some officers, who called up afterward to *thank*
us. I was the one who answered the phone, and I was flabbergasted. Then
Mistler came to tell us a story about bromides that is absolutely hilarious.
Here it is. Only I don't know whether the censor will let it pass this time
because it has to do with confidential documents. Who cares. In any case,
I'll tell it to T., too, which means one more chance that it will get through.
If it's chopped out, ask her for it. I'm telling her too to ask you for it in case
of excision. So then, this morning Lieutenant Munot comes into the clerks'
place intrigued and amused: "What's all this about bromides?" The entire
general staff got the same confidential note today. It contains the report of a
police commissioner: a soldier approaches a prostitute, agrees on price—fifteen
francs for the trick—pumps her for two hours, and, despite obvious goodwill
of both parties, which no one contests, nothing happens. On leaving this
inconclusive event the soldier refuses to pay the fifteen francs and says that,
unable to fulfill his part of the agreement because of circumstances beyond
his control, he is released from the contract. There's a struggle, and they're
hauled off to see the commissioner, who asks him what exactly is the cir-
cumstance beyond his control. At which point the soldier replies that everyone
knows that every morning bromide is put in their coffee. The commissioner
made a report to the Minister of War, who orders an inquiry. Following which
each of the headquarters received the same note. They are asked if they knew
what this was all about. No one has said what became of the soldier.

Quiet, faintly lyrical afternoon. I didn't accomplish much but was in
an exquisite mood. I'm happy to find the daily rhythm of your letters restored.
Understanding why one isn't getting them is all well and good, but it still
makes one sad. And there was a big one and a very tender one, my love.
Tonight we ate a gugelhupf and drank a liter of white wine. Tomorrow is
Armistice Day and the army will give us *choucroute*, white wine, red wine,
and a cigar. There will be movies, and I suppose I'll go. There was one
tonight too, but I didn't feel up to it. My love, that's all, but I'm afraid this
letter is rather curt, because people are talking all around me. Yet I want you

to know, since you liked it when I said I was "perfumed," that I'm all perfumed with you. I love you as much as possible, dear little one.

To Simone de Beauvoir

Saturday, November 11

My darling Beaver

I'm so pleased you're working so well (your Wednesday letter told me so). But you neglect to say if it's *good* work. And what exactly are you doing? Progressing or revising? For me, the work is scarcely moving; and writing is less fun now that I know Marcelle has to be redone. Everything I'm doing seems provisional. Still, I'm going on with chapter XVII. You know, I'm really a bit bored today. Yesterday I was in a divine mood, this morning too, but this afternoon weighs a bit heavily. That's because it's a holiday. November 11. At the division kitchen, they gave us a meal so Pantagruelish that, for once, I didn't go to L'Écrevisse. Hors d'oeuvre, *choucroute garnie*, brioche, stewed plums, two kinds of wine, coffee, vintage Alsatian brandy, and a cigar. In fact, it was the only commemoration of this strange day on which we celebrate in the very midst of the war to end all wars the end of the preceding war to end all wars. But we paid for it by loafing around all day in the deserted school, with the vague feeling that it was a holiday and we should be doing something but didn't know what. I read Berlioz's *La Vie amoureuse*, wrote a bit in my notebook while waiting for the mail, and then came the letters. One from you, one from Tania, who writes very regularly at this point (tell me the story about Arlette Jacquart, about which she said, significantly, "I don't dare write it to you"). Tania must be dissuaded from taking out false registrations at the Sorbonne. It could be extremely dangerous for her.

News of the day: once more they are beginning to say we'll be leaving. No doubt we will withdraw some thirty kilometers for a rest period. It also seems that we won't begin to benefit from the system of leaves until December 1st. But that doesn't necessarily delay the date of my arrival in Paris, because if the cutoff date remains March 1st, as seems likely because of the possibility of spring operations, they'll have to let more go off at a time. Finally, here is the day's physiognomy: thick haze around the school, rumors, emptiness. We didn't even do a reading, the weather was so awful. Actually the characteristics of these days in general are rather strange; in good times and bad, they're always the same: up to 1:30 it goes like clockwork, seven lively, interesting hours. I could never get up too early to suit myself. And then from 1:30 to 9, it drags a bit. I think I'll finally get your package tomorrow morning. You may have to send me a few more books this month. You could buy me *La Vie de Baudelaire* by Porché and also Marivaux's *Théâtre* (all or in part) in the Garnier collection, and then *Le Diable amoureux* by Cazotte in the same collection—*Provinciales* by Giraudoux—*Fermé la nuit [Fancy Goods/Open All Night]* by Morand—*Les Croix de bois* ["The Wooden Crosses"] by Dorgelès—*Tradition de minuit* ["Midnight Tradition"]—*Sous la lumière froide* ["Under Cold Light"]—*Quai des brumes* ["Port of Shadows"]—*Le Nègre Léonard et Maître Jean Mullin* by Mac Orland—Mérimée's short stories (spare me *Carmen* and *La Venus d'Ille*. But I would like *Colomba*)—Flaubert's *L'Éducation sentimentale* and then, as soon as you have the cash, the Pléiade Shakespeare, that's what I'm burning to read just now. Let's add *La Négresse du Sacré-Coeur* by André Salmon—and also *L'Inquiète Paternité* and *Le Camarade infidèle* and *Un Homme heureux* by Schlumberger—and also the novels of Louis Codet—and *Aimée* and *Florence* by Jacques Rivière—and *L'Allemand*—and then *Saint-Saturnin*, why not, by Schlumberger also—*As I Lay Dying* by Faulkner. Naturally not all at once, that would cost too much. But if you like, you could copy the list on a piece of paper—the sequence isn't very important, they'll all please me equally— in whatever order you may buy them for me. From the various books, you can see that I'd like to dip back into the atmosphere of 1919–1929. If you see something entertaining on that era,* add it on, even if you think I've read it, that would make me happy (I have read most of these books). I want you to know, my little flower, that simply listing all the books gave me a lot of pleasure, and I'm trembling with impatience. That gives me an idea. In a while I'm going to dig around in my brain for all the books I might like, and will make a list of them that I'll send you tomorrow with my letter.

My little one, my darling Beaver, listen to me: I miss you. Very much. Now I know what I lack, what I've lost, and it is completely insidious, I can't protect myself against it as well. But don't be anxious, it's very sweet, and I'm happy to be missing you like this.

I send you all my love.

---

*Add to the list: *Au temps du Boeuf sur le toit* by Maurice Sachs (that *is* the title, isn't it?).

To Simone de Beauvoir

November 12

My darling Beaver

I have just given a long speech on literary prizes and publishers' commercial activity to Mistler and Pieter—it interested one of them as a rebel and the other as a businessman. The problem is, it's now eight-thirty. I'll still have the time to write you a little letter, but the other two will have to do without. It's not important, really, I can blame the mails. I'll write tomorrow morning. Today I deliberately took an hour's rest because my eyes were tired, and right now they're still bothering me. It's this electric light. But you, my little one, for nothing in the world would I want the slightest delay with my letters. Writing to you seems like innocent, easy chatter, exactly as though I were beside you with your little hand in mine, or your arm, and then I tell you what's going through my head from whatever perspective I like, according to what the day brings. Whereas for the others, they are *composed* letters. I love you so much. Ah, today I was moved to tears, because I had to talk about Saint-Cloud in my journal, and I thought back to your little bed, where you were so skinny and shy. How I love you, little Beaver, how I wish you were here. You know I love you just as much and as poetically as though it were the beginning of an affair, and yet there is so much more that you know. My love, how dear you are to me, and how much I need you.

We are leaving. It's almost certain. Actually we won't go far away— still on the front line, it seems, but in a quiet sector. For me it makes no difference, though it does complicate certain matters. Here, all is agitation, we look at maps, we make comments, we cite sources, but basically the guys don't give the slightest damn about it all, it amuses them instead, because it provides a change. I was in an excellent mood today, and then I got your books (the Romains) but *no halva*. Is there another package? No Saint-Claude (tobacco), nor above all any cartridges for my fountain pen. If you forgot, my love, send me quickly at least the cartridges. There are none here, and my supply is dwindling. Send 3 of them: 1 for Pieter and 2 for me. When you have the chance you could also send a little notebook similar to yours but in the next smallest size (you saw mine) and with red edges (ruled in squares, of course). I'm reading Romains's little books (excuse "little books") with the *greatest* of interest. There are lots of totally apt observations about the war of '14. And at times he almost achieved a being-in-the-war. There is a description of fear in the trenches, in the abject style of a practitioner, but it *achieves* the feeling of being in that position. When I've finished them, if the rest is as good as the first 100 pages, I'll send them back for you to read. Aside from that, lunch at L'Écrevisse, reading to 3,000 meters, a few notes in my notebook, and then work on my novel, which has finally started to move again. Since it's Sunday, the acolytes were taking a walk, and the first sergeant and Hang were at the window, gazing through binoculars at the young beauties of the region. I haven't felt this as Sunday. The guys, exhausted by yesterday's festivities, weren't overly reeking of Sunday. It was rather more weekday. Now I'm going to bed. 2 letters from Tania dated the same day. Right at the moment, I'm full of good feelings for her. I wrote to her yesterday to postpone her efforts on Emma's behalf by a few days. Anyway I think she's off to some very small burg, and communications will be more difficult. That wouldn't stop you, won't stop you, but I don't know how poor T. will manage.

My dearest, my little sweet. I love you very much.

To Simone de Beauvoir

November 16

My darling Beaver

First some *excellent news*, but undoubtedly you will already know it: the NRF writes me that it is sending you 5,000 francs, and it seems that there's still a small balance, which you'll get later in the year. That pleases me rather a lot because it proves after all that *The Wall* and *Nausea* have sold rather well. Then, and most important, you will simply have to transmit the above-mentioned check (marked "pay only to the undersigned") with endorsement to M. Bienenfeld and your signature: and there's your Bienenfeld affair all in order. Given that your overtime will pay your taxes, you'll only have to put aside a franc or two here and there for the Lady, and the debts will finally vanish. They've stopped all talk of cutting our salaries as government employees in the army, and Paul, who is usually the pessimist, believes that if it were going to happen it already would have. Naturally the idea of sending the five thousand francs to M. Bienenfeld in one fell swoop is simply a suggestion, do whatever is best, you are the little head of finance and I don't want to interfere with your plans.

I was delighted to read today in your letter that you received the first of mine since your trip. That feels like a renewal of contact. You're so affectionate, my love, and I love you so much. What you say about Bienenfeld is interesting though somewhat nebulous. What I ultimately deduced is that she had a Platonic concept of the human condition as a form including happiness in its essence. Actually that's rather more Aristotelian, it's even what they call eudaemonism. Is that what you mean? Nothing is more foreign to me. At her age I "refused" happiness with a comic indignation—while actually enjoying perfect happiness. But from that era I still retain this, that happiness never seemed a necessity of that condition. I do not see that I have a right to last year's happy life any more than to the twenty cubic meters of blue air in this schoolroom. But it seems to me that there too you must understand her better than I, since you told me that for a long time happiness for you had consisted of a privileged position for perceiving the world. That is no longer your opinion, since you are the totally perfect Beaver, but you were extremely shocked at the beginning of this war (which the proprietress of Le Boeuf Noir delicately calls the present crisis). I was amused by Merleau-Ponty's letter. Particularly what he has to say about the bookstore owner and about Brunschvicg. The passage about the commandment and the *hylé*[1] is rather shaky, to tell the truth, and that's what removes some of the comic aspects from Brunschvicg's incomprehension. But I like it that Brunschvicg speaks of "holding fast" as in 1914. I am returning the letter.

We are still waiting for our departure. I'm in an excellent mood, but my eyes hurt, this blue light combined with the electric light all day long wears me out. There's nothing I can do about it: I cannot and do not want to write less; when I've finished my novel I'll rest a bit. The halva arrived in good order, with the ink cartridges and the Saint-Cloud and *Le Canard Enchaîné*.[2] Thank you very much, my little sweet. We ate a whole box at lunch, the acolytes, Mistler, two soldiers we had just met, and the waitress at L'Écrevisse. The other one I'll eat all alone, like a Dullin, little by little. It's scrumptious and the almonds seem to add a certain something.

I'm having trouble writing this chapter. First, it is difficult in itself, and then there's the problem of showing a sudden and intermittent glimpse of liberty, and I can say almost nothing, since the essence will be given in the second volume, and then finally I'm caught between a Husserlian theory and an existential theory of liberty, I'm unsure of my thoughts. In fact, originally Mathieu was to steal from Lola out of passion for Ivich and not because of

---

[1]Greek word for "matter." Hylomorphism, the central doctrine of Aristotle's philosophy of nature, viewed every natural body as consisting of two intrinsic principles: one potential, viz., primary matter *(hylé)*, and one actual, viz., the substantial form, *morphē*. Brunschvicg was the teacher of both Merleau-Ponty and Beauvoir, who felt he was stuck in an archaic mind-body quandary they had transcended with phenomenology.

[2]Weekly magazine satirizing politics and culture.

liberty, and it is to make him less of a poor specimen that I give him this slight insight. There is also a technical difficulty: when Mathieu dashed out at the end of the last chapter, it was *action*. And in this new chapter it seems to me that the reader would expect more action, a spare account à la Mérimée. Whereas he is necessarily given a woolly poetic style. There you have a whole bundle of problems. I'm trying to make something out of all that, but I'm shuffling my feet a bit. All the same, I think I'll have the thing solved in a day or two. Then I will have to talk about Daniel, and that will amuse me, you have encouraged me.

I am going on with *Les Hommes de bonne volonté*,[3] and it is really good. It isn't a novel, but for once, despite the broad scattering of characters, you really get the impression of a splendid unity. Of course, the war is an ideal subject for that, but no matter, it takes talent. It actually remains very intellectual, and you *feel* nothing. Even in the very midst of war, interested in the war as I am and necessarily sensitive to the various massacres and mutilations, the tale of an attack in the trenches leaves me cold. On the other hand, the depiction of a mediocre general is altogether amusing. I'll send it to you. Soon you will have to send me some books; go ahead with a big bundle, since the NRF paid up. Of course you don't have much cash left. So then, don't: with the Ellery Queen and the Cassou and perhaps one other little book from the list, I'll get through till the end of the month. Then on December 1st you could send me two hundred francs' worth of books.

There, my little dearest. I'm stopping because my eyes hurt. Alas, I still have two letters to write, and I have to make them long, because yesterday I sent little scraps. With all my love.

To Simone de Beauvoir

November 14

My darling Beaver

I got two letters from you at the same time, Saturday's and Sunday's, which keenly interested me. Reading your account in two installments of the Lucile-Leccia[1] affair gave me an oddly cruel sense of repugnance and jealousy. Jealousy, you ask? Not jealous of Lucile or Leccia, but somehow disturbed

---

[3] A multivolume novel by Jules Romains (pen name of Louis Farigoule, 1885–1972) published in the period 1932–47; translated into English as *Men of Good Will*.

[1] Both women were students at Dullin's drama studio.

by that weird lewdness of intimacy between women: the sense of a zone forbidden to man. Aside from that it is rather beautiful: Lucile cradling the dirty laundry.

Here, it now appears that we aren't about to leave. At least it is put off a few days (?). It annoys me, I don't know anymore what to say to T. I'm afraid she'll take it as a deliberate dodge. On the other hand, our leaves are indeed beginning on November 20th, and there is much turmoil among the clerks, who are preparing departure lists. Alas, my poor-dear-little Beaver, I am next to last, which puts me down for February 1st.

Aside from that, a fierce argument yesterday between Pieter and me on the following subject: I said I felt lousy being safely ensconced here. Pieter: "You don't mean that. If you really were sincere, you'd sign up for the infantry." It is all covered at length in my journal. But I won't tell you the whole thing, because I still have two letters to do and my eyes are beginning to hurt seriously, I think I'll have to stop writing for a few days. But how about this little anecdote. The chaplain's orderly tells a guy who repeats it to Courcy, the clerk, that we're soon leaving for X. What's more, Lieutenant Munot asks his laundrywoman for his linens to be ready on Wednesday. The rumor immediately crystallizes: We're leaving on Wednesday for X. That evening Courcy accosts Lieutenant Munot: "We are leaving for X on Wednesday, aren't we, Lieutenant?" The lieutenant gives a start: "First I've heard of it!" "That's great!" thinks Courcy. "He's just great." "Actually, it wouldn't be impossible," said Lieutenant Munot. "There could be good reasons. If so, you'll have to pack up." Lieutenant Munot goes out and meets Lieutenant Ullrich. "It seems," he tells him, drawing him aside, "that we're leaving for X on Wednesday." Lieutenant Ullrich goes into the clerks' room: "Let's see a general staff map." "What are you looking for, Lieutenant?" asks Courcy craftily. "I'm looking for X. It seems we're heading there." Courcy gets up discreetly and comes in to us: "That does it. It was hard, but I dragged it out of Lieutenant Ullrich, he's more naive, and so, my friends, we are leaving for X on Wednesday." Immediately Paul gets up and goes to get his hair cut by a civilian barber—in case X has been evacuated (we later learn that X has not been evacuated), and on the way he gives everyone the information, which comes back to us through a dozen different intermediaries an hour later. Today, counter-rumor: we are not leaving for X. A few obstinate souls say that the order was given and then countermanded. Paul, winking: "It must be because of the Dutch affair."[2]

---

[2]Hitler had set November 12 as the date for his attack on France and the Low Countries, but bad weather caused repeated cancellations.

My love, I would love to go on indefinitely talking to you about whatever comes to mind, but I must stop. You cannot know how I love you, I'm a bit choked up, I'd like to see you again.

Goodbye, good little face, good little cheeks. Love.

To Simone de Beauvoir

November 15

My darling Beaver

I am so touched and moved by your dear letters. And I'm so pleased to think of you with a solid happiness anchored deep within your little being. If I'm to be calm, I absolutely have to feel that you're happy. I love you so much.

I received tons of mail today. No letter from Tania, who's been keeping her silence for 3 days, but a letter from my mother—one from Poupette, who was moved to write by a dream in which I appeared as a nutcracker; she picked up a pen the moment she woke up, under the effect of that tender image—an appealing letter from Kanapa, who writes: "There are few situations so delicate as mentioning the war to anyone who has been called up"; and he clearly still believes himself to be in 1916, an era in which, so they say, a gulf separated the most understanding civilian from the soldier. As for me, I still feel I'm on an even footing with civilians, and I have no new sensitivity that would make me jump up if people didn't speak correctly about the war. It's that we haven't been pounded day and night like our fathers— and finally, guess who else (I'm taking advantage of the end of a page to ask you the riddle): one from Nizan. 15 lines on a blue card. He's holed up in some general staff with a lieutenant who "loves nothing in the world so much as *The Wall* and *The Conspiracy*."[1] He has all the time in the world to write the sequel to *The Conspiracy*, hopes to go on leave soon (because he has two children), and asks to be remembered to you. He perfidiously adds at the end of the letter (and I can imagine his ferocious look): "What has become of Aron? He must have some stripes by now, if memory serves."

The whole thing amused me enormously. Aside from that, my eyes are better. Yesterday things were getting a bit worrisome, but today I'm on the road to recovery. I worked on my novel because the fly specks I leave in my notebook wear my eyes out—and then, to be quite frank, I had nothing to put in it, other than a proper critical attack on myself, but I'm beginning to

---

[1] A novel by Nizan published in 1937.

tire of those little games. I was in great good humor because the novel isn't
going badly, and then really *Verdun* and *Prelude to Verdun*[2] are *excellent*.
You shouldn't expect to find fully realized protagonists in it or individual
stories or—except in a few rare cases—visual scenes, but a terrific re-creation
of that enormous event, with multiple points of view and yet profound unity,
and then finally, what I have found nowhere thus far, a true sense of *being-
in-war*. There is a march of relief troops for Verdun that is truly *tremendous*.
Of course, unanimism[3] is fitting here as nowhere else. I'll send it to you. But
for your part, do send me some books immediately and before anything else.
Really it is an astonishing pleasure, and one that I had forgotten, to read a
book when it is good. And I can easily see that I am a scribbler heart and
soul, for this is the only thing I can sincerely *admire* (not the author, the
book). I read that march on Verdun with feelings as close as possible to
admiration. He's an odd guy, Romains. He wrote so many bad books before
those two. You have to read it in great chunks, mind you, at about the speed
and rhythm of a detective story, since almost every detail is awkward, but the
ordering of the whole, the rhythm, the shifts, and the choice of points of
view are done with surprising skill. He has a phrase that's a refreshing departure
from *All Quiet on the Western Front*[4] or *Feu*,[5] and constitutes a précis of his
whole book: "In war there are no innocent victims." It seems quite natural,
but I imagine it took twenty years of distance and the attitude of a historian
to discover it.

Since we are talking about war, by the way, let's turn to this one. Guess
what our division will be doing tomorrow? *Maneuvers!* A fictitious enemy is
supposed to fire on the village. Therefore we have to bring together the artillery
batteries and the infantry regiments. Just imagine in 1914, three kilometers
from enemy lines, a division playing little war games. You must admit it has
a certain Gallic humor. "Odd war," writes Nizan without other commentary.
I imagine that, for a multitude of reasons, he must find it even odder than
I do.

Aside from that, lunch at L'Écrevisse with Mistler, Paul, and Pieter,
read newspapers, jokes and military pranks (by the way, Bouglé's letter is a
lovely joke. In short, always the good school principal, he wants to retrieve
our library books in case we should be killed.) That's all.

---

[2]Novels in Romains's *Men of Good Will.*
[3]A movement cofounded by Romains and the poet Georges Chennevière, combining
belief in universal brotherhood with the psychological concept of group consciousness.
[4]*By Erich Maria Remarque. (SdB)* Published 1929.
[5]By Henri Barbusse (1873–1935), 1916 (*Under Fire,* 1917), a novel about a French
squadron.

I'm stopping here, my sweet Beaver, it's six o'clock, and great commotion reigns in this room because Pieter wants to cook some green peas over Courcy's alcohol lamp. I'm going to eat some of those peas. My sweet little Beaver, I feel such tenderness toward you, I love you. Never have I felt so forcefully that our lives have no meaning outside of our love and that nothing changes that, neither separation, nor passions, nor the war. You said it was a victory for our morality, but it is just as much a victory for our love.

I love you.

(1) Would you buy

   2 little cardboard basins
   100 grams of hyposulfite of soda
   2 frames, 4½ × 6
   2 packets of strong self-toning paper, 4½ × 6 (preferably Seltona)
   25 grams of chlorhydrate of diamidophenol
   50 grams of anhydrous sulfite of soda

It's for developing our photos—there are still more for you. You can send this whenever you like.

(2) Recently the opening of my fly was widening and Pieter was finding me grosser and grosser. Today in the schoolyard I pass the infantry colonel: "Hey there, private!" "Colonel, sir?" "Your fly, my friend." "Yes sir, I just noticed it, and I'm about to sew it up." "Sew it up, sew it up, please!" He was laughing to himself about it as he went off. The story cheered up the 27 soldiers who are in the schoolyard around the clock, and it made the rounds of the building. I tried to fix it, but the damage turned out to be so severe I finally put on my fatigue pants and took the others to the tailor.

To Simone de Beauvoir

November 16

My darling Beaver

The things you tell me about Bourdin really entertained me. I don't deny she can be crazy, but watch out that you don't get used to her vocabulary and all her shenanigans. All told, almost everything she says she could have said a year ago (except perhaps for that strange story that he is *following* her). That leaves her ravaged face still to be explained. You must understand that if she says it out of imbecilic lyricism and gratuitous lies as she always has, it's not madness: it is *she*, no more no less. But if you think there's something stunted and hopeless behind it, then it does begin to resemble Renée Ballon. I am very surprised you say nothing at all about the 5,000 francs. Perhaps they're still at the Hôtel Mistral, and the proprietor hasn't forwarded them. If not, protest a bit. Or are you already so secure? Talk to me about it. I am really moved that Z. speaks about me with infinite warmth. On the other hand, I'm a bit surprised that Tania, after her profuse repentance and tenderness, has suddenly stopped writing to me for four days. Can you cast some light on this?

I really liked how you tried to describe for me the hazy days of Paris at war, and the way it's taking on a populist, German cast.[1] I felt it all very clearly and it made a strong impression. My dear love, do as much of that as you can, it moves me, and I feel I'm seeing it; you know what I told you: little flower, you live for me. Your letters are very comforting because they are beginning to radiate happiness again, my wise little one. I love you so much. I received a letter from Hadjibelli (Tchimoutchine),[1] who has the nerve to be asking me for a bibliography for the second year of his graduate studies. In fact I will send him one. But later. I have to write to Kanapa, to Poupette, to Nizan, it's too much, in addition to the daily letters. My eyes are actually better, and then I ask myself whether the little drinks I have with impressive regularity aren't the indirect cause of the problem. All the more so because this morning Pieter said in a tone of gentle reproach, "You're tippling!"—which earned him a chewing-out but is slightly true.

This morning Paul set out on a mission by bicycle. They'd wanted to burden him with a rifle, but fear made him violently irritable: "In that case, no! I'll refuse to go!" I thought his convictions prevented him from carrying an instrument of destruction, but no: it's his semicircular canals, which are faulty, and if his back is loaded down he goes head over heels. Finally the colonel took pity and lent him an obsolete, nonworking revolver (the rules specify going out armed because of the mysterious "parachutists"). He left wearing his helmet, looking like an old Englishwoman. An hour later he was back. I first saw his helmet and glasses, then his face, which was livid, and his lips were trembling. He was walking the bicycle back and said curtly: "The pedal got twisted, the chain snapped." Then we noticed that the whole left side of his jacket and pants were splattered with mud. His right wrist was

---

[1]The Paris streets seemed to have taken on a neat and uncluttered look like some blue-collar streets of Berlin, lending a new abstraction to the gray autumnal poetry of Paris (*Lettres à Sartre*, Vol. 1, p. 263).
[2]*A former student of Sartre's. (SdB)*

half sprained, his left hand scraped. We asked him what had happened, and at first he said, untruthfully, "It's the chain." Then he admitted that a car had scared him as it passed and he'd taken a dive, onto his helmeted head and his hands. A prank by his semicircular canals, probably, but he'd set out convinced that some disaster would befall him. I'm beginning to understand what hidden organic basis underlies his profound conviction that he'll be killed in the war: it's that he's afraid of his body. It's easy for Pieter, Keller, and me to be optimistic, with our docile, uncomplaining bodies. But Paul's body must be a gloomy prankster that goes off from time to time on charming caprices, such as taking a dive, falling in the mud. And to keep things in hand, Paul needs a narrow, well-ordered little life, with a solicitous wife at his side. Even at that, he sometimes finds himself at night huddled in the fireplace. So war is a terror for him, because he's there among rough men and all alone with that body prone to getting carried away. He feels pursued. Odd fellow. Did I tell you that for five years he'd hidden from his wife, a good socialist like himself, that he'd been made a corporal? She heard of it by chance: "And did I ever get a tongue-lashing!"

Let's get down to the chronological account. Awoke at 6:30, breakfast at La Rose, finished *Verdun*, which I'll send back to you in a day or two (I have *nothing left to read*), a reading from 8:00 to 9:00 for the division's "field maneuvers" (it was while going to report the results three kilometers away that Paul busted his ass), work—this damn section on freedom is giving me problems, I still have twenty-five lines to go, but they're fighting me all the way. Reading—lunch with Pieter at L'Écrevisse: each reads to himself or daydreams, like the eternal old couple. Return, 2nd reading, I read, work— Paul, in a corner, pale from the morning's emotion and his bandaged hand.

That's it. I've written nothing in the little notebook, to spare the eyes. My love, I love you with all my might, and I'm in ecstasy at the thought of seeing you soon. I kiss you on your dear little face, every darling centimeter.

Send me some books, my little flower. If the photographic materials cost too much, send me the books first and wait till December 1st for the materials.

To Simone de Beauvoir

November 17

My darling Beaver

No letters from you today. I'd foreseen it for one of these days, because the day before yesterday I inexplicably received two at the same time. Since I have no anxieties and even find this gap *natural*, for the reason I've just mentioned, it allows me to understand all the better what I miss when a day goes by without anything from you: it is a sort of Goethesque wisdom that allows me to *attend* the various events of my life without actually partaking of them. With your letters, I feel Olympian at little cost, because I regain a world we hold in common, which is *good*, be it in war or peace, like a tormented novel that ends happily. I think that it comes from the absolute and total regard I have for you: the moment that exists, there is that absolute, the rest must clearly follow, even the worst. I imagine that is what you must be feeling when you call me your "little absolute." My darling, I love you very much.

I got an exalted letter from Dumartin spontaneously proclaiming himself my disciple, avowing an admiration that is not intellectual but human, and ending by asking me to correct twenty pages of a novel he has just written. There are a few pages of subtle humor in it that I liked very much, as when he says, "I spent two months of isolation and *individuality* in England." But I am even more amused by this shower of former students that still associate me with their little concoctions, one (Hadjibelli) asking me for a bibliography, another (Kanapa) a definition of Aristotle's physics, the third that I read his literary work. Alas, I'll have to answer them all. I'll devote one whole day to it. I've finished the difficult passage in my novel and in a way that pleases me. But will you be satisfied, little judge?

Another letter, which explains Tania's silence: she wrote it on Sunday night after getting drunk with some Poles, like a true Polishwoman, and had slept chastely in one of their beds. Then, having written it to "tell everything, even the half-assed stupidities," she didn't dare mail the letter and undoubtedly hauled it around in her purse for two days. Then on the third day, appalled at not having written to me, afraid that you might tell me about it, she must have tossed it into a mailbox with her eyes closed and the feeling of jumping off a bridge. In fact, I find the story rather charming and am going to send her a friendly reply.

Nothing new. They are going to give us a physical, stick their fingers up our rears and in our mouths, make us pee in a glass. A lot of the guys want to hide their clap so their pensions won't be denied if they contract a kidney infection. Pieter, who has a hernia, is afraid they might operate on him, which would oblige him to trust to military hands, but he is also somewhat tempted, because that would give him 18 convalescent days + 10 of the regular leave. You can just imagine the abundance of flowery speeches born of this dilemma. On top of that he has a miserable long-standing case of the clap that he doesn't expect to keep hidden. Paul, thinking we were headed for the medical officer this afternoon, fussed about, saying, "I have on yesterday's socks, I'll smell."

At noon we lunched at L'Écrevisse. There was a light infantryman just back from the front line. He held forth with the following very typical talk: "We can see the Germans very well, they're two hundred fifty meters away, they have a good time lolling on the grass and playing the accordion . . . at night they go about their little chores and we provide them with light—and they did the same for us till—two weeks ago—an ass, a Moroccan on our side, downed one of theirs with his rifle. Since then you can't stick out your neck without them banging away at you." He concluded, bitterly, "There's always someone that'll fuck things up, and it's the other suckers that's gotta pay." A speech common to the military species but usually heard when a drunken soldier has committed some outrage and the bars are consequently put off limits for the troops.

My eyes are still tired—probably a bit less, but I've gone back to my notebook anyway, and it has given me great pleasure. There's absolutely no more question of our leaving here. On the other hand the leaves are indeed beginning on the 20th, and I might be in Paris around January 18.

Goodbye, my dearest, my little flower, I send you all my love, no one—not even you—could be fonder of someone than I am of you.

To Simone de Beauvoir

November 18

My darling Beaver

Excuse me for today—yours is the second letter I've written. This is the first time it has happened and it won't again soon, but Tania had sent me a very pleasant, touching letter. So I began with her. But that will do it for some time.

Yet I am melting with gratitude to you, my little dearest: this morning

I received the handsome Shakespeare and Cassou's 48,[1] and then this after-noon such a long and pleasant letter in which you told me of being moved because I wanted to read. And your emotion moved me in turn. And then I thought how you had immediately run to the post office to mail those two books, and at that my heart melted. You are so kind to me, my love. Quite kind enough. To change the feeling without dropping the level, I laughed till I cried on learning that you'd read *L'Oeuvre* with amusement, skepticism, and complicity because you'd just read *Le Canard Enchaîné*. I see you so clearly, laughing all by yourself at Le Dôme in front of a big article entitled "Terrible repression after the Munich attempt." You are a little wonder. (Today I'm enjoying my daily ration of Olympianism; it has me very chipper.)

This morning, so-called induction medical. In a barroom of the tavern they had us urinate into beer steins. The Acolytes stripped. Me too. I shall say nothing about myself, except that as I tried to seem relaxed in front of six soldiers seated at a table, buttoned up to the chin and shuffling papers, I was very aware of *having a back*. But the Acolytes surprised me: stark naked they didn't seem nuder than usual. Paul's butt and the slight curvature of his spine didn't make me feel odd. It was as though I'd always known them. Nor the enormous belly Keller displayed as though saying, "That's a fact," while the doctor dictated to his aides, "Obesity o-b-e-s-i-t-y." It's as though I've always been seeing them nude. I think that despite the jackets and the heavy blue pants, we live in the state of total nudity. The dignified gathering took on a melancholy cast from so many naked sexual apparatuses. Wrinkled, jaded, ashamed, they vainly tried to hide below their little tufts of hair. The doctor palped them with an elegant finger, saying, "Cough." And I understood and wholeheartedly endorsed André Breton's phrase "I'd be ashamed to appear naked before a woman unless I had an erection." No question about it, it's a matter of good taste. True, it may not be much prettier erect. But at least it's justifying its existence. As for draping it with forget-me-nots,[2] no! Better a sprig of parsley. After the medical, a walk in the countryside. It made me think, I don't know why, of the walk in *Faust*, when he meets the spaniel (not according to Baty, according to the text).[3] I walking in front, with the Acolytes following along. Vague disgust, from having seen so many penises. But what is there about them that is disgusting? It was sexual, I suppose. A

---

[1]Jean Cassou, *Quarante-huit* (Paris, 1939), about the revolution of 1848.

[2]*Allusion to Lawrence's* Lady Chatterley's Lover. (*SdB*)

[3]In Goethe it was a poodle; Sartre's spaniel comes from his reading of Nerval's translation. Jean- Baptiste-Mary Gaston Baty (1885–1952), playwright and producer-director at the Théâtre Montparnasse (where he staged *Faust*) and the Comédie Française.

way of proving to oneself that one doesn't have "those tastes." But perhaps I calumniate myself; in any case the reaction was minor and spontaneous. Perhaps the odor of urine played some part in it. Paul's smells sour, but I had already noticed that when he was peeing out our landlady's window. He himself is dull and gray, but the humors of his body have some pungency.

Afterward, dinner at L'Écrevisse. Around 11 they'd notified me that there was a package; I ran to the postal clerk and found the splendid Shakespeare, with lots of plays I've never read and others I was bursting to reread. I read *King Lear*, which bored me for one act, then thrilled me. The character of old Lear is delightful. I really like it when he gets angry because they've tied his man in the stocks and he keeps repeating, "Who put my man i' th' stocks?" There is lots of melodrama in it, but astonishing nonetheless—and altogether fresh and new. You didn't read 48, you, you lazy one, yet it looks entertaining. After lunch I worked on my novel, received and read the letters, and replied. It's now eight o'clock.

Mistler just came in. Now he's almost certain that we're going off twenty kilometers from here on Monday or Tuesday. This is one of those events that should, I think, leave us totally unaffected.

My love, I'm so pleased that you feel my love, I wish you'd have the feeling constantly, that it would never leave you, as it never leaves me. You are my pure dear little flower.

To Simone de Beauvoir

November 18

My darling Beaver

Two letters from you today, an immense one and a very short one. That means I won't get one from you tomorrow, but it gives me enormous pleasure nonetheless to have 6 long pages from you. But tell me, naughty one, did you forget that you had a rendezvous with Bourdin? There is no trace of her in your Friday schedule.

My love, is the Lady coming back to Paris? You say you'd like it if I saw her again during my leave. I deduce that she wrote you saying she was coming back. Certainly I'll see her, gladly. It seems to me that it must still be peacetime where she is, and I really have a strong affection for her, which has borne up very well during the war. The war is very precious: it provides a classification system. The Lady has persisted, Tania and Bost have risen, and you . . . I have never loved you more. But perhaps it would be unjust (except for you) to take this catastrophic classification for the *real* classification. Doubtless there is no real classification. At any rate, I'll really enjoy seeing the Lady, if things turn out that way. But nobody else; that doesn't interest me at all. I am not in the least coming back to Paris to *rediscover something left behind*. I think I will never again rediscover anything. Something has ended. Even in peacetime, it will be something different. In Paris there is *you*, as well as Tania and my mother. That's all. And then there is wartime Paris, which I want to *know* and not rediscover. Did the Lady get my photos? Write me about all of this.

My love, I can't imagine how I could have seemed sad in my recent letters, when I wasn't at all. It's just that the trouble with my eyes diminished my vitality. I am hardly writing in my notebook anymore, to save my eyes—and I'm doling it out in dribbles. If these eyes would just clear up, I'd be peaceful and content again. What I was jotting the other day in the now-neglected notebook is that eye troubles are harder to bear than war problems because they're unjustified and also because they're prolonged by *civilian* concerns: "What if I had to give up writing," etc. And then I realized that I think *with my eyes*. If I cannot *focus* them, I cannot focus my thoughts. In fact, things are improving, but they are still strained, and that gives me slight but constant nausea. However, it is neither a serious concern nor unbearable. When I've finished my novel, I'll take a rest for ten days or so and that will be the end of it.

You asked me for a historical rundown of last year. You'd do better to go to the Bibliothèque Nationale to consult the newspapers; that way you'd get the atmosphere.

That's the best I can do for you, my dear love. But having said that, I *urge* you to do a little research; you can't let yourself off that easily.

My love, I must stop here. Fortunately absolutely nothing happened today. I love you passionately, my most precious little flower. Your letters are so nice, they are little elixirs for my heart. Adieu. We are leaving tomorrow, apparently.

To Simone de Beauvoir

November 20

My darling Beaver

No letter from you today, exactly as expected. But I miss your little daily greeting, my love. I had a note from Paulhan explaining the Alain escapade: he had signed the famous Communist manifesto for Peace. He is charged, interrogated at home very politely. He replies: "I saw the word Peace, I signed without reading the rest." Without a doubt he will be acquitted. I also got a long letter from my mother, very optimistic and predicting, according to a certain "highly placed" person whose name she prudently withholds, the end of the war by Christmas. I sincerely hope she is right but have my doubts. At any rate, my little one, at any rate I do not believe that we will be facing it for long. Till spring perhaps—till autumn? Things seem to be going really badly in Germany, and the affair in Holland (so I was right, wasn't I?) proves their disarray.

What is there to tell you so you'll have your long daily letter? Alas, almost nothing. That we didn't leave, of course. But that we may be leaving tomorrow. And tomorrow I will tell you that we didn't leave. That I have gone from Mathieu to Daniel. This part interests me a great deal and is moving along much faster; I'm on a roll. I've done, I think, six good pages on his relationship with Ralph. In the gloomy mode—but that isn't stated. I've read *Troilus and Cressida* again and, you know, liked it less than the last time. On the other hand, I'm enchanted by *Antony and Cleopatra*, a little gem. It's true that the guy is astounding. I'll read the whole thing carefully and send it back with *Verdun* and *Prelude to Verdun*. Unfortunately the print is very tiny for my poor eyes.

Aside from that, what to tell you? Really nothing's going on here anymore and I'm not writing in my notebook, I have nothing left to say. But I'm very happy. Particularly now that my novel is going well. It isn't wasted time.

Your letters give such pleasure. They are so tender, my darling Beaver, and I feel you so close. My love, this separation is a very minor test, since we will see each other again and love each other so much.

I love you.

To Simone de Beauvoir

November 21

My darling Beaver

What to tell you? We are forgetting the war here. Never has it been harder to grasp than these past few days. Never was life more workaday. All day long it's nothing but one mass of complaints and gossip. There's a running battle between the 3 guys at the Artillery Intelligence Service, who accuse one another of being shirkers, then each one proclaims that he is requesting transfer to "the boom-boom," then winds up impressing himself with his own heroism, and the whole thing ends on a note of exhausted torpor from which they rouse themselves to gossip innocently. Next door in the clerks' office, they are squabbling over some trifle: Mistler is cross at Courcy. Between us harmony reigns. I'm working well and my eyes are better, I've taken the opportunity to write and read all day, tomorrow can look out for itself. It has put me in the most marvelous mood. First I put the all-but-final touches on the scene between Ralph and Daniel, and then I drew up an outline of Daniel's "guilt feelings." I think that it's the most delicate part of the whole book. After that I read Cassou's 48, somewhat hazy but it helped me to understand humanitarianism, the forefather of our humanism. Therefore I wrote in my notebook. I'm always happy when I can write in it, but these days, because of my eyes, I'd ask myself, for each little idea, "Is it worth the pain?" And of course it never was. After that I read the 4th act of *Antony and Cleopatra*, which is stupendous, better than *Julius Caesar*. And Gide translated like a god. Only, what small type they used. Alas, here I sound like an old fogy grumbling about type being too small. But this will pass, I hope. This morning it wasn't going too well, and then later, not so badly. These days I'm writing my drafts with my eyes closed, to rest them, and when I open my eyes I see lines that rise and fall, a rather beautiful effect.

There were two long letters from you, my love. Naturally I won't get anything tomorrow, but who cares? I really like having a big chunk of your days—of your life—this way. How well-ordered it is, how regular. You bring tears to my eyes, my little sweet. I love you so. I'm overjoyed at the thought of reading your novel on my leave. There will be a good chunk of it. True, it will be only the next-to-last draft, but no matter. Read the newspapers, my little flower, for the whole year, so you can be totally familiar with it and find an echo of what was on people's minds.

I have been interrupted by Pieter, bringing me a tract some German planes dropped this morning two hundred meters from here. A peasant brought it in, and we're passing it around. The paper is in the form of a leaf, a beautiful rust color. On one side there is a brief text:

> Autumn
> The leaves are falling and we will too.
> The leaves fall because God wills it.
> But we'll fall because the English will it.
> Next spring no one will remember either dead
> leaves or soldiers slain! Life will go on
> above our graves.

Below this madrigal, a skull wearing a helmet.

I've just been disturbed again, but this time more civilly: all the officers enter in single file, giggling and animated. They've come in quest of a pair of binoculars to look at Saturn's rings. Paul, Hang, Keller, and Naudin are following them. I suspect Keller had a hand in it, because in civilian life you have to pay to see the moon through binoculars and here the spectacle is free.

Tania writes to me very regularly. There was yet another letter from a student, this one named Blanchet, asking me for a bibliography. That really stretches professional obligations a bit far. Did I tell you that it flatters me, because they don't imagine I might have changed. It's half due to laziness of intellect, I suppose—like that girl who wanted to do a drawing of you dressed as a bohemian but couldn't go so far as to imagine that you might not have a desk pad and a telephone—half out of faith in me. It makes me feel alive, carrying the weight of so many little confidences, most of which lack the slightest self-awareness. But I'll have to answer, that's the devil of it.

My dearest, how happy I am about your self-confidence and because my letters can give you some happiness. You know, I'd accept a lot of bad things if you could remain happy. But don't be afraid, I know that would be the worst way to give you happiness. It's more a manner of speaking. It's marvelous how it makes the world seem optimistic and good, whatever happens around here, just to think that you are even slightly blissful, back there in that weird Paris. And it seems something like a promise of happiness for myself. My love, my eyes are completely misted over as I write this, because I'm thinking of your dear little smile. I love you with all my might.

As you see, we are still right here.

Simone de Beauvoir

November 22nd

My darling Beaver

I'm really moved by your dear little letter. I'll have to tell you which one, otherwise you won't know. It's the one in which you talked about Saint-Exupéry. Written Monday the 20th. My love, your "tender sufferings"[1] are

---

[1] A phrase from *Terre des Hommes* (*Wind, Sand and Stars*), by Antoine de Saint-Exupéry (1900–44).

so precious to me. I don't mind if you get them from time to time. It's not unlike what I call "little whiffs." I wish you a cast-iron well-being, staunchly insolent, and then from time to time, because of human frailty, a small bouquet of tender sufferings. I can so clearly picture the little expression that must be crossing your face. It has to be the one I picture as you wake up. The tenderest, most flickering, most beautiful. I love you, my dearest. You mustn't pity me in the least, you know. I'm unfeeling (except for you, my dear love, but that doesn't sadden me, on the contrary, it is my form of gaiety), I conjure up no images—unless they are the tender sufferings I just mentioned, there are traces of them in my notebook. This very day, around 12:30, at L'Écrevisse, there was a guy who turned on the radio in the next room (this is the first copy, not from my notebook), and I got the impression they were playing jazz. I say I had the impression because there was also a racket of plates and voices. I felt I couldn't bear it—you know I don't use words lightly, that must be taken in the strong sense—and suddenly a cruel, poetic Paris was surging up before my eyes, the very thing a jealous exiled lover can feel about his mistress, you know what I mean, you yourself have felt it. And yet I was jealous of nobody, neither of Tania, who is all charm and tenderness, nor of you, above all, my dear little one. Nonetheless, it is basically all of you, you as much as Olga or Tania or even the Gérassis, all of those consciousnesses that I envied. But it was all a haze. And then the guy turned up the music and it was some cheap tune. I heard snatches of the words "Pa-pa-pa-pa—Pa-pa-Paris." There was only piano and violin, nothing to fear in the way of a saxophone or little trumpet, which generally wring a tear from me. And yet that trashy music could still be humiliated, and it was, by the noise of plates and the filthy voices and the guys twirling the radio knobs, turning the volume up and down, stopping the song, starting it up again, etc. And I was in an odd state, vaguely tempted nonetheless to see a cruel resurging image of Paris, which even that music could have given me—and consequently irritated to see it shredded and dispersed—and on the other hand pleased to be spared it. As you wisely say in your own case, Alsatian wine is perhaps not totally estranged from these subtle impressions. And then it stopped, they gave the communiqués and commentaries, it turned funny. Paul was across from me reading *Le Populaire*; I got back to reading the first act of *Coriolanus*, which is very enjoyable. In the end, I didn't know Shakespeare at all. This is a sort of discovery and it's made a strong impression.

And then I came back, I did a reading for some officers elegant as butterflies. It's a type I hadn't encountered before: the ready wit, the sally, the biting phrase, the faintly homosexual grace tempered by a martial virility. There were two of them who eventually plunked themselves right in front of the theodolite, making us lose the balloon. One of them is Lieutenant Z., of whom I've already spoken, the other a captain in the light infantry. It was the latter who said to Paul: "Married? And not wearing your wedding ring?" "N-no, Captain." "Hmm! And how many children?" "One." "Married how long?" "5 years, Captain." "Well! You aren't in any hurry, my boy!" And he turns his back on him. As a matter of fact he is a bachelor and chases women here with a captain in the air force.

And then—one more tender suffering—what do I find but your little letter, which brings tears to my eyes. But that's not all, there are five others, each one with a phrase that moves me:

Lévy:[2] "You are just as present now among us as in past times; we speak of you just as often, and you inspire many discussions."

My mother: "It gives me great joy to see the Beaver again, and to talk with her in all confidence about my dear little child—my only worldly goods."

Tania: "Montparnasse seems washed out this evening and ordinary. I would have liked some flair, because that's how I am, confronting things and in my relationship with you. I bow low before you."

Martine Bourdin: (I'm sending you her letter, which will make you die laughing). But it's too long to write out, you'll read it—in particular it was seeing you as seen by her that struck me, and these words: "It is quite clear that only you exist for her."

The fact remains that these letters, with their discreet or expansive little compliments, have reduced me to a state of oddly tender humility and embarrassment. I don't easily recognize myself in them, me the bearded one—so grubby that the waitresses at L'Écrevisse burst out laughing when I enter, and the patroness has to shoosh them, and the worst of it is that it doesn't bother me—in the odd character, also somewhat pompous, that all those individuals think me. It brought a lump to my throat. And I found myself in a strange state, moved, reproaching myself for being moved, not knowing what to do with that tender feeling and strongly suspecting it of being inauthentic, and yet altogether delighted, so much so that I still am, my love. It is in that state that I write you, in order to give you that little emotion, and in fact the only use of it I could see as authentic is to pour it into a little burst of love for you (which is why I'm writing to you at 2:30 instead of at 5 o'clock). I love you.

I can't yet send *Barnaby Rudge*[3] to Bost because I've lent it to a slob of an orderly who's in raptures over it, claims he's never read anything better

---

[2]The historian Raoul Lévy had been a student of Sartre's at the Lycée Pasteur.
[3]*By Dickens. (SdB)*

since *Ton corps est à toi* ["Your Body Is Yours"]. But I'll send *Verdun* to-morrow. Ultimately, the Cassou is pitiful, enough to give you a stomachache. Give me Bourdin's address (she's in Paris, the letter testifies to that). When you know it, I'll write her a note. There's a hilarious moment in her letter when, after voluptuously evoking my kisses on her arm, she asks, "Are they giving you bromides?"

Aha! I've got a "good piece of news," as my old grandfather used to say: my eyes are just about back to normal. I'm ecstatic. I worked at the little notebook and found loads of ideas for Daniel's remorse. That's it, till to-morrow, my love. When you say that each of my letters surprises you because you didn't think it could give you as much happiness as the previous one, that delights and bothers me because it almost seems to lay a responsibility at my door. But I won't give in to that temptation: I always want to write to you spontaneously without thinking of your expectations, I know that's the way you like my letters best. I don't know whether this one will give you as much pleasure as the others, but you know, just take the one that seems tenderest and reflect that I was loving you no more than today.

With all my love.

When you have the money to buy some books, send me *two small notebooks* with red edges, the size just below yours.

My Beaver

In writing to Tania I reworked and literaried the fleeting emotion I had at L'Écrevisse. I pretended that it was of her I was jealous, which holds up. It strikes me as a pitiful little sacrilege,* and I relieve myself of it in confessing it to you. It's five o'clock now, I've written and read a bit, and I still hold on to that "tender suffering" as a blessing. I am very happy.

I love you.

Rereading Bourdin's letter, I get the impression that she is a bit mad when she writes, "You know, I think it'll take several days for you to untangle my head."

---

*Slightly abashed too at being so morally crass.

To Simone de Beauvoir

November 23

My darling Beaver

No letter from you today. Nor from anyone except Tania. One solitary letter, that's a very meager delivery. And what's more it was late. And besides, I don't have much to tell you, except that I love you very much. This will be a very short letter for lack of material. I got up at six o'clock, went to La Rose. Mistler was there, looking stupid, because I'd loaned him the Heidegger and he doesn't understand a word of it. So I explained being-in-the-world while I had breakfast. And we walked back through beautiful dry cold weather, -3° C. I had put on the handsome fur-lined gloves my mother sent me. After which there was an interminable argument between the first sergeant, Hang, Paul, and Pieter about the goals of the war. I said my piece while drinking some coffee, another "bromide" coffee, then worked rather well on my novel. Lunch at L'Écrevisse; I forgot to tell you I'd discovered a little idea on will during the night (a violent desire to urinate had seized me and, awake and unable to satisfy it, I did some philosophy to get my mind off it), I thought over this little idea, wide-eyed, while Pieter chattered away beside me, and I wrote *"tu"* because I had just spoken to Pieter, who is as boring as steady rain and talking of going off on leave before the others. The idea panned out somewhat, and this afternoon after the reading, I began to write it down in my little notebook. It's a complex mixture of the botched passage in notebook #2, of my courses, of things I told you last year—that passive resistance is necessary for will (otherwise there would be nothing but wishes), and finally the Spinozan idea that consciousness and will are one. You can see just about what that leads to. Or perhaps it doesn't make any sense to you at all. (My love, it's awful trying to write to you while Pieter, mad with self-important niggling, is distractedly blaring away with completely false reasoning right beside me.) I went to phone in the reading, it took me from 2 to 3 o'clock, then the rest of the time I worked. And then around seven o'clock Pieter began his yammering. It is odious, having to do with a mixup that they have created, to his disadvantage—so he says—between his mobilization classification and his recruitment classification. You get the drift. It's been going on for two hours. It is impossible to continue writing—please forgive me. I hate him, but what can I do, I told him right out: "Shut up, you are reasoning like a woman, you're an ass." He keeps on.

Another interruption: I get up and this time I set him straight. But do you suppose he'd keep quiet? Now he's explaining why he was wrong. This time I give him a proper bawling out. After which Paul, completely panicky because there's going to be a night reading and the colonel will be there, begs me to straighten out my pack. On the off-chance he might come here. In short, it's pretty ear-splitting. I imagine this letter is disjointed, but I am seething with rage. Do forgive me, little one, I'd begun it so tenderly, but you know these brief rages that sometimes get the better of me. So, that's where I am. My love, I'm stopping here. I love you just as much as yesterday, but it irritates and humiliates me not to be able to tell you so calmly. I love you with all my heart.

To Simone de Beauvoir

November 24

My darling Beaver

Today I'm taking my time. The acolytes have left for a walk and I'm alone here with a few soldiers and officers who are working dutifully. You must have thought me quite mad when you got my last letter. You weren't mistaken: I was furious. And then I calmed down because we did a night reading for the colonel and the captains, the scene was pretty as can be, you could see the small reddish star (the light attached to the balloon) slipping away between the yellow stars, and we had to work hard to get past the moon's reflection. It was $-4°C$, and the moonlit, frozen countryside was most appealing. The officers didn't look so bad either, all draped in their capes, stamping the ground to warm their feet and from time to time giving off jabbing flashlight rays. It was about 9:15; we went home to bed right afterward. Paul had a bout of sleepwalking around one in the morning. He suddenly began to cry out, "Ho Ho Ho Ho Ho! Oh!" the last "Oh" slow, quivering, and horrified. I said, "Paul!" since we had agreed that I would wake him, because of the landlady, who might get frightened. In a sleep-ridden voice he said, " 'S a matter?" I: "Paul!" Then, with a politely embarrassed giggle (the tone you might use when someone comes up to you pretending to know you—"I'm afraid I don't really know who you are"): "I don't in the least know where I am!" And making the most of his own quandary, with a sort of psychological relish: "No, I really don't!" He bursts out laughing. Me: "You're at X." He, very irritated: "Hey, I know that!" Me: "Why did you holler?" He, in very bad faith: "Me? I hollered?" Silence. Then I hear a stirring, rustling of silk, heavy objects being dragged about, a gasp. Me: "What're you doing?" Paul, dignified, offended: "Nothing. I'm simply awake." And immediately after that, a strong, even breathing that soon changes into light snoring. We agreed this morning that throughout the conversation he was totally and profoundly asleep, even when he said, "I'm awake." Sleep, after all, is an odd thing. That conversation with a guy who was sound asleep seems much more poetic, even, than a conversation with a madman.

This morning, I went to La Rose to read *Coriolanus*, and then Mistler came in and we exchanged impressions of Pieter with shrugs and nods. He was very put out, because Pieter had called him a "happy woman." "When Sartre talks, you brighten up like a happy woman." Then I worked till ten o'clock, on the topic of will, but there's still something tangled. Still, it's already better than the last time. The next time through will do it. Then I went to take a bath—but not at the public bath, which happens to be the former prison, but at a barber's. It is the barbers around here who'll let you have a bath. Then L'Écrevisse, then roll call, then a reading, and on my return two letters from you. I don't agree that you write me bad letters, my little one. Quite the opposite, they are so tender, little beloved, so full of gracious touches, and you explain so well how you love me. It isn't your fault if your dear little life is so well ordered. And it is rather to the good, because the novel will move along at a fast clip. Accept your pain patiently; this war will end sooner than we might think. From time to time buy a copy of Valois's *Nouvel Âge*,[1] it's a little daily whose ideas are basically quite wise. So wise, in fact, that it is mercilessly censored. Therefore you don't get your money's worth.

My love, I *beg* you not to say that you are going to see Emma at Christmas. If Tania could go, it might get by, but as her incompetence will surely prevent her, the result will be on one hand that she will hate you all the time you are with Emma, and on the other hand that it will be impossible to make her understand later that Emma is seeing you two days out of five, whereas you will actually have seen her twice in three months. Do spare me that, because I'm the one who will pay for Emma, and I don't *at all* like the idea. On the contrary, I'm very satisfied with my relationship with her: she may deceive me, but for the moment I've become mythic to her, she reverences me, as you know, and that provides her with her solemn, romantic little myth. Don't destroy that for me, please.

Another thing: we can perfectly well get photos developed here, my

---

[1]Georges Valois (1875–1945), journalist and politician, founded a fascist movement in France in 1925, but later broke with fascism and took part in the Resistance.

good little person; however, doing it themselves will keep the acolytes busy. Therefore, would you be kind enough to send the ingredients as soon as possible. It can hardly come to more than thirty-five francs outlay.

Yet another thing: we know the numbered order of our leaves. That, in fact, was what Pieter made such a scene about last night. I'm in a much better slot than I had dared hope: 121 out of 230, so almost the middle. If the departures were normal, that would mean mid-January, but they're letting us out drop by drop, one a day, so you can see what that means. True, they might accelerate the rate in a few weeks.

Received two charming little notes from the Lady, one inside the other. She had written at the time of the photos but didn't have my address.

So there's the day. Right now I'm off to pick up a package of books from the postal clerk—yours, my sweet. And then I'll come back to write to T. and my mother. I'd also like to find a bit of time to work on my novel.

My love, I love you so much, and it is a joy for me to know you are so wise and, all in all, happy. I was delighted to think that you were going to hear *Alceste*. I only hope Z. wasn't late. I'll know tomorrow. This is like a little serial.

I love you.

If Emma leaves Toulouse for Biarritz, I'm afraid she won't have time enough to make new friends in her new lodging. Does that matter?

To Simone de Beauvoir

November 25

My darling Beaver

I won't be writing much to you today. Really the days are so alike that they almost seem one. They gave Paul a shot today (against typhoid). He's walking up and down in his blue overcoat like a soul in torment. The rest of us will get shots later, and stronger ones (in two weeks). Naturally that means that we aren't yet leaving. They wouldn't drag around fifty feverish soldiers. I've hardly been out more than he; I'm out of money and I lunch here. By great good fortune a package stuffed with victuals arrived from my mother, and I consume them right here. This is not to ask you for cash: Pieter would lend me some if I needed it. It's just that I want to finish the month without shelling out anything: I haven't been a good little financial manager, but who cares. I won't borrow from Pieter except for tobacco. I got loads of packages this morning: two from my mother, with a small can of

Sterno and some cotton. The Sterno was to heat water and the cotton to soak in the hot water and make compresses for my eyes. I was touched. There was also soap, a replacement battery, and food, sausage, tuna, foie gras, and countless caramels. In addition to that, your little package, with Saint-Exupéry and *The Spanish Testament*.[1] Thank you, dear one. *The Spanish Testament* looks excellent. I've scarcely glanced at the other; Paul, the patient, seized on it. But why didn't you send the Ellery Queen? Is it really that awful? If it's at all readable, add it to the large bundle of books you'll send me soon. And then a package from Bost, can you imagine, consisting of *Dead Souls*, *Sous la lumière froide*, and *La Cavalière Elsa*,[2] but not *Moll Flanders*. I glanced at *La Cavalière Elsa* and find it unreadable. Nonetheless it's what peple liked circa 1923. The first chapter is excellent, but after that come prophecies, plus dubious and "very modern" characters and anticipations etc. Uninteresting. He knows how to tell a story, but that's not what he *wants*, he thinks it's beneath his subject. Well, anyway, I have something to read. I began *Hamlet*, which is terrific, and I haven't finished 48. Tomorrow I'll send you *Verdun* and *Prelude to Verdun*. I'll send them to your place, at the hotel, which is easier.

At two o'clock, a weather reading. Mail at the same time, but nothing from you, my love. It always gives me the same sad disappointment, and the world always seems slightly hostile. No doubt I'll get two tomorrow. Merely a note from Tania. The end was slapdash, she had hurriedly scribbled that she loved me passionately, because Blin, from the Atelier, was coming to her place. Blin is hanging around, trying for an affair. She is flattered, and I suppose it will work out, but I have to say I find it very disagreeable. But what what can I do? You can't fight at a distance, and besides, in this sort of thing, struggle is rather undignified. All I can do is think of something else. I was on edge for an hour or two, but now I've calmed down. It's an oddly hollow passion. I suppose that had there been a letter from you, I wouldn't have given this a second thought. But it was almost as though you had left me alone facing T. Fortunately that isn't true, my little one, fortunately it's a small nightmare of the passions, and I've waked up. Now it's over, and I know I'll have two letters from you tomorrow, you who are my life, and I'm joyfully looking forward to tomorrow, because we're already on the far slope of the day. It's quite obvious that these little love crises come from the fact that we are living on our own resources all day long. That hasn't

---

[1]*By [Arthur] Koestler. (SdB)*
[2]*[The latter two] by [Pierre] Mac Orlan. (SdB)*

prevented me from writing my novel, and rather well. This whole chapter will be good. But I'll have to rework it. On the subject of Marcelle, T.—to whom I had mentioned that you thought her character would have to be changed, asking her advice so as to seem to be treating her as a grown-up— naturally said it should be preserved intact. She offers arguments that aren't too stupid: "With that nasty little impression at the outset, how could you make her strong?—and besides, her situation doesn't lend itself to strength— and above all, if in addition to being strong and appealing, she keeps an underhanded side, which becomes disturbing, wouldn't she become practi- cally a sister to Ivich, who would stand out less?" The fact remains that Marcelle isn't too good. But I could turn her around totally, to weakness. Only then no one would understand how Mathieu could be interested in her. There's a difficulty there that I don't yet know how to address. Anyway, there is no hurry about it.

That was the day, my love. I would like to go on with my letter and tell you whatever comes to mind, because I feel so comfortable with you, little joy of the world. But what can I tell you, except that I love you with all my might, and that I feel you near me. You know, it is because of you that I formulated the theory of presences. Basically, other people are nothing to me now. But you, my little flower, you are a very warm presence, right up against me. You are my love. You are as real and as "transcendent" as though you were here.

I kiss you on your dear little eyes, little one.

Paul gave me back the Saint-Exupéry. I'm going to read the passage on "tender sufferings" thinking of you.

I set Mistler off on a very interesting inquiry, on the real fate of the Alsatian refugees. I'm noting down the results in my little notebook.

To Simone de Beauvoir

November 26

My darling Beaver

Today is a very dull and plodding Sunday with nothing going on. It's raining, no readings. Last night Paul slept at the school, so as not to catch cold, and I slept alone in the bed, under six blankets. For the first time in three months, I had an erotic dream. I was going out with a little brunette who brought to mind Gégé's sister, Kay Francis, and Jacqueline Audry all rolled into one. Impossible, you will say. But true. In a dream. But that young person's flesh was tender, so tender, so very tender. She told me she had a bruise on her haunch—I don't know why, but it was shocking, she had been beaten or knocked to the ground—and, leaning over, she lifted her skirts and showed me a derrière that was only slightly bruised but trembling, almost liquid, like apple jelly. I touched it and kissed it. After which we went off to meet you, quite jauntily—and you, meanwhile, were telling us you'd just slept with some unknown noble or other in a hotel room. Still somewhat distracted by the dream, I woke up at six and went to La Rose for breakfast, where I met Mistler, looking important and armed with a tiny notebook. In that tiny notebook he is taking down the results of a sociological inquiry I can't describe to you but which interests him very much and which I entrusted to him, as much to give him something to do as out of real curiosity. I came back here and worked, rather well all in all, first on my notebook, then on my novel. At 11:15, Pieter started fidgeting. Yesterday noon he had been bored all alone at a restaurant because I hadn't gone along for lack of money. He had offered to lend me some money but I refused. The prospects of going off alone to lunch or eating army rations here seemed equally intolerable. So in the end he timidly said, "Come on, my treat." "Absolutely not!" I said, curtly and with feigned surprise. "There's no reason for that." Fortunately for him, he remembered just in time that I'd treated him a while back: "Yes, yes, it's to return your October invitation." "OK, if that's the reason!" I got up and we went off to eat at Le Boeuf Noir, in a back room, rather unappealing stuff, as you know, but served by nice people. I gave a friendly greeting to the proprietress, but I don't know if she recognized me with my beard (forgive me, little one). After lunch we came back here through the rain, and I read *Sous la lumière froide*. It seemed odd. That era is certainly dead. The book gave the impression of historic testimony, like Sénancour's *Obermann*,[1] and because of that was difficult to read, much more like straight history than Shakespeare's plays are. At the same time I recognized all the quirks of style I'd invested so much time eliminating—overabundance of comparisons, the insertion of an ironic subordinate clause in the middle of a rather serious principal clause, the very rhythm of the sentence; I'd complete it in my head before I'd finished reading it through, it was that close to my own rhythm. And then sentences like the one I'll copy out for you, which are anonymously *of the period* and could just as readily be found in Morand, Mac Orlan, or Giraudoux: "At the end of the block a woman from the Île d'Ouessant, her

---

[1]Étienne Pivert de Sénancour (1770–1846), French author of the epistolary novel *Obermann*, which influenced the Romantics Balzac, Sand, and Matthew Arnold.

Tom Thumb umbrella tucked under her arm and her hair tossing in the wind, managed to give temporary significance to the minute particle of the world whose view belonged to my room." Nothing is missing, not even the intellectual awkwardness of the execution or the high-pitched whine of the prose. It is also like Nizan—I mean the Nizan of '22–23, in his college preparatory years; I was more melodious and woolly. And this definition of books from Mac Orlan seems to suit almost all the literature of the time: "My writing stayed lean. That way I kept to my earlier approaches and the curious physical insubstantiality of those who possess nothing."

How strange it is to see books that existed in my mind as adventure novels now freezing up and slowly turning into classics. In that book I seemed to be catching unawares a metamorphosis into the classic. Even now, you can't read much of it without being quietly brushed by memories of the dresses of that era and masses of details that are gone forever.

I got two letters from you, my sweet, and I'm so happy, they are so nice, and then you are living such a moral life, my love, I can easily laugh over it. Work, concerts, the opera. While I think of it, I suppose that Gluck imagined a still shabbier staging and execution of his operas than what you saw on Wednesday, since ultimately opera came out of tragedy. He would surely have licked his chops with satisfaction and been delectably scandalized by the *realism* of the staging and of Lubin's approach (a realism that far surpasses what he—and many others—was reproached for having introduced into that noble art). I love you so much, my dear little one, I am completely one with you, and I well understand what you say about launching ourselves toward the same future. That is certainly the way it is with you, most beloved little one. Six scribbled lines from Tania: "I've been reading and drawing all day," which seems fishy, I think there's "something new going on." But today that hardly moves me—precisely because I have your two long letters, and this locates the petty affair at the right level. But I think I told you, yesterday there were no other letters and I had to face her alone.

That's all for today, little one. Paul is well again, thank you very much. Yesterday he didn't want to read *The Spanish Testament* for fear that it would affect him, but this evening, as his temperature is down to normal, he picked it up with only slight hesitation.

I love you, my love, my little dearest, I love you passionately. Ah! I had said I wouldn't use that word anymore. In any case, you are my most dear little Beaver.

To Simone de Beauvoir

November 27

My darling Beaver

I got no letters from anybody today, neither from you, nor from T. Just a short note from my mother—including a charming detail. But I'll have to explain, it is in several stages. 1st stage: Two weeks ago she writes: "Do me this favor—find me the names of 20 needy soldiers to whom we could send packages. Your Aunt Marie Hirsch asked for them, and I undertook to furnish them." —I reply that it won't be easy, given that in the General Staff there's hardly anything but solid citizens, but anyway I would do what I could. 2nd stage: She writes to me: "Yes, basically it is a bother. Forget it." Meanwhile I had found a way, by asking Mistler to speak about it to the officers. The officers alerted the noncommissioned officers, and more than six notes had been typed out and distributed to the corps. Eventually I had 24 names and quickly sent them along. 3rd stage: Here's the reply from my mother: "I have the list. Aunt Marie will devote tomorrow afternoon to making up some cards. If you would kindly send her a note *to thank her*, she would be pleased." What do you think of that, my little Beaver?

Here there's a tornado brewing. Paul hates me. We had a quarrel this morning, but his hatred began yesterday. I hesitate to tell you the story because it is full of aerological details and basically not very funny. But since I tell you everything . . . ! Well then, every day we hand on the results of our reading to various batteries that ask for it. This takes a good hour, because the telephone lines are constantly busy. It's all right when there is a reading. But when it's raining? At first glance it would seem pointless to phone the batteries to tell them about the rain, given that they can perceive it all by themselves and thereby conclude, with no great effort, that the reading has not taken place. Fine. But Paul told us a while back with a self-important, worried air that in such cases the authorities require us to pass on at least the temperature and barometric pressure. Which supposes that we will waste an hour and tie up the lines that whole time. But Paul has so often spoken with the same worried importance about the "authorities," he has so often taken shelter behind them, that in the end we don't believe it anymore. Well then, yesterday it was raining cats and dogs, no reading. At two-thirty Paul gets worked up: we must telephone, what are you waiting for? Doubtless he could have done it all alone—but he had to stay in our room, since his injection had been just the day before. Irritated, I say to him: "Hold on. Calm down!"

And he, finicky: "Oh! But the thing is that . . ." Lieutenant Renato was there, bending over a general staff map, with his aristocratic behind toward us. Pieterkowski suddenly gets up and goes over to him: "Lieutenant, do you believe it does much good to encumber the lines to tell the batteries that it's raining?" So Lieutenant Renato finds himself in the painful situation of a man who suspects that an absurd order has been given by a certain authority and he doesn't remember which authority it was, whether it was one of his superiors or even himself. He gets out of it elegantly, saying: "Oh well . . . it's Sunday, don't bother them." And with that, he leaves the room. Pieter returns to his seat, laughing at Paul, who is basically irascible, and briefly fills me in. I shrug and simply say: "If at least he'd learn a lesson from this. But he's incorrigible." Paul goes ashen and not a word passes his lips. He sulked all evening, but I didn't notice. It was Mistler who said to me at breakfast: "Paul was really fuming all last night." Thereupon this morning another incident: Paul insists on asking the army meteorological post for the "forecasts." Those "forecasts" regularly turn out to be false, but since he is asking for them— out of vague fear of a big attack and in spite of the fact that it is absolutely not our concern—he doesn't want to agree that they are false. Last night at six o'clock, making the calls for him, I asked for them. I was told: "Heavy rain morning and afternoon, improvement toward evening." This morning the weather was fine, and clearly it hadn't rained since midnight. I point this out to Paul, who answers, evasively, "They didn't say that the rain wouldn't be intermittent." I tell him, "You're not answering in good faith, Paul. You can't speak of intermittent when the last rain is so far off that there's no more trace of water on the ground than a beard on a hen." That's when he exploded: "It's you that's dishonest. You never answer in good faith." "Then you're in real trouble," I said, "because I, who you say am in bad faith, I have a reputation around here for honesty, while everyone says that you, honest as the day is long, reek of hypocrisy." "And why is everything blamed on me, while Pieter's shameful conduct in going to beg for authorization from Lieutenant Renato is considered good?" "I don't find his conduct shameful." "I do. And anyway it's part of his character, always going begging from everyone. And on top of that, when he got his answer, as a slap in the face you turn to me with a triumphant laugh." Upon which Pieter shows up, he is brought up to date, and the argument heats up still further. What a gang-up Paul brought on himself! They went off to lunch together, and Pieter explained his personality to him. There was yet another episode after lunch that I'll spare you, which ended in embarrassment for him (in a word, he told us that regulations required asking the army corps weather unit for certain information, which later turned out to be optional). In short, he's sure to sleepwalk tonight. He actually girds himself in bad faith. He is embarrassed, being authoritarian by nature and provided with an authority he wouldn't hesitate to use, out of a liking for it and out of fear, were it not, to his misfortune, conferred on him by a social institution his principles condemn. So that's the story. He's been sulking in the corner for fifteen minutes. The whole thing, as I realize in telling it to you, is totally insane, except that it represents a mass of others, still less recountable, that constitute the basis of our relationship. That's what we've been giving each other hell for, that's what's become the butt of my moral force, etc.

This morning I wrote at great length in my notebook about stoicism and authenticity—authenticity and Gide-derived fervor—and about a slight joy that has settled on me without any cause. I've finished *Sous la lumière froide*, charmingly old-fashioned, with a complete stereotype cast of sailors, pimps, and women about whom are we constantly told, "You see, I'm talking about them without stereotyping." Classic as hell. I read some Saint-Exupéry and did indeed find lots of easygoing, pleasant remarks about his calling and the world seen through his calling. I lunched in on cheese and sausage, while Paul and Pieter lunched out, and then we did a reading and I worked a bit more. There was a big shot in the area today—an important general—and it seems we are leaving tomorrow or the day after. But we've heard that one before. I'd still like to know for sure, one way or another, because of Emma.

And that's that, my little flower, absolutely everything. I reread the 17 pages of the Mathieu-Daniel chapter and see there's still work to do. That upsets me somewhat, but I'll get back to it and patch it up. For the moment it interests me much less. The last chapter will interest me more, I think. But above all now I'm dying to write a play. If I do, you'll just take it to Toulouse and Dullin. Someday do go and see the Boxers, my little flower; they certainly deserve your visit as reward for their perseverance. I'd be much obliged.

I love you with all my might, my little heart, you are me, you are my life. Till tomorrow.

Remember to send me some books *the moment* you have some cash, as I'll soon have nothing much left: the Shakespeare is almost squeezed dry, *Sous la lumière froide* is read, as is 48, and the Saint-Exupéry begun. And *Dead Souls* tells me nothing worthwhile.

Did you notice that one of Mermoz's exploits is very similar—and even sassier—than one that Barthelmess pulls off in *Only Angels Have Wings*?

To Simone de Beauvoir

November 28

My darling Beaver

I'm still a bit bothered by that Blin business. Tania's letters are still constrained and devious. She often sees him, tells me that she's going to see him—and the next day sends me six embarrassed lines in which he goes unmentioned. Actually she has stopped telling me much about her life. For instance, she didn't breathe a word about that military type who was in Zazoulich's room. Who was it? Jacquart's lover? I've just written her a letter asking her for frank explanations, and if those explanations don't satisfy me, I'll send her packing. While I think of it, my little sweet, would you please *immediately retrieve* the manuscript of my novel you entrusted to her. Say you want to send it to the Lady. I'm not petty enough to protect myself in the event things go to pieces between us, but the thought came to me this morning all on its own: if it stays with her too long, it's lost. Don't worry, the thing generally worries me from 2 to 4, and afterward I'm completely calm, but it's the same thing over and over: it's as an aftermath of taking her *too* seriously for awhile that I'm disappointed now. Of course, I've just consummated the umpteenth breakup in my mind. But I'm slightly more sensitive to the blow here, because I'm alone and away from all entertainment.

As a slight change from all these recriminations, I want you to know that last night, after writing to you, I spent a very sentimental, very pure evening, reading Saint-Exupéry. It's not that it is so good (though it is certainly very worthy and excellent in places), but it made me feel homesick. For once I wasn't missing my real past life, you, Paris, my era, the places I've known. It was some something quite different, far more tender and submissive: I was missing Argentina, Brazil, the Sahara, the world I don't know, a whole life in which neither you nor anyone else had a place, a life I haven't had, which I might have had at the time when I was "a thousand Socrateses," as Lévy says.[1] I felt childish and alone, moved like a very young man by a glimpse of his future—and at the same time knowing that it would nevermore be my future. It was metaphysical and without jealousy—with the intense feeling of that meal he has with two young Argentines, not that it's terribly original

---

[1] Sartre applied to his period of youthful optimism, 1921–29, this description bestowed on him by Raoul Lévy for the dazzling, iconoclastic magnetism he displayed in the lycée classrooms.

or well written, but because, well, I was in the guy's skin, it was incredibly alive. And then it was an odd life without that savor of death now shared by all things, stymied by the war, a fresh new life, far beyond war and peace, because it did not exist. I believe it's the first time in ten or twelve years that I've dreamed about a life unrelated to mine. Ordinarily I'm steeped in my own and regret nothing. Anyway, I scarcely need to tell you that when I was thinking "I could have had that life," it wasn't even in the sense of the little boy in the Gide who said: "I *could* have screwed that woman yesterday, because I had a hard-on." I'm one-eyed and clumsy, and that alone keeps me from ever being an airline pilot. Rather, it was more a sort of general human reality within me that could have been so. Toward evening I went out in the dark to buy some bread, and I was tinged with melancholy, because I'd walked with you through those dark streets to your train. It all seemed so close, because I hadn't so much as laid eyes on them since you left. From time to time I lit up a closed store window with my flashlight, looking for a bakery.

When I got up this morning it was very cold, and I felt the cold *via my occupation*, under the influence of *Wind, Sand and Stars*, or rather noticing that I felt that way. I wrote in my notebook: "This time it's *my* cold, the substance of my work, a cold I'll be charged with measuring in an hour or so. It is much less painful to bear than the other sort, because I don't endure it passively. It doesn't bite, it caresses and scratches me, almost as a cat might play with me. At the same time, unlike the other sort, it isn't a little frozen pool that seeped into the bedroom through the cracks around the windows to stagnate there. It is the sign of good weather, it *is* the good weather. Into this bedroom, through closed shutters and the yellow glow of light bulbs, it has filtered in, a ray of sunlight, a dry rosy dawn. I don't need to open the windows, I'm already in good weather, and there's no longer anything ominous in this awakening of two soldiers with red eyes, they're getting up in the fields, the walls no longer count. They haven't fallen, but they can do nothing against this dimension of cold, my new medium. And the morning cold is no local adventure of mine or my comrades. For now it is charged with exotic poetry like a flight of migrating birds."

After that I lunched at La Rose while reading *Hamlet*; I had a good laugh, suddenly remembering that Gide attributed his whole character to a stay in Wittenberg and the influence of Schopenhauer. Mistler came in and gave me a mass of information for our inquiry (you know: on the sociological phenomenon represented by the evacuation of the Alsatians to Haute-Vienne, Dordogne, and Charente). Then I worked to patch up my chapter, and it rolled along as though on wheels. I lunched heroically on bread and chocolate

WITNESS TO MY LIFE

(hoping to lose weight), and then after lunch, a reading and 2 long letters from you. 2 letters from Tania. Ah, something else: I sent you the books (the Romainses and Dabit's *Journal*. Read Dabit's *Journal*, it's dreadful but makes extremely entertaining reading in 1939).

We are leaving, it's settled. Some officers came to our room to reconnoiter their new location. It gave me somewhat the impression that an old tenant wanting to move out of his apartment would get from the visit of people who want to rent it. We're not moving far: still in this sector. The annoying part for us is that *perhaps* we might stay there for only 21 days— just long enough to get activated—and then go elsewhere to rest. But nothing is less certain: here, as far as we're concerned, the periods of active service and rest have differed only on paper. So don't worry about it. *At the latest*, I'll be on leave by January 20th. I'm beginning to be terribly eager for it.

Goodbye, my little sweet, my little dearest. With all my love.

To Simone de Beauvoir

November 29

My darling Beaver

I had not one letter today, neither from you, nor from T. Just a note from Kanapa criticizing my article on the Transcendental Self. My God, but that article seems from far away and long ago! Not because it was written in peacetime, but because my view on all that has changed. Without my gaining a definitive one. Aside from that, well, it was a pleasant happy day. I slept alone last night, because Paul was on guard duty. I crept into the landlady's house like a sleepwalker going home: she'd gone to bed before I came in, and with the help of my flashlight I found the keys where she had left them hidden. And then I slept, poetically alone. I have finally acquired a total spiritual solitude here, but as for *physical* solitude—I mean being alone in a room or lost in a crowd that doesn't know me—by my careful calculations it doesn't add up to more than *one half hour* a day, counting moments of obligatory solitude, which I'd actually have to call instants of accompanied solitude. And what of La Rose? you will ask. But these days Mistler comes to join me at La Rose. He talks to me, and we converse about Heidegger. Note that these continual presences don't bother me anymore. But an unexpected fifteen minutes of solitude seems like a godsend, quite enough to make me feel altogether poetic. This morning I went to La Rose and ate three rolls, because I'd fasted last evening. But don't worry: tomorrow morning is December 1st, and I'll borrow a hundred francs from Pieter. Afterward I did excellent work all morning and wrote up my love crisis, now ended, in my notebook. The annoying thing is that it will pass through so many hands I have to disguise it a bit. Conclusion: I waver, I've told nothing but the truth, but not *the whole* truth. As for my novel, I'm putting the final touches on this chapter. I'll have worked on it a whole month, but ultimately it is the most difficult, the one with the big decisions (Mathieu's Decision— Daniel's Decision). Note that it is as difficult to have a *decision* feel like a decision in a novel as it is to have an act feel like an act. You can say all you like that X or Y has decided that . . . but it always runs the risk of seeming like a determined psychic phenomenon, tossing around in the flux of consciousness and followed by movements of the body. It runs the risk of appearing to be a *passion*. For example, Mathieu *decides* to steal from Lola. But he could just as well do it out of passionate despair because of Ivich's scorn.[1] How to give *the impression* of the difference? You too will find this difficulty when your Françoise decides to poison Xavière. Particularly since decisions are never wholly pure, and from a certain angle one can detect signs of passion. In short, I think I've just about succeeded. You'll see soon enough.

Aside from that, nothing new. At noon I enjoyed a physical semi-solitude because I had lunch with the oafish Keller. When he has an audience of one, he waxes cheery and babbles on. More than two, and he clams up out of fear of overdoing it. So he put in a few innocent words here and there, but he never requires anyone to listen or answer. So I did neither. Then I went back to work (no readings because of rain), I read a bit of Gide's *Journal*, which has just been returned to me, and here I am. We aren't leaving before Monday, but it's in earnest, many of the batteries have already gone.

The first sergeant comes in, he tells us about Russia's attack on Finland; it's very bad.

That, my little sweet, is all I can get out of an empty day. I thought very intently about you this morning as I got up. I was thinking about the cold, as I told you yesterday, and of skiing, and then I saw you again on the slopes, in your little white jacket, and tears almost came to my eyes, my dearest. When will we go skiing again?

I love you with all my might.

---

[1] In *The Age of Reason*, Lola is a cabaret singer in her forties in love with the young student Boris. Mathieu has much the same relationship with Boris's sister Ivich as Sartre was having with Tania.

To Simone de Beauvoir

November 29

My darling Beaver

Today very skimpy mail. One short letter from you and nothing else. But no matter, you will write me a full account of the evening at Le Poisson d'Or. As for Tania, I'm answering silence with silence. I feel more and more friction between us. Early in the week I was angry with her for allowing that annoying pinprick of passion to compromise the balanced calm I'd counted on maintaining throughout my monastic retreat. But since then I reflected that *first* it wasn't an unjustified dirty kick or even a minor piece of bad luck *tacked on* to the war. Instead it was one of the natural consequences of the war, to attribute to that and to live through within it and in accordance with it. It's natural to be forgotten and deceived when you are away and defenseless—while quite the contrary, it's our own mutual security, little one, that is abnormal. Once more—and this time thanks to you—I am seeing things in their true proportions. But nowadays there can be no lack of poor guys who have one woman only, one support, and who are extremely uneasy imagining the total liberty of that consciousness. So it becomes part of the general price. And then I also thought that this love crisis might actually be a direct effect of the war, like an escape valve, an unacknowledged way of wearing me down because I've been a captive too long. For ultimately this little emotional crisis is not absolutely justified: cither through the value I attribute to T. when I see her, or by the facts themselves (there's scarcely a doubt that an affair's going on at this moment, but that she's stuck like a leech to my future seems scarcely doubtable either, as you were saying so rightly). So that I blame myself severely for the whole to-do. But what can I do? The thing that doesn't jibe here is that I cannot say that these relationships are worth much more than a stupid fit of jealousy. Outside of these crises, all is sweetness and languor. The value I place on that young woman comes mainly from moments of passion. So there's never a plenitude. In a word, as you can see, all these considerations indicate rather clearly that the crisis is on the mend. I really think that it is a captive's minor impatience, aggravated perhaps by a tricky liver. It annoys me, because the whole time I'm chafing about this emptiness, I'm distracted from thinking of you, who are my plenitude and joy. Fortunately it lasts just part of the day (generally coming after the mail) and the rest of the time I can enjoy our own relationship, read peacefully, and write. While I think of it, I received the book Lévy sent me:

the German translation of *Pylon*.[1] It's the gesture that charmed me. But I'd bet it was you who gave him the idea. It's difficult, incidentally—I don't understand it all, not by a long shot. You must quickly send me some books, good little one, I'm running out. And while I'm at it, also thank my students Marcel Orion, René Saurat, and Bertrand for their kind letters. Rémy and Octave Nys sent me a card too, for the moment they are in Rouen at Mme Naquet's,[2] but I'll answer them myself. I am still reading *Wind, Sand and Stars* but finding it less entertaining. On the other hand, I am completely bowled over by *Hamlet*, which I finished this morning at La Rose. I worked very dutifully and did a complete reconstruction of the chapter I'm working on. I'll begin the other in our new vacation spot.

For the big event is our departure. In forty-eight hours for sure. I want you to know that we'll be in a village with a population of 500, rather evacuated,* to be precise we'll be living five or six hundred meters from the village in a requisitioned hotel where they have provided for *a bedroom* with a *bed* and *sheets* for each of us. I'll no longer be sleeping with the somnambulist, which delights me. We will also have a room in the hotel where we can stay during the day, with a telephone. There's no central heating, mind you, but good stoves stocked with real coal. We'll be there for seven weeks— it's the period for our "sector"—and perhaps after that we'll simply come back here, since our predecessors there are coming to settle in here. So there's the future all but settled as far as March, barring snags. Pieter is contemplating the idea of going out daily to lunch, for a small consideration, at the house of some local lady. That decision strongly appeals to me, and I'll go along with it. Thanks to which, she will undoubtedly show us great devotion. But the whole thing will take looking-into on site.

And that's all, my Beaver. This morning I stayed here again for lunch. And I had no dinner. Consequently over the past few days I must have lost some of the excess fat engirdling me. I am reading—I almost forgot to tell you—*The Spanish Testament*, which impresses me very much. To tell the truth, the prison days interest me less, precisely because *I could have* imagined it all from my armchair (as you say, *The Wall* is in the same general vein), but the part that grips me is the account of the defense of Málaga and its

---

[1] *By Faulkner. (SdB)*

[2] *The initials of these names spell the word Morsbronn, where Sartre was then located.* (SdB) After several postponed departures, the artillery division to which his unit was attached finally got there on December 5.

*But there's been no official evacuation. And a good number of inhabitants are still there.

capture. It is astonishing, and it certainly conveys the odd, lazy, heroic, cowardly, cruel, and disorderly nature of the Spanish war. It very clearly confirms what Boubou told us, but definitely not that great bombastic machine *L'Espoir*.[3]

Would you believe there are some artillery guys here who've been sent off to *Versailles* for their rest period? Those pigs—lucky bastards!

My love, if you only knew how I long to see your little face and your dear smile.

I love you.

It would surprise me if you ever get this drowsy hasty letter, which you'll have to pardon in advance. I need to write to you as much as I need to get your letters.

Return the tax sheet to its sender with a finely turned note explaining that whilst I certainly do not refuse to pay, I have been mobilized and request an extension. Or *better yet*, stop by there. That's Pieter's advice.

To Simone de Beauvoir

December 1st

My darling Beaver

I'm in the midst of entering into my notebook things involving the various ethics I have adopted since the École Normale. And there are any number of them. Once when I was writing a line or two about Olga, I said, "I put her on such a pedestal then that, for the first time in my life, I felt humble and disarmed before someone." And then, my love, I reflected that it was in regard to you, the little paragon, that I should have felt completely humble at that time, and that in any case I was very much so nowadays. Oh! my dear love, what a beautiful, precious little one you are. Truly precious. I love you so much. You know, I still see you with your little turban—or rather I don't see you but there is something warm and strong and tender which is here now—and it is you, little one. You are my *dear* love.

Listen, here are two pieces of news: one bad, which has to do with Emma, and the other good, which concerns me. Here it is: I think you'll have to gently prepare yourself not to spend your Christmas vacation with

---

[3]By André Malraux (1901–76); Paris, 1937. *Man's Hope*, trans. S. Gilbert and A. Macdonald (New York, 1938).

her. She writes me that this rather shatters her, but she'll be in some god-forsaken hole with only herself and her parents, no doubt, the railroad doesn't go there, and her mother doesn't in the least like the idea of someone visiting her in a place like that. Naturally Emma said that *she'll do her best*, but she thinks it would be better for you to wait till the 1st of February, when she'll be back in Toulouse, even if it entails taking three or four days off at that time. There, you see, it will be for certain. Whereas by asking permission right away from your/her parents, you run the risk of antagonizing them. And then again, she won't be there before the 5th or 6th, and that will give her very little time to turn around. Of course, all this remains speculative, but I know that the people around her are pessimistic—particularly those who know that backwater.

Here, on the other hand, is a good piece of news, but this time one that concerns me. Because of the war, the status of the weather guys is rather paradoxical. The young ones, in the active army, are doing their military service in posts behind the lines (Tours, Bordeaux, etc.), and the old guys like us, the reservists, are at the front, in the reading posts. So there is a projected order officially under study that would *bring back* the meteorologic reservists to the territorial units and replace them at the front with the active-duty weather groups. It will, of course, take two or three months to accomplish this. But just think, little Beaver, I'll be in Tours or in Rouen, you could come to see me whenever you want and without needing the slightest authorization, spend vacations near me, etc. Doesn't this make up for the first news? And on top of that, every two weeks I'll have 48-hour leaves. Undoubtedly more work, but I'll still have enough time left to write my facta. This plan has an *excellent chance* of being approved.

Today I got loads of letters. A charming one from young Bost, who's with Amselem and the dancer. He doesn't seem too cheery, the poor guy. A letter from an admirer. 4 pages. A certain Borne—without one thing in common, it seems, with the Borne we know. He lives in Montélimar. "Sir," he writes (speaking of *The Wall*), "I could write pages and pages about this absolutely repellent but admirable collection." Two very dutiful letters from Tania. I seem to have withdrawn somewhat from my recent delirium. Not that I've stopped thinking about the possibility of a little affair between her and Blin. But what difference can it make to me? It's obvious that it is only one thing in her life and that her life is me—less perhaps through the tenderness I inspire in her than through the intellectual and material need she has for me. And this need must of course be embellished, topped by a thousand fabled and poetic superstructures which she seems to construct more easily because I'm not there. So that affair is over. Obviously, it resulted from entirely different causes: it was the only possible outcome, I believe, available in a minor crisis of the blues for which my pride closed off all other exits. Since yesterday morning I've been in an excellent mood, which Paul craftily explains today by the fact that I went back to eat at L'Écrevisse. "It's too bad," he sighs, "our boy is such a slave to material things." I also got a letter from a student named Mergier. Uninteresting. Yesterday I worked a great deal on my novel. Today I didn't touch it, I spent the whole time writing in my notebook. In it I'm trying to define my previous moral attitudes. I'm having a very good time with it. I'll work on it some more tomorrow. Don't forget to tuck one or two little notebooks into your package of books—otherwise I'll never be able to find any, either here or there.

My love, for your students 20 francs a day may be very slightly exaggerated, but 15 francs is extremely reasonable, that would make 1,200 francs more, a handsome figure. My little flower, if ill luck has it that you can't visit Emma, nonetheless I hope you have a very nice Christmas vacation. The Lady writes that I should pressure you to go to her. Will you? Or else, will you go skiing? I've read that some ski resorts will undoubtedly be open and functioning. What are you going to do?

I'm overwhelmed because I have to answer so many people:

> Kanapa
> Dumartin
> the Lady
> Poupette
> Borne
> Mergier (a student)
> Hadjibelli

It will take me a whole day to do it.
My love, my dear love, you are my dear little flower. With all my love.

Don't forget to retrieve my manuscript from Tania.
Yes, I would like *Le Concept d'angoisse.*[1]
Don't tell Z. yet that I may be brought back to the interior. There will be time enough when it is done, and maybe even afterward, so that we'll have time to get organized. In short, *don't tell anyone* (except my mother).
My fan, Borne, asked me for my photo!

---

[1]By Søren Kierkegaard (1813–55); 1844. *The Concept of Dread,* trans. W. Lowrie (1944).

To Simone de Beauvoir

December 2

My darling Beaver

I haven't done anything good all day. I wrote in my notebook but was a bit tired from guard duty last night, and just scribbled. It's a pity, the subject was interesting: the vicissitudes of my moral theories.

No letter from you today. But doubtless it's a delay in the mails, which are extremely irregular these days. Often a day goes by without a letter from you or T. then I get two the next day, but from what you wrote me yesterday, I gather it's about the same for you. But I did have news about you through my mother. She told me she'd spoken to you about spas for rheumatics and you'd found it discouraging. Alas, my good little one, I think you'll be very discouraged on that score. But the happiness I mentioned yesterday seems to be shaping up. It would be so nice.

Today I went to take a bath at the barber's. The mother looks like a courtesan, and the son paints his eyelids blue and powders his cheeks ocher; he looks like a hustler from the Zanzi Bar. It's rather odd to see that here. After the bath I worked on my notebook, I didn't go to L'Écrevisse because I was on guard duty, and lunched with Keller on bread and chocolate. The day before, I'd eaten a bit of the macaroni he'd gone to fetch from the kitchen, and that saddened him for 24 hours: "He takes me for his servant," he'd said to Paul. "I've never been anyone's servant." I had taken a quarter portion and he had treated himself to 3¾ portions. So today I ate my bread and my chocolate with great ceremony. On hearing about it, Mistler hurried in with a half a log of goat cheese and gave it to me. He spoils me. This morning, as I was on guard duty and couldn't go to La Rose, he brought me back two rolls he'd buttered himself. Here's a story Keller told about himself, it's him to a T: "At the Fort de Saint-Cyr," he said, "they gave me an injection against typhoid and handed me 3 quinine tablets in case it gave me a fever. The shot didn't do a thing to me and I didn't get a fever, but I downed the 3 tablets anyway so they wouldn't go to waste."

This afternoon only a little weather reading, because the ceiling was so low. I wasted an hour phoning it in. Then I worked some more. My notebook. That's when things weren't working at all. And now I'm writing to you. I put some little tributes to you in the notebook. My love, send the books soon and retrieve my manuscript from Tania. No one can accuse me of underhandedness there, because I'm on the best of terms with her: the

delirium is over. But I'll breathe easy only when you've repossessed the novel.
I send you all my love, my little flower.

This is a wretched little letter, but I'm dropping from weariness, and I still have two to write. I love you very much, my little sweet.

To Simone de Beauvoir

December 3

My darling Beaver

How tender your little letters are. They stir my heart. I read them a first time on arrival around two o'clock, and then I reread them in the evening before writing. But oh my, how badly you scrawl, little one. It's nearly illegible. That isn't a reproach, since I can decipher you, but I wonder if it's due to fatigue, nervous tension, or quite simply because—having a notebook, novel, letters to write every day—you have acquired the habit of doing short-hand. Here, for example, is the way you write "impression": imp〰︎. Just try to figure that one out. I must be reading you with the eyes of love, for I never make a mistake. Yet to try me even further, you misplace letters within words. Here is how you write "crains" [fear]: 〰︎. It doesn't matter, I read all of it. And today it was two letters, two long and tender letters. My love, how much and how well you love me. But you know I return it. You too are my whole life; you are a perfection. I'm happy you're growing very fond of Sorokine, that gives you a little companion, and she seems so charming, according to your letters. But take care of yourself, wretched little one. What is this great swollen bubo? You seem very tired in your last three letters. Thanks so much for sending me some books. Nothing has come yet. I can't remember any of my list, it will give me a real surprise. About five days ago I sent the Romains and the Dabit. If nothing has arrived, complain. To finish up answering you, I want you to know I'm disgusted with my stepfather. Because he doesn't know how to behave, to the point of constantly making scenes with my mother these days, whereas the poor woman—mistakenly, of course—is worrying about me. I'd like to haul off and smack him one. It's made me sad. And then it's the same thing over and over; you write me that it won't be much fun on my leave, and I immediately begin to rebel within, thinking, don't let's see him get going on that one, etc. But right after that I reflect that if I bawl him out it's my mother who'll pay. So he'll do as he likes, naturally, and I'll be "very nice," just as she wants me to. But you'll admit that for a guy who has just spent five months under military authority, it's not a dazzling atmosphere for a leave. In two weeks you should tell my mother, quietly and as though it were nothing, that I'll sleep "in town," and will come to them at noon, so she doesn't have any false hopes. I'll try to take her out one day, all the same. It will be the three of us together, it will be gently boring, but I pity her deeply, poor woman. She didn't deserve this. You know, Paul has many of my stepfather's traits: physicist's temperament, pessimism, underhandedness, bitterness. And I think I make him pay a bit, for my stifled bitterness against my stepfather—I don't remember when I realized that. My love, I'm so sad that there's so little hope you'll get to see Emma, I don't like to think of the letter I'll get from you in response to mine of the day before yesterday. But you know that within two months you will see her—right after my leave. In general, I suppose that we have to differentiate between the times when her work absorbs her and those when she is almost on a little vacation. In the second she is accessible—in the first, no. But what do you say to the good news I gave you? In any case, if it doesn't work out, go off and get in some skiing, my little sweet. But be careful, don't leave the side of the good Colette Audry, I couldn't go on.

We are leaving Tuesday morning around 7 o'clock, and we'll reach our new abode at 9 o'clock. Paul went to size up the place with the lieutenant; it seems it isn't too bad. There are three cafés and a restaurant *which can do as a hotel.* We will have a small living room surrounded by three bedrooms, one with 2 beds and 2 with 1 bed. It will be quiet. We'll have a stove, the telephone, and a private entrance. No doubt a bit more work: 3 readings a day. But you know, that's still nothing. I think that I will work well. We'll be there only about seven weeks. After that, our rest period.

Today is Sunday, but I hadn't noticed that at all. In an aquarium fish forget about the tides. I had lunch at La Rose and talked about Heidegger with Mistler, then I went to the school, to write some twelve pages or so in my notebook about Gide's *Journal.* On rereading it I was struck, in fact, by the religious and quasi-sacred character of this journal, and I saw that he had a nature all his own, worlds away from the journals of Stendhal or the Goncourts. The model is the old family register, where they copy down the dates of marriages, of births and deaths in the family, a few maxims and certain memorable events. The rest is icing. Later I went to lunch at Le Lion d'Or, again with Mistler, and there, timid and blushing, Mistler said, "Since I've known you I'm a different man. I had gone off to war despondent, thinking, that's two years or more down the drain, and I'll come back ruined—and you explained that it was *my* war, you made me feel it, and it's amazing how much I've changed, now that it interests me and I understand that it's part of my life." My nose twitches as I tell you this, but right then and there I blushed too and, though flattered, I had the odd feeling—as I often do in such cases—that those thanks were addressed not to me, but to some character I was pretending to be, that I was some wretched joker playing his role. Yet at the same time I thought it was a beautiful test for my new morality if my example and a few conversations alone could totally restore serenity to a forty-year-old man of goodwill. You will admit that's a very different thing from inspiring enthusiasm in a few adolescents. Suddenly, on my return, I *saw* that morality, which I have been practicing for three months now without ever working it out theoretically—in direct contradiction to habit. I haven't yet written it down, but you can guess it, and, to make it a bit more explicit, here is what I wrote in my journal: "I see how metaphysics and values relate, humanism and contempt, our absolute liberty and our condition in a life unique but bounded by death, our inconsistency as creatures without a God and yet not our own makers, and our dignity, our autonomy as individuals and our historicity." Everything revolves naturally around ideas of liberty, life, and authenticity. Tell me whether, from the first little notebook and our conversations, you can get an inkling of what I mean. And incidentally, within a week or so, when I'll have it all down lucidly, I'll copy it out for you, because it is extremely important and I'm sure you'd be eager to discuss it. But I think we are on the right track.

Incidentally, after those few days of depression, I'm back to a more serene version of the tension I felt during the early days of the war, which this lotus-eating atmosphere had gradually made me forget. In short, I am happy and busy.

I bought two handsome little notebooks with green edges. They are ruled for larger handwriting, so my eyes will be less strained, because in the long run it is those fly tracks in my notebook that are ruining my eyes.

My love, I'll stop here. I won't write to T., since she is in Laigle. Did you know that she had used up all her money in eight days and had to borrow from Jacquart. That's what kept her glued to her, though she loathes her. The moment she got her November allowance, T. threw it all in her face and is making a dignified exit toward Laigle now. There are always such shabby tales involving spinelessness and money. But she writes me charming notes professing love, and I feel comfortable with her, though keeping her at the proper level.

You, my little absolute, my swollen blossom. Take good care of yourself.

On second thought, in your place I would try to see Emma anyway. I mean, you can still ask her mother. That way you'll know for sure.

Have you had my students over, as I asked you to the day before yesterday?

I got an oddly embarrassed letter from Hirsch (NRF), asking me to kindly agree to a cut in my royalties on *L'Imaginaire*, from 10% to 7%, as an exception. And announcing the publication of the book for mid-January.

To Simone de Beauvoir

December 4

My darling Beaver

We are leaving. Tomorrow morning at 4 we will load our baggage onto trucks and after a bit we're off. We'll doubtless arrive around nine or ten o'clock. This whole day has been chaos, bundles piled one atop the other, first done up carefully, then undone. Nervousness, arguments. Yet we're only going 20 kilometers away. And, as Mistler says, they've known it for a month now, no one could complain of being taken by surprise. But it reminded me of my grandparents' departures for July vacations: you couldn't really say that they'd been taken by surprise either. But they would get worked up, and twenty-four hours ahead of time, the family would be caught up in the fever of departure. That same familial fever has reigned here since this morning, for more and more relationships within the artillery must be explained through *family* rather than *camaraderie* or team spirit. I must add that the acolytes have been among the least nervous, though Paul was determined to buy canned goods out of fear of dying of hunger there. We explained to him at length that the army would still have to provide for the men's alimentary needs, that the village where we're going possessed three restaurants, and that what's more we possessed enough cans to go into business, but he would have none of it. Then Pieter said gently, "Well, we'll see," and he calmed down. I worked anyway in the midst of a hellish racket, and I let them do up the packages. About that, I have to admit that they are angelic: Paul never wants to leave anything for others to do, out of impatience and panic; as for Pieter, he always tells me, "Well, what can I say, I've got nothing to do. Let me do the packing, it'll help pass the time." So for the umpteenth time I went back to the end of chapter XVII, it's almost finished, and I'm in a hurry to be done with it. I think that over there I'll begin the XVIIIth and last, which ought to be more fun. After that I'll go back to this one. In any case, the novel will be finished by the time I come home on leave. I lunched at Le Lion d'Or, alone at first and thinking over my morality, and then with the acolytes afterward, then roll call and mail when we got back. There was a long letter from you and a package of books. Thank you, my little sweet. I am absolutely delighted to be rereading *L'Education sentimentale*[1] and the Mérimée. This will last a good long time. On top of all that, I found *Jacques le Fataliste*[2] at the tobacco shop for 100 cents. It's a real classic. It doesn't surprise me at all that Morand is unreadable, but I'd like to know why. Because after all he was popular in 1925—even met with enthusiasm. Buy the books secondhand if possible. Also received the mail order. I think that I'll ask you for another 200 francs near the end of the month (the 15th or 16th). Will that be OK? Also received a tenderly contrite letter from Tania. She says she's been through lean confusing times, had felt a need for a *person*, had seen Blin only in the same way she saw Mouloudji, out of liking for his physical being and some lunar attraction between them, that it was "magical," that she loves me alone and wants an affair only with me. And I can well understand the kind of state she's in, a mixture of despair, of listlessness, of boredom, the taste for something new, with the sleazy business of borrowing from Jacquart and that final decision to leave for Laigle, motivated, or so she says, by her lack of money (after returning everything to Jacquart, there was nothing left). But it must also come from the same need to break free that Zazoulich sometimes felt in her bad Paris days. What surprises me is that in today's letter you spoke of going out with the 2 Z's next Friday. That's the very day, so you wrote me, that Tania left. So they didn't fill you in either out of indifference or because there's still something fishy behind it and Olga, scalded by that business in July, doesn't want to be drawn into it again. After all, they'll certainly have to tell you about her leaving. But that's enough about T. I don't want you to think that she is on my mind now as much as this letter would indicate. I'm telling you all this by way of winding up the business. Through your letters and hers, I am reconstructing her life in Paris.

---

[1]Gustave Flaubert's *Sentimental Education* (1869). In 1953 Sartre began writing his unfinished multivolume study of Flaubert, *L'Idiot de la famille* (*The Family Idiot*), published in 1971.

[2]A mock-picaresque novel by Denis Diderot (1713–84), editor of the vast *Encyclopédie*, playwright, and critic, in many ways the enlightenment intellectual par excellence.

I'm still delighted with my ethics, which is duly somber and deeply felt. Since September I've been quietly slipping that way: the war, *The Spanish Testament*, *Wind, Sand and Stars*, *Verdun* all inclined me toward it. It's particularly the collapse of stoicism that brought me there; right now I consider it a "morality of complaisance." We've come a long way, my dear little one, since the time when we were rationalists, Cartesians and anti-existential. And here we are. I feel a bit sad about leaving this town,[3] where I have memories of you; again today the other has been first to leave me.[4] This schoolroom, which had become a little "home," stands there ice-cold, all our things that were lying all over the place are in boxes now, and the boxes are piled on top of each other, dutifully waiting in a corner. But on the other hand a change is fun. There's a lot to be said in favor of our new place. And it is poetic; from our windows, it seems, we can see two little blue heights twenty kilometers away, German hills. In fact, every day we must give the Army Corps information on their health: "They're a bit hazy today," "Bluer than usual," etc.

Till tomorrow, my love. I would really like to read one of your books, but they are piled in Pieter's box. I'm going to write to T., to my parents. But what are you going to do with that strange Sorokine in the clutter of your little life?

With all my love

To Simone de Beauvoir

December 5th

My darling Beaver

I'm totally exhausted. Up at 4 in the morning, in the truck till 7, I manned the phone from 7 on. Maybe you know what it's like: there's this board with holes and pegs hanging from green cords. It rings and a little flap above a hole drops down. You have to insert the peg into the hole: "Who are you calling?" "So-and-so." You pull out, with great dexterity, the peg you'd inserted in the 1st hole and put it in so-and-so's hole, if I may put it that way, then you take the peg hanging under so-and-so's hole and plug it in the caller's hole. "Go ahead please, you are connected to so-and-so."

---

[3] *Brumath. (SdB)*
[4] In the French, the feminine pronoun *elle*—"she"—refers to the town, which seems to be deserting him, while also evoking his feelings just stated for Tania, a gender trope only half conveyed in the English through substitution of "the other."

That's no problem, but when you have six calls at a time coming in, you don't know where to turn. There are 200 calls in a day. It's 19:00 right now, and I haven't stopped once in twelve hours—and I still have the night to get through, on a day bed beside this infernal apparatus. But I haven't, God be praised, committed overly gross foul-ups. In rare moments of respite, the officers would come in to mess around with the object and, out of pure wonder, insert random pegs in the odd holes, which would then begin to ring. Or else the clerks would come in to have the thing explained. Of course, I wasn't able to get in a lick of reading or writing or really get anything done, and now that I have a bit more time to myself, my three acolytes are visiting, romping around sticking their noses into everything. This little game is going to last till tomorrow noon. And it'll start up again once a week for forty-eight hours. But I suppose we'll get set up a bit better. In any case, the four other days we won't have much more to do than before, and I'll still be able to work. I'm actually not overwhelmed, rather more amused by this new occupation, but worn out and with a splitting headache. Excuse me for not writing a longer letter. Tomorrow I'll send you a long one with details of the trip and description of the area. —My poor darling Beaver, I'm really afraid you'll be badly disappointed. Today they gave me two fat letters from you, one is Saturday's, the other Sunday's, and my heart fell because you explained how happy it made you to think you would see Emma again, and how that sustained you. Incidentally, she has written to say there's little she can do, but she'll do her best.

I was highly entertained by your stories about Minder,[1] Wahl,[2] and Toulouse. Like you, I was impressed by Minder's intellectual charm. As for Wahl's idea, it is absolutely unrealizable: theses must absolutely be unpublished material, and the first hundred pages of *L'Imaginaire* have already appeared in *La Revue de Méta*. Between two phone calls I laughed to myself, just thinking of you in the Métro with Wahl.

In the teachers' room at Camille Sée, get hold of the 15 August 39 issue of *La Revue des Deux Mondes* and read an article signed XXX called "The Peace-War." It's extremely intelligent, and based on it, anyone can clearly understand what our war is, the war-peace. Read it, I urge you.[3]

---

[1] *A specialist in German who had just married Colette Audry. (SdB)*

[2] Jean Wahl, a Sorbonne professor very impressed by Sartre's upcoming publication, *Imagination*, suggested that he submit it, unchanged, to the Sorbonne as a thesis, which would qualify him for teaching there.

[3] In Sartre's précis of the article (*The War Diaries*, trans. Quintin Hoare [New York, 1983], pp. 96–99), a state of "war-peace" evolves from the specter of total war along the dense European frontiers. Instead, the author advocates a political war of intervention in the internal politics of the aggressor nation or an economic war of sanctions to undercut its war capabilities.

My love, never have you explained to me so well just how you love me. Never have I felt it so strongly and never have I been so bowled over. Yet today I felt slightly blue till 2 o'clock—and I didn't expect any mail, because of the forwarding of our mail. And then your two letters arrived and from then on everything was better, I felt completely serene and blissful. I love you.

Count on a beautiful long letter, full of details, for tomorrow. I whole-heartedly approve your budget, and I don't even understand why you are concerned about having twenty silly francs more than the Z's. Actually I feel that 50 francs a day aren't much to live on, my little flower.

To Simone de Beauvoir

December 6

My darling Beaver

To you, I'm going to write a long letter, but to the others I'll say I've been at the telephone again all day and I'm in a daze. It's not true, I slept very well, and I only worked the phone till noon. After lunch I stayed with Mistler, today's operator, because I wanted to keep warm beside the only stove in the place, and theoretically to instruct him. I read Flaubert's *Sentimental Education*, taking notes on his style, which is *execrable*. What do you think of this sentence: "It descended to the depths of his temperament and almost became a general way of feeling, a new mode of existing"? Yet that's writing from a guy with the reputation of an able stylist. It's actually stupid enough to make you weep. But interesting, despite him, somehow. After that I had to update my journal, which needed it, then evening tiptoed in and I'm writing to you.

My little dearest, I'm pleased you aren't too disappointed at the idea of not seeing Emma. Your letter was so calm. I trembled some as I opened it. I was scared you might say, "All my happiness has been shattered." But not so. Oh my wise little one, my little flower, my love. So I'll have nothing but happiness through you.

Well then, yesterday I left at six o'clock, after getting up at four and loading boxes onto the trucks till six. In the breaks, I perched my butt on the edge of a school bench and copied out passages from that remarkable article by XXX, which gave me a complete understanding about the reasons and ways of being of this war. It's too long to describe, but do read it. After which, we poured into a bus. I was beside Mistler. Dawn was rising across a flat and graceless countryside. I explained to him what the war is, from my newfound knowledge, and it was a real revelation: "Aren't you pleased," I said to him, "you lowly second-class shit, to know what even important folk in Paris don't know?" "Ha!" he said, delirious with joy. "My memory of you will be forever linked to my image of this war." We unloaded at 7 in front of a rather shabby hotel across from a German-style gray-to-black public bath, with light green shutters. Hotel and baths stand on a rise about 700 meters from the village. We went into the hotel; they immediately shoved me and Mistler at the telephone while "the relief" proceeded, meaning the replacement of the officers of the old division with ours. It was haunting, because we could somehow see our own *image* from the outside: a division set up exactly like ours, with a lieutenant symmetrical to one of our lieutenants; a colonel symmetrical to our colonel, even right down to my own symmetrical other, the weather readers, a big, red-faced Fatty Arbuckle with glasses and a precious look on his bon-vivant flesh, another thin and pale, with a rim of a beard. We gazed at the image of ourselves with hostility and curiosity, with a vague feeling of solidarity with *our* officers against *their* officers. The room has felt very inhuman and transitory throughout the day, we were ill at ease, and then I had that ringing malevolent beast on my hands. Then today everything generally fell into place. And I find a poetic feeling to this place that the other lacked and that you would not even suspect, oh you, who know the war better than other Parisians. First of all, our hotel is much more like a wartime HQ than our peaceful school was. All the services are together here. The soldiers and the officers all stay in the hotel, the officers eat their lunch in a small dining room on a round table covered with oilcloth. Almost all day it bears their cutlery, with napkin rings on which they've scratched their initials with a knife. It's a beehive, this hotel, all day long buzzing with the military. It bears all the characteristics of both peace and war. From the outside it's still a hotel. A second-class hotel (it seems that only people of modest means come here, social security pensioners, etc.). But the moment you walk in you get the whiff of neglect and decay so characteristic of evacuated houses. The bedrooms smell more like mushrooms. They're full to bursting with military stuff, packs, overcoats, musette bags, etc. And yet there's a stale smell of civilian miseries wafting about, too. Under their heavy red comforters the mattresses are thick and the box springs exquisite, just right for rheumatics. The dirty, torn wallpaper, with its flowers, is more civilian, more individualized than the enamel of the school walls, so amenable to military socialism. The bedrooms evoke—if untruthfully—the wretched, seedy rooms in the workers' hotels along the Canal de la Villette, you remember, my little flower? The clerks' room, with the telephone, has really become a very special, unique object, where these various layers of signification intermingle. It is a rectangular, extremely dirty room opening onto the main road, which it overlooks from above through a long bay window. The wooden ceiling, with its exposed beams, once painted white but now a dirty gray, slants down steeply from the back wall to the bay. At night they black out the window with blankets and rugs, creating an impression of oriental luxury: tent, animal skins, etc. Against the wall they've pushed a sideboard, a mirrored-front oak cupboard (which our predecessors riddled with nails), and a small, low Boulle-style chest of drawers, with a marble top. That's the flea-market side, reinforced by 2 still-lifes in a style you can just imagine—and also, on the first day, by a heap of flotsam, mattresses, chairs, armchairs, etc. left by our predecessors, which we've since cleared out. But as I mentioned, it is a former dining room for rheumatic pensioners. Whence the presence of ads on the walls: Suze, Mandarin, Cithia, Dubonnet, Pernod fils, Carola table water, Dolfi. In a gilt frame on white paper, under glass: "Lanson père et fils, Reims." But below it, on a slate hung from a nail, a chalk inscription: "Guard duty: Mistler—Orderly: Hantziger." In the middle of the room, a German stove from Nuremberg. Against the bay window, seven rectangular tables with typewriters, file cabinets, folders: the General Staff. But right beside that, there's a small round table covered with a red-and-white cloth, which, together with the nearby officers' dining room, suggests the sweet pleasures of alimentation. And on that table, a large vase with tacky artificial irises. On the wall near the door, a coatrack. Gas masks, khaki overcoats hang from the hooks. The five newspaper-shaded lamps bathe the scene in filtered domestic light. You see the layers of signification: Tartar camp, pensioners' restaurant, family dining room, flea market, General Staff HQ, war. The whole thing melded. And then in the middle of all that, malevolent, surrealistic objects: the phone with its wires dangling sadly from the ceiling like stiff hair, matted with filth, and then in the middle of the ceiling, right above the stove, a ventilator that starts up pitilessly each time you want to turn the lights on or off. The whole thing is appealing, and, though I can't really work there, I do like to be in the room.

A bit farther on there's another hotel for rheumatics similarly occupied by the military, and still farther, a café-restaurant, perched high up—you enter up a flight of steps—where I breakfasted this morning awash in humanism and surrounded by soldiers who are sleeping all around the place in barns or nondescript shelters and will move up to the lines tomorrow. I know nothing about the village, I drove through it yesterday morning in the bus.

It was actually charming—the soldiers were asking one another in the bus, "You're going to the Hôtel Bellevue?" "No, I'm at the Hôtel Beausite." "Oh, then I'd better pack my things," like vacationers busing from the train to the beach resort and getting ready to have the bus stop in front of their hotel.

Goodbye, my love. It's a quarter to ten, in the dining room there is a piano, and I'm going to play it for a moment so the clerks can dance.

Till tomorrow, little flower. With all my love,

To Simone de Beauvoir

December 7th

My darling Beaver

So now life is settling down in this Hôtel Bellevue. An odd hotel, completely isolated, right beside the main road. Military socialism thus far— in the town halls, the schoolrooms, all the public offices where they parked us—had a touch of Prussian state socialism—of the anthill variety, where individuality disappeared or took refuge in our thoughts and dreams. Here it is more idyllic, Fourieriest. It is really the story of a handful of men (who loathe each other, actually) who share a *destiny*. It is beginning to smell bittersweet, the gossip and backbiting, but it is awfully poetic. Just one nuisance, the cold. And not here, in this beautiful warm clerks' room I described yesterday, but at our weather unit, a constricted annex where we naturally have to stay put from time to time. But Pieter made a fuss, and they'll probably give us a stove. This whole household lives on its own resources, we hardly go out except to get our food or take a walk to the café, near the station. I haven't yet set foot in the village. Pieter says it's "tripe." He had dizzy spells, the little angel, went to the medical officer this morning, who gently booted him out. This morning he was well again and very happy. But do we ever have work: three readings a day, to do and then phone in, observations, telephone duty one day out of four, rooms to sweep and fire to lay one day a week. I haven't gotten back to my novel. I'm waiting till we get a stove. It would be pretty rude to bring my papers here and quietly write while the clerks are busy at the typewriters. I am writing in my journal. This afternoon I began to lay out my ethics. It holds up. I'll copy it out for you tomorrow or the next day, to get your opinion. I can't read any more of *Sentimental Education*, it's too stupid, and besides I loathe the great delicacy of that era—

it smacks of the gallantry of the bearded gentleman, conscious of his good breeding, the pudgy white fingers. And then, beyond all that, it's devilishly dull. And badly written. I'm going to turn to Marivaux.[1]

I received no letter from you today. But that doesn't surprise me, I had two yesterday. I was almost sure that would happen today.

The thing I've conveyed to you badly is that there's been something tiresome about these last few days. Tiresome but not unpleasant: between readings we come in here to warm up, talk a bit, pause a moment, undecided, around the stove, smiling vaguely, without thinking of a thing. And then I settle down, write four lines, read ten, and something distracts me and I let myself be distracted. It's some sort of odd bliss. Tonight, for instance, there are five or six of us in this large silent room, the officers are eating in the next one, we hear the sounds of their knives and forks on the plates, and then from time to time a little burst of the radio. And I'm writing to you while anticipating with pleasure a warm night under the covers and a pleasant day tomorrow, deep in dry winter nature, in alternating cold and warmth, with the sort of giddiness imparted by this uninspired, crowded hotel, something like the giddiness given off by Tania's soul. Here's a simple thing that's enough to charm me: while I write, an orderly sat down on the other side of the table, it's the guy who was snoring, whom I woke up by whistling, who then accused me of whistling in my sleep. He's a fat wheezer. He says nothing, breathes loudly and watches me with leaden eyes. It's nothing, but it gives me vertigo because I'm sure there's absolutely nothing in that head but my face seen from above looking down, foreshortened.

The staff sergeant returned *The Castle*. I'll send it to you very soon. Give me news of Bost as soon as you have some.

All my love, my little sweet.

To Simone de Beauvoir

December 8

My darling Beaver

I'm writing to you in a warm and cozy spot, from the clerks' room, while the officers are dining. Billows of radio waft out of their dining room. It's classical music, not bad, and I'm rather pleased to be hearing it, even

---

[1]Pierre Marivaux (1688–1763), playwright and novelist.

though it is distorted by the door and Captain Orcel, who likes to laugh, is accompanying it with his "pom-pom-pom-poms." You take what you can get. My sweet little Beaver, we might well go to a concert, the two of us, when I'm home on leave. Mistler seemed to want to give me his turn for leave because his girlfriend won't be in Paris except at the end of January. That would put me in Paris around the 3rd or 4th, but he hasn't spoken of it since. I'll mention the matter to him.

My love, after beating your brains to figure out what rheumatics I was alluding to, you frightened me by suddenly saying, "I've got it!" Heavens, what on earth could you have understood, after all that brain work? I was simply talking about authentic bathhouses for rheumatics.

Emma writes me that she'll do her level best. But what can she do? She's isolated from the village and knows nobody. She does have someone in mind. But you would do just as well to find a way on your own. (The officers have just come out, they've left the dining room door open, the classical music is pouring out in pleasant billows, a slight cold draft is pouring out along with the music, but we accept the latter in consideration of the former.)

Aside from that, it's still the cramped life of the phalanstery. Of a phalanastery nearing its end, when the experiment has failed, and they don't yet want to admit it completely, but people are hating each other in every nook and cranny. Here there are solid warmed-over hatreds and cabals. A revolt was stirring today because they wanted to assign a clerk or a meteorologist to clean the offices and light the fires every morning. Pieter protested vehemently to a lieutenant and had them agree to assign the orderlies "on principle," so he said. But the orderlies aren't pleased at all. On principle, of course. Again the whole thing is a matter of human dignity. I, who am without dignity, win out, for I'll be able to go to an isolated little café every morning from 7 o'clock to 8:30 to eat buttered bread and drink a cup of coffee while I read. You cannot imagine a more insubstantial and more lowly form of humanity than the clerks whose lives I share. Nippert is a Protestant accountant, the Puritan sort, his great civilian pastimes are *Bibelforschingen*, Protestant gatherings centering on a pastor, in which they comment on the Bible while drinking tea. He is a small redheaded bull terrier, youthful, almost bald, with thick tortoiseshell glasses. Hantziger seems like something out of the movies, a visionary dreamer, but he's beginning to get on my nerves. Courcy, whom I very mistakenly likened to Nizan, is also an accountant or office worker somewhere in Neuilly. The main occupation of all of the above is to pillory the fat staff sergeant, Thibaud, behind his back and while brown-nosing him to his face, so to speak. But the particularly striking thing is the extreme insubstantiality of their recriminations and their toadying. Really they scarcely exist. They are even protected from an esprit de corps by their insubstantiality. They are not there. As for me, fat Staff Sergeant Thibaud has been running after me since yesterday because I got two votes for the Théophraste-Renaudot literary prize (it's getting to be like a hex). I gave him a tongue-lashing today, but he just came back, all sweetness, as I was about to leave: "I was hoping for a bit of piano," he told me in confidence (because I play the piano a little in the evening in the officers' dining room), "but I think those gentlemen are in no hurry to leave." He wants to drive me to Paris in a car, because he is going off on leave the same day as me, but my guess is that we'll have been on bad terms for a long time by then. He also wants to introduce me to a M. Gateau-Gaillard, or something like that, a scholarly sort who's writing an amiable research work on the "Ghosts of Trouville" and who happens to be his landlord. On the other hand, I almost never see the weather unit and the first sergeant, my former fellow students in the schoolroom. They are swallowed up in the group. Rather more so the officers. We can see them living, we hear them living more. We still have no stove, and all of this is not a normal life. (I'm not writing my novel, and I loiter around here all day—still happy.) We'll have one tomorrow, and it will be giving off heat no doubt by the day after. Today a big event: Keller is going off on leave. They came to tell him tonight. It will take him twenty-six hours to get to Paris. It will seem to you that this in no way concerns us, and yet it does: he is the first of us to really go, it makes things palpable now. Incidentally, and in a less magic fashion, he is the 31st on the list, so there are still 90 before me, or 45 days dating from the 9th. I'll be in Paris on January 23rd, barring the unexpected (among others, the possibility of Mistler giving me his turn).

I am still writing on morality, and I think I'll copy it all out for you tomorrow. It is abstract but true to life.

My love, today I got your two delightful letters; how much I love you, how happy I am to be seeing you again soon. Can you imagine that I'm completely absorbed by the atmosphere here and by my work on morality, and that nothing counts more than you, aside from here. You, just you, are what matters when nothing else does. I am interested, *along with you*, in this hotel and this atmosphere.

Today, on my way back from a little café at the bottom of the hill, I heard the sound of cannon to my right—deep, heavy explosions. It seemed a peaceful, ordinary sound, a sort of administrative necessity; I imagined the land plowed up by the explosion, but because of the nature of this war, I could not imagine that men had died.

Till tomorrow, I love you, my little flower.

To Simone de Beauvoir

December 9

My darling Beaver

Today has been quite uneventful. Too much so—I haven't received my daily note from you. But yesterday I got two and doubtless there'll be two more tomorrow. I picked up the packages you thoughtfully sent me, my little flower. I read some Marivaux, then other duties claimed me, such as doing readings and carrying a stove upstairs, piece by piece, to our common room, between which I finished my writing on morality. I'll copy it out for you here. It's very long. If I can't finish it now, I'll continue tomorrow. But I'm really eager to discuss it with you.

First question: morality is the system of ends; therefore, toward what end must human reality act? The only answer: to its own end. No other end for human reality can be proposed. Let us first establish that an end cannot be proposed except by a human being, who is his own possibilities, which is to say, he pro-jects himself toward these possibilities in the future. For an end can be neither altogether transcendent to the one who advances it as an end nor altogether immanent. If transcendent, it would not be *his* possibility. If immanent, it would be dreamed but not willed. So the linkage between the agent and the end presupposes a certain bond of a being-in-the-world variety—that is, a human existence. The moral problem is specifically human. It presupposes a limited will—it has no meaning outside of that, involving either animals or the divine spirit. But in addition, an end has a very specific existential type: it could not be a given existent, or, by that very fact, it would cease to be an end. But neither can it be a pure virtuality, in the sense of a simple transcendent possibility, or it would lose its attracting power. It has a plenary and affective existence, but one that is yet to come, which returns from the future back onto human reality by demanding to be realized by it in a present. From this fact an eternal and transcendent existence, like God or divine will, could not be an end for the human will. On the contrary, human reality can and must be the end for itself because it is always on the side of the future, it is its own reprieve.

But, in addition, human reality is itself bounded on all sides by itself, and whatever the end it sets itself, that end is always itself. One cannot grasp the world except through a technology, a culture, a condition; and in turn the world so apprehended reveals itself as human and refers back to human reality. I wrote in *Nausea*: "Existence is a plenum that man cannot leave." I do not retract what I said, but it should be added that the plenum is human. The human is an existential plenum that human reality discovers again and again as far as the eye can see. Man rediscovers his own project everywhere, and he finds nothing but his project. On this subject, the strongest thing one can can say for a morality without God is that human reality is moral to the very extent that it is without God, and a morality is moral only when it is for man and intended for human reality, even Christ's morality. But this doesn't mean that the morality must be *either* an individualism in which the individual considers himself an end *or* a social utilitarianism *or* an extended humanitarianism in the sense that men, as individual particles of humanity, would be an end for all men. It simply means that human reality is of a particular existential type, as constituted by its existence in the form of value to be realized through its freedom. This is what Heidegger expresses when he says that man is a being of distances. But let it be clearly understood that this being-value which constitutes us, taken as the value of our horizons, is neither you nor I nor all men nor a *fully developed* human essence (in the sense of Aristotelian eudaemonism), instead it is the ever-moving reprieve of human reality itself (at the same time and completely indifferently, it is me, you, all of us). Human reality exists expressly for the purpose of itself. And it is this *self*, with its specific type of existence (as that which is waiting for it in the future to be realized through its freedom), that is *value*. But let us agree that human reality is *constituted* by the relationship to self in the future. Therefore human reality is neither a fact nor a value, it is the relationship of a fact to a value, a fact that is explained by a value. There is no other value than human reality for human reality. And the world is what separates human reality from its express intention. No world, no value. Man sometimes believes he would be *more* moral if he were relieved of the human condition, if he were God, if he were an angel. He does not realize that morality and its problems would vanish with his humanity. From this it follows that to determine the strictures of this morality, there is no other way than through discovering the nature of human reality. We must be careful here not to fall into the error of disclaiming the value of the fact, for human reality is a fact as much as a value.

The characteristic aspect of human reality that concerns us here is that it is self-motivated without being its own foundation. What we call its freedom is that it never is anything without motivating itself to be so. Nothing can ever happen to it *from the outside*. This is because human reality is consciousness first and foremost, or, to put it another way, whatever it is, it is also consciousness of being so. Human reality motivates its own reaction to the event within that reality, and that reaction is the event, and it becomes aware of the event only through the reaction. So human reality is free in the sense that its reactions and the way it sees the world are totally attributable to it. But total freedom can exist only for a being who is his own foundation, by which I mean responsible for his own facticity. Facticity means nothing but the fact that in the world at every moment there is human reality. It is a *fact*. As such it derives from nothing and is reducible to nothing. And everything—the world of values, necessity and freedom—depends on that primitive, absurd fact. If we were to examine any consciousness whatsoever, we would find nothing that is not attributable to it. But the fact that *there is* a consciousness that motivates its own structure is irreducible. This facticity is not something external, nor is it something within. It is not the passivity of an object created and sustained, but neither is it the total independence of the *ens causa sui*. But on closer examination, it is quite clear that this facticity does not mean that consciousness is founded on anything other than itself—on God, for instance—since any transcendent foundation of consciousness would kill consciousness at the point of origin. Consciousness simply exists *without* any foundation. It is a sort of nothingness inherent in consciousness which we call its gratuitousness. This gratuitousness might be compared to a fall in the natural world, and the motivations to a sort of acceleration that the falling stone might freely apply to itself. In other words, the speed of fall depends on the consciousness, but not on the fall itself.

Consciousness is structured so as to propel itself forward in the world, to escape this gratuitousness, but it does so for its own purpose in order to be its own foundation in the future. To say that human reality exists for its own purpose is the same as to say that consciousness thrusts itself forward into the future in order to be its own foundation there. That is, it undertakes to project, to the horizon and beyond the world, a certain future for itself in the illusion that when it becomes that future it will be so as its own foundation. Thus the primary constitutive value of human nature and source of all values is to-be-the-self's-own-foundation. Consciousness is pure facticity, but human reality is constituted by this value on the horizon, or from this facticity. This is because consciousness, the free basis of its possibilities, is the basis of its future being without being able to be the basis of its present being. That is what is called will. (I wrote about this on December[1] 23 and 24.) What consciousness fails to perceive is that when this future becomes the present, even if it is exactly as it should be, it will be consciousness and will therefore draw its motivation from itself, while still overcome by the consequent gratuitousness and nothingness.

Thus through all his undertakings man seeks neither growth nor self-preservation but rather self-foundation. And after each undertaking, he remains just as he was: gratuitous to the core.

My love, I'll stop there. This is clearly no more than the merest beginning. I'll copy out the rest tomorrow and the day after. But here already is material we can discuss. Rest assured that I love you, little one; tomorrow I'll copy out a shorter section and I'll talk to you of me and thee. You are my little flower.

To Simone de Beauvoir[1]

[date uncertain—
probably December 10]

My darling Beaver

Just a brief note to tell you that I love you with all my might. But I don't know how to arrange for you to come here. You be the judge: I'm at Morsbrunn, five or six hundred meters from the village. I know absolutely no one there. Nor do the soldiers. They're billeted in hotels or the public baths. In this region rife with spyitis, I can hardly ask a favor point-blank of anyone of the slightest importance (for in effect he would have to answer for you). I'll try through the postal clerk's landlady, but he's not all that obliging. You try from your end. I'm at the Hôtel Bellevue, six hundred meters from the town, opposite the public baths.

I love you.

---

[1]Sartre meant to say November 23 and 24.

[1]*This very explicit letter must have reached me by unusual means.* The letter was probably tucked in with the two notebooks that Sartre entrusted to Mistler as he left for Paris on leave, which were delivered to Beauvoir. The last of the two books survived, to appear as the first section published in *The War Diaries*.

To Simone de Beauvoir

December 10

My darling Beaver

I have a bit of good news for you, but I can't say it because of censorship. Well anyway, generally speaking, after our two-month assignment here, I think we may go to an entirely different place, much more pleasant, mountainous and accessible. It seems likely. Rejoice and be gay at heart thinking of the long vacation and the Easter vacation. It puts me in a good humor, a very good humor, my little dearest. I'd so like to have you here, like a very good, very appealing little Beaver. My God, then I wouldn't keep my notebook anymore, I'd tell you everything that very moment, that's what I'd do.

Mistler is off on leave—while we're on the subject of notebooks. It suddenly dropped into his lap yesterday. He was 41st on the list, and we were up to 31. But he's replacing a guy who can't get away. He began to tremble when he heard about it, especially since his friend, a married woman with a kid (you might expect it of him), is in Paris and just about to leave. She wasn't to get back again after that till the end of January. *But,* out of pure idiocy and for the sake of appearance, he promised his turn to that trash Nippert, who has 2 kids. Pangs of conscience, guilt. I immediately put the thing in perspective, being the official keeper of his conscience, and settled the question of principles and practical questions, and finally he was able to leave. But today, till the 3 o'clock departure hour, he was nuts, going through such a terrible crisis of passive joy, with an idiotic look in his eyes and a sweet, gentle smile, that we got worried. I gave him my two black notebooks to give to you, because I can't wait for you to read them. Tell me in detail in a long letter what you think of the ideas. In one you'll find the continuation of my thoughts on morality, but it doesn't end there; I'll copy out the end of it, but not today. Today was Sunday. I didn't notice it, but evidence suggests that the Sabbath rites persist for others, because the little station restaurant was packed with light infantrymen. Half of them were forced to stay on their feet, and blocked the way. They are young, all from the active service, and most have splendid beards, which they started after September 1st. About mine, they tell me to keep on hoping. For several days I'd noticed that they considered themselves *our* proletariats. We were the Ariels of the General Staff, and they nudged each other when we came in. This very morning Captain Munier was telling me, "You should go and have a little chat with the light infantrymen. I suspect they would have quite a few interesting things to tell you." Because he knows I keep a journal. I answered, "They won't talk. They scorn us because we're General Staff." And he, irritated: "Ah yes! General Staff! They think they're at war, and they scorn us. Yet we are a very small General Staff." Whence I concluded that this ironic scorn also existed among the officers of the light infantry in regard to our officers. Today we were nine at the table, squeezed in like sardines, four light infantry sergeants, two privates, Mistler, Pieter, and me. We struck up a general conversation, and Pieter leaped at the first opportunity to tell them we were reservists. "Oh, reservists? We thought you guys were regular army." That raised us a peg in their opinion. Right away, Pieter said, with the air of an old flirt, "Mistler is 37. And I'm 38. And Sartre 34. We don't look too much like old geezers?" A rather odd question, somewhat embarrassing to me at that table of buck privates, which reestablished the generational difference and the harlotry of the older generation in respect to the younger generation. But the three of us were all solidarity, awaiting the verdict. They protested ever so politely and with a touch of irony, and one of them said as he pointed me out, "Even that one, we took him for an army brat." Whereupon a tall dark-haired one from the class of '35 said to me, "Weren't you at the Lycée Pasteur?" I said yes. He must have seen me going by from time to time in Neuilly, when he'd been a student there. He spoke to me formally, unlike the others—because I had been a teacher. Upon which, to great bursts of laughter, I spilled my plate of green peas and mashed potatoes onto my lap. I went out to wash off, and they poked fun at me a bit—for my beard, my grubby appearance. Mistler told me that then the former student from Pasteur intervened to say, wide-eyed with amazement, "Even so, that guy could've been an officer if he liked. Just think, he's a Norm-Sup grad!" I sat down again and we exchanged digs of all sorts, and once more I adopted that odd tone and role I assume among groups of men: a pathetic sort of guy, ugly, filthy, dressed somewhat repellently, his ideas somewhat revolting, but making people laugh anyway, stirring them up a bit.

After lunch I worked on my journal and read Marivaux. I went back to the phone again, but finally it's a sinecure if you know how to go about it. And I'll be at it till noon again tomorrow and the day after. But, an excellent piece of news, our room—the meteorologists'—has finally been given a stove, and it's spreading a lovely warmth. I'll never leave it again, and I'll get back to work on my novel, no holds barred.

What do you think of this letter I got today?

Professor
    Les Nouvelles Littéraires have assigned me to query personalities in the literary world. I ventur [*sic*] to send you this questionnaire, soliciting the favor of a reply.
    I hope you will be favorably disposed toward my request, and I beg you to believe, Professor, in the expression of my high consideration.
    Yours extremely truly
Signature [*sic*] Jacqueline Lignot.
Address: Mme R. Roux 10 bis rue Vavin.

    And here are the questions:

    (1) Did the war cause great perturbation or a great change in your way of seeing and thinking?
    (2) Have you been able to continue working?
    (3) On what and under what conditions?

Pretty weird, eh? Koyré's letter no less so.

Dear Sir
    I am writing to you (a) for news of you (b) to hear news of the paper you were to give at the Recherches Philosophiques.

    There, dear little one, the news from this sector. Right now I must write to my *stepfather*—pity me.
    I love you, my ever so charming little Beaver.

To Simone de Beauvoir

December 11th

My darling Beaver
    Here I am at the phone again, but by now I carry out my task with the nonchalance of a specialist—which incidentally leads to an occasional error. I confess I get a kick out of extracting voices from that magic box by inserting pegs in holes. But you humiliate me by comparing me to the fat lady at Le Dôme. Mine has 12 holes, and communicates by relays with over 200 stations. Tonight I'm sleeping here on the daybed, on watch over that box of tricks. And tomorrow I'm on duty till noon. From noon on, I'll try out the little home, the little *querencia* where Pieter and Paul, looking blissful and relaxed, simmer away on a low fire.
    Today I wrote a lot in my journal. Pages and pages on life, on the

essence. I finished the contemptible *Sentimental Education,* and I tired of Marivaux. Mind you, Marivaux is charming, but only in small doses. I'll go back to Shakespeare, I still have *Othello, Macbeth,* and *The Tempest* to read, and then I'll send it back to you. Any time now you can send *Quai des brumes* and the *Carnets de moleskine,* and even think ahead to another mailing, should the occasion arise, around December 25 if you aren't going off to see Emma, poor little Beaver. Tomorrow afternoon I'll go to the village on your behalf.

Emma writes me that she is overcome with longing to see you, but she feels a sort of resigned torpor. She'll do her very best, but she has little hope. It's the same thing for a telegram: she has to find someone, since her mother forbids her to send a telegram. If you don't go to see her, I hope you'll go off for some skiing in Mégève. I wish you could take along Bienenfeld. It would be a bit of fun for you. And then some two weeks later I'll be home on leave. And then a month or two after that, I'm counting on big changes.

Did you retrieve my novel? Hurry up and do so, also tell me so in writing, my little sweet. I'm all atremble. Tomorrow is correspondence day— I don't know how many letters I'm late in answering. And the day after tomorrow I'm getting back to the writing. I want to finish before my leave.

Would you like to spend your Easter vacation around Annecy or near Culoz?[1] Or your summer vacation? Duraton[2] writes me that it is pleasant and not too expensive around there. And it is accessible, I think. It isn't an army zone, or not anymore. There is simply the fortified sector of the Jura. You write to tell me whether you like the idea.

My love, how well you explain that you are alone, but alone *with* me. I totally agree. And like you I think that this separation will do *us* good from many points of view, so long as it doesn't go on too long. It toughens us, because in order to be happy, we usually need each other *so much.* And then it deprived you—for a short time, actually—of the presumption of happiness. I think you'll make as much progress as you did in Marseilles. But then you'll be frighteningly perfect. Yes, my little flower, I know just exactly how you are with others, without any self-perception. And that's what makes you so pure. But in fact I'd like to talk about it with you. There is much to be said about it. You know, I'll willingly eat a "truffle in ashes"[3] when I'm home on leave.

---

[1] *Sartre was hoping to be sent to the rear, in the Alps. (SdB)*

[2] *A fictitious character. (SdB)*

[3] Beauvoir had described the elaborate dish—a truffle buried in pastry-wrapped pâté and served in ash-covered paper—being consumed at the next table at La Coupôle (*Lettres à Sartre,* Vol. 1, p. 335).

I love you passionately, my love. I long to hold your skinny little body in my arms. And I want to see your coat. You know, they know just when the trains for the guys on leave come in, and you could simply wait for me in the station. I'll come without a mustache but with a *necklace beard* trimmed by the army barber, which I'll do away with the very next day.

Goodbye, my little flower.

When this letter reaches you, you'll probably have received my notebooks. I think you'll find them entertaining. Write me all about it, in detail.

To Simone de Beauvoir

December 12

My darling Beaver

I wanted to do my correspondence today. Poupette, the Lady, Kanapa, Paulhan, Hirsch, etc. And then I chickened out and this was followed by a long conversation with Paul and Pieter on the value of an oath. Mistler had promised to give up his turn for going home on leave to that worthless young Nippert, who's married and a father. And then finally he didn't do it. Was he right or wrong? We have a court of morality here, it reminds me of the good times at the Lady's, with our Department of Wit. But here the participants are easier to confuse, they lack the tenacity of the bulldog in sheep's clothing. Anyway, I maintained that you should never commit yourself (this is the result of my several months of flirtation with the morality of oaths) and in addition that if you break your word with a little ass, a despicable object like Nippert, it serves him right. Obviously they upheld the opposite, but I pulverized them. They reassure themselves by saying to each other, he's too clever for us. You see, it's basically the theory of sophism[4] still pursuing me. Just one slightly amusing thing came out of the whole long argument. It's that I suddenly understood why Mistler likes me so much. He had already said once, "I've changed a lot, it was a revelation, the day you said in front of them that legitimate households are less valuable than free associations." And that day I had indeed noticed that he was lapping it up and thinking with his heart. And then again, when I showed him my surprise the other day that he had even for one instant considered giving in to Nippert, he who thought as I do that a liaison requires more consideration, more self-

---

[4] *A theory that Guille and I used against Sartre's reasoning.* (SdB)

observation, than marriage, and has more real value, he replied with embarrassment, "Oh, but I've changed a lot since then." Linking that to the
fact that he is a sad and nervous guy, and a scrupulous one, and to the other
fact that his friend is a married woman with a kid, I suddenly understood
that for a long time he must have been torn by the illegitimacy of his love,
to the point of contracting a real inferiority complex, and that what drew him
to me and fascinated him was to see a guy in the same situation as he at
peace and even proud of it. As Pieter says—aptly, for once—I am the justification of his life. That entertained me while also reducing me to greater
modesty, for I had thought that it was the strength of my reasoning that had
drawn him to me. There was that also, you will say. Yes, but *also*.

Aside from that, I was on telephone duty all morning long, reading
Fermé la nuit, and writing about Morand's style in my new notebook. I think
it is dated, but about the first two nights I'm less critical than you, it's readable.
The third is vile, and I didn't read the fourth. But it gave me a violent desire
to read V. Larbaud's *Barnabooth*. Would you kindly buy it for me, little one?
And while you're at it, *immediately buy*, read quickly, and send me André
Maurois's *Les Origines de la guerre de 1939*. For the reasonable price of 7.50
francs. It's probably superficial and empty but there must be scraps here and
there for the gleaning, because he must know the English point of view rather
well. Can you believe that the fat Thibaud loaned me *Les Croix de bois* ["The
Wooden Crosses"],[5] which I had never read. It isn't badly done, but though
loads of details ring true (how they go about their labors, the way they sleep
on straw, make up their bundles, etc.), it doesn't tremendously impress me.
While we're on the subject, what do you think of J. Romains? And on that
subject, send me Bost's address, I've lost it and he didn't include it on his
last note.

After the telephoning I went to lunch at the station restaurant. It's
always packed with army guys, there's a pretty young girl—something between
Martine Bourdin and Rirette Alphen,[6] does that give you the picture?—
reserved with the soldiers and yet quite likable, who puts on a dab of perfume
when she feels like it. And so, you will ask? Are you being soldierly, like
friend Bidasse? Like the soldier Ouvrard sings about, and his romance with
the cashier at Le Grand Café? What can I say, my little flower, we have to
live the military life authentically. Incidentally, there is a laundress there who
could be useful to us. We'll see.

After lunch I took possession of the "home." But that great ass of a

---

[5] By Roland Dorgelès.
[6] *Rirette Nizan's maiden name.* (SdB)

Paul had let the fire go out as a welcome for me. I got it going again, and, well, it really *is* a home. There I peacefully read *Les Croix de bois* and the *NRF*, which they obligingly send me from Gallimard. And then all of a sudden I was seized by a hunger to write. But something altogether new. It was a sort of freedom for-writing that I suddenly became aware of. Don't worry, wise little adviser, I'll first finish my novel, and after a short period of restraint, the urge will be all the livelier, toward the end of January. So then, the little "home": three tables, four chairs, flowered wallpaper, a mirrored wardrobe, a stove, and all our meteorological stuff. It doesn't have much impact, it's just insidiously comfortable. Corrupting, as Nizan would say. As for Nizan, I got a little note from him on his return from leave. I am sending you that note, which made me laugh. And a long, long letter from you, my dear little one, so entertaining, with your tales of the Moon Woman. You know, perhaps I'm really becoming a little Ghéon.[7] The stories about Youki absolutely made me feel sick with disgust, and I don't understand how the Moon Woman could have agreed to "get her off," after the stories about Pierre and the washbasin.[8] You, the objective one, you didn't tell me whether you felt slightly offended. Perhaps it is simply because those stories took place between fat women of a certain age and that I remember only too well the Moon Woman's breasts and what the Z's said about Youki's stomach. A note from Tania. Then that little speech on morality, and finally I'm writing to you.

My dearest, I am so happy to think that by now you have the little black notebooks in your possession and that it must give you something a bit more concrete—at least for a while—than my letters, because it isn't addressed to you by name, but is instead a little fragment of my solitude. But, my little flower, you said it so well, in speaking about yourself, even my solitude is with you.

With all my love, my little sweet.

[7]Henri Ghéon (1875–1944), French religious playwright and poet.
[8]Beauvoir had reported, third-hand, on a wild party with lots of drink and sex and a washbasin used as a bidet.

To Simone de Beauvoir

December 13

My darling Beaver

Today was uneventful. I did the readings and then I wrote in detail about Mistler's life in my notebook, with background I spared you yesterday, and then I got your dear little letter, my little flower, and a letter from my mother, who enclosed an article by Thérive in *Le Temps* in which he writes, about the Prix Goncourt: "Should we be surprised that the Goncourt judges have not discovered an incomparable masterwork? Such obligations weigh upon them! The best books of this year are signed by authors beyond [. . .][1] or else circumstances are really unfavorable for spotlighting works that are too bold, too cruel, too immoral. That is why they could not include M. Alexandre Arnoux or M. Billy or M. Sartre, who, in ordinary times, would have furnished an ideal laureate." That gave me pleasure anyway, but the reasoning is strange. In my journal I'll have to ponder the officially established link between war and morality—so habitual that we no longer watch out for it and yet so paradoxical—whereas, without even speaking of the *fact* of war, everyone knows that it is the time of shady profiteering, debauchery, and panic.

Emma wrote you a quick note, so I was told. Go through the procedures, in any case. But she *assures me*, my love, that you will see her just as you are hoping before two months are up. You'll have to resign yourself to distinguishing her cloistered moments—when she really can't see anyone—from her worldly periods, when she can openly meet others. The last time you saw her, it was in just such a worldly period. Also, alas, her place is so small, she wouldn't really know where you could stay. Anyway, she tells me that she'll try something else. But don't despair. You'll see her first in January. And the hardest part of the separation is behind you, I assure you. After this it will be easier.

Goodbye, my little sweet, till tomorrow. I don't like knowing that you are all nervous and frosty, as you were when you wrote that letter. I love you so much. Till tomorrow.

I wrote to Paulhan, to Hirsch (who wants to dock 3% of my author's rights for *L'Imaginaire*. Naturally I gave him my consent). On that subject, you tell me that according to Wahl the book will be published in five months.

---

[1]*Illegible word. (SdB)*

Whereas in his letter of November 30, Hirsch writes, "I hope we will be able to come out in mid-January, which is incidentally an excellent launching date." How do you reconcile that? And from whom did Wahl hear it and when did he learn it?

To Simone de Beauvoir

December 14

My darling Beaver

I received a brief letter from you in which you send me word that you received my notebooks, and it pleased me very much to know that they were in your hands and that you are reading them. I so like to have you know everything I think. For instance, you must talk about them *in minute detail* in your letters, and criticize and discuss them—and, since they seem rather like the work of a stranger, say what kind of a guy he seems to you. Appealing, that much we know, since you say so. But in what way? What sort of a man? And doesn't he make a whole lot of noise for the small amount of war he's waging?

Today I did scarcely anything but work. I took up the novel again and drafted away all morning (I can imagine the word "drafted" setting your nerves on edge, and you'd be right). Horrible arguments are arising between Paul and me because he wants to keep the temperature of our office at 15°C and I at 24°. We each storm out of the room in turn, to show our disapproval to the other. This morning, since he was making me waste my time lighting the stove, I went off to work by the telephone. Then around 11 o'clock I took possession of the office, put a few briquettes on the fire, and instantly raised the temperature from 15° to 24°. Paul, who was absent, came back a while later, caught a blast of the fiery furnace in the face, and stalked off haughtily to go and eat in his frigid room. When he came back I'd gone out for lunch with Pieter, the abandoned stove was burning like hellfire, and the room was at 31 degrees, so it seems. During the afternoon we showed a little more consideration for one another: Paul would add briquettes to the stove on his own, and I would open the window the moment the temperature approached 20 degrees. I "worked up a theory" on the war and morality, drawing inspiration from [Roger] Caillois's theory on *La Fête*. I half believe in it, it's brilliant stuff. But while I was writing, it came to me how I'd been able to conceive a theory a minute in the wild days of my youth, and the kind of personal beliefs they corresponded to.

Toward evening, Pieter brought in a pie, there were fried potatoes on the menu, we ate and we drank. With dessert he offered a little glass of brandy, and recounted things he remembered from the last war, when he hung around with the pimps and drug lords of the Rue de Lappe and the Place des Vosges. "Several of us have turned out all right, we've led acceptable lives," he says modestly. Because his father, a Polish Jew like Bienenfeld, lived on the Rue des Rosiers. In those days the Rue de Lappe was in its heyday, the Americans hadn't yet discovered it. Real live pimps held card parties, with a blanket stretched across their knees, in the park at the Place des Vosges. They played for big money. Pieter and a buddy were the lookout men, to warn them if the cops showed. The buddy became a banker, Pieter became an angel. It's really poetic, hearing these memories of lowlife from the other war while we're waging this one. It must have been an odd Paris. Yours is more austere. Right now Pieter is playing cards with the radio guys next door, and I'm writing to you.

My love, I too am so longing to see you. So much, so much. And to talk to you for a long, long time, and to sleep in your little arms. But in any case the rhythm of the home leaves has noticeably speeded up, and you can firmly count on me for the 20th of January. Scarcely more than a month away. They read us a circular urging the guys on leave to raise morale behind the lines. So is it that low? At any rate I'll raise yours, my little flower. I love you with all my might.

Listen: you carefully tell me the date in my notebook and talk of a day when I was pompous and then repented. But I have absolutely no idea what that refers to. Till tomorrow. You didn't say whether you got my novel back from our Cossack girl. You must do so immediately.

To Simone de Beauvoir

Wednesday, December 15

My darling Beaver
There you are, reconciled with the Gérassis, and you're going to their house? I thought that the "old friendship was dead. . . ." Those people are marionettes. Actually, I have no need to write to Gérassi, and the old friendship can stay dead so far as I'm concerned. You amused me with the glimpse of T.-Sorokine. Here's the other point of view (which incidentally meshes admirably with the one you heard).

"Finally, stuffed with all sorts of fried food, we sat down in an outdoor café, where an accordionist was playing delightfully. At that point I collapsed inside. I even hated Sorokine a little bit because she asked me too many questions. I think she's worse than you when it comes to questions. It's that sort of plain, precise question, clear as spring water, that requires a plain, clear, precise answer. My whole life was put to the test: if I liked painting, if I was happy like this, if I was broadening my mind, what I was doing spending all that time alone in cafés, etc. All these questions pierced me like so many jabs of a stiletto. On top of which I don't know stuff that precisely, or the little ploys I should have instantly used to answer it all, it was all my little everyday torments put on the mat, and I realized, through the strange distaste and sadness that came from answering them, that my life is con- temptible and that a thousand things in me aren't put to good use. I have only embryos of knowledge, not one of which is developed. From that moment on, I didn't like Sorokine anymore, the accordion was tearing at my heart, and I wanted to go home. Otherwise, one can have a good time with her."

So it was a shambles. Nonetheless, does Sorokine understand the class- iness of the Z. sisters? Perhaps it's something she's too young to feel. T. was careful not to tell me that the Moon Woman had read my letters (because I had duly warned her not to leave them lying around), I find that story fascinating, and you must tell it to me *in minute detail*, my little sweet. What did the Moon Woman say? Was she irritated, did she rage about me, etc.?

As for me, yesterday was dead calm (I'm writing to you at 6 in the morning). For me it was a day of rest, and I dutifully worked all day. The Daniel-Marcelle conversation will probably be done today. They make us carry helmet and mask now, and also since last night a gun, because para- chutists dressed as French soldiers landed somewhere in the region. So Nippert inspects every soldier he doesn't know with a very wary eye. Yesterday he called me twice to point out suspects. We found an air rifle in the house, and we're having a great time killing flies by firing the air charge at them point-blank. I wasted 45 minutes that way, playing the Indian in the room downstairs, walking on tiptoe with my rifle under my arm, stalking flies.

And that's everything, dear little one, I realize that it's meager, but what can I do? I'm afraid they might evacuate my troops. Charlotte had already put out lots of mattresses and bedding, baby carriages, wardrobes in the courtyard on the off chance. Alas, we'll no longer be able to go to her place for lunch. But it's a small loss, at that. You'll send me nice preserves instead of money, that's all, and we'll certainly economize.

Here are a few books to send, my little sweet:

Meredith: *The Egoist*

Claudel: plays *(La Ville—Tête d'Or—L'Annonce faite à Marie) Le Soulier de satin.* ["The City"—"Golden Head"—"The Annunciation to Mary," "The Satin Slipper"]

Lucas Dubreton: *Louis-Philippe* (published by A. Fayard)

Radclyffe Hall: *The Well of Loneliness*

In the Pléiade collection: Verlaine's *Les Chroniqueurs et Poésies complètes.*

The ones that are underlined are particularly dear to me; a package including Claudel, Lucas Dubreton, and Verlaine would melt my heart in joy.

That's what's up, dear little one. I realize that this is a slightly dry letter. But I am nonetheless hardly dry at heart. Only I didn't hear the alarm clock, I woke up 15 minutes late, and I'm hurrying, I'm galloping, so this letter will get off in time. I love you so much, my little sweet. I'll put it properly in writing this evening. I kiss you passionately.

Don't forget; the 20th: 14.4 Sg

To Simone de Beauvoir

December 15

My darling Beaver

I too think there's no longer much hope for Emma, and that saddens me also. But I don't in the least want you to contemplate my leave with that moroseness, dear little one. I swear to you that everyone, including my mother, will get a chance only after you, and that our time together will be long and full. On the contrary, I'm overjoyed, and I'm absolutely sure that it will be a really good time, time that will count for the two of us. Sure, we'll have to hide a bit, which will complicate things some. But as for us, little flower, let's not confuse hiding and being hemmed in. To hide is an act, and to be hemmed in is a character trait, but you won't be so with me at all, I am determined to take the necessary precautions, and beyond that I won't worry about a thing. And we'll go to Montmartre and along the Boulevards and to the Porte d'Orléans, and take long walks. Only the Latin Quarter and Montparnasse will be forbidden to us, but basically, for you it's simply a certain daily activity that will be lacking. I think I'll push my audacity to the point of taking you by cab to dinner at Lipp. There you have it. For—reassure me on one point—there must still be taxis in Paris? No, my dearest, have no fear, *I want to have a good time* in Paris, and have a good time with you. I don't want to come back from my leave feeling jostled about and hampered, hardly daring to think, "Is that all it was?" That's not my style. Nor yours, and I'll be as ruthless about enjoying its benefits as I once was—do you remember?—on searching Paris high and low for a copy of V*erve*. And you said, "How determined you are, my man. Just like me, but not about the same things." This time it will be about the same thing. My love, I so long to see you.

I got your letter on the notebooks, and it made me very happy to hear that you find them interesting. Tomorrow go into greater detail on the ideas. I'm pleased you find it new, because I wasn't thinking in the least about newness, but about expressing myself as well as possible, simply. My love, you know I was very moved when I read that we have sharp edges, you and I, and that we have grown hard, because I thought that we had grown hard together and that this was our life, and the love we have for each other seemed like something old already, and very moving, like La Argentina—remember?—the first evening you saw her, in Rouen I think. My dear little Beaver, I love you so much this evening. Except that you have made me fall into abysses of perplexity and into a deluge of notes in my journal: am I simply taking stock of myself, or is it that I hope to slough off that hardened, slightly deadened personality along with the peace? And what more do I want? To progress, of course, that's my usual bent, but to what end? I concluded that it was not so much a question of changing myself as of trusting in nothing but myself, and that in that sense you're right, it is a stock-taking. And that it was not moral to want anything else. On the subject of morality, you are left in suspense at the end of the notebook. I'll copy out the rest tomorrow.

Today I was calm and blissful, writing away at my journal, when they came to tell me that Nippert had just been given a typhoid shot and that consequently I must replace him, which I did unwillingly. Ultimately we never get away from that telephone. It's not unpleasant, mind you, but I can hardly work on my novel. Today I read Ellery Queen's *Four of Hearts*, which was a lot of fun, and then I wrote in my notebook. Then came your letter, so dejected, poor little flower, which made me a little downhearted. How I would like to hug you in my arms. Nothing from Tania, but I'm quite astonished by the complete indifference it leaves me with, after my fit of jealous passion in Brumath. I think something in my mental economy went out of whack for a day or two.

Enough of that. People around me are more and more contemptible, except for Pieter, who is a fine person, but it simply doesn't bother me. Tomorrow afternoon I'll get back to my novel.

I love you, my little sweet, I love you so much, you hardened little being, you little sharp edges.

Ah! I was about to forget the main thing: my love, *I beg you* not to go off skiing *all by yourself*, as you're intending to do. That's pure madness. At least consider that even if nothing happened to you, I wouldn't be really living. Can't you go with Colette Audry and Pelletier? It seems to me that it would be far less austere than the terrible solitude that must grab you when the sun goes down, the sort of thing we scared Boubou with, last year. You'll be moping around. Tell me quickly how you see it all. —*Don't forget to get my novel back from Z.*

To Simone de Beauvoir

December 16

My darling Beaver

I've just written to M. Koyré and to an admirer I'd promised myself to write to for almost a month. It is nine o'clock, it's blowing like hell outside, whistling, grinding, banging, but here we are, cozy in our little home, in a uterine warmth. Pieter isn't here. Paul is darning his socks beside me. And oh, my little one, how I love you, in this comfortable night scene with the wind at my window; how close we'd be, chatting away here together. You know, I was happily anticipating your long letter on the notebooks, and then the mail brought me nothing, just one of its little jokes. I had just a scrap from Tania and a long letter from my mother, which is really very fine. She explained that the day before was a *really* good day for her, because she got a letter from me and she saw you.

Well, as for me, last night I slept by the phone. Before that, Hantziger, a tall guy with gray hair and a porcelain face, a stupid look about him, and unfathomable light-blue eyes, with white eyelashes, the one who plays the same waltz every night on the piano—did I tell you that I play some too: Beethoven's sonatinas and the little works for children by the masters, and also "The Beautiful Blue Danube" and the Waltz from *Faust*, anything we could turn up in old closets. Well, Hantziger said, with the reserved manner of someone trying not to influence someone, "Here, Sartre, you the philosopher, what d'you think of this?" And he handed me a letter from his wife, a pious creature, whom he'd married at 23 and dumped for an English typist after thirteen years of marriage. He totally abandoned the conjugal hearth two months before the war and wanted to start divorce proceedings when, on September 1st, he was sent to Nancy, then to Ceintrey and here to see whether his divorce had come. His wife is holding on to him, since she writes that she won't refuse the divorce, though it breaks her heart and violates her religious principles—but what wouldn't she do for her dear Arthur, even if it cost her own happiness—except that he really can't require her, on her own and as though on her own initiative, to take the steps most totally opposed to her happiness, her religion, and her best interest. And so there's Arthur, screwed, for as a private 2nd class here, he can't go to Paris and do what is necessary to get a divorce. Screwed, cornered. May, the blond stenographer, sends him letters in English—but the legitimate one has undertaken a vigorous offensive, sending very few letters and substantial packages. He has accepted them, since he's a glutton, thanked her, the correspondence has picked up again, and with it the beginning of his classic indecision, which has become the *cause célèbre* among the clerks: which one should he keep? It is so all-consuming that he goes around all day looking off into space, his mouth bloated with a puzzled melancholy. And the other day, out walking a dog, which I'll tell you about all in good time, on the end of a rope, he came back with the rope but no dog, unaware that he was missing something. Except that yesterday, the wife had gone too far: she had enclosed in the letter a mail order for fifty francs, a present all the odder in that Hantz is well provided with money on the side. It made him suspicious, and he offered me the pious, frigid letter, which reminded me of a hair shirt. I read it: a letter cloaked in the dignity of a spouse and a believer, but very studied, it seemed to me. It wasn't unlikely that the money order was a trap aimed at establishing, in case of divorce proceedings, that Mme Hantziger supports her mobilized husband. So I advised him to send the money order back to his wife, and he listened approvingly but without snapping out of his torpor, which has become chronic. "You know, my friend, I don't know what I'll do. Sometimes I say to myself: we'd just rented a beautiful apartment, bought new furniture, a piano, it will mean starting over, is it really worth the trouble? And at those moments I feel like going home to her."

After which I slept on the divan. And here's the shaggy dog story. On the road, the clerks picked up a year-old dog, stricken with distemper and more than three-quarters dead. He is now a permanent fixture in one corner of the veranda, where he drools and coughs, slowly expiring. I hated him last night, the moribund wretch, for he coughed and rattled away from midnight to four o'clock without a break. It was a strange noise that I vaguely compared to something or other, in my semisomnolent state. This morning, getting up, I saw that I had a belly. No sooner seen than decided: till I see you again, I'm going on a rigid diet; only one meal a day with no bread or alcohol. I jotted it down in my journal to make the decision unshakable. I manned the phone all morning long, and then had a "free afternoon." I began the last chapter of my novel, and I think that it will go like a breeze, because it's all dialogue. No notable incident, except for a mysterious chimney fire, which sent off splendid rockets into the dark night and had the whole hotel dashing into our place crying out, "It's gotta be the weather guys." But it wasn't at our place; we had a tiny cadaver of a fire that was scarcely giving off any heat, simply a couple of red embers. "That's OK," the officer said reluctantly. But since something had to be done nonetheless, he came back fifteen minutes later and became hypnotized by our fire, which, by this time, was about to give up the ghost, till he had persuaded himself that it was too much. "You'll have to put it out," he finally declared. But anger caught up with me, and I refused outright. "Oh, I see," he said. We kept our fire and the sparks stopped. But all evening Paul talked about a fire he had witnessed when he was twelve which was caused by a few glowing cinders. God knows what he'll dream about. Well, that's it, dearest. I'm reading *Colomba*,[1] which is awfully well done, and *The Concept of Dread*, in which there are countless things within theologic terms that are obviously a bit forbidding. His influence on Heidegger is undeniable. I filled yet another notebook. I'll have this one delivered to you by Pieter. I've begun notebook 5. I'm pleased as Punch with it.

With all my love, my darling little one, my little flower.

Send me the books, please. *And get back my factum from Z.*

To Simone de Beauvoir

December 17

My darling Beaver

This evening I had hoped to copy out for you the rest of my ethics, since you want to know all of it, but it's late and the notebook is with Pieter.

---

[1] By Prosper Mérimée.

413

There is another finished notebook, and there'll undoubtedly be yet another before Pieter goes off on leave. I'll get him to deliver them to you. Today I'll write you a brief letter, and won't write anyone else. Tania writes me a slapdash little note every four days; I'm dumbfounded when I think that two weeks ago I had a brief love crisis about this creature who means absolutely nothing to me today. I don't conclude anything from that, I know I'll still see the charm in her and go crazy again some time or other because of her. But before I give it another try, I'll at least have to see her again. For the moment, it's dead. I'm all alone with you, my love, and interested in only the essential.

I have two letters from you, my little one, one long, one short. I'm so sorry you feel numb and glum, like the weather.

Since my presence would warm you up a bit, you should know I may have a chance to come earlier: perhaps before the 10th of January. I argued doggedly with a lieutenant for them to admit the principle of the weather unit's independence from the Artillery Division when it comes to leaves. It really isn't logical for us to be part of the AD list, since we don't do the same work as the clerks and, consequently, nothing stands in the way of a weather guy being on leave at the same time as a clerk. Of course, the clerks are backing me up. Under this hypothesis the weather guys would go off one after the other, with no intervals—I right after Pieter. Without making any promises, the lieutenant stated that he would give me satisfaction "insofar as possible." Of course, we have to expect disappointments, but things could still turn out well, since for us the list must be closed before February 15, meaning all those on leave must be back by that date.

This morning I worked on the novel with relish. And then Pieter took me out for lunch with a Jewish infantryman he knows who happens to be stationed near here. It was uninteresting. Next I came back here and worked on my notebook, but the leave question was the order of the day. Everyone said to me, "Go talk to the lieutenant," and I wasted an unbelievable amount of time shuttling back and forth before finding him. This evening I eagerly dived into the journal again, so much so that it's now eleven o'clock. What you told me about precedents[1] has me completely fired up to write about it, and I'm putting down whatever comes into my head. Oh my little judge, I write by turns either in my novel or my notebook according to the things you have to say about them. I have so much confidence in you. But tell me: if you aren't going to Provins, how can you reclaim the journal you loaned to

---

[1]After a first incomplete reading, she had evoked Bergson and Kant in her appraisal of his thoughts on morality and will (*Lettres à Sartre*, Vol. 1, p. 350).

the Boxer? And also *get my novel back from Zazoulich.* You must quickly send me some books, little one. No need to send me 300 francs. 150 will easily get me through to the end of the month. Then devote some of the rest to buying me books. I'm going to send you back the others, or else give me Bost's address right away. He doesn't put it on his letters.

I wonder with some concern if your stay in Mégève might not be a bit gloomy, and if you aren't going to feel isolated. It's true that the skiing will pick you up. I'm pleased you're going with Kanapa.[2] Yesterday I was apprehensive, imagining you lost in the snow.

My dearest, I leave you with that; I'm exhausted. For some time now I've been trying to make up in the evening for the hours I lose at the telephone. I'll be there again tomorrow. I get very little sleep. But I love you so much, my little one, I love you with all my might. You are a sweet little flower.

To Simone de Beauvoir

Monday, December 18

My darling Beaver

We're in the process of fighting like hellcats for the HQ to accept the principle that the weather guys leave one after the other without gaps. It looks hopeful. Last night I'd somewhat lost hope because I'd jumped all over someone from around here, an ass, but today it's beginning to take shape, and I have a good chance of getting to Paris around the 8th of January. That would be awfully pleasant. Meanwhile, to put the principle into practice Pieter will have to leave the moment Keller gets back, that is to say the 23rd. As he said this morning with good common sense and charming naiveté, "You see, the important part is for me to leave."

There was no letter from you today. They've been coming by twos, every two days. Tell me, my little Beaver, there are loads of things you could talk to me about in my notebooks: Flaubert's style, Gide's *Journal*, the article about the war in *La Revue des Deux Mondes*, the conclusions I drew from it,* etc.

I would have liked to know your view on all of it. But perhaps you'd rather talk to me about it face to face, since we also might just be twenty

---

[2] Jean Kanapa, Sartre's former student, happened to be going to Mégève.

*M. Chevalier's song and his commentary.

days or so from seeing each other—only fifteen by the time you get this letter. In fact, you'll hardly have time to return from skiing, when there I'll be stepping off the train in Paris. Such walks we'll take, my love, we'll go everywhere. If Dullin and Toulouse are there, I think we'll spend an evening at their place anyway, it would give me a good laugh to see them in wartime. To the Gérassis', of course, mystery, etc. etc. It annoys me a bit, because these days I long to be in Montparnasse with you, and that's what I won't have. But at any rate, don't worry, I'll be ruthless enough.

It's getting more and more comfortable around here. They got in a guy from the Engineers to replace us at the phone, so we never leave home anymore. So I wrote sixty pages in two days in my journal, and I'm working very dutifully on the last chapter of my novel, which will go quickly, since I've been thinking about it a lot for a long time. I've discovered new ideas on liberty, facticity, and motivation and I'm coming up with, God forgive me, bold new ideas about human nature. All this will be communicated to you in good time. The weather's cold and dry, and the sky completely gray, but it's pleasant out, a pleasant winter landscape (on the ugly side). There's no more gunfire at all, from either side. No planes, of course, because of the low ceiling. Absolute calm. This, right now, is my good hour. Pieter's playing cards next door with the radio guys. Paul is fussing around the place, getting ready for tomorrow before going to bed; it's nine o'clock, and till eleven I'll be alone. At that point I'll go to bed. I'll write to my parents and then read a bit in *The Concept of Dread*, which I'll send or bring back to you, and which you'll read with the greatest of interest, if only to understand Kierkegaard's influence on Heidegger and on Kafka (you know that Kafka feathered his nest through that book). I'll have you send back *Wind, Sand and Stars* and *48* and *The Spanish Testament*, since you refuse to give me Bost's address. Shakespeare and Gide will follow with *Fermé la nuit*, but I'm keeping them to tide me over till you've sent me a few books, because I have nothing left to read, particularly since you'll be in Mégève from the 25th to January 2nd and won't be able to send me anything. Please add the Cazotte, *Les Carnets de moleskine*, and *Quai des brumes*, which you already have, and then buy me one or two books chosen at random from the list, as a surprise. Will you have time to do this? the moment you get this letter? Thank you, my little sweet.

I love you so, my little dearest. I was so happy about what you told me yesterday, that your happy disposition is slightly altered, slightly muted, but that it's still very much the way you see the world around you. I love you with all my might.

The fact that Z. has the manuscript is already a mark of progress. *Now you must get it from her.*

Add a hundred *envelopes* to the package of books, because I'm out.

To Simone de Beauvoir

December 19

My darling Beaver

I've just had a long conversation with Pieter and Paul about Morality. Paul was cagey, saying little but understanding very clearly, Pieter charming, an angel but really a bit of an ass too. I'm not entirely sure why I enjoy doing this. Perhaps because a person has to talk a bit. Otherwise I wouldn't open my mouth all day. By speaking I mean just that: exercising my vocal cords—because when it comes to mental solitude, I don't have it: I write to you, I'm with you. Incidentally, I've given a lot of thought—and have written in my journal—about what you have written me: that I seem more solitary to you right now. As for my relationship with you, that's odd. Yet I tend to believe you, because in November you'd figured out that I was depressed long before I'd felt it myself. It amazes me, and it seems almost as though my letters actually had faces for you, and I feel your love even more tenderly than when you say it, though you say it well, my little flower. You seem to have a surer sense of me than I do. All of this to describe the spirit in which I proceeded with this self-examination. Well, here you have it: first of all, what I'm about to tell you is simply a historic interpretation, an empty hypothesis, more or less. During November something strange happened within me. I lost my sense of equilibrium. I suppose it was from seeing you: it was like a delayed-action bomb, jarring my calm, and then in the opposite direction, the approaching leave, which gave a meaning to my time here. Because there was something to wait for, it removed the patience that you described so well as an "indulgence of war" (you'll say, "That's very pretty, indulgence of war, but I never said it"—oh modest little flower). Well—my eyes were hurting as well—it resulted in that emotional crisis, with T. as its pretext and object but going far beyond that. And then the uprooting, the settling in here, robbed my passions of a home base, which was the last straw. And now I think I'm in a sort of "convalescence"; you know, I've already been through the same sort of thing once before, a much longer aftermath of an affair out of all proportion to this one, the Olga affair. I feel a bit reticent in such cases, a bit set on my little ideas and pursuits. So there, perhaps that's the state I'm in. What makes me think so is that T.—while she never writes, which should rather bother me—really seems nonexistent. But I have no other proofs. I rather thought I felt entirely drawn toward your little self, full of concern for you. But you must know, little judge. Besides, it's quite clear that my journal is absorbing much of my attention, that I'm pleased to be back at work on my novel; I'm so swaddled in this warm *querencia* that I shudder with pleasure when I enter it, at the very prospect of reading or writing here. But through all that, how much I am with you, my dearest. Oh no, you know, I've just examined these past few days, how I think of you and await your letters, the rest just isn't true. I love you so. Now, perhaps there's also this: I write my letters later now, from ten to midnight, and they may bear the marks of the day's fatigue. If you aren't too pleased with the recent ones, tell me, and I'll write them during the day—yours, at least, my dearest, I never want you to have pathetic little letters from me.

As for doings here, there's nothing: I work, we've been taken off the phone, I've done a lovely little theory on freedom and nothingness, I'm rather pleased with the way my last chapter's shaping up. And I did get the books, thank you, my little Beaver, they bring real joy. *Les Carnets de moleskine* is disappointing—I've only read the opening—but I find Giono's preface very beautiful. Is he still in prison? You must have that information through the Audrys? It wasn't *Le Diable boiteux* ["The Lame Devil"] by Lesage but *Le Diable amoureux* ["The Devil in Love"] by Cazotte that I'd asked for. No matter: I read the first page of this one and was enchanted, I'm delighted to be rereading it. It's fraud for M. Maurois to be calling his book *Les Origines de la guerre de 39*, while merely dealing with the diplomatic moves immediately preceding it.

I leave you there, my dearest little Beaver. I'm off to bed. My little one, my little dearest, I am near you and love you with all my heart.

Your little husband.

Ask Zazoulich for my novel.

To Simone de Beauvoir

December 20

My darling Beaver

I received two letters from you.

I'm amused that the Gérassis are reading my notebooks, it's sort of like an official reading, because in my eyes they represent all the incomprehension and malevolence of the general public. Incidentally, how has Gérassi reacted to the events in Finland? Is he still bouncing back? I myself find it a shameful mess and, worse still, ridiculous. Ask him and relay his reply.

I'm also happy that you have got some letters from me not "cloaked in solitude." In actual fact, that must be a little illusion of yours. You who read *L'Oeuvre* with a *Canard* outlook, I wonder whether—on receiving my most recent letters while you were reading my notebooks, which are, after all, more solitary—you might not have read them from a notebook perspective. My dear little Beaver, since your visit here, I honestly don't believe I've been cut off from you, not even for some solitude with you. I love you so much.

I'm very pleased about your relationship with Sorokine. That girl seems a real jewel. You're just as good at making a person love the people you find appealing, as you are at cooling them toward the ones who've offended you. But don't worry, I'm not hatching any plot in my head. It's curious how this war has bromized my infamous desire for flirtations that you used to see. As I say, there is no one but you, and I contemplate nothing but that when I think of peace. To be exact, when T. is very nice, I can feel tenderly toward her. (I think she was merely a *pretext* for that crisis of the passions, which had a deeper source. It seems—according to Paul and Pieter—that I was in a rotten mood during the crisis. They attributed it to the fact that I'd given up eating at the restaurant. And thereby conclude with satisfaction that just like them, I have my weaknesses.) But aside from that faint shadow of affection, there's only you in my future and in my dreams. It's really marvelous, little one, to have the relationship we have.

As for my life, it is uneventful and studious. This morning I went for a bath in the bathhouse. It too is occupied from top to bottom by the army; there are at least 12 rooms where you can still take baths, and the guys set up beds in the tubs or right beside them. It too has an odd look now: all green, with that aquarium light so appropriate to baths. Low hallways, sea-green lighting, thick walls. And from one end to the other, stalls. I don't know why, it smacks of bordello and ancient palace, from the mere fact that you know it's *inhabited* by guys with their histories and destinies. Of course, you run into soldiers all over the place. The water is naturally sulfurous, hot, and smells like rotten eggs. Pieter had a bath there yesterday, and he kept dropping off all through the day—simply because he's fat, I think. Paul had woken him up and he said, the minute he was awake, "It must be the bath. The radio guys told me they went there the other day, and that it made them feel queasy." He boasts of not snoring, whereas last night he went on like a blacksmith's bellows, and when I pointed it out to him, he anxiously blurted, "Well, you see, it's the bath. It tired me out. You made a point of telling me the other day that I'd snored. D'you remember if that coincided with my last bath?" But I didn't feel anything of the sort after my bath today. It seems it's because I didn't stay in long enough. The rest of the time, work and reading. We didn't even do a reading, because it was foggy. I began all the books at once, greedily, finished the Maurois, which is a swindle. Began *Barnabooth*. I'm in the middle of *Carnets de moleskine*, but as you say, the guy [Lucien Jacques] isn't at all interesting.

That's all for today, little Beaver. The novel is moving along beautifully and will soon be finished.

I love you very much, my little flower.

Send me some paper like this (2 or 3 pads) with your next package of books.

To Simone de Beauvoir

December 21

My darling Beaver

This will be a very quick letter to welcome you to Mégève. Hey there, my love, I can just imagine you in our little Idéal Sport chalet, which was such a treat. Do at least be careful. You'll be progressing without me. But you'll teach me everything some other winter. Go at least once to Isba, if it's open this year, to tell me what it's like. Have a good time, dear little one, take the Mont d'Arbois trail very fast. Do you remember how fast we went at the end? I envy you a bit. But just as in my dream, I feel I have no right to do so. I don't ski well enough, and when I had the chance to do it, I took a good bit of coaxing. Well, that's too bad for me.

I can't give this much time today, because Klein, the driver, attracted by our loud voices, came in to warm up just as I was getting down to writing.

I'd been telling Pieter that he had the personality of a gossipy old woman, and that made him mad. Klein told several interesting stories, but the censor wouldn't let them by. So you'll hear them later. Only, he lingered for an eternity and now it's eleven. Fortunately it was a quiet day—poor in events, fertile in ideas—and I have nothing to recount. Do you remember what I once told you about "presexual" states and situations: how, right from the start, certain states or situations are significant for man (*holes*, for instance); and, though presexual in itself, that significance would eventually be preempted by sexuality. Well, I've come up with the theory. I also found a theory of nothingness while reading Kierkegaard. Good work, these days, I think the journals I've done here are by far the best. More philosophical perhaps, but without any stammering.

Otherwise, humdrum routine. Tomorrow I'll be making a pilgrimage. Do you get my meaning?[1] I got the letter from young Bost that you're having me hold on to, and I find it intelligent and terrifically appealing. He has made notable progress. I'll copy the whole thing down in my journal. I was amused by V.'s[2] as well. Send her my address via the Moon Woman.

And there you have it, my little sweet. I'm happy right now: I'll be seeing you soon, I sense that you're on an even keel, and I'm working well. It all seems pretty pleasant, and besides, I'm like Bost, this war still interests me. Nothing happens, but as he very correctly says, you feel as though you're participating in an enormous social event, and you wouldn't want to miss it for the world. I wish it would end, but I wouldn't want to be "sent back home" before it's over. I think you can understand that.

My love, I'm stopping here, this is a wretched little letter, please excuse me. But you know, I love you so much, so much, as much as possible, my dear little you who are me.

To Simone de Beauvoir

December 22

My darling Beaver

Nothing from you today. One letter from Paulhan, one from Gisèle Freund. I would really have liked a little letter from you, my love. They are

---

[1]Beauvoir would know that he was near Pfaffenhoffen, the cradle of his mother's family, so he believed, and where as an eight-year-old in 1913, he with his mother had visited his aunt, Caroline Biedermann, who had the best lingerie shop in town.

[2]Louise Védrine.

so full, so gracious, so appealing, and I love it so much when they're thick and puffed up with anecdotes.

Today I went on the pilgrimage. At 7:30 sharp, a truck took me off to get some hydrogen tanks from a few kilometers away. It was −9°C, with bright sunshine, the countryside was dry and powdered white. The ground was hard as wood, and the truck raised clouds of dust ahead and behind, just as in summer. The mission consisted almost entirely of drinking. We got there, we loaded on the tanks of hydrogen, and then we went to a little café where there happened to be a weather guy who was going off on leave that very night. He paid for a round of schnapps, then I did, then the orderly who helped me load the tanks, then the driver and the weather guy again, and finally me again. Thereupon the weather guy took me to their office, they're in a bank, the BNC, where I used to have an account. They have a tiny corner of a large open room, separated from the airmen only by a counter. I thought of the snug, well-heated little room assigned solely to us, the readings guys, and understood our priceless good fortune. Then I wandered around town searching for anything familiar. In vain. I only managed to pick up two terry-cloth towels for the captain, some writing paper for the lieutenant, a bottle of fine wine for Paul (he has had the ridiculous and almost touching idea of celebrating his 30th birthday here), a national lottery ticket for Naudin. Turning a corner I found myself facing a great ocher edifice, with a store selling lingerie on the ground floor. Without a ray of recognition, I knew that this was it. I remembered a novel I'd written in one of its rooms when I was 8, a novel called *Pour un papillon* ["For a Butterfly"].[1] I went to buy some envelopes in the store across the street, as I did in those days (I used to buy notebooks). But the whole thing was unemotional. And yet at one point as I stood, glued there, in front of the lingerie store, the face of some unknown woman moved up close to the display window, and that touched me deeply. That was all. I left, went back to the café; the driver stood us a round of schnapps—and then Grener and then I, and we drove back to "our hotel" around noon. A failed pilgrimage, but a delightful morning. I was completely surprised and disappointed that there was still a whole afternoon to go. It actually turned out to be a very decent one, *I finished my novel* in rough draft and wrote that phrase I've been saying to myself from time to time for a whole year now: "I have attained the age of reason." In a couple of weeks it'll be finished, finished. It's about time; it doesn't interest me very

---

[1]See *The Words*, p. 88: "A scientist, his daughter, and an athletic young explorer sailed up the Amazon in search of a precious butterfly."

much anymore. Still and all, I believe the ending will be fine. I recorded the pilgrimage in my journal and read a bit of *Les Carnets de moleskine*, which, in fact, is damn impressive in the second part. All the more impressive, perhaps, in that the guy who lived it is *very nondescript* and unappealing. He isn't even redeemed by the strength of his feelings or ideas, like for example Romains's characters, who are human beings—not even saved by our sympathy. It is absurd that the guy exists and absurd that he's immersed in that insignificant massacre. When you buy me some books, my little sweet, don't forget to buy me *Blaise* by Drieu la Rochelle, which has just come out. I'm delighted in advance. (Research reveals it's not called *Blaise*, but *Gilles*.) And then *Le Boeuf clandestin*[2] is just out too.

Goodbye, my little sweet, I'm dog-tired. I get a poetic sort of feeling from the thought that this letter will find you deep in your snow. In *our* snow. I know so well where you'll go to pick it up. I remember the post office and the lines we went through there, I don't really remember why. It is varnished and spotless as a clinic. Have a good time, be reasonable, and make progress.

With all my love.

To Simone de Beauvoir

December 23

My darling Beaver

I'm writing to you from a furnace. Paul let the stove go out, and Keller rekindled it recklessly, tossing in armloads of coal, the flame shot skyward, a pair of Paul's socks burned up, the wall cracked, and some mice piled out of their hole to warm up. It was thirty degrees at least, a fact you might appreciate. Paul was livid with anger—at me, of course, though I had nothing to do with it. We shouted at each other—then made up, because it was his birthday and we had to be on good terms to eat the pie and drink the wine he was offering around. But we're all stewed in our own juices; crimson and wilting, I can't put one idea in front of the other. Still, I did work a bit.

So Keller came back from leave. He seemed poetic and irritating, because on the one hand he had totally and completely been right in the middle of Paris, no more nor less than I when I get there. But on the other hand, I knew I wouldn't get a thing out of it, and in fact I didn't get a thing out of it. Pieter was to leave immediately afterward, but he's still here, there

---

[2]*By Marcel Aymé. (SdB)*

is some drawing of straws involving his leave. You'd do well, my dearest, not to count on me for one set date: let's say between the 6th and the 20th. Paulhan, who has not the least doubt about it, writes, "Would you come for tea at my place on the 26th?" I think he considers himself the godmother of the mobilized *NRF* authors. It suits him to a T.

Today there were two big letters from you, lovely and plump, my darling Beaver, such a joy. And so tender. You tell me so beautifully how you love me. And you're repaid in return. You amuse me, you and your harem of women. I warmly encourage you to be very affectionate with Sorokine, who is so delightful. But, you'll say, "I'll have to give her up at the end of the war." Don't be naive, my love: either you won't have cared enough and then—given the way you are—after the war or some other time, you'll drop her like a hotcake, or else it may turn out that you become attached to her, and at that point I know you are dogged enough to want to keep her, come what may. It would be a crying shame to sacrifice that pure and lovely heart.

I worked a bit on my journal. I'm starting a VIth, four and five are filled, Pieter will drop them off at your place and you'll find them when you get back. Then I went out to the restaurant for lunch, went to pick up bags of coal with the colonel's driver, who is likable. Then I worked a bit more. The ruckus about the stove, Keller's return, Paul's birthday, all took up some time. Too much time. And now I'm writing to you. Along with *Gilles*, please send me the two most recent Romains: *Quinette contre Vergé* and *La Douceur de vivre* ["The Joy of Living"]. They're about 1919 and '20. I'll send back the Shakespeare posthaste, though you won't be there when it arrives, and the same for some other books. It's great that you can put aside 1,500 francs in addition to the daily 50 francs. That will give us enough to have a really good time, my love, and we won't be caught short for cash if we feel like seeing any particular place together again. I'll contribute 95 francs to the kitty: it's the travel money they give the guys going home on leave. Have you read *Barnabooth*? Do you want it? It's entertaining because of the period.

Have a good time, you good little skier. I'm aware that this letter is idiotic, but simply lay it to the 29 degrees still pervading this room; with all my love, my little flower.

When you get back, don't fail to go by Monnier's. G. Freund's photographic exhibition will be showing there every day from 2 to 6. You'll see the gorgeous one of me where I look like an angel.

To Simone de Beauvoir

December 24

My darling Beaver

It's Christmastime, and you're surely on the train, my little dearest, perhaps you're already asleep, your entire face screwed up with the effort of sleeping. I know you well, so many times I've watched you in the corner across from mine, all wrapped up in sleep, little one, so serious and serene. You who have been on so many trips with me. I think there are crisscrossed skis in the netting above your head, or perhaps even interlaced straps, and sleepers lying on the woven network. And when you wake up, your eyes are red and you're all excited. I love you, I love to recall each detail of your personality, all your transports and asperities. They make me laugh and tug my heartstrings, all in tenderness for you. But do be careful.

Here's a bit of a bother in the offing: that pig of a Louis Marin has just introduced a bill before the Chamber of Deputies that would cut the salaries of mobilized government employees by two-thirds, so he can raise the soldiers' pay by 2 francs. Naturally this still has to be voted on, but we should already think about some adjustments in my finances. What will happen to T.? How will you get by? Give it a moment's thought. And above all, if the bill becomes law, buy the newspapers and show the article to Z., because, since this comes at a time when I'm on the worst of terms with T., I wouldn't want anyone to accuse me of leaving her in Laigle out of pettiness. In any case she'll be able to come in January, since they've already paid you my whole salary. I've decided not to write to her anymore (unless she writes herself, but she must have come to the same decision on her own) till my trip to Paris. With no official break-off or anything like that.

So it was Christmas Eve today; astonishing how much it means to the guys here. Some of them said to me, around the 15th of December, "This time it's going to be tough, it's the big holiday season and we won't be home." All through the night, the owner of the Café de la Gare dreamed about cooking, because her bistro is going to be packed to the rafters without a break, today and tomorrow. And in some branches of the army, the officers passed the hat to put on a Christmas Eve feast for their men. But now, something to make you laugh. Believe it or not, the clerks bought a Christmas tree with candles, ornaments, and all the trimmings. A tiny fir tree in a pot on a table. The colonel and officers were happy enough to preside at the gathering, and they kindly invited the weather unit. And so at 6:45 tonight, we trooped down to the veranda, which was swarming: clerks, telephone people, drivers, orderlies, cooks. The officers arrived and the lights were turned off, and the colonel made a benevolent little speech by the light of the tree candles: "Under these circumstances it would not seem right to mention the usual joyful wishes for your families. At least for the moment they are happy, knowing that you are safe. For the time being you are merely being asked to be patient, but we must win, and I do not imagine that we can do so without a military effort. I am completely satisfied with you as a team. You get along well together, but only a baptism of fire will give you perfect cohesion." Then he added, "It's true that you are more likely to do battle with your typewriters, but one never knows." Thereupon Corporal Courcy declared, "We would like you to know, Colonel, that we are very much aware of the honor you pay us in consenting to preside over our little gathering, and that this evening will remain among our best memories." And the colonel said, "Very good. Well now, that's very nice. Well then, gentlemen, let's move on to the next room." In the next room six bottles of champagne were waiting for us and some cookies. The colonel offered me the first glass, which caused much comment. He said to me, "Well then, Sartre, aren't you finding anything for your novel in this curious war?" "Well, no, sir," I said. "Oh, I'm sure you will." The officers asked for a volunteer for some music, and everyone said—this is the part that will make you laugh—that I knew how to play the piano. So I went over to play, with great feeling, a waltz called "Grossmütterchen" ["The Little Grandmother"]. Captain Orsel did nothing to hide the fact that he would have preferred some marches, but there was no sheet music for them. Thereupon they clamored for Naudin, the staff sergeant. He sang a love song to the tune of "Temps des cerises" ["Cherry Blossom Time"]. In it he explained to a faraway maiden that in winter he would send her some snowdrops, in the spring some periwinkle, and—he was supposedly in the trenches—in summer some flowers stained with the blood of our heroes, poppies. The colonel came up to me and said, "You have a most appealing talent." Meanwhile Hantziger, ever sad, who plays waltzes at night till eleven, had a crafty look about him as he sidled up to the piano bench. He finally sat down and, unasked, played *his whole* repertory. The colonel moved from one group to another, with an amiable word for everyone. To wind it up, and giving in to Captain Orsel's entreaties, I sang "The Toreador's Song" and made everyone join in the chorus. Then we went back to the veranda, and they lit some sparklers hidden among the pine needles. Soon after that I came up to write to you.

Yesterday Keller came back from his leave. Mistler today. Pieter is leaving tomorrow. He'll be back on the 7th. If I leave right after that, I'll be in Paris at the Gare de l'Est at 17:30 on the 9th. If they slip in another guy before me—which is possible: Hang—I'll be in on the 20th at the same time. You could very well come to meet me at the station, because the military leave trains arrive right on schedule, on condition that you tell me, 1st, a place to rendezvous between 5:30 and 7:30—for example, a café near the Gare de l'Est—and 2nd, another meeting place for the evening in case we miss each other. In any case you'll be alerted at the appropriate time. So I'm going to see you again and talk to you about everything in great detail, my darling Beaver, and I'll take you by the arm and watch the expressions flicker across your face. The whole thing is firm and imminent now. I love you. Mistler said that on arriving, when he first caught sight of Paris he was overcome by a deep serenity and joy, and that in the long run ten days of leave are extremely satisfying. So worry not, I won't let anything spoil my own.

Farewell, good little skier, tell me about all your exploits. Give Kanapa my best and tell him that if I'm not writing to him, it's because I'd have to answer his questions in Aristotelian Physics and the Transcendence of the Ego, which would constitute a monumental letter. But that his Theory of the Ego is intelligent, though still incomplete, and I'll write him as soon as I've finished my novel. Within about two weeks. About his lecture on the Philos. of Quality, he must read Metzger on the "Philosophy of the Concept."*

Till tomorrow.

You Little Naughty, you probably left without picking up my manuscript from Z.

I love you.

To Simone de Beauvoir

December 25

My darling Beaver

Today I dashed off a note to my parents so as to be able to write you a leisurely letter. It's ten o'clock, the charmed moment when I'm all alone (or almost: Paul is in bed. Keller is asleep over a book beside me; I have no idea why he doesn't go off to bed too). Only, I realize that I have nothing at all to tell you.

---

*He might also look at Daudin's work on classification. Does he understand that the physics of quality is the physics of classification? That's the essential consideration.

It's Christmas. I gathered from your letter that you left earlier than I'd thought, Saturday, as was your every right, and not Sunday evening. So yesterday, when I'd imagined you on the train, you had already had a whole long day of skiing, and were already enjoying the sleep of the just in a slightly cold room. I wonder what sort of odd accommodations you'll set up with Kanapa.

Today Pieter left on leave. After him comes my turn. Even now, there's a certain happy excitement when we see a guy go off; we "identify" with him. We burden him with advice, with cans of food, we help him, and finally he stands us to a round of drinks. He seemed very precious to me today, because he was headed off toward Paris. In twenty hours or so he'll get off at the Gare de l'Est, and then he'll take the Métro to Gambetta, and from there at 255 Rue des Pyrénées, he'll go into a store called Chez Gaston, where he'll find his wife and kid. But he was irritating, he whose principal virtue is being natural—which is partly why we call him the angel—because for some unexplained reason he'd adopted a pose: he wanted to be "the guy who," as he puts it, goes off on leave with a calm indifference, laced, of course, with good humor. There was no way for us to celebrate with him. Yet all through the night he tossed about and coughed and cleared his throat—a sign of intense nervousness in his case—and this morning, when I played dead to the world after reveille, he anxiously wanted to know what I was up to, for fear that I'd gone back to sleep and would let him fall asleep again. At eleven o'clock I accused him of adopting a pose; he got mad, and we came to words that hurt, he telling me, "You observe others but don't know yourself, you're pretentious." And I replied, "You're an old woman and a weakling." But between the two of us it never goes very far. We went off together, reconciled, to get our grub, which was reputed to be magnificent—so much so that we elected to forgo a restaurant in order to take advantage of it—and what a disappointment. A lousy *choucroute* swimming in dishwater, and some sour oranges. A bottle of third-rate champagne was added to the regular fare— but you can just imagine what that was like. We drank it nonetheless while smoking cigars, also furnished by the quartermaster and the cause of no small commotion, and then we set off—Keller, Paul, Mistler, and I clustered around the fortunate one, who stood us a round. He suddenly took on the expression of a greedy child, with a vaguely furtive cast to his air of deep inner pleasure. For the moment he looked like pictures of his son and like Charles Laughton in *The Private Life of Henry VIII* when, in his old age, he devours a leg of mutton in the absence of his last wife. We drank up. Mistler has read *The Wall* and liked "Childhood of a Leader" but feels that

"The Wall" itself adds nothing if you've read *The Spanish Testament*. We came back and I dutifully—oh so dutifully—went to work. I'm feeling a renewed interest in the novel, and right now I'm working with intense pleasure on the big scene between Daniel and Mathieu. I believe that what I'm doing is good (I've already done the last Mathieu-Ivich scene, when he kisses her, and the Mathieu-Lola scene; in a week it'll be done). This evening Pieter's absence, along with the thousands of little noises he makes with his mouth, lent a monastic calm to our space. It was voluptuous.

My dearest Beaver, I'm eagerly awaiting your first letter from Mégève, to know where you're staying and whether you're having enough fun. I'm delighted that you seemed to be leaving in a daze of anticipation. All my love.

To Simone de Beauvoir

December 27

My darling Beaver

Today I dashed off six lines to Tania so as to write you a better letter. I prefer it, this way I have all the time I need, I don't tuck in little stupidities at the tail end of your letter. You know, by dint of great mental effort, after writing to you yesterday, I found two or three small fresh items. What were they? Ah yes, there's one I did put down in my journal, I'll copy it out for you. Not that it's essential, far from it, and I'll have infinitely more entertaining things in my journal to show you when I'm back on leave. But here's my entry: "From time to time Keller drums out marches on the table with the tips of his fingers. A civilian habit. I can see him at home, with his plate pushed back, eyes unfocused, tapping away on the oilcloth while his wife stacks the dishes. But the curious thing about it is that until recently he didn't do it. I imagine he always used to do it before the war, but with the September mobilization, abruptly taking off for unknown adventure, he forgot in his haste to bring along most of his little tics. They stayed at home and, on his return from leave, he brought them with him because he knew the monastic and administrative kind of life he'd find waiting here. By and large, the guys coming back from leave are more like their civilian selves." That's all—and then I said too that when I've finished the novel, I'll make some high literary fantasy for a while. You understand: the novel is a serious matter, the journal is a serious matter, there's no writer more serious than myself; one American even reproached me for that. But generally speaking, since it's wartime and

I shouldn't even be able to work, this almost provides me with a justification to venture into any flight of free creative imagination whatsoever. That, rather than drama, is what I'll do: experiments in free association. They'll be whatever they'll be, but I'll dare anything, since this time is a gift, and I'm very sure I'll gain thereby. Does that worry you?

You know, Pieter's absence is a luxury. I work, I read, as though I were a monk. I read *La Comédie de Charleroi*[1] and began *Provinciales*.[2] I'm amused by *Provinciales* because I read in some paper that Jules Renard said about them, "They're not giving the Prix Goncourt to Giraudoux because they don't want to give it to Renard." And in fact Renard's influence on G. is quite clear. This sentence, for instance: "The cat goes off again, tying a knot in his tail to remind himself that he is furious," and you can gradually see the classic Giraudoux taking shape *based on* Renard. Of course, I wrote about that in the notebook. And I also began Rauschning. It's very interesting, and I had a good laugh because, do you remember, Aron had offered us the trilogy of *"charismatic power, Machiavellian elitism, mass"* as what he had discovered in Nazism from his own personal meditations. Whereas it is the *concerted* theme of Rauschning's 400 pages. I despair of ever finding a personal idea in Aron.

What more to tell you? I'm *four* pages from the end of my novel, do you realize that? I've strained my eyes today by writing too small in my new notebook, so I'm writing larger. I'm thinking loads of things and I'm happy, I just have to say it: you sent a big fat letter from Mégève, and, without exaggerating, all day long it's made me feel *as though I were there*. Particularly since we have snow here, and silence. I was taken with the skiing and with you, you seemed strangely present, almost a materialization. My how I do love you, little one. You know, it really gets to me when I know you are thoroughly happy, truly it makes me happy myself, everything falls into place. And I can virtually see you there. Reserve a room on the off chance for next year, and on from year to year, and—perhaps next year, or at any rate one fine day—we'll go skiing together, and we'll be all alone in the chalet in the evening, and we'll turn on the radio. My love.

Incidentally, there's a little jazz tune floating up through the floor from the officers' dining room, and I find it very touching. Tania has written two letters of excuses, I can't hold out against her, so I answered in a friendly tone. But you and I will go to the Hôtel Mistral.

---

[1] *By Drieu la Rochelle.* (SdB)
[2] *By Giraudoux.* (SdB)

I love you, little sylph, little minx.

It's time to think about sending me some dough, since it's almost the end of the month.

To Simone de Beauvoir

December 28

My darling Beaver

Yet another lovely letter from you, completely at ease, how nice your little chalet seems. And the ski lift is so handy. But I'm impatient because you say you haven't yet altogether caught up with your last year's level. Do write about all your progress *in detail*, with no fear of adding technical details; they *interest me*. I was so excited to hear that you'd skied down Mont d'Arbois. It must seem lovely to you because you have a *reason* to go down: to get the mail. It almost puts you on a par—thumbing your nose impudently—with the peasants, for whom skiing is a means of transportation. I imagine that if we were together we wouldn't be saying, "Let's try to ski very well down the slopes of Mont d'Arbois." Instead, with a cool wink: "Shall we go get our mail?" But I'm furious that the mail—mine at least—isn't reaching you. I've written most scrupulously since the 22nd, I think, and I get your letters from Mégève very quickly—only one day longer than those from Paris. I can't understand why you aren't getting mine. Could it be because I put "Mégève" without the Département? I would willingly ask you to tell me which one it's in, but that would be a new variation on the tale of the man who writes letters that reach a mailbox to which nobody has a key, in order to explain where to find the key, etc. So God help us. In any case, if you receive this letter, it must be at least the *fifth* I've written to Mégève. My pen stopped just in time to remind me to tell you to send me *posthaste* and even from Mégève, where they must be available, 2 packs of ink cartridges. Otherwise I'll go quite mute and you will think I don't love you anymore. I have 4 left.

Here, a studious day. I read the Rauschning, which fascinates me. Am I reading something into it? I have no idea. You tell me. Anyway, it has inspired sound reflections on violence as a means to promote morality, and I've concluded that violence must be used. I was really like Hercules at a crossroads between vice and virtue. Violence was on one side, gentleness on the other, I had to choose. But it seemed clear to me that violence is necessary. Whence, as you've already surmised, forty pages in the journal. What else have I done? My novel, but not much, given my total absorption in violence.

I lunched here on a plate of lentils, because I like lentils and because I was so absorbed by my topic. Paul had indigestion, he turned green and went to bed, and then later Mistler came in to hear the good word. He's a disciple in all senses of the word. I'll soon have disciples all over the place. He had brought along a full bottle of schnapps, which we proceeded to empty— Keller, he, and I—he went off again, totally tongue-tied, in a cloud of ideas and alcohol. And now I'm writing to you. I'll scribble a letter to T., who is writing dutifully every day for the moment, but it bores me to write to her. You know, I'm still and always closely linked *with you*, so very passionately, and I think for you and you seem present, and so as to leave nothing unsaid, I love you with all my heart. But other people have rather faded into the background right now, I am wholly absorbed by this war, in which nothing is really happening, but in which I am thinking so well. You'll see the journals; I believe they're far more interesting than the previous ones.

My love, I have nothing else to say, but I wouldn't want you to think that this is a dry little letter from a guy who's isolated in his own petty thoughts. If you only knew how strongly I am *feeling* you at your skiing, how much I am with you. You are my sweet little flower, the only thing that counts in my life, and it counts a damn lot—though actually, it doesn't count "in," since you are simply one with my life, my darling Beaver. I tell you that this war makes a person more harshly and clearly aware of hierarchies. There is no one but you, my dear little one (right now I'm going to write to T. that I love her passionately, which sickens me somewhat).

I send you my tender love, good little skier.

Give Kanapa my best. It seems that Lévy has let me down all along the line. He says I don't understand a thing in Kant.

To Simone de Beauvoir

December 29

My darling Beaver

Well, Mistler came in again this evening. I'm really up against it, because it's ten o'clock and, after your letter, I have to write *two* to T., since I couldn't make the effort to write to her last night, so she will still think I'd written. This grind of daily letter writing is really wearing if the heart isn't in it anymore. I don't even have the right to complain, actually, since I'm still delighted to get letters. They entertain me, there are little anecdotes, it gives a sense of movement. So I'm screwed, as they say around here, like a rat in a trap.

There's nothing to say about today, my dear. I didn't even get a letter from you. I'm not anxious, but it wouldn't take two days' delay for me to imagine that your leg is broken or you've bashed your skull. Besides, a day without a letter from you always creates a real little void: the day lacks your sanction. In other respects nothing happened. I didn't even write in my journal, because the novel drew me in, and then as a sort of health measure: when you shut yourself up alone with your journal the way I did yesterday, without the corrective of other people, you begin to boil and end up needing a safety valve. That was the case yesterday, I had a concept of the world as completely closed in on me, and dark. Ordinarily I'm a bit above my theories, but then, no: I was right in them. So today I wanted to do something entirely different. And there's another reason too, a less serious one: I'm nearing the end of the notebook, and if I write too much in it, it will be done *before* January 1st. Whereas I wrote in my most beautiful script on the flyleaf "December–January '39," and it annoys me to strike things out. I already became a bit disgusted at the last notebook because I made a huge stain on it.

It's −12°C. It is no small matter to carry off a reading at that temperature. Paul puts on a balaclava, helmet, overcoat, gloves, and thus done up looks scarcely human. As for me, I put on gloves, but remain coatless and without a balaclava. Keller doesn't even put on gloves. But it hurts, honestly. I thought of unfortunate young Bost, who mustn't be having a good time of it. The countryside is frozen solid and the sky exceptionally clear. I went to take a bath this morning in the sulfurous water, then worked, did the reading, lunched at the Café de la Gare. Corporal Courcy, the Joseph Prudhomme[1] of the clerks, a great reader of A. France, came to pester me at the end of the meal. I buried myself in my reading of the Rauschning, to show I wanted to be alone. Seeing this, he used the ploy of offering me a schnapps in celebration of his stripes as corporal first class. You can't refuse that, but while drinking *his* schnapps, I had to listen to *his* conversation, laced with "like father, like son," "A foreign liar is usually believed," etc., or this one: "We must adapt to different personalities." "There are some worse off than ourselves." "Why worry, when we can't do anything about it?" We came back together, and I did more work and another reading, then read Stendhal's *Journal*, lent to me by Mistler, since the supply of books is almost zero. I

---

[1] A familiar figure of lower-middle-class banality, full of pompous, self-satisfied nonsense, as drawn by Henri Monnier in *Les Memoires de Joseph Prudhomme*, 1857.

made up two packages for Bost and one for you, but it's lack of money that's keeping me from sending them. I'll tap Paul for a hundred francs while waiting for your money order. A bit later I'll send you the Rauschning, which you must read. The first 80 pages of the Romains aren't the best. The pleasant part is rather the unstinting pains he takes to observe the situation from every angle, and also what he has to say about Verdun. Looking forward to your opinion. This evening Mistler came in, all swathed in his overcoat because he was dying of the cold—and had cramps in his gut. We comforted him, he always goes off cheered by these encounters, though we take a few jabs at him, tease him, are gently rough with him. For example I say to him: "You should be ashamed: you make fun of Hantziger because his name is Arthur—whereas you, you're called Edgar." Then he says: "Oh, yes. Yes! Yes!" and then he slips into a reverie for a time. That's what he likes. He's becoming more and more like an old Englishwoman. And also like Grock,[2] if you please. That's all, my dearest. Till tomorrow, I'm all eagerness to get your letters, and I love you with all my heart. Have a good time.

To Simone de Beauvoir

December 30

My darling Beaver

So yesterday no letters from you, and now today the mail hasn't come. It means a good long time without you, dear one. You will have made lots of progress with your skiing meanwhile. It is eight o'clock now, you're dining with Kanapa while listening to the radio, you're completely done in and maybe even yawning, however discreetly. I would so like to be with you. What a joke, this war, which goes only so far as to deprive men of their women without doing them any other harm.

You know, you must surely be less freezing than I am. It was −18°C this morning. And last night −4° and −5° in our bedrooms. Just imagine this: sleeping warmly (our blankets and comforters are very warm) in a room where the water freezes. But if we so much as poke a little finger out from under the covers, it gets frozen, too. I still had some trouble getting to sleep, because I hadn't managed things very well with the covers, and there were several insidious drafts down my back. And then everything was fine after that (around one in the morning), and unfortunately I had to get up at six-

---

[2] A Swiss clown (1880–1959) whose blunders with the piano and violin became proverbial.

thirty. I went to the Café de la Gare and breakfasted while reading the Rauschning, then went back to the journal. Today, theory on bad faith: it was so ripe, it fell right into my lap; I'll go on with it tomorrow. I also had lunch there, and the proprietor explained, tearing his hair, that the officers have caused an incredible rise in prices in the town, where they gather provisions, because they pay without checking the total. Just at the moment when they could do a "good bit-a bizniz," he told me sadly. And he added, "In the long run, it's the privates who'll get the worst of it." Which inspired some economic reflections in my journal. This afternoon I went to fetch a heavy bag of coal for us weather guys; it's there in the corner, fat-bellied, inspiring confidence. Then I worked on my novel, did a reading, fasted, drank a glass of wine. Mistler came over and lent me Stendhal's *Journal*, which I'm delighted to be reading, and now I'm writing to you. Alas, my poor Beaver, my letter is going to end here. If they are ordinarily so long, it's that I stuff them with answers to yours. But I don't know anything about you anymore. And my life here is absolutely monastic. Right now it seems to me that a severe God has taken away all the pleasures of my life so I can dedicate myself for a brief time to culture, to thought, and to meditations on myself. I don't even sense the war anymore, I'm cultivating my mind. It's a curious life, and if it continues, a curious benefit for me.

My love, I still love you very deeply. There would be a perfect place for you in this monastic life, only it stays empty. We'd work and we'd both cultivate our minds, and we'd love one another very much.

I love you so much.

The mail came in at last, six hours later, but there's nothing in it from you.

From tomorrow on, I think it wise to begin sending letters for you to Paris again, general delivery.

I love you. And I wish you a happy new year, my dearest.

To Simone de Beauvoir

December 31

My darling Beaver

I got three long letters from you today. You can't imagine what lively pleasure that gives my days, to know that you're so happy in the snow. It truly transforms the world. I suppose it's because I see so few and such monotonous things—I'm not saying that to complain, since my mind is alert and I'm very content—that I'm left with more place and enthusiasm for imagined pleasures; reality doesn't work in a reductive way, and I'm completely surrounded by your mountains. My love, how present you are to me in your slightest activity. Your life in the open air up there seems so marvelous, and it's easy to understand how happy you are. As for my leave, my little sweet, this is the moment for patience, the date will shuttle back and forth from day to day, for the very reason that it is almost upon me. At any rate it's not for the 6th. They're talking now of the 13th or the 14th. Perhaps even a bit later. But, as you say, in the long run a week or two of waiting is nothing, because it will come about. As it turns out, I don't think we can conceivably hide it from Tania, particularly since for the moment we're on good terms again. It's moving along, sweetly. She wrote three letters, then no more. And I'm not going to write tonight, not to be vindictive, but out of fatigue. But finally, this mutual cooling off cannot justify such measures of retaliation. So we'll adhere to our original plan. We'll go to the Hôtel Mistral. I'm not allowed to send a telegram; in any case I'll get the necessary information. But you'll be alerted in time anyway, about the date and hour of my arrival. For the moment there's nothing to say to Z. I'll go to the headquarters after the New Year's festivities, and I'll ask for all the particulars. Now that I think of it, little one, don't forget the ink cartridges, and along with the books, as soon as possible, send two notebooks, larger than the last ones (the same size as the ones I've given you) but *ruled*. Don't worry if you didn't get the notebooks, I didn't give them to Pieter, finally, because I was soon going to see you. You'll get four all at once when I get to Paris, and a completely new theory on *nothingness*. Another on *violence*. Another on *bad faith*.

Do you realize that I've actually *finished* the novel? I put the words "The End" at the bottom of a page. After which—I was very serious and dignified because I'd finished it—I painstakingly tore up that page into small scraps along with the two preceding ones. Then I threw them all into the coal scuttle. I only noticed my mistake ten minutes later. I had to retrieve the bits of paper from the bucket, smudging up my fingers, and fit together the puzzle's pieces. I succeeded, and copied out the whole thing. Then below "The End" I wrote: "The next volume will be called *September*." Do you like "September"? It strikes me as being quite strong, and I don't think we ever spoke about that title. I like it so much that I'm undecided about whether to start in right away on the second book. Ultimately I'm weary of *The Age of Reason*, but that doesn't have to mean that *September* will disgust me, since it's something entirely different. I won't do the whole thing, actually.

Just episodes: Sarah killing her kid, Boubou at the dance hall with Mathieu. Mathieu meeting a woman in a brawl, Nancy's last night, etc. And then all the lives of guys who finally meet up with him in the railway car. Yes, yes, this makes me determined to write it for you, and I'll begin in two or three days. From now till then I'll tinker with the ending a bit, so I'll be able to bring it to you in January.

This morning Mistler came along with me for breakfast at the Café de la Gare, and he was dazzled by the intimacy I had reached, eating in the kitchen with the waitresses, among the leftovers from the day before and cuts of red meat destined for the noon meal (which is not the part that enchants me most), whereas the café is off-limits to the military before 11. He asked by what learned politics I had reached that point, and I explained: it's that the proprietors, contemplating me in their kitchen, are struck by the privilege that it constitutes and think there must be some reason for it but seem to have forgotten what. So then they redouble their attention to make up for their forgetting. To the point that at noon, when all the army guys are driven out, I stay there lingering peacefully over my coffee and go off only when I'm ready. In fact, hearing one day that the café was to be off-limits the following day, I wandered in that next day with a calm impudence I'd be far from displaying in civilian life and said to the waitress, "Oh, but you're not going to send *me* away, now are you?" She did send me packing, and I took off. The following day the owner was there, and I held out a five-franc note to pay. She had no change, it was 2.50 francs. So I guilefully remarked, "Well, that'll be for tomorrow." Here Pieter would say, "You see . . . the perfect touch." And thus the habit was set. Of course it's devilishly poetic, that deserted kitchen in the morning, with the meat on the table, huge basins full of potatoes, sausages hanging from a rod, and a congenital idiot, drooling slightly as he lights the fire. Then along comes the first waitress, the one who—as I must have told you—voluntarily shows off her behind to the idiot, who doesn't seem exactly moved by the exhibition. And the two of them gossip in German about the proprietors, sounding like the opening scenes and exposition in a comedy by Labiche[1] (the lady's maid and valet talking together); they freely call on me as witness. After which comes a second waitress. Then the military cook from the law officers' mess, which is held in one of the rooms of the café, then the army truck driver in charge of provisions, all these folk drink their coffee around me, reading away, then the proprietress too, slovenly, still disheveled from sleep, and finally at eight-

---

[1]Eugène Labiche (1815–88), prolific playwright of vaudeville comedies.

thirty, her daughter Charlotte, the young beauty of the place. Around 8:35, I leave. Mistler came in after me and they wanted to kick him out, but I raised a protective hand above him and said, "Serve him, he's with me." And it was done. He was full of respect, and I explained to him that in the struggle begun between the military authority, which wishes to deprive me of my breakfasts, and me, who am sternly bent on having them (you well know me on that point), doubtless I will regularly win out, because I stand ready for anything. But it may well lead to my having poetic and clandestine breakfasts in back rooms, kitchens, bedrooms, who knows where else?

After which we went back up and I worked all morning on a theory of bad faith, which didn't turn out as well as I'd hoped. Then I went back for lunch at the Café de la Gare, and Mistler, who is beginning to cling a bit, came along too. We were packed in like sardines, because it was Sunday and the last day of the year. I recounted thousands of things to Mistler, whom I interest, instruct, and frighten somewhat; I let him in on my idea of installing a dictatorship of liberty to force people, through a regime of tortures and arguments, to be free. Then we went back up, and I worked on my novel, which I finished. I fasted, and now I'm writing to you. And since I wrote yesterday to my parents and am not writing to T., I'll be able to go to bed almost as soon as I've finished writing. It's only $-2°C$ in the bedrooms, and since I heat my covers in here, I'm not cold anymore at night.

I love you, my little sweet, my thoughts hardly leave you, you are my strength and joy. Till tomorrow, my darling Beaver, I'm sleepy, and you, after your day of skiing, must already be asleep.

I haven't said any more about your vacation in Annecy[2] because I don't know anything more about it, which isn't to say anything for or against your plan.

---

[2]*In case Sartre was withdrawn to the Alps. (SdB)*

Select Bibliography

Sartre's Works

L'Imagination. Paris: Presses Universitaires Françaises, 1936. *Imagination: A Psychological Critique*, trans. Forrest Williams. Ann Arbor: University of Michigan Press, 1979.

La Transcendance de l'égo. Paris: Vrin, 1937. *The Transcendence of the Ego*, trans. Forrest Williams and Robert Kirkpatrick. New York: Noonday Press, 1957.

La Nausée. Paris: Gallimard, 1938. *Nausea*, trans. Lloyd Alexander. New York: New Directions, 1964.

Le Mur. Paris: Gallimard, 1939. *The Wall*, trans. Lloyd Alexander. New York: New Directions, 1948.

Esquisse d'une théorie des émotions. Paris: Hermann, 1939.

L'Imaginaire. Paris: Gallimard, 1940. *The Psychology of Imagination*. New York: Philosophical Library, 1948; New York: Washington Square Press, 1966.

L'Être et le Néant. Paris: Gallimard, 1943. *Being and Nothingness*, trans. Hazel Barnes. New York: Philosophical Library, 1956; New York: Washington Square Press, 1966.

Les Chemins de la liberté, Vol. I, *L'Âge de raison*. Paris: Gallimard, 1945. *The Age of Reason*, trans. Eric Sutton. New York: Vintage Books, 1973.

Les Chemins de la liberté, Vol. 2, *Le Sursis*. Paris: Gallimard, 1945. *The Reprieve*. New York: Knopf, 1947; New York, Vintage Books, 1973.

Les Chemins de la liberté, Vol. 3, *La Mort dans l'âme*. Paris: Gallimard, 1949. *Troubled Sleep*. New York: Knopf, 1950; New York, Vintage Books, 1973.

Les Mots. Paris: Gallimard, 1963. *The Words*, trans. Bernard Frechtman. New York: Braziller, 1964; New York: Vintage Books, 1981.

Oeuvres romanesques, ed. Michel Contat and Michel Rybalka. Bibliothèque de la Pléiade, Paris: Gallimard, 1981.

Les Carnets de la drôle de guerre. Paris: Gallimard, 1983. *The War Diaries*, trans. Quintin Hoare. New York: Pantheon, 1985.

Lettres au Castor et à quelques autres, Vols. 1 and 2. Paris: Gallimard, 1983.

Écrits de jeunesse, ed. Michel Contat and Michel Rybalka. Paris: Gallimard, 1990.

General Bibliography

Bair, Deirdre. *Simone de Beauvoir: A Biography*. New York and London: Summit Books, 1990.

Beauvoir, Simone de. *La Cérémonie des adieux*, suivi de *Entretiens avec Jean-Paul Sartre*. Paris: Gallimard, 1981. *Adieux: A Farewell to Sartre*, trans. Patrick O'Brian. New York: Pantheon, 1984.

———. *La Force de l'âge*, Vols. 1 and 2. Paris: Gallimard, 1960. *The Prime of Life*, trans. Peter Green. Cleveland and New York: World, 1954.

———. *L'Invitée*. Paris: Gallimard, 1943. *She Came to Stay*. Cleveland and New York: World, 1954.

———. *Lettres à Sartre*, Vol. 1. Paris: Gallimard, 1990. *Letters to Sartre*, trans. Quintin Hoare. New York: Arcade Publishing, 1992.

Cohen-Solal, Annie. *Sartre 1905–1980*. Paris: Gallimard, 1985. *Sartre: A Life*, trans. Anna Cancogni, ed. Norman MacAfee. New York: Pantheon, 1987.

Gerassi, John. *Jean-Paul Sartre: Hated Conscience of His Century*. Chicago: University of Chicago Press, 1989.

Hayman, Ronald. *Sartre: A Biography*. New York: Simon & Schuster, 1987.

Acknowledgments

The translators wish to thank Arlette Elkaim Sartre for her perceptive eye; Constance Jewett Ellis; Katherine Cheremeteff Davison; Matthew Ward, Irene Ilton, and Marilyn Myatt; our editors at Scribner's, Erika Goldman and John Glusman; Charles Flowers; Christianne Baudry and Francis Baudry; Brenda Riddick; and the Florence Gould Foundation and The New York Foundation for the Arts for a helpful grant.

Index